PHILIP'S

STR  5

Staf ....e

First published in 1995 by

Philip's, a division of
Octopus Publishing Group Ltd
2–4 Heron Quays, London E14 4JP

Second colour edition 2002
Second impression with revisions 2003

ISBN 0-540-08118-3 (pocket)

© Philip's 2003

OS Ordnance Survey®

This product includes mapping data licensed from Ordnance Survey® with the permission of the Controller of Her Majesty's Stationery Office. © Crown copyright 2003. All rights reserved. Licence number 100011710.

Printed and bound in Spain
by Cayfosa-Quebecor

Contents

III **Key to map symbols**

IV **Key to map pages**

VI **Route planning**

VIII **Administrative and Postcode boundaries**

1 **Street maps** at 2½ inches to 1 mile

282 **Street maps of centres of Stoke-on-Trent, Longton and Newcastle-under-Lyme** at 5 inches to 1 mile

285 **Town maps** of Congleton, Macclesfield, Buxton, Chesterfield, Derby and Matlock

288 **Index** of towns and villages

289 **Index** of streets, hospitals, industrial estates, railway stations, schools, shopping centres, universities and places of interest

Digital Data

The exceptionally high-quality mapping found in this atlas is available as digital data in TIFF format, which is easily convertible to other bitmapped (raster) image formats.

The index is also available in digital form as a standard database table. It contains all the details found in the printed index together with the National Grid reference for the map square in which each entry is named.

For further information and to discuss your requirements, please contact Philip's on 020 7644 6932 or james.mann@philips-maps.co.uk

Key to map symbols

III

(22a)	**Motorway** with junction number		Walsall	**Railway station**
	Primary route – dual/single carriageway			**Private railway station**
	A road – dual/single carriageway			**Bus, coach station**
	B road – dual/single carriageway			**Ambulance station**
	Minor road – dual/single carriageway			**Coastguard station**
	Other minor road – dual/single carriageway			**Fire station**
– – –	**Road under construction**			**Police station**
	Pedestrianised area			**Accident and Emergency entrance to hospital**
DY7	**Postcode boundaries**		H	**Hospital**
	County and unitary authority boundaries		+	**Place of worship**
	Railway		i	**Information Centre** (open all year)
– – –	**Railway under construction**		P	**Parking**
	Tramway, miniature railway		P&R	**Park and Ride**
	Rural track, private road or narrow road in urban area		PO	**Post Office**
	Gate or obstruction to traffic (restrictions may not apply at all times or to all vehicles)			**Camping site**
– – –	**Path, bridleway, byway open to all traffic, road used as a public path**			**Caravan site**
	The representation in this atlas of a road, track or path is no evidence of the existence of a right of way			**Golf course**
58				**Picnic site**
230	**Adjoining page indicators**		Prim Sch	**Important buildings, schools, colleges, universities and hospitals**
237	The map area within the pink band is shown at a larger scale on the page indicated by the red block and arrow		River Medway	**Water name**
				River, stream
				Lock, weir
				Water
				Tidal water
				Woods
				Houses
			Church	**Non-Roman antiquity**
			ROMAN FORT	**Roman antiquity**

Acad	**Academy**	Mkt	**Market**
Allot Gdns	**Allotments**	Meml	**Memorial**
Cemy	**Cemetery**	Mon	**Monument**
C Ctr	**Civic Centre**	Mus	**Museum**
CH	**Club House**	Obsy	**Observatory**
Coll	**College**	Pal	**Royal Palace**
Crem	**Crematorium**	PH	**Public House**
Ent	**Enterprise**	Recn Gd	**Recreation Ground**
Ex H	**Exhibition Hall**	Resr	**Reservoir**
Ind Est	**Industrial Estate**	Ret Pk	**Retail Park**
IRB Sta	**Inshore Rescue**	Sch	**School**
	Boat Station	Sh Ctr	**Shopping Centre**
Inst	**Institute**	TH	**Town Hall/House**
Ct	**Law Court**	Trad Est	**Trading Estate**
L Ctr	**Leisure Centre**	Univ	**University**
LC	**Level Crossing**	Wks	**Works**
Liby	**Library**	YH	**Youth Hostel**

■ The small numbers around the edges of the maps identify the 1 kilometre National Grid lines ■ The dark grey border on the inside edge of some pages indicates that the mapping does not continue onto the adjacent page

The scale of the maps on the pages numbered in blue is 3.92 cm to 1 km • 2½ inches to 1 mile • 1: 25344

0	¼	½	¾	1 mile
0	250m	500m	750m	1 kilometre

The scale of the maps on pages numbered in red is 7.84 cm to 1 km • 5 inches to 1 mile • 1: 12672

0	220 yards	440 yards	660 yards	½ mile
0	125m	250m	375m	½ kilometre

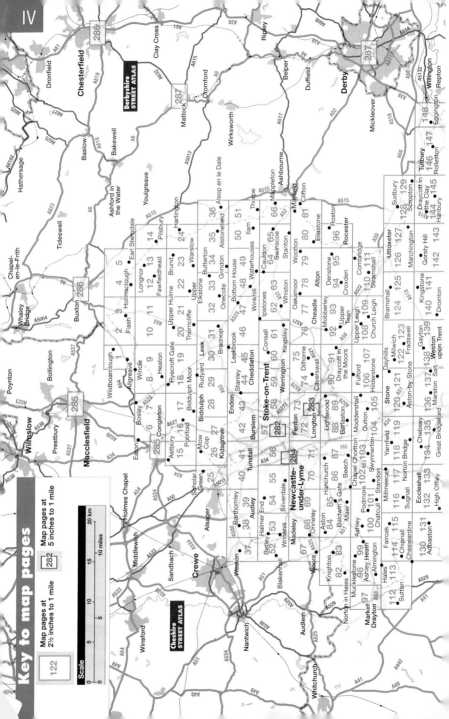

Route planning

Scale

0 1 2 3 4 5 6 7 8 km
0 1 2 3 4 5 miles

Cheshire

Shropshire

Telford and
Wrekin

Shropshire

Worcestershire

Derbyshire

Warwickshire

Staffordshire

**Staffordshire
Moorlands**

**City of
Stoke-
on-Trent**

**Newcastle-
under-Lyme**

Stafford

**East
Staffordshire**

**Cannock
Chase**

**South
Staffordshire**

Lichfield

Tamworth

Walsall

Sandwell

Dudley

Birmingham

City of Wolverhampton

Major administrative and
Postcode boundaries

County and unitary
authority boundaries

District boundaries

Postcode boundaries

Area covered by this atlas

Scale

0   5   10   15 km

0   5   10 miles

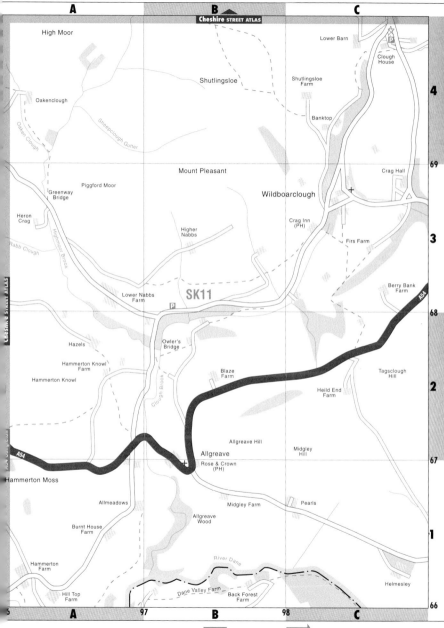

High Moor

Shutlingsloe

Lower Barn

Clough
House

Oakenclough

Shutlingsloe
Farm

Banktop

4

Oaken Clough

Sheepclough Gutter

69

Mount Pleasant

Crag Hall

Greenway
Bridge

Piggford Moor

Wildboarclough

Heron
Crag

Highmoor Brook

Higher
Nabbs

Crag Inn
(PH)

Firs Farm

3

Rabb Clough

Berry Bank
Farm

Lower Nabbs
Farm

SK11

P

Owler's
Bridge

68

Hazels

Tagsclough
Hill

Hammerton Knowl
Farm

Blaze
Farm

Heild End
Farm

2

Hammerton Knowl

Clough Brook

A54

Allgreave Hill

Midgley
Hill

Allgreave

67

Hammerton Moss

A54

Rose & Crown
(PH)

Allmeadows

Midgley Farm

Pearls

Burnt House
Farm

Allgreave
Wood

1

River Dane

Hammerton
Farm

Helmesley

Hill Top
Farm

Dane Valley Farm

Back Forest
Farm

66

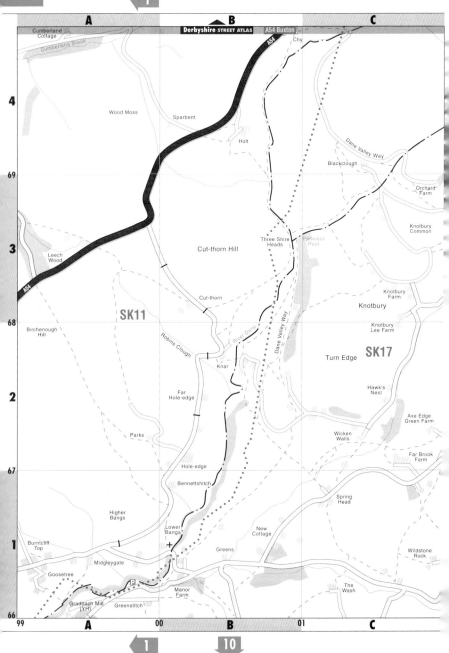

A54 Buxton

Cumberland
Cottage

Cumberland Brook

Wood Moss

Sparbent

Holt

Chy

Dane Valley Way

Blackclough

Orchard
Farm

Leech
Wood

Cut-thorn Hill

Three Shire
Heads

Panniers
Pool

Knotbury
Common

Knotbury
Farm

Knotbury

SK11

Cut-thorn

Birchenough
Hill

Robins Clough

River Dane

Dane Valley Way

Knotbury
Lee Farm

Turn Edge

SK17

Knar

Far
Hole-edge

Hawk's
Nest

Axe Edge
Green Farm

Parks

Wicken
Walls

Far Brook
Farm

Hole-edge

Bennettshitch

Higher
Bangs

Lower
Bangs

Spring
Head

New
Cottage

Burntcliff
Top

Midgleygate

Greens

Wildstone
Rock

Goosetree

Gradbach Mill
(YH)

Greenstitch

Manor
Farm

The
Wash

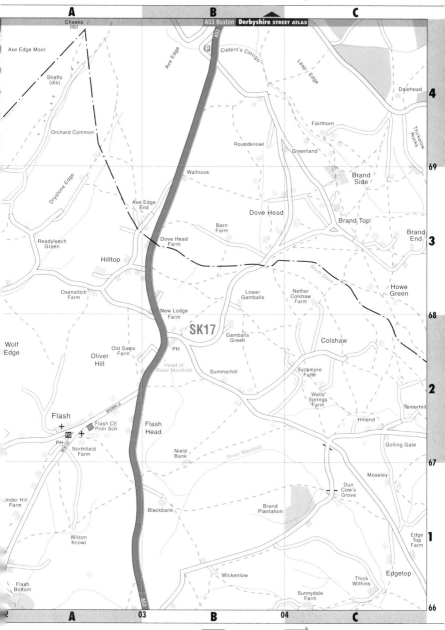

A   B   A53 Buxton **Derbyshire** STREET ATLAS   C

Cheeks Hill

Axe Edge Moor

Shafts (dis)

Axe Edge

Cistern's Clough

Leap Edge

Orchard Common

Dalehead

Fairthorn

Roundknowl

Greenland

Thirkelow Rocks

4

69

Wallnook

Drystone Edge

Brand Side

Axe Edge End

Dove Head

Brand Top

Brand End

3

Readyleech Green

Barn Farm

Dove Head Farm

River Dove

Hilltop

Howe Green

Oxenstitch Farm

Lower Gamballs

Nether Colshaw Farm

68

New Lodge Farm

SK17

Gamballs Green

Colshaw

Wolf Edge

Old Sams Farm

PH

Summerhill

Sycamore Farm

2

Oliver Hill

Head of River Manifold

Wells Springs Farm

Tenterhill

Flash

BROWN LA

Hillend

Golling Gate

Flash CE Prim Sch

Flash Head

PO

PH

Nield Bank

River Manifold

67

NEW RD

Northfield Farm

Moseley

Under Hill Farm

Dun Cow's Grove

Blackbank

Brand Plantation

Wilson Knowl

Edge Top Farm

1

Wickenlow

Thick Withins

Edgetop

Flash Bottom

Sunnydale Farm

66

A   03   B   04   C

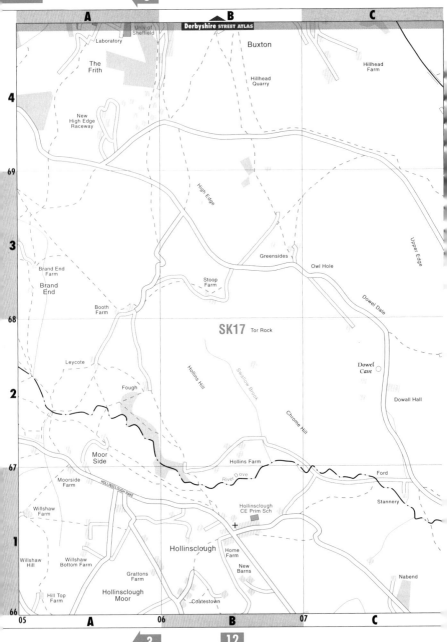

A   B   **Derbyshire STREET ATLAS**   C

Univ of
Sheffield

Laboratory

Buxton

The
Frith

Hillhead
Quarry

Hillhead
Farm

4

New
High Edge
Raceway

69

High Edge

3

Greensides

Owl Hole

Upper Edge

Brand End
Farm

Stoop
Farm

Dowel Dale

Brand
End

Booth
Farm

68

SK17 Tor Rock

Leycote

Hollins Hill

Swallow Brook

Dowel
Cave

Fough

2

Chrome Hill

Dowall Hall

Moor
Side

Hollins Farm

Ford

67

Moorside
Farm

HOLLINSCLOUGH RAKE

River Dove

Stannery

Willshaw
Farm

Hollinsclough
CE Prim Sch

+

1

Hollinsclough

Home
Farm

Willshaw
Hill

Willshaw
Bottom Farm

Grattons
Farm

New
Barns

Nabend

Hill Top
Farm

Hollinsclough
Moor

Coatestown

66

05   A   06   B   07   C

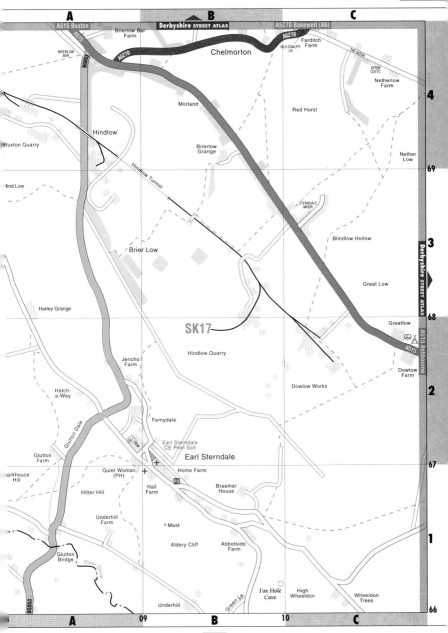

A515 Buxton

A5270 Bakewell (A6)

Brierlow Bar Farm

Chelmorton

Farditch Farm

OLD COALPIT LA

THE DITCH

DITCH COTTS

Netherlow Farm

BRIERLOW BAR

B5053

A5270

A515

Morland

Red Hurst

Hindlow

Brierlow Grange

Nether Low

Buxton Quarry

Hindlow Tunnel

Hind Low

STERNDALE MOOR

Blindlow Hollow

Brier Low

Great Low

Harley Grange

Greatlow

SK17

A515

Derbyshire STREET ATLAS

Hindlow Quarry

Dowlow Farm

Jericho Farm

Hatch-a-Way

Dowlow Works

Glutton Dale

Fernydale

Earl Sterndale CE Prim Sch

B5053

Earl Sterndale

Glutton Farm

Quiet Woman (PH)

Home Farm

Braemar House

arkhouse Hill

Hall Farm

Hitter Hill

Underhill Farm

Mast

Aldery Cliff

Abbotside Farm

Glutton Bridge

River Dove

Fox Hole Cave

High Wheeldon

Wheeldon Trees

B5053

Underhill

Green La

A 09 B 10 C

4

69

3

68

2

67

1

66

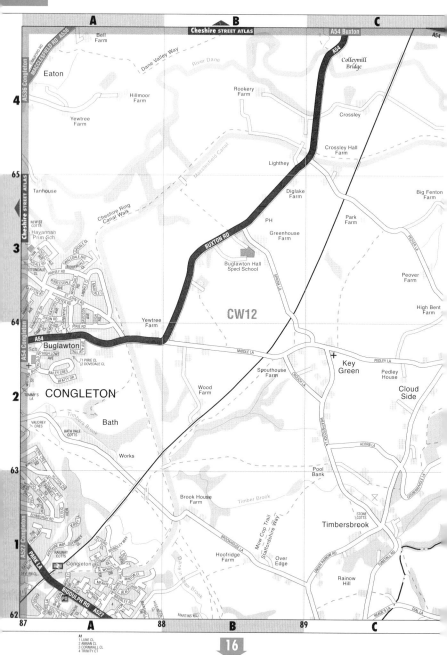

A535 Congleton
MACCLESFIELD RD A535

Bell Farm

Eaton

Dane Valley Way

River Dane

Colleymill Bridge

Rookery Farm

Hillmoor Farm

Crossley

4

Yewtree Farm

Crossley Hall Farm

Macclesfield Canal

Lighthey

65

Cheshire STREET ATLAS

Tanhouse

Big Fenton Farm

Diglake Farm

Cheshire Ring Canal Walk

NEW ST COTTS

BUXTON RD

PH

Park Farm

Hayannah Prim Sch

Greenhouse Farm

Peover Farm

3

MIDDLEWALE LA

Buglawton Hall Specl School

CW12

High Bent Farm

64

Yewtree Farm

A54 Congleton

Buglawton

MIDDLE LA

Sch

HIGH LOWE AVE

1 PIRIE CL
2 DOVEDALE CL

Key Green

PEDLEY LA

Pedley House

BAILEY DR

BEATTY DR

Cloud Side

2

TOMMY'S LA

CONGLETON

Timbers Brook

Spouthouse Farm

Bath

VAUDREY CRES

BATH VALE COTTS

Wood Farm

ACORN LA

Works

63

Brook House Farm

Timber Brook

Pool Bank

A527 Congleton

PARK LA

EDINBURGH RD

Brook House Farm

Mow Cop Trail

Staffordshire Way

STONE COTTS

Timbersbrook

1

RAILWAY COTTS

Congleton

Hoofridge Farm

Over Edge

Rainow Hill

BIDDULPH RD

A527

MARTINS HILL

62

A1
1 LUNE CL
2 ANNAN CL
3 CORNWALL CL
4 TRINITY CT

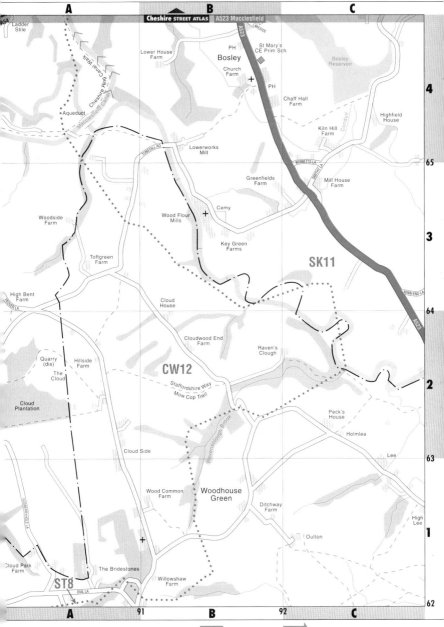

Cheshire STREET ATLAS | A523 Macclesfield

A | B | C

4

65

3

64

2

63

1

62

A | 91 | B | 92 | C

Ladder Stile

A54

Canal Walk

Macclesfield Canal

Cheshire Ring

Aqueduct

Lower House Farm

Bosley

Church Farm

PH

PH

St Mary's CE Prim Sch

Bosley Reservoir

LAKESIDE

A523

Chaff Hall Farm

Kiln Hill Farm

Highfield House

Conduit

Lowerworks Mill

TUNSTALL RD

BENNETTS LA

SMITH LA

Greenfields Farm

Milf House Farm

Woodside Farm

Wood Flour Mills

Cemy

Key Green Farms

SK11

Toftgreen Farm

High Bent Farm

PEDLEY LA

Cloud House

Cloudwood End Farm

Raven's Clough

DUNN END LA

A523

Quarry (dis)

The Cloud

Hillside Farm

CW12

Staffordshire Way
Mow Cop Trail

Ravensclough Brook

Peck's House

Holmlea

Cloud Plantation

Cloud Side

Lee

Wood Common Farm

Woodhouse Green

Ditchway Farm

High Lee

Oulton

Cloud Park Farm

ST8

GOSBERRYHOLE LA

DIAL LA

The Bridestones

Willowshaw Farm

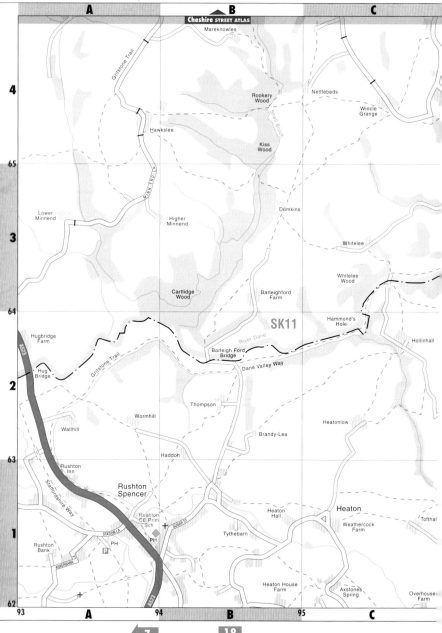

4

Mareknowles

Gritstone Trail

Rookery Wood

Nettlebeds

Wincle Grange

Hawkslee

Shell Brook

Kiss Wood

65

MINNEND

Dumkins

Lower Minnend

Higher Minnend

Whitelee

3

Whitelee Wood

Cartlidge Wood

Barleighford Farm

Hammond's Hole

64

Hollinhall

Hugbridge Farm

River Dane

SK11

Gritstone Trail

Barleigh Ford Bridge

Dane Valley Way

Hug Bridge

2

A523

Thompson

Wormhill

Heatonlow

Wallhill

Brandy-Lea

Haddon

63

Rushton Inn

Staffordshire Way

Rushton Spencer

Heaton

Tofthal

Heaton Hall

Weathercock Farm

1

Rushton CE Prim Sch

SUGAR ST

Tythebarn

STATION LA

PH

Rushton Bank

P

PH

A523

AXKENBANK

Heaton House Farm

Axstones Spring

Overhouse Farm

62

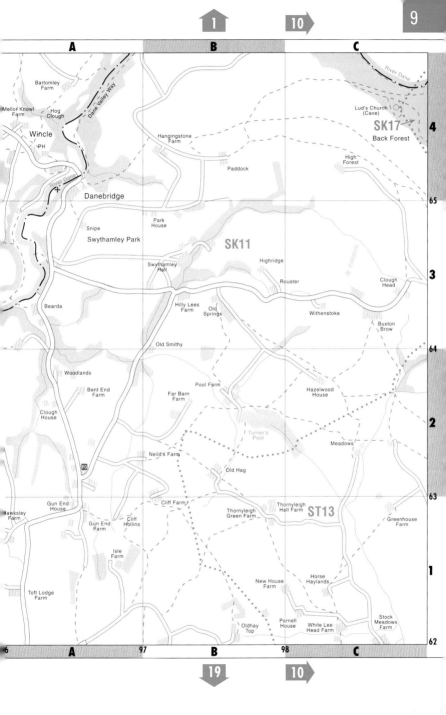

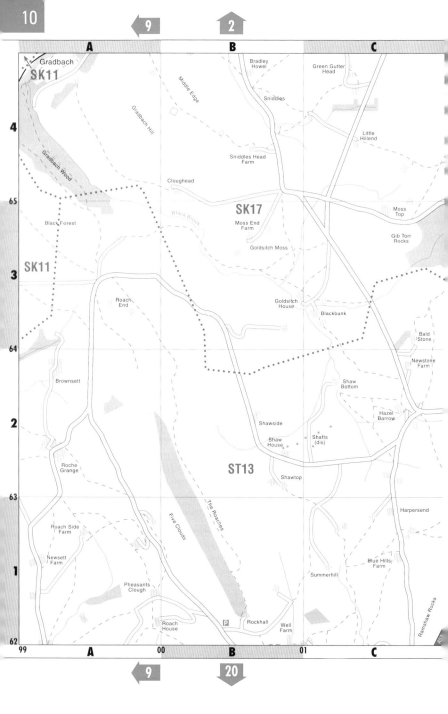

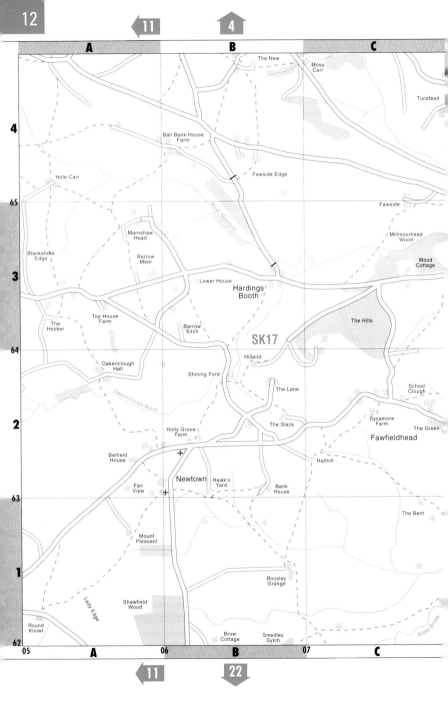

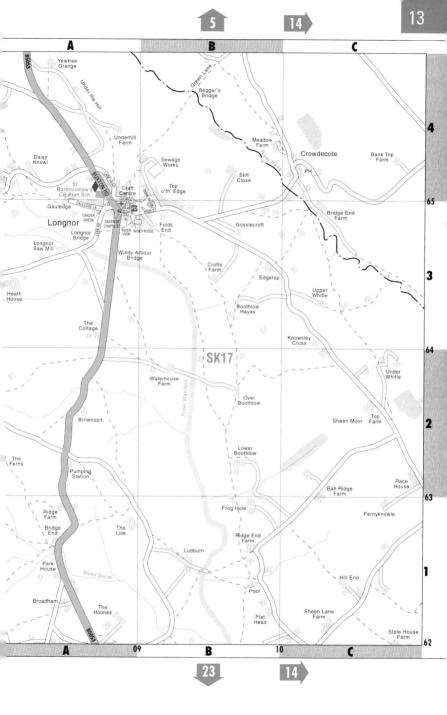

5　14

A　B　C

4

Yewtree Grange
Under the Hill
B5053
Beggar's Bridge
Green Lane
Meadow Farm
River Dove
Crowdecote
Bank Top Farm
Underhill Farm
Daisy Knowl
St Bartholomew's CE Prim Sch
BUXTON RD
LANE HEAD
Craft Centre
CHURCH ST
PO
KING RIDGE
HIGH ST
Sewage Works
Top o'th' Edge
Stiff Close
PH
Gauledge
GAULEDGE LA
MARKET PL
QUEEN ST
CHAPEL ST
CARDER GREEN
RIVER VIEW
WINDYRIDGE
Bridge End Farm
65
Longnor
Gosslecroft
Longnor Bridge
Folds End
Longnor Saw Mill
Windy Arbour Bridge
Crofts Farm
Edgetop
Upper Whittle
Heath House
3
The Cottage
Boothlow Hayes
Knowsley Cross
Under Whittle
64
SK17
Waterhouse Farm
Over Boothlow
Brownspit
Sheen Moor
Top Farm
2
The Ferns
Lower Boothlow
Pumping Station
Ball Ridge Farm
Race House
63
Ridge Farm
Frog Hole
Fernyknowle
Bridge End
The Low
Ridge End Farm
Park House
Ludburn
Blake Brook
Hill End
1
Broadham
Pool
The Holmes
Sheen Lane Farm
Flat Head
Slate House Farm
62

River Manifold
B5053

A　09　B　10　C

23　14

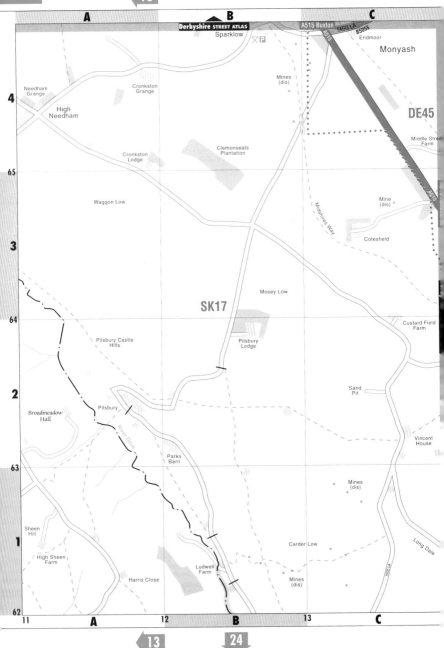

Derbyshire STREET ATLAS
Sparklow
A515 Buxton
TAGG LA
B5055
Endmoor
Monyash

Needham
Grange
Cronkston
Grange
Mines
(dis)

High
Needham
DE45

Cronkston
Lodge
Clemonseats
Plantation
Middle Street
Farm

65

Waggon Low
Mine
(dis)

Mightshires Way
Cotesfield

3

64
Mosey Low

SK17
Custard Field
Farm

Pilsbury Castle
Hills
Pilsbury
Lodge

2
Sand
Pit

Broadmeadow
Hall
Pilsbury
River Dove
Vincent
House

Parks
Barn

63
Mines
(dis)

Sheen
Hill

1
Carder Low
Long Dale

High Sheen
Farm
Mines
(dis)

Harris Close
Ludwell
Farm

62

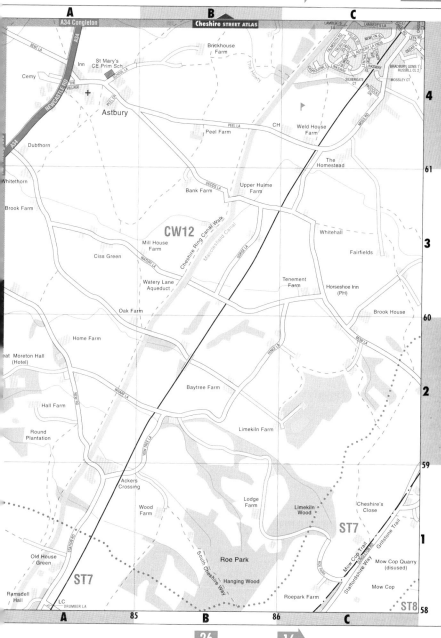

A   B   C

BENT LA
Inn
St Mary's
CE Prim Sch
Cemy
THE VILLAGE
NEWCASTLE ROAD
Astbury
Dubthorn
Whitethorn
Brook Farm

Brickhouse
Farm

The Hovel

LAMBERT'S LA
LAMBERT'S LA
LEEK RD
NEWLYN
ASTBURY LA ENDS
CHESHIRE CL
LINKSWAY
BRADBURY GDNS 1
RUSSELL CL 2
SILVERGATE CT
MOSSLEY CT
PADDOCK DR

4

Weld House
Farm
CH
Peel Farm
PEEL LA

The
Homestead

61

Bank Farm
DODDS LA
Upper Hulme
Farm

CW12
Mill House
Farm
Ciss Green
WATERY LA
Cheshire Ring Canal Walk
Macclesfield Canal
GOSE LA
Whitehall
Fairfields

3

Watery Lane
Aqueduct
Tenement
Farm
Horseshoe Inn
(PH)
Oak Farm
Brook House

60

Home Farm
Great Moreton Hall
(Hotel)
WHARF LA
NEW RD
FENCE LA
MOW LA

Baytree Farm

2

Hall Farm
Round
Plantation
YEW TREE LA
Limekiln Farm

59

Ackers
Crossing
Wood
Farm
Lodge
Farm
Limekiln
Wood
Cheshire's
Close
ST7

South Cheshire Way
Mow Cop Trail
Staffordshire Way
Gritstone Trail
ROE PARK

1

Old House
Green
STATION RD
ST7
Roe Park
Hanging Wood
Roepark Farm
Mow Cop Quarry
(disused)
Mow Cop
Ramsdell
Hall
LC
DRUMBER LA
ST8
58

A   B   C
85   86

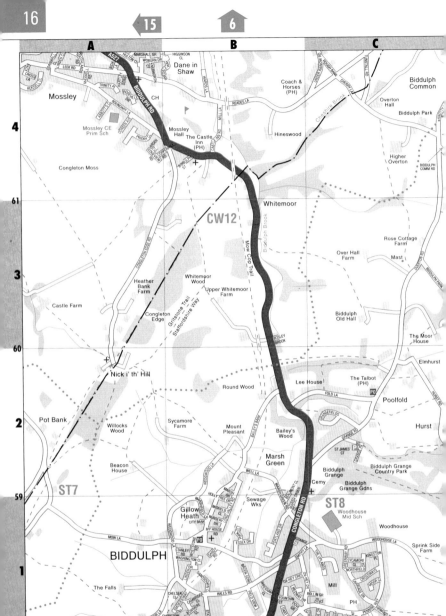

A

B

C

MARSHALL GR.

HIGGINSON CL.

WOBURN DR.

LEEK RD.

Dane in Shaw

Coach & Horses (PH)

Biddulph Common

Mossley

TRINITY PL.

CH

Overton Hall

Biddulph Park

READES LA.

Mossley CE Prim Sch

Mossley Hall

The Castle Inn (PH)

Hineswood

Higher Overton

BIDDULPH COMM RD

4

Congleton Moss

61

Whitemoor

CW12

Rose Cottage Farm

Mast

Over Hall Farm

Heather Bank Farm

Whitemoor Wood

Upper Whitemoor Farm

Biddulph Old Hall

3

Castle Farm

Congleton Edge

Gritstone Trail

Staffordshire Way

Mow Cop Trail

Biddulph Brook

The Moor House

Elmhurst

60

Nick i' th' Hill

Round Wood

Lee House

The Talbot (PH)

Poolfold

FOLD LA.

2

Pot Bank

Willocks Wood

Sycamore Farm

Mount Pleasant

Bailey's Wood

Marsh Green

Hurst

Beacon House

Biddulph Grange

Biddulph Grange Country Park

ST7

Cemy

Biddulph Grange Gdns

ST8

Woodhouse Mid Sch

59

Gillow Heath

Sewage Wks

Woodhouse

CITY BANK

IVY HOUSE

WOODHOUSE LA.

Sprink Side Farm

MOW LA.

PO

BIDDULPH

Mill

1

The Falls

PH

CONGLETON RD

Oxhey Fst Sch

Hollylane

Moorland Rd

THOMAS ST.

A527

58

87

A

88

B

89

C

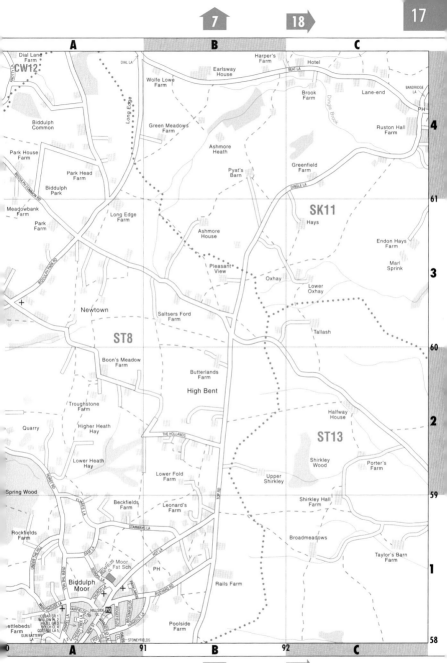

Dial Lane Farm
CW12
Dial La
Long Edge

Harper's Farm
Earlsway House
Hotel
BEAT LA
Wolfe Lowe Farm
Brook Farm
Lane-end
Dingle Brook
BANDRIDGE LA
PH

Biddulph Common

Green Meadows Farm
Ashmore Heath
Ruston Hall Farm
4

Park House Farm

BIDDULPH COMMON RD

Park Head Farm
Pyat's Barn
Greenfield Farm

Biddulph Park
DINGLE LA

Meadowbank Farm
SK11
61

Long Edge Farm
Ashmore House
Hays

Park Farm
Endon Hays Farm

BIDDULPH PARK RD
Marl Sprink

Pleasant View
3

Newtown
Oxhay
Lower Oxhay

Saltsers Ford Farm

ST8
Tallash

60

Boon's Meadow Farm
Butterlands Farm

Troughstone Farm
High Bent

Halfway House
2

Higher Heath Hay

Quarry
THE HOLLANDS
ST13

Lower Heath Hay
Shirkley Wood
Porter's Farm

Spring Wood
Lower Fold Farm
Upper Shirkley

TOP RD

Beckfields Farm
Leonard's Farm
Shirkley Hall Farm
59

ROEST RD
STANWAYS LA
ELLKER LA

Rockfields Farm
UNDER THE LANE
OVER THE LANE
Broadmeadows

BEELOW LA
DALE LA
Biddulph Moor Fst Sch
PH
Taylor's Barn Farm
1

Biddulph Moor
SCHOOL LA
BACK LA
NEW ST
PARK LA
SOUTH BANK RD
Rails Farm
RUDYARD RD

WOODHOUSE LA
FAIRFIELDS
HILLSIDE
PO
CEDAR GR 1
WILLOW PL 2
HAZEL GR 3
BEECH LA 4
COTTAGE LA 5
ettlebeds Farm
GUN BATTERY
POOLES RD
DALES
STONEYFIELDS
Poolside Farm

0
91
92
58

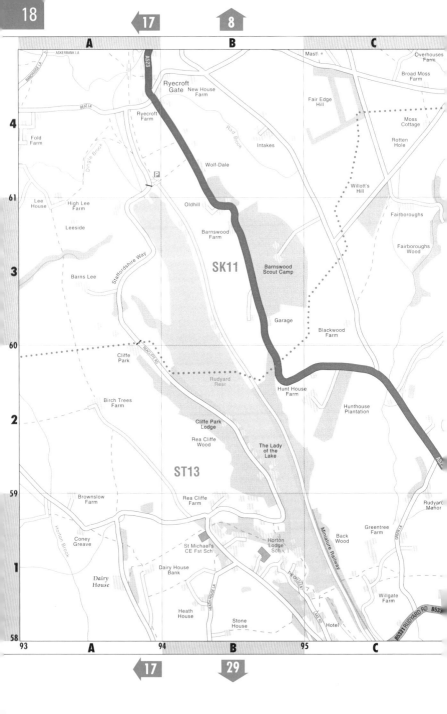

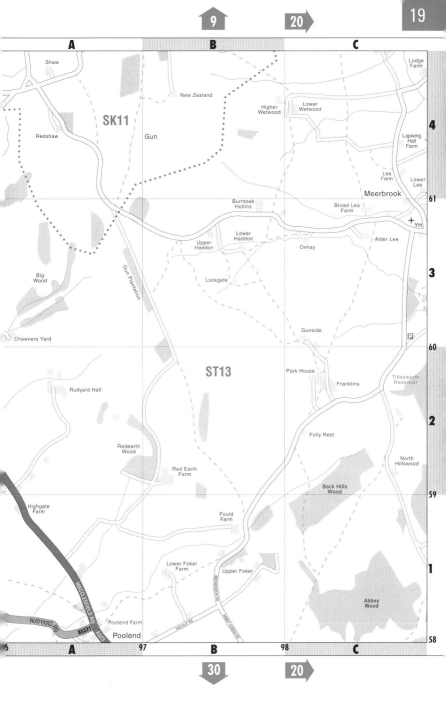

9
20

A   **B**   **C**

Shaw

Lodge Farm

New Zealand

SK11

Higher Wetwood

Lower Wetwood

4

Redshaw

Gun

Lapwing Hall Farm

Lea Farm

Lower Lee

Meerbrook

61

Burntoak Hollins

Broad Lea Farm

+ YH

Lower Haddon

Upper Haddon

Oxhay

Alder Lee

Big Wood

Gun Plantation

Lockgate

3

Chawners Yard

Gunside

60

ST13

Park House

Franklins

Tittesworth Reservoir

Rudyard Hall

2

Folly Rest

North Hillswood

Redearth Wood

Red Earth Farm

Back Hills Wood

59

Highgate Farm

Fould Farm

MACCLESFIELD RD A523

Lower Foker Farm

Upper Foker

1

MEERBROOK RD

Abbey Wood

RUDYARD RD

B5331 A523

Poolend Farm

Poolend

HIGHUP RD

FORD GREEN RD

58

A   97   **B**   98   **C**

30
20

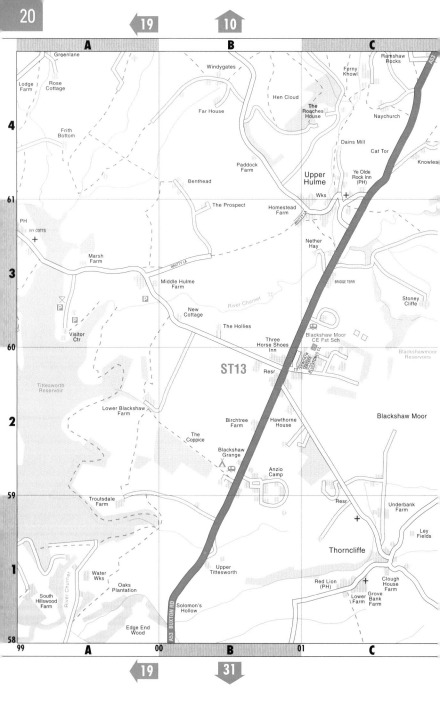

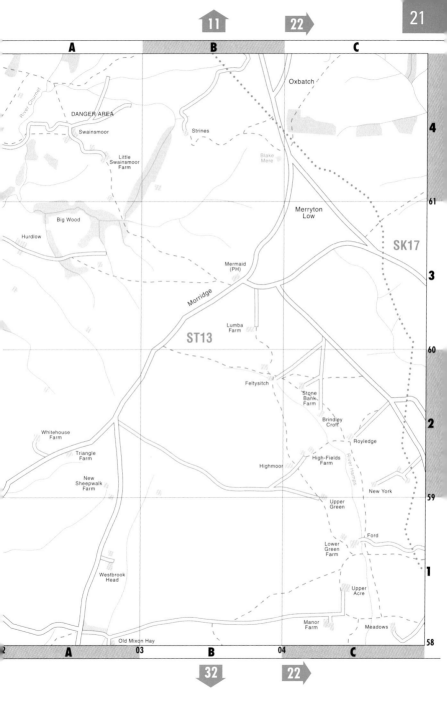

A **B** **C**

Oxbatch

River Churnet

DANGER AREA

Swainsmoor

Strines

4

Little
Swainsmoor
Farm

Blake
Mere

Merryton
Low

61

Big Wood

Hurdlow

SK17

Mermaid
(PH)

3

Morridge

Lumba
Farm

ST13

60

Feltysitch

Stone
Bank
Farm

Brindley
Croft

Whitehouse
Farm

Royledge

2

Triangle
Farm

High-Fields
Farm

Highmoor

River Hamps

New
Sheepwalk
Farm

New York

59

Upper
Green

Ford

Lower
Green
Farm

1

Westbrook
Head

Upper
Acre

Manor
Farm

Meadows

58

A 03 **B** 04 **C**

A
B
C

Sherwood
Farm

Shawfield
Wood

Shawfield

Upper Fleet
Green

Heath
Hillock

Gee's Farm

Fleet
Green

Little
Fernyford

4

Lower
Fleetgreen

Blake Brook

Lumpool
Plantation

Great
Fernyford

61

Swallowmoss
Plantation

Shawfields
Farm

Top Swallow
Moss

Cuckoostones

Upper Hay
Corner

Lum Edge

Swallow Moss

3

Herbage
Barn

SK17

60

Herbage

Averhill Side

Revidge

Forkhill
Plantation

2

Hob Hay

Manor
House

Warslow Brook

Upper
Elkstone

Moorside
Farm

59

Moorside

Cowhay
Head

WELL A

Hill
House

Mount
Pleasant
Farm

Oils
Heath

Hoarstones

1

Under the
Hill

Townhead

ST13

Ryecroft

Greenside
Farm

Lower
Elkstone

Heath
House

B5053

Sha
Sid

Little
Brownlow

Breech

58

05
A
06
B
07
C

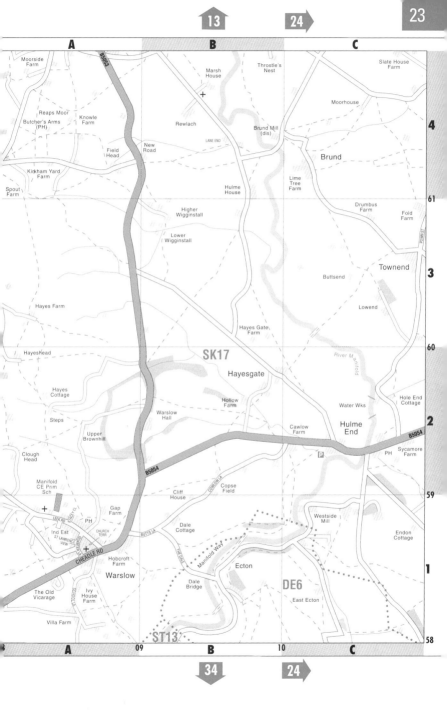

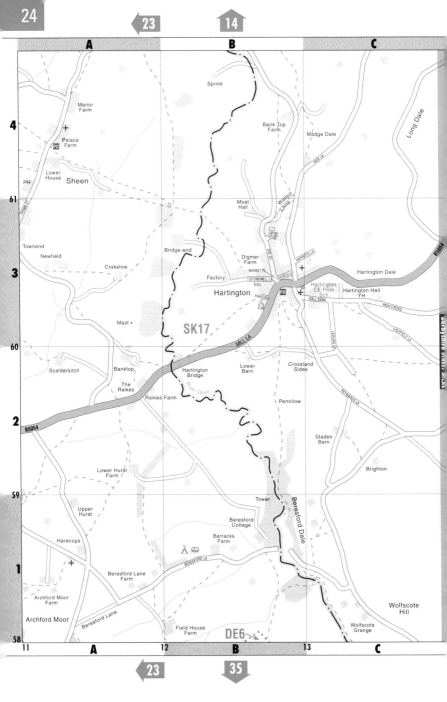

A   B   C

Sprink

Manor
Farm

Bank Top
Farm

Madge Dale

Long Dale

4

Palace
Farm

Lower
House

Sheen

PH

61

Moat
Hall

Walton Lane

B5054

Townend

Newfield

Crakelow

Bridge-end

Digmer
Farm

Hartington Dale

MARKET PL

STONEWELL LA

Factory

Inn

Hartington

Hartington
CE Prim
Sch

Hartington Hall
YH

HIGH CROSS

CHURCH ST

PARSONS

HALL BANK

HIGHFIELD LA

3

Mast

SK17

MILL LA

60

Scaldersitch

Banktop

The
Raikes

Hartington
Bridge

Raikes Farm

River Dove

Lower
Barn

Crossland
Sides

Pennilow

RICHARDS LA

Staden
Barn

Brighton

2

B5054

Lower Hurst
Farm

Tower

Beresford Dale

59

Upper
Hurst

Beresford
Cottage

Barracks
Farm

BERESFORD LA

Harecops

1

Beresford Lane
Farm

Staden
Barn

Wolfscote
Hill

Archford Moor
Farm

Archford Moor

Beresford Lane

Field House
Farm

DE6

Wolfscote
Grange

58

11   A   12   B   13   C

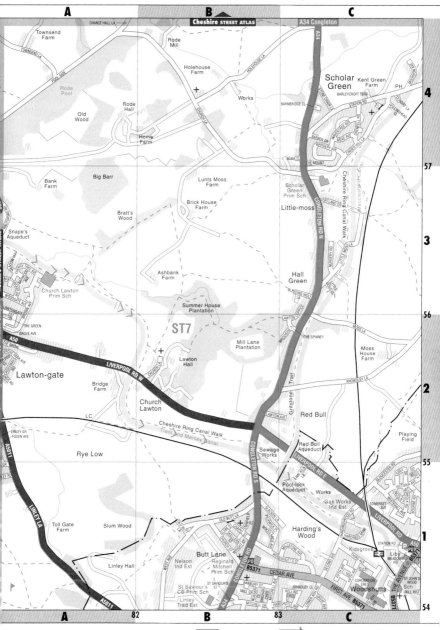

A34 Congleton

A **B** **C**

Townsend Farm

CHANCE HALL LA

TOWNSEND LA

POOL SIDE

HOLEHOUSE LA

Rode Mill

Holehouse Farm

Scholar Green

Kent Green Farm

PH

BARLEYCROFT TERR

STATION RD

Rode Pool

Old Wood

Rode Hall

CHURCH LA

Works

BARNBRIDGE CL

4

BARBER DR

MARGERY AVE

MEAD AVE

MAGE AVE

UNDER HILL LA

Home Farm

ALMA CL

THE MOUNT

57

Bank Farm

Big Barr

Lunts Moss Farm

Scholar Green Prim Sch

Little-moss

CONGLETON RD N

COURTLAND DRIVE

Cheshire Ring Canal Walk

Brick House Farm

Bratt's Wood

Snape's Aqueduct

3

Church Lawton Prim Sch

Ashbank Farm

Hall Green

BLEEDING WOLF LA

THE GREEN

GROVE AVE

Summer House Plantation

ST7

56

A50

LAWTON

WOODSOCK

THE SPINNEY

ROSE LA

Moss House Farm

LIVERPOOL RD W

Lawton Hall

Mill Lane Plantation

Gritstone Trail

KNOWLEY LA

Lawton-gate

Bridge Farm

Church Lawton

Red Bull

Playing Field

2

LC

Cheshire Ring Canal Walk
Trent and Mersey Canal

LAWTON AVE

CONGLETON RD S

LINLEY GR

FODEN AVE

Rye Low

Sewage Works

Red Bull Aqueduct

LIVERPOOL RD E

55

LINLEY LA

Pool-lock Aqueduct

Works

Gas Works Ind Est

SOMERSET AVE

LIVERPOOL RD

Toll Gate Farm

Slum Wood

OLD BUTT LA

Harding's Wood

Kidsgrove

STATION RD

Lib

PO

1

A50

Linley Hall

Nelson Ind Est

Butt Lane

Reginald Mitchell Prim Sch

CONGLETON RD

B5371

CEDAR AVE

Woodshutts

MILL RISE

A5011

St Saviour's CE Prim Sch

ST SAVIOURS ST

Linley Trad Est

BANBURY ST

HOLLINS

MITCHELL

BRINDLEY CL

FIRST AVE

B5371

54

A 82 **B** 83 **C**

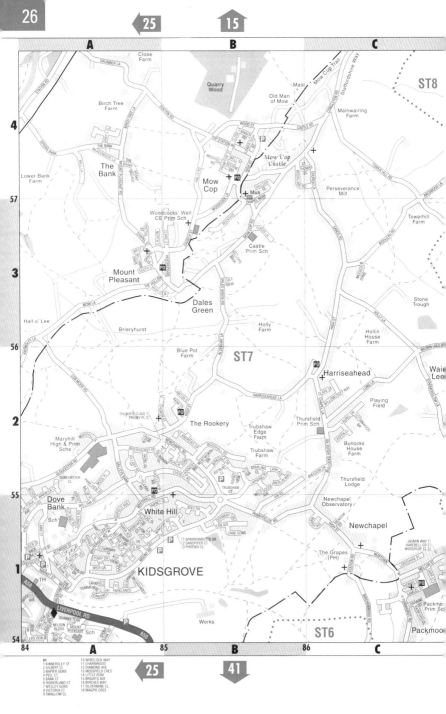

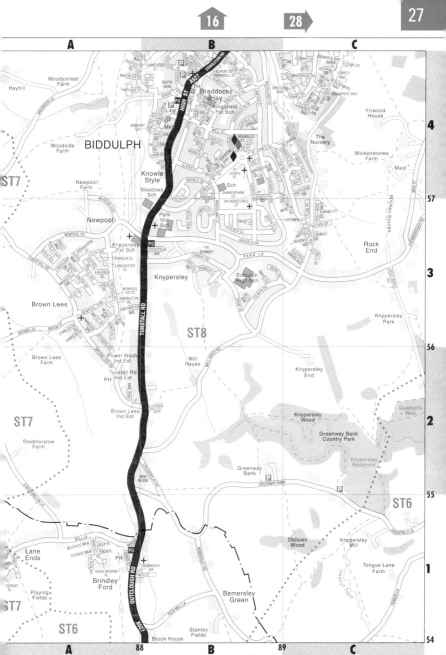

A   B   C

Moodystreet
Farm

Hayhill

Firwood
House

The
Nursery

Wickenstones
Farm

Mast

4

Woodside
Farm

BIDDULPH

ST7

Braddocks
Hay

Kingsfield
Fst Sch

Brambles
Ct

St
John's
Pl

Sch

Wickenstones
Ct

Shakespeare
Ct

Wicken Stones

57

Newpool
Farm

Knowle
Style

Meadows Sch

Rock
End

Newpool

Park Mid
Sch

Knypersley
Fst Sch

Greenfield

Knypersley Fst Sch

The
Spinney

Park La

Knypersley
Park

3

Knypersley

Newpool
Cotts

Biddulph
High Sch

Brown Lees

ST8

Brown Lees
Farm

Mill
Hayes

Knypersley
End

56

Power Wash
Ind Est

Tunstall Rd
PH Ind Est

ST7

Brown Lees
Ind Est

Victoria
Row

Knypersley
Wood

Gawton's
Well

2

Stadmorslow
Farm

Greenway Bank
Country Park

Greenway
Bank

Knypersley
Reservoir

ST6

55

ST6

Dallows
Wood

Knypersley
Mill

ST6

Lane
Ends

PH

Brindley
Ford

Tongue Lane
Farm

1

Playing
Fields

Bemersley
Green

Head of Trent

ST7

ST6

Stanley
Fields

Brook House

54

A   88   B   89   C

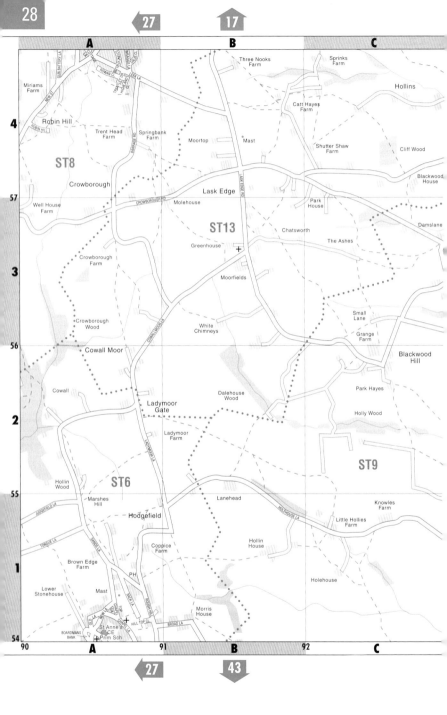

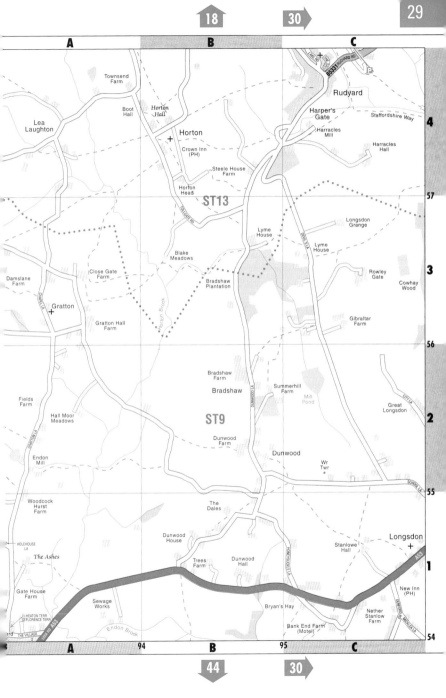

A
B
C

4

Rudyard

Townsend Farm

Boot Hall

Horton Hall

Horton

Lea Laughton

Crown Inn (PH)

Steele House Farm

Horton Head

Harper's Gate

Harracles Mill

Staffordshire Way

Harracles Hall

ST13

57

Lyme House

Longsdon Grange

Lyme House

Blake Meadows

Close Gate Farm

Damslane Farm

Bradshaw Plantation

Rowley Gate

Cowhay Wood

Gratton

3

Gratton Hall Farm

Horton Brook

Gibraltar Farm

56

Bradshaw Farm

Bradshaw

Summerhill Farm

Mill Pond

Great Longsdon

Fields Farm

Hall Moor Meadows

ST9

2

Dunwood Farm

Endon Mill

Dunwood

Wr Twr

SCHOOL LA

55

Woodcock Hurst Farm

The Dales

Dunwood House

Dunwood Hall

Stanlowe Hall

Longsdon

1

HOLEHOUSE LA

The Ashes

Trees Farm

New Inn (PH)

Gate House Farm

Sewage Works

Bryan's Hay

Nether Stanlow Farm

1 HEATON TERR
2 FLORENCE TERR

THE VILLAGE

Bank End Farm (Motel)

Endon Brook

54

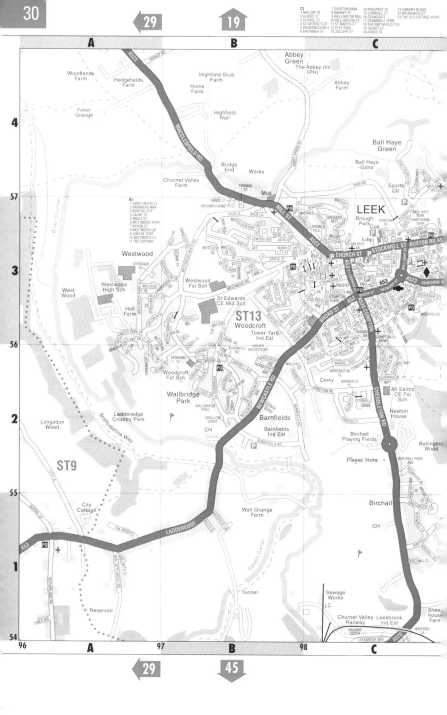

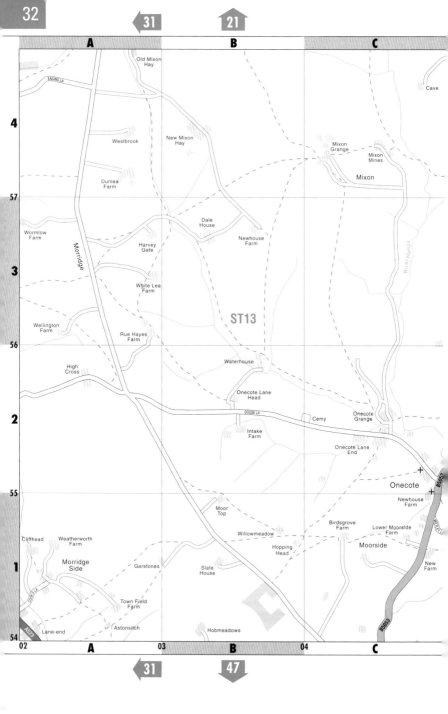

A
B
C

LASHNU LA

Old Mixon
Hay

4

Westbrook

New Mixon
Hay

Mixon
Grange

Mixon
Mines

Cave

Mixon

Dunlea
Farm

57

Wormlow
Farm

Dale
House

Newhouse
Farm

Morridge

Harvey
Gate

3

White Lea
Farm

River Hamps

Wellington
Farm

Rue Hayes
Farm

ST13

56

Waterhouse

High
Cross

Onecote Lane
Head

2

DOUSE LA

Cemy

Onecote
Grange

Intake
Farm

Onecote Lane
End

55

Moor
Top

Onecote

Newhouse
Farm

Cliffhead

Weatherworth
Farm

Willowmeadow

Birdsgrove
Farm

Lower Moorside
Farm

Moorside

Hopping
Head

1

Morridge
Side

Garstones

Slate
House

New
Farm

Town Field
Farm

Lane-end

Astonsitch

Hobmeadows

54

02

A

03

B

04

C

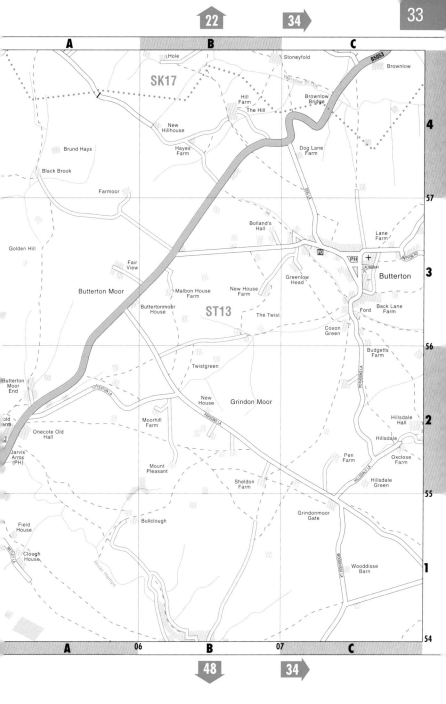

A B C

Hole
Stoneyfold
Brownlow
B5053

SK17
Warslow Brook
Brownlow
Bridge

Hill Farm
The Hill

New Hillhouse

Brund Hays

Black Brook

Dog Lane Farm

Farmoor

4

57

Bolland's Hall

Lane Farm

Golden Hill

PO

PH

Fair View

CAUSEWAY PL

Butterton

3

Butterton Moor

Malbon House Farm

New House Farm

Greenlow Head

Buttertonmoor House

ST13

The Twist

Back Lane Farm

Ford

Coxon Green

56

Budgetts Farm

Twistgreen

Butterton Moor End

New House

Grindon Moor

Hillsdale Hall

old arm

TITTERTON LA

Moorhill Farm

Hillsdale

2

Onecote Old Hall

PARSONS LA

Pen Farm

Oxclose Farm

Jarvis Arms (PH)

HILLSDALE LA

Hillsdale Green

Mount Pleasant

Sheldon Farm

55

Field House

Bullclough

Grindonmoor Gate

Clough House

River Hamps

WOODDISSE LA

Wooddisse Barn

1

54

A 06 B 07 C

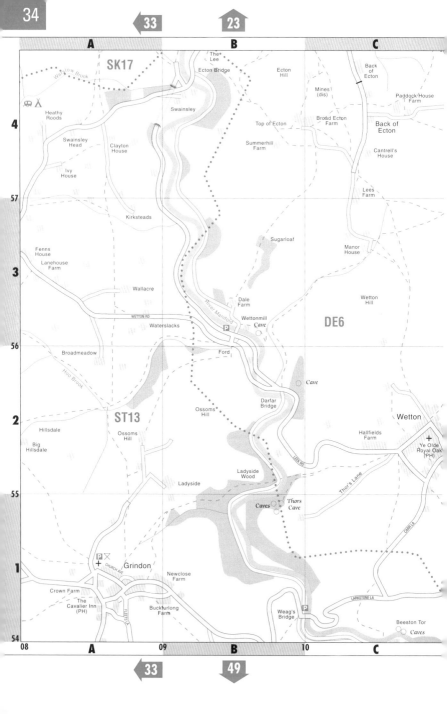

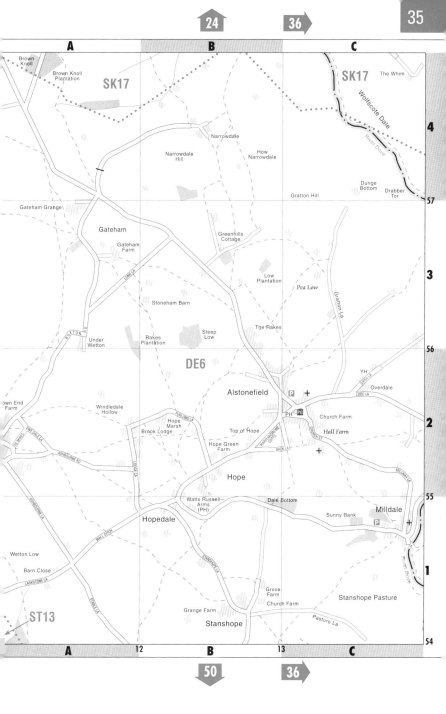

A
B
C

Brown Knoll

Brown Knoll Plantation

SK17

SK17

The Whim

Wollscote Dale

River Dove

4

Narrowdale

Narrowdale Hill

How Narrowdale

Dunge Bottom

Drabber Tor

57

Gratton Hill

Gateham Grange

Gateham

Greenhills Cottage

Gateham Farm

LONG LA

Low Plantation

Pea Low

Gratton La

3

Stoneham Barn

Under Wetton

BUXTON

Rakes Plantation

Steep Low

The Rakes

56

DE6

YH

Overdale

LODE LA

Alstonefield

P

PH

P

Church Farm

own End Farm

Windledale Hollow

FURLONG LA

Hope Marsh

Brook Lodge

Top of Hope

Hall Farm

HARDPLOW VIEW COTTS

BACK LA

CHURCH ST

2

FIVE DALE LA

ASHBOURNE RD

LODE LA

Hope Green Farm

Hope

MILLWAY LA

ASHBOURNE LA

Watts Russell Arms (PH)

Dale Bottom

Sunny Bank

Milldale

P

55

Hopedale

MILL DITCH

STANSHOPE LA

Wetton Low

Barn Close

River Dove

LARKSTONE LA

1

Grove Farm

Stanshope Pasture

STABLE LA

ST13

Grange Farm

Church Farm

Pasture La

Stanshope

54

A
12
B
13
C

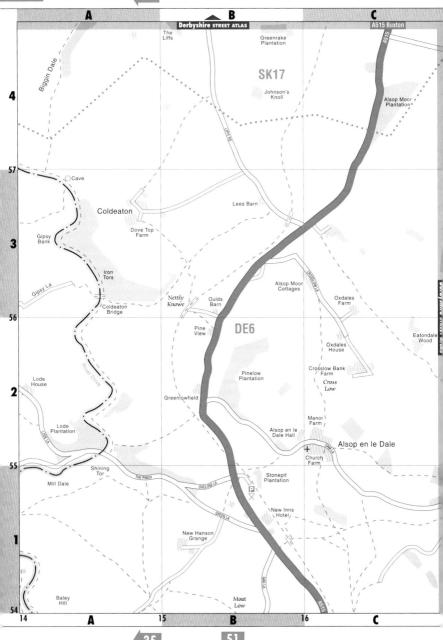

35

A

B

C

A515 Buxton

The Liffs

Greenrake Plantation

SK17

Johnson's Knoll

Alsop Moor Plantation

4

57

Cave

Coldeaton

Lees Barn

Gipsy Bank

Dove Top Farm

3

Iron Tors

Alsop Moor Cottages

Oxdales Farm

Gipsy La

Coldeaton Bridge

Nettly Knowe

Ould's Barn

DE6

56

Pine View

Oxdales House

Eatondale Wood

River Dove

Pinelow Plantation

Crosslow Bank Farm

Cross Low

Lode House

2

Greenlowfield

Lode Plantation

Manor Farm

Alsop en le Dale Hall

Alsop en le Dale

55

Shining Tor

THE PINCH

OXCLOSE LA

Church Farm

Mill Dale

Stonepit Plantation

GREEN LA

New Inns Hotel

1

New Hanson Grange

Baley Hill

Moat Low

54

14

A

15

B

16

C

35

51

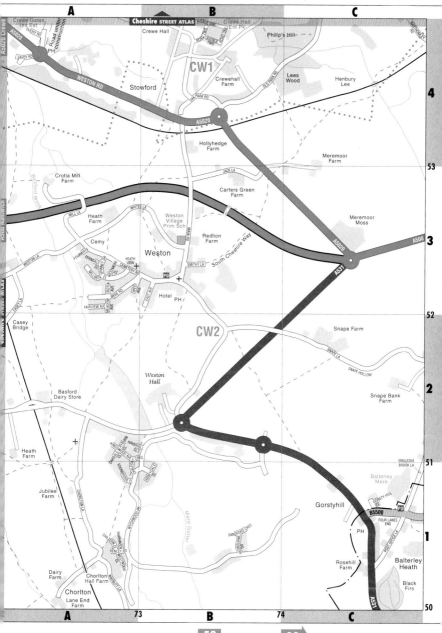

Cheshire STREET ATLAS

A | B | C

CW1

Crewe Gates Ind Est
Crewe Hall
Crewe Hall Ent Pk
Philip's Hill
DUDLEY RD
SAVOY RD
WESTON RD
A5020
PH
Stowford
Crewehall Farm
Lees Wood
Henbury Lee
OLD PARK RD
A5020
4

Hollyhedge Farm
Meremoor Farm
53

Crotia Mill Farm
JACK LA
Carters Green Farm
Meremoor Moss
MILL LA
WHITES LA
Heath Farm
Weston Village Prim Sch
South Cheshire Way
A5020
A500
3
A531

Cemy
WESTON LA
FOUNTAIN
FERNDALE
OLD RECTORY
Weston
Redlion Farm
MAIN RD
SMITHY LA
HEATH VIEW
CEMETERY RD
EAST AVE
MEADOW
PO
FAIRVIEW AVE
Hotel
PH

Casey Bridge
CASEY LA
CW2
Snape Farm
SNAPE LA
SNAPE HOLLOW
52

Basford Dairy Store
Weston Hall
Snape Bank Farm
2

Heath Farm
Mere Gutter
ENGLESEA BROOK LA
51

Jubilee Farm
CHORLTON LA
HAWKSEY
KINGSWOOD
EDERINGTON
WYCHWOOD PK
Balterley Mere
GORSTY HILL
Gorstyhill
B5500
PO
FOUR LANES END
POST OFFICE RD

Dairy Farm
Heath Farm
CHILL LA
HAREFIELD
PENDLE
OLD VICARAGE
SANDFORD CRES
PH
Rosehill Farm
Balterley Heath
Black Firs
A531
1

Chorlton Hall Farm
Chorlton
Lane End Farm

A | B | C
73 | 74

Cheshire STREET ATLAS

M6 The North West

Top End Farm

Valley Brook

LC

Walnut Tree Farm

Mill Farm

Bridge House Farm

Foxley Farm

Toad Hole Farm

4

MILL LA

Flash House

Smith Green Farm

Daisy Bank Farm

Smith's Green

RADWAY GREEN RD

New Farm

SMITHY LA

53

Monneley Farm

BARTHOMLEY RD

Cherrytree Farm

Churchfield Farm

Bluemire Farm

Motel

A500

SMITHY LA

Barthomley

RADWAY GREEN RD

White Lion (PH)

16

A500

3

Town House Farm

Englesea Brook

Old Hall Farm

HUNGERFORD PL

Glebe Farm

Valley Farm

Domvilles Wood

CW2

Bayley-Lane Farm

52

Basford Coppice

Domvilles Farm

DEANE LA

Manor Farm

Englesea-brook

ENGLESEA BROOK LA

SHADE LA

Dean Rough

The Limes Farm

Knowl End

2

Mus

Dean Brook

ST7

MARTHALL LA

FACKLEY RD

Balterley Green Farm

Spring Farm

51

Balterley Green

Mill Dale Farm

Mill Dale

B5500

Pear Tree Lake Farm

Shortfields Farm

1

Pear Tree Farm

Hall o' th' Wood

Balterley

B556

Black Mere

Bell Farm

BACK LA

Waggon and Horses (PH)

NANTWICH RD

LIMBRICK RD

50

Cheshire STREET ATLAS

Bank Top

CW2

Bradeley Rd

Lower
Foxley

Foxley

Mosshouse

Foxley
Gorse

Foxley
Farm

Eardleyend Rd

Foxley
Drumble

4

High Foxley
Farm

Wrench's
Coppice

53

Brockwood
Hill Farm

Eardleyend

Park Manor
Farm

Alsager Rd

Eardley
Hall

Brockwood Hill

The Fields

Millend

MILLEND LA

3

HULLOCK'S POOL RD

A500

Crown St

Cross
Farm

Poole
House

Hullock's
Pool

52

Brook
Farm

ST7

Great Oak
Farm

Park Lane
Farm

Sewage
Wks

Park La

Yewtree
Farm

New
Farm

Alsager Rd

Park End

Park
Farm

Bignall End Rd

2

Moat Farm

Moat La

Townhouse

Pear Tree
Farm

Ravensmead
Prim Sch

Edward St
Woods St

Bignall
End

Tibb St

Firs
Farm

Community
Ctr

Chapel St

Ravens La

B5500

New Peel
Farm

Wilbraham's Wlk

New Rd

Watlands

51

Raven's La

Kent Hill
Farm

Church Rd

St James St

Liby

Mckellin Cl
Boyles Hall Rd

Younger's Rd
Gresley Way

Westlands

Barthomley Rd

Peel Hollow

Audley

Dean Hollow

Chapel
St

Hillside Cres

Cherry Tree Rd 1
Cedar Cres 2
Wedgewood Ave 3

The Quarry

Hartwich Rd

Wereton

Westfield Rd

Lemon Gdns
Edge Dr

New King St

Queen St

King St

Mellard St

Heath Ave

Grang.y Green La

1

Boon Hill Rd

Hawthorne Ave

Grange
Farm

Boon
Hill

Old Peel
Farm

B5367

Camb La

Quarry New
Farm

Shraleybrook

Greenbutts
House

Rye
Hills

Ryehill
Farm

Ryehills

Rye Hills

Wood Lane
Prim Sch

50

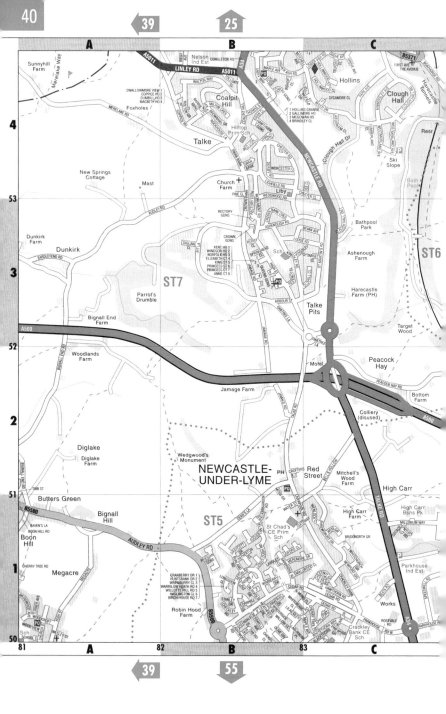

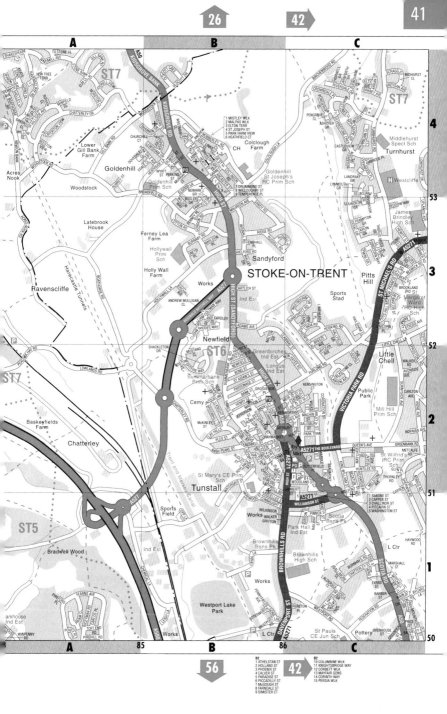

A   B   C

SHAKESPEARE   TILSTONE CL
YEW TREE TERR   ST7
KIDSGROVE BANK

4

Acres Nook   Lower Gill Bank Farm   Goldenhill   Woodstock   CHURCHILL CT   Goldenhill Prim Sch   PO   1 MISTLEY WLK
2 MAS WLK
3 ELTON TERR
4 ST JOSEPH ST
5 PARK FARM VIEW
6 HEATHFIELD CT   Colclough Farm   CH   ST7

Goldenhill St Joseph's RC Prim Sch   Middlehurst Specl Sch   Turnhurst
H Westcliffe

Latebrook House   BROADFIELD RD   7 DRUMMOND ST
8 WILLOUGHBY ST
9 TEMPERENCE PL   James Brindley High Sch   53

Ravenscliffe   Ferney Lea Farm   Hollywall Prim Sch   Holly Wall Farm   Sandyford   STOKE-ON-TRENT   Pitts Hill   Margaret Ward RC High Sch   Brodkand Rd   3

Harecastle Tunnels   Works   BARTLETT ST   Ind Est   ANDREW MULLIGAN   Sports Stad   Little Chell

Newfield   ST6   ADAMS AVE   52

P   Baskeyfields Farm   Chatterley   SHACKLETON DR   LOWLANDS RD   Greenbirches Ind Est   Longus Ind Est   Public Park   Mill Hill Prim Sch

ST7   Summerbank Prim Sch   Cemy   KENSINGTON   2

McKINLEY ST   JEFFERSON   St Wilfrid's RC Prim Sch

HAYMARKET   SALISBURY ST   1 RABONE ST
2 CAPPER ST
3 CHALLINOR ST
4 PITCAIRN ST
5 WASHINGTON ST   51

A527   St Mary's CE Prim Sch   Tunstall   A5271 THE BOULEVARD   Scotia Bsns Pk

ST5   Bradwell Wood   Sports Field   Ind Est   WILKINSON ST   WALKER ST   GRIFTON ST   Park Hall Ind Est   Brownhills Bsns Pk   Brownhills High Sch   L Ctr   MARSHALL   1

Works   Works   BRERETON PL   Pottery   OVERHOUSE   50

arkhouse Ind Est   FEARNS AVE   Westport Lake Park   Works   L Ctr   St Pauls CE Jun Sch

WINPENNY RD   PIREHILL RD   85   DANEBRIDGE ST   86   A5271

A   B   C

B2
1 ATHELSTAN ST
2 HOLLAND ST
3 PHOENIX ST
4 CALVER ST
5 PARADISE ST
6 PICCADILLY ST
7 McGOUGH ST
8 FARNDALE ST
9 SIMISTER CT

B2
10 COLUMBINE WLK
11 KNIGHTSBRIDGE WAY
12 CORBETT WLK
13 MAYFAIR GDNS
14 CORINTH WAY
15 PERSIA WLK

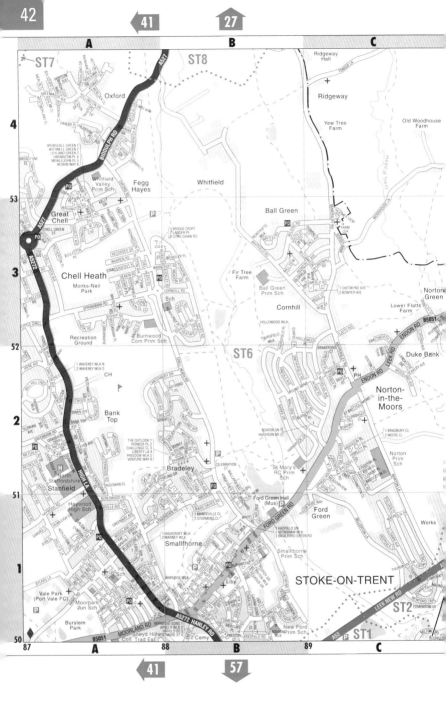

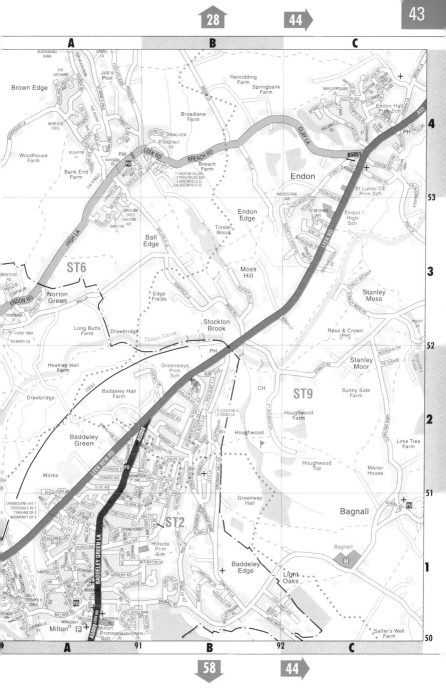

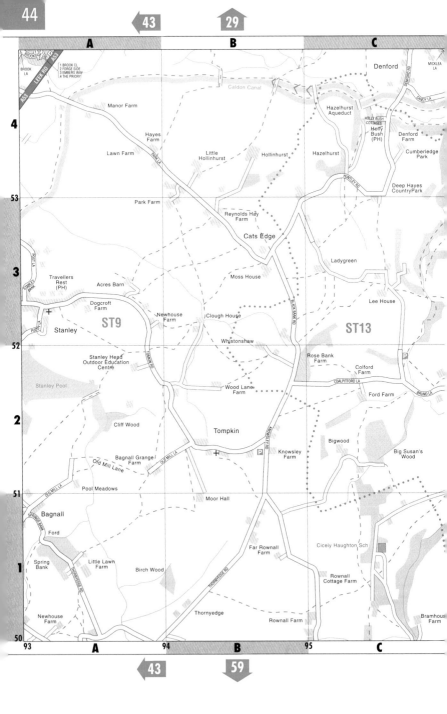

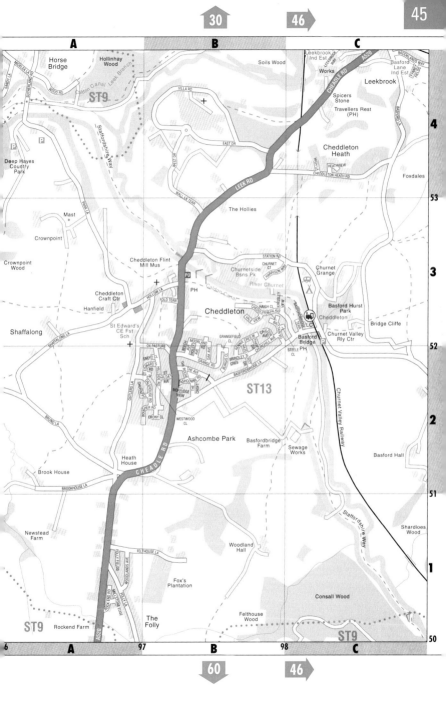

A   B   C

Horse Bridge
Hollinhay Wood
Soils Wood
Leekbrook Ind Est
Works
Basford Lane Ind Est
MUCK FALL LA
SANDY LA
SUTHERLAND
WOOD RD
Caldon Canal   Leek Branch
ST9
Staffordshire Way
VILLA RD
CHEADLE RD
A520
BACKLANDS WAY
Leekbrook
BEDFORD RD
Spicers Stone
Travellers Rest (PH)

P
P
Deep Hayes Country Park
P
POST LA
EAST DR
WEST DR
LEEK RD
WALL LA TERR
Cheddleton Heath
HIGH LA
HEATHVIEW
CHEDDLETON HEATH RD
Foxdales

4

53

Mast
Crownpoint
Crownpoint Wood
Cheddleton Flint Mill Mus
The Hollies
STATION RD
CHURNET CT
HARRISON RD
Churnetside Bsns Pk
River Churnet
Churnet Grange
Churnet Grange

3

Cheddleton Craft Ctr
Hanfield
Shaffalong
St Edward's CE Fst Sch
OX PASTURE
SHAFFALONG LA
MILLSIDE LA
FOLD TERR
Caldon Canal
PH
P.O
PH
Cheddleton
HAIGH CL
CTRL VIEW
KINGSLEY RD
ETRURIA AVE
GRANGEFIELD CL
DEANE CL
RAVE
Basford Hurst Park
Cheddleton
Bridge Cliffe
Churnet Valley Rly Ctr

52

MOORLAND
GRANGEFIELD CL
GRANGE CRES
THE JINNY
BRINDLEY
CL
DALE
PH
Basford Bridge
STEELE CL
Basfordbridge
LC

BRUNO LA
OSTLERS LA
SNEYD'S CL
LEONARD'S RD
HILLSIDE RD
ST HILDA'S AVE
CHAPEL LA
WALKER RD
CRONY CL
ASHCOMBE
MOORSIDE VIEW
THE DRIVE
THE GROVE
WESTWOOD CL
ST13
Ashcombe Park
Basfordbridge Farm
Sewage Works
BASFORDBRIDGE LA
Basford Hall

2

Heath House
CHEADLE RD
Brook House
BROOKHOUSE LA

51

Newstead Farm
FELTHOUSE LA
FOLLY FIELDS
Woodland Hall
Shardloes Wood
Staffordshire Way

1

ST9
A520
Rockend Farm
NURSERY CL
OAK LA
MILLSTONE EDGE
GRACE LA
Fox's Plantation
The Folly
Felthouse Wood
Consall Wood
ST9

6   97   98   50

A   B   C

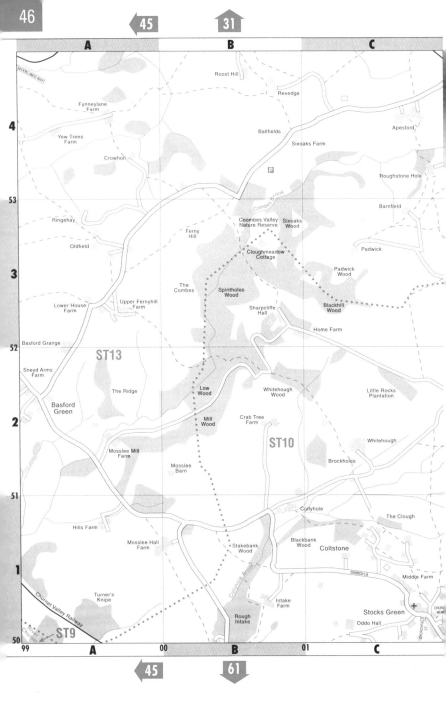

WOODLANDS WAY

Roost Hill

Revedge

Fynneylane Farm

Apesford

4

Yew Trees Farm

Ballfields

Sixoaks Farm

Crowholt

Roughstone Hole

P

53

Combes Brook

Barnfield

Ringehay

Coombes Valley Nature Reserve

Sixoaks Wood

Ferny Hill

Padwick

Oldfield

Cloughmeadow Cottage

Padwick Wood

3

The Combes

Spiritholes Wood

Lower House Farm

Upper Fernyhill Farm

Sharpcliffe Hall

Blackhill Wood

Home Farm

52

Basford Grange

ST13

Sneyd Arms Farm

The Ridge

Low Wood

Whitehough Wood

Little Rocks Plantation

Basford Green

2

Mill Wood

Crab Tree Farm

ST10

Whitehough

Mosslee Mill Farm

Mosslee Barn

Brockholes

51

Collyhole

The Clough

Hills Farm

Blackbank Wood

Mosslee Hall Farm

Stakebank Wood

Coltstone

CHURCH LA

1

Turner's Knipe

Middle Farm

Churnet Valley Railway

Intake Farm

Stocks Green

CHURCH MDW

ST9

River Churnet

Rough Intake

Coltbrook Brook

Oddo Hall

CHURCHFIELD CT

50

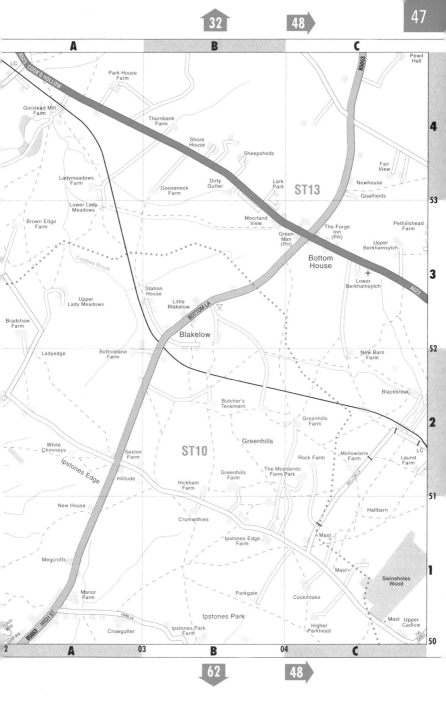

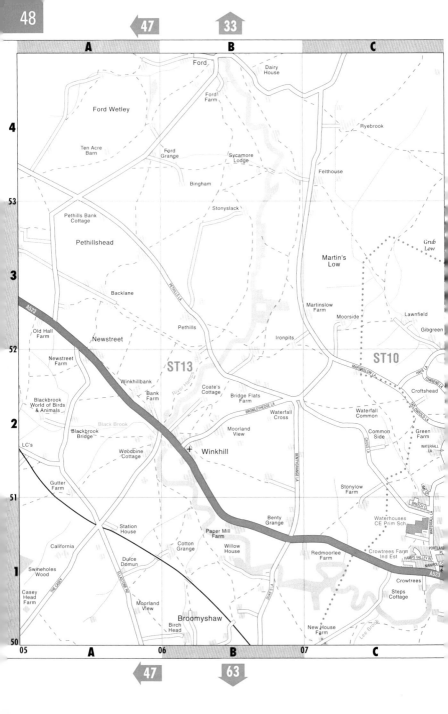

A   B   C

4

Ford

Dairy House

Ford Wetley

Ford Farm

Ten Acre Barn

Ford Grange

Sycamore Lodge

Ryebrook

Felthouse

Bingham

53

Pethills Bank Cottage

Stonyslack

Grub Low

Pethillshead

Martin's Low

3

Backlane

Martinslow Farm

Moorside

Lawnfield

Gibgreen

Pethills

Ironpits

ST10

Old Hall Farm

Newstreet

52

Newstreet Farm

MARLMOLLOW LA

Croftshead

Winkhillbank

Bank Farm

Coate's Cottage

Bridge Flats Farm

Blackbrook World of Birds & Animals

Waterfall Cross

Waterfall Common

2

Blackbrook Bridge

Black Brook

BROMLEYHEDGE LA

Moorland View

Common Side

Green Farm

WATERFALL LA

LC's

Woodbine Cottage

Winkhill

51

Gutter Farm

Stonylow Farm

Waterhouses CE Prim Sch

Station House

California

Benty Grange

Paper Mill Farm

Cotton Grange

Willow House

Redmoorlee Farm

Crowtrees Farm Ind Est

HAMPS VALLEY RD

A523

1

Swineholes Wood

Dulce Domun

Moorland View

Crowtrees

Casey Head Farm

Broomyshaw

Birch Head

New House Farm

Steps Cottage

Lee Brook

50

05   A   06   B   07   C

A   B   C

Manor Farm
Weag's Barn
Beeston Tor Farm
River Manifold
ST13
Mayfurlong
Oldpark Hill
Deepdale Farm
Soles Coppice
4
Deepdale
The Lows
Old Soles Wood
Oldfields Farm
53

River Hamps
Soles Hill
Soles Hollow
Mere Hill
Throwley Hall
3
Hell Hole
Throwley Moor
DE6
Manifold Way
Throwleymoor Farm
Waterfall Low
Back o' th' Brook
52
Redwayclose Barn
Little Wood
Woodhead Farm
Throwley Cottage
Ford
RACE LA
Red Lion Inn (PH)
Lee House
Hole Shades
2
Pike Low
TATLOWFOLD LA
Pikelow Farm
Sparrowlee
Waterfall
PIKELOW LA
Sparrowlee Bridge (foot)
Farwall
Cart Low
Slade House
51
The Flatts
Lamber Low
FARWALL LA
FieldHouse Farm
Pitchings Farm
WHITELEES LA
BOGGSTER LA
NFIELD
1
Waterhouses
Calton
BACK LA
Calton Green
Caldon Mill
The Budds
STONY LA
PO
BACK LA
Ye Olde Crown Hotel
A523
DOGMOOR LA
GREEN LA
50

3   A   09   B   10   C   50

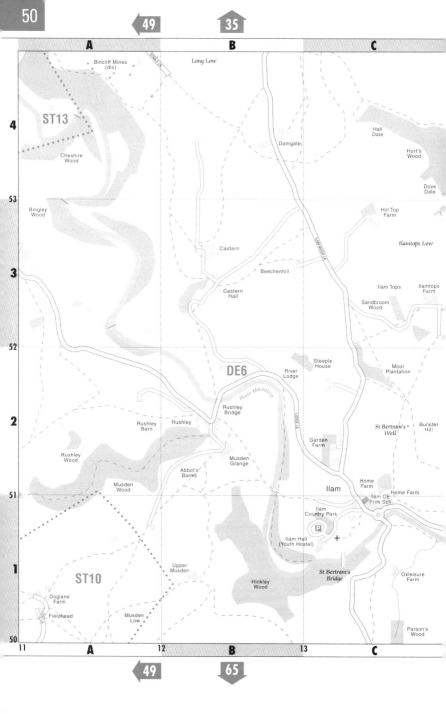

A   B   C

Bincliff Mines
(dis)

Long Low

STYLE LA

ST13

4

Cheshire
Wood

Hall
Dale

Hurt's
Wood

Damgate

Dove
Dale

53

Bingley
Wood

Hill Top
Farm

Castern

Ilamtops Low

Beechenhill

3

CASTERN LA

Castern
Hall

Ilam Tops

Ilamtops
Farm

Sandbroom
Wood

52

DE6

Steeple
House

Moor
Plantation

River Lodge

River Manifold

Rushley
Bridge

St Bertram's
Well

Bunster
Hill

2

Rushley
Barn

Rushley

LODGE LA

Garden
Farm

Rushley
Wood

Musden
Grange

Home
Farm

Abbot's
Banks

Ilam

Home Farm

51

Musden
Wood

Ilam CE
Prim Sch

Ilam
Country Park

P

Ilam Hall
(Youth Hostel)

+

1

ST10

Upper
Musden

St Bertram's
Bridge

Oxleisure
Farm

Hinkley
Wood

Doglane
Farm

Fieldhead

Musden
Low

Parson's
Wood

50

11   A   12   B   13   C

A   B   C

4

49

3

Cheshire STREET ATLAS

48

CW5

2

47

1

46

72   A   73   B   74   C

West Heath
The Elms
A531
MAIN RD
CW2
The Anchorage
WAYBUTT LA
Doddlespool Hall
DODDLESPOOL BARNS
Doddlespool Farm
Buddileigh
Elmer Riddings
The Slum

Swan Brook

Betley Common
Mere Gutter
Oak Tree Farm
COMMON LA
Green Valley Farm

WRINEHILL RD
Half Moon Farm
Gonsley Green Farm
Gonsley Cottages
Blakenhall Moss
Coppice Bank
Lower Den Farm

Manor Farm
Betley Mere

DEN LA
CW3
Higher Den Farm
Den Bridge
Cracow Moss

West View
Blakenhall
MILL LA
New Farm
Yew Tree Farm
Ash Tree Farm
Fog Cottages
Hayes Farm
Blakenhall Farm
Dairy Farm
Bunkers Hill

Shaw's Rough
Ash Coppice
Randilow Farmhouse
Grange Farm
Checkley Brook
Checkley Brook Farm
The Coppice
Checkley Bridge
CHECKLEY LA
Checkley Hall
Checkley
Little Meadow

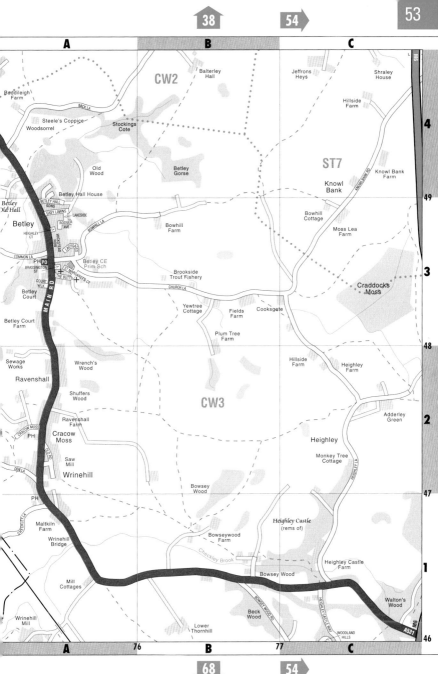

CW2

Balterley
Hall

Jeffrons
Heys

Shraley
House

M6

Baddileigh
Farm

BACK LA

Hillside
Farm

Steele's Coppice

Woodsorrel

Stockings
Cote

4

Old
Wood

Betley
Gorse

ST7

Knowl Bank
Farm

KNOWL BANK RD

Betley Hall House

Knowl
Bank

49

Betley
Old Hall

BETLEY HALL
GDNS

EASY LAWNS

LAKESIDE

RODGER
AVE

Betley

HEIGHLEY
CT

BOWHILL LA

WHITCHURCH RD

LADY LA

Bowhill
Farm

Bowhill
Cottage

Moss Lea
Farm

COMMON LA

PH PO

BRASSINGTON
ST

Betley CE
Prim Sch

ST MARGARET'S CT

Brookside
Trout Fishery

MAIN RD

COURT
WALK

THE BUTTS

CHURCH LA

3

Craddocks
Moss

Betley
Court

Yewtree
Cottage

Fields
Farm

Cooksgate

Betley Court
Farm

Plum Tree
Farm

48

Sewage
Works

Wrench's
Wood

Hillside
Farm

Heighley
Farm

Ravenshall

Shuffers
Wood

CW3

Adderley
Green

Ravenshall
Farm

CRACOW MOSS

2

Cracow
Moss

PH

Heighley

DEN LA

OLD RD

Saw
Mill

Monkey Tree
Cottage

Wrinehill

47

PH

Bowsey
Wood

CHECKLEY LA

Maltkiln
Farm

Heighley Castle
(rems of)

Wrinehill
Bridge

Bowseywood
Farm

Checkley Brook

Heighley Castle
Farm

HEIGHLEY CASTLE WAY

1

Bowsey Wood

BOWSEY WOOD RD

Mill
Cottages

Walton's
Wood

A531 M6

Wrinehill
Mill

Lower
Thornhill

Beck
Wood

WOODLAND
HILLS

46

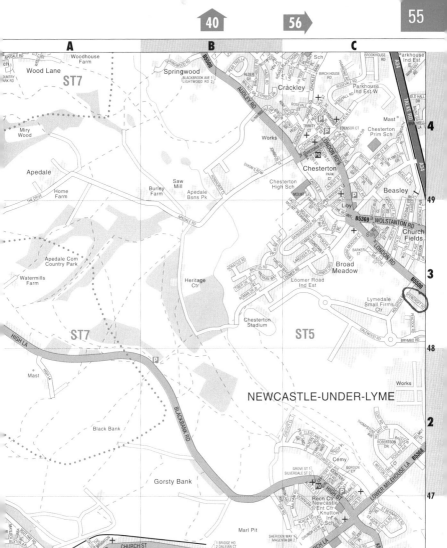

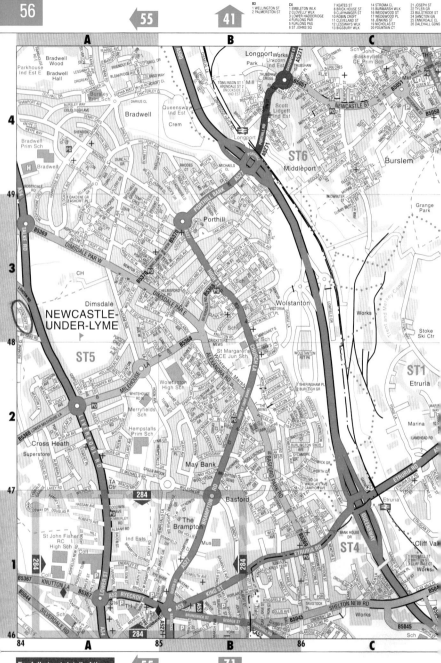

55

41

B3
1 WELLINGTON ST
2 PALMERSTON ST

C4
1 EMBLETON WLK
2 CLOVELLY WLK
3 LOWER HADDERIDGE
4 FURLONG PAR
5 FURLONG PAS
6 ST JOHNS SQ

7 KEATES ST
8 BRICK HOUSE ST
9 CLAYHANGER ST
10 ROBIN CROFT
11 CLEVELAND ST
12 LESSWAYS WLK
13 BIGSBURY WLK

14 STROMA CL
15 BURMARSH WLK
16 WEDGWOOD ST
17 WEDGWOOD PL
18 JENKINS ST
19 NICHOLAS ST
20 FOUNTAIN CT

21 JOSEPH ST
22 TYLER GR
23 BULSTRODE ST
24 SANCTON GN
25 ENNERDALE CL
26 DALEHALL GDNS

Longport Works
Unicorn Ind Est

ST6
Middleport

Burslem

Grange Park

Porthill

NEWCASTLE-
UNDER-LYME
ST5

Dimsdale

Wolstanton

Stoke Ski Ctr

ST1
Etruria

Cross Heath
Superstore

Marina

May Bank

Basford

ST4

The Brampton

St John Fisher
RC
High Sch

Cliff Vale
Works

Etruria

KNUTTON LA

284

55

71

For full street detail of the
highlighted area see page 284.

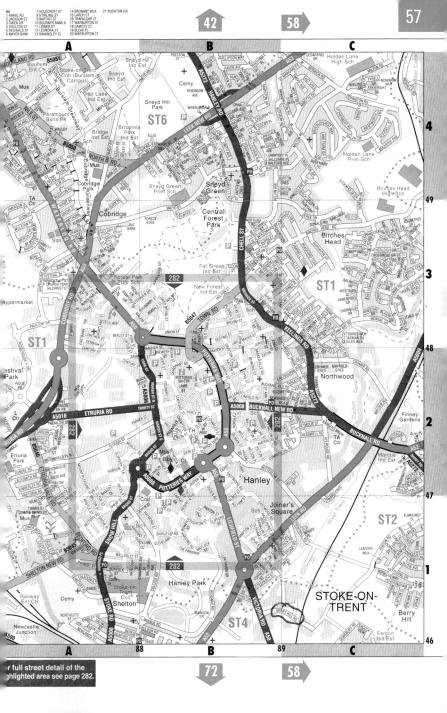

57
43

STOKE-ON-TRENT

ST2

ST1

ST3

Jack Hayes

Jack Hayes Farm

Greenfields Farm

Carmounthead

Woodhead

Mast

Kerry Hill Farm

Kerry Hill

Works

Carmountside

Cemy

Crem

Abbey Farm

PH

Carmountside Prim Sch

Holehouse Farm

Moorside Farm

Wetley Moor

Abbey Hulton

Little Eaves

Firtree Farm Nursery

Abbey Hill Specl Sch

Eaves La

Great Eaves

Launders Bank

Brookhouse Wood

Heath View

Blackfriars F Ed Unit

Bucknall

Bucknall

Hanley Hayes Farm

Bucknall Park

Townsend Prim Sch

Werrington Rd

Mulliner Cl

Stewart's Farm

Ash Hall

Ash Bank

Brookhouse

Mitchell High Sch

Ash Bank Rd

Ash Way

Townsend

Simfields

Eaton Park Prim Sch

Bentilee

Duddy Rd

Sundorne

Berry Hill Greenway

Berry Hill High Sch

Liby

Dereham Way

Widow Fields Farm

Berry Hill

Ubberley

Ford Hayes

A5009

Leek Rd

A52

A5272

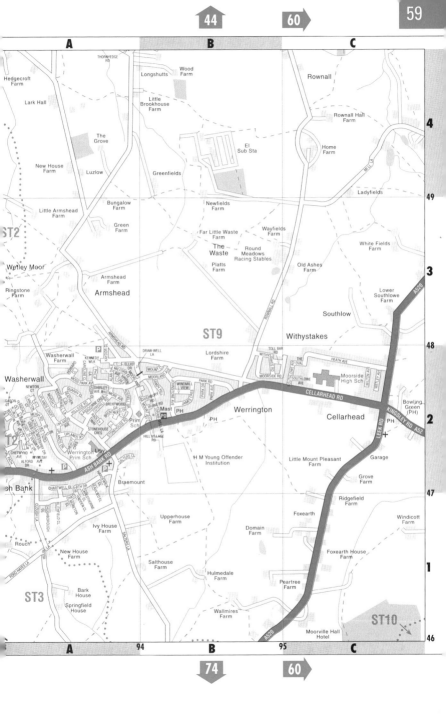

A
B
C

THORNYEDGE RD

Hedgecroft Farm

Longshutts
Wood Farm

Rownall

Lark Hall

Little Brookhouse Farm

4

Rownall Hall Farm

The Grove

El Sub Sta

New House Farm

Luzlow

Greenfields

Home Farm

Ladyfields

49

Little Armshead Farm

Bungalow Farm

Newfields Farm

ST2

Green Farm

Far Little Waste Farm

Wayfields Farm

White Fields Farm

Wetley Moor

The Waste

Round Meadows Racing Stables

Old Ashes Farm

3

Ringstone Farm

Armshead Farm

Platts Farm

Lower Southlowe Farm

Armshead

Southlow

A520

ST9

Withystakes

Washerwall Farm

DRAW-WELL LA

Lordshire Farm

KENNEDY WLK

MOUNT

TOLL BAR RD

WITHYSTAKES RD

48

P

Washerwall

MOORLAND

WINDMILL VIEW

MOORSIDE RD

THE OVAL

SOUTHLOWE RD

HEATH AVE

WHITLEY AVE

Moorside High Sch

Bowling Green (PH)

NEWTON

SHIRLEY AVE

PARK RD

PARK AVE

JAMES CRES

CELLARHEAD RD

Cellarhead

2

T2

BRENTWOOD

Werrington

LEEK RD

PH

Prim Sch

Mast

PO

PH

Garage

KINGSLEY RD A52

PH

HILL VILLAGE RD

Little Mount Pleasant Farm

Werrington Prim Sch

Liby

P

ASH BANK RD

P

H M Young Offender Institution

Grove Farm

CHARTWELL CL

FRITH DR

Braemount

Ridgefield Farm

47

sh Bank

Foxearth

Windicott Farm

Rouch

New House Farm

Upperhouse Farm

Ivy House Farm

Domain Farm

SALTERS LA

Foxearth House Farm

1

RODD MERES LA

Salthouse Farm

Bark House

Hulmedale Farm

Peartree Farm

ST3

Springfield House

Wallmires Farm

ST10

A520

Moorville Hall Hotel

46

A
94
B
95
C

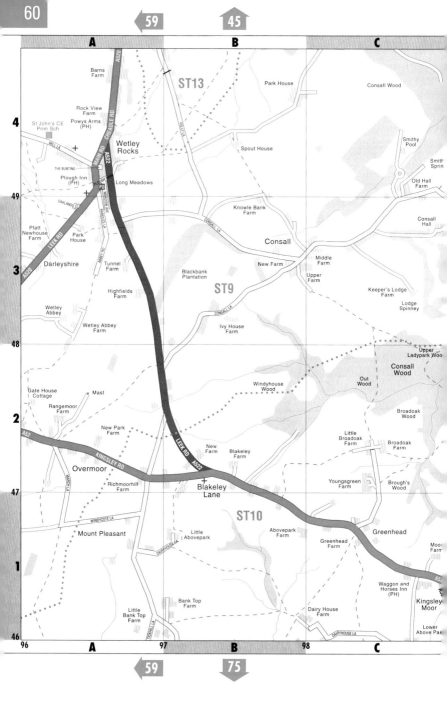

A
B
C

Consall
Wood
ST13
Chase
Wood
Coalpit
Wood
Belmont Farm
Belmont
Hall
Hay
House
Heath House
Farm
Noonsun
Common
BELMONT RD

Staffordshire Way
E2

Ash
Sprink
Price's
Cave
Stones
Farm

4

Consallforge
PH
Devil's
Staircase
Crowgutter
Wood

49

Consall
Lawn Farm
ST9
Glenwood
House
Booth's Hall
Farm
Booth's
Wood

Wildacres
Lawn
Wood
Flint
Mill
Booth's
Wood
Caldon Canal
Ruelow
Wood

3

Consall Nature
Park
Churnet Valley Railway
River Churnet
Far Kingsley
Banks
Cherryeye
Bridge

Lower Ladypark
Wood
Hazles
Hazles
Wood

48

Hollins
Wood
Hazlescross
Coldlea
Farm
Churnet
Valley Wildlife
Sanctuary

HOLLINS LA
Staffordshire Way
E2
Bank
Sprink

2

Hollins
ST10

Church Gorse
Farm
Breach
Farm
Hallcroft
Wks
HAZLESCROSS
Kingsley
Wks
A52

THE GREEN
HIGH ST
CROSS ST 1
CHAPEL ST 2
NEWHALL ST 3
HOLT LA
PO
DOVEDALE RD
47

Kingsley Moor
Farm
Duke's
Plantation
Barnfields
Farm
St Werburgh's
CE Prim Sch

VICTORIA
COTTS
HASTE
HILL LA
HOLT LA

1

Kingsley
Moor

Hazlewall
Barn
Waste
Wood
Highcroft
Rookery
SHAWE PARK RD
BURTON CRES
PH
46

9
A
00
B
01
C

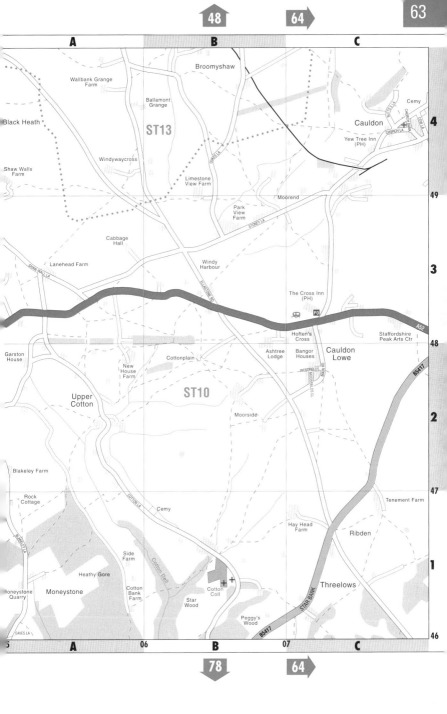

A   B   C

Broomyshaw

Wallbank Grange
Farm

Ballamont
Grange

Cemy

ST13

Cauldon

Black Heath

Yew Tree Inn
(PH)

4

Windywaycross

Shaw Walls
Farm

Limestone
View Farm

Moorend

49

Park
View
Farm

STONEY LA

Cabbage
Hall

SHAW WALLS LA

Lanehead Farm

Windy
Harbour

3

The Cross Inn
(PH)

FLASHING RD

PO

Staffordshire
Peak Arts Ctr

A52

Garston
House

Hoften's
Cross

48

Cotton plain

Ashtree
Lodge

Bangor
Houses

Cauldon
Lowe

B5417

New House
Farm

WESTFIELDS

MOORFIELDS CL

2

ST10

Moorside

Upper
Cotton

Blakeley Farm

47

Rock
Cottage

Tenement Farm

COTTON LA

Cemy

Hay Head
Farm

Ribden

BLAKE LA

Side
Farm

1

Heathy Gore

Cotton Dell

STAR BANK

Threelows

Moneystone
Quarry

Moneystone

Cotton
Bank
Farm

Cotton
Coll

Star
Wood

Peggy's
Wood

EAVES LA

B5417

46

A   06   B   07   C

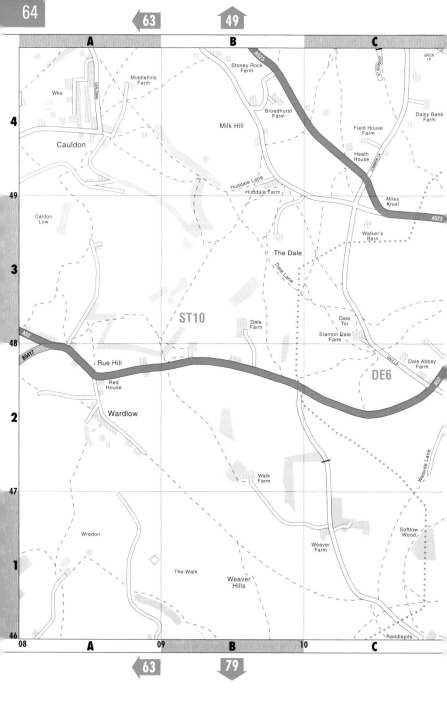

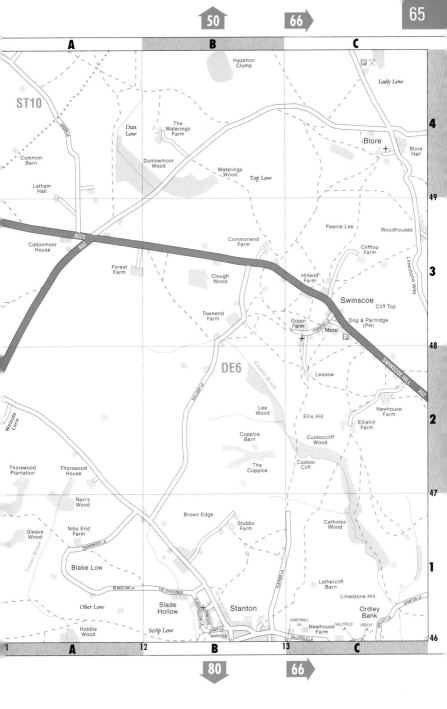

A
B
C

ST10

Hazelton Clump

Lady Low

Dun Low

The Waterings Farm

Dunlowmoor Wood

Waterings Wood

Top Low

Blore

Blore Hall

4

Common Barn

Latham Hall

49

A523

A52

Commonend Farm

Feenie Lee

Woodhouses

Clifftop Farm

Limestone Way

Caltonmoor House

Forest Farm

Clough Wood

Hillend Farm

Swinscoe

Cliff Top

3

Townend Farm

Green Farm

TOWNEND LA

Motel

Dog & Partridge (PH)

P

SWINSCOE HILL

A52

48

DE6

Ellishill Brook

Leasow

Newhouse Farm

2

Welside Lane

BELGREY LA

Lee Wood

Ellis Hill

Ellishill Farm

Coppice Barn

Cuckoocliff Wood

The Coppice

Cuckoo Cliff

Thorswood Plantation

Thorswood House

47

Nan's Wood

Brown Edge

Stubbs Farm

Catholes Wood

Gleave Wood

Nibs End Farm

THORSWOOD LA

Tinsell Brook

Blake Low

Latherdiff Barn

Limestone Hill

STANTON LA

1

BLAKELOW LA

THE STITCHINGS

CROFT LA

PARK LANE

CHAFF LA

FLAXFIELD LA

Ober Low

Slade Hollow

Stanton

Ordley Bank

ORDLEY LA

ORDLEY

Hobble Wood

Scrip Low

MARSH LA

HONEYWALL LA

Newhouse Farm

SALLYFIELD LA

SALLYFIELD LA

46

A
B
C

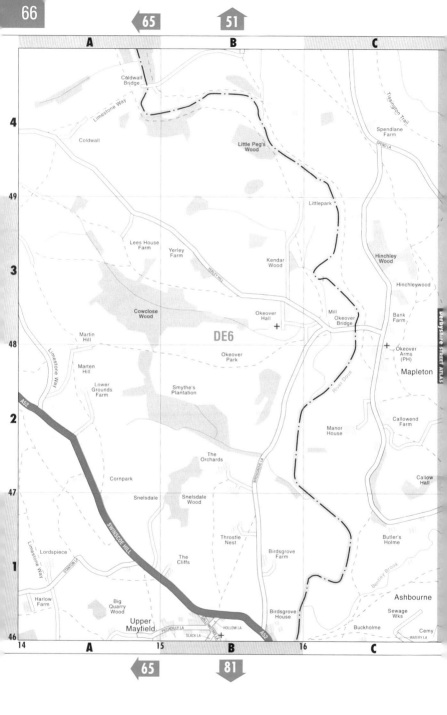

A   B   C

4

49

3

48

2

47

1

46

14   A   15   B   16   C

Derbyshire Street Atlas

Caldwall Bridge

Limestone Way

Coldwall

Little Peg's Wood

Tissington Trail

Spendlane Farm

SPEND LA

Littlepark

Lees House Farm

Yerley Farm

YERLEY HILL

Kendar Wood

Hinchley Wood

Hinchleywood

Cowclose Wood

Okeover Hall

Mill
Okeover Bridge

Bank Farm

DE6

Martin Hill

Okeover Park

Okeover Arms (PH)

Mapleton

Limestone Way

Marten Hill

Lower Grounds Farm

Smythe's Plantation

River Dove

A52

Manor House

Callowend Farm

BRIDGE HILL LA

The Orchards

Cornpark

Callow Hall

SWINSCOE HILL

Snelsdale

Snelsdale Wood

Throstle Nest

Birdsgrove Farm

Butler's Holme

Bentley Brook

Ashbourne

Limestone Way

STANTON LA

Lordspiece

The Cliffs

Sewage Wks

Harlow Farm

Big Quarry Wood

Upper Mayfield

PICCADILLY LA

SLACK LA

DEAD TREE

HOLLOW LA

A52

Birdsgrove House

Buckholme

Cemy

WATERY LA

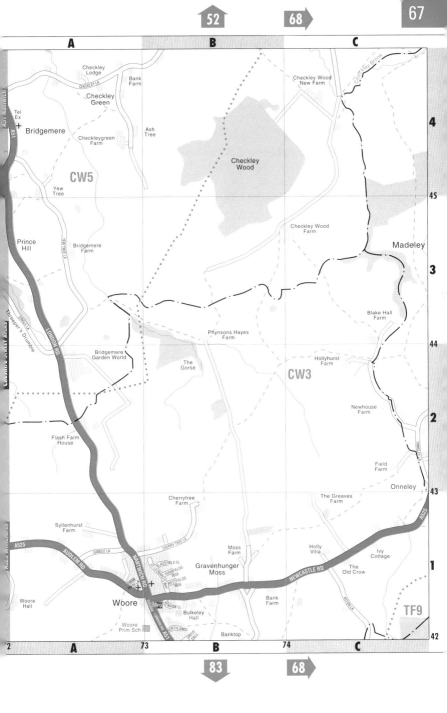

A
B
C

Checkley
Lodge

Bank
Farm

CHECKLEY LA

Checkley
Green

Ash
Tree

Checkley Wood
New Farm

Checkley Brook

Tel
Ex

Bridgemere

Checkleygreen
Farm

Checkley
Wood

4

A51 NANTWICH

CW5

Yew
Tree

45

Prince
Hill

Bridgemere
Farm

YEW TREE LA

Checkley Wood
Farm

Madeley

LONDON RD

3

DOBELL LA

Blake Hall
Farm

Thrasher's Drumble

Bridgemere
Garden World

Phynsons Hayes
Farm

Hollyhurst
Farm

44

CW3

The
Gorse

Newhouse
Farm

2

Flash Farm
House

ONNELEY LA

Field
Farm

Onneley

43

A525

Cherrytree
Farm

The Greaves
Farm

Syllenhurst
Farm

CHERRY TREE LA

A525

Holly
Villa

Ivy
Cottage

1

AUDLEM RD

CANDLE LA

NANTWICH RD

Moss
Farm

Gravenhunger
Moss

NEWCASTLE RD

The
Old Crow

ASPEN LA

BLAZEFIELD CL
FARMFIELDS RISE
WESTFIELDS RISE

Woore
Hall

Woore

A51

Bulkeley
Hall

Bank
Farm

TF9

Woore
Prim Sch

BRICK CL

ORCHARD CRES

Banktop

A525

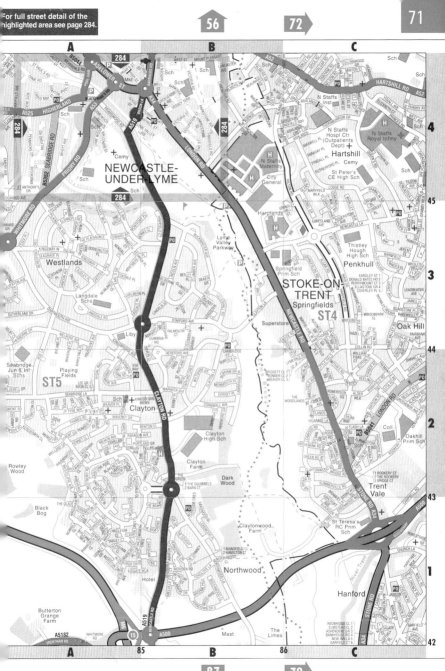

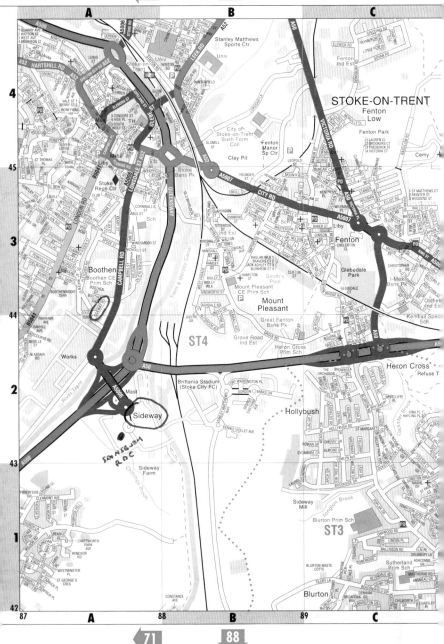

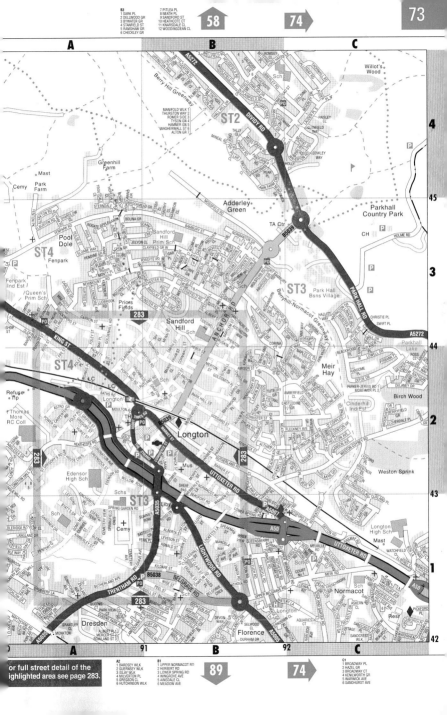

B3
1 SARK PL
2 DELLWOOD GR
3 BYWATER GR
4 STANFIELD ST
5 RAMSHAW GR
6 CHECKLEY GR
7 PITLEA PL
8 NEATH PL
9 SANDFORD ST
10 HEATHCOTE CT
11 KNARSDALE CL
12 WOODINGDEAN CL

58
74

4

45

3

44

2

43

1

42

A2
1 BARDSEY WLK
2 GUERNSEY WLK
3 ISLAY WLK
4 MILVERTON WLK
5 GREGSON CL
6 HUTCHINSON WLK

B1
1 UPPER NORMACOT RD
2 HERBERT RD
3 LOWER SPRING RD
4 WINGROVE AVE
5 AINSDALE CL
6 MEADOW WAY

89
74

C1
1 BROADWAY PL
2 HAZEL GR
3 BROADWAY CT
4 KENILWORTH GR
5 WARWICK AVE
6 SANDHURST AVE

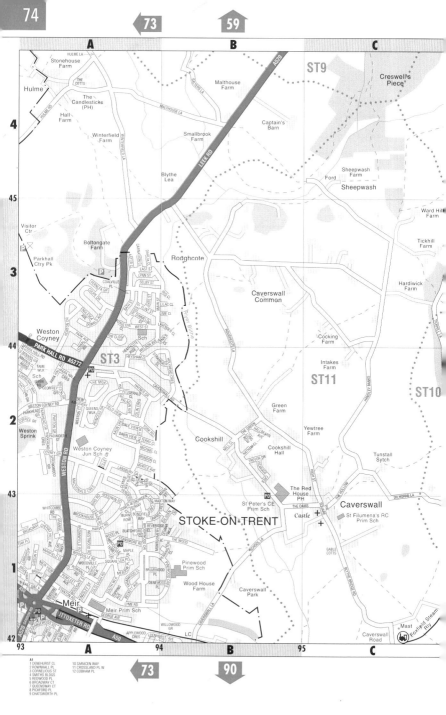

ST9

Creswell's Piece

Stonehouse Farm

HULME LA

THE COTTS

Hulme

The Candlesticks (PH)

Malthouse Farm

MALTHOUSE LA

Captain's Barn

Hall Farm

Winterfield Farm

Smallbrook Farm

4

Blythe Lea

Sheepwash Farm

Ford

Sheepwash

Ward Hill Farm

45

Visitor Ctr

Tickhill Farm

Parkhall Ctry Pk

Bottongate Farm

Roughcote

Hardiwick Farm

3

Caverswall Common

River Blithe

Weston Coyney

44

ST3

Cocking Farm

PARK HALL RD A5272

Intakes Farm

ST11

ST10

Weston Coyney Jun Sch

Green Farm

Yewtree Farm

2

Weston Sprink

WESTON RD

Cookshill

Cookshill Hall

Tunstall Sytch

43

The Red House PH

Caverswall

St Peter's CE Prim Sch

Castle

St Filumena's RC Prim Sch

STOKE-ON-TRENT

Pinewood Prim Sch

GABLE COTTS

1

The Square

Briarwood

Wood House Farm

Meir Prim Sch

Caverswall Park

Mast

Foxfield Steam Rly

Meir

ITTOXETER RD

A50

GEORGE AVE

CRESSWALL LA

LC

Caverswall Road

42

93

94

95

A

B

C

A1
1 DENEHURST CL
2 ROWNHALL PL
3 CORNELIOUS ST
4 SMITHS BLDGS
5 REDWOOD PL
6 BROADWAY CT
7 QUEENSWAY CT
8 PICKFORD PL
9 CHATSWORTH PL

10 SARACEN WAY
11 CROSSLAND PL W
12 COBHAM PL

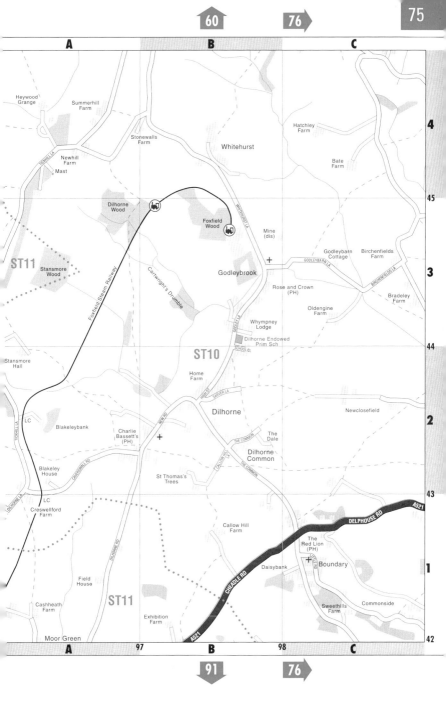

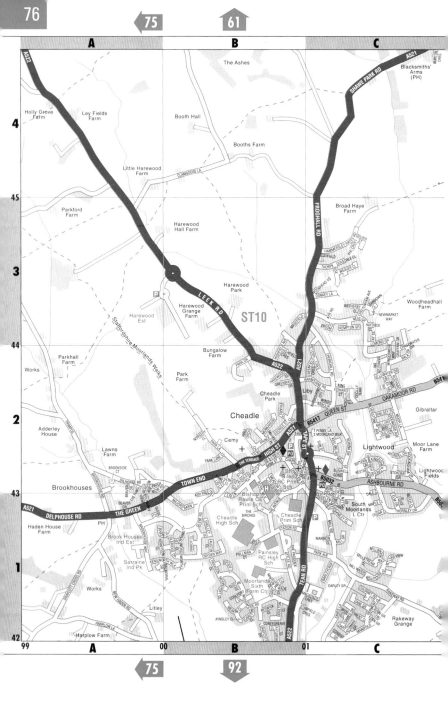

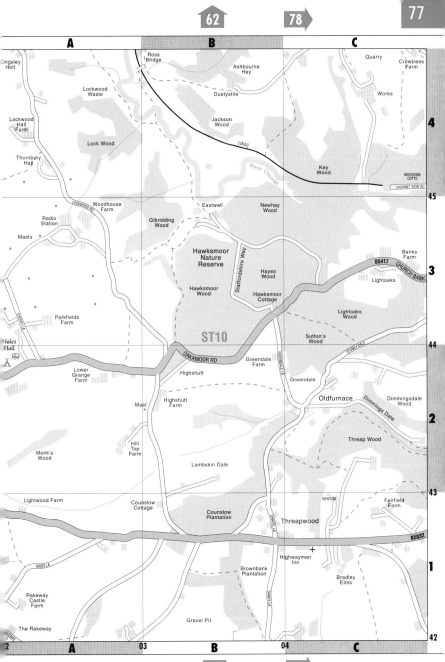

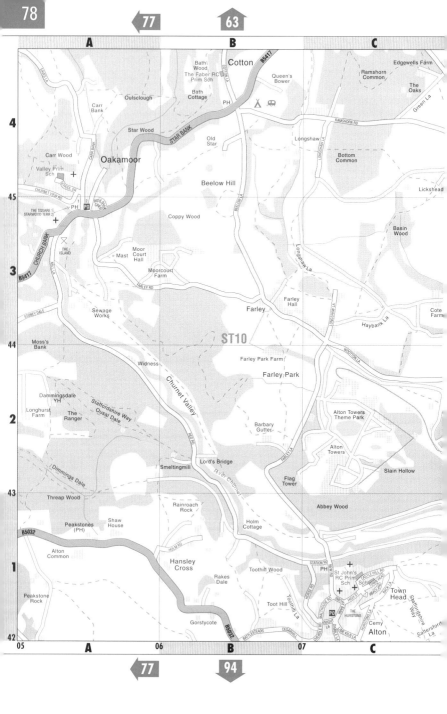

A B C

Sycamore Farm

Ramshorn

RAMSHORN RD

Gander Well

Uplands Farm

Eid Low Farm

4

Weaver Lane

Gidacre Lane

HALL LA

Wootton

HALL LA

Delbert

45

Parkside

icks Wood

Eid Low

Ridding Side

Delbert Farm

DE6

Wootton Park

Banks Farm

Canada Lake

Eid Low Plantation

THE AVENUE

PARKGATE LA

Parkgate

3

44

ST10

Lower Grounds Farm

WOOTTON LA

Holly Wood

Wootton Lodge

HAYA LA

Brookleys

WASTE LA

Plumpton Banks Plantation

Brookleys Lake

Waste Wood

Waste Farm

Alton Park

P

WESTHOUSE LA

MARSH LA

2

Alton Towers Hotel

Green Lane

43

Park Banks

Ina's Rock

Sand Pit

Paul's Lane

ST14

BROOMHILLS LA

LITTLEFIELD LA

Churnet Valley

River Churnet

Hole Brook

Crumpwood Farm

HENDING LA

Prestwood

BOGMILL LA

CHELTWOOD LA

1

Fargelow

affordshire Way

42

A 09 B 10 C

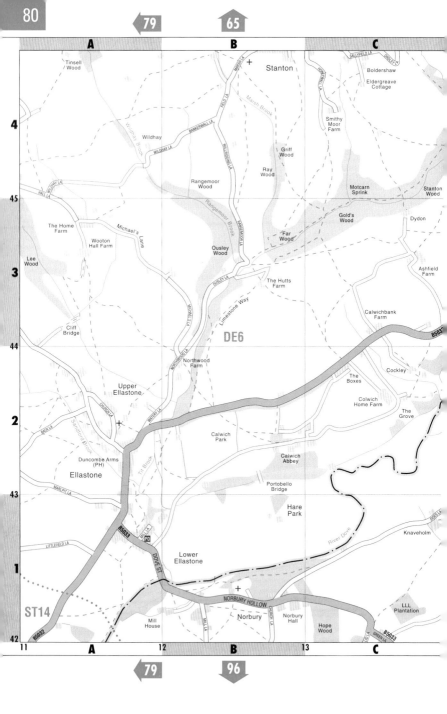

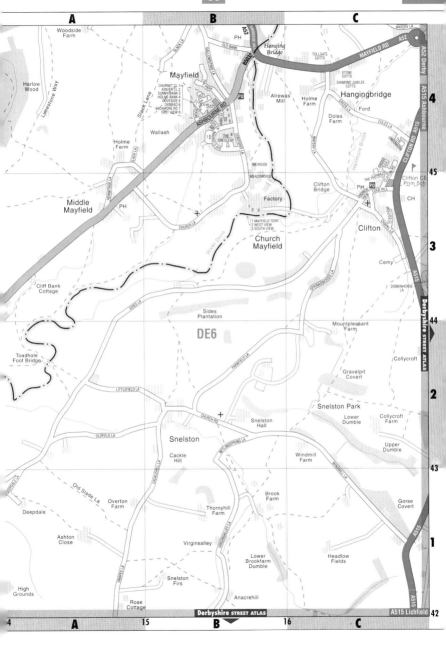

A B C

Woodside Farm

Harlow Wood

Limestone Way

A52

PH

OLD BANK

GALLOWSTREE LA

SLACK LA

Mayfield

CHURNET CL 1
KINVER CL 2
SUNNYBANK 3
HOLME BANK 4
DOVESIDE 5
OXMEAD 6
SYCAMORE RD 7
ERST VIEW 8

Slack Lane

THE PARK

Wallash

Holme Farm

SLACK LA

HERMITAGE LA

Middle Mayfield

PH

ASHBOURNE RD

PO

SCH

THE CRESCENT

CHURCH LA

River Dove

WEIRSIDE

MEADOWSIDE

Factory

1 MAYFIELD TERR
2 WEST VIEW
3 SOUTH VIEW

Church Mayfield

Cliff Bank Cottage

SIDES LA

Sides Plantation

DE6

Toadhole Foot Bridge

LITTLEFIELD LA

OLDFIELD LA

Snelston

Cackle Hill

Old Slade La

Deepdale

Overton Farm

Ashton Close

High Grounds

Rose Cottage

OLDFIELD LA

DAKERS LA

COCKSHEAD LA

Snelston Firs

Thornyhill Farm

CHURCH RD

FAIRFIELD LA

Snelston Hall

MILL LINDSPRING LA

Virginsalley

Anacrehill

Brook Farm

Lower Brookfarm Dumble

Windmill Farm

WINDMILL LA

Hanging Bridge

B5032

TOLLGATE COTTS

MAYFIELD RD

STONE COTTS

DIAMOND JUBILEE COTTS

Hangingbridge

Alrewas Mill

Holme Farm

Ford

Doles Farm

DOLES LA

GREENLANE

Hinmore Brook

Clifton Bridge

SPRINGWOOD LA

PH

PO

Clifton CE Prim Sch

COCK HILL

CH

Clifton

Cemy

DOBBINHORSE LA

Mountpleasant Farm

Collycroft

Gravelpit Covert

Snelston Park

Lower Dumble

Collycroft Farm

Upper Dumble

Gorse Covert

Headlow Fields

A52

WATERY LA

A52 Derby

A515 Ashbourne

A515 Old Hill Rd

Clifton Rd

A515

Derbyshire STREET ATLAS

A515

A515 Lichfield

Derbyshire STREET ATLAS

4

15

B

16

C

42

1

2

43

44

3

45

4

66

81

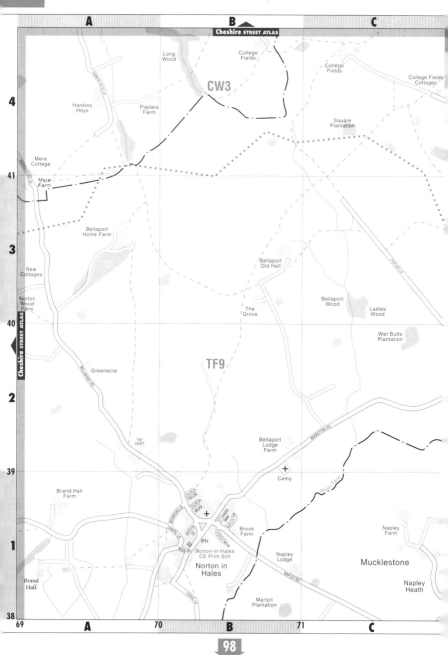

A **B** **C**

4

CW3

Long Wood

College Fields

College Fields

College Fields Cottages

Hankins Heys

Poplars Farm

Square Plantation

41

Mere Cottage

Mere Farm

Bellaport Home Farm

3

Bellaport Old Hall

New Cottages

Norton Wood Farm

The Grove

Bellaport Wood

Ladies Wood

40

Wet Butts Plantation

TF9

Greenacre

2

THE CROFT

Bellaport Lodge Farm

BEARSTONE RD

River Tern

39

Brand Hall Farm

Cemy

CHURCH FIELDS

CHURCH WLKS

Napley Farm

1

PH

Brook Farm

Napley

Norton-in-Hales CE Prim Sch

Mucklestone

Brand Hall

Main Rd

Norton in Hales

Napley Lodge

NAPLEY RD

Napley Heath

Marlpit Plantation

38

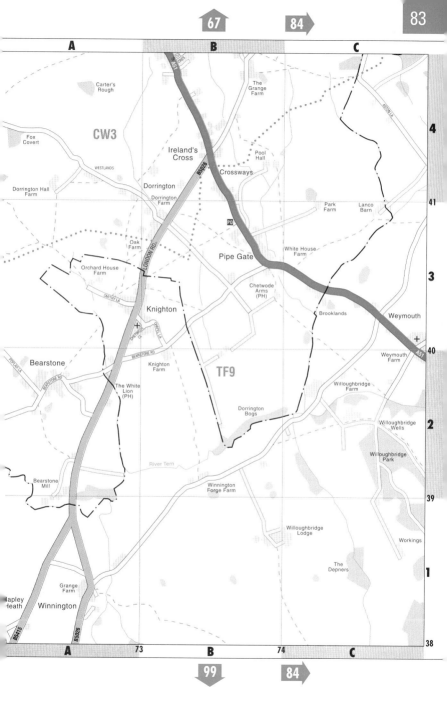

A
B
C

4

Carter's
Rough

The
Grange
Farm

BASTON LA

Fox
Covert

CW3

Ireland's
Cross

Pool
Hall

WESTLANDS

Crossways

41

Dorrington

B5026

Dorrington Hall
Farm

Dorrington
Farm

Park
Farm

Lanco
Barn

PO

Oak
Farm

LONDON RD.

White House
Farm

Pipe Gate

3

Orchard House
Farm

Chetwode
Arms
(PH)

SMITHY LA

Brooklands

Weymouth

Knighton

CHETWODE

DIMSELLA

+

Bearstone

BEARSTONE RD.

+

40

POPLAR LA

Weymouth
Farm

Knighton
Farm

TF9

BEARSTONE RD.

The White
Lion
(PH)

Willoughbridge
Farm

Dorrington
Bogs

Willoughbridge
Wells

2

Willoughbridge
Park

River Tern

39

Bearstone
Mill

Winnington
Forge Farm

Willoughbridge
Lodge

Workings

Grange
Farm

The
Depners

1

apley
Heath

B6415

B5026

Winnington

A
73
B
74
C
38

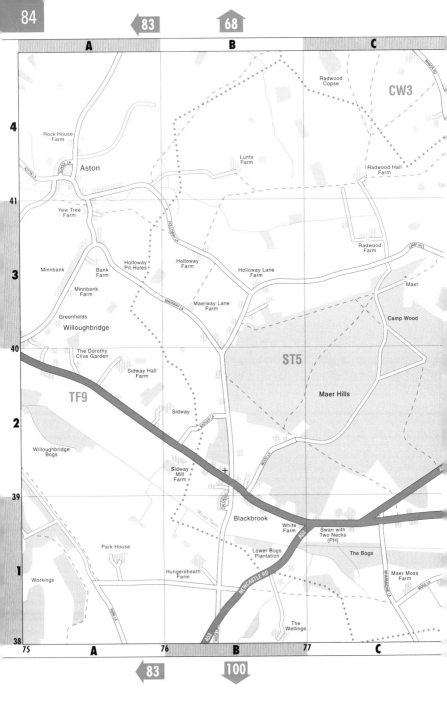

83
68

A
B
C

4

Rock House
Farm

Aston

Lunts
Farm

Radwood
Copse

CW3

Radwood Hall
Farm

41

Yew Tree
Farm

ASTON LA

HOLLOWAY LA

Radwood
Farm

CAMP HILL

3

Minnbank

Bank
Farm

Holloway
Pit Holes

Holloway
Farm

Holloway Lane
Farm

Mast

Minnbank
Farm

MAERWAY LA

Maerway Lane
Farm

Camp Wood

Greenfields

Willoughbridge

40

The Dorothy
Clive Garden

ST5

Sidway Hall
Farm

Maer Hills

TF9

Sidway

BADGER LA

2

Willoughbridge
Bogs

WOOD LA

Sidway
Mill
Farm

+

39

River Tern

Blackbrook

White
Farm

Swan with
Two Necks
(PH)

A53

The Bogs

Park House

Lower Bogs
Plantation

1

Workings

Hungersheath
Farm

NEWCASTLE RD

Maer Moss
Farm

WHARMADINE LA

MOSS LA

PARK LA

A53

ROCK LA

The
Wellings

38
75
A
76
B
77
C

83
100

A
B
C

CW3

Moat Wood

Whitmore Wood

Limepits

Hillside Lodge

Hillside Farm

4

Madeley Park Farm

Snapehall Farm

Whitmore Heath

PARK WOOD DR
EASTWOOD RISE
WILL WOOD
MANOR GLADE

41

Madeley Park Wood

BIRCH TREE LA
SNAPE HALL RD
HEATH RD

A53
QUARRY LA
PH

Swallow Hill

Whitehouse Wood

New House Farm

White House

The Hill

The Old Rectory

Coney Greave

3

amp Hall

Slymansdale

Shropshire's Wood

ST5

COMMON LA
CONEY GREAVE LA
APPLETON DR

PH
PO

SNAPE HALL

MANOR RD

HOLLY BUSH LA

MS MEADOW WAY
SANDOLES
DALE
MOSS LA
HERON WAY
GRANGE WAY
WHITFIELD
WHITE BRIDGE
CASTLE CROFT
FAIRVIEW
FAIRWEW RD

Baldwin's Gate CE Prim Sch

40

Maer Hills

Red Hill

Berry Hill

Baldwin's Gate

Chorlton Moss

Moss Farm

Works

Bungalow Farm

2

WESSON LA
KEMP LA

War Hill

Hill Chorlton

A51

Berth Hill Fort

Maerfield Gate Farm

39

Coombe's Rough

COOMBE LA

Little Lane

Broughton Plantation

1

HADDON LA

Maer Pool

Maer Hall

Maer

The Old Rectory

TF9

The Ridding

Bates Farm

38

A
B
C

4

41

3

40

2

39

1

38

Holbrook's Wood

A5182

A53

New Hayes Farm

Rook Hall Farm

A5182

TRENTHAM RD

Acton Hall Farm

Acton

Whitmore Hall

The Rookery

Whitmore

A53

Actonhill Farm

Model Farm

WHEEL LA

Little Paddocks

Hobgoblin Gate

Hanchurch Hills

Newhouse Farm

ST5

Hanchurch Heath

HARLEY THORN LA

Swynnerton Old Park

Water Tower

Hanchurch Hills Circular Wlks

BENT LA

Shelton under Harley Farm

ST4

DIMS LA

Byatt's Common

Cloud End

Shelton under Harley

Keepers Cottage

Springfields

Harley Thorns

Nursery Common

Stableford Bridge

Cock Inn (PH)

A51

Stableford

Common Lane

STABLEFORD BANK

Rowe Farm

The Rowe

Hatton Common

ST21

Hatton Rough

Little Lane

Bluebell Bank

A51

81
82
83

A
B
C

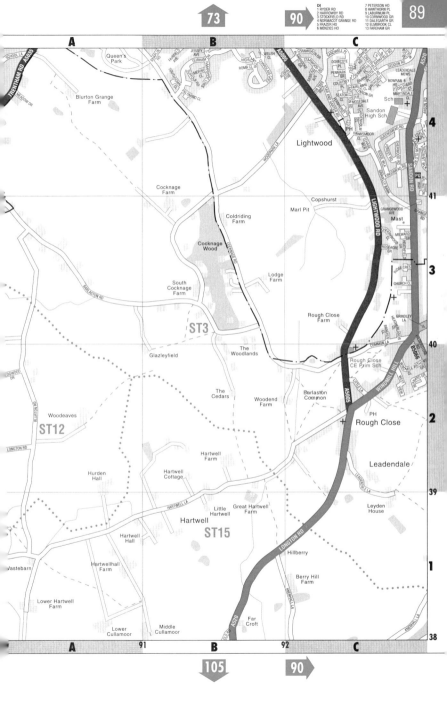

90

A
1 DUDLEY PL
2 CROSSLAND PL E
3 COBHAM PL
4 KINGSFORD PL
5 BURGUNDY GR
6 BRIDESTONE CL

7 GRISEDALE CL
8 VISCOUNT WLK
9 HOBBY CL
10 PARTRIDGE CL
11 TREGENNA CL
12 POLPERRO WAY
13 LINHOPE GR

14 ASHURST GR
15 GOOSEMOOR GR
16 LINDALE GR
17 RUSHMOOR GR

89

74

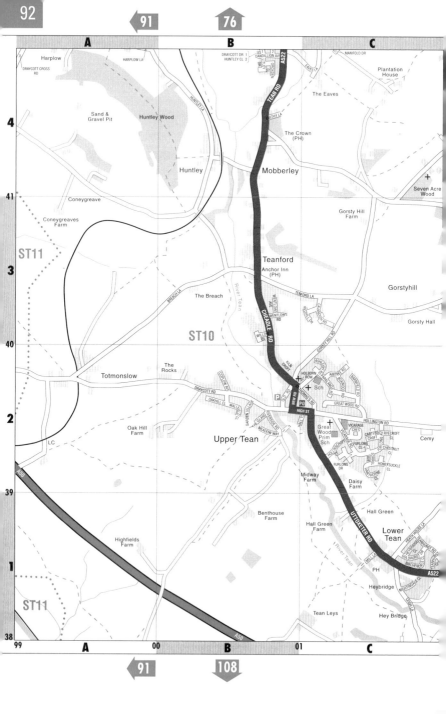

A

B

C

RAKEWAY RD

Rakeway

PH

Cheadle
Common

Freehay

Sand and Gravel Pit

Brown Bank
Farm

Lightoaks
Farm

Coneydale
Farm

Lord's
Coppice

Coneydale
Farm

Beech
Farm

Dale Bank
Farm

Spring
Farm

Winnothdale

Pad
Plantation

ST10

Temple Wood

North Plantation

The Temple

HOLLINGTON RD

Paradise
Cottage

Lodgedale
Farm

Goldhurst

Hollybush

Broadview

Common
End

HEATH HOUSE LA

Heath
House

Broadgate Hall

TEANHURST
RD

Checkleyfields
Cottage

Highridges

Broadgatehall Drumble

ST14

Checkleyfields
Farm

Fourtrees

UTTOXETER RD

Overton

BADGERS HOLLOW 1
CRANBERRY AVE 2

A522

Overton
Farm

A

03

B

04

C

4

41

3

40

2

39

1

38

A B C

New Farm

B5032

Tithebarn

DENSTONE LA

B5032

Turnditch Farm

4

Bradley in the Moors

Spond Farm

Gallows Green

Newhouse Farm

BABB LA

41

Bradley Hall Farm

Jeffreymeadow

Eatonflats

Fields House

Wood Farm

3

Greatgate Wood

Greatgate

Highfields Farm

SANDY LA

Ford

40

ST10

Croxden Brook

Abbey Farm

Croxden

Croxden Abbey

Abbey

QUARRY BANK

QUARRY RD

Broadmoor Wood

PH

2

ST14

Abbey View Farm

Pointhorne

High Ridge Farm

Vicarage

Butterley Bank Farm

39

Upper Whitley

Hollington

MOUNT FIELDS

SCHOOL LANE

RECTORY RD

Holly Grove

Birchendale

The Long Close

Woottons

Lower Whitley

1

A50 SHUTS LA

Chipperlee Coppice

ST14

Hollingtonfields

Madeleypark

Gravelly Bank

38

05 A 06 B 07 C

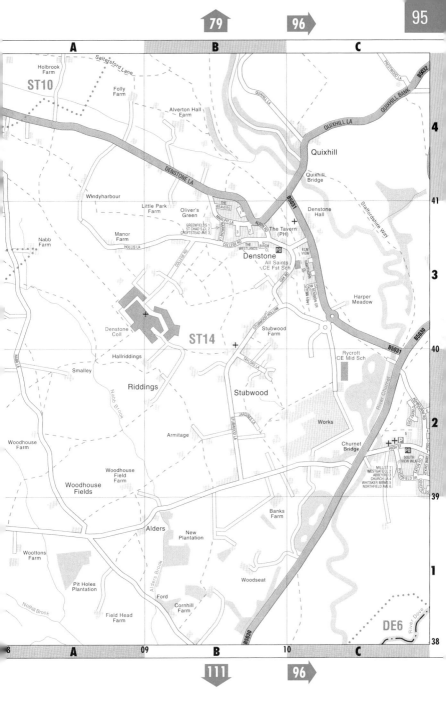

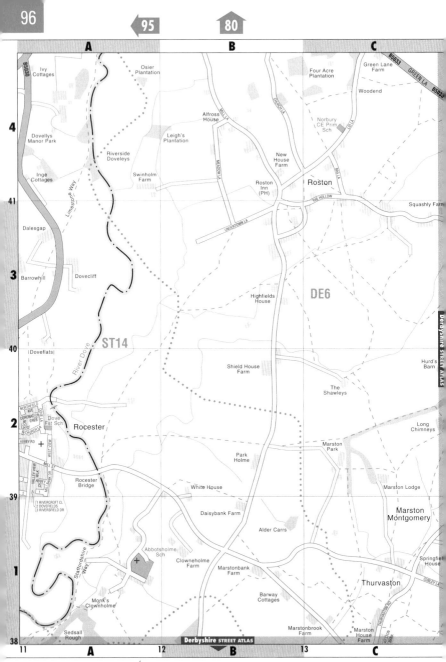

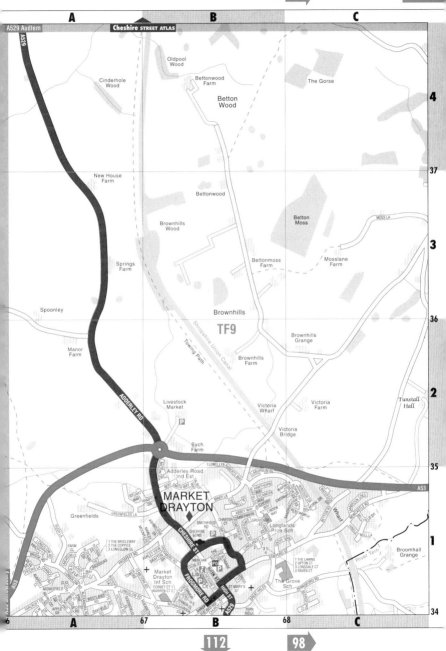

A · B · C

4

37

3

36

2

35

1

34

Greenhill Farm

Betton Hall Farm

Betton Hall

Betton

Betton Farm

River Tern

Marlpit Wood

Drayton Spinney

Tunstall Hall

The Rough

The Park

Shifford's Bridge

NEWCASTLE RD

A53

Clod Hall

NEW COUNCIL HOS

Little Heath Green

Coal Brook

FORGE LA

Norton Forge Farm

Devil's Ring & Finger

Oakley Park

Oakley Hall

Oakley Park Farm

Oakley

Bache Pool

Old Pool Plantation

TF9

Oakley Lodges

Daisy Lake

Red Bull

B5415

SANDY LA

PINFOLD LA

Bloreheath Farm

Almington

Upper House Farm

Almington Hall

Sand Pit

The Arbour

MAER RD

Napley

B5415

The Haven

Park House

Oakley Folly

The Folly

A53

Audley's Cross Farm

Audley's Cross

Bloreheath

BLORE RD

Blore Heath Farm

Sand Pit

Hales Farm

Hales

BLORE LA

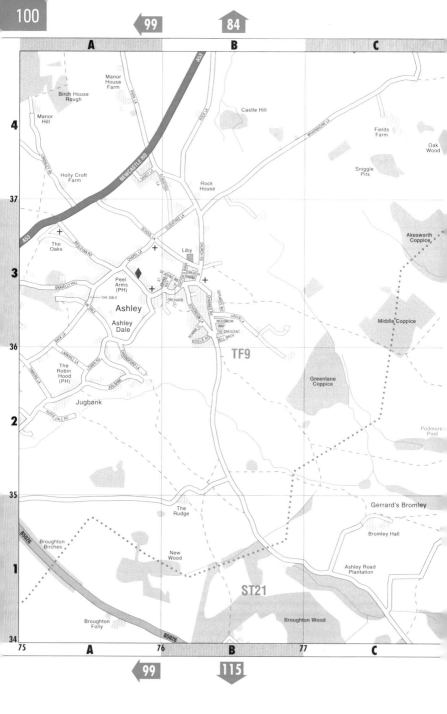

A
B
C

4

37

3

36

35

2

1

34

A53

NEWCASTLE RD

PARK LA

A53

BIRCH HOUSE ROUGH

Manor House Farm

Manor Hill

Birch House Rough

Holly Croft Farm

Castle Hill

WHARMADINE LA

Fields Farm

Oak Wood

Sniggle Pits

Rock House

The Oaks

WOLFORD RD

CHAPEL LA

SCHOOL LA

ELDERTREE LA

CHURCH RD

Liby

Akesworth Coppice

GRAVELLY HILL

Peel Arms (PH)

THE DALE

THE DALE

Ashley

Ashley Dale

ST JOHN'S RD

MILL RD

ORCHARD CL

GERARD'S WK

GREEN LA

WOODROW WAY

THE CRESCENT

BELL ORCH

MURREE CL

EGGE LE JEAN

CHARNES RD

SOVEREIGN WY

Middle Coppice

Greenlane Coppice

TF9

BACK LA

LAGHILL LA

LOWER RD

CHRISTSONGS LA

AXIS BANK

HAWES LA

HORSE DALE RD

The Robin Hood (PH)

Jugbank

Podmore Pool

35

The Rudge

Gerrard's Bromley

B5026

Broughton Birches

New Wood

Bromley Hall

Ashley Road Plantation

ST21

Broughton Folly

B5026

Broughton Wood

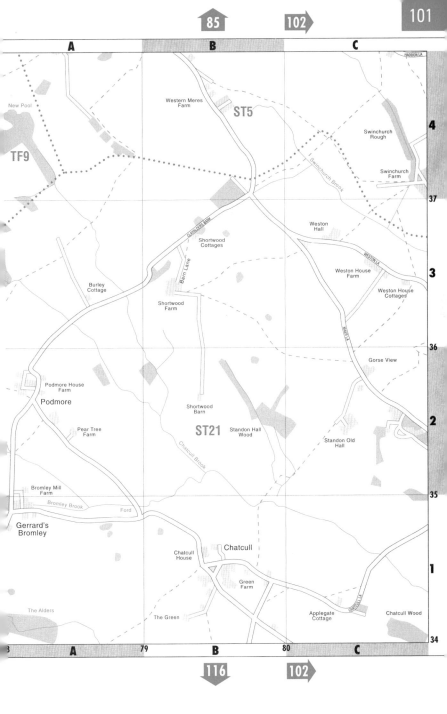

HADDON LA

New Pool

TF9

Western Meres Farm

ST5

Swinchurch Rough

Swinchurch Brook

Swinchurch Farm

4

37

CLAYDUGGS BANK

Shortwood Cottages

Weston Hall

WESTON LA

Barn Lane

Burley Cottage

Weston House Farm

Weston House Cottages

3

Shortwood Farm

36

Podmore House Farm

Gorse View

Podmore

Shortwood Barn

ST21

Standon Hall Wood

Standon Old Hall

2

Pear Tree Farm

Chatcull Brook

35

Bromley Mill Farm

Bromley Brook

Ford

Gerrard's Bromley

Chatcull House

Chatcull

1

The Alders

Green Farm

The Green

Applegate Cottage

CHATCULL LA

Chatcull Wood

34

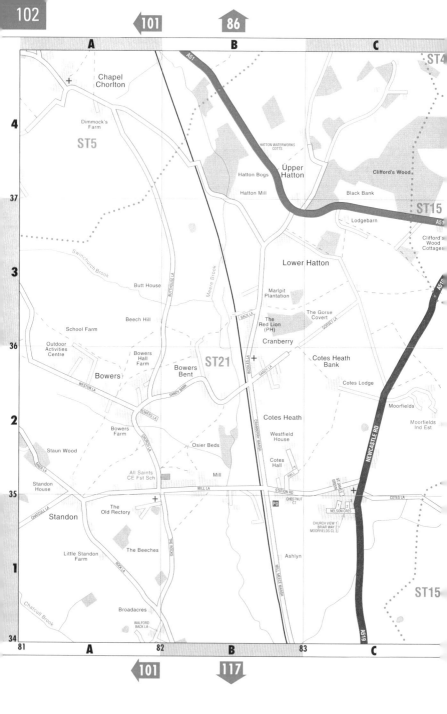

A B C

101 86

ST4

Chapel
Chorlton

Dimmock's
Farm

ST5

4

37

HATTON WATERWORKS
COTTS

Upper
Hatton

Hatton Bogs

Clifford's Wood

Hatton Mill

Black Bank

ST15

Lodgebarn

Clifford's
Wood
Cottages

Swinchurch Brook

Butt House

Lower Hatton

3

Marlpit
Plantation

Beech Hill

BACK LA

The Gorse
Covert

GORSES LA

School Farm

The
Red Lion
(PH)

Outdoor
Activities
Centre

36

Bowers Hall
Farm

Bowers
Bent

Cranberry

ST21

Cotes Heath
Bank

Cotes Lodge

Bowers

WESTON LA

SANDY BANK

BIDDLES LA

LANSEY LA

Moorfields

Moorfields
Ind Est

BOWERS LA

CROSS LA

Bowers
Farm

2

Cotes Heath

CRANBERRY MARSH

NEWCASTLE RD

Staun Wood

Osier Beds

Westfield
House

CROSS LA

Standon
House

All Saints
CE Fst Sch

Mill

Cotes
Hall

HALL LA

ST JAMES
GREEN 1

COTES LA

MILL LA

STATION RD

35

The
Old Rectory

PO

CHESTNUT
CT

3

NELSON CRES

Standon

Little Standon
Farm

CHATCULL LA

ROCK LA

THE ROCKS

The Beeches

CHURCH VIEW 1
BRIAR WAY 2
MOORFIELDS CL 3

1

Chatcull Brook

Broadacres

Ashlyn

MILL MEECE MARSH

ST15

WALFORD
BACK LA

34

81 A 82 B 83 C

101 117

A   B   C

New Waste
Plantation

A519

BEECH DALE LA

Beech House
Farm

ST4

Groundslow
Fields

H

Groundslow

ST12

Green Lane

The
Greathills

4

M6

37

wynnerton
eath Farm

The
Stretters

Cash's
Pit

Calloway
Pit

Wing House
Farm

Green Birch
Farm

Sandyford

WINDMILL LA

DUSE LA

Eastwood

Long Compton
Farm

3

Whitehouse

Closepit
Plantation

Sandyford
Farm

Wood Cottage
Farm

A51

Lodge
Covert

36

ST15

Kennels
Cottages

ST21

Fitzherbert
Arms
(PH)

Swynnerton

FITZHERBERT CL 1
THE ORCHARD 2
BERNARD CHEADLE LA 3

PO

WILLIAMS WK

ISLANDS WK

REAVERS WK

Flash
Pit

THE
HAY BARNS

STONE RD

CHURCH RD

2

Our Lady's
RC Prim Sch

PARK VIEW

Swynnerton
Hall

HALL LA

Blakelow

Swynnerton
Park

The
Dixons

Grange
Cottages

35

Cotes

COTES LA

The
Crossash

Swynnerton
Grange

Cotes House
Farm

BIRCH HOUSE LA

1

The
Doles

Withy
Bed

Highlowbank

34

A   B   C

85   86

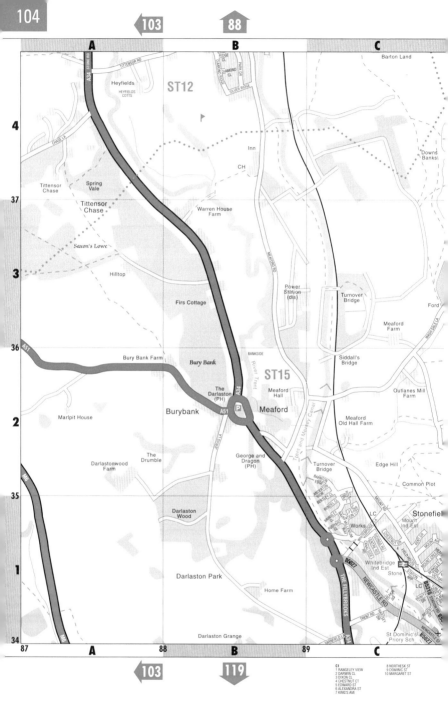

A

B

C

ST12

Barton Land

Heyfields

HEYFIELDS
COTTS

TITTENSOR RD

STONE RD

A34

RIDGE

DIAMOND RIDGE

DIAMOND CL

PARK DR

SILVER RIDGE

Downs
Banks

Inn

CH

4

Tittensor
Chase

Spring
Vale

Tittensor
Chase

CHASE LA

37

Warren House
Farm

MEAFORD RD

Saxon's Lowe

Hilltop

3

Firs Cottage

Power
Station
(dis)

Turnover
Bridge

Ford

Meaford
Farm

HIGH DELLA

A51

36

Bury Bank Farm

Bury Bank

BANKSIDE

River Trent

ST15

Siddall's
Bridge

Outlanes Mill
Farm

A51

A34

The
Darlaston
(PH)

P

Meaford
Hall

Meaford

2

Marlpit House

A51

Burybank

George and
Dragon
(PH)

Trent and Mersey Canal

Meaford
Old Hall Farm

Turnover
Bridge

Edge Hill

M6

The
Drumble

Darlastonwood
Farm

Common Plot

35

Darlaston
Wood

Works

LC

Stonefiel

Mount
Ind Est

1

Darlaston Park

Home Farm

B5027

Whitebridge
Ind Est
Stone

THE FILLYBROOKS

NEWCASTLE RD

LC

B5027

M6

Darlaston Grange

St Dominic's
Priory Sch

WHITEBRIDGE

TRENT RD

A34

87

A

88

B

89

C

C1
1 RANGELEY VIEW
2 DARWIN CL
3 DIXON CL
4 CHESTNUT CT
5 EDWARD ST
6 ALEXANDRA ST
7 KING'S AVE

8 NORTHESK ST
9 DOMINIC ST
10 MARGARET ST

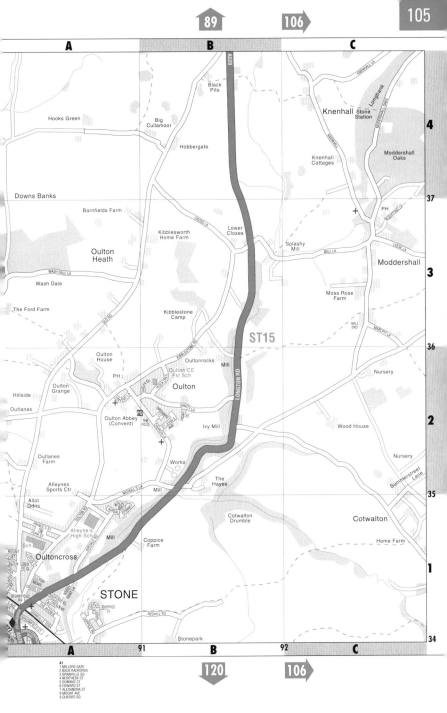

A
B
C

Hooks Green

Big Cullamoor

Black Pits

Knenhall
Stone Station

4

Hobbergate

Knenhall Cottages

Moddershall Oaks

Downs Banks

37

Barnfields Farm

Kibblesworth Home Farm

Lower Closes

Splashy Mill

Moddershall

Oulton Heath

WASH DALE LA

Wash Dale

3

The Ford Farm

Kibblestone Camp

Moss Rose Farm

OLD RD

HALL END

MARLPIT LA

ST15

36

Oulton House

Oultonrocks

Mill

Nursery

KIBBLESTONE RD

Oulton CE Fst Sch

PH

Oulton Grange

Oulton

Hillside

Oulton Abbey (Convent)

THE FOLD

Ivy Mill

Wood House

2

Outlanes

VANITY LA

Nursery

Outlanes Farm

Works

Summerstreet Lane

Alleynes Sports Ctr

Mill

The Hayes

35

Allot Gdns

Cotwalton

Cotwalton Drumble

Alleyne's High Sch

Mill

Home Farm

Oultoncross

Coppice Farm

1

STONE

Coppice CL

REDHILL RD

Stonepark

34

A
91
B
92
C

A1
1 MILLERS GATE
2 BACK RADFORDS
3 GRANVILLE SQ
4 NORTHESK ST
5 DOMINIC CT
6 EDWARD ST
7 ALEXANDRA ST
8 MOUNT AVE
9 QUEEN'S SQ

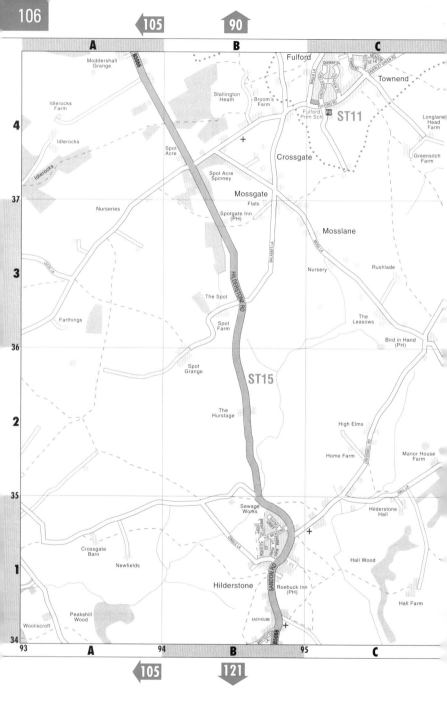

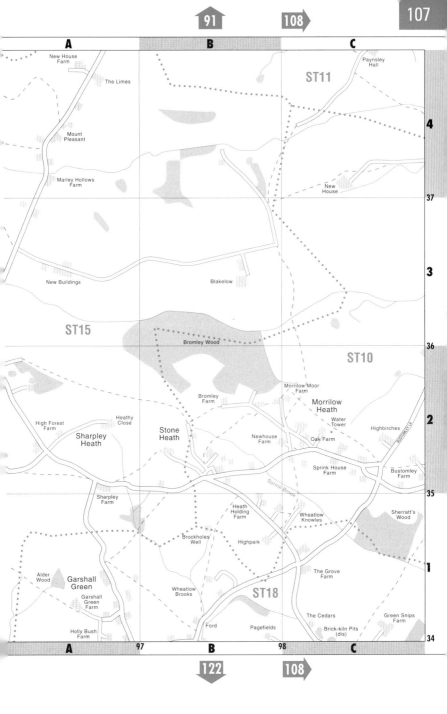

91
108

A   B   C

New House Farm

The Limes

Paynsley Hall

ST11

4

Mount Pleasant

Marley Hollows Farm

New House

37

New Buildings

Blakelow

3

ST15

Bromley Wood

36

ST10

Morrilow Moor Farm

Bromley Farm

Morrilow Heath

High Forest Farm

Heathy Close

Stone Heath

Sharpley Heath

Newhouse Farm

Oak Farm

Water Tower

Highbirches

2

Sprink House Farm

Bustomley Farm

Sharpley Farm

Sprink Brook

35

Heath Holding Farm

Wheatlow Knowles

Sherratt's Wood

Brockholes Well

Highpark

Alder Wood

Garshall Green

The Grove Farm

1

Garshall Green Farm

Wheatlow Brooks

ST18

Holly Bush Farm

Ford

Pagefields

The Cedars

Green Snips Farm

Brick-kiln Pits (dis)

A   97   B   98   C

34

122
108

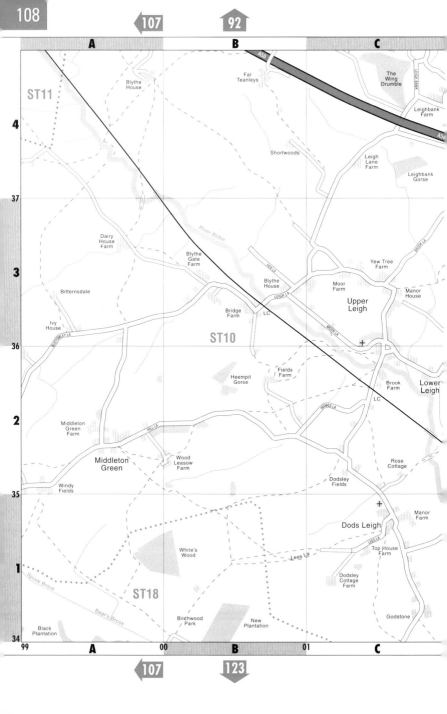

A   B   C

Checkley

Checkleybank
Farmhouse

CRABMILL HOLLOW

A522

Hutchinson Meml
CE Fst Sch

New Broom
(PH)

GREEN
PK

St MARY'S CL

Rectory
Farm

Green
Farm

OLD LA

LY

**Deadman's
Green**

UTTOXETER RD

River Tean

Sewage
Works

Broadgatehall Brook

TILE LA

Folebank
Farm

FOLEBANK
BARNS

Dairy

Fole

A522

Fole
Bridge

4

37

BROOK LA

Park Hall
Farm

Hell
Clough

Fole
Farm

Fole
Hall

ST14

3

Parkhall
Cottage

RECTORY CL

PARKHALL LA

LIME CL

Amesbury

New
Farm

A50

36

All Saints CE
Fst Sch

PH

**Church
Leigh**

ST10

Crossways
Farm

Nobut
Hall

High
Farm

Upper
Nobut

BAGOTS
VIEW

COUNCIL
HOS

Wellcroft
Cottage

Brook House
Farm

REDFIELD LA

DOWNSLOW LA

Heath
Cottage

Withington

HOLLY
MOUNT

Farmers Arms
(PH)

**Withington
Green**

Nobut
Farm

2

35

The Bents
Farm

Cuckoo
Lane
Farm

Cuckoo Lane

Benter
Farm

Manorhouse
Farm

Lower
Nobut

**The
Bents**

MONSELL LA

FIELD LA

River Blithe

Headlands

Hothill
Farm

1

Hayes
House

ST14

34

A   03   B   04   C

A   **B**   **C**

Oldwood

Hollywood Farm

ST10

Nothill Wood

HOLLINGTON LA

Cotton's Wood

Nothill Farm

4

Pale Flatts Farm

A522

Madeley Farm

High Farm

Dove House

Old Turnpike

The Alders

37

Lawn Farm

Creighton Park Farm

Townend Farm

WATERLOO LA

New House Farm

Beamhurst

Beamhursthall Farm

3

Oldwood

Overfole

Beamhurst Hall

Spar Flat Farm

ST14

Flashes Farm

Newhouse

HOLLINGTON LA

PH

River Team

Mill Farm

Mount Pleasant

CEDAR DR 1
CHURCH FARM 2

Beamhurst Bridge

Springfields

ST MICHAEL'S RD

36   A50

Beamhurst Lane

POPPY'S LA

V.CARAGE DF

Waterloo Farm

Deggs Leasow

2

Park View

FEEDER LA

35

Broadoak Farm

Lightwoodfields

Parks' Farm

The Parks

THOMAS GR

FRADLEY GR

A522

A5

BURTON MEWS 1
DERBY MEWS 2
NOTTINGHAM CT 3
LINCOLN CT 4
SHEFFIELD CT 5
LEICESTER CT 6
MANCHESTER CT 7

Dagdale Farm

Banktop

1

Dagdale

GRENVILLE

Moss Beds

Sch

Yew Tree Farm

LIGHT FOOT

34

05   **A**   06   **B**   07   **C**

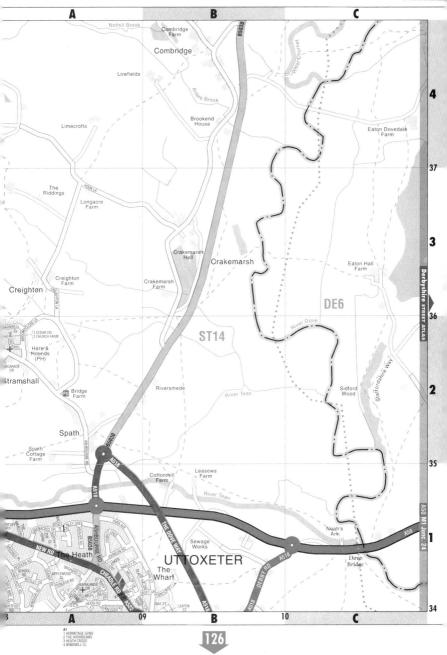

Nothill Brook
Combridge Farm
Combridge
Lowfields
Brookend House
Limecrofts
River Churnet
Eaton Dovedale Farm
The Riddings
HOOK LA
Longacre Farm
Crakemarsh Hall
Crakemarsh
Eaton Hall Farm
Creighton Farm
CREIGHTON LA
Creighton
Crakemarsh Farm
DE6
BARNWELL CL
1 CEDAR DR
2 CHURCH FARM
Hare & Hounds (PH)
ST14
River Dove
VICARAGE DR
Stramshall
Bridge Farm
Riversmede
River Tean
Sidford Wood
Staffordshire Way
Spath
B5030
Spath Cottage Farm
ASHBOURNE RD
A518
Cottonmill Farm
Leasows Farm
River Tean
35
A50 M1 Junc. 24
NEW RD
The Heath
B5030
ASHBOURNE RD
PARK AVE
THE DOVE WAY
CHEADLE RD
B3522
UTTOXETER
The Wharf
Sewage Works
Noah's Ark
A50
A518
DERBY RD
Dove Bridge
A518
EATON ST
GAS ST

A1
1 HERMITAGE GDNS
2 THE HORNBEAMS
3 HEATH CROSS
4 WINDMILL CL

97

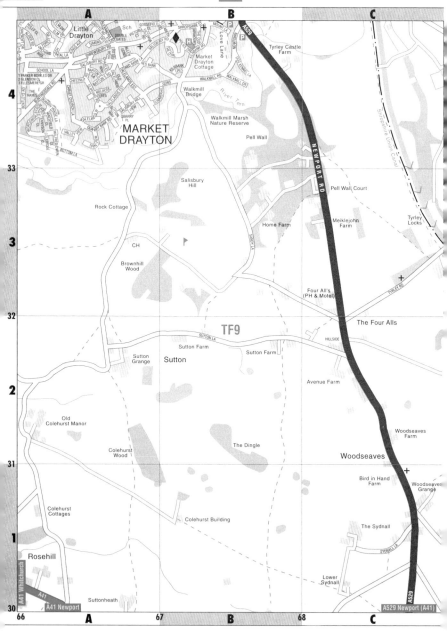

MARKET DRAYTON

Little Drayton

Walkmill Bridge

Walkmill Marsh
Nature Reserve

River Tern

Tyrley Castle
Farm

Pell Wall

Market
Drayton
Cottage

Salisbury
Hill

Rock Cottage

Pell Wall Court

Shropshire Union Canal

Tyrley
Locks

Meiklejohn
Farm

Home Farm

Brownhill
Wood

CH

Newport Rd

Four All's
(PH & Motel)

The Four Alls

Tyrley Rd

TF9

Sutton La

Sutton Farm

Sutton
Grange

Sutton

Sutton Farm

Hillside

Avenue Farm

Old
Colehurst Manor

The Dingle

Woodseaves
Farm

Woodseaves

Colehurst
Wood

Bird in Hand
Farm

Woodseaves
Grange

Colehurst
Cottages

Colehurst Building

The Sydnall

Sydnall La

Rosehill

Lower
Sydnall

A41 Whitchurch

A41

A41 Newport

Suttonheath

A529 Newport (A41)

A529

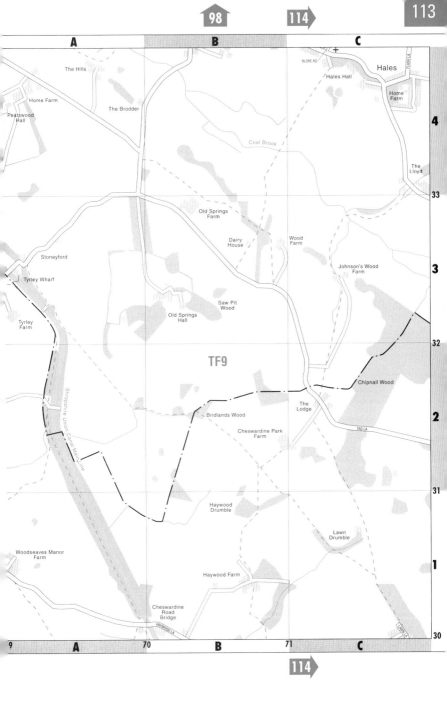

A   **B**   **C**

The Hills

Home Farm

Peatswood Hall

The Brodder

BLORE RD

Hales Hall

+

Hales

FLASH LA

Home Farm

4

Coal Brook

The Lloyd

33

Old Springs Farm

Dairy House

Wood Farm

Stoneyford

Johnson's Wood Farm

Tyrley Wharf

3

Saw Pit Wood

Tyrley Farm

Old Springs Hall

32

Shropshire Union Canal Main Line

TF9

Chipnall Wood

Bridlands Wood

The Lodge

2

Cheswardine Park Farm

TAG LA

31

Haywood Drumble

Woodseaves Manor Farm

Lawn Drumble

1

Haywood Farm

Cheswardine Road Bridge

HAYWOOD LA

30

9   **A**   **70**   **B**   **71**   **C**

A **B** **C**

ST21

4

Park Springs

Burntwood
Farm

Burnt Wood

Lloyd
Drumble

Keeper's
Lodge

Smith's Rough

Bishop's Wood

Park
Springs
Farm

Knowleswood

The
Lloyd
Farm

33

The
Nook
Farm

Goldenhill
Farm

Glass
Houses

Dales
Wood

The
Lees

3

Coal Brook

Chipnall Lees

Heatherdale
Farm

Chipnall
Mill
Farm

TF9

32

Lipley
Heath
Farm

Rushymoss
Wood

2

Chipnallhall
Farm

Chipnall Farm

Lipley
Farm

Bishop's Wood

TAG LA

Chipnall

MOSS LA

Lipley

Moss
Lane
Farm

31

Cheswardine Hall

Sycamore
Cottage

1

Lipley Hall
Farm

Lipley
Cottages

Lipley
Villa

Greaves
Plantation

Marsh
House

30

ST20

ST20

72 **A** **73** **B** **74** **C**

A   **B**   **C**

B5026

Broughton Hall

Broughton

Charnes

Fairoak Grange

Charnes Home Farm

Charnes Park

4

Bishop's Wood

Wetwood Farm

Wetwood

33

Green Farm

B5026

TF9

Fairoak

ROOKERY COTTS

Buttersbank

COPSY DALE

FAIROAK BANK

PH

Pennyquart Well Farm

Moss Farm

Lower Farm

Greatwood Lodge

Blackwaters

3

Park House

ST21

Armsdale

32

Gorse Farm

WINDMILL LA

Cave

2

Bishop's Wood

River Sow

LINGER LA

TF9

Greatwood Farm

Little Blorepipe

31

Greatwood House

Blorepipe

1

White Farm

Mill Barn Farm

ST20

Mill Pond

The Mount

NEW IN BANK

Outlands

30

5 **A** **76** **B** **77** **C**

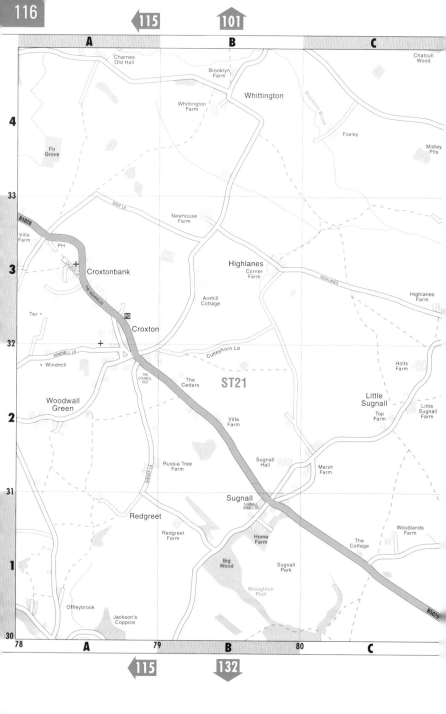

A B C

New Birch House

Pilstones Wood

The Highlows

4

Mast

Beatty Hall

British Telecom Technical College

Swynnerton Training Area

Howard Hall

High Lows Lane

Springfields Fst Sch

33

ST15

TIMBERFIELDS 1
HOLLY FIELDS 2
THE WILLLOWS 3

Yarnfield

Meece House

COBHAM CL 1
SOPWITH CL 2
YEAGER CT 3

Cold Meece Ind Est

Works

3

Coldmeece

Eastfields

The Broom

Brookside Bsns Pk

32

Hill Farm

Baden Hall Lodge

HILTON DR

The Rookery

Upper Heamies Cottages

2

Baden Hall

Middle Heamies

Baden Hall Cottages

Drake Hall (HM Prison)

Upper Heamies

Meece Brook

31

ST21

Lower Heamies

B5026

Pool Plantation

Lower Heamies Wood

1

Magpie Wood

Hilcote Cottages

Oxleasows

Norton Bridge

Hilcote Farm

B5026

30

84 A 85 B 86 C

A4
1 NEWCASTLE ST
2 MILLERS GATE
3 REDHILL GDNS
4 CHURCH CL
5 CLAREMONT CL
6 ASHDALE CL
7 THE GLEN
8 ERNALD GDNS
9 CLINTON GDNS
10 DOWNING GDNS

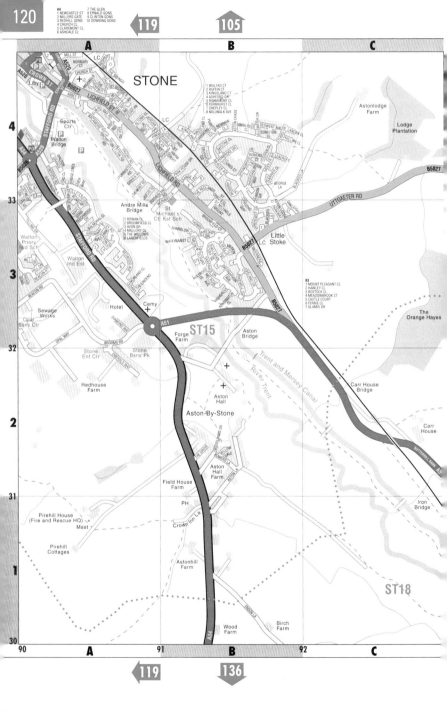

STONE

1 WULFAD CT
2 RUFFIN CT
3 KINGSLAND CT
4 ASHFORD GR
5 RIGBEMONT CL
6 FERNHURST CL
7 SHEPLEY CL
8 MILLWALK AVE

Astonlodge Farm

Lodge Plantation

B5027

UTTOXETER RD

Andre Mills Bridge

St Michael's CE Fst Sch

1 ROWAN CL
2 BROOMFIELD CL
3 AVON GR
4 MALLORY CL
5 THE WILLOWS
6 LARCHFIELDS

Little LC Stoke

B3
1 MOUNT PLEASANT CL
2 HAWLEY CL
3 BOSTOCK CL
4 MEADOWBROOK CT
5 CASTLE COURT
6 FERNIE CL
7 GLAMIS DR

Walton Priory Mid Sch

Walton Ind Est

The Orange Hayes

Sewage Works

Opal Bsns Ctr

Hotel

Cemy

ST15

Forge Farm

Aston Bridge

Carr House Bridge

Stone Ent Ctr

Stone Bsns Pk

Trent and Mersey Canal

River Trent

Carr House

Redhouse Farm

Aston Hall

Aston-By-Stone

Field House Farm

Aston Hall Farm

PH

Pirehill House (Fire and Rescue HQ)

Mast

Crown Inn La

Iron Bridge

Pirehill Cottages

ST18

Astonhill Farm

Wood Farm

Birch Farm

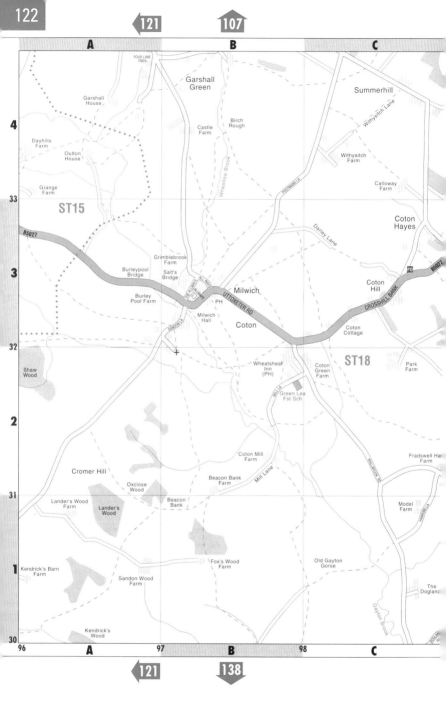

121
107

A **B** **C**

4

Garshall
Green

Summerhill

Garshall
House

Withysitch Lane

Castle
Farm

Birch
Rough

Dayhills
Farm

Oulton
House

Withysitch
Farm

Calloway
Farm

Grange
Farm

33

ST15

Coton
Hayes

B5027

Darley Lane

Wheallow Brook

Postmans La

Grimblebrook
Farm

3

Burleypool
Bridge

Salt's
Bridge

Milwich

Coton
Hill

PO

B5027

Burley
Pool Farm

THE GREEN
THE LANES

UTTOXETER RD

PH

CROSSHILL BANK

Coton Bank

Milwich
Hall

Coton

Coton
Cottage

SANDON LA

32

Shaw
Wood

Wheatsheaf
Inn
(PH)

Coton
Green
Farm

ST18

Park
Farm

GREEN LA

Green Lea
Fst Sch

2

Coton Mill
Farm

Fradswell Ha
Farm

WALKBROOK RD

Cromer Hill

Oxclose
Wood

Beacon Bank
Farm

Mill Lane

Lander's Wood
Farm

31

Lander's
Wood

Beacon
Bank

Model
Farm

HIXON LA

Kendrick's Barn
Farm

1

Fox's Wood
Farm

Old Gayton
Gorse

The
Dogland

Sandon Wood
Farm

Kendrick's
Wood

Gayton Brook

SOOLE LN

30

96   97   98

A **B** **C**

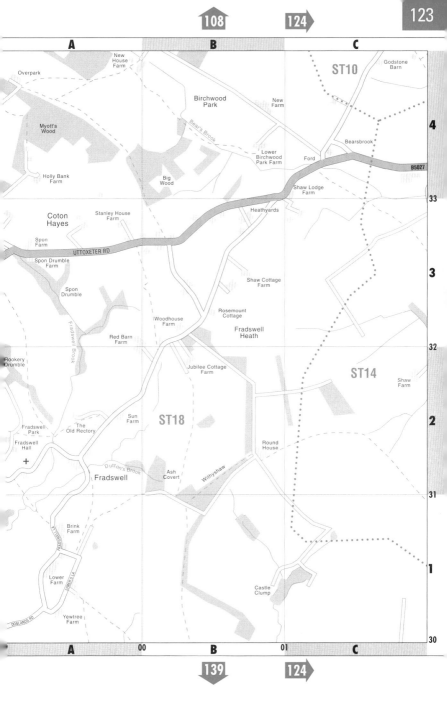

A B C

ST10

The Gorse
Longleys

Painleyhill Farm
Hobbhill

Bank Farm
Painleyhill

4

Field Farm

Fieldmill Farm

Spring Farm

B5027

B5027

Field

Moor House

33

Carry Coppice

Carry Coppice

Carry Lane

3

Round Wood

32

ST14

River Blithe

Church Farm

Brook House

+ Gratwich

Road Island Farm

2

The Rectory

Caverswall

Burndhurst Mill

A518

A518

BOURNE LA

MILL LA

SHORT LA

31

Banktop Farm

COMMON LA

Gratwichwood Farm

Poolfields

Stony Lane

WOOD LA

1

Manor Farm

Hand Leasow Wood

Leafields

ST18

A518

30

02 A 03 B 04 C

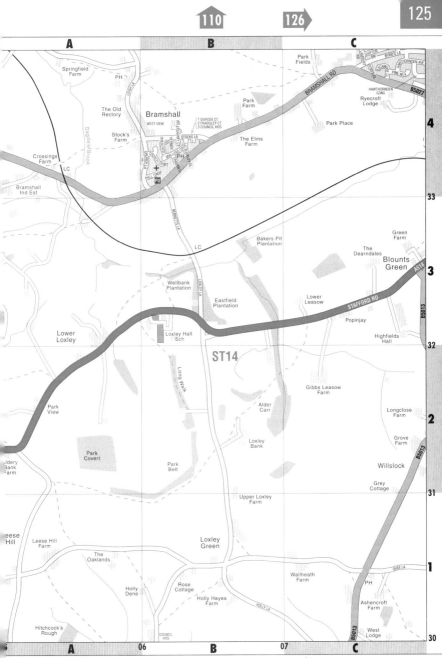

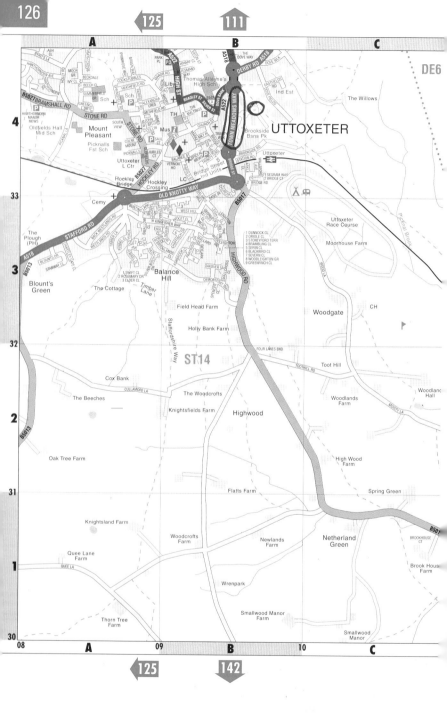

125
111

A   B   C

DE6

The Willows

UTTOXETER

4

Mount Pleasant
Oldfields Hall Mid Sch
Picknalls Fst Sch

Uttoxeter L Ctr

Hockley Bridge   Hockley Crossing

33   Old Knotty Way   Uttoxeter Race Course

Cemy   Moorhouse Farm

The Plough (PH)

Stafford Rd

Blount's Green

1 DUNNOCK CL
2 ORIOLE CL
3 STONEYFORD TERR
4 BRAMBLING CL
5 SERIN CL
6 BLACKBIRD CL
7 SEVERN CL
8 WOODLEIGHTON GR
9 GREENFINCH CL

3   Balance Hill
The Cottage   Timber Lane

32   Field Head Farm   Woodgate   CH

Holly Bank Farm

ST14

Cox Bank   Four Lanes End   Toot Hill

The Woodcrofts   Woodlands Farm   Woodland Hall

The Beeches   Knightsfields Farm   Highwood

2   Oak Tree Farm   High Wood Farm

31   Flatts Farm   Spring Green

Knightsland Farm   Woodcrofts Farm   Newlands Farm   Netherland Green   Brookhouse Ct

1   Quee Lane Farm   Brook House Farm

Wrenpark

Thorn Tree Farm   Smallwood Manor Farm   Smallwood Manor

30
08   A   09   B   10   C

125
142

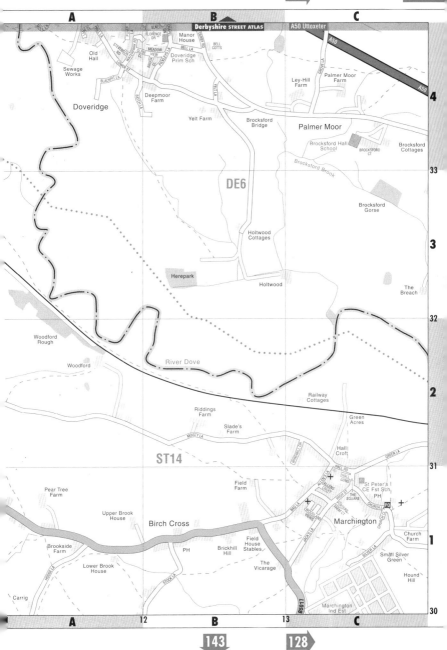

Sewage Works

Old Hall

Doveridge

Manor House

Doveridge Prim Sch

Bell Cotts

Ley-Hill Farm

Palmer Moor Farm

Deepmoor Farm

Yelt Farm

Brocksford Bridge

Palmer Moor

4

Brocksford Hall School

BROCKSFORD CT

Brocksford Cottages

DE6

Brocksford Brook

33

Brocksford Gorse

Holtwood Cottages

3

Herepark

Holtwood

The Breach

32

Woodford Rough

River Dove

Woodford

Railway Cottages

2

Riddings Farm

Green Acres

Slade's Farm

MOISTY LA

ST14

Hall Croft

31

Field Farm

St Peter's CE Fst Sch

PH

Pear Tree Farm

THE SQUARE

Upper Brook House

Birch Cross

Marchington

Church Farm

1

Brookside Farm

PH

Brickhill Hill

Field House Stables

Small Silver Green

Lower Brook House

STOCK LA

The Vicarage

Hound Hill

Carrig

B5017

Marchington Ind Est

30

127

Derbyshire STREET ATLAS | A515 Ashbourne

A

B

C

Cave
Cottage

Heath House
Farm

Somersal
Heath

Merefield
Gorse

Parkside

A515

Sudbury Park

Brickyard
Farm

Oaks
Green

Sudbury Park
Farm

Gorse
Covert

A50

4

FLACKETTS LA

Flacketts Lane
Farm

SUDBURY PK

Grove
Plantation

Halfway
House

A515

33

West
Broughton

Broughton Brook

HM
Prison

The Grove

Sewage
Works

Home
Farm

Fiddlers
Farm

Portway
Head

Deercote

DE6

West Broughton
Farm

Oak
Cottage

P

Square
Pond

3

The
Decoy

PH

SCHOOL LA

VERNON LA

32

Sudbury
Hall

Mus

PO

Aston

Sudbury

MAIN RD

A5

MAIN RD

Sudbury
Prim Sch

Rectory
Farm

A515

Aston
House
Farm

Dovebank

2

Weir
Plantation

River Dove

LEATHERSLEY LA

Dovefields
Crossing

LC

GREEN LA

Dove
Fields

Aston
Bridge

31

ST14

Sudbury
Dairy

LC

Hotel

1

Houndhill
Farm

Moat
Farm

Draycott
Mill

Densey
Lodge

A515

30

14

A

15

B

16

C

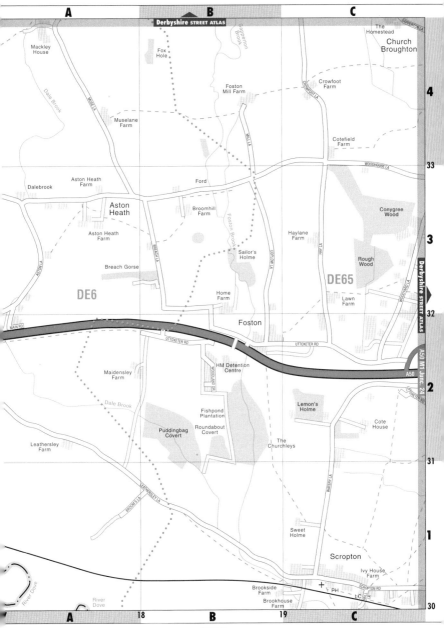

Derbyshire STREET ATLAS

A **B** **C**

4

33

3

32

2

31

1

30

Mackley
House

Fox
Hole

The
Homestead

Church
Broughton

Sapperton Brook

Foston
Mill Farm

Crowfoot
Farm

Dale Brook

NELL LA

Muselane
Farm

MILL LA

Cotefield
Farm

WOODHOUSE LA

Dalebrook

Aston Heath
Farm

Ford

Aston
Heath

Broomhill
Farm

Conygree
Wood

Foston Brook

Haylane
Farm

HAY LA

Aston Heath
Farm

Breach Gorse

BREACH LA

Sailor's
Holme

Rough
Wood

CORLOW LA

DE6

DE65

Home
Farm

Lawn
Farm

Foston

Derbyshire STREET ATLAS

MAIN RD

UTTOXETER RD

UTTOXETER RD

A50 M1 Junc. 24

A50

Maidensley
Farm

WOODLAND LA

HM Detention
Centre

Lemon's
Holme

Dale Brook

Fishpond
Plantation

Cote
House

Puddingbag
Covert

Roundabout
Covert

The
Churchleys

Leathersley
Farm

LEATHERSLEY LA

BROOM'S LA

MATERY LA

Sweet
Holme

Scropton

Ivy House
Farm

PH

SCROPTON RD

River Dove

River
Dove

Brookside
Farm

Brookhouse
Farm

18 **19**

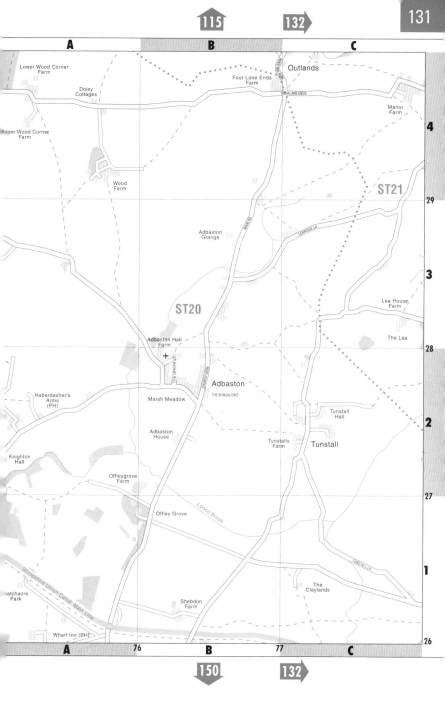

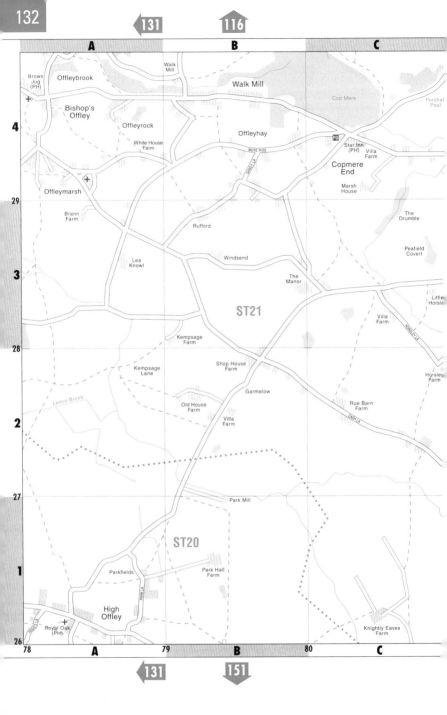

A   B   C

Brown
Jug
(PH)
Offleybrook
Walk
Mill
Walk Mill
Cop Mere
Pershal
Pool

Bishop's
Offley
Offleyrock
Offleyhay
PO
Star Inn
(PH)
Villa
Farm

4
White House
Farm
MERE RISE
Copmere
End
Marsh
House
The
Drumble

Offleymarsh
29
Peafield
Covert

Brann
Farm
Rufford
Windsend
The
Manor
Little
Horsle

3
Lea
Knowl
ST21
Villa
Farm
HORSLEY LA

28
Kempsage
Farm

Kempsage
Lane
Shop House
Farm
Horsley
Farm

Lonco Brook
Old House
Farm
Garmelow
Rue Barn
Farm
CASH LA

2
Villa
Farm

27
Park Mill

ST20

1
Parkfields
Park Hall
Farm
PARK LA

High
Offley

Royal Oak
(PH)
Knightly Eaves
Farm

26
78   A   79   B   80   C

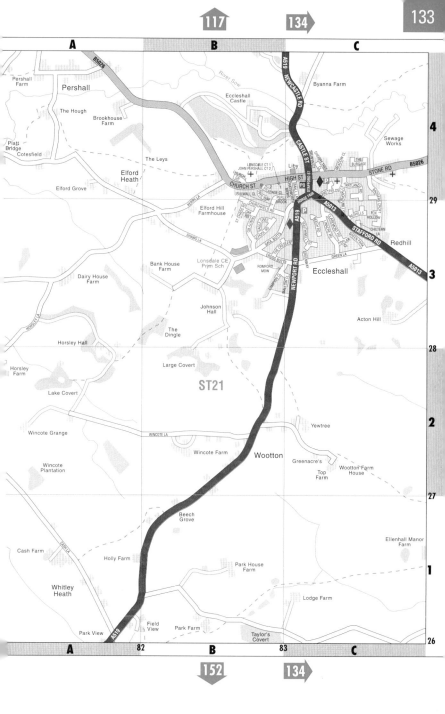

A B C

B5026

Scamnel Farm

Smallwood Pit

Hillcote Hall

Hillcote Wood

ST15

The Leas

STONE RD

4

B5026

Rodgeley Lodge

Fletchers Wildlife Ctr

SCAMNEL LA

The Vicarage

29

Fieldhouse Farm

Drumble Wood

Mill Farm

Chebsey

The Dingle

River Sow

MILL LANE

Riverside Farm

MILL LA

3 STAFFORD RD A5013

FOUR LANE ENDS

Walton Hall Sch

Walton Gorse

ST21

Pyebirch Manor

PYEBIRCH LA

Long Covert

Walton Farm

Walton

Waltonbank Wood

28

Round Covert

WALTONHURST LA

Walton Grove

Waltonbank

A5013

2

Spurleybrook Farm

27

Waltonhurst

Oncote Covert

ST18

Brook Covert

Gamesley Brook

1 Ellenhall Manor Farm

Seggersley Farm House

Ladfordfields Ind Est

Ladfordfield

Cocktails Gorse

B5405

Ellenhall

GRANGE CL

The Marsh

MARSH LA

ST20

Ladford Covert Ind Pk

BIRCH LA

Ladford Trad Pk

B5405

26

84 A 85 B 86 C

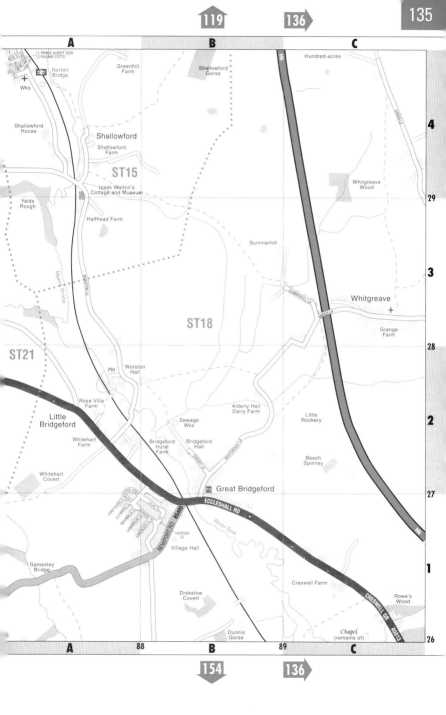

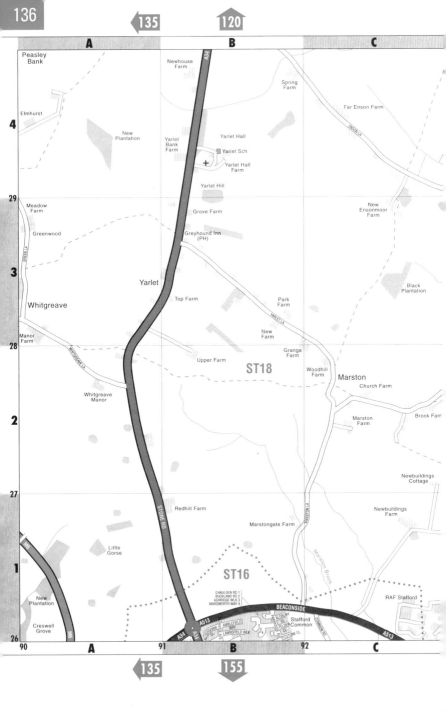

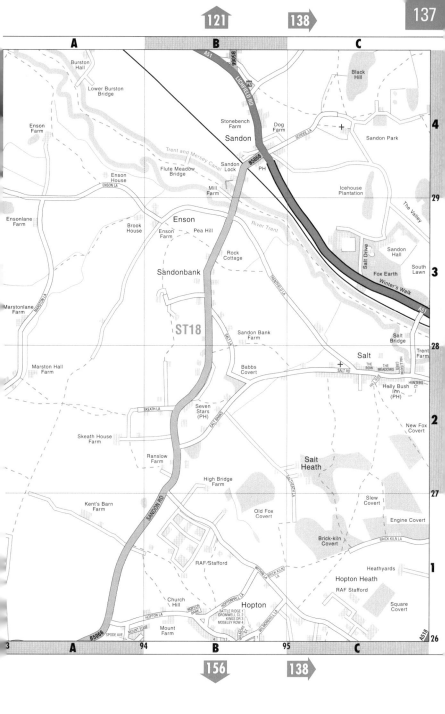

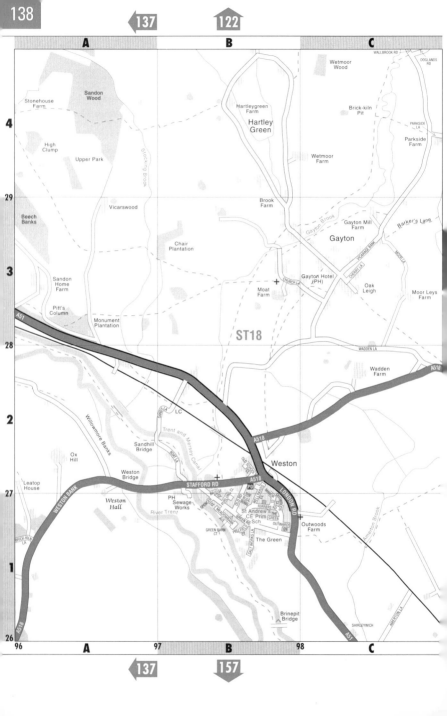

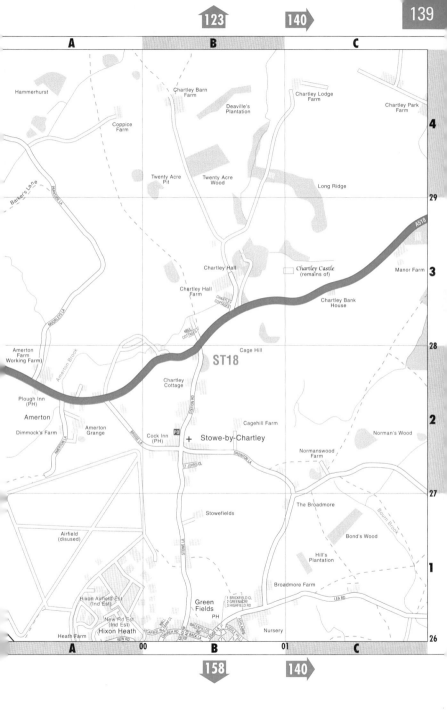

A   B   C

Hammerhurst

Chartley Barn
Farm

Deaville's
Plantation

Chartley Lodge
Farm

Chartley Park
Farm

4

Coppice
Farm

Barker's Lane

Marsdell La

Twenty Acre
Pit

Twenty Acre
Wood

Long Ridge

29

A518

Moorley La

Chartley Hall

Chartley Castle
(remains of)

Manor Farm

3

Chartley Hall
Farm

CHARTLEY
COTTAGES

Chartley Bank
House

MILL
COTTAGES

Amerton Brook

Cage Hill

28

Amerton
Farm
(Working Farm)

ST18

Chartley
Cottage

Plough Inn
(PH)

STATION RD

Amerton

BRIDGE LA

Cock Inn
(PH)   PO

+ Stowe-by-Chartley

Cagehill Farm

Norman's Wood

2

Dimmock's Farm

Amerton
Grange

AMERTON LA

ST JOHNS CL

DRAYTON LA

Normanswood
Farm

27

The Broadmore

Bourn Brook

Airfield
(disused)

Stowefields

STOWE LA

Bond's Wood

Hill's
Plantation

1

Broadmore Farm

LEA RD

Hixon Airfield Est
(Ind Est)

Green
Fields

1 BRICKFIELD CL
2 GREENACRE
3 HIGHFIELD RD

New Rd Est
(Ind Est)
Hixon Heath

Heath Farm

VICARAGE RD
MILL
CHURCH RD
BACK LA
GREENFIELD
1 2 3
PH
PUDDLE HILL
JOHN KING
POST KINGS

Nursery

NEW RD

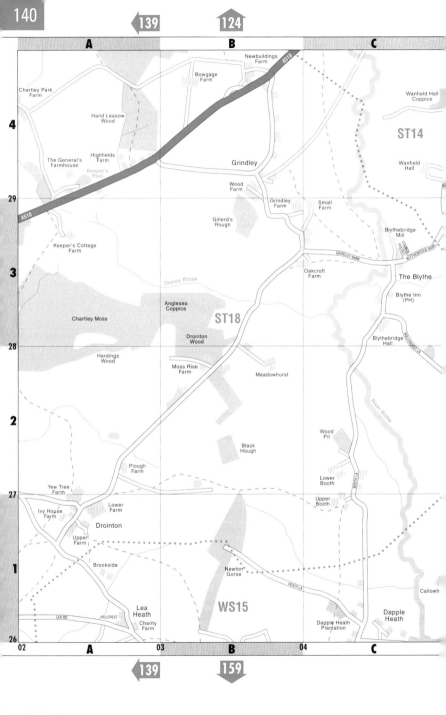

A   B   C

4

Chartley Park Farm

Hand Leasow Wood

Newbuildings Farm

Bowgage Farm

A518

Wanfield Hall Coppice

ST14

The General's Farmhouse

Highfields Farm

Keeper's Pool

Grindley

Wanfield Hall

29

A518

Wood Farm

Grindley Farm

Small Farm

Keeper's Cottage Farm

Gillerd's Rough

Grindley Bank

Blythebridge Mill

COACH & HORSES

BLYTHEBRIDGE BANK

3

Stoney Brook

Oakcroft Farm

The Blythe

Anglesea Coppice

Blythe Inn (PH)

Chartley Moss

ST18

Blythebridge Hall

28

Drointon Wood

Hardings Wood

Moss Rise Farm

Meadowhurst

HOLT FORREST LA

River Blythe

2

Wood Pit

Plough Farm

Lower Booth

Yew Tree Farm

Black Hough

BOOTH LA

27

Lower Farm

Upper Booth

Ivy House Farm

Drointon

Upper Farm

1

Brookside

Newton Gorse

Callowh

Lea Heath

WS15

HEATH LA

Dapple Heath

LEA RD

HILLCREST

Charity Farm

Dapple Heath Plantation

26

02   A   03   B   04   C

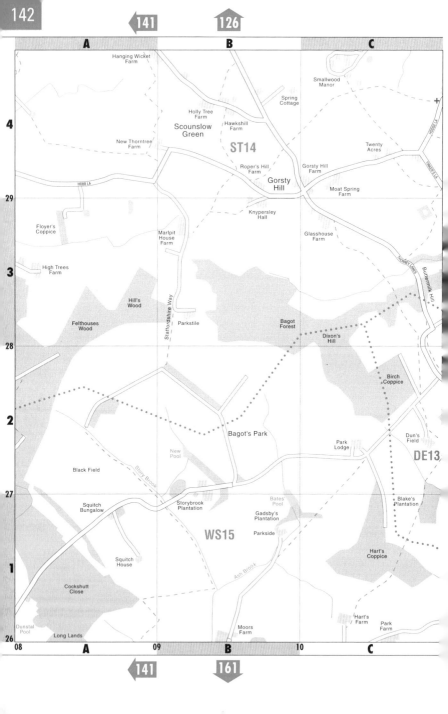

A | B | C

4

Scounslow Green

ST14

Hanging Wicket Farm

Holly Tree Farm

Hawkshill Farm

Spring Cottage

Smallwood Manor

New Thorntree Farm

Twenty Acres

Roper's Hill Farm

Gorsty Hill Farm

Gorsty Hill

29

HOBB LA

Floyer's Coppice

Marlpit House Farm

Knypersley Hall

Moat Spring Farm

Glasshouse Farm

3

High Trees Farm

Hill's Wood

Felthouses Wood

Staffordshire Way

Parkstile

Bagot Forest

Dixon's Hill

TURNEY LANE

Buttermilk Hill

28

Birch Coppice

2

Bagot's Park

Black Field

Story Brook

New Pool

Park Lodge

Dun's Field

DE13

27

Squitch Bungalow

Storybrook Plantation

Bates' Pool

Gadsby's Plantation

Blake's Plantation

WS15

Parkside

Hart's Coppice

1

Squitch House

Ash Brook

Cockshutt Close

Hart's Farm

Park Farm

Dunstal Pool

Long Lands

Moors Farm

26

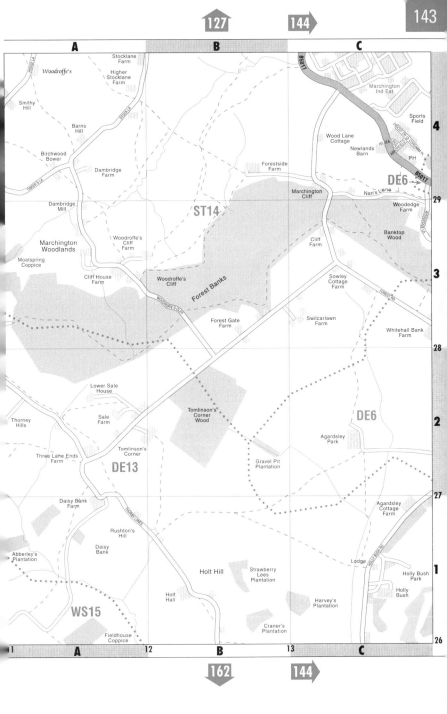

A
B
C

Woodroffe's
Stocklane Farm
Higher Stocklane Farm

Smithy Hill

Marchington Ind Est

Barns Hill

STOCK LA

Sports Field

4

Wood Lane Cottage

Birchwood Bower

Newlands Barn

PH

Dambridge Farm

UTTOXETER RD CHEADLE RD

Forestside Farm

HILL SIDE

DE6

29

Dambridge Mill

ST14

Marchington Cliff

Nan's Lane

Woodedge Farm

Marchington Woodlands

Woodroffe's Cliff Farm

Cliff Farm

Banktop Wood

Moatspring Coppice

Cliff House Farm

Woodroffe's Cliff

Forest Banks

Sowley Cottage Farm

3

WOODROFFE'S CLIFF

FOWEL'S RD

Whitehall Bank Farm

Forest Gate Farm

Swilcarlawn Farm

28

Lower Sale House

Thorney Hills

Sale Farm

Tomlinson's Corner Wood

DE6

2

Agardsley Park

Three Lane Ends Farm

Tomlinson's Corner

DE13

Gravel Pit Plantation

27

Daisy Bank Farm

Agardsley Cottage Farm

THORNEY LANES

Rushton's Hill

Abberley's Plantation

Daisy Bank

Lodge

HOLLY BUSH RD

Holly Bush Park

1

Holt Hill

Strawberry Lees Plantation

Holly Bush

WS15

Holt Hall

Harvey's Plantation

Fieldhouse Coppice

Craner's Plantation

26

1
A
12
B
13
C

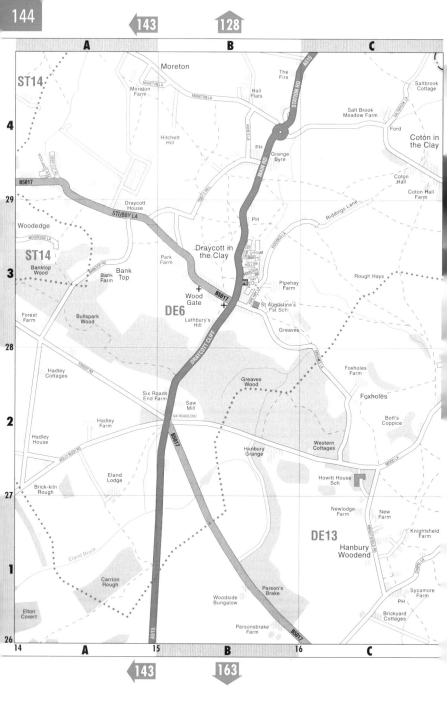

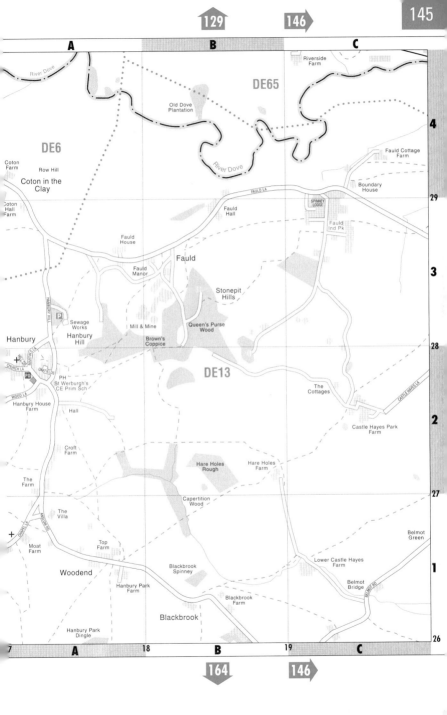

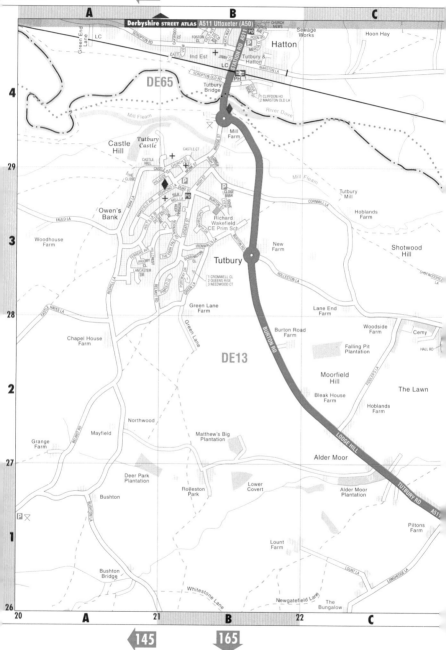

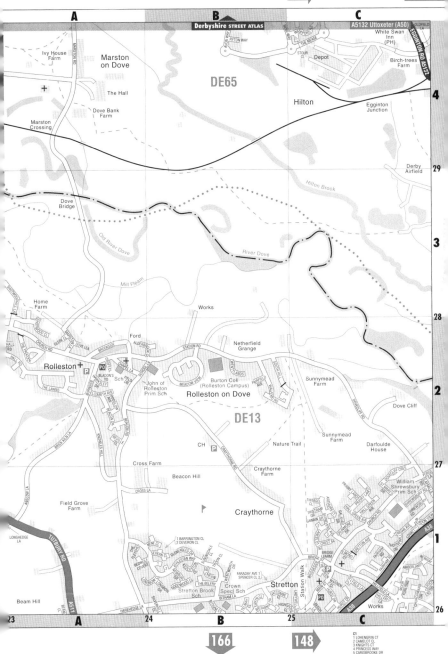

Derbyshire STREET ATLAS

A5132 Uttoxeter (A50)

White Swan Inn (PH)

EGGINTON RD A5132

OLDFIELD

Ivy House Farm

MARSTON RD

Marston on Dove

RYTON WAY

AVON WAY

WASHFORD CL

THE BEACH

STOUR CL

Depot

Birch-trees Farm

DE65

The Hall

Hilton

Dove Bank Farm

Marston Crossing

Egginton Junction

4

Derby Airfield

29

Hilton Brook

Dove Bridge

Old River Dove

River Dove

3

Mill Fleam

28

Home Farm

Works

COPSIDE CL

GREEN LEA

DOVE LEA

BROOKSIDE

Ford

ALDERBANK

Netherfield Grange

STATION RD

HALL RD

THE STREET

CHURCH RD

Rolleston

Sch

P

BLADON'S YD

CROFT CL

P

MOORLEY RD

CHAPEL LA

MEADOW VIEW

John of Rolleston Prim Sch

Burton Coll (Rolleston Campus)

THE LANDS

FAIRISLE CL

FAIRISLE AVE

Sunnymead Farm

THE LAWNS

ELIZABETH AVE

DONWESTON AVE

BEACON RD

NEVILLE CL

HILLARY WAY

BLACK LA

KNOWLES HILL

DE13

Rolleston on Dove

WALNUT CL

Sunnymead Farm

Dove Cliff

Darfoulde House

BRICK KILN LA

CH

P

CRAYTHORNE RD

Cross Farm

Nature Trail

Craythorne Farm

27

DOVECLIFF CRES

William Shrewsbury Prim Sch

MARLOW LA

Beacon Hill

CROSS LA

Cross La

Field Grove Farm

A38

Craythorne

VINTAGE CL

TINTAGEL CL

TRISTRAM

GAWAIN CL

FRIARS LANE

HALL LODGE

PERCY LA

CREST CL

DOVE LEY CL

AMERLAND

1

LONGHEDGE LA

TUTBURY RD A511

1 BARRINGTON CL
2 DEVERON CL

DEVERON CL

BLAKELEY CL

CHRISTIAN WAY

FAIRWAY

MEDWYN CL

COVEN

GOODWOOD CL

LONGDON CL

FAIRISLE CL

CRESTON

FARADAY AVE 1
SPENCER CL 2

BRIDGE FARM

Stretton Walk

P

Works

A38

Beam Hill

A511

Stretton Brook Sch

THE BELFRY

Crown Spec Sch

BITHAM LA

Stretton

BRIDGE

PO

26

HAREHEDGE LA

23 A 24 B 25 C

C1
1 LOHENGRIN CT
2 CAMELOT CL
3 KNIGHTS CT
4 PRINCESS WAY
5 CARISBROOKE DR
6 ALDERHOLME DR
7 MANTON CL

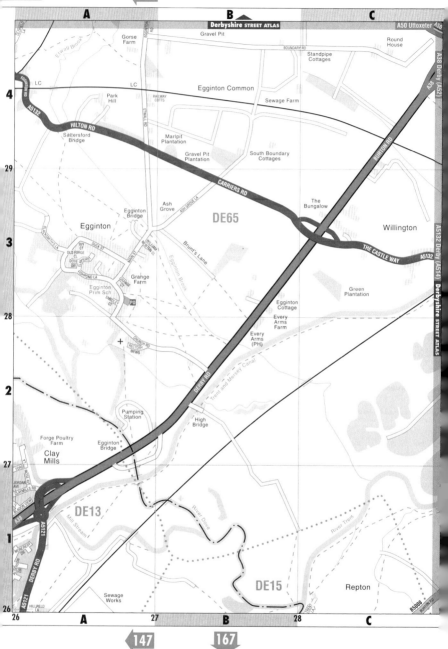

A

B

Derbyshire STREET ATLAS

C

A50 Uttoxeter

Gravel Pit

Gorse
Farm

Round
House

BOUNDARY RD

Standpipe
Cottages

LC

LC

Egginton Common

Park
Hill

4

RAILWAY
COTTS

Sewage Farm

HILTON RD

Saltersford
Bridge

Marlpit
Plantation

29

Gravel Pit
Plantation

South Boundary
Cottages

CARRIERS RD

Ash
Grove

DE65

The
Bungalow

Egginton
Bridge

Egginton

Willington

3

Brunt's Lane

THE CASTLE WAY

A5132

Grange
Farm

Green
Plantation

Egginton
Prim Sch

PO

28

Egginton
Cottage

Every
Arms
Farm

Every
Arms
(PH)

CHURCH RD

RECTORY
MEWS

DERBY RD

Trent and Mersey Canal

2

Pumping
Station

High
Bridge

Forge Poultry
Farm

Egginton
Bridge

Clay
Mills

27

River Dove

DE13

River Trent

Mill Stream

1

DERBY RD

DE15

Repton

Sewage
Works

B5008

26

26

A

27

B

28

C

A
B
C

ST20

Ellerton
Grange

Flashbrook
Manor

4

Lower Camp
Farm

25

Camp Farm

Banqueting
Farm

Showell
Grange

Ovens Bottom

Flashbrook
Wood

Mow Cop

Flashbrook
Grange

3

TF10

Chetwynd Airfield

New Houses

24

Whitleyford
Bridge

Puleston
Common

GIPSY LA

Manor
Cottages

2

Pickstock
Farm

Whitley Manor
Farm

Lonco Brook

Pickstock

23

Brook Farm

Pickstock
Manor

etwynd
eath

River Meese

Puleston
Hill

1

Taylor's
Wood

Puleston Hill
Covert

Lane End

CHESTER RD

Puleston

Puleston Park

22

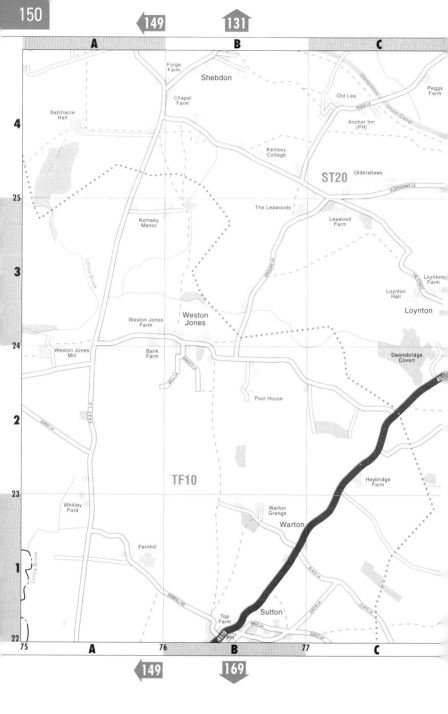

A

B

C

Forge Farm

Shebdon

Chapel Farm

Old Lea

Peggs Farm

Shropshire Union Canal

PEGGS LA

Batchacre Hall

Anchor Inn (PH)

4

Kemsey Cottage

ST20

Oldershaws

OLDERSHAWS LA

25

The Leawoods

Kemsey Manor

Leawood Farm

Lonco Brook

3

GREGORY LA

THE STREET

Loynton Farm

Loynton Hall

Loynton

Weston Jones Farm

Weston Jones

24

Weston Jones Mill

Bank Farm

BAKERS LA

Deansbridge Covert

A5c

MILL LA

Pool House

2

GORSEY LA

SHAY LA

23

TF10

Heybridge Farm

Whitley Ford

Warton Grange

Warton

Fernhill

BLACK LA

1

Lonco Brook

CLIFFS LA

FERNHILL RD

Top Farm

Sutton

GREEN LA

GUILD LA

BACK LA

A519 (PH)

22

75

A

76

B

77

C

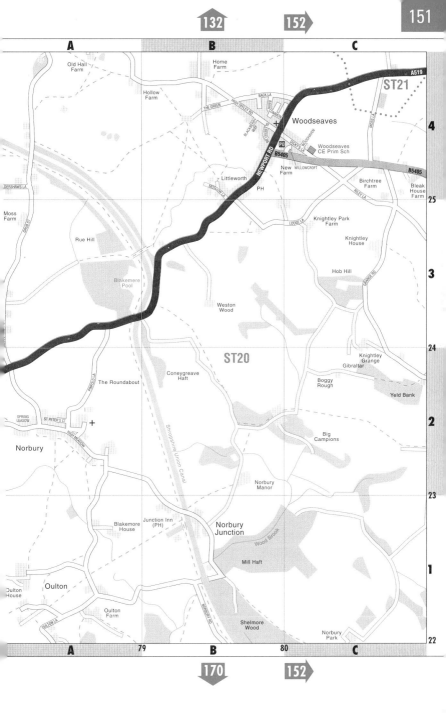

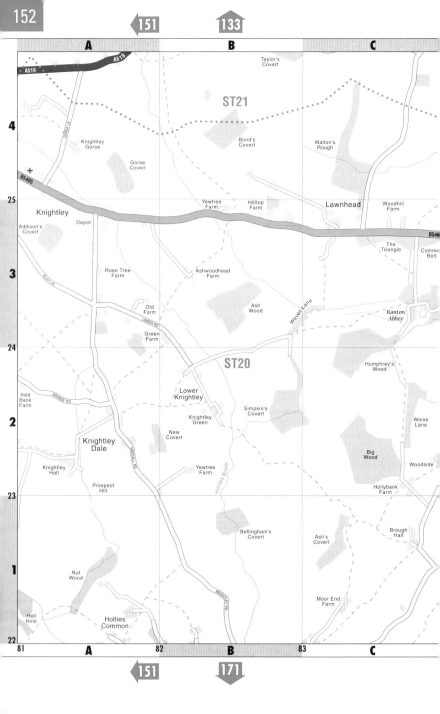

A   B   C

A519

A519

Taylor's
Covert

ST21

4

Knightley
Gorse

Bond's
Covert

Walton's
Rough

Gorse
Covert

B5405

25

Yewtree
Farm

Hilltop
Farm

Lawnhead

Woodhill
Farm

Knightley

Depot

B54

Addison's
Covert

The
Triangle

Comme
Belt

3

BULL LA

Rose Tree
Farm

Ashwoodhead
Farm

Wavell Lane

Ranton
Abbey

Old
Farm

Ash
Wood

LOWER RD

Green
Farm

24

ST20

Humphrey's
Wood

Lower
Knightley

Yeld
Bank
Farm

GRANGE RD

Simpkin's
Covert

Woise
Lane

2

Knightley
Green

GNOSALL RD

New
Covert

Big
Wood

Woodside

Knightley
Dale

Knightley
Hall

Yewtree
Farm

Hollies Brook

Hollybank
Farm

Prospect
Hill

23

Bellingham's
Covert

Ash's
Covert

Brough
Hall

1

Nut
Wood

KNIGHTLEY RD

Moor End
Farm

Hell
Hole

Hollies
Common

22

81   A   82   B   83   C

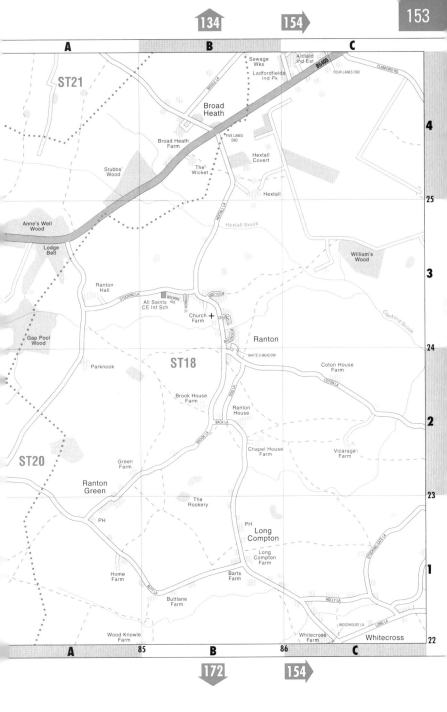

153
135

A   B   C

CRESWELL GRO
A5013

Bullockscroft Brook

Creswell

Edwards
Covert

Floss
Bridge

Lower
Cooksland
Farm

The
Grove

Cooksland
Hall
Farm

Love Lane

Wilke's
Wood

Cooksland

4

Ashpit
Covert

The
Mount

Seighford
Hall

Ansell's
Covert

Seighford

Ford

Moor
Covert

Millian Brook

25   +

THE
CLIMBERS

PH
Cooper Perry
Prim Sch

Ashes
Covert

Clanford
Covert

Haynes's
Covert

3

Clanford Hall
Farm

SEIGHFORD RD

Oldford
Covert

Clanford
Bridge

GRASSMERE
HOLLOW

24

Oldford
Farm

Wassage
Covert

ST18

DOXEY
FIELDS

Ashton Hill
Farm

ASTON DR

Aston
Bank
Farm

Coton
Clanford

Presford Brook

2

COTON LA

CORSTY LA

Barn
Farm

Sunnyside
Farm

Little Aston
Farm

ASTON HILL

Aston
Hall

Aston

Aston
Farm

ST16

Coton
Hall
Farm

Green
Farm

Glen
Farm

Holly Bush
Farm

Butterbank
Bridge

Presford
Bridge

Doxey Brook

Mill
Farm

Wks

Hill
Farm

23

Villa
Farm

Presford
House
Farm

Oak
Farm

BLACKHEATH LA

TWEMLOW
CL

+

Butterbank Brook

Red Lion
(PH)

PO

WILLOW
BROOK

LONG LA

CROSSING LA

1

The
Handfords

The Way for the Millennium

Stallbrook
Hall

MAPLE DR

Derrington

CASTLE VIEW
EST

Bungalow
Farm

Longlane
Farm

Boons
Ind Est

M6

22

87   A   88   B   89   C

153
173

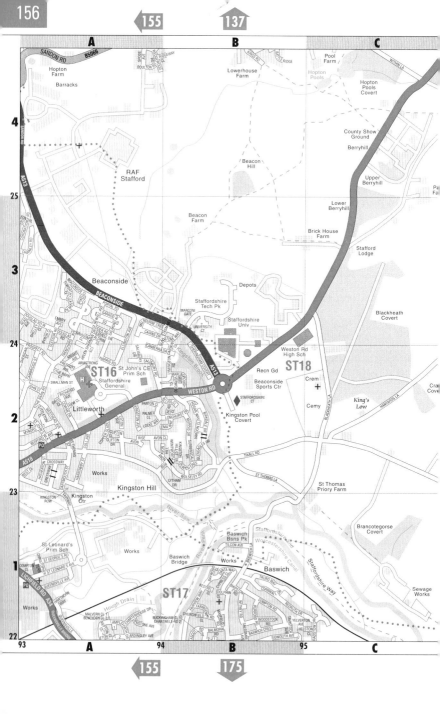

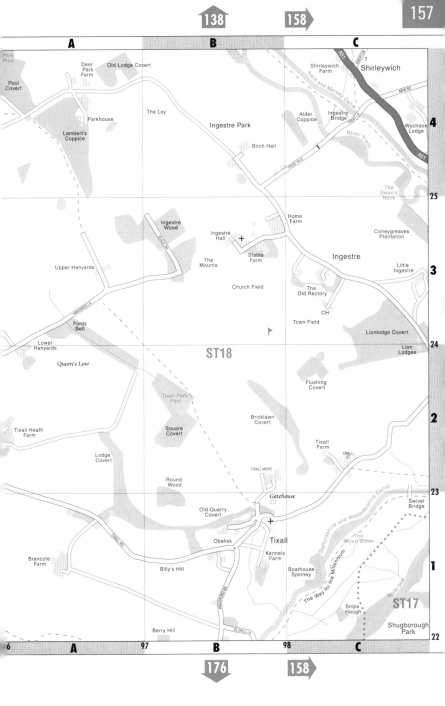

A **B** **C**

Park
Pool

Pool
Covert

Deer Park
Farm

Old Lodge Covert

Shirleywich
Farm

Shirleywich

A51

LIMEKILN LA

NEW RD

Parkhouse

The Ley

Ingestre Park

Trent and Mersey Canal

Alder
Coppice

Ingestre
Bridge

Wychdon
Lodge

4

Lambert's
Coppice

Birch Hall

River Trent

A51

TRENT WLK

25

The
Swan's
Neck

Ingestre
Wood

Home
Farm

Coneygreaves
Plantation

BLACK DR

Ingestre
Hall

✝

Upper Hanyards

The
Mounts

Stable
Farm

Ingestre

Little
Ingestre

3

Church Field

The
Old Rectory

HANYARDS LA

CH

Fords
Belt

Town Field

Lionlodge Covert

Lower
Hanyards

▶

ST18

24

Lion
Lodges

Queen's Low

Flushing
Covert

2

Tixall
Park
Pool

Bricklawn
Covert

Tixall Heath
Farm

Square
Covert

Tixall
Farm

TIXALL
CT

Lodge
Covert

Round
Wood

23

TIXALL RD

Old Quarry
Covert

TIXALL MEWS

Gatehouse

Staffordshire and Worcestershire Canal

Swivel
Bridge

✝

Obelisk

Tixall

The
Broad Water

Brancote
Farm

Billy's Hill

Kennels
Farm

1

Boathouse
Spinney

The Way for the Millennium

River Sow

ST17

HOLDIFORD RD

Berry Hill

OLDMILL LA

Snipe
Haugh

Shugborough
Park

22

6 **A** 97 **B** 98 **C**

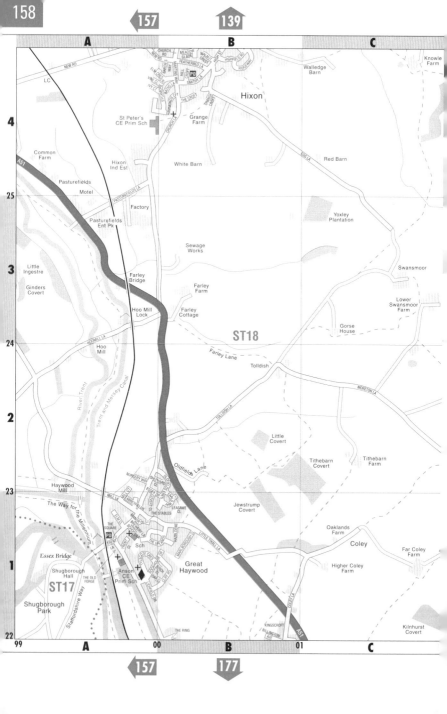

A B C

Lower Lea
Farm

Lea
Heath

Lea Heath
Farm

Newton
Bridge

Lea
Farm

The Wicket
(PH)

shaw's
Rough

Manor
Farm

Newtonhurst
Farm

River Blithe

Newton

Newbuildings
Farm

Middle
Farm

Bourn Brook

4

Vaughan's Lane
Farm

Newton
Farm

VAUGHAN'S LA

25

Long
Plantation

Blithfield
Reservoir

3

Dairy
House
Farm

Dairy
House

Blithfield
Hall

24

Rectory

ST18

Rectory
Farm

WS15

Blithfield
Park

Moreton Barn
Farm

Moreton Brook

2

Oakfields

SCHOOL LA

Moreton
Farm

Admaston
Lodges

Moreton
House

B5013

23

LEA LA

Blithfield
Gorse

Wilderley
Barn

Moreton
Grange

Lea Hall
Farm

MORETON LA

SHERBROOK LA

1

Spencer's
Plantation

Flint's
Barn

Upper
Moreton

Jongham's
Cottage

Moreton
LA

B5013

22

A 03 B 04 C

Newton Hurst

Dimsdale Plantation

Dimsdale

Bagots' Bromley
* Mon
B5013

Bagots' Bromley Cottages

The Warren

Stansleywood Saw Mills

Duckley Plantation

B5013
B5014

UTTOXETER RD

Dunstal Hall Farm

Dunstal Brook

HALEY LA

25

Stanley Wood

Barn Farm

Yeatsall Cottages

Leafields Farm

GRANGE

SALTERS

ST ALFRED

BAGOT ST

LINTAKE DR

3

Yeatsall

YEATSALL RD

Wilversall House

Narrow La

Milne Brook

DOSSE LA

Highash

24

Blithfield Reservoir

WS15

PORT LA

Highelms

Halfhill La

Causeway

WATERY LA

Black Wood

Yenbrook

STOCKBY LA

2

Admaston Farm

Portfields

Mickledale

WALTERS RD

Seedcroft

B5013

Admaston

23

St Stephen's Hill

STEENWOOD LA

Round Plantation

Staffordshire Way

Tad Brook

1

Steenwood Cottages

Boat House

Medleywood Barn

River Blithe

SHERRACOP LA

Newlands Cottage

Sherracop Plantation

Park Barn Farm

NEWLANDS LA

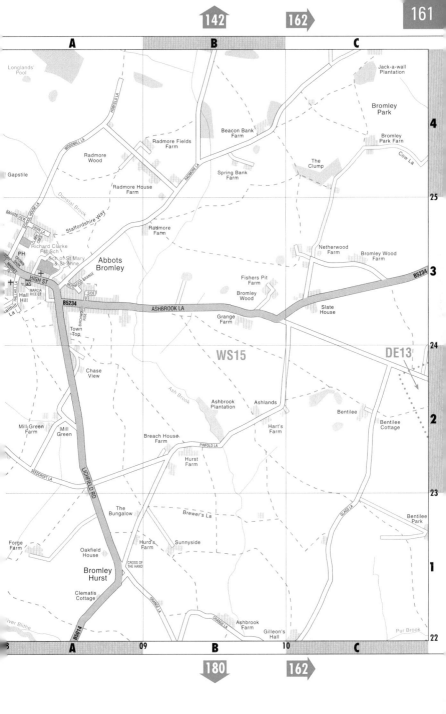

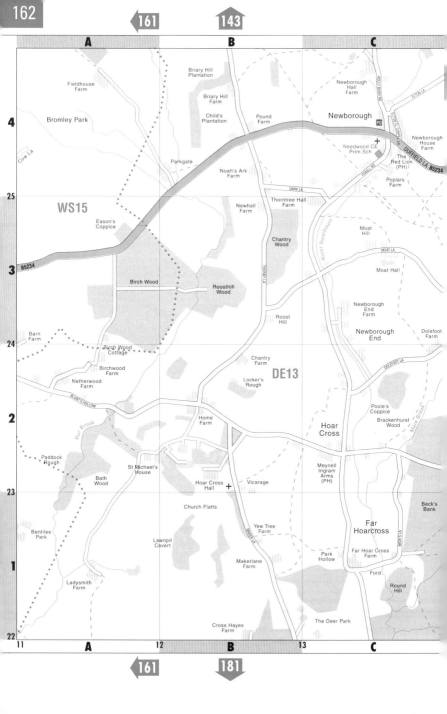

A   B   C

Stockley Park

Stockley Plantation

Whitestone Lane

Newgatefield Lane

PH

BEAMHILL RD

LONGHEDGE LA

Hill Top Farm

Upper Outwoods

Mount Pleasant Farm

Poplars Farm

Anslow Park Farm

Upper Outwoods Farm

MAIN ST

4

Morley Prim Sch

Mill Hill Farm

Anslow

FIELD LA

OUTWOODS LA

Bell Inn (PH)

OUTWOODS LA

25

Riddings Farm

Bungalow Farm

Mayfields Farm

Mast

Outwoods Lane

Henhurst Field

Lower Outwoods

Anslow Common

MAIN ST

MARPLE RD

CHAPEL LA

LOWER OUTWOODS RD

ST GEORGE'S RD

TERRERSON'S RD

3

Snobnall Brook

Henhurst Wood

Redhouse Farm

PH

Henhurst Wood Farm

HENHURST FARM

Leys Farm

Shobnall Dingle

DIMBLE DR

FRED BREWER WAY

Oaks Wood

24

HENHURST HILL

FOREST RD

ROBERSON RD

Shobnall Prim Sch

PO

Nursery

Shobnall Brook

Rough Hay

DE13

HENHURST RIDGE

AVALON LA

SHOBNALL RD

Rough Hay Farm

Depot

SINAI CL

Shobnall Grange

B5017

POSTERN RD

Sandyford Dingle

DE14

Brewery

Shobnall

Postern House Farm

Glenfield

Sinai Park

Lord's Well

23

CALLINGWOOD LA

Trent and Mersey Canal

The Way for the Millennium

Pool Green Farm

The Rough

Pool Green Bridge

The Thorns

Prince's Covert

The Bungalows

1

School Bridge

NEW ROW

MAIN ST

Tatenhill

Battlestead Hill

Lawns Farm

Towing Path

WILLINGTON RD

DARK LA

22

20   A   21   B   22   C

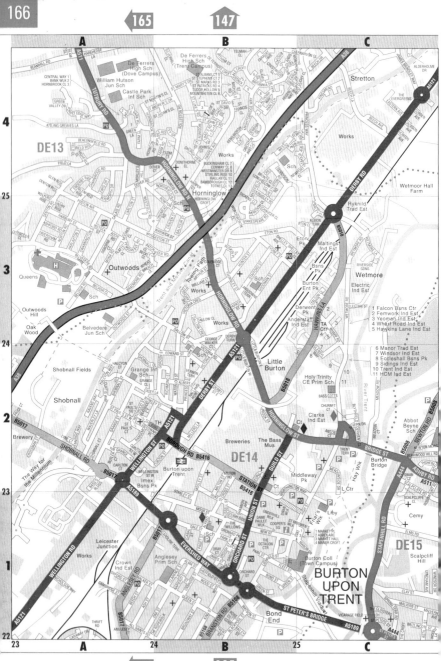

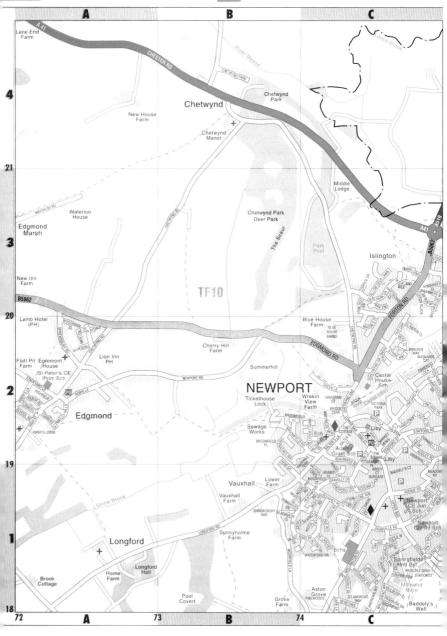

A   B   C

Lane End Farm

A 41

CHESTER RD

River Meese

CHETWYND PARK

Chetwynd

Chetwynd Park

New House Farm

Chetwynd Manor

4

21

Waterloo House

WATERLOO RD

Chetwynd Park Deer Park

The Scaur

Park Pool

Middle Lodge

A41

A519

B5062

Edgmond Marsh

3

Islington

SUNNY

FORTON RD

TF10

New Inn Farm

B5062

20

Lamb Hotel (PH)

Blue House Farm

BLUE HOUSE BARNS

Cherry Hill Farm

EDGMOND RD

Flatt Pit Farm
Egremont House

Lion Inn PH

St Peter's C E Prim Sch

Summerhill

NEWPORT RD

Castle House Sch

Edgmond

2

NEWPORT

Tickethouse Lock

Wrekin View Farm

HAWISHAM CT

VICTORIA PARK

Liby

P

19

Vauxhall

Lower Farm

Adams Gram Sch

Liby

P

MEADOW RD

BADDELY'S CT

Strine Brook

Vauxhall Farm

SHREWSBURY WAY

BLACKMORE

Newport C E Jun Sch

Newport Girls' Inf Sch

1

Longford

LONGFORD RD

Sunnyholme Farm

WATERFORD DR

Sch

Springfields IND EST

STATION CT

Millwood Mere

PRINCESS GDNS

Brook Cottage

Home Farm

Longford Hall

Pool Covert

Grove Farm

Aston Grove PINEWOODS

ST ANDREWS WAY

RICHMOND

Baddely's Well

18

72   A   73   B   74   C

A   B   C

ST20

Sutton Bank
Farm

Forton
Monument

Windswell
Pool

Sheepsley La

A519

4

Forton

Swan Inn
(PH)

Thistlefield
Covert

River Meese

21

New
Guild

Meretown

Meretown
Farm

Moss
Pool

Clark's
Plantation

Aqualate
Mere

3

LOUGH LA

KESTREL CL

BEECHFIELDS WAY

TF10

20

Broom
Hill

WALKLEY BANK

Boathouse
Wood

The
Spectacles

Roundabouts

Aqualate
Hall

BEN JONSON AVE

WATERS EDGE CLOSE

1 TOMKINSON CL
2 AQUALATE CL
3 HENLEY DR
4 FISHERS LOCK
5 SUMMERHOUSE GR
6 THE OVAL BGLWS

Aqualate
Castle

Aqualate Park
Deer Park

The
Shrubbery

2

PLOUGHMANS

GRO

Castle
Wood

Gardener's
Wood

HAMPTON AVE

HAZELTON

STAFFORD RD

HIGH
MDWS

MEADOW RD

BROADWAY

BARNMEADOW

A518

A518

BARNMEADOW CL

BARNMEADOW RD

Parson's
Barn

19

AUDLEY MDWS

AUDLEY HO

AUDLEY AVE

Cemy

The Burton
Borough Sch

Park
Wood

Audley Ave
Bsns Pk

Park
Farm

1

Lime Tree
Cottage

A518

Park
Bank

A518

A41

A   76   B   77   C   18

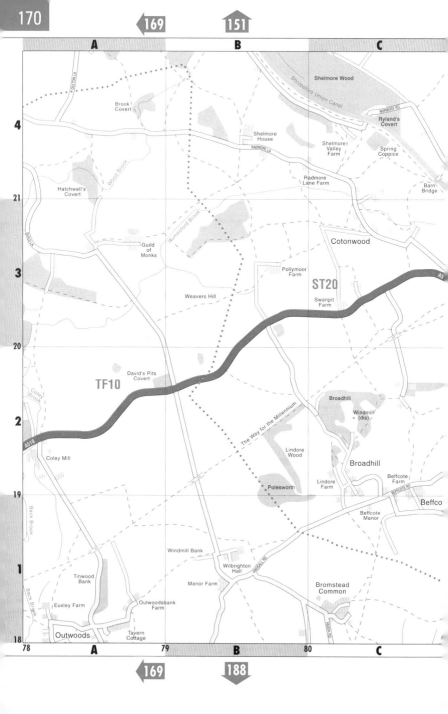

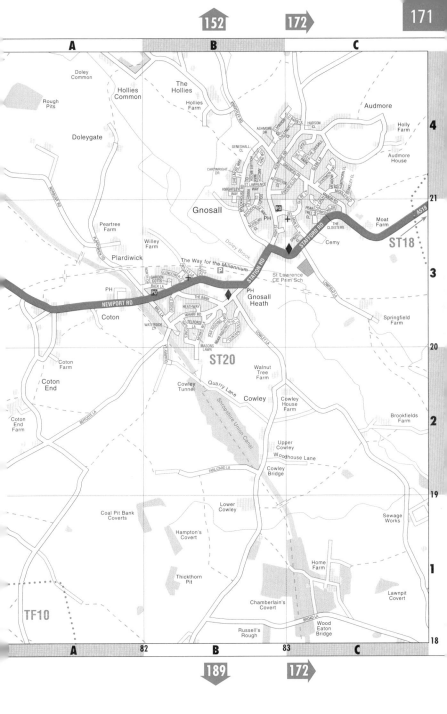

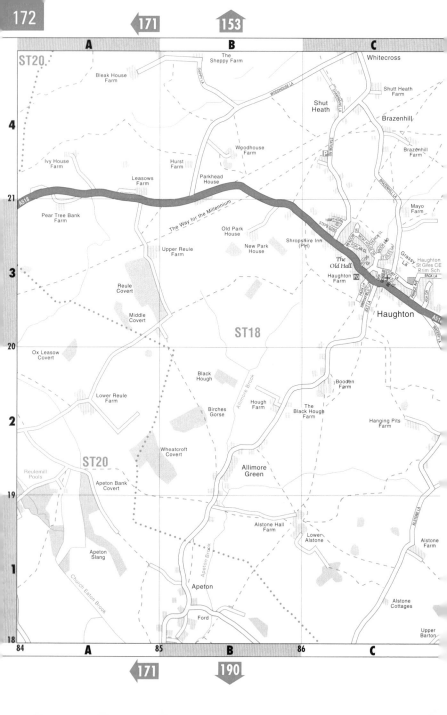

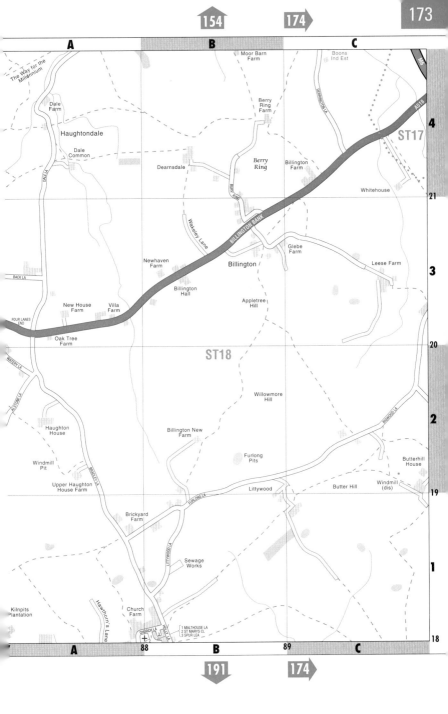

The Way for the Millennium

Moor Barn Farm

Boons Ind Est

M6

Dale Farm

A518

Haughtondale

Berry Ring Farm

ST17

4

Dale Common

Dearnsdale

Berry Ring

Billington Farm

BURY LANE

Whitehouse

21

Wakeley Lane

BILLINGTON BANK

Glebe Farm

Leese Farm

Newhaven Farm

Billington

BACK LA

Billington Hall

Appletree Hill

3

New House Farm

Villa Farm

FOUR LANES END

Oak Tree Farm

20

ST18

Willowmore Hill

WATERY LA

ALSTONE LA

2

Haughton House

Billington New Farm

PENKWOOD LA

Windmill Pit

Furlong Pits

Butterhill House

Upper Haughton House Farm

BRADLEY LA

FURLONG LA

Littywood

Butter Hill

Windmill (dis)

19

Brickyard Farm

LITTYWOOD LA

Sewage Works

1

Kilnpits Plantation

Hawthorn's Lane

Church Farm

CHURCH LA

MILL LA

1 MALTHOUSE LA
2 ST MARYS CL
3 SPUR LEA

18

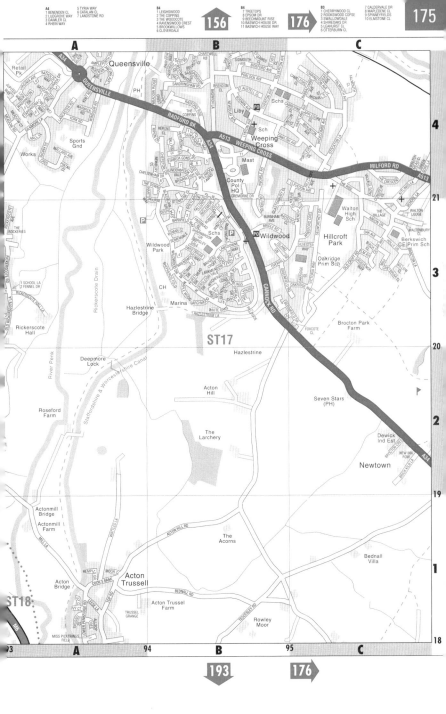

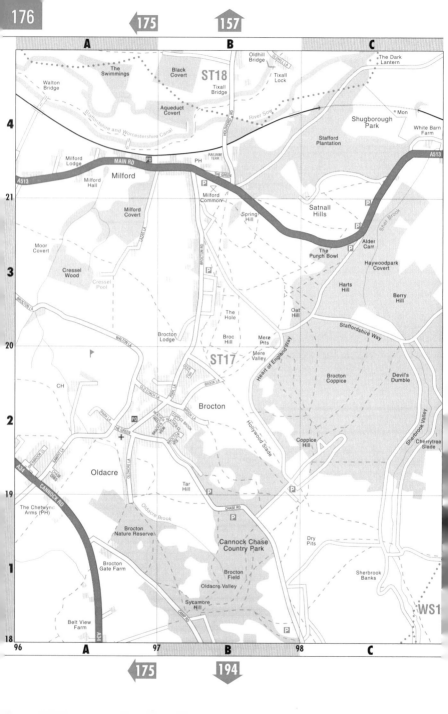

A   B   C

The Swimmings

Walton Bridge

Black Covert

ST18

Oldhill Bridge

Tixall Bridge

Tixall Lock

The Dark Lantern

Aqueduct Covert

Staffordshire and Worcestershire Canal

River Sow

Mon

Shugborough Park

White Barn Farm

4

Stafford Plantation

A513

Milford Lodge

MAIN RD

PO

PH

THE GREEN

Milford

Milford Hall

Milford Covert

RAILWAY TERR

Milford Common

Satnall Hills

A513

A513

21

Spring Hill

Shell Brook

Moor Covert

BROCTON RD

The Punch Bowl

Alder Carr

Haywoodpark Covert

Cressel Wood

Cressel Pool

Harts Hill

Berry Hill

3

BROCTON LA

WALTON LA

The Hole

Oat Hill

Staffordshire Way

Brocton Lodge

Broc Hill

Mere Pits

Brocton Coppice

Devil's Dumble

20

Mere Valley

ST17

Heart of England Way

OLD COACH LA

POOL LA

BROOK LA

Sherbrook Valley

Cherrytree Slade

2

CH

FARM LA

Brocton

PO

THE GREEN

Hollywood Slade

Coppice Hill

SHERBROOK LA

Oldacre

OLDACRE LA

Oldacre Brook

Tar Hill

CHASE RD

A34

CANNOCK RD

19

The Chetwynd Arms (PH)

Brocton Nature Reserve

Cannock Chase Country Park

Dry Pits

1

Brocton Gate Farm

Brocton Field

Oldacre Valley

Sherbrook Banks

Sycamore Hill

CAMP RD

WS1

18

96   A   97   B   98   C

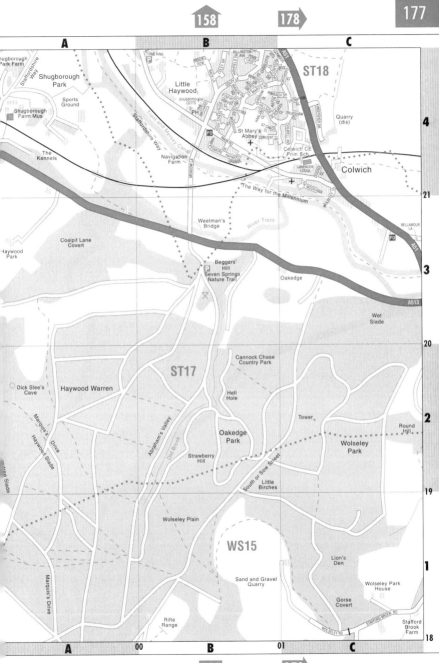

A **B** **C**

Shugborough
Park Farm

Shugborough
Park

Staffordshire Way

Sports
Ground

THE RING
P

BILLINGTON

Little
Haywood

WINDSOR'S ROW

HIXON CL

ST18

Shugborough
Farm Mus

SHUGBOROUGH
COTTS

PH

RIMBAGE DR

Quarry
(dis)

4

The
Kennels

Staffordshire Way

PO

St Mary's
Abbey

MEADOW LA

HAYWARD
GRANGE

ST CHADS

CONVENT CL

Colwich CE
Prim Sch

CHAPEL RD

KINGFISHER DR

LAVENDER
LODGE

Colwich

Navigation
Farm

The Way for the Millennium

MOORINGS

21

Weetman's
Bridge

River Trent

BELLAMOUR
LA

PO

A513

Coalpit Lane
Covert

Haywood
Park

Beggars'
Hill
P   Seven Springs
Nature Trail

Oakedge

3

Wet
Slade

20

Haywood Warren

ST17

Cannock Chase
Country Park

Hell
Hole

Tower

Round
Hill

2

Dick Slee's
Cave

Marquis's Drive

Abraham's Valley

Old Brook

Oakedge
Park

Wolseley
Park

Haywood Slade

Strawberry
Hill

South or Sow Street

Little
Birches

19

erey Slade

Wolseley Plain

WS15

Lion's
Den

1

Marquis's Drive

Sand and Gravel
Quarry

Wolseley Park
House

Gorse
Covert

STAFFORD BROOK RD

Rifle
Range

WOLSELEY RD

Stafford
Brook
Farm

18

A   00   **B**   01   **C**

A   B   C

Crabtree Farm

Park Barn Farm

Newlands

Newlands Grange

Lower Newlands Farm

NEWLANDS LA

amley House Farm

Stockwell Heath

SHERBROOK LA

PARK LA

MOOR LA

Pool Farm

Ash Hill

4

Staffordshire Way

FAIR MDWS

MARLTON LA

HEATHWAY

NEWLANDS LA

Long Mets La

Oxclose Plantation

Gorse Hill

PH

SANDON WAY

ASPEN PL

AREAR

CLOSE

Finners Hill

21

HIGH ST

Longley La

Colton

LISCROFT

SEAMOUR WAY

HOLLOW LA

MARTLIN LA

VAM RD 15

Martlin Hill

Banktop

Bank Top Farm

Hurst Wood

Hurst Wood Farm

Rosewood Farm

Hadleygate

3

BLITHBURY RD

WS15

20

Old Wood Farm No 2

Old Wood Farm No 7

New Barn

Old Wood Farm No 8

Black Flatts Farm

Stonyford Covert

STONYFORD LA

Stonyford Farm

Parchfield House Farm

2

B5014

Parchfield Farm

BLITHBURY RD

Colton Hall Farm

Stone Cottages

19

Rugeley Junction

1

Rake End

RAKE END CT

UTTOXETER RD

River Trent

Rectory

Cawarden Springs Farm

WADE LA

WADE CROFT

B5014

A 06 B 07 C

18

179

161

DE13

A   B   C

4

Blithford
Farm

NEWLANDS LA

B5014

Mount
Pleasant

Poplar
Farm

ORANGE LA

Rookery
Farm

Old Lane

Ash
Hill

The
Willows

The
Hurst

Little Blithe

Porter's
Hill

21

NUNS LA

Priory
Farm

Old Lane

PEARTREE LA

Bank House
Farm

UTTOXETER RD

3

Blithbury
Farm

River Blithe

Braddocks
Barn

Pur Brook

Manor
Farm

BLITHBURY RD

Blithbury

Longacres

WS15

Hayend
Wood

20

New
House
Farm

Hayend

PIPE WOOD LA

Westwood
Sch

B5014

Pipewood Cottage
Farm

Pipe
Wood

Town End
Farm

BLITHBURY RD

Hamstall
Hall
✠

2

Coatfield

Hamstall
Ridware

✠

19

Bentley Hall
Farm

Goldhayfields

Hunger
Hill

Cowley
Hill

LICHFIELD RD

PH

BLYTHE
VIEW

Woodhouse
Farm

Cowley
Hill Farm

1

Quintin's
Orchard

Blythe House
Farm

CHADWICK CRES

18

OAKLANDS
CL

A   09   B   10   C

08

179

198

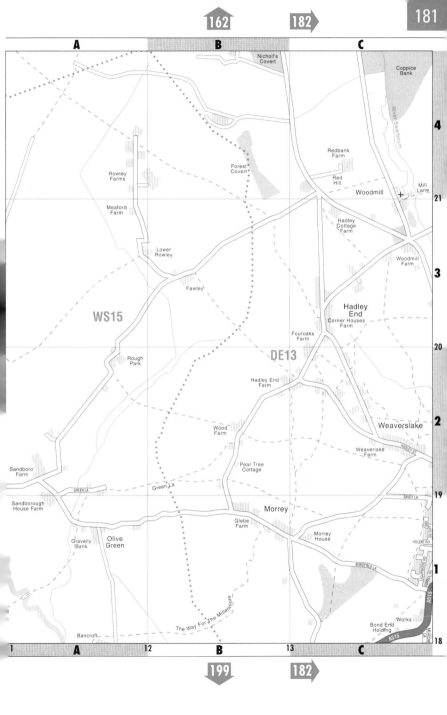

A B C

4

Nicholl's
Covert

Coppice
Bank

River Swarbourn

Redbank
Farm

Red
Hill

Woodmill

Mill
Lane

21

Forest
Covert

Rowley
Farms

Meaford
Farm

Hadley
Cottage
Farm

Lower
Rowley

Woodmill
Farm

3

Fawley

WS15

Hadley
End

Corner Houses
Farm

Fouroaks
Farm

DE13

20

Rough
Park

Hadley End
Farm

Weaverslake

2

Wood
Farm

Weaverlake
Farm

HADLEY RD

Pear Tree
Cottage

Sandboro'
Farm

Green La

GREEN LA

Green La

SAVEY LA

19

Sandborough
House Farm

Morrey

Glebe
Farm

Morrey
House

ASH RD

FRYS RD

HOLLINS RD

Gravelly
Bank

Olive
Green

BONDFIELD LA

LIGHTWOOD RD

A515

1

The Way For The Millennium

Bancroft

Bond End
Holding

Works

A515

MEADOW RD

18

164
184

A   B   C

Home Farm

Deanery
Plantation

Bannister's
Hollies

Highlands
Park

Rockets
Oak

TATENHILL LA

4

Deanery
Farm

The
Exchange

The
Oaks

Hobholes
Dingle

The
Caves

HARDGROVE HILL

Fernhill
Farm

Sprinks Barn
Farm

Bikersdale
Wood

21

DUNSTALL CROSS

DUNSTALL HILL

The
Larches

The
Hills

Yew Tree
Farm

DUNSTALL
CROSS

FOREST RD

Dunstall

Dunstall Home
Farm

Greenlane
Plantation

3

Old
Hall

Dunstall
Hall

The Park

Forest
Thorn

Mill
Pond

Saw
Mill

Gravel
Pits

20

Forest
Barn

Smith Hills
Cottages

DE13

The
Pool

ASHBROOK HILL

Lower
Farm

Needwood
Rise

Smith
Hills

BRICK KILN LANE

Woodside
Farm

2

The Bell
(PH)

Barton
Gate

Small
Meadows

Silver Hill

The Knoll

SMALL MDWS

19

BARTON GATE

Barton-under-
Needwood

Barton
Hall

MANOR
CT

DUNSTALL RD

BAT LE

Barton
Park

MAIN ST

P

PO

Liby

John Taylor
High Sch

Telephone
Exchange

PH

Thomas
Russell
Inf Sch

STATION RD

B5016

1

Blakenhall

Barton
Cottage

H

MEADOW

GILMOUR LA

Thomas
Russell
Jun Sch

Sewage
Works

Marina

Gorsey Hill
Farm

THE ALDERS

ASH TREES RD

CEDAR
RD

18

7   A   18   B   19   C   18

201
184

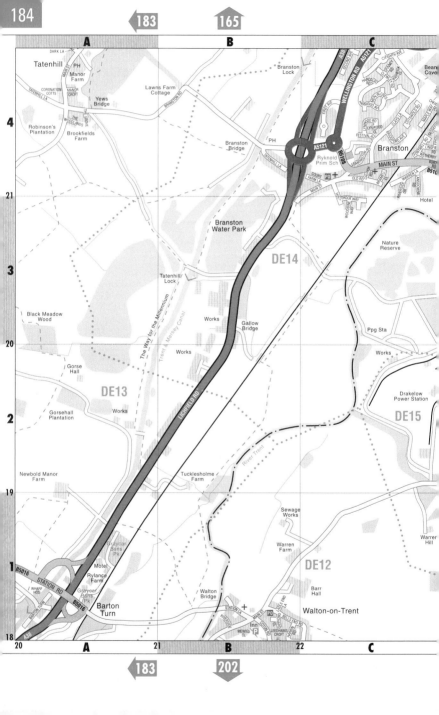

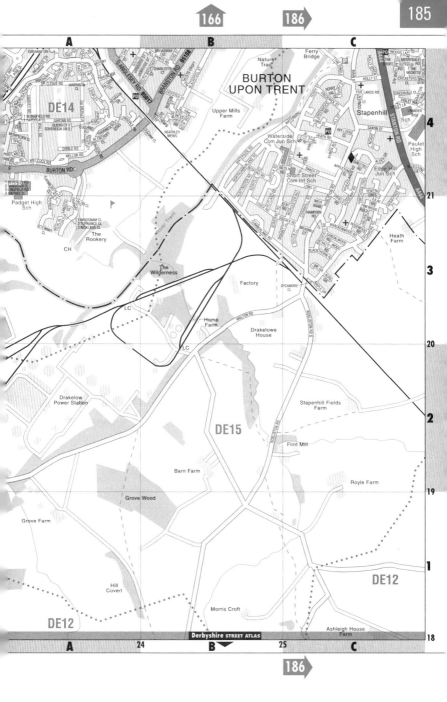

BURTON
UPON TRENT

DE14

Stapenhill

Padget High
Sch

The
Rookery

CH

The
Wilderness

Factory

Home
Farm

Drakelowe
House

Drakelow
Power Station

Stapenhill Fields
Farm

DE15

Flint Mill

Barn Farm

Royle Farm

Grove Wood

Grove Farm

DE12

Hill
Covert

Morris Croft

DE12

Ashleigh House
Farm

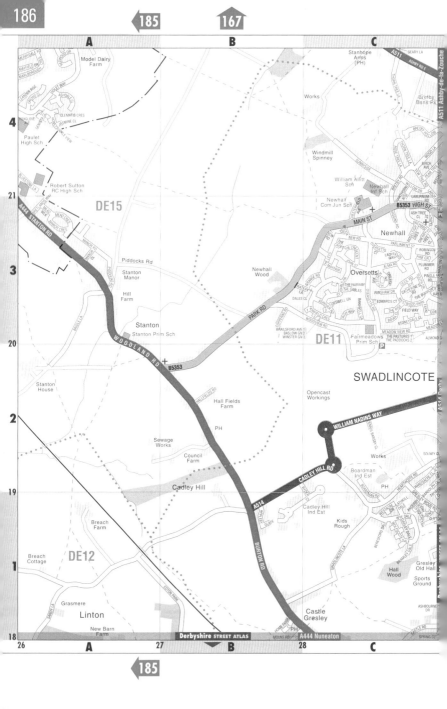

A | B | C

A56 to Telford (A442) | A41 | A518

Chetwynd
Aston
Field
Aston
Wheatsheaf
(PH)
Aston
Manor
Resr

New
Plantation

Back Brook

4

Pave
Lane
Yew Tree
Manor

Stockton
Roughs

Stockton
Grange

17

COUNCIL
HOS

Fox
& Duck
(PH)
Resr
Pave Lane
Farm

LITTLEHALES RD

PUDDNOT LA

TF10

Stockton

Stockton
House

3

Muster Hill

16

Cotes
Pool

Greens
Wood

Broomfield
Plantation

Ash Pit

Lynn
Cottages

Coach House
Cottages

Woodcote
Hall

The
Marlpits

2

Child Pit
Farm

Woodcote

Springpool

CHADWELL A

Riding
School

Childpit
Lane

15

The
Roundabout

Barbers
Gorse

Woodcote Hill

B4379

Lilleshall Hall
National Sports
Ctr

TF11

Nutty
Hills

1

Nutty Hills
Farm

Heath Hill
Lodge
Heath Hill

Bloomsbury

Grange Acre

Cherry Tree
Farm

B4379

HEATH HILL

HAND LA

A41 Wolverhampton

A41

14

5 | A | 76 | B | 77 | C

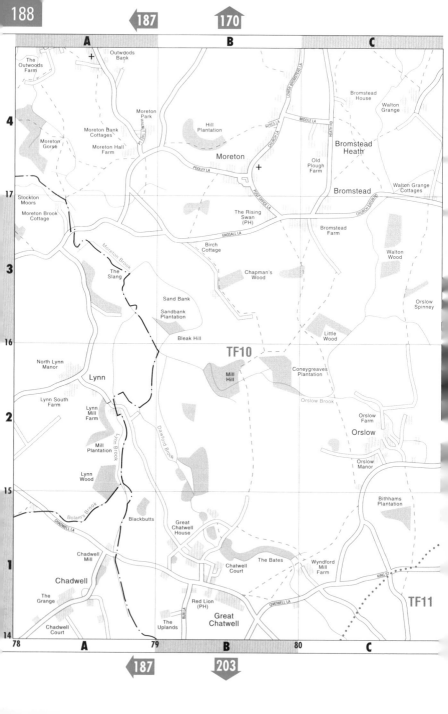

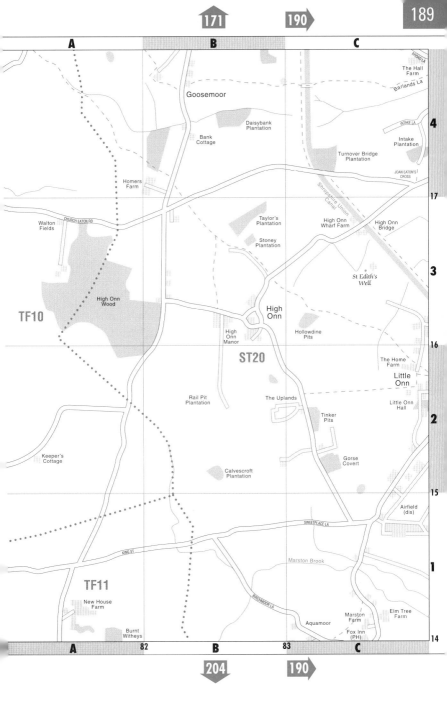

171

190

A

B

C

BRAND LA

The Hall Farm

Barlands La

INTAKE LA

4

Goosemoor

Daisybank Plantation

Bank Cottage

Intake Plantation

Turnover Bridge Plantation

JOAN EATON'S CROSS

Homers Farm

CHURCH EATON RD

Shropshire Union Canal

17

Walton Fields

Taylor's Plantation

High Onn Wharf Farm

High Onn Bridge

Stoney Plantation

St Edith's Well

3

High Onn Wood

TF10

High Onn

High Onn Manor

Hollowdine Pits

16

The Home Farm

ST20

Little Onn

Rail Pit Plantation

The Uplands

Little Onn Hall

2

Tinker Pits

Keeper's Cottage

Gorse Covert

Calvescroft Plantation

15

Airfield (dis)

SWEETPLACE LA

Marston Brook

1

KING ST

TF11

New House Farm

BIRCHMOOR LA

Marston Farm

Elm Tree Farm

Aquamoor

Burnt Witheys

Fox Inn (PH)

14

A

82

B

83

C

204

190

A   B   C

Bradley

ALMSHOUSE CROFT
Goring
Farm PO

Whitehouse
Farm

BARTON LA

Old Lane

FORGE
RISE

LEVEDALE RD

The Wells
Farm

Pigstockheys
Covert

4

OAK LA
Hayes
Farm

SHREDICOTE LA

MITTON RD

17

Willow Farm

Levedale

Bradley Hall

Levedale
Farm

+

ST18

Field House
Farm

Shredicote Hall
Farm

3

Priory
Farm

Down House
Farm

Shredicote
Farm

New House
Farm

16

Spion
Kop

ST20

2

Upper Mitton
Farm

Church Eaton Brook

Mitton

Lower Mitton
Farm

Staffordshire Way

15

ST19

Mitton
Manor

Whiston Brook

Whiston
Hall

The Swan
(PH)

Bickford

Ivy House
Farm

Pear Tree
Farm

Whiston

Longnor Farm

1

14

A   88   B   89   C

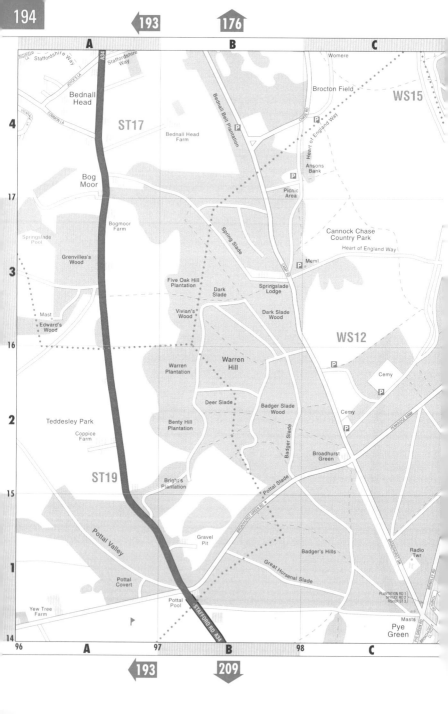

193
176

A   B   C

WS15

RICHFIELD LA
Staffordshire Way
JOYCE'S LA
A34
Staffordshire Way

Womere

Bednall
Head

Brocton Field

4

VICARAGE LA
COMMON LA

ST17

Bednall Head
Farm

Heart of England Way

Bednall Belt Plantation

P

P

17

Bog
Moor

Bogmoor
Farm

Ansons
Bank

CARR RD

P

Picnic
Area

Springslade
Pool

Grenvilles's
Wood

Cannock Chase
Country Park

Heart of England Way

3

Five Oak Hill
Plantation

Spring Slade

CARR RD

Meml

P

Mast

Dark
Slade

Springslade
Lodge

Edward's
Wood

Vivian's
Wood

Dark Slade
Wood

WS12

16

Warren
Plantation

Warren
Hill

P

Cemy

P

Teddesley Park

Deer Slade

Badger Slade
Wood

Cemy

FANSIDE LANE

2

Coppice
Farm

Benty Hill
Plantation

Badger Slade

P

Broadhurst
Green

ST19

Bright's
Plantation

Pottal Slade

BROADHURST DR

15

Pottal Valley

Gravel
Pit

BROADHURST EAST RD

Badger's Hills

Radio
Twr

1

Pottal
Covert

Great Horsenal Slade

PYE GREEN RD

Masts

Yew Tree
Farm

Pottal
Pool

STAFFORD RD A34

PLANTATION RD 1
SPRUCE RD 2
FISHER ST 3

BIRCH ST 1
HILL TOP

Pye
Green

14

96   A   97   B   98   C

193
209

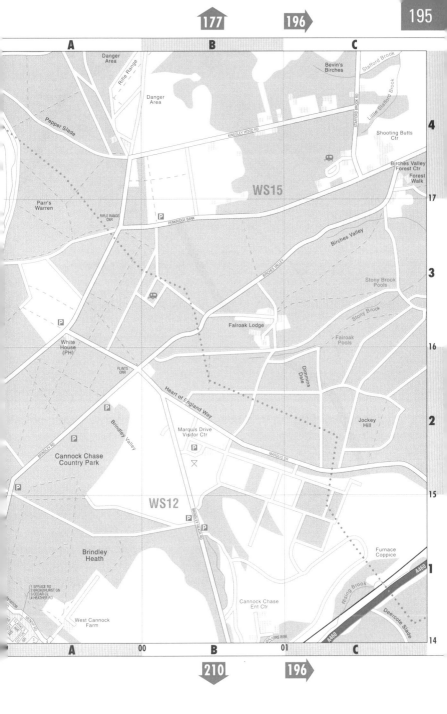

A   B   C

Danger Area

Rifle Range

Bevin's Birches

Stafford Brook

Little Stafford Brook

Danger Area

KINGSLEY WOOD RD

Pepper Slade

Shooting Butts Ctr

STAFFORD BROOK RD

4

Birches Valley Forest Ctr

Forest Walk

WS15

Parr's Warren

RIFLE RANGE CNR

17

P PENKRIDGE BANK

Birches Valley

Birches Valley

Stony Brook Pools

3

Fairoak Lodge

Stony Brook

Fairoak Pools

White House (PH)

P

16

FLINTS CNR

Dimmins Dale

Heart of England Way

Jockey Hill

2

Marquis Drive Visitor Ctr

P

P

Brindley Valley

MARQUIS DR

BROADHURST RD

Cannock Chase Country Park

P

WS12

15

P

BRINDLEY HEATH RD

Brindley Heath

P

Furnace Coppice

A460

1

Rising Brook

1 SPRUCE RD
2 BROADHURST GN
3 CEDAR CL
4 HEATHER RD

West Cannock Farm

Cannock Chase Ent Ctr

Deercote Slade

A460

ELLERS RISE

14

A   00   B   01   C

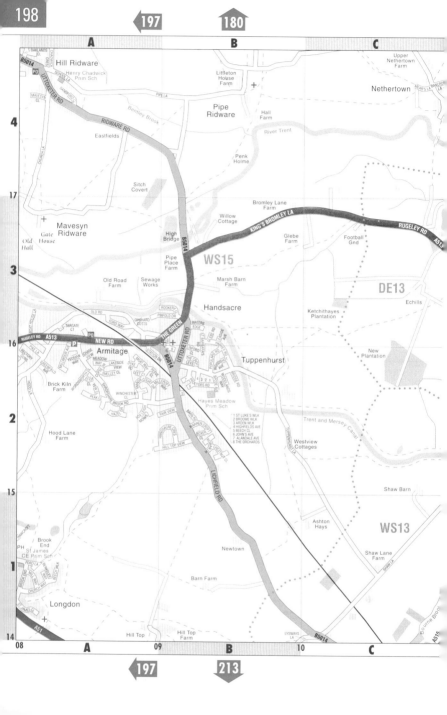

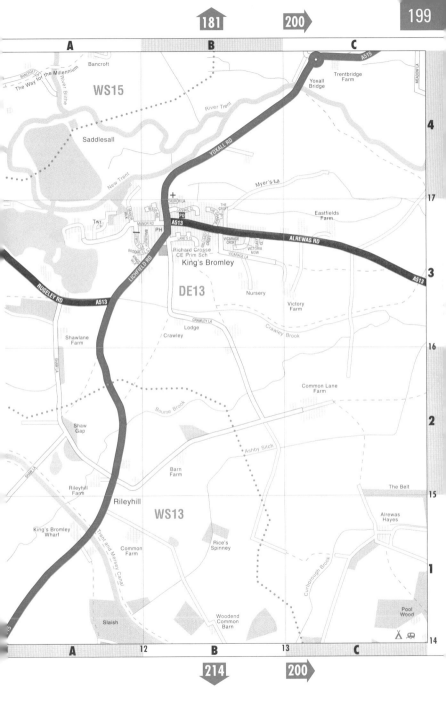

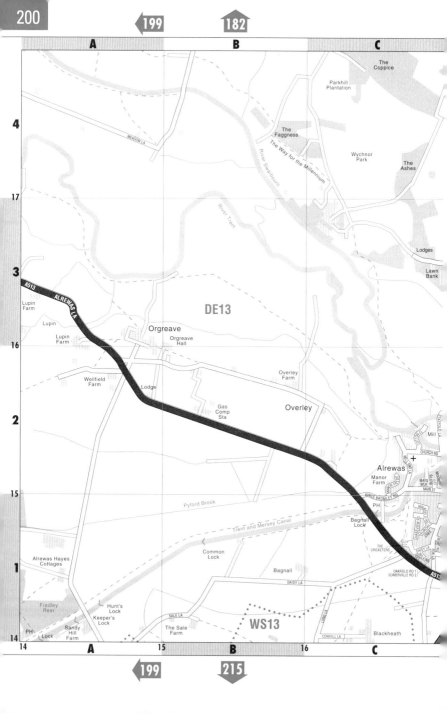

199
182

A B C

4

17

3 A513 ALREWAS LA

DE13

Lupin
Farm

Lupin

Lupin
Farm

Orgreave

Orgreave
Hall

16

Wellfield
Farm

Lodge

Overley
Farm

Overley

2

Gas
Comp
Sta

Mill

CHURCH RD

Alrewas

Manor
Farm

MAYS
WLK

MAIN ST

15

Pyford Brook

KINGS BROMLEY RD

PH

Trent and Mersey Canal

Bagnall
Lock

THE
CRICKETERS

Common
Lock

Alrewas Hayes
Cottages

Bagnall

DAISY LA

OAKFIELD RD 1
SOMERVILLE RD 2

A513

1

Fradley
Rear

Hunt's
Lock

Keeper's
Lock

Sandy
Hill
Farm

SALE LA

The Sale
Farm

WS13

LONG LA

COWHILL LA

Blackheath

PH
Lock

14

14 A 15 B 16 C

The
Coppice

Parkhill
Plantation

The
Faggness

The Way for the Millennium

Wychnor
Park

The
Ashes

River Swarbourn

River Trent

Lodges

Lawn
Bank

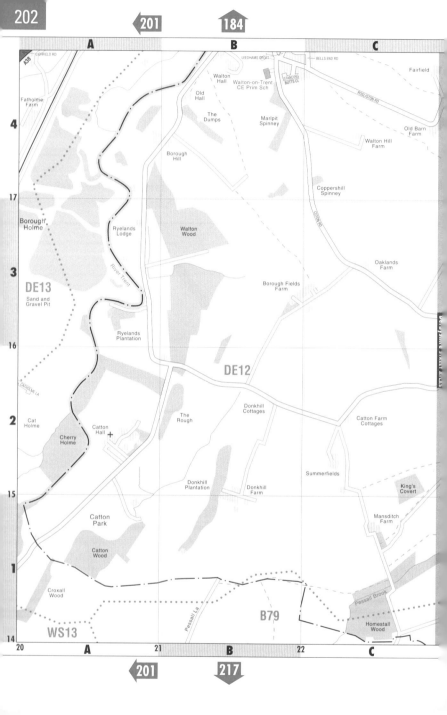

A B C

LICHFIELD RD
A38
Fatholme
Farm

LEEDHAMS CROFT
BELLS END RD
Walton
Hall
Walton-on-Trent
CE Prim Sch
STANDING
BUTTS CL
Fairfield

Old
Hall
The
Dumps

ROSLISTON RD

Marlpit
Spinney

Old Barn
Farm

Walton Hill
Farm

4

Borough
Hill

Coppershill
Spinney

17

Borough
Holme

Ryelands
Lodge

Walton
Wood

River Trent

Oaklands
Farm

3

DE13

COTON RD

Sand and
Gravel Pit

Borough Fields
Farm

Ryelands
Plantation

16

DE12

CATHOLME LA

Donkhill
Cottages

Catton Farm
Cottages

2

Cat
Holme

The
Rough

Catton
Hall

Cherry
Holme

Summerfields

King's
Covert

Donkhill
Plantation

Donkhill
Farm

Mansditch
Farm

15

Catton
Park

Catton
Wood

1

Croxall
Wood

Pessall Brook

Pessall La

B79

Homestall
Wood

WS13

14

20 A 21 B 22 C

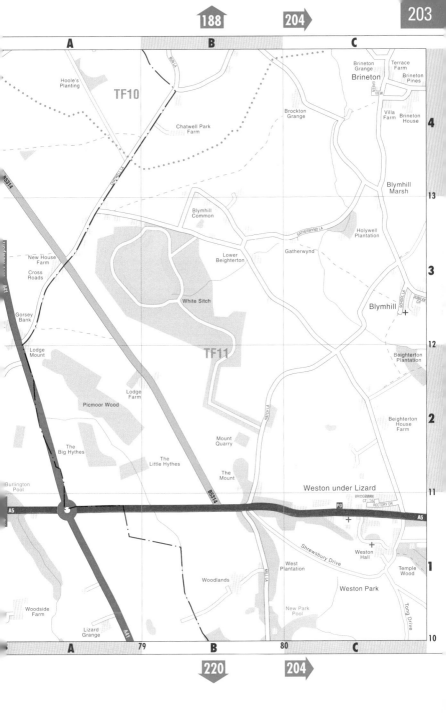

A B C

Hoole's Planting

TF10

Chatwell Park Farm

Brineton Grange

Terrace Farm

Brineton

Brineton Pines

Brockton Grange

Villa Farm

Brineton House

4

Blymhill Marsh

13

New House Farm

Cross Roads

Blymhill Common

GATHERWYND LA

Holywell Plantation

Gatherwynd

Lower Beighterton

Gorsey Bank

White Sitch

Blymhill

3

Lodge Mount

TF11

12

Beighterton Plantation

Lodge Farm

Picmoor Wood

BIRCH LA

Beighterton House Farm

2

The Big Hythes

The Little Hythes

Mount Quarry

The Mount

Weston under Lizard

11

Burlington Pool

A5

B5314

BRIDGEMAN CT

PO

RECTORY DR

A5

Shrewsbury Drive

Weston Hall

West Plantation

MILL LA

Temple Wood

1

Woodlands

Weston Park

Tong Drive

A41

Woodside Farm

New Park Pool

Lizard Grange

10

A 79 B 80 C

203

189

A   **B**   **C**

BIRCHMOOR LA

Marston

Manor
Farm

ST20

4

Wet Croft
Plantation

Wrestlers
Farm

Wrestlers
Wood

Ryefield Lane

Mottymeadows Brook

13

Motty Meadows

Broadholes Lane

BROADHOLES LA

Beaudesert
Plantation

3

Lincoln Brook

Lower
Brockhurst

Lucknow
Farm

Brick Kiln
Lane

Hartley's
Gorse

Grove
Farm

Brockhurst
Coppice

Blymhill
Grange

TF11

12

High Hall

Brockhurst

2

Blymhill
Lawn

ST19

New Buildings
Farm

Blymhill Lawn
Farm

Hurst
Plantation

Hurst
Farm

IVETSEY RD

Lawn
House

Ivetsey
Bank

The
Hurst

Brickyard
Plantation

11

Wheaton Aston
New Hall

A5

Bradford
Arms
Hotel

Wall Plantations

A5

Wheaton Aston
Old Hall

1

Temple
Pool

Cottage
Wood

Lichfield Drive

East Park

Dogkennel
Wood

Ivetsey Bank
Farm

Weston
Park

Weston Park
Farm

10

81   **A**   82   **B**   83   **C**

203

221

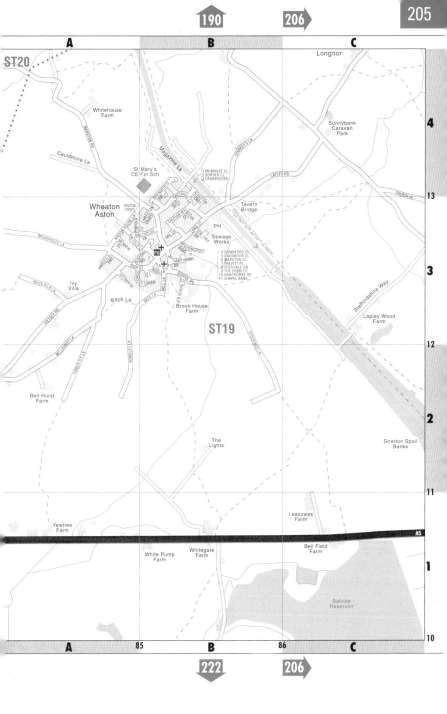

190 206

ST20

Longnor

Whitehouse
Farm

Sunnybank
Caravan
Park

4

Cauldmore La

Magazine La

MARSTON RD

St Mary's
CE Fst Sch

BEARLEY'S LA

LAPLEY RD

CHURCH LA

13

1 PRIMROSE CL
2 BORDEN CL
3 CRANBROOKS

Wheaton
Aston

FENTON
CROFT

Tavern
Bridge

Staffordshire Union Canal

PH

CASTRAN WAY

Sewage
Works

BROADHOLES LA

MEADOWCROFT

4 DOWNFORD CL
5 OAKSMOOR CL
6 MARSTON CL
7 TREVITT PL
8 FESTIVALE GN
9 THE COBBLES
10 HAWTHORNE RD
11 CHAPEL BANK

Staffordshire Way

HAWTHORNE
DR

PO

HIGH ST

SCHOOL RD

Lapley Wood
Farm

BRICK KILN LA

Ivy
Villa

Back La

BACK LA

WESLEY RD

BELMONT LA

DARBY PIT LA

Brook House
Farm

STOCKWELL LA

ST19

12

Bell Hurst
Farm

2

The
Lights

Stretton Spoil
Banks

11

Yewtree
Farm

Leasowes
Farm

A5

Bell Field
Farm

1

White Pump
Farm

Whitegate
Farm

Belvide
Reservoir

A   85   B   86   C   10

222 206

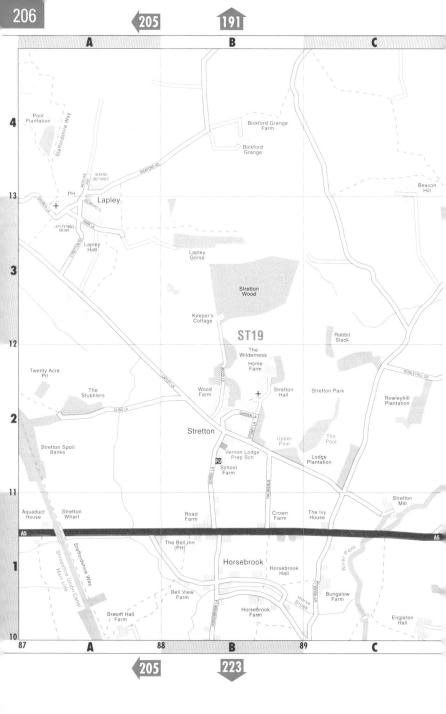

205
191

A   **B**   **C**

Pool
Plantation

Staffordshire Way

4

Bickford Grange
Farm

Bickford
Grange

QUEENS
COTTAGES

MEECE LA

BICKFORD RD

Beacon
Hill

PH

13

CHURCH LA

Lapley

BICKFORD CL

STRETTON RD

LAPLEY HALL
MEWS

PARK LA

Lapley
Hall

Lapley
Gorse

3

Stretton
Wood

Keeper's
Cottage

ST19

Rabbit
Slack

12

The
Wilderness

Home
Farm

LAPLEY LA

ROWLEYHILL DR

Twenty Acre
Pit

The
Stubblers

SLING LA

Wood
Farm

WOOD LA

Stretton
Hall

Stretton Park

Rowleyhill
Plantation

2

Stretton Spoil
Banks

GARDEN LA

STONEY LA

Stretton

Upper
Pool

The
Pool

SCHOOL LA

Vernon Lodge
Prep Sch

PO

School
Farm

Lodge
Plantation

THE AVENUE

11

Aquaduct
House

Stretton
Wharf

Road
Farm

Crown
Farm

The Ivy
House

Stretton
Mill

A5

A5

Shropshire Union Canal
Main Line

Staffordshire Way

The Bell Inn
(PH)

Horsebrook

Horsebrook
Hall

River Penk

1

HORSEBROOK LA

IVY HOUSE LA

Bungalow
Farm

Bell View
Farm

Horsebrook
Farm

Horse
Brook

Breom Hall
Farm

Engleton
Hall

10
87   **A**   **88**   **B**   **89**   **C**

205
223

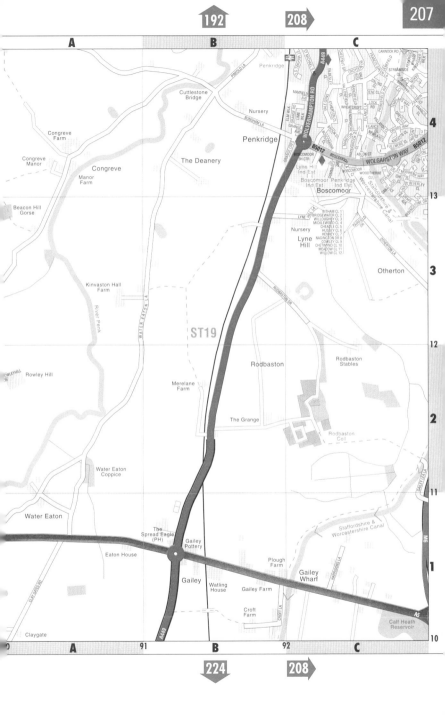

A **B** **C**

4

Penkridge

Cuttlestone
Bridge

Nursery

Congreve
Farm

Penkridge

Congreve Manor

Congreve

The Deanery

Manor
Farm

Beacon Hill
Gorse

13

Boscomoor

Moscomoor

Lyne Hill
Ind Est

Boscomoor Penkridge
Ind Est Ind Est

WOLGARSTON WAY

Woodtherne

BITHAM CL 1
BRIDGEWATER CL 2
WILLOUGHBY CL 3
MICKLEWOOD CL 4
CHEADLE CL 5
HUSSEY CL 6
HENNEY CL 7
NAGINGTON DR 8
COWLEY CL 9
CHETWND CL 10
MEADOW CL 11
WILLOW CL 12

Nursery

Lyne
Hill

Otherton

3

Kinvaston Hall
Farm

River Penk

Water Eaton La

ST19

12

Rodbaston

Rodbaston
Stables

Rowley Hill

Merelane
Farm

The Grange

Rodbaston
Coll

2

Water Eaton
Coppice

11

Water Eaton

The
Spread Eagle
(PH)

Gailey
Pottery

Staffordshire &
Worcestershire Canal

M6

Eaton House

Plough
Farm

Gailey
Wharf

1

Gailey

Watling
House

Gailey Farm

A5

Croft
Farm

Calf Heath
Reservoir

Claygate

10

A 91 **B** 92 **C**

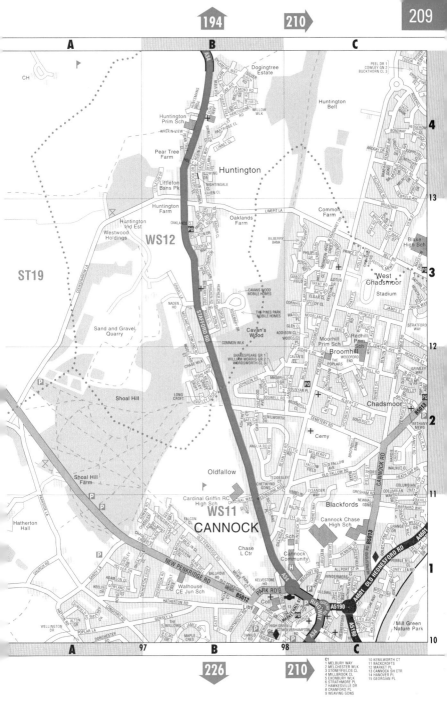

A · B · C

CH

Dogingtree Estate

PEEL DR 1
COWLEY GN 2
BUCKTHORN CL 3

Huntington Belt

Huntington Prim Sch

Pear Tree Farm

Littleton Bsns Pk

Huntington

Huntington Farm

Common Farm

Oaklands Farm

West Chadsmoor

Blake High Sch

Huntington Ind Est
Westwood Holdings

WS12

Bilberry Bank

THE PINES PARK MOBILE HOMES

Moorhill Prim Sch

Redhill Prim Sch

ST19

Sand and Gravel Quarry

CAVANS WOOD MOBILE HOMES

Cavan's Wood

Broomhill

COMMON WLK

SHAKESPEARE GR 1
WILLIAM MORRIS GR 2
WORDSWORTH CL 3

THE POPLARS
WOODFORD END

Moorhill End

Chadsmoor

B5013

Shoal Hill

CHASE WLK

LONG CROFT

Cemy

BETHANY MEWS

Oldfallow

OLD FALLOW AVE
OLD FALLOW RD

Shoal Hill Farm

Cardinal Griffin RC High Sch

Blackfords

Cannock Chase High Sch

Hatherton Hall

WS11
CANNOCK

CANNOCK RD

OAKHILL

Chase L Ctr

Cannock Community

NEW PENKRIDGE RD

Walhouse CE Jun Sch

B5012

Liby

RING WAY

A5190

A34

A4601

OLD BEDFORD RD

Mill Green Nature Park

WELLINGTON DR

B · 97 · B · 98 · C

C1
1 MELBURY WAY
2 MELCHESTER WLK
3 STONEYFIELDS CL
4 MILLBROOK CL
5 EXONBURY WLK
6 STRATHMORE PL
7 HAWKESVILLE DR
8 CRANFORD PL
9 WEAVING GDNS
10 KENILWORTH CT
11 BACKCROFTS
12 MARKET PL
13 CANNOCK SH CTR
14 HANOVER PL
15 GEORGIAN PL

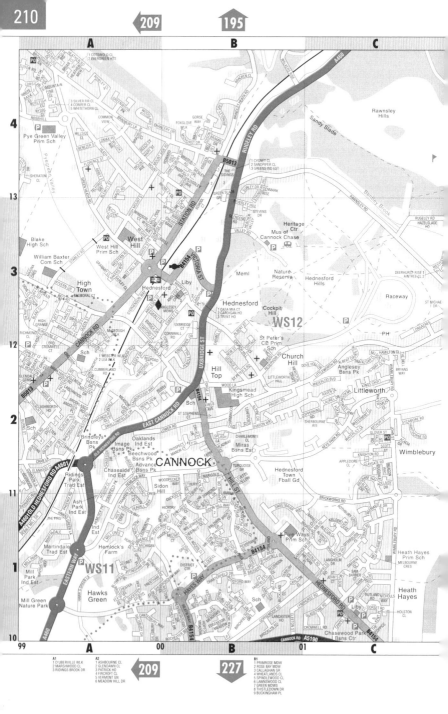

Mutchills Gutter

Horsepasture
Pools

CH Sukers
Lodge

Rawnsley Hills

Beaudesert
Old Park

Stonepit Green

Horsepasture
Covert

4

The Lawn

WS15

Hazel Slade
Com Prim Sch

13

PO

PH

Hazelslade
Nature
Reserve

Castle Ring
Fort

Broad Hazels

P

Cannock Wood
Ind Est

Hazelslade

PH

JENKINSTOWN

Bentley Brook La

UPLANDS CL 1
HIGH MDW 2

Spoil Heap

Cannock
Wood

3

P

Rawnsley

The
Grange

+

CHAPEL LA

CUMBERLEDGE HILL

PO

Cannockwood
Farm

CANNOCK WOOD RD

CHETWYND DR

1 SLADE VIEW RISE
2 SANDOWN CL
3 JESMOND CL
4 KEMPTON CL
5 GOODWOOD CL
6 ST FRANCIS CL

New Hayes

P

12

NEW HAYES RD

New Inn
(PH)

Cooper's
Cottages

SUMMERSIDE
AVE

ST BERNARDS

Court Hayes
Farm

Covert
Lane

Hayfield
Hill

WS12

RUSHTON
MEWS

Redmoor Brook

Wimblebury
Farm

Prospect
Village

PAGETS CROFT

IRONSTONE RD

Hawthorn
Farm

Red Moor

2

P

Geptieshaw
Hill

Noddyfield Valley

SEVENS RD

Redmore Inn
(PH)

HAYFIELD RD

BENSON RD

P

P

Old Lodge
Hill
Country Park

11

Opencast Workings

BYRON CL 1
SCOTT WAY 2
ALBION WAY 3
COTTON WAY 4
MOUNTBATTEN CL 5
WESLEY CL 6

Ironstone Road
Farm

Coney
Lodge
Farm
Boney Hay
Prim Sch

1

WS7

MOWBRAY
CROFT

Cuckoo Bank

BALMORAL
WAY

KINGSDOWN

Sch

MELFORD RISE

SANDOWN

MAY CL

Caravan
Site

CONISTON OR AVE

ASHLEY
CROFT

ANGEL
CROFT

HIGH ST

SPINNEY LA

4 3 2

10

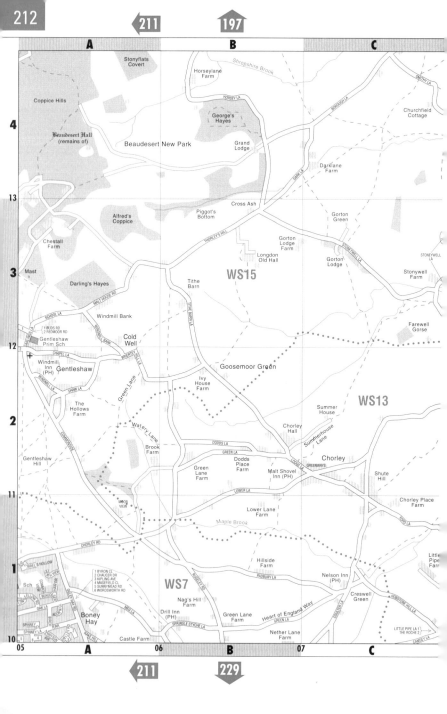

A   B   C

Stonyflats
Covert

Horseylane
Farm

Shropshire Brook

SMITH'S LA

Coppice Hills

HORSEY LA

Churchfield
Cottage

BURROUGH LA

4

George's
Hayes

Beaudesert Hall
(remains of)

Beaudesert New Park

Grand
Lodge

Darklane
Farm

PARK LA

13

Alfred's
Coppice

Piggot's
Bottom

Cross Ash

Gorton
Green

Longdon
Old Hall

Gorton
Lodge
Farm

STONEYWELL LA

STONEYWELL
LA

Chestall
Farm

THORLEY'S HILL

Gorton
Lodge

3   Mast

Darling's Hayes

Tithe
Barn

WS15

Stonywell
Farm

Farewell
Gorse

MALT HOUSE RD

TITHE BARN LA

Windmill Bank

SCHOOL LA

BRIERLEY LA

1 BUDS RD
2 REDMOOR RD

Cold
Well

12

Gentleshaw
Prim Sch

CHAPEL LA

Goosemoor Green

Windmill
Inn
(PH) Gentleshaw

BRIERLEY LA

Green Lane

Ivy
House
Farm

WS13

Summer
House

The
Hollows
Farm

SHAW LA

REDMOOR LA

Watery Lane

Chorley
Hall

Summerhouse
Lane

2

Gentleshaw
Hill

COMMONSIDE

Brook
Farm

DODDS LA

GREEN LA

Dodds
Place
Farm

LODGE LA

Chorley

GREENWAYS

Shute
Hill

Green
Lane
Farm

Malt Shovel
Inn (PH)

LOWER LA

Chorley Place
Farm

11

MOOR
VIEW

Lower Lane
Farm

FORD LA

Maple Brook

CHORLEY RD

Hillside
Farm

Little
Pipe
Farm

1 BYRON CL
2 CHAUCER DR
3 KIPLING AVE
4 MASEFIELD CL
5 SUNNYMEAD RD
6 WORDSWORTH RD

PADBURY LA

Nelson Inn
(PH)

Creswell
Green

1

PRILL'S HOLLOW

Sch

WS7

RUGELEY RD

HORSTONE HILL LA

OAK LA

Nag's Hill
Farm

Drill Inn
(PH)

MILL LA

Boney
Hay

Green Lane
Farm

Heart of England Way

CHORLEY RD

GREEN LA

CAMSEY LA

LITTLE PIPE LA 1
THE ROACHE 2

BANK HILL

Castle Farm

SPRINGLE STYCHE LA

Nether Lane
Farm

10

05   A   06   B   07   C

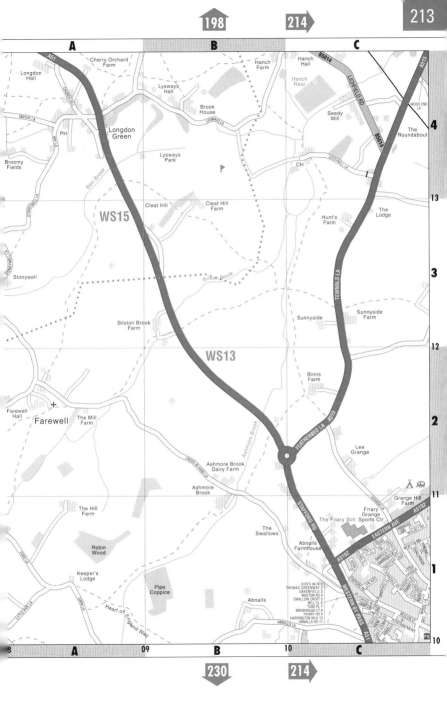

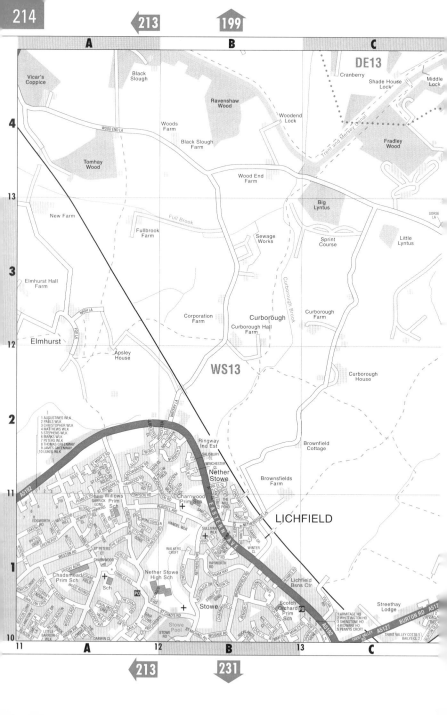

215

201

DE13

A513

Croxall

CROXALL RD

Dovecote

The
Hall

RIDGE LA

BADLEY GREEN LA

Chetwynd or
Salter's Bridge

Roddige

Whitemoor
Haye

Brown's
Island

Oakley
Farm

RODDIGE LA

River Meece

4

WS13

Broadfields

Croxall
Mill

13

River Tame

3

New Buildings
Farm

A513

Sittles

Lady
Walk

Elford
Park

12

STOCKFORD LA

Sand & Gravel
Pit

Park
Farm

The
Bungalow

2

Bisphill
Plantation

B79

11

Home
Farm

Greendales
Farm

A513

Elford

BROWNSDALE LA

Howard
Prim Sch

THE SQUARE

1

OLD MILL DR

THE GARDENS

CROSS KEYS RD

PH
PO

THE BECK

CAT'S LA

THE CAUSEWAY

RIDGET LA

Raddle
Farm

The
Hill

BURTON RD

A513

Old
Orangery

10

17

A

18

B

19

C

215

233

A
B
C

Pessall Farm

Raddle
Farm

The
Grange

4

WS13

13

Wayside

Croxall
Mill

Pessall Brook

Brook House
Farm

Broadfield's
Farm

3

PESSALL LA

RADDLE LA

CROXALL RD

Edingale
PH

Mary Howard CE
Prim Sch

CROXALL RD

FIELD FARM DR

CHURCH

MAIN RD

LULLINGTON RD

BLAKE RD

WOODYARD DR 1
CHURCH WLK 2
CHURCH HOLLOW 3

SCHOOL LA

MOOR LA

HATCHETTS LA

SCHOOL LA

2
1
3

BEECHFIELD

HOLLAND
CT

12

Wks

B79

Poplars
Farm

Crabtree
Farm

Grange
Farm

2

MILL LA

River Mease

MAIN RD

Rose
Cottage

HAUNTON RD

11

Haselour

Haselour
House

Haselour
Hall

CHURCH RD

PH

Harlaston

PO

MANOR LA

MAIN RD

Acacia
Grove

MANOR RD

Little
Harlaston

1

Model
Farm

Coppinshill
Barn

Well
Barn

Twizles Lane

10

0
A
21
B
22
C

A   B   C

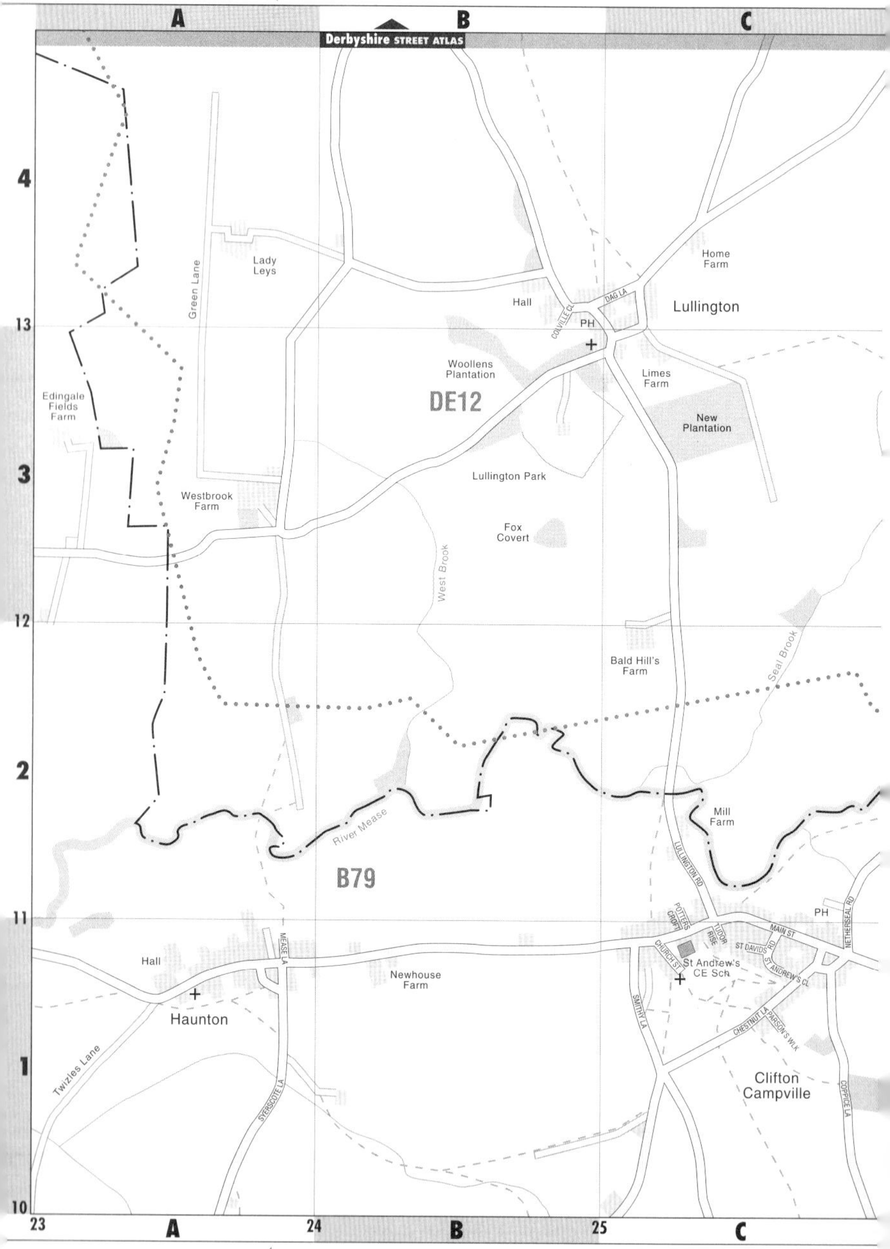

4

Home
Farm

Lady
Leys

Green Lane

Hall

COLVILLE CL

DALE

PH

Lullington

13

Woollens
Plantation

Limes
Farm

DE12

New
Plantation

Edingale
Fields
Farm

3

Westbrook
Farm

Lullington Park

Fox
Covert

West Brook

Seal Brook

12

Bald Hill's
Farm

2

River Mease

Mill
Farm

PH

B79

LULLINGTON RD

NETHERSEAL RD

11

Hall

MEASE LA

CLARKE'S LA

MAIN ST

ST DAVIDS

Newhouse
Farm

POTTER'S
ST ANDREW'S
CL

St Andrew's
CE Sch

CHESTNUT LA

ANDREW'S WLK

Haunton

Twizles Lane

STRESSOLL LA

SMITH'S LA

COPPICE LA

1

Clifton
Campville

10

23   A   24   B   25   C

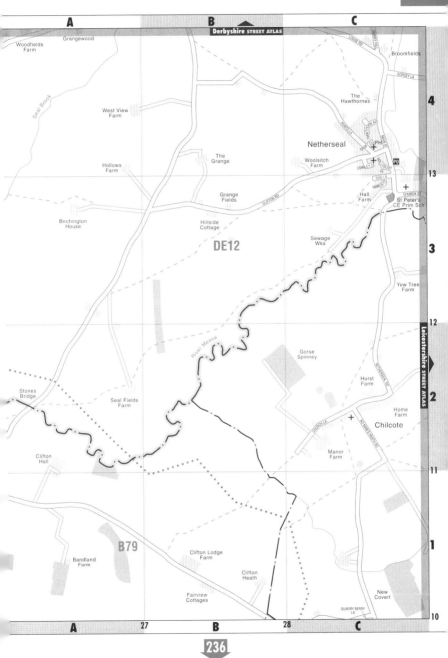

A   B   C

Woodfields Farm

Grangewood

Broomfields

GORSEY LA

LODGE RD

BURY HILL

The Hawthornes

4

West View Farm

Netherseal

PH

Seal Brook

The Grange

Woolsitch Farm

PO

Hollows Farm

STANLEY CL

13

Grange Fields

CLIFTON RD

Hall Farm

St Peter's CE Prim Sch

DOG LA

MANOR CT

CHURCH SQ

Birchington House

Hillside Cottage

DE12

Sewage Wks

3

Yew Tree Farm

12

River Mease

Gorse Spinney

Hurst Farm

Stones Bridge

Seal Fields Farm

Home Farm

2

CHURCH LA

Chilcote

ROBESSEAL RD

ROBINS HEATH RD

Clifton Hall

Manor Farm

11

B79

Bandland Farm

Clifton Lodge Farm

Clifton Heath

New Covert

1

Fairview Cottages

QUARRY BERRY LA

A   27   B   28   C

10

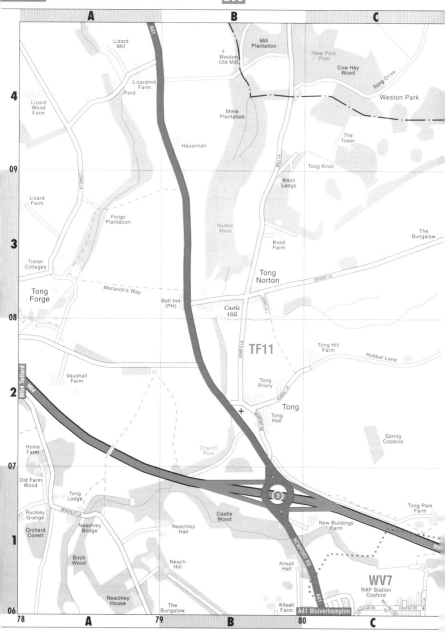

A   B   C

4

09

3

08

2

07

1

06

78   A   79   B   80   C

Lizard Mill

Weston Old Mill

Mill Plantation

New Park Pool

Cow Hey Wood

Tong Drive

Weston Park

Lizardmill Farm

Ford

Lizard Wood Farm

Mere Plantation

Havannah

The Tower

Tong Knoll

Knoll Lodge

The Bungalow

Lizard Farm

Forge Plantation

Norton Mere

Knoll Farm

Timlet Cottages

Monarch's Way

Tong Forge

Bell Inn (PH)

Castle Hill

Tong Norton

OFFOXEY LA

TF11

Tong Hill Farm

Hubbal Lane

Vauxhall Farm

Tong Priory

Tong

M54 Telford

Home Farm

Old Farm Wood

Church Pool

Spring Coppice

Tong Lodge

Castle Wood

New Buildings Farm

Tong Park Farm

M54

Ruckley Grange

BEACHLEY LA

Neachley Bridge

Neachley Hall

Orchard Covert

Birch Wood

Neach Hill

Kilsall Hall

WV7 RAF Station Cosford

Neachley House

The Bungalow

Kilsall Farm

A41 Wolverhampton

MILL LA

NEWPORT RD

FRIAR S LA

SHARP LA

MILL LA

Tong Hall

A   B   C

The Hawkshutts

Belvide Reservoir

Top Barn Farm

Hag Wood

Birk's Barn

SHUTT GREEN LA

4

Bridleways Farm

Black Ladies

Drybrook Plantation

ST19

09

Chambersfield

Kiddemore Green

KIDDEMORE GREEN RD

Oakley

Paradise

New Inns (PH)

Wet Hay Wood

FORDS LA

Strangleford Birch Farm

Pearse Hay Farm

3

Coldham

Harvington Birch Farm

Cream Pot

Big Hyde Rough

The Whitemoor

Peckerfield Wood

08

Hungary Hill Farm

Old Coppice

Monarch's Way

Wyrley Low Plantation

2

Plant's Hagg

Bath Farm

Robinson's Plantation

Chillington Farm

Horse Paddock Wood

Langley Plantation

WV8

07

Brick Kiln Plantation

Langley Lawn Farm

Langley Pit

Chillington Hall

Upper Avenue

Chillington Street

Brick Kiln Lane

1

RENSHAW WOOD LA

The Charlemagne

Sham Bridge

The Park

Big Wood

The Canal

06

The Pool

84   A   85   B   86   C

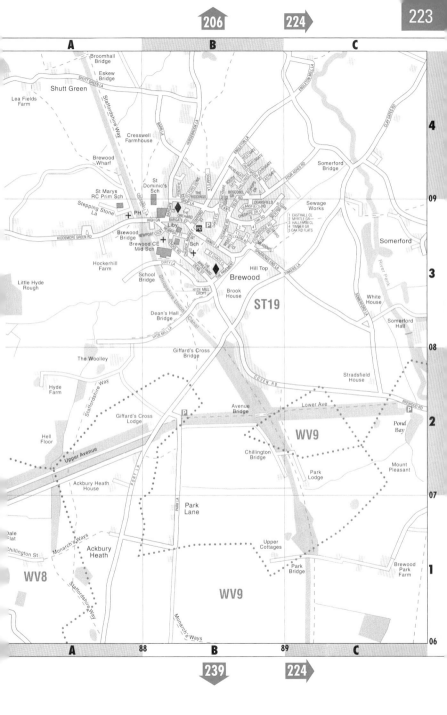

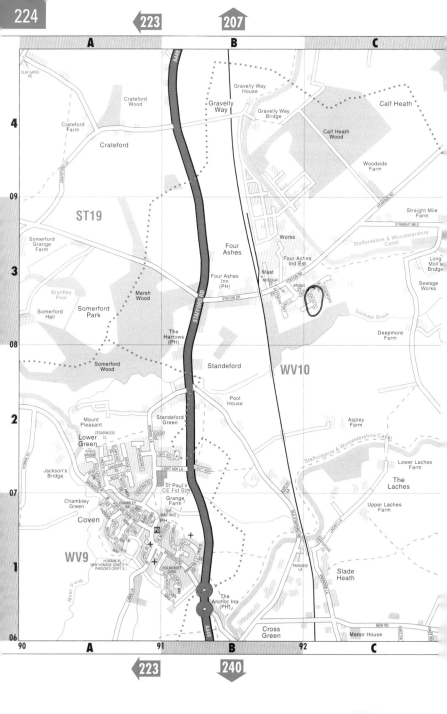

A   **B**   **C**

A49

CLAY GATES RD

Crateford Wood

Gravelly Way House

Gravelly Way

Gravelly Way Bridge

Calf Heath

4

Crateford Farm

Crateford

Calf Heath Wood

Woodside Farm

HOMARD RD

09

ST19

Straight Mile Farm

STRAIGHT MILE

Somerford Grange Farm

Works

Staffordshire & Worcestershire Canal

Four Ashes

Four Ashes Ind Est

Long Moll's Bridge

3

Brantley Pool

Marsh Wood

Four Ashes Inn (PH)

Mast

MODULAR CT

STATION RD

BRUNEL CT

Sewage Works

STATION DR

LACHES CL

CROFT END

Saredon Brook

Somerford Hall

Somerford Park

The Harrows (PH)

Deepmore Farm

08

STAFFORD RD

Somerford Wood

Standeford

WV10

Pool House

2

Mount Pleasant

Standeford Green

Aspley Farm

Lower Green

CEDARWOOD CL

SCHOOL LA

SUNSET CL

Staffordshire & Worcestershire Canal

KINGS BRIDGE

OAKSHAW

LIGHT ASH LA

LIGHT ASH CL

LIGHT ASH

Lower Laches Farm

Jackson's Bridge

HOMAN RD

WOOD AVE

The Laches

07

Chambley Green

St Paul's CE Fst Sch

LACHES LA

Upper Laches Farm

Coven

CHAMBLEY

Grange Farm

THE MALTINGS PH

PO

GUILDFORD RD

1

WV9

HOMAGE PL
NEW HOMAGE GDNS
PARSON'S CROFT

HOLMCROFT GDNS

BREWOOD RD

PARADISE LA

PARADISE LA

Slade Heath

River Penk

The Anchor Inn (PH)

A49

Cross Green

NEW RD

Manor House

DRUID LA

06

90   **A**   **91**   **B**   **92**   **C**

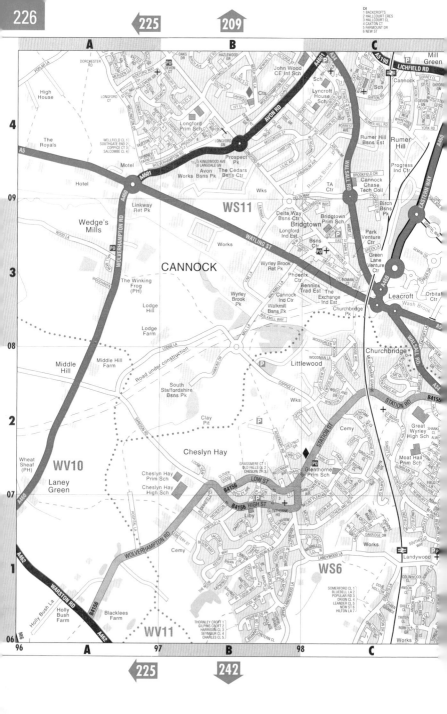

225

209

C4
1 BACKCROFTS
2 HALLCOURT CRES
3 HALLCOURT CL
4 CAXTON CT
5 FARMOUNT DR
6 NEW ST

A   B   C

POPLAR LA

High
House

The
Royals

A5

Hotel

Motel

DORCHESTER
RD

LONGFORD
CT

WELLFIELD CL 1
SOUTHGATE END 2
COPPICE CT 3
SALCOMBE CL 4

OAKS
DR

HAZELWOOD
GR

DEVON
CT

Longford
Prim Sch

Longford
GR

Prospect
Pk

5 KINGSWOOD AVE
6 LANGDALE GN

Avon
Works

The Cedars
Bsns Ctr

John Wood
CE Inf Sch

Lyncroft
House
Sch

Sch

Sch

A5190
LICHFIELD RD

Mill
Green

Cannock

Rumer Hill
Bsns Est

Rumer
Hill

Progress
Ind Ctr

A460

Cts

4

09

WOLVERHAMPTON RD

A460

A460

Linkway
Ret Pk

Wedge's
Mills

WS11

Delta Way
Bsns Ctr

Bridgtown
Prim Sch

Longford
Ind Est

Bsns
Ctr

Cannock
Chase
Tech Coll

Park
Venture
Ctr

Green
Lane
Venture
Ctr

Birch
Bsns
Pk

EASTERN WAY

A460

WATLING ST

Works

Bridgtown

TA
Ctr

BROOKFIELD DR

WALSALL RD

3

CANNOCK

The Winking
Frog
(PH)

Lodge
Hill

Wyrley Brook
Ret Pk

Phoenix
Ctr

Wyrley
Brook
Pk

Bennick
Trad Est

Cannock
Ind Ctr

Walkmill
Bsns Pk

The
Exchange
Ind Est

WALKMILL WAY

Churchbridge
Pk

Leacroft

Orbital
Ctr

A5

08

Middle
Hill

Middle Hill
Farm

Lodge
Farm

Road under construction

LODGE LA

South
Staffordshire
Bsns Pk

Littlewood

Churchbridge

STATION RD

B4156

A34

2

WV10

Wheat
Sheaf
(PH)

Laney
Green

Clay
Pit

Cheslyn Hay

Cheslyn Hay
Prim Sch

Cheslyn Hay
High Sch

GRASSMERE CT 1
OLD FALLS CL 2
CHESLYN DR 3

Wks

Cemy

STATION ST

Glenthorne
Prim Sch

Great
Wyrley
High Sch

Moat Hall
Prim Sch

07

A460

WOLVERHAMPTON RD

B4156

LOW ST

B4156 HIGH ST

Liby

Glenthorne
GR

Cemy

Works

Landywood

1

A462

WARSTON RD

B4156

Holly Bush La

Holly
Bush
Farm

Blacklees
Farm

WV11

THORNLEY CROFT 1
GILPINS CROFT 2
HARRISON CL 3
SEYMOUR CL 4
CHARLES CL 5

WS6

SOMERFORD CL 1
BLUEBELL LA 2
POPULAR RD 3
ORION CL 4
LEANDER CL 5
NEW ST 6
HILTON LA 7

Works

M6

06

96   A   97   B   98   C

225

242

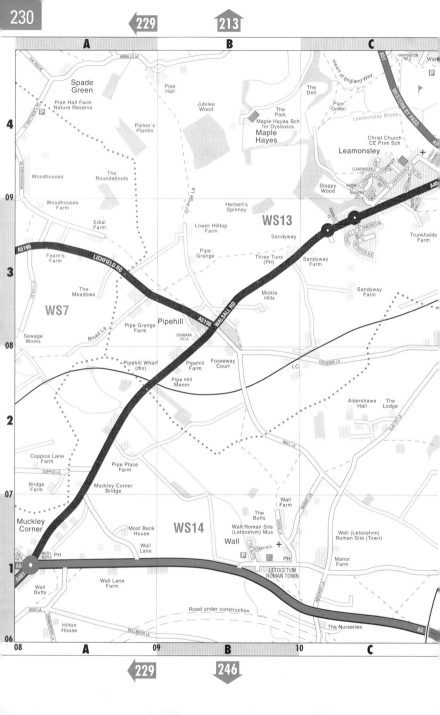

B4
1 HOULBROOKE HO
2 WILLIAM LUNN'S HOMES
3 THE CHEQUERS
4 DRAKE CROFT
5 MALLARD CROFT
6 MERCIAN CT

214   232

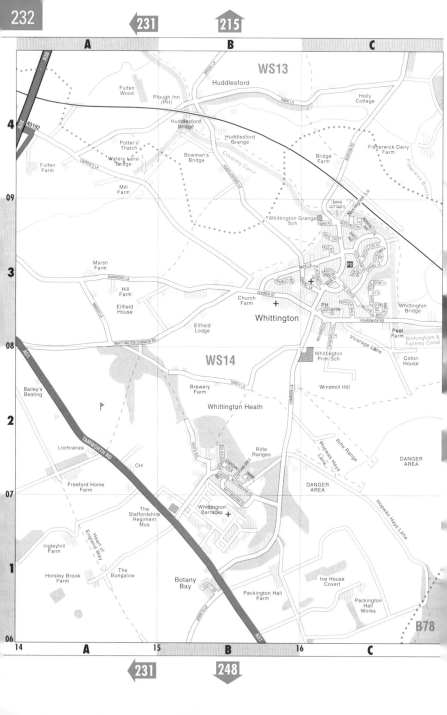

WS13

Huddlesford

Fulfen
Wood

Plough Inn
(PH)

PARK LA

Holly
Cottage

Huddlesford
Bridge

Huddlesford
Grange

Bridge
Farm

Fisherwick Dairy
Farm

Potter's
Thatch

Bowman's
Bridge

Coventry Canal

Fisherwick Brook

Fulfen
Farm

CAPPER'S LA

Watery Lane
Bridge

HUDDLESFORD LA

BURTON RD

Norington La

Mill
Farm

SWAN
COTTAGES

Whittington Grange
Sch

SWAN RD

WOODINGTON RD

Marsh
Farm

SEAL CROFT

BACK LA

PASS

Hill
Farm

DARNFORD LA

FRAMLEY RD

LANGTON CRES

PO

GRINE CL

Whittington
Bridge

Ellfield
House

MAIN ST

CHURCH ST

CHAPEL LA

BLACKSMITH

ST JOHNS RD

KESTREL CL

Church Farm

Whittington

PH

TOE GREEN

CLOISTER WALK

FISHERWICK RD

Ellfield
Lodge

WHITTINGTON COMMON RD

PARRINGTON

WINDMILL HILL LA

Peel
Farm

Birmingham &
Fazeley Canal

WS14

Whittington
Prim Sch

Vicarage Lane

Coton
House

A51

Bailey's
Beating

Brewery
Farm

SANDY LA

COMMON LA

Windmill Hill

Rifle Range

Hopwas Hays
Lane

DANGER
AREA

Lochranza

TAMWORTH RD

CH

HEATH RD

Whittington Heath

Rifle
Ranges

Hopwas Hays Lane

Freeford Home
Farm

RALPH CL

STAFFORD CRES

OWENS

DANGER
AREA

Heart of England Way

UNION

CHESTER RD

NOTTINGHAM RD

Ingleyhill
Farm

The
Staffordshire
Regiment
Mus

Whittington
Barracks

Ice House
Covert

Horsley Brook
Farm

The
Bungalow

Botany
Bay

NOTTINGHAM RD

Packington Hall
Farm

Packington
Hall
Works

BURNT LA

EXETER RD

A51

B78

216
234

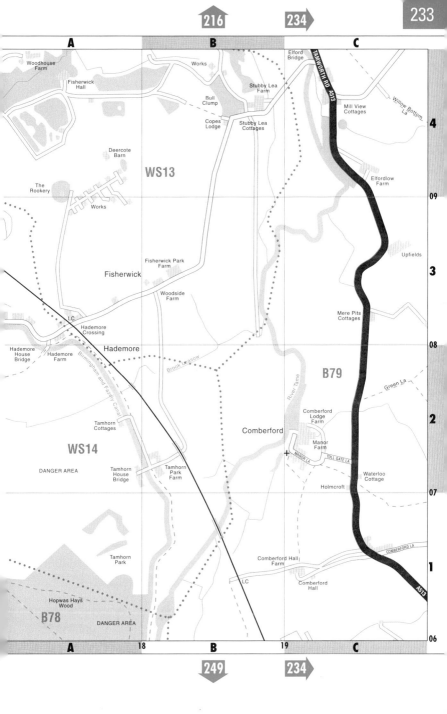

A   B   C

Woodhouse
Farm

Fisherwick
Hall

Works

Bull
Clump

Stubby Lea
Farm

Elford
Bridge

Copes
Lodge

Stubby Lea
Cottages

Mill View
Cottages

Willow Bottom
La

4

Deercote
Barn

WS13

Elfordlow
Farm

The
Rookery

Works

09

Upfields

Fisherwick Park
Farm

Fisherwick

3

Woodside
Farm

Mere Pits
Cottages

LC

Hademore
Crossing

Hademore

08

Hademore
House
Bridge

Hademore
Farm

Brook Langsow

B79

Green La

River Tame

Birmingham and Fazeley Canal

Comberford
Lodge
Farm

Tamhorn
Cottages

Comberford

2

Manor
Farm

WS14

Manor La

Toll Gate La

Waterloo
Cottage

DANGER AREA

Tamhorn
House
Bridge

Tamhorn
Park
Farm

Holmcroft

07

Comberford La

Tamhorn
Park

Comberford Hall
Farm

1

Hopwas Hays
Wood

LC

Comberford
Hall

B78

DANGER AREA

A513

A   18   B   19   C   06

249
234

233
217

A B C

4

09

3

08

2

07

1

06

Fishpits
Barn

Twycros
La

Portway La

Dunimere
Farm

Hogs Hill

Willow Bottom La

Portway

Winterdyne
Farm

Birdsley
Farm

Green La

Mere Pits

Cherryfield
Cottages

Wiggington
Fields
Farm

B79

Hanging Hill

Syerscote
Manor

Watergate
Cottage

Pessote La

Wigginton
Manor

Syerscote Barn

COMBERFORD LA

PH

Wigginton

St Leonard's CE
Prim Sch

Bridge Cottages

World's End
Cottages

BIRCH RD

WALRAND
CL

Arkall Farm

A513

Rawlett Sports
Ctr

SILL
GREEN

ASHBY RD

Amington
Hall
Cottages

B5493

Rawlett
High Sch

20 A 21 B 22 C

A   B   C

COPPICE LA

4

09

Far Barn

Thorpe
Constantine

Home
Farm

The Dale

Thorpe Hall

+

3

Highfields

Old Gorse

Gorse
Farm

B79

Clifton
Rough

08

Podmore
Cottages

Lonkhill
Farm

Statfold
Farm

B5493

2

Statfold

+

07

Thorpegorse
Cottages

Statfold
Cottages

Poplars
Farm

Shuttington
House

Copnill
Farm

Poplar
Cottage

1

Statfold
Barn
Farm

A   24   B   25   C

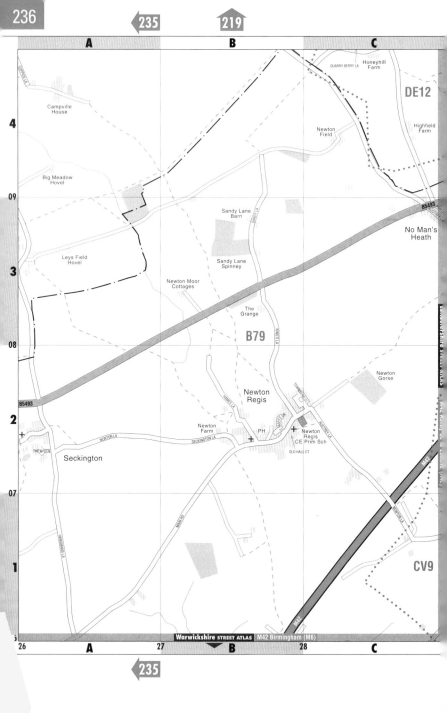

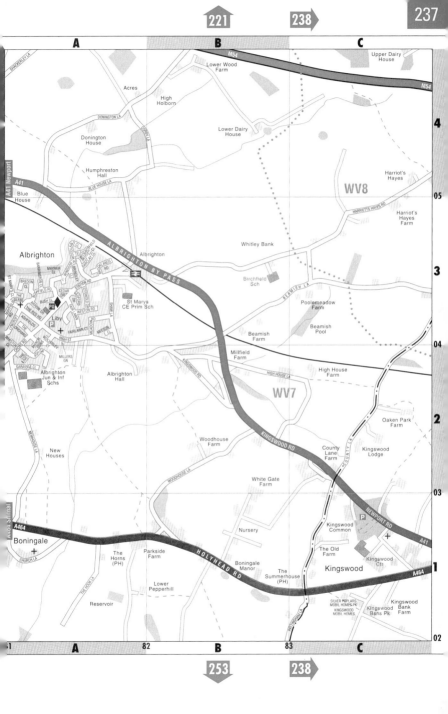

221
238

A   B   C

M54

Upper Dairy House

Lower Wood Farm

Acres

High Holborn

DONINGTON LA

Lower Dairy House

4

Donington House

Humphreston Hall

BLUE HOUSE LA

Harriot's Hayes

WV8

05

A41 Newport

A41

Blue House

HARRIETTS HAYES RD

Harriot's Hayes Farm

ALBRIGHTON BY PASS

Whitley Bank

Albrighton

Albrighton

3

MAYFAIR CL

ORLANDS RD

St Marys CE Prim Sch

Birchfield Sch

BEAMISH LA

Poolemeadow Farm

PO

CEDAR DR

Liby P

FAIRLAWN CT

Beamish Farm

Beamish Pool

04

MILLERS GN

HIGH ST

Albrighton Hall

Millfield Farm

High House Farm

HIGH HOUSE LA

Albrighton Jun & Inf Schs

KINGSWOOD RD

WV7

2

New Houses

Woodhouse Farm

County Lane Farm

KINGSWOOD RD

Oaken Park Farm

Kingswood Lodge

COUNTY LA

WOODHOUSE LA

White Gate Farm

03

A464 Shifnal

NEWPORT RD

P

A464

Boningale

A464

Nursery

Kingswood Common

The Old Farm

Kingswood Ctr

CHURCH LA

The Horns (PH)

Parkside Farm

HOLYHEAD RD

Boningale Manor

The Summerhouse (PH)

Kingswood

A464

1

THE HOOK LA

Lower Pepperhill

SILVER POPLARS MOBIL HOMES PK

KINGSWOOD MOBIL HOMES

Kingswood Bsns Pk

Kingswood Bank Farm

Reservoir

02

81   A   82   B   83   C

253
238

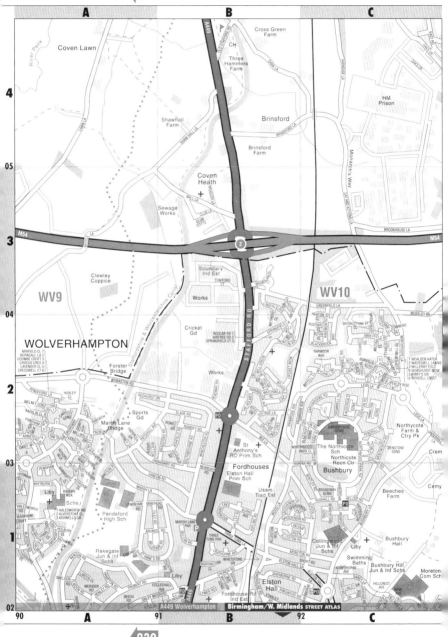

A   **B**   **C**

Coven Lawn

River Penk

Cross Green Farm

CH

Three Hammers Farm

4

Shawhall Farm

Brinsford

HM Prison

Brinsford Farm

Monarch's Way

05

Coven Heath

Sewage Works

BALL LA

CLUB LA

CLUB COTTS

BRINSFORD LA

BROOKHOUSE LA

3

M54

M54

②

Clewley Coppice

Boundary Ind Est

STAFFORD CT

BROADFOOT

GREENFIELD LA

WV9

WV10

Works

HEATON ST

MOSELEY RD

04

Cricket Gd

REDCAR RD 1
AINTREE RD 2
SPRINGFIELD CT 3

RUDYARD CL

BRICHSTONE ST

BILTON CL

ABBEYFIELD RD

GRANGE

TOWNEND

WOLVERHAMPTON

1 MIRFIELD CL 1
BURNSALL LA 2
COOMBE CROFT 3
CROCUS CRES 4
LAVENDER CL 5
CRESSWELL CT 6

BLACKBROOK

FARMBROOK WAY

1 WEALDEN HATCH
2 WADESMILL LAWNS
3 WILLERBY FOLD
4 WINBSHURST MDW
5 BIRBY'S GN
6 WENDELL CREST

Forster Bridge

WOBASTON RD

Works

STAFFORD RD

MILL LA

RONVILLE

PEBBLE LA

PEBBLEY RISE

2

PENDEFORD LA

HUXLEY

WELNEY GDNS

HAZLIN CL

SLADE RD

REDHURST DR

ROMSEY RD

ROMSEY GR

FARMER

WATERMILL

COTTAGE LA

FARRAM

LEGS LA

LEGS LA

Sports Gd

Marsh Lane Bridge

PADBURY

Northcote Farm & Ctry Pk

CARISBROOKE GDNS

DENSTONE GDNS

Crem

03

DAISY WLK

ROMSEY WAY

NEWBURY RD

SANDON RD

MARSH LA

CARBERRY RD

BRETON CL

PIRAMBOOK

NORTHWOOD PARK CL

TAIRFAX RD

The Northcote Sch

Northcote Recn Ctr

Bushbury

Cemy

HALESWORTH RD

PENSHAW

WHITBURN RD

Liby

FYNFOE WLK

Schs

1 HALESWORTH RD
2 ALVERSTOKE CL
3 ASHWELLS GR

St Anthony's RC Prim Sch

Fordhouses

Elston Hall Prim Sch

BROADWAY GDNS

RUSHALL RD

Beeches Farm

HAREHOME CROFT

HOLBURY

LEWISHAM RD

MINEHEAD

Pendeford High Sch

Usam Trad Est

GROSVENOR RD

SCHOLARS

1

Rakegate Jun & Inf Schs

SANDWELL

ARUNDEL RD

ST ANNE'S RD

MARSH LANE PAH

THREE TUNS PAR

WHETSTONE GN

ALLESTON RD

MORETON RD

ELSTON HALL GN

Collingwood Jun & Inf Schs

Liby

Swimming Baths

KEMPTHORNE AVE

Bushbury Hall

Bushbury Hill Jun & Inf Schs

Moreton Com Sch

SHELDON RD

CLARSON CR

MERIDEN AVE

PROBERT RD

BEECH RD

OXLEY MOOR RD

ECCLESHALL AVE

Liby

BARRINGTON RD

CHURCH RD

SHERBORNE RD

Fordhouse Rd Ind Est

Elston Hall

HINCHWOOD RD

LINLEY DR

HILLCREST AVE

02

LYMER RD

A449 Wolverhampton   **Birmingham/W. Midlands** STREET ATLAS

A   **90**   **91**   **B**   **92**   **C**

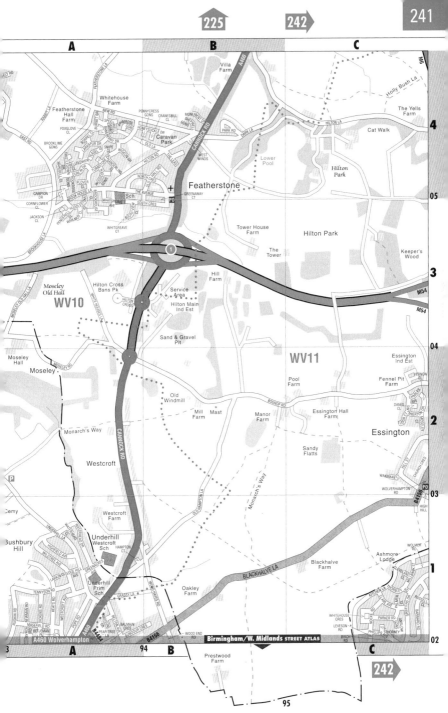

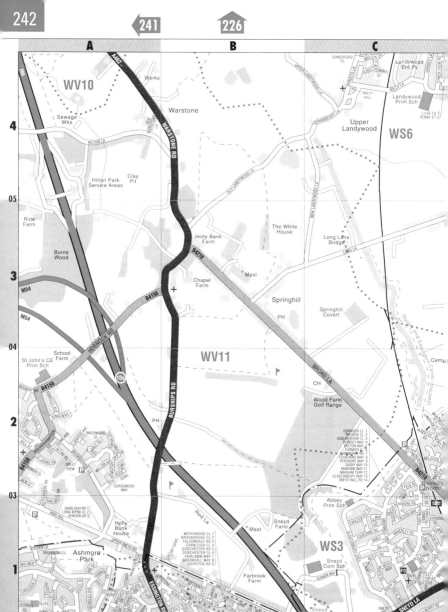

WV10

Works

Warstone

Sewage
Wks

Hilton Park
Service Areas

Clay
Pit

Ride
Farm

Burns
Wood

M54

M54

School
Farm

St John's CE
Prim Sch

HOBNOCK RD

B4156

10a

BURNSNIPS RD

PH

BIRCHWOOD

HOLLY
VIEW

P

GORSEMOOR
WAY

GAIRLOCH RD 1
LONG MYND CL 2
HEBDEN GR 3

P

Holly
Bank
House

Ashmore
Park

WOLMER

Sch

PERKS RD

SANDY
CRES

ESSINGTON RD

Red La

WITHYWOOD CL 1
BROCKERIDGE CL 2
FALCONDALE RD 3
CRANLEIGH CL 4
DORCHESTER RD 5
DORCHESTER CL 6
FAIRLAWN WAY 7
BROOKHILL WAY 8
GRIFFITHS RD 9

Mast

Sneyd
Farm

Farbrook
Farm

WARSTONE RD

B4210

Holly Bank
Farm

Chapel
Farm

+

B4156

PH

Mast

WV11

Springhill

PH

Springhill
Covert

The White
House

Long Lane
Bridge

BROAD LA

CH

Wood Farm
Golf Range

SOMERFORD
CL

Landywood
Ent Pk

+

HOLLY
HILL

Landywood
Prim Sch

LILAC LA 1
PENNY CT 2

Upper
Landywood

WS6

OLD LANDYWOOD LA

N.W. LANDYWOOD LA

Upper Landywood

STRAWBERRY LA

LONG LA

WS3

COXMOOR CL 1
TREVOSE CL 2
COALMEADOW CL 3
RUMSEY WAY 4
HOLTON WAY 5
FURNESS 6
BURBERRY RD 7
FOUNTAINS WAY 8
PERSHORE WAY 9
EASBY WAY 10
MARGAM WAY 11
MARGAM TERR 12
GLASTONBURY WAY 13
SNEYD HALL RD 14

Abbey
Prim Sch

P

Sneyd
Com Sch

Sneyd
Resr

VERNON WAY

WV12

Sneyd
Ho

PO
Sch

SNEYD LA

A4124

MULBERRY

CHEPSTOW CL

Wyrley and Essington Canal (disused)

Cemy

WS11

Wyrley
Common

Engine Lane
Spinney

Clay
Pit

Coppice
Side Ind
Est

4

Wyrley
Hayes

Beck's
Bridge

BROWNHILLS

Mast

Big House
Farm

The
Slough

Coopers
Bridge

Works

05

WS8

High Bridge
Bridge

Catshill
Junction
Bridge

York's
Bridge

Highbridge

Holy
Trinity
CE Prim Sch

Brownhills
Bsns Pk

3

Recn
Gd

Clayhanger

St Davids

Ryder's Hayes
Farm

Sewage
Works

Maybrook
Ind Est

Oak
Park

04

Sch

L Ctr

Walsall
Wood

Ryder's Hayes
Crossing

WS3

Railswood
Farm

Grange
Farm

Dairy
Farm

2

Pelsall

WS9

Woodfield
Ho

Works

03

Pelsall
Common

High
Heath
Shelfield
Com Sch

Highfield
Farm

Vigo

Hotel

Lathams
Bridge

Pit
(dis)

1

WS4

Brick Kiln
Pool

Clay
Pit

Heath
End

Brick
Works

Rushall
JMI Sch

Shelfield

Works

Clay
Pit

Empire
Ind Est

02

Nursery

02   A   03   B   04   C

A
B
C

Lawton
Grange

Chesterfield
Farm

Barn
Farm
Road under construction

Hilton

Chesterfield
Road under construction

Bullmoor Lane
Covert

Chesterfield
Lodge

4

Hilton
Farm

Crane Brook

Raikes
Covert

Ashcroft
Farm

Cranebrook
Farm

05

Gayley
Cottage

Poultry
Houses

Keeper's
Cottage

Malkin's
Coppice

ESSINGTON
CL

Ppg
Sta

PO

Lynn Lane
House

3

The
Bungalow

Lynn

Owlett Hall
Farm

Footherley
Rough

Dairy
Farm

Birchbrook
Ind Pk

Shenstone

LYNN LA

The
Nurseries

04

Laurels
Farm

Swan
Farm

Keeper's
Cottage

WS14

Lower
Stonnall

Spinney
Farm

FOOTHERLEY LA

Shenstone
Court

2

Footherley
Hall

Home
Farm

Footherley

GRAVELLY LA

HOOK LA

WS9

New Barns
Farm

Footherley Brook

03

Griffin's
Covert

Cockheath
Coppice

Footherley
Farm

Croft
Farm

White's
Farm

1

Bagot's
Barn

MOOR LA

Biddle's Field
Wood

Bosses

02

FORGE LA

08

A

09

B

10

C

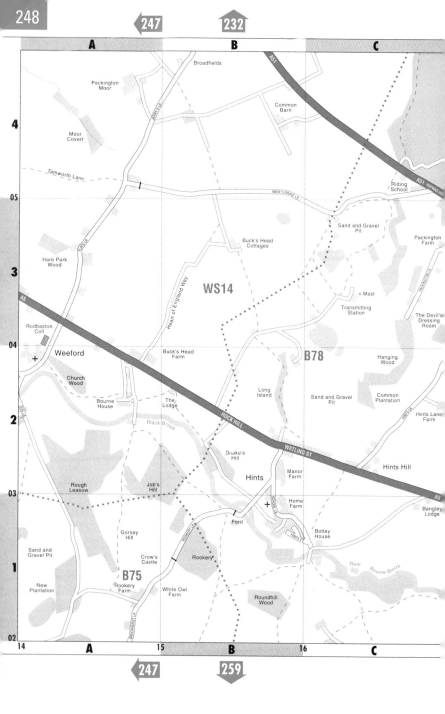

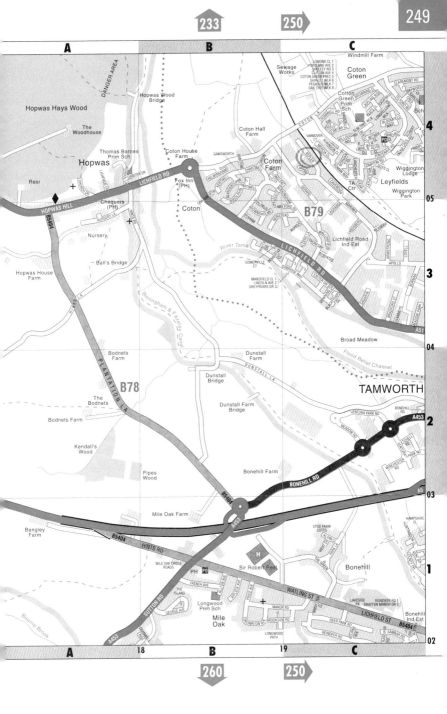

Warwickshire STREET ATLAS

M42 Ashby-de-la-Zouine (A42)

Amington Hall

Decoy Barn

Cow Barn

The Decoy

Amington Old Hall

New Rd

PEARTREE CT

WESSEX CT

CORONATION CRES

PEARTREE CL

Wolferstan Arms (PH)

Shuttington

Church Farm

Shuttington Bridge

The Pretty Pigs (PH)

SHUTTINGTON RD

B79

Alvecote

ALVECOTE COTTS

PO

Nature Reserve

SHACKLEFORD WAY

LANGDALE

ALDRIDGE

DOLLERY

BARRINGTON

LEVETT RD

Askew Bridge

Greenacres Prim Sch

Cemy

HODGE LA

TREFOIL

SKINNER

LYTHAM

CARNOUSTIE

Coventry Canal

River Anker

Marina

Alvecote Priory

P

1 SUNNINGDALE
2 MUIRFIELD

CRESTWOOD

HIGHFIELD AVE

LINDERA

WOODLAND RD

MAPLE RISE

MADRONA

Amington

KERRIA

MAGNOLIA

PO

B77

EAGLE DR

CH

Amington Heath Com Prim Sch

Amber Bsns Village

Tamworth Bsns Pk

FAIRWAY CT

AMBER

MERCURY CT

QUINCE

Quince Tree Sch

Alvecote Wood

Priory Farm

B78

BROOMWEED

BRIAR

SAND WAY

Tamworth Bsns Ctr

Lodge Farm

Amington Ind Est

Mercian Pk

War Meml

Works

PULHAM

SEDGE

STEPHENSON

BRANSTON

GLASCOTE RD

Darwell Pk

B5000

ABBERLEY

PENNINE WAY

DULCE

MICA CL

DEEPDALE

Pooley Hall and remains of Hall

POOLEY LA

River Anker

THE LIMES

Playing Field Stoneydelph Prim Sch

EALING GR

CORBEN

CHEVIOT

CROSDON

BELLINGHAM

CHILTERN RD

Priory Farm

Sports Gd

TAMWORTH RD

The Hermitage

TAMWORTH RD

B5000

Stoneydelph La

P

PO

LINTLY

GATON

LOUGHSHAW

MALHAM RD

LOWFORCE

BUCHTEN

MOORCROFT

MALLERSTANG

PIKE CL

SAXON CL

THE DALES

B5000

TF11

A

B

C

4

Bishton
Cottages

Bishton
Manor

RUSHEY LA

WV7

Shropshire
Lodge

Rous's
Covert

Home
Farm

HOME FARM RD

Patshull
Park

Albrighton
Lodge

Wildicote

01

Snowdon
Pool

Monkey
Bridge

Wilderness
Hill

Patshull
Hall

Bennetts
Wood

Monkeybridge
Plantation

Burnhill
Green

Lower
Snowdon

SNOWDON RD

Dartmouth
Arms (PH)

Decoy
Wood

Church
Pool

Old Park

3

Half Moon
Plantation

Middle
Ley

Shepherds
Buildings

Old Park
Plantation

Shepherds
Plantation

Cut
Spinney

The
Great Pool

WV6

00

Far Ley

Oulton
Garden

Green's
Coppice

Jubilee
Plantation

Plant's
Neck

Mill
Pond

Hotel
CH

2

Bridgenorth
Plantation

Pasford
Farm

Stanlow
Farm

Pasford

99

Kingslow
Cottages

Kingslow

Pasford
Farm

Kingslow
Farm

1

Kingslow
Hall

Pasford
House

Nun Brook

WV15

Chesterton
Cottage

Birchley
Farm

98

78

A

79

B

80

C

237
254

A **B** **C**

New Brook
Plantation

Upper
Pepperhill

The Hooks

WV7

Simmond's
Wood

Wrottesley
Lodge
Farm

4

Horse
Rail

Scott's Bank
Plantation

Hawk's
Well

Birch
Coppice

Bickley's
Rough

01

Wrottesley Old Park

Spring
Coppice

High Park

The
Beeches

Deers Leap

Mere Oak
Corner

3

Rifle Range
Plantation

The
Butts Spinney

Westbeech

West Logan
Farm

HOLLIES LA

The
Meadleys

Westbeech
Farmhouse

00

Nore
Hill

Westbeech
House

Nurton
Hill

The
Hollies

The Slangs
Plantation

WV6

WARSTONE HILL RD

Grange
Farm

Woodhouses

WOLVERHAMPTON RD

2

PATSHULL RD

COLLEGE FARM
CL

St Chads
CE Prim
Sch

Nurton Hall
Farm

Nurton

Tuters
Hill

HIGH ST

Nurton Brook

CORVE LA

PH
WD

THE RETREAT GARDENS

99

Tanhouse
Farm

BROADWELL LA

THE
SQUARE

Pattingham

Sewage
Works

HALL END

Moor Lane
Farm

GREAT MOOR RD

Copley
Farm

CHESTERTON RD

BRAEMAR RD

CLIVE RD

ELMR BROOK

MOOR LA

MOOR LA

1

RUDGE RD

Great
Moor

Madame's
Coppice

Hamley
Park

Ford

BENNETTS LA

Little Moor

98

A 82 **B** 83 **C**

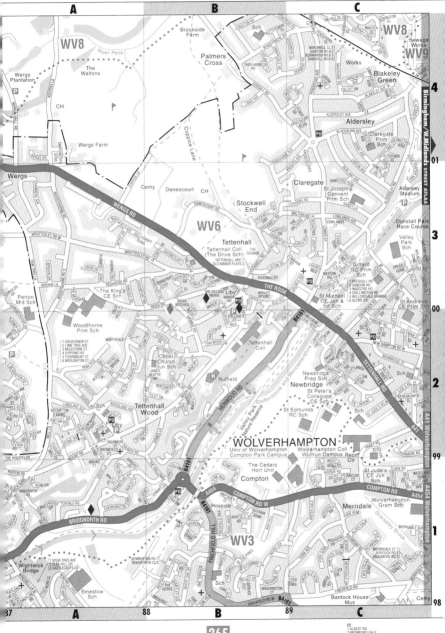

WV8

River Penk

Wergs
Plantation

The Waltons

Brookside
Farm

Palmers
Cross

WV8

Sewage
Works

WV9

CH

Wergs Farm

Blakeley
Green

Aldersley

Claregate
Prim Sch

Wergs

Claregate

St Joseph's
Convent
Prim Sch

Aldersley
Stadium

Danescourt

CH

Stockwell
End

WV6

Tettenhall

Dunstall Park
Race Course

Valley
Park
Sch

Tattenhall Coll
(The Drive Sch)

THE ROOK

Giffard
RC Prim
Sch

The King's
CE Sch

The Village
Mews

Liby

St Michael
CE Jun &
Inf Sch

St Andrews
CE Prim Sch

Perton
Mid Sch

Regis
Beeches

COLLEGE

Woodthorne
Prim Sch

Tettenhall
Coll

Christ
Church
Jun Sch

H

Nuffield

Newbridge
Prep Sch

Newbridge
St Peter's
Collegiate
CE Sch

Tettenhall
Wood

Valley Park
Nature Reserve

St Edmunds
RC Sch

WOLVERHAMPTON
Univ of Wolverhampton
Compton Park Campus

Wolverhampton Coll
Wulfrun Campus

Recn
Ctr

Sch

The Cedars
Hort Unit

Compton

St Jude's
CE Jun
Sch

Wolverhampton
Gram Sch

Merridale

BRIDGNORTH RD

Hospice

COMPTON RD

A454

Wightwick
Bridge

Smestow
Sch

FINCHFIELD HILL

WV3

Bantock House
Mus

Cemy

C2
1 ALBERT RD
2 BROMFORD DALE
3 SLADE HILL
4 ST JUDE'S CT
5 THE CEDARS
6 BRIMFIELD PL
7 SALFOUR CT
8 NEWBRIDGE MEWS
9 GRAFTON CT

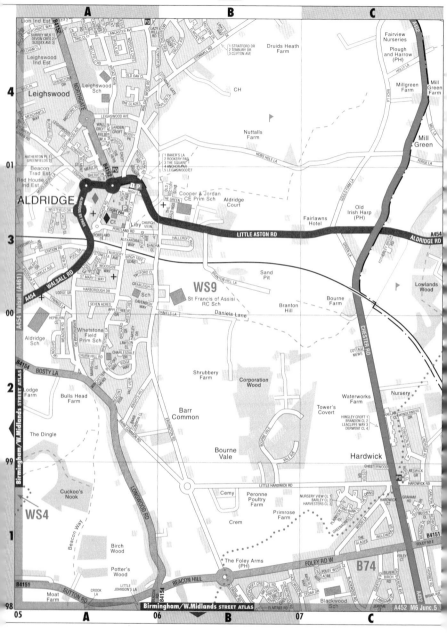

245

A B C

4

01

3

00

2

99

1

98

05 A 06 B 07 C

Lion Ind Est
B1152
Surrey Wlk 1
Devon Cres 2
Sussex Ave 3
Precham Cl
Leighswood
Ind Est

Leighswood Sch

Leighswood

Merchants Way

Hatherton Pl 1
Greenfields 3
B1152
Beacon Trad Est
PO
Red House Ind Est

ALDRIDGE

Court Par
Ct
Liby
CHURCH VIEW

WS4

WS9

St Francis of Assisi RC Sch

Aldridge Sch

BOSTY LA

Lodge Farm

Bulls Head Farm

The Dingle

Cuckoo's Nook

Beacon Way

Birch Wood

Potter's Wood

Moat Farm

SUTTON RD

CROOK LA

LITTLE JOHNSON'S LA

LONGWOOD RD

B4154

Leighswood Ave

Whetstone Field Prim Sch

CHARLESDALE DR

CHURN HILL RD

Daniels Lane

Daniels La

Branton Hill La

Sand Pit

Barr Common

Shrubbery Farm

Corporation Wood

Bourne Vale

Cemy

Crem

Peronne Poultry Farm

Primrose Farm

BEACON HILL

The Foley Arms (PH)

1 STRATFORD DR
2 TENBURY DR
3 CLIFTON AVE

Druids Heath Farm

CH

Nuttalls Farm

HOBS HOLE LA

1 BAKER'S LA
2 ROOKERY PAR
3 THE SQUARE
4 ANCHOR PAR
5 LEIGHSWOOD CT

Cooper & Jordan CE Prim Sch

Aldridge Court

THE GREEN

LITTLE ASTON RD

Branton Hill

Bourne Farm

Fairlawns Hotel

CHESTER RD

Fairview Nurseries

Plough and Harrow (PH)

HENLY LA

Millgreen Farm

Mill Green Farm

Mill Green

FORGE LA

Old Irish Harp (PH)

A454
ALDRIDGE RD

Lowlands Wood

Waterworks Farm

Tower's Covert

HINGLEY CROFT 1
BRANDON CL 2
LEACLIFFE WAY 3
DERWENT CL 4

Nursery

WINDERMERE DR

Hardwick

CHESTERWOOD

PO
KESWICK GR
HARDWICK DR

LITTLE HARDWICK RD

NURSERY VIEW CL 1
BARLEY CL 2
HARVESTERS CL 3

HARDWICK CT

GRAHAM RD

B4151

THE GLADES

FOLEY RD W

B74

FOLEY WOOD CL
ACRE

Blackwood Sch

A452 M6 Junc.5

A454 Walsall (A461)

WALSALL RD
A454

Birmingham/W.Midlands street atlas

B4151

Birmingham/W.Midlands STREET ATLAS

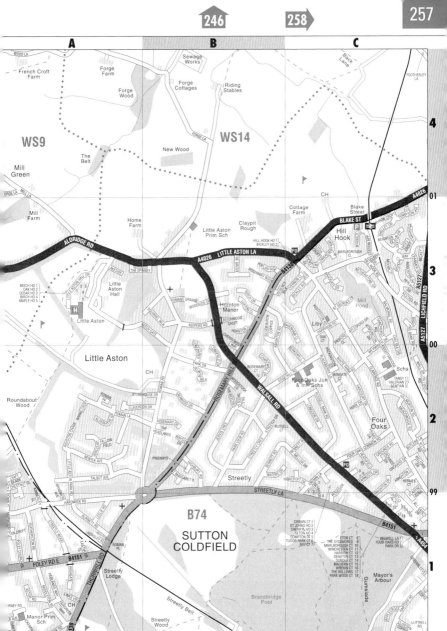

WS9

WS14

Mill
Green

Mill
Farm

WOOD LA

French Croft
Farm

Forge
Farm

Sewage
Works

Forge
Cottages

Riding
Stables

FOOTHERLEY
LA

Back
Lane

Forge
Wood

FORGE LA

New Wood

The
Belt

ORGE LA   BELL LA

Home
Farm

Little Aston
Prim Sch

Claypit
Rough

Cottage
Farm

CH

Blake
Street

BLAKE ST

Hill Hook

Hill
Hook

A4026

A4026

ALDRIDGE RD

A4026   LITTLE ASTON LA

HILL HOOK HO 1
BICKLEY HO 2

MARLBOROUGH
WAY

PO

B4138

A5127 LICHFIELD RD

A5127

BEECH HO 1
OAK HO 2
CEDAR HO 3
BIRCH HO 4
MAPLE HO 5

Little Aston
Hall

THE SPINNEY

LITTLE ASTON PARK RD

LAKESIDE

Little Aston

Mill
Pond

ROMANS GRANGE
WOODSIDE DR

Horinton
Manor

BEECHWOOD
CROFT

BEECH GATE

KEEPERS RD

HORINTON CL

Liby

Schs

TANSY 1
VALERIAN 2
GENTIAN 3

Little Aston

CH

Roundabout
Wood

ROMAN RD

STONEHOUSE DR

CLAVERDON DR

ROMAN LA

ROSEMARY DR

The
Headlands

WAYSIDE
DR

PARK DR

BSLK

ROSEMARY CT

Four Oaks Jun
& Inf Schs

WINGATE

Four
Oaks

ROSEMARY HILL RD

WALSALL RD

RUSSELL CT

PINEWAYS

ST MARGARET'S RD

HIGHCROFT

Streetly

PO

B4151

HERMES
CT

B4138

FOLEY RD E

B4151

Roman
PL

HARDWICK RD

THORNHILL RD

STREETLY LA

STREETLY LA

B74

SUTTON
COLDFIELD

Streetly
Lodge

CROWN CT 1
ST JOHNS HO 2
CHERRYLS HO 3
SETON HO 4
COMPTON DR 5
TUDOR PARK CT 6
BAY CT 7

ETON CT
THE SYCAMORES
MARLBOROUGH CT 10
WINCHESTER CT 11
HARROW CT 12
DENSTON CT 13
QUIGLE CT 14
MALVERN 15
WREKIN CT 16
THE WILLOWS 17
PARK WOOD CT 18

BELWELL LA 1
FOUR OAKS RD 2
PARK DR 3

Mayor's
Arbour

Gumslade

Manor Prim
Sch

RNEY RD

LINDS VIEW

CH

Streetly
Belt

Streetly
Wood

Bracebridge
Pool

LUTTRELL
RD

PARKSIDE WAY

A   B   C

4

WS14

01

B74

3

00

Hill

B75

2

Mere
Green

Roughley

99

SUTTON
COLDFIELD

1

B74

Ley
Hill

Moor
Hall

98

A B C

Brockhurst
Cottages

Fordway
Farm

Woodside
Farm

Lower Bangley
Farmhouse

Weeford
Park

Stockfields

Brockhurst
Farm

Brock Hurst

White House
Farm

WAGGONER'S LA

4

Heart of England Way

Hints
Farm

01

BROCKHURST LA

Three Parish
Wood

Great Bangley
Farm

BANGLEY LA

Draytonlane End
Farm

SUTTON RD

A453

Brick Kiln
Plantation

Canwell
Hall

DRAYTON LA

3

Home
Farm

CANWELL DR

Pithole
Plantation

CRANEBROOK HILL

Shirrall
Coppice

Loddy
Wood

B75

Meadow
Farm

CARROWAY HEAD HILL

Middle Park
Plantation

B78

Shirrall
Hall

00

Heath
Plantation

Carroway Head

LONDON RD

Lamb
Farm

B4151

Carroway Head
Farm

SHIRRALL DR

SLADE RD

SLADE LA

Trickley
Coppice

2

Bassett's Pole
(PH)

A446

Shirrall
Gorse

A453

TAMWORTH RD

Trickley
Coppice

Slade
Farm

FOX HILL RD

COLLETS BROOK

HILL LA

Trickley
Coppice
Farm

99

Collets
Brook
Farm

COPPICE LA

Fox Hill
House

Woodlands

Parkwood
House Farm

Woodside
Farm

Crem

TAMWORTH RD

LONDON RD

Middleton
Wood
Farm

1

Road under construction

Collets Brook

New Park
Wood

A38

A446

Woodlands
Farm

A   15   B   16   C

98

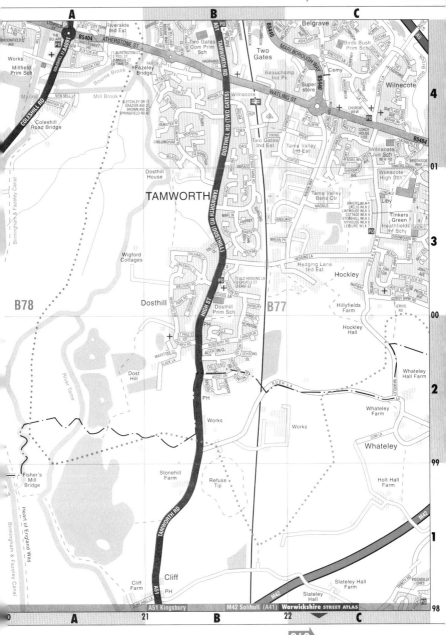

A
B
C

Rudge Hall

The Shubberies

The Clive Farm

Black Brook

BENNETT'S LA

4

Rudge

Rushy Marsh

Lower Barn

RUDGE RD

CLIVE RD

97

A454

Alder Coppice

The Triangle Covert

WV6

3

Cannebuff

Fox Cottage

Garden Centre

Garden Village

BRIDGNORTH RD

Naboth's Vineyard

The Fox (PH)

Little Burbrook

96

A454

Clive View

Blakeley Pool Farm

Smestow Brook

Foxlands

FOX RD

2

Staffordshire Way

POST OFFICE RD

Woodcote

95

Seisdon

WOLMORE LA

Moat Rough

Wolmore Farm

Staffordshire

Seven Stars (PH)

PO

EBSTREE RD

CROSSHILL LA

WV5

Little Round Hill

Home Farm

1

Woodman Inn (PH)

Abbot's Castle Hill

TINKER'S CASTLE RD

Wilderhope

Seisdon Common Rd

B4176

Upper Aston

Long Common

Staffordshire Way

Tinker's Castle Farm

Upper Aston Farm

The White House

B4176

94

A
82
B
83
C

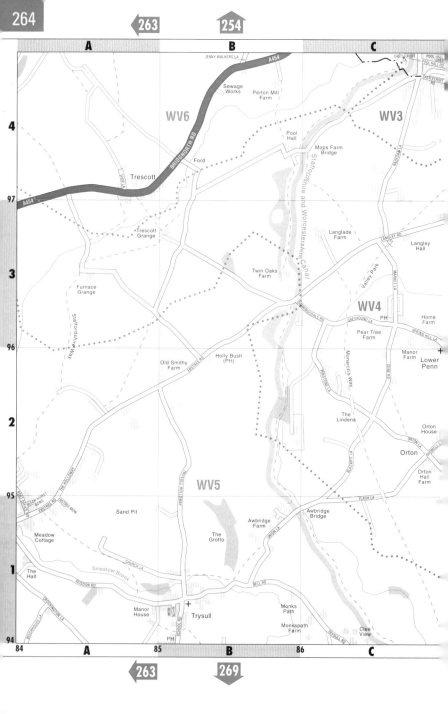

A   **B**   **C**

JENNY WALKERS LA   A454

CASTLECROFT
POOL HALL CRES
POOL HALL RD
CASTLECROFT RD

Sewage
Works

Perton Mill
Farm

WV6

WV3

BRIDGNORTH RD

4

Pool
Hall

Mops Farm
Bridge

Ford

Trescott

97

A454

Staffordshire and Worcestershire Canal

Langlade
Farm

LANGLEY RD

Langley
Hall

Trescott
Grange

Twin Oaks
Farm

Valley Park

MARKET LA

3

Furnace
Grange

WV4

COMMONSDALE RD

GREYHOUND LA

PH

Home
Farm

Staffordshire Way

Pear Tree
Farm

SPRING HILL LA

96

Old Smithy
Farm

Holly Bush
(PH)

ERSTREE RD

Monarch's Way

DENE RD

Manor
Farm

Lower
Penn

2

The
Lindens

MILL HILL HOLLOWAY

LA LINCH LA

Orton
House

ORTON LA

POWELL LA

Orton

WV5

95

BEECH HURST GDNS
POST OFFICE RD
ERSTREE MDW

Sand Pit

The Grotto

Awbridge
Farm

CRUSH LA

Awbridge
Bridge

FLASH LA

Orton
Hall
Farm

Meadow
Cottage

CHURCH LA

WEBB RD

Smestow Brook

1

The
Hall

BELL RD

CROCKINGTON LA

BELLENCROFT LA

Manor
House

WHITE
TOAD RD

Trysull

Monks
Path

Monkspath
Farm

TRYSULL RD

Clee
View

PH

94

84   85   86

A   **B**   **C**

265

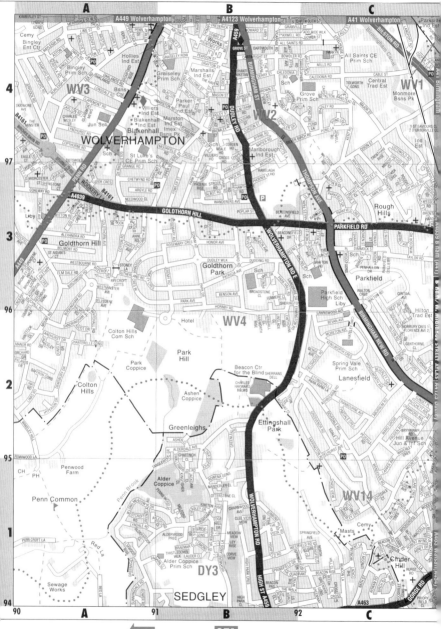

268

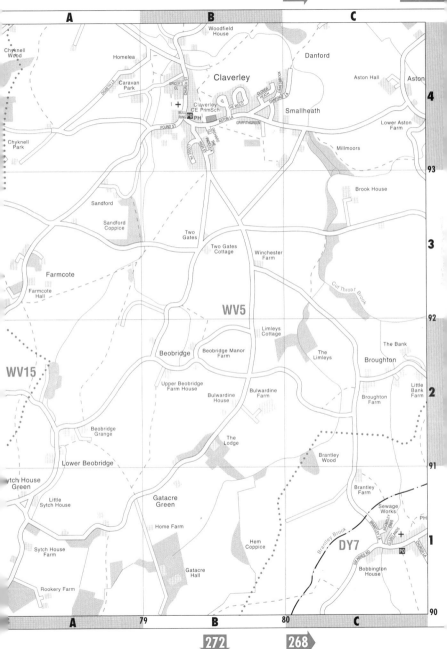

A B C

Woodfield House

Chyknell Wood

Homelea

Danford

Aston Hall

Aston

Caravan Park

Claverley

DRURY LA

SPICER'S CL

CHURCH ST

CLOVER HEATH

Smallheath

Lower Aston Farm

Chyknell Park

Claverley CE PrimSch

THE WOLD

ASTON LA

DANFORD LA

LIGHTWOOD LA

PO PH

BULL RING

POUND ST

THE CROFT

THE PADDOCK

ORCHARD CL

GRIFFITHGREEN

Millmoors

4

93

Sandford

Brook House

Sandford Coppice

Two Gates

Two Gates Cottage

Winchester Farm

3

Farmcote

Cut Throat Brook

92

Farmcote Hall

WV5

Limleys Cottage

WV15

Beobridge

Beobridge Manor Farm

The Limleys

The Bank

Broughton

Little Bank Farm

2

Upper Beobridge Farm House

Bulwardine House

Bulwardine Farm

Broughton Farm

Beobridge Grange

The Lodge

Brantley Wood

91

Lower Beobridge

ytch House Green

Gatacre Green

Brantley Farm

Sewage Works

PH

Little Sytch House

Home Farm

Brantley Brook

BRANTLEY LA

BRANTLEY DRIVE

SIX ASHES RD

LODGELANDS

CHURCH LA

PO

DY7

1

Sytch House Farm

Hem Coppice

Bobbington House

Rookery Farm

Gatacre Hall

A B C

79 80 90

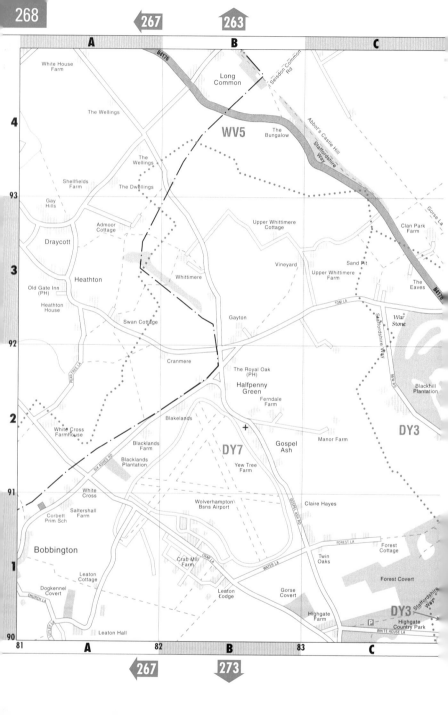

A
B
C

4

3

2

1

White House
Farm

The Wellings

Shellfields
Farm

Gay
Hills

Admoor
Cottage

Draycott

Heathton

Old Gate Inn
(PH)

Heathton
House

Swan Cottage

The Wellings

The Wellings

The Dwellings

Whittimere

Cranmere

White Cross
Farmhouse

Blakelands

Blacklands
Farm

Blacklands
Plantation

SKY ASHES RD

White
Cross

PERR HILL LA

Saltershall
Farm

Corbett
Prim Sch

Bobbington

Leaton
Cottage

Dogkennel
Covert

CHURCH LA

Leaton Hall

Long
Common

B4176

Seisdon Common Rd

WV5

The Bungalow

Abbot's Castle Hill

Staffordshire Way

Upper Whittimere
Cottage

Vineyard

Upper Whittimere
Farm

Sand Pit

Gorse La

Clan Park
Farm

The Eaves

B4176

TOM LA

War
Stone

Staffordshire Way

WAR LA

Blackhill
Plantation

DY3

Gayton

The Royal Oak
(PH)

Halfpenny
Green

Ferndale
Farm

DY7

Gospel
Ash

Manor Farm

Yew Tree
Farm

Wolverhampton
Bsns Airport

GOSPEL ASH RD

Claire Hayes

FOREST LA

Forest
Cottage

Forest Covert

Twin
Oaks

CRAB LA

WATER LA

Crab Mill
Farm

Leaton
Lodge

Gorse
Covert

Highgate
Farm

P

Staffordshire Way

DY3

Highgate
Country Park

WHITE HOUSE LA

93

92

91

90

81
82
83

A
B
C

A B C

All Saints CE Prim Sch
The Plough (PH)
Hunters Green
Nursery
The Bratch
Bratch Bridge
The Beeches
Woodford Grange
BRIDGEWATER DR
4
Fiershill Farm House
WV5
Smestow Brook
Smestow Barn Farm
Ounsdale High Sch
Westfield Prim Sch
Wombourne
93
The Park Farm
Courtenay House
FEIASHILL CL
Works Wombrook Ind Est
St Bernadettes RC Prim Sch
Ounsdale
GORSE LA
Smestow Bridge Ind Est
Works
Giggetty
Cherry Trees Sch
Smestow Gate
Smestow Bridge
BRIDGNORTH RD
3
Wombourne Ent Pk
Brickbridge
Smestow Gate Farm
Works
92
Blakeley
CHAPEL LA
B4176
CH
The Nine Iron (PH)
Smestow
WOODLAND VIEW
Amptronik Trad Est
Heathmill Ent Ctr
New Road Farm
Mill Lane
Church Cottage Farm
New Lodge
NEW RD
Church Farm
Himley Plantation
91
DY3
P
St John's Prim Sch
Swindon
DY7
Whitehouse Plantation
Staffordshire Way
The Old Bush (PH)
1
Highgate Country Park
Whitehouse Farm
DY6
Hinksford Farm
P
Old Plantation
Swindon Rough
85
86
90

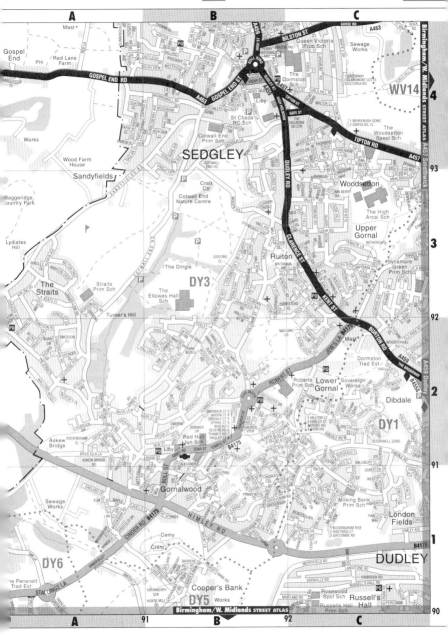

A   B   C

Birmingham / W. Midlands STREET ATLAS   Smethwick   A457

Mast

Gospel
End

PH   Red Lane
Farm

GOSPEL END RD   A463   GOSPEL END ST

BILSTON ST   GORSE RD   A463   ROCK

Queen Victoria
Prim Sch

The
Dormston
Sch

Sewage
Works

WV14

Greenway
2 CLAREMONT COTTS
3 VICTORIA RD

Works

Wood Farm
House

Sandyfields

SEDGLEY

St Chads
RC Sch

Cotwall End
Prim Sch

TIPTON RD

1 BERRYBUSH GDNS
2 DAFFODIL CL

The
Woodsetton
Spec Sch

A457

93

Cotwall End
Nature Centre

Craft
Ctr

Woodsetton

The High
Arcal Sch

Baggeridge
Country Park

DUDLEY RD

Lydiates
Hill

The Dingle

Ruiton

Upper Gornal

NETHERGATE

Sycamore
Green
Prim Sch

3

The
Straits

Straits
Prim Sch

The
Ellowes Hall
Sch

DY3

Britannia

CLARENCE ST

Turner's Hill

KENT ST

BURTON RD

A459

92

Mast

Woodsetton
Trad Est

THE BROADWAY

A459 Dudley

Askew
Bridge

Roberts
Prim Sch

Lower
Gornal

Sovereign
Works

Dibdale

DY1

2

Red Hall
Jun Sch

BULL ST

ZOAR ST

Gornalwood

B4175

WARWICK CT 1
ARDEN CT 2
DIBDALE CT 3
SPIRAL CT 4
SEVERN HO 5
SEVERN HO 6
THAMS HO 7
HAGLEY CT

1 HILLTOP CT
2 HIMLEY CT
3 TRENT HO
4 AVON HO

Milking Bank
Prim Sch

London
Fields

91

Sewage
Works

CINDER RD   B4175   HIMLEY RD

1 BUCKINGHAM RISE
2 HASTINGS CT
3 GATCOMBE RD

DUDLEY

B4176

1

DY6

STALLINGS LA

Cem

Crem

Cooper's Bank

DY5   Works

Rosewood
Spcl Sch

Russell's
Hall

Russells Hall
Prim Sch

90

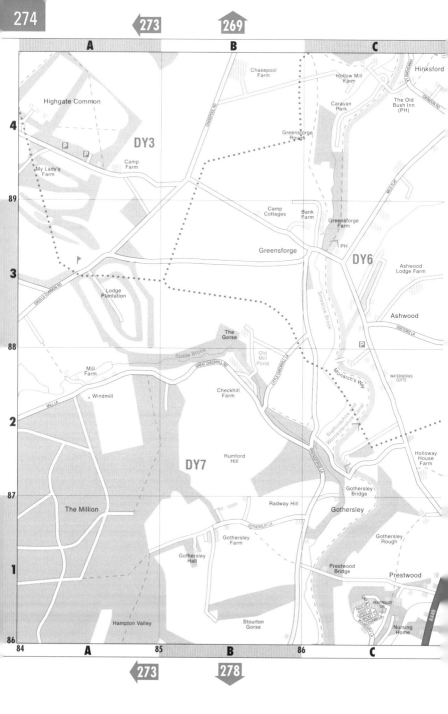

270

B4
1 CHARTERFIELDS SH CTR
2 FRANCIS CL
3 TRESHAM RD
4 CORRIN GR
5 WATERFORD RD

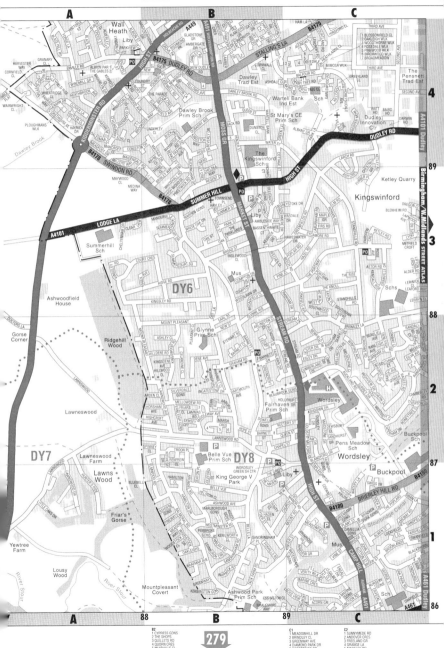

279

B2
1 CYPRESS GDNS
2 THE SHOPS
3 QUILLETS RD
4 QUOPIN CRES
5 MUIRVILLE CL
6 QUALE GR
7 ROSE COTTAGE DR
8 CROSS ST

C1
1 MEADOWHILL DR
2 BRINDLEY CL
3 GREENWAY AVE
4 DIAMOND PARK DR
5 SWEETBRIAR DR
6 MAGNOLIA WAY
7 WHITETHORN RD
8 DEWBURY RD

C2
1 SUNNYMEDE RD
2 ANDOVER CRES
3 FREELAND GR
4 GRANGE LA
5 MADELEY RD

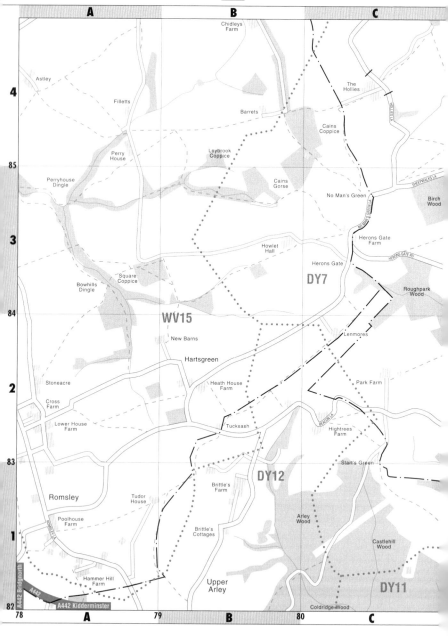

A   B   C

4

Astley

Filletts

Chidleys
Farm

The
Hollies

Barrets

Cains
Coppice

85

Perry
House

Leybrook
Coppice

Perryhouse
Dingle

Cains
Gorse

No Man's Green

SHEEPWALKS LA

Birch
Wood

HOLLIES LA

3

Howlet
Hall

Herons Gate
Farm

Herons Gate

HERONS GATE RD

DY7

NEW MAN'S GREEN LA

Square
Coppice

Bowhills
Dingle

Roughpark
Wood

84

WV15

New Barns

Lenmores

Hartsgreen

Park Farm

2

Stoneacre

Heath House
Farm

Cross
Farm

Lower House
Farm

Tucksash

BEACON LA

Hightrees
Farm

83

Start's Green

DY12

Brittle's
Farm

Romsley

Tudor
House

Arley
Wood

Poolhouse
Farm

Castlehill
Wood

1

Brittle's
Cottages

DY11

Hammer Hill
Farm

Upper
Arley

A442 Bridgnorth

A442

82

A442 Kidderminster

Coldridge Wood

78   A   79   B   80   C

MAMBLE LA

A B C

A458
COTE LA
A458

Essex
Wood

Home
Farm

Temple
Pool

Falcon
Farm

Broom
Hill

4

The Sheepwalks

Priest
Wood

Lyndon Covert

Lord Grey's
Gorse

Heathlands

CLANBROOK RD

CHESTER RD

EXCEL LA

Staffordshire Way

85

SHEEPWALKS LA

Compton Court
Farm

WIGLEY BANK RD

Little Brook

Brindley's
Heath

Little Birch
Copse

Compton

Union Hall
Farm

HUNTSMANS
WLK

Kinver

3

Brindley
Hall

BARKNLL TREE LA

BATH LA

Sandy La

Barn Piece
Farm

WHITE HILL

Staffordshire Way

Potter' Cross
Farm

84

Compton Hall
Farm

Pigeonhouse
Farm

DY7

HERONS GATE RD

ROCKY WALK

Redcliffe
Covert

CHURCH VIEW
GDNS

The
Wilderness

Dodson's
Farm

Iron
House

COMPTON RD

RED HILL

COMPTON RD

HEATH

2

Lydiates
Farm

GREENFIELD RD

Gorse
Covert

P

Holy Austin
Rock

FOREST RD

COMBES RD

Holly Rise
Cottage

BEACON LA

Valehead
Farm

Kinver Edge

83

Greyfields
Court

Brown's
Farm

BIRD'S BARN LA

KINGSFORD LA

Kingsford
Cottage

Nanny's
Rock

CHURCH RD

Cemy

SANDY LA

1

DY11

Kinver Edge
Farm

Castle
Hill

Castle Hill
Farm

P

Vale's
Rock

Kingsford
Country Park

Lodge
Farm

GIPSY LA

82

A 82 B 83 C

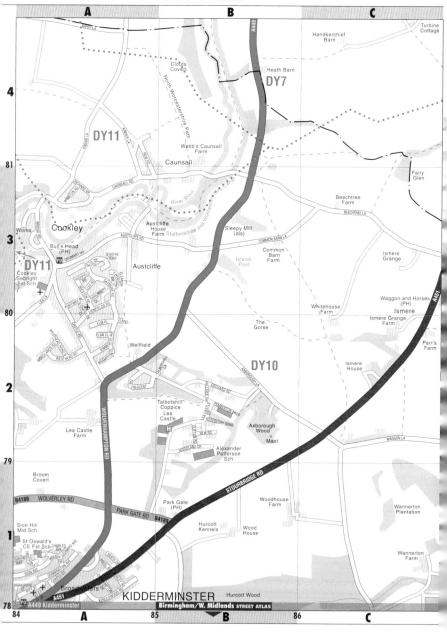

A B C

DY7

Sugarloaf
Farm

DUNTY JOHN
LA
Burys
Hill

A451

4

Mast
Crown Inn
(PH)

KIDDERMINSTER RD

Iverley

Iverley Hay
Farm

DRUM LA

SUGAR LOAF LA

The Birches

81

Iverley House
Farm

Highdown
Cottages

North Worcs Path

Upper Brake
Farm

Haybridge
High Sch

STOURBRIDGE RD

DY8

BRAKE LA

Hagley
RC
High Sch

THE
BRAKE

THE COPPICE

FIVE
WAYS

Common
Farm

IVERLEY LA

Palmer's
Hill

Hagley

WOODLAND AVE

HAYBRIDGE AVE

HOARSTONE

SUMMERVALE
RD

THE CRESCENT

3

Pumping
Station

Brakemill
Plantation

Brakemill
Farm

Sewage
Works

THE SYCAMORES 1
THE HAZELS 2
THE SPRUCES 3
THE HAWTHORNS 4
THE BRIARS 5
THE GREEN 6
LONG CL 7
SPRING CL 8

80

STAKENBRIDGE LA

Stakenbridge
Farm

BEECHES MEWS 9
PINEWOODS CT 10

PINEWOODS RD

DY10

Stakenbridge

Bridge
Farm

WAGGON LA

Churchill

STONEY LA

Harborough
Farm

Falconry
Ctr

Nursery

KIDDERMINSTER RD S

THICKNALL LA

A456 Birmingham

A450

DY9

2

CHURCHILL LA

Churchill
Farm

Harborough
Hill

WORCESTER RD

79

WHEATMILL CL

THE CROFT

BIRMINGHAM RD

Harborough
Hall

Broome
Mill

Windmill
Pool

BROOME LA

CH

MILL LA

LC

Blakedown

STNHN
DR

Monarch's Way

STOURBRIDGE RD

Wannerton
House

Downs
Plantation

Blakedown
CE Prim Sch

B4188

Broome Lodge
Farm

BROOME LA

1

Sewage
Works

Swan
Pool

Forge
Pool

New House
Farm

BELBROUGHTON RD

Knoll Hill
House

B4188

Hackman's
Gate

Hundred Acre
Farm

A 88 B 89 C

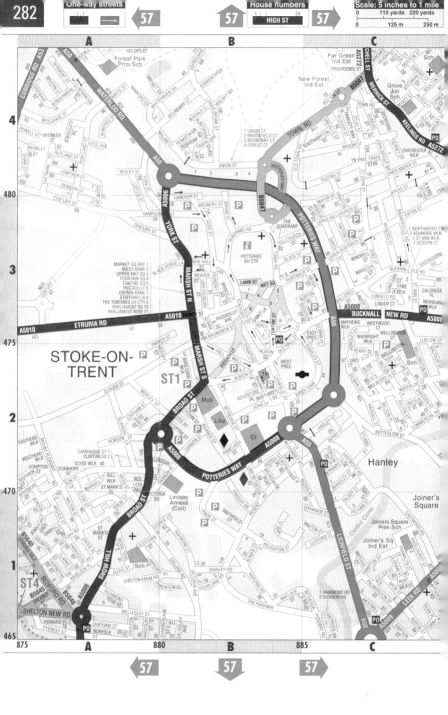

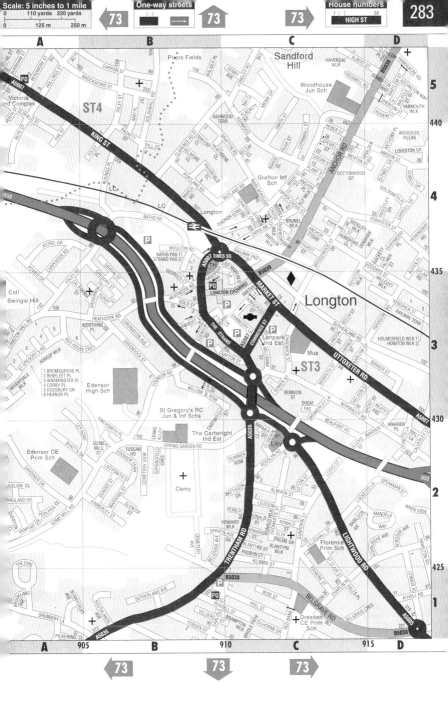

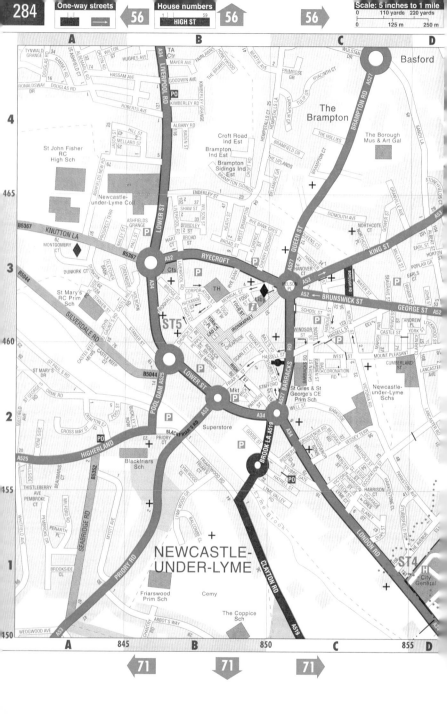

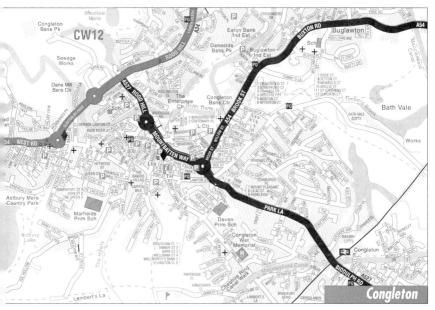

Congleton

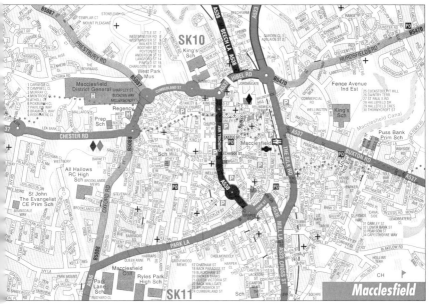

Macclesfield

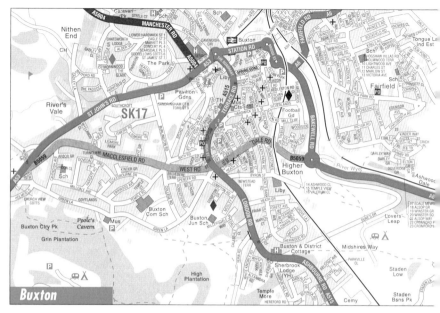

Buxton

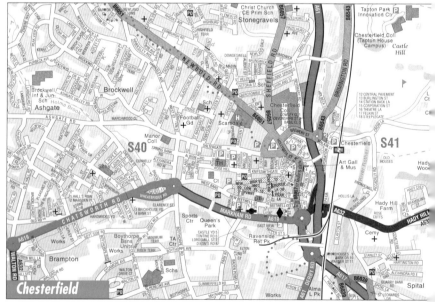

Chesterfield

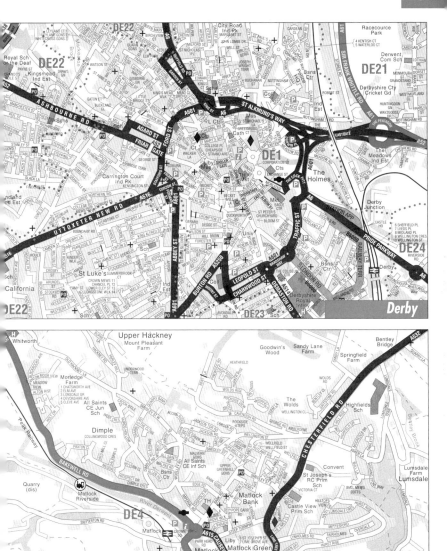

Derby

Matlock

Index

Church Rd **6** Beckenham BR2..........**53** C6

Place name	Location number	Locality, town or village	Postcode district	Page and grid square
May be abbreviated on the map	Present when a number indicates the place's position in a crowded area of mapping	Shown when more than one place has the same name	District for the indexed place	Page number and grid reference for the standard mapping

Public and commercial buildings are highlighted in magenta. Places of interest are highlighted in blue with a star★

Abbreviations used in the index

Acad	Academy	Comm	Common	Gd	Ground	L	Leisure	Prom	Prom
App	Approach	Cott	Cottage	Gdn	Garden	La	Lane	Rd	Road
Arc	Arcade	Cres	Crescent	Gn	Green	Liby	Library	Recn	Recreation
Ave	Avenue	Cswy	Causeway	Gr	Grove	Mdw	Meadow	Ret	Retail
Bglw	Bungalow	Ct	Court	H	Hall	Meml	Memorial	Sh	Shopping
Bldg	Building	Ctr	Centre	Ho	House	Mkt	Market	Sq	Square
Bsns, Bus	Business	Ctry	Country	Hospl	Hospital	Mus	Museum	St	Street
Bvd	Boulevard	Cty	County	HQ	Headquarters	Orch	Orchard	Sta	Station
Cath	Cathedral	Dr	Drive	Hts	Heights	Pal	Palace	Terr	Terrace
Cir	Circus	Dro	Drove	Ind	Industrial	Par	Parade	TH	Town Hall
Cl	Close	Ed	Education	Inst	Institute	Pas	Passage	Univ	University
Cnr	Corner	Emb	Embankment	Int	International	Pk	Park	Wk, Wlk	Walk
Coll	College	Est	Estate	Intc	Interchange	Pl	Place	Wr	Water
Com	Community	Ex	Exhibition	Junc	Junction	Prec	Precinct	Yd	Yard

Index of localities, towns and villages

Abbots Bromley 161 A3
Acton Trussell 175 A1
Adbaston 131 B2
Admaston 160 A2
Alberighton 237 A3
Aldridge 256 A3
Alrewas 200 C1
Alsop en le Dale 36 C2
Alstonefield 35 B2
Alton 78 C1
Alveley 272 A1
Anslow 165 B4
Armitage 198 A2
Ashley 100 A3
Astbury 15 A4
Audley 39 B1
Bagnall 43 C1
Barlaston 88 C1
Barthomley 38 B3
Barton Turn 184 A1
Barton-under-Needwood 183 B1
Betley 53 A3
Biddulph 27 A4
Blakedown 281 B1
Blakenhall 52 A2
Blore 99 A1
Blymhill 203 C3
Blythe Bridge 90 C4
Bobbington 268 A1
Boscobel 221 C3
Bosley 7 B4
Bradley 191 B4
Bradnop 31 C2
Branston 184 C1
Bretby 167 C1
Brewood 223 B3
Bridgemere 67 A4
Brierley Hill 279 C4
Brocton 176 B2
Brownhills 245 A3
Bucknall 58 A2
Burntwood 229 B3
Burslem 56 C4
Burton upon Trent 166 C1
Butterton 33 C3
Buxton 4 B4
Cannock 209 B1
Caverswall 74 C1
Chapel Chorlton 102 A4
Cheadle 76 B2
Chebsey 134 C3
Cheddleton 45 B3
Chell Heath 42 A3
Chelmorton 5 B4
Cheslyn Hay 226 B2

Cheswardine 130 A4
Chetwynd 168 B4
Chetwynd Aston 187 A4
Chilcote 219 C2
Chorlton 37 A1
Church Broughton 129 C4
Church Eaton 190 A4
Church Leigh 109 A2
Claverley 267 B4
Clifton 81 C3
Clifton Campville 218 C1
Codsall 238 C2
Colton 179 A3
Colwich 177 C4
Congleton 6 A2
Consall 60 B3
Cookley 280 A3
Coppenhall 174 B2
Cotton 78 B4
Croxden 94 B2
Denstone 95 B3
Dilhorne 75 B2
Dordon 262 C3
Doveridge 127 A4
Draycott in the Clay ..144 B3
Draycott in the Moors ..91 C3
Drayton Bassett 260 B3
Dudley 271 C1
Dunstall 183 B3
Earl Sterndale 5 B2
Eaton 6 A4
Eccleshall 133 C3
Edgmond 168 A2
Edingale 217 B3
Egginton 148 A3
Elford 216 B1
Ellastone 80 A2
Ellenhall 134 A1
Elmhurst 214 A3
Endon 43 C4
Enville 273 B1
Essington 241 C2
Farewell 213 A2
Fawfieldhead 12 C2
Fazeley 260 C4
Featherstone 241 B4
Fenton 72 C3
Flash 3 A2
Forsbrook 91 A4
Forton 169 A4
Foston 5 B3
Fradswell 123 A2
Gayton 138 C3
Gnosall 171 B3
Gorstyhill 37 C1

Great Chatwell 188 B1
Great Wyrley 227 A2
Grindon 34 A1
Hademore 233 A2
Hagley 281 C3
Hamstall Ridware 180 C2
Hanbury 145 A3
Hanchurch 87 A4
Hanley 57 B2
Harlaston 217 B3
Hartington 24 B3
Hatton 146 B4
Haughton 172 C3
Heath Hill 187 B1
Heaton 8 C1
Hilderstone 106 B1
Hill Ridware 198 A4
Hilton 147 C4
Himley 270 A2
Hints 248 B2
Hixon 158 B4
Hollinsclough 4 B1
Hopton 137 B1
Hopwas 249 A4
Huntington 209 B4
Ilam 50 C2
Ingestre 157 C3
Ipstones 62 A4
Keele 69 C4
Kidderminster 280 A1
Kidsgrove 26 A1
King's Bromley 199 B3
Kingsley 61 C2
Kingstone 141 B4
Kingswinford 275 C3
Kinver 278 A2
Lawton-gate 25 A2
Leek 30 C3
Lichfield 231 B4
Linton 186 A1
Little Aston 257 A2
Longdon 197 C1
Longford 168 A1
Longnor 13 A3
Longsdon 29 C1
Longton 73 B2
Lower Penn 265 A2
Lullington 218 C4
Madeley 67 C3
Maer 85 B1
Mapleton 66 C2
Marchington 127 C1
Market Drayton 97 B2
Marston 136 C2
Marston Montgomery ..96 C1

Marston on Dove 147 A4
Mayfield 81 B4
Meerbrook 19 C4
Meir 74 A1
Middleton 260 A1
Millmeece 117 C4
Milwich 122 B3
Monyash 14 C4
Mount Pleasant 26 A3
Mow Cop 26 B4
Mucklestone 99 A4
Netherseal 219 C4
Newborough 162 C4
Newcastle-under-Lyme ..71 A4
Newport 168 B2
Newton Regis 236 B2
Newton Solney 167 C4
Norbury 151 A2
Norton Canes 227 C3
Norton in Hales 82 B1
Norton-in-the-Moors ..42 C2
Oakamoor 78 A4
Onecote 32 C2
Packmoor 26 C1
Pattingham 253 B1
Penkridge 192 C1
Perton 254 B2
Polesworth 262 C4
Ranton 153 B3
Repton 148 C1
Rocester 96 A2
Rolleston 147 A2
Romsley 276 A1
Roston 96 C4
Rudge 263 A4
Rudyard 29 C4
Rugeley 196 C4
Rushton Spencer 8 A1
Salt 137 C2
Sandon 137 B4
Scholar Green 25 C4
Scropton 129 C1
Seckington 236 A2
Sedgley 271 B4
Sedgford 154 A4
Seisdon 263 C1
Shareshill 225 B1
Sheen 24 A4
Shenstone 247 A3
Shuttington 251 C4
Snelston 81 B2
Stafford 155 C2
Standon 102 A1
Stanton 65 B1
Stoke-on-Trent 72 C4

Stone 120 A4
Stourbridge 279 C2
Stramshall 111 A2
Streethay 215 A1
Sudbury 128 C2
Sutton 112 B2
Sutton Coldfield 258 C1
Swadlincote 186 C2
Swindon 269 C1
Swinscoe 65 C3
Swynnerton 103 A2
Talke 40 B4
Tamworth 250 A2
Tatenhill 165 A1
The Bank 26 A4
Thorncliffe 20 C1
Thorpe 51 B1
Thorpe Constantine ..235 C3
Tissington 51 C3
Tittensor 88 A1
Tixall 157 B1
Tong 220 B2
Trentham 88 A3
Tunstall 41 B2
Tutbury 146 B3
Upper Arley 276 B1
Upper Tean 92 B2
Uttoxeter 126 B4
Wall 230 B1
Walsall 243 A1
Walton-on-Trent 184 C1
Warslow 23 A1
Waterhouses 49 A1
Weeford 248 A2
Weston 37 B3
Weston 138 B2
Weston-under-Lizard ..203 C2
Wetton 34 C2
Wheaton Aston 205 A3
Whitgreave 135 C3
Whitmore 86 A3
Whittington 232 B3
Wigginton 234 A1
Wildboarclough 1 C3
Willington 148 C3
Wincle 9 A4
Wolverhampton 266 A4
Wombourne 269 C3
Wood End 262 B1
Woodcote 187 B2
Woodhouse Green 7 B1
Woodseaves 151 C4
Woore 67 A1
Wootton 79 C4
Yoxall 182 A1

Aarons Dr ST7 ....39 C1
Abberley B77 ....251 B1
Abberley Rd DY3 ....271 B2
Abbey Arc DE14 ....166 C1
Abbey Cl Penkridge ST19 .208 A4
  Rocester ST14 ....96 A2
Abbey Ct Bucknall ST2 ....58 A3
  Newport TF10 ....168 C1
Abbey Dr Colwich ST18 ...177 B4
  Walsall WS3 ....234 A3
Abbey Green Rd ST13 .....30 B4
Abbey Hill Specl Sch ST2 .58 B3
Abbey Hulton Prim Sch
  ST2 ....58 A3
Abbey La ST2 ....58 A3
Abbey Prim Sch WS3 .....242 C1
Abbey Rd Bucknall ST2 ....58 A3
  Cheddleton ST9 ....60 A3
  Sedgley DY3 ....271 B2
  Tamworth B77 ....250 B2
Abbey Sq WS3 ....242 C1
Abbey St Bucknall ST2 .....58 A3
  Burton u T DE14 ....166 B1
  Cannock WS11 ....210 A4
  Newcastle-u-L ST5 ....55 B1
  Sedgley DY3 ....271 B2
  Stafford ST5 ....120 A4
Abbey Way TF9 ....97 B1
Abbey Wood Cl ◆ ST13 ..30 B3
Abbeydale Cl CW2 ....37 B3
Abbeyfield Rd WW10 ....240 C2
Abbeyfields ST18 ....158 A1
Abbeyside ST18 ....153 B3
Abbot Beyne Sch DE15 ..167 A2
Abbot's Rd ST11 ....31 A4
Abbot's Way ST5 ....71 A3
Abbots Bromley Hospl
  WS15 ....160 C3
Abbots Field WS11 ....209 C3
Abbots Pl ST2 ....58 A3
Abbots Rd ST2 ....58 A3
Abbots Way WV3 ....255 C1
Abbots Wlk
  Rugeley WS15 ....197 A3
  Stafford ST16 ....155 C3
Abbotsford Rd WS14 ....231 C4
Abbotsholme Sch ST14 ...96 A1
Abbott's Cl CW12 ....16 A4
Abbotts Ct ST2 ....58 A4
Abbotts Dr ST1 ....57 C4
Abbotts Rd WS3 ....243 B1
Abbotts St WS3 ....243 B1
Abella B77 ....250 C2
Aberford Gr ST1 ....57 C3
Abingdon Rd WS3 ....242 C1
Abingdon Way
  Trentham ST4 ....88 A4
  Walsall WS3 ....242 C1
Ablon Ct ST13 ....207 C4
Ablow St WV2 ....266 B4
Abnalls Croft WS13 ......213 C1
Abnalls Ho WS13 ....213 C1
Abnalls La WS13 ....213 C1
Abney Dr WV14 ....266 C1
Acacia Ave ST5 ....55 C1
Acacia Cres WV8 ....239 A2
Acacia Ct DY8 ....279 C3
Acacia Gdns ST7 ....26 B2
Acacia Gr Cannock WS12 .210 C2
  Newcastle-u-L ST5 ....55 C1
Achilles Cl WS6 ....226 C1
Achilles Way ST17 ....57 C1
Ackelton Gdns WV3 .....265 C4
Acorn Cl Ashley TF9 ......99 B3
  Burntwood WS7 ....212 A1
  Cannock WS11 ....210 B1
  Great Wyrley WS6 ......227 A4
Acorn Gr
  Brierley Hill DY8 ....275 C1
  Codsall WV8 ....238 C1
Acorn La CW12 ....6 C2
Acorn Rd WV11 ....242 A1
Acorn Rise ST5 ....89 C4
Acorn Starter Units
  WS7 ....228 B4
Acorn View B77 ....229 B3
Acres Nook Rd ST7 ....41 A3
Acres The
  Newcastle-u-L ST5 ....55 B1
  Wolv WV3 ....255 B1
Acreswood Rd ST6 ....42 A1
Acton Ct ST18 ....174 C1
Acton Dr DY3 ....271 A2
Acton Hill Rd ST17 ......175 B1
Acton St ST1 ....57 B3
Adam Ct WS11 ....209 B1
Adams Ave ST6 ....41 B3
Adams Cl TF10 ....168 C1
Adams Cres TF10 ....168 C1
Adams Gr ST13 ....30 B2
Adams Gram Sch TF10 ..168 C2
Adams Rd
  Brownhills WS8 ....245 A3
  Wolv WV3 ....265 B4
Adams St
  Newcastle-u-L ST5 ....56 B2
  Norton-in-t-M ST2 ....43 A1
Adamson Cl WS11 ....209 A1
Adamthwaite Cl ST11 ....90 B4
Adamthwaite Dr ST11 ...90 B4
Adderley Green Inf Sch
  ST3 ....73 B3
Adderley Pl ST12 ....88 C2
Adderley Rd
  Market Drayton TF9 ......97 A2

Adderley Rd continued
  Norton-in-t-M ST6 ....42 C2
Adderley Road Ind Est
  TF9 ....42 C2
Addie Rd DE13 ....166 A3
Addington Way ST3 .....283 D5
Addison Cl WS11 ....209 C3
Addison Croft DY3 ......271 A3
Addison Rd WV11 ....241 A1
Addison Rd WV3 ....265 C4
Addison St ST1 ....57 B3
Adelaide Cres DE15 .....167 B1
Adelaide Dr WS12 ......210 C2
Adelaide St ST6 ....57 A4
Adelaide Wlk WV2 ......266 C4
Adkins St ST6 ....57 B4
Admiral Parker Dr
  WS14 ....246 C3
Adonis Cl B79 ....250 B4
Adrian St ST4 ....72 C3
Advance Bsns Pk WS11 .210 A2
Adventure Pl ST1 ....282 B2
Adwalton Rd WV6 ......254 C2
Aegean Cl ST14 ....48 B3
Aelfgar Ct WS15 ....178 C1
Aelfgar Ho WS15 ....178 C1
Affleck Ave B78 ....249 B1
Agenoria Dr DY8 ....279 C3
Agger Hill ST5 ....54 B1
Ainsdale Cl ⑧ Meir ST3 .73 B1
  Stourbridge DY8 ....279 C1
Ainsley Cl ST2 ....58 A3
Ainsworth Ave WV10 ....61 B1
Ainsworth Rd WV10 ....240 C2
Ainsworth St ST14 ....72 B3
Aintree Cl
  Burton u T DE14 ....185 A4
  Cannock WS12 ....210 C3
  Trentham ST4 ....88 A4
Aintree Rd
  Upper Tean ST10 ....92 C2
  Wolv WV10 ....240 B2
Aintree Way DY1 ....271 C1
Airdale Gr ST15 ....105 A1
Airdale Rd ST15 ....105 A1
Airdale Spinney ST15 ....105 A1
Airfield Ind Est ST18 ....153 C4
Aitken Cl B78 ....250 A1
Aitken St ST6 ....56 C4
Ajax Cl WS6 ....226 C1
Ajax Way ST2 ....57 C1
Akesmoor La ST7,ST8 ....27 A4
Alan Dale ST9 ....59 A2
Alan Rd ST2 ....58 B2
Alanbrooke Gr ST3 ......89 C4
Alandale Ave WS15 .....198 B2
Alanley Cl ST6 ....42 B1
Alastair Rd ST14 ....71 C2
Alaxandra Dr DE13 .....182 A2
Albany Dr Cannock WS12 .210 C2
  Rugeley WS15 ....178 B2
Albany Gr
  Kingswinford DY6 ......275 C4
  Stoke-on-T ST4 ....71 B4
  Walsall WV11 ....242 B1
Albany Rd
  Newcastle-u-L ST5 ......284 B4
  Stoke-on-T ST4 ....71 B4
Albany St ST6 ....41 B4
Albemarle Rd
  Newcastle-u-L ST5 ......56 A2
  Stourbridge DY8 ....279 C1
Albert Ave ST3 ....73 C2
Albert Cl WV8 ....238 C2
Albert Davies Dr WS12 ..210 C2
Albert Dr ST3 ....269 C1
Albert Rd
  Burton u T DE15 ....167 A2
  Stafford ST16 ....73 C1
  Market Drayton TF9 .....97 A1
  Newcastle-u-L ST5 ......56 B2
  Stafford ST17 ....155 C3
  Wolv WV4 ....266 A3
Albert St ⓵ Wolv WV6 ..255 C2
Albert St Audley ST7 ....39 C2
  Biddulph ST8 ....27 B4
  Burton u T DE14 ....166 B2
  Cannock, Chadsmoor
  WS11 ....209 C2
  Cannock, Church Hill
  WS12 ....210 B3
  Kingswinford DY6 ......275 A4
  Leek ST13 ....30 C3
  Rugeley WS15 ....178 C1
  Tamworth B79 ....250 B3
Albion Rd WS8 ....244 C4
Albion Sq ST1 ....282 B2
Albion St Hanley ST1 ....282 B2
  Kingswinford DY6 ......275 A4
  Leek ST13 ....30 C3
  Rugeley WS15 ....178 C1
  Tamworth B79 ....250 B3
Albion Way WV7 ....211 C1
Albrighton By Pass
  WV7 ....237 A3
Albrighton Jun & Inf Schs
  WV7 ....237 A2
Albrighton Sta WV7 ....237 A3

Albutts Rd WS11 ....228 A2
Alcester Cl ST6 ....42 A3
Alcove The WS3 ....243 B1
Aldbury Cl ST16 ....156 B3
Aldbury Pl ST1 ....72 C1
Aldeburgh Cl WS11 .....243 A2
Aldeburgh Dr ST5 ....71 A1
Alden Hurst WS7 ....228 C4
Alder Cl Ashley TF9 .....99 C3
  Kidsgrove ST7 ....41 A4
  Lichfield WS14 ....231 C4
Alder Coppice DY3 .....266 B1
Alder Coppice Prim Sch
  DY3 ....266 B1
Alder Dale WV3 ....255 C1
Alder Gr Burton u T DE15 .185 C4
  Newcastle-u-L ST5 ....55 B4
  Stafford ST17 ....174 A4
Alder Rd
  Kingswinford DY6 ......275 C3
  Market Drayton TF9 ....112 A4
Alder Way WS12 ....211 A3
Alder Wlk ST14 ....71 C2
Alderbrook Cl
  Rollaston DE13 ....147 A2
  Sedgley DY3 ....266 A1
Alderdale Ave DY3 .....266 B2
Alderflat Dr ST14 ....88 B3
Alderford Cl WV8 ......255 C4
Aldergate B79 ....250 A3
Alderhay La ST7 ....26 B3
Alderhithe Gr B74 ......257 A2
Alderholme Dr ⑥ DE13 .147 C1
Alderney Cl ST5 ....70 C2
Alderney Cres ST13 .....72 C2
Alders La B79 ....249 C3
Alders The DE13 ....183 B1
Aldersea Cl ST6 ....41 C1
Aldershaw Cl ST16 .....136 B1
Aldersleigh Dr ST17 ....175 B3
Aldersley Ave WV6 .....255 C4
Aldersley Cl WV6 ....255 A3
Aldersley High Sch
  WV8 ....239 B1
Aldersley Rd WV6 ......255 C3
Aldersley Stad WV6 ....255 C3
Alderson Dr DE13 ......147 C1
Alderton Dr WV3 ....265 C4
Alderton Gr ST3 ....90 A3
Alderwood Prec DY3 ...266 B1
Alderwood Rise DY3 ...271 A3
Aldin Cl B78 ....249 C1
Aldridge By Pass WS9 ..256 A3
Aldridge Cl
  Brierley Hill DY8 ....279 C4
  Polesworth B78 ....261 A4
Aldridge Rd Aldridge B74 .256 B1
  Little Aston B74,WS9 ...257 A3
Aldridge Sch WS9 ......256 A2
Aldrin Cl Meir ST3 ......90 B4
  Stafford ST16 ....156 A3
Aldwich Dr WV3 ....265 A4
Aldwych Cl WS9 ....256 A4
Aldwych Dr WS9 ....256 A4
Alexander Cl WS13 .....215 B3
Alexander Patterson Sch
  DY10 ....280 B2
Alexander Rd WV8 .....239 B2
Alexandra Cres ST14 ...126 A4
Alexandra Ct
  Burton u T DE15 ....167 A2
  Sedgley DY3 ....271 B2
Alexandra Inf Sch ST3 ..73 C1
Alexandra Mews B79 ...250 B3
Alexandra Rd
  Burton u T DE15 ....167 A2
  Stafford ST16 ....73 C1
  Market Drayton TF9 .....97 A1
  Newcastle-u-L ST5 ......56 B2
  Stafford ST17 ....73 C1
  Wolv WV4 ....266 A3
Alexandra St ⑥ ST15 ...104 C1
Alexandra Way WS9 ....256 A4
Alford Dr ST12 ....59 A2
Alfred Lyons Cl WS15 ...160 C3
Alfred St Burton u T DE14 .166 B1
  Fenton ST4 ....72 C4
  Tamworth B79 ....250 A3
  Walsall WS3 ....243 A1
Alfreton Rd ST4 ....73 A3
Algar Rd ST14 ....71 C3
Alicia Way ST17 ....43 C3
Alison Dr DY8 ....279 C2
All Saints CE Fst Sch
  Church Leigh ST10 ....109 A2
  Denstone ST14 ....95 C3
  Leek ST13 ....30 C2
  Standon ST21 ....102 B2
All Saints CE Inf Sch
  ST18 ....153 B3
All Saints CE Prim Sch
  Acton Trussell ST17 ...193 C4
  Alrewas DE13 ....166 A4
  Seisdon WV5 ....269 A4
  Tatenhill DE13 ....164 B1
  Wolv WV2 ....266 C4
All Saints Croft DE14 ..185 B4
All Saints Dr B74 ......258 A1
All Saints Rd
  Burton u T DE14 ....185 B4
  Stoke-on-T ST4 ....72 A3
  Wolv WV2 ....266 B4
Allan Cl DY8 ....279 C4
Allan St ⑧ DY8 ....279 C4
Allard St DE14 ....166 C2
Allen Birt Wlk WS15 ...178 B2
Allen Gdns TF9 ....112 A4
Allen Rd WV6 ....255 C2

Allen St Cheadle ST10 ....76 C2
  Stoke-on-T ST4 ....71 C4
  Tamworth B77 ....250 B1
Allen's La ST14 ....127 C1
Allenby Ct ST5 ....70 C2
Allenby Sq ST14 ....71 C2
Allendale ST16 ....155 A4
Allendale Wlk ST3 ......72 C1
Allens Croft ST14 ......127 C1
Allens La WS3 ....243 C1
Allens Rough Prim Sch
  WV12 ....242 B1
Allensmead B77 ....250 B1
Allensmore Ave ST4 ....73 A3
Allensway ST5 ....70 C2
Allerdale Rd WS8 ......244 C4
Allerton Rd ST4 ....87 C4
Alleston Wlk WV10 ....240 B1
Alley The DY3 ....271 A2
Alley's La ST20 ....190 A4
Alleyne's High Sch
  ST15 ....105 A1
Alleynes Sports Ctr
  ST15 ....105 A2
Alliance St ST14 ....155 B3
Alliss Cl ST16 ....156 B2
Allport Rd WS11 ....209 C1
Allport St WS11 ....209 C1
Allsop Cres ST17 ....175 A1
Allthorpe Pl ST5 ....70 C2
Allton Ave B78 ....249 B1
Allton Ct B77 ....250 C2
Allways Cl ST18 ....122 B3
Allways The ST18 ......122 B3
Alma Cl ST7 ....25 C4
Alma Rd DE11 ....156 C4
Alma St Burton u T DE14 .166 B1
  Fenton ST4 ....72 B3
  Leek ST13 ....30 B3
  Stoke-on-T ST4 ....104 C1
  Walsall WS3 ....42 A3
Almond Cl
  Cannock WS11 ....210 B1
  Walsall WS3 ....243 A1
Almond Ct DE13 ....147 C1
Almond Gr Fenton ST4 ..72 C2
  Swadlincote DE11 ......186 C3
Almond Pl ST5 ....40 C1
Almond Rd
  Huntington WS12 ......209 B4
  Kingswinford DY6 ......275 C3
Almshouse Croft ST18 ..191 A4
Almshouses Madeley CW3 .68 C3
  Newton Solney DE15 ...167 C4
  Wolv WV4 ....265 C2
Alnwick Cl WS12 ....210 C1
Alnwick Rd WS3 ....243 A2
Alpha Way WS6 ....243 A4
Alpine Dr ST4 ....210 B2
Alpine Way WV3 ....255 B1
Alrewas Rd DE13 ......199 C3
Alsager Rd ST7 ....39 B3
Alsop St ST13 ....30 C3
Alston Cl Cannock WS12 .210 C1
  Sutton Coldfield B74 ...258 A4
Alstone La Bradeley ST18 .172 C1
  Haughton ST18 ....172 C1
Alstonefield YH* DE6 ...35 C2
Alswitch Gr ST12 ....58 B3
Althorp Way DE13 ......166 B4
Althrop Gr ST3 ....73 B2
Alton Cl Newcastle-u-L ST5 .55 B1
  Wolv WV10 ....240 C2
Alton Gr Bucknall ST2 ...73 B4
  Cannock WS11 ....209 C1
  Wolv WV10 ....168 C1
Alton Rd ST14 ....95 B3
Alton Towers Theme Pk*
  ST10 ....78 C2
Altona Cl ST15 ....120 A4
Alvaston Cl WS3 ....243 B2
Alvecote Cotts B79 ....251 B3
Alverley Cl WV9 ....240 A1
Alverton Cl B77 ....261 B2
Alvis Cl B79 ....249 C4
Alwen St DY8 ....275 C1
Alwyn B77 ....261 C4
Alwyn Cl WS6 ....227 A2
Alwyn Cres ST6 ....57 B4
Alwyn Rd ST4 ....88 A4
Amanda Ave WV4 ......265 C2
Amber Bsns Village
  B77 ....251 A2
Amber Cl B77 ....251 A2
Amber Ct Endon ST9 ....42 C3
  Tamworth B77 ....251 A2
Amber Gn WS11 ....210 B1
Amberfield Cl ST3 ......73 C2
Ambergate Cl WS3 .....243 B2
Ambergate Dr DY6 .....275 B4
Amberlands Cl B74 ....257 C3
Amberley Way B74 ....256 C1
Amblecote Dr ST3 .....73 A2
Amblecote Prim Sch
  DY8 ....279 C4
Amblefield Way ST16 ..136 B2
Ambleside Cl WV11 ....242 A1
Ambleside Dr DE15 ....120 B4
Ambleside Pl ST16 .....42 A2
Ambleside Way DY6 ...275 B3
Ambrose Cres DY6 .....275 B4
Ambrose Pl ST17 ....41 C4
Amelia Cl ST2 ....43 C3
America St ST6 ....41 B2
Amerton La
  Weston ST18 ....138 C1

Amerton La continued
  Weston, Amerton ST18 ..139 A2
Amerton Working Farm*
  ST18 ....139 A2
Amicable St ST6 ....56 C4
Amicombe B77 ....251 B1
Amington Cl B75 ....258 B2
Amington Heath Com Prim
  Sch B77 ....251 A2
Amington Ind Est B77 ..251 A2
Amington Rd B77 ......250 B2
Amison St ST3 ....73 B2
Ampleforth Dr ST17 ...156 A1
Ampthill Pl ST4 ....71 C1
Amptronik Trad Est
  DY3 ....269 B2
Ancaster St ST14 ....41 B4
Anchor Cl B77 ....250 C2
Anchor Par WS9 ....256 A3
Anchor Pl ST3 ....283 C4
Anchor Rd Aldridge WS9 .256 A3
  Longton ST3 ....283 C4
Anchor Terr ST3 ....283 C4
Anchor Way ST20 ......171 B4
Ancient High House Mus*
  ST16 ....155 C2
Anderby Gdns DE11 ....186 C1
Anders B79 ....250 A3
Anders Sq WV6 ....254 C2
Anderson Pl ST16 ......42 A2
Anderstaff Ind Pk DE14 .166 C3
Anderton View ST12 ...104 C2
Andover Cl ST13 ....73 B3
Andover Cres ⑤ DY6 ..275 C2
Andover Pl WS11 ......210 A2
Andrew Mulligan Cl ST6 .41 B3
Andrew Pl ST5 ....284 D3
Andrew St ST6 ....41 B4
Andrews Ho WS13 .....231 A4
Andrews Rd WV6 ......245 A2
Aneurin Bevan Pl WS15 .178 B1
Angel Croft WS7 ....211 C1
Angelica B77 ....250 C2
Angle St ⑥ ST13 ....30 B3
Anglesea Dr ST3 ....73 A2
Anglesey Bsns Pk WS12 .210 C2
Anglesey Cl WS7 ......228 C2
Anglesey Cres
  Brownhills WS8 ....228 C1
  Cannock WS12 ....210 B3
Anglesey Ct DE14 .....166 A1
Anglesey Mews WS12 ..210 B3
Anglesey Prim Sch
  DE14 ....166 B1
Anglesey Rd
  Brownhills WS8 ....228 C1
  Cannock WS12 ....210 A3
  Lichfield WS13 ....214 A1
Anglesey St
  Burton u T DE14 ....165 C2
  Cannock WS12 ....210 A3
Anglia Rd WS11 ....209 B2
Angorfa Cl WS13 ......230 C4
Angus Cl ST2 ....58 B2
Anker Cl WS7 ....229 B3
Anker View B77 ....250 B2
Ankerdrive B79 ....250 A3
Ankermoor Prim Sch
  B77 ....250 B2
Ankerside Sh Ctr B79 ..250 A2
Anna Wlk ST6 ....56 C4
Annan Cl ⓶ CW12 .....6 A1
Anne Cres WS11 ....209 C3
Anne Ct ST7 ....40 B3
Anne Rd WV4 ....266 A3
Annette Rd ST4 ....73 A3
Anslow Gdns WV11 ....241 C1
Anslow La DE13 ....147 A1
Anslow Rd DE13 ....145 A1
Ansmead Gr ST3 ......72 C1
Anson Ave WS13 ......214 A1
Anson CE Prim Sch
  ST18 ....158 A1
Anson Cl Burntwood WS7 .229 B4
  Great Wyrley WS6 .....226 C3
  Perton WV6 ....254 C1
Anson Ct Burton u T DE14 .166 C2
  Fazeley B78 ....261 A4
Anson Dr ST17 ....175 C3
Anson Gr ST15 ....178 C1
Anson Rd Alrewas DE13 .201 A1
  Great Wyrley WS6 .....226 C1
  Meir ST3 ....90 A4
Anson St WS15 ....178 C1
Anson's Row ST18 .....177 B4
Ansons Cl DE14 ....226 B1
Ansty Dr WS12 ....210 B1
Anthony Gr ST3 ....89 C2
Anthony Pl ST13 ......283 D4
Antler Dr WS15 ....178 A1
Apedale Bsns Pk ST5 ..55 A3
Apedale Com Ctry Pk*
  ST5 ....55 A3
Apedale Rd
  Audley, Wood Lane ST7 ..55 A4
  Newcastle-u-L ST5 .....55 B3
Apex Bsns Pk WS11 ....227 C2
Apex Rd WS8 ....244 B4
Apley Pl ST14 ....87 C4
Apley Rd DY8 ....279 C4
Apollo B79 ....249 C3
Apollo Cl WS11 ....210 A3

Apollo Wlk ST6 .....42 B1
Appian Cl B77 .....261 B4
Apple Croft CW3 .....68 B4
Apple Gr TF9 .....97 A1
Apple Wlk WS12 .....210 B1
Appleby Gdns WV12 .....242 B1
Appleby Glade DE11 .....186 B1
Applecroft ST5 .....40 C1
Applecross B74 .....257 C1
Appledore Cl
  Cannock WS12 .....210 C2
  Great Wyrley WS6 .....227 A2
  Stafford ST17 .....175 C4
Appledore Gr ST7 .....41 C4
Appleford Pl ST4 .....72 C1
Applegarth Cl ST14 .....156 B1
Appleton Cl Biddulph ST8 .....27 C3
  Burton u T DE15 .....185 C4
  Congleton CW12 .....15 C4
  Swadlincote DE11 .....186 C3
Appleton Cres WV4 .....266 A3
Appleton Dr ST5 .....85 B3
Appletree Gr WV9 .....256 A3
Applewood Cl ST14 .....111 A1
Applewood Cres ST3 .....90 B4
Appleyard Cl 1 ST16 .....155 C2
Appleyard The ST10 .....223 B3
Apse Cl WV5 .....269 C4
Apsley Gr ST12 .....88 A1
Aqualate Cl TF10 .....169 A2
Aqualate Ho ST17 .....174 C3
Aquaries Ct ST3 .....73 C1
Aquinas St ST4 .....72 A4
Arbor Cl B77 .....250 B2
Arbor Gate WV9 .....245 A2
Arborfield Rd ST14 .....143 C4
Arbour Cl CW1 .....68 C4
Arbour Mews WS11 .....227 C3
Arbour St Hanley ST1 .....282 C3
  Talke ST7 .....40 B3
Arbourfield Dr ST12 .....58 A1
Arbourtree Ct WV5 .....270 A4
Arbury Dr DY8 .....275 B2
Arcade The DY3 .....271 C3
Arcadia Pk WS15 .....197 A4
Arcal St DY3 .....271 C4
Arch Ct WS15 .....196 C4
Archid Way ST12 .....58 A1
Arctic Pl ST4 .....88 A4
Arden Cl
  Kingswinford DY8 .....275 B2
  Leek ST13 .....31 A3
  Rugeley WS15 .....178 B1
  Stourbridge DY8 .....279 C4
  Tamworth B77 .....250 B2
Arden Rd
  Barton-u-N DE13 .....201 B4
  Tamworth B77 .....261 C3
Arden Wlk WS15 .....198 B2
Ardgay Dr WS12 .....209 C4
Ardingley Ave ST17 .....156 A1
Argles Rd ST13 .....31 A4
Argosy Cl ST3 .....90 A4
Argyle Ave B77 .....250 B2
Argyle Cl DY8 .....275 C1
Argyle Way WV4 .....266 A3
Argyle St Hanley ST1 .....282 A1
  Tamworth B77 .....250 C2
Argyll Cl ST11 .....90 C3
Argyll Rd ST3 .....73 B1
Ariane B79 .....249 C4
Aries Cl ST16 .....41 C3
Arion Cl B77 .....250 B3
Arkall Cl B79 .....250 B4
Arkle B77 .....261 B2
Arkle Cl ST14 .....126 B4
Arkwright Gr ST1 .....57 C4
Arlescote Cl B75 .....258 B1
Arley Dr DY8 .....279 C2
Arley Gr WV4 .....265 B3
Arley Rd WV4 .....266 A3
Arleygh Way ST6 .....275 B2
Arlington Way ST3 .....89 C4
Armishaw Pl 2 WS15 .....197 A3
Armitage Gdns ST4 .....197 A3
Armitage Hill DE13 .....183 C2
Armitage Ho WS13 .....214 C1
Armitage La WS15 .....197 A3
Armitage Rd WS15 .....197 A3
Armshead Rd ST9 .....59 A3
Armside Cl WS3 .....244 A2
Armstead Rd WV9 .....240 A2
Armstrong B79 .....249 C3
Armstrong Ave ST16 .....156 A2
Armstrong Gn ST6 .....57 B4
Arnold Cl B79 .....250 A3
Arnold Gr ST5 .....56 A4
Arnold Rd ST4 .....185 A4
Arnotdale Dr WV12 .....209 C4
Arps Rd WV8 .....238 C2
Arran Cl WS11 .....210 A2
Arran Dr Chell Heath ST7 .....41 C4
  Tamworth B77 .....261 C4
Arrow Dr WV7 .....237 A3
Arthur Evans Cl WS15 .....197 A3
Arthur St Burton u T DE14 .....166 B3
Cannock, Chadsmoor
WS11 .....209 C2
Cannock, Wimblebury
WS12 .....210 C2
Newcastle-u-L ST5 .....55 C1
Stone ST15 .....105 A1
Tunstall ST6 .....41 C2
Wolv WV2 .....266 B4

Arthur Terry Sch B74 .....258 A2
Arthur Wood Pl WS15 .....178 B1
Arthurs Ct DE13 .....147 C1
Arundel B77 .....261 A4
Arundel Dr ST10 .....76 C2
Arundel Gr WV6 .....254 C2
Arundel Rd
  Kingswinford DY8 .....275 B1
  Wolv WV10 .....240 A1
Ascot Cl Burton u T DE15 .....167 A2
  Lichfield WS14 .....231 B4
Ascot Dr Cannock WS11 .....226 B4
  Sedgley DY1 .....271 C1
  Tamworth B77 .....261 B2
  Wolv WV4 .....266 A2
Ascot Gdns DY8 .....275 B1
Ash Bank Rd ST2,ST9 .....59 A2
Ash Cl Cheadle ST10 .....76 C1
  Codsall WV8 .....239 A2
  Uttoxeter ST14 .....126 A4
Ash Cres DY6 .....275 A3
Ash Ct DE16 .....172 C3
Ash Gr Albrighton WV7 .....237 A2
  Barlaston ST12 .....88 B1
  Blythe Bridge ST11 .....90 B4
  Brewood ST19 .....223 B3
  Cannock WS11 .....209 C2
  Caverswall ST12 .....58 C2
  Fenton ST3 .....72 C1
  Lichfield WS14 .....231 C4
  Newcastle-u-L ST5 .....55 A1
  Sedgley DY3 .....271 C3
  Tamworth B77 .....261 C3
  Wheaton Aston ST19 .....205 B3
Ash Green Cl ST4 .....88 A4
Ash Green Prim Sch ST4 .....88 A4
Ash Gr Cl Se Da DE65 .....148 B3
Ash Hill WV3 .....255 B1
Ash La Great Wyrley WS6 .....227 A2
  Newton Regis B79 .....236 C3
  Swynnerton ST15 .....118 C3
Ash Park Ind Est WS11 .....210 A1
Ash Rd ST15 .....120 A4
Ash Rise ST17 .....174 C2
Ash St Burton u T DE14 .....166 A1
  Walsall WS3 .....243 B1
Ash Tree Cl DE11 .....186 C3
Ash Tree Ct WS11 .....209 B2
Ash Tree Hill ST10 .....76 B1
Ash Tree La WS13 .....215 A1
Ash Tree Rd DE13 .....183 B1
Ash View
  Huntington WS12 .....209 B4
  Kidsgrove ST7 .....26 A1
Ash Way Caverswall ST12 .....58 C2
  Newcastle-u-L ST5 .....71 A2
Ashbourne Cl 1 WS14 .....210 A2
Ashbourne Dr
  Market Drayton TF9 .....97 B1
  Newcastle-u-L ST5 .....55 A1
  Swadlincote DE11 .....186 C1
Ashbourne Gr ST1 .....282 B4
Ashbourne La DE6 .....35 A1
Ashbourne Rd
  Alstonefield DE6 .....35 A2
  Cheadle ST10 .....76 C2
  Leek ST13 .....31 A2
  Mayfield DE6 .....81 B4
  Rocester ST14 .....95 C2
  Uttoxeter ST14 .....111 A1
  Walsall WS3 .....243 B2
  Wolv WV4 .....266 C2
Ashbrook DE15 .....167 A1
Ashbrook Cl
  Gnosall ST20 .....171 B4
  Uttoxeter ST14 .....126 B3
Ashbrook La WS15 .....161 B3
Ashburton St ST6 .....57 A4
Ashby Cres ST3 .....72 C1
Ashby Rd
  Burton u T DE15 .....167 A1
  Tamworth B79 .....250 B4
Ashby Rd E DE15 .....167 C1
Ashcombe Gn ST13 .....72 C1
Ashcombe Rd ST13 .....45 B2
Ashcombe Way ST13 .....30 C2
Ashcott Wlk ST3 .....58 B1
Ashcroft Ave ST4 .....71 C1
Ashcroft Cl ST5 .....56 A3
Ashcroft Gr ST5 .....56 A3
Ashcroft Inf Sch B79 .....250 B4
Ashcroft La
  Shenstone WS14 .....246 C4
  Wall WS14 .....246 C4
Ashcroft Oval ST5 .....56 A3
Ashcroft Pl ST5 .....56 A3
Ashcroft Rd ST5 .....56 A3
Ashdale Cl
  Burton u T DE15 .....186 A4
  Kingswinford DY6 .....275 B4
  3 Stone ST15 .....120 A4
Ashdale Dr ST16 .....155 B4
Ashdale Pk ST15 .....118 C3
Ashdale Rd Fenton ST4 .....72 B3
  Leek ST13 .....31 A4
  Tamworth B77 .....250 B3
Ashdale Rise ST5 .....71 A2
Ashdene Gdns DY8 .....275 B1
Ashdown Dr DY8 .....275 C2
Ashe's La DE6 .....266 B2
Ashen Cl DY3 .....266 B2
Ashenden Rise WV3 .....265 A4
Ashendene Gr ST4 .....87 C4
Ashenhurst Way ST13 .....30 C2
Ashenough Rd ST7 .....40 B3
Ashfield Cl ST5 .....284 A4

Ashfield Gr WV10 .....240 B2
Ashfield Rd
  Wolv, Compton WV10 .....240 B2
  Wolv, Compton WV3 .....255 B1
Ashfield Sq ST2 .....58 A1
Ashfields WV7 .....237 A3
Ashfields Grange ST5 .....284 B3
Ashfields New Rd ST5 .....284 A4
Ashfiats Rd ST17,ST18 .....174 C2
Ashford Dr DY3 .....271 C4
Ashford Gr ST15 .....120 B4
Ashford Rd DE13 .....166 A3
Ashgrove ST4 .....72 B4
Ashgrove WS7 .....228 C3
Ashland St WV3 .....266 A4
Ashlands ST18 .....139 B1
Ashlands Ave ST4 .....71 C4
Ashlands Cres ST4 .....71 C1
Ashlands Gr ST4 .....71 B4
Ashlands Rd ST4 .....71 C4
Ashlar Cl ST6 .....42 A4
Ashlea B79 .....262 C3
Ashlea Dr DE16 .....81 B4
Ashleigh Ave DE14 .....186 C3
Ashleigh Cres ST19 .....205 B4
Ashleigh Dr
  Tamworth B77 .....261 C4
  Uttoxeter ST14 .....110 C1
Ashleigh Rd
  Rugeley WS15 .....196 C4
  Upper Tean ST10 .....92 C2
Ashley Cl
  Kingswinford DY6 .....275 B2
  Newcastle-u-L ST5 .....155 A2
  Stourbridge DY8 .....279 B1
Ashley Croft ST20 .....190 A4
Ashley Cres ST15 .....167 A2
Ashley Gdns WV8 .....238 C2
Ashley Gr ST5 .....56 B2
Ashley Mount WV6 .....255 B3
Ashley Rd
  Burntwood WS7 .....211 C1
  Kidderminster DY10 .....280 A1
  Walsall WS3 .....242 C1
  Wolv WV4 .....265 C3
Ashley View TF9 .....97 B1
Ashmall WS7 .....229 B2
Ashman St ST6 .....42 B1
Ashmead Rd WS7 .....229 A4
Ashmole Ave WS7 .....229 C4
Ashmole Cl WS14 .....231 C3
Ashmore Ave WV11 .....242 A1
Ashmore Dr ST20 .....171 B4
Ashmore Wlk WS11 .....282 C3
Ashoale Cl WS12 .....209 B4
Ashover Gr ST7 .....41 C4
Ashover Rd DE11 .....186 C3
Ashridge Ave WS5 .....71 A1
Ashridge Gr ST13 .....73 B3
Ashridge Wlk ST16 .....136 B1
Ashton Cl CW12 .....15 A2
Ashton Ct Caverswall ST9 .....59 A2
  Newcastle-u-L ST5 .....71 A1
Ashton Dr WS4 .....244 B2
Ashtree Bank WS15 .....197 A3
Ashtree Ct ST18 .....177 B4
Ashtree Rd WS3 .....244 A2
Ashurst Gr 14 ST17 .....90 A4
Ashwell Rd ST4 .....71 B4
Ashwells Gr WV9 .....240 A1
Ashwood ST3 .....283 C4
Ashwood Dr DY8 .....275 B1
Ashwood Cl TF9 .....97 A1
Ashwood Gr
  Forsbrook ST11 .....91 A3
  Wolv WV4 .....266 A3
Ashwood Park Prim Sch
  DY8 .....275 B1
Ashwood Terr ST3 .....283 C5
Ashworth Ave DE15 .....167 B1
Ashworth Gr WS12 .....210 A2
Ashworth St ST4 .....72 B3
Ashworth Way TF10 .....168 C1
Askerbank La SK11 .....8 A1
Askern Cl ST13 .....72 C1
Askew Bridge Rd DY3 .....271 A2
Askew Cl DY3 .....271 C3
Aspen Cft ST17 .....174 A4
Aspen Cl ST7 .....26 C2
Aspen Ct WS12 .....211 A3
Aspen Gr WS7 .....228 C3
Aspen Rd DE13 .....201 B4
Aspen Way TF10 .....168 C1
Aspley Cl WV10 .....224 C3
Aspley La WV10 .....224 B2
Asquith Cl ST18 .....210 B1
Asquith Dr WV10 .....224 C3
Astbury Cl Kidsgrove ST7 .....26 B2
  Walsall WS3 .....243 A2
Astbury Lane Ends CW12 .....15 C4
Aster Cl ST3 .....74 A3
Aster Wlk WV9 .....240 A2
Astil St ST5 .....166 C1
Aston Chase ST15 .....120 B4
Aston Cl Colwich ST18 .....177 B4
  Penkridge ST19 .....208 A4
  Shenstone WS14 .....246 C3
Aston Dr TF10 .....168 C1
Aston Grove ST15 .....120 B4
Aston La Claverley WV5 .....267 B4
  Maer TF9 .....83 C4
  Stone ST15 .....120 B2
  Sudbury DE6 .....129 A3
Aston Lodge Parkway
  ST15 .....120 B3

Aston Rd ST5 .....40 B1
Aston St WV3 .....266 A4
Aston Terr ST16 .....155 C3
Astonfields Ind Est
  ST16 .....155 C3
Astonfields Rd ST16 .....155 C3
Astonfields Road Bsns Pk
  ST16 .....155 C3
Astor Rd Aldridge B74 .....257 A1
  Kingswinford DY6 .....275 C3
Astoria Cl WV12 .....242 B1
Astoria Dr ST17 .....174 C3
Astoria Gdns WV12 .....242 B1
Astro Gr ST3 .....283 A4
Athelney Ct WS3 .....244 A2
Athelstan Cl ST19 .....208 A4
Athelstan Gr WV6 .....254 C3
Athelstan St ST16 .....41 B2
Athelstan Way B79 .....249 C4
Athena Rd ST1 .....57 C3
Atherstone Rd ST4 .....185 A4
Atherstone St B77,B78 .....261 A4
Athlestan Way DE13 .....147 B1
Athlone St ST6 .....42 A1
Atholl Rd ST3 .....283 D1
Atkins Way ST14 .....95 C2
Atlam Ct ST2 .....58 A2
Atlantic Gr ST4 .....88 A4
Atlas St ST4 .....72 C3
Attingham Dr WS11 .....210 A1
Attlee Cres
  Rugeley WS15 .....196 C4
  Stafford ST17 .....174 B4
Attlee Gr WS11 .....210 B3
Attlee Rd ST10 .....76 B1
Attwell Pk WV3 .....265 B4
Attwood Gdns WV4 .....266 C3
Attwood Rd WS7 .....228 B4
Attwood St ST7 .....26 A1
Aubrey St ST6 .....41 C4
Auchinleck Dr WS13 .....214 B1
Auckland Rd DY6 .....275 C2
Auden Ct WV6 .....254 C2
Auden Pl ST13 .....283 D4
Auden La WS7 .....174 B4
Auden Way ST17 .....174 B4
Audley Ave TF10 .....169 A1
Audley Ave Bsns Pk
  TF10 .....169 A1
Audley Pl ST5 .....71 A3
Audley Rd Audley ST7 .....39 C3
  Newcastle-u-L ST7,ST5 .....40 A1
  Newport TF10 .....168 C2
  Talke ST7 .....40 A3
Audley St
  Newcastle-u-L ST5 .....55 C2
  Tunstall ST6 .....41 B2
Audmore Rd ST20 .....171 B4
Audnam DY8 .....275 C1
Augustine Cl ST15 .....120 B4
Augustine Gr B74 .....257 C3
Augustines Wlk WS13 .....214 C1
Aukland St ST6 .....57 A4
Aulton Rd B75 .....258 C1
Aumbry Cl TF9 .....97 A1
Austcliffe Rd DY10 .....280 A3
Austin Ct Cheadle ST10 .....76 B1
  Sedgley DY1 .....271 C1
  Stone ST15 .....120 A4
Austin Cote La WS14 .....231 C4
Austin Friars ST17 .....155 C1
Austin St ST1 .....282 C1
Austrey La
  Newton Regis B79 .....236 C2
  Newton Regis, No Man's Heath
  B79 .....236 C3
Austwick Gr ST4 .....72 A4
Autumn Berry Gr DY3 .....271 C3
Autumn Cl WS4 .....244 B1
Autumn Dr
  Lichfield WS13 .....214 B1
  Sedgley DY3 .....271 B2
  Walsall WS4 .....244 B1
Avarne Pl 15 ST16 .....155 C2
Aveling Gn ST1 .....57 C4
Aveling Rd ST1 .....57 C4
Avenue One CW1 .....37 B4
Avenue Rd
  Cannock WS12 .....210 C1
  Newport TF10 .....168 C1
  Stoke-on-T ST4 .....57 B1
  Wolv WV4 .....265 C3
Avenue Rd S TF10 .....168 C1
Avenue The Bagnall ST9 .....43 C2
  Blakedown DY10 .....281 A1
  Cheadle ST10 .....76 B1
  Chedleton ST13 .....45 B3
  Endon ST9 .....43 C4
  Envile DY7 .....273 B1
  Featherstone WV10 .....241 A4
  Forsbrook ST11 .....91 A4
  Newcastle-u-L, Basford ST5 .....56 B2
  Newcastle-u-L, City General Hospl
  ST4 .....71 B4
  Stone ST15 .....105 A1
  Wheaton Aston ST19 .....206 B2
  Wolv, Fenchfield WV4 .....265 C2
  Wolv, Penn WV4 .....265 C2
  Wootton DE6 .....79 C4
Avenue Two CW1 .....37 B4
Averill Dr WS15 .....178 B1
Averill Rd ST13 .....174 B4

Aviation La DE13 .....165 C3
Avill B77 .....262 A3
Avington Cl DY3 .....271 B4
Avoca St ST13 .....90 B4
Avoca St ST1 .....282 C4
Avocet Cl ST14 .....126 B3
Avon B77 .....262 A3
Avon Bsns Pk WS11 .....226 B4
Avon Cl Kidsgrove ST7 .....26 A1
  Newcastle-u-L ST5 .....71 A2
  Perton WV6 .....254 C2
  Stafford ST16 .....156 A2
Avon Cres WS3 .....244 A1
Avon Dale TF10 .....168 C1
Avon Gr Ashley TF9 .....99 C3
  Cheadle ST10 .....76 C1
  Stone ST15 .....120 A3
Avon Hill ST16 .....156 B2
Avon Pl ST15 .....271 C2
Avon Rd Burntwood WS7 .....228 C3
  Cannock WS11 .....226 B4
  Stourbridge DY8 .....279 C2
  Walsall WS3 .....243 C1
Avon Rise ST16 .....156 A2
Avon Way
  Burton u T DE15 .....167 A1
  Marston on D DE65 .....147 B4
Avondale Cl DY6 .....275 C4
Avondale Rd WV6 .....255 C2
Avondale St ST6 .....56 B4
Avonlea Gdns WS15 .....178 B1
Avonside Ave ST6 .....41 C2
Avonwick Gr ST1 .....58 A3
Axborough La DY10 .....280 B2
Axbridge Wlk ST4 .....42 B1
Axon Cres ST3 .....74 A2
Aylesbury Rd ST2 .....58 B1
Aylesford Cl DY3 .....266 B1
Aylesford Dr B74 .....257 C3
Aynsley Ave ST5 .....71 A2
Aynsley Cl ST10 .....76 B1
Aynsley Rd ST4 .....57 A1
Aynsley Specl Sch ST11 .....90 C4
Aynsley's Dr ST11 .....90 C4
Ayr Rd ST10 .....76 C3
Ayrshire Gr ST3 .....73 B1
Ayrshire Way CW12 .....6 A1
Ayrton Cl WV6 .....255 A2
Ayshford St ST3 .....283 B3
Azalea Cl WV8 .....239 A2

B

Babbacombe Ave ST17 .....175 C4
Babbington Cl
  Tutbury DE13 .....146 B3
  Whittington WS14 .....232 C3
Babworth Cl WV9 .....240 A1
Back Browning St ST16 .....155 B2
Back Bunt's La ST9 .....43 B2
Back Cross La CW12 .....16 A4
Back Ford Green Rd ST6 .....42 B1
Back Garden St ST5 .....284 C2
Back Heathcote St ST7 .....26 A1
Back La Aldridge WS9 .....256 C4
  Alton ST10 .....78 C1
  Ashley TF9 .....100 A3
  Betley CW2,CW3 .....53 A4
  Colwich ST18 .....177 B4
  Ellastone DE6 .....82 A2
  Endon, Brown Edge ST6 .....43 A4
  Endon, Hodgefield ST6 .....28 A1
  Forton TF10 .....150 B1
  Gnosall ST20 .....171 A3
  Haughton ST18 .....173 A3
  Hixon ST18 .....139 B1
  Leek ST13 .....30 B3
  Millmeece ST21 .....102 B3
  Ranton ST18 .....153 B2
  Shenstone WS14 .....246 C1
  Uttoxeter ST14 .....126 B4
  Waterhouses ST10 .....49 C1
  Wheaton Aston ST19 .....205 B3
  Whittington WS14 .....232 C3
  Woodseaves ST20 .....151 B4
  Wootton DE6 .....79 C4
Back Radfords 2 ST5 .....105 A1
Back Rd DY6 .....275 B4
Back Westlands Rd
  ST14 .....126 A3
Backcester La WS13 .....231 A4
Backcrofts WS11 .....209 B1
Baddeley Green La ST2 .....43 A2
Baddeley Hall Rd ST2 .....43 B2
Baddeley Rd ST2 .....43 A1
Baddeley St Burslem ST6 .....41 C1
  Cheadle ST10 .....76 C1
Baddeley's Ct TF10 .....168 C1
Baden Powell St WS15 .....211 C3
Baden St ST3 .....284 B4
Bader Rd WV6 .....254 C2
Badger Brow Rd TF9 .....99 B3
Badger Cl WS12 .....209 B3
Badger Gr ST3 .....90 B4
Badger La WV5 .....267 C4
Badger St ST5 .....284 B3
Badger's Dr3 .....271 C3
Badger's End ST19 .....205 A3
Badgers Bank Rd B74 .....257 C3
Badgers Brow ST1 .....57 C2
Badgers Cl WS13 .....244 A3
Badgers Croft
  Ecclesfield ST21 .....133 C3
  Stafford ST17 .....175 B3
Badgers Hollow ST10 .....93 A1
Badgers Rise ST13 .....30 C3

Badgers Sett ST13 ......30 C3
Badgers Way WS12 ....210 B1
Badgery Cl ST14 ......111 A1
Badminton Cl DY1 ....271 C2
Badnall Cl ST13 ....30 C3
Badnall St ST13 ....30 B4
Bag La Admaston WS15 ..159 B4
  Marchington ST14 ....127 C1
  Roston DE6 ....96 C4
Baggeridge Cl DY3 ....271 A4
Baggeridge Ctry Pk*
  DY3 ....270 C2
Baggott Pl ST5 ....70 C4
Baggott St WV2 .....266 B4
Bagnal Hospl ST9 .....43 C1
Bagnall Rd Bagnall ST9 ..43 B1
  Norton-in-t-M ST2 ....43 B1
Bagnall St ST1 ......282 B2
Bagot Gr ST1 ....57 C4
Bagot St WS15 ....160 C3
Bagots Oak ST17 .....174 B4
Bagots View
  Abbots Bromley WS15 ..161 A3
  Church Leigh ST10 ...109 A2
Bagridge Cl WV3 .....265 A4
Bagridge Rd WV3 .....265 A4
Bailey Ave B77 ......261 C3
Bailey Cl Burntwood WS7 ..228 B4
  Cannock WS11 ......210 A2
Bailey Cres CW12 .....6 A2
Bailey Rd ST3 ....72 C2
Bailey St Burton u T DE14 ..166 B1
  Newcastle-u-L ST5 ...284 A3
  Stafford ST17 ......155 C1
  Stoke-on-T ST4 ......56 C1
Bailey's Bank ST8 .....16 B2
Bailye Cl WS13 ......214 C1
Bain Ho ST17 ....174 C3
Bainbridge Rd ST4 .....88 A4
Bains St ST5 ....55 C4
Baird Ho DY6 ....275 C4
Baker Ave WV14 .....266 C1
Baker Cres ST2 ....43 B2
Baker Cres N ST2 .....43 B2
Baker Cres S ST2 .....43 A2
Baker Dr WS13 ......215 B4
Baker St Burntwood WS7 ..228 C3
  Burton u T DE15 ....185 C4
  Fenton ST4 ....72 C3
Baker's La Aldridge WS9 ..256 A3
  Lichfield WS13 ......231 B4
  Norbury FT10 ......150 B2
Bakers Gdns WV8 ....238 C2
Bakers Way
  Cannock WS12 ......210 A3
  Codsall WV8 ....238 C2
Bakers Wlk B77 .....261 C3
Bakewell Cl
  Newcastle-u-L ST5 ....55 A1
  Walsall WS3 ....243 B2
Bakewell Dr ST15 ....120 B3
Bakewell Gn DE11 ...186 C3
Bakewell St ST4 ....71 C3
Bala Gr ST4 ....76 C2
Bala Ho ST17 ....174 C3
Balaam's La ST15 .....106 B3
Balance Hill ST14 ....126 B4
Balance St ST14 .....126 B4
Balcombe Cl ST5 ....284 B1
Baldwin Gr WS11 ....210 B1
Baldwin Way DY3 ....269 C1
Baldwin's Gate CE Prim Sch
  ST5 ....85 B3
Balfour B79 ....250 A2
Balfour Cres WV4 ....255 C2
Balfour Ct
  Sutton Coldfield B74 ..258 A2
  [7] Wolv WV6 ......255 C2
Balfour Gr ST8 ....27 C4
Balfour Rd DY6 .....275 C4
Balfour St
  Burton u T DE13 ....166 B3
  Hanley ST1 ....282 C2
Balgrove Ho WS11 ...209 B1
Balk Pas ST16 ......155 B2
Ball Green Prim Sch ST6 ..42 B3
Ball Haye Gn ST13 ....31 A4
Ball Haye Rd ST13 ....30 C3
Ball Haye St ST13 ....30 C3
Ball Haye Terr ST13 ...30 C3
Ball Hayes Rd ST6 ....42 B3
Ball La Brewood WV10 ..240 B3
  Leek ST13 ....30 C3
  Norton-in-t-M ST6 ....43 A3
Ball's Yd ST5 ....284 B3
Ballarat Wlk DY8 ....279 C3
Ballington Gdns ST13 ..30 C3
Ballington View ST13 ..30 C2
Ballinson Rd ST17 .....72 C4
Balliol Bsns Pk WV9 ..239 C2
Balliol St ST4 ....72 A4
Balmain Cres WV11 ..241 A1
Balmoral Cl
  Lichfield WS14 .....231 B3
  Stone ST15 ....120 A3
  Tamworth B79 ......250 A4
  Trentham ST4 ....72 A1
Balmoral Ct WS11 ...210 A3
Balmoral Dr
  Cannock WS11 ......209 C4
  Cheadle ST10 ....76 A1
  Market Drayton TF9 ...97 C1
  Wombourne WV5 ....265 A1
Balmoral Rd
  Burton u T DE15 ....167 A2
  Kingswinford DY8 ...275 B1
  Stafford ST17 ......156 B1

Balmoral Rd continued
  Sutton Coldfield B74 ..257 C3
  Wolv WV4 ....266 A3
Balmoral View DY1 ...271 C2
Balmoral Way WS7 ...211 C1
Baltic Cl Cannock WS11 ..209 C1
  Trentham ST4 ....88 A4
Balvenie Way DY1 ...271 C2
Bamber Cl WV3 .....265 C4
Bamber Pl ST5 ....55 C3
Bamber St ST4 ....72 A4
Bamborough Cl DE13 ..166 B4
Bamburgh B77 ......261 B4
Bambury St ST3,ST4 ...73 B3
Bamford Cl WS13 ....243 B2
Bamford Gr ST1 .....282 A4
Bamford Ho WS3 ....243 B2
Bamford Rd Walsall WS3 ..243 B2
  Wolv WV3 ....266 A4
Bamfont St B77 ......250 B2
Bampton Ave [4] WS7 ..229 A4
Bampton Cl ST9 ......43 C4
Banbury Dr WV5 ....269 C2
Banbury Dr ST3 .....271 C3
Banbury Gr ST13 .....27 C4
Banbury Rd WS11 ...226 B4
Banbury St ST17 .....25 B1
Bancroft B77 ....250 C2
Bancroft La
  Forsbrook ST11 ......90 C3
  Hamstall Ridware WS15 ..199 A4
Bandridge La SK11 ....18 A4
Baneberry Dr WV10 ..241 A4
Banford Gr ST14 ....110 C1
Bangley La
  Drayton Bassett B78 ..260 A4
  Hints B78 ....259 C3
Bank Cl ST14 ....126 B4
Bank Cres WS7 .....228 C3
Bank Cl [3] ST17 .....26 A1
Bank End ST6 ....43 A4
Bank Hall Rd ST6 .....42 A1
Bank House Dr ST5 ...56 C1
Bank Pas [9] ST16 ...155 C2
Bank Rd DY3 ....271 B1
Bank Side Hartington SK17 ..24 B3
  Stone ST15 ....119 C3
Bank St Cannock WS12 ..210 C1
  Cheadle ST10 ....76 B2
  Kidsgrove ST7 ....26 B2
  Tunstall ST6 ....41 B2
Bank The Gnosall ST20 ..171 B3
  The Bank ST7 ....26 A4
Bank Top WS15 .....178 B1
Bank Top Ave ST10 ...62 A3
Bank Wlk DE13 .....166 A4
Bankerwall La DE6 ....80 B4
Bankfield Gr ST3 .....54 C2
Bankfield Rd ST3 .....89 C4
Bankhouse Dr CW12 ...6 A3
Bankhouse Rd
  Forsbrook ST11 ......91 A4
  Trentham ST4 ....87 C4
Banks La ST10 ....61 C2
Bankside
  Newcastle-u-L ST5 ...284 C2
  Stanton DE6 ....65 B1
  Stone ST15 ....104 B2
  Wombourne WV5 ....269 C4
Bankside Way WS9 ..245 A1
Bankton Rd ST3 ......73 B4
Banktop Rd DE6,ST14 ..144 A3
Banky Brook Cl ST6 ...42 B2
Bannut Tree La DY7 ..277 B3
Banstead Cl WV2 ....266 C4
Bantock Ave WV3 ...265 C4
Bantock Ct WV3 ....265 C4
Bantock Gdns WV3 ..255 C1
Bantock House Mus*
  WV3 ....255 C1
Baptist St [8] ST16 ...177 C4
Bar Hill CW3 ....68 B2
Bar La DE13 ....183 A1
Bar Wlk WS9 ....245 B1
Barbara St B79 .....250 A3
Barber Cl WS12 ....210 C1
Barber Pl ST6 ....25 C4
Barber Pl ST6 ....41 C3
Barber St ST6 ....41 C3
Barber St ST6 ....41 C3
Barber's Sq ST5 .....56 B2
Barbridge Rd ST5 ....40 B1
Barbrook Ave ST3 ....73 C2
Barclay Cl WV7 .....237 A3
Barclay St ST3 ....73 B3
Barcliff Ave ST3 ....250 C2
Bardell Cl WS3 .....243 C2
Bardolph Cl DE11 ...186 C2
Bardsey Wlk [1] ST3 ..73 A2
Bardwell Cl WV4 ....255 C4
Bardy La Armitage WS15 ..197 C2
  Longdon WS15 ......197 B1
Barfoot St ST3 ....54 B3
Barford Rd ST5 ....70 C2
Bargate La ST19 ....223 B3
Bargate St ST19 ....223 B3
Bargery Rd WV11 ...242 A1
Bargrave Dr ST15 .....56 A4
Bargrave St ST1 ......58 B1
Barker St ST16 ......155 B2
Barker St Longton ST3 ..283 C3
  Newcastle-u-L ST5 ...55 C3
Barks Dr ST6 ....42 B2
Barlaston CE Fst Sch
  ST12 ....88 C1
Barlaston Cl ST15 ...155 B4
Barlaston Old Rd ST4 ..88 A3

Barlaston Rd
  Barlaston ST3 ....89 A3
  Stoke-on-T ST3 .....88 C4
Barlaston Sta ST12 ...88 B1
Barley Cl Aldridge WS9 ..256 C1
  Burton u T DE14 ....166 C3
  Cannock WS12 ......210 A3
  Sedgley DY3 ....269 C2
  Wolv WV8 ....239 C1
Barley Croft Perton WV6 ..254 B2
  Whittington WS14 ...232 C3
Barley Ct ST16 ......155 A3
Barley Gn WV8 ......224 A1
Barley Green La WS13 ..201 B1
Barley Grech ST20 ..171 C3
Barley Rd ST10 ....62 A4
Barleycorn Cl DE15 ..167 A1
Barleycroft ST10 ......76 C1
Barleycroft Terr ST7 ...25 A3
Barleyfield Rise DY6 ..275 A4
Barleyfields Audley ST7 ..39 B1
  Chell Heath ST6 .....42 B2
Barlow Dr ST3 ....73 B3
Barlow Cl B77 ......250 C2
Barlow St ST3 ......283 C3
Barlstone Ave ST11 ...90 C3
Barmouth Cl ST4 .....27 C3
Barmouth Gr ST6 .....27 A1
Barn Ave DY3 ....271 B1
Barn Bank La S17,ST18 ..174 B3
Barn Cl Dordon B78 ..262 C3
  Lichfield WS13 .....214 A2
  Rugeley WS15 ......197 A3
  Stafford ST17 ......174 C3
Barn Comm ST20 ...151 B4
Barn Croft
  Burntwood WS7 ....229 A2
  Great Wyrley WS6 ..227 A2
Barn Ct ST5 ....73 B4
Barn End Rd ST17 ...193 A4
Barn La ST19 ....265 C4
Barn La ST19 ....223 B4
Barn Owl Dr WS3 ...243 C2
Barn Rd WS15 ......198 B2
Barnaby Sq WV10 ...240 C2
Barnard Pl WV2 ....266 C3
Barnard Rd WV11 ...241 C1
Barnard Way WS11 ..209 C1
Barnbridge B77 .....250 B1
Barncroft Rd ST6 .....42 B3
Barnes Croft ST15 ...106 B1
Barnes Rd
  Shenstone WS14 ....247 A3
  Stafford ST17 ......174 B4
Barnes Way ST3 ......73 B1
Barnett Cl DY6 .....275 B2
Barnett Gn DY6 ....275 B2
Barnett Gr ST6 ....41 C3
Barnett La DY6,DY8 ..275 B2
Barnett St B77 ......275 B2
Barnetts La WS8 ....228 C1
Barnfield ST4 ....71 C3
Barnfield Cl
  Lichfield WS14 .....231 A3
  Stone ST15 ....119 C4
Barnfield Pl ST13 .....30 C2
Barnfield Rd Burslem ST6 ..57 A4
  Leek ST13 ....30 B2
  Upper Tean ST10 ....92 C2
Barnfield Way
  Cannock WS12 ......211 A3
  Stafford ST17 ......175 B3
Barnfields La DE13 ...30 B2
Barnfields La Ind Est ST13 ..30 B2
Barnfields La ST10 ....61 B1
Barnfields Prim Sch
  ST17 ....175 B3
Barngate St ST13 .....30 C3
Barnhurst La WV8 ....239 C3
Barnlea Gr ST3 ....90 A3
Barnmeadow Cl TF10 ..169 A2
Barnmeadow Rd TF10 ..169 A1
Barns Cl WS9 ....244 C2
Barns Croft B74 .....257 A2
Barnsdale Cl ST4 .....88 B3
Barnswood Cl WS11 ..226 A4
Barnwell Cl ST14 ....111 A2
Barnwell Gr ST4 .....72 A1
Barnwood Rd WV8 ..239 C1
Baron Cl WV10 .....240 B1
Baron St ST4 ....283 A5
Baron's Way ST18 ...158 B4
Barr Common Cl WV9 ..256 A2
Barr Common Rd WV9 ..256 A2
Barr St DY3 ....277 C2
Barracks La WS14 ...245 B4
Barracks Rd ST5 ....284 C2
Barracks Way [2] ST13 ..30 B3
Barrage Rd ST18 .....28 A4
Barrar Cl DY8 ......279 C4
Barratt Gdns ST2 .....58 A4
Barratts Croft DY5 ..271 B1
Barrett Cres ST6 .....57 A3
Barrett Dr ST6 ....57 A3
Barrett St ST7 ....40 B4
Barrington
  Albrighton WV7 ....237 A3
  Burton u T DE13 ...147 B1
  Wolv WV10 ....240 B1
Barrington Cl ST5 ....56 C2
Barrow Hill Rd DY5 ..271 B1
Barry Ave ST2 ....58 A2
Bartholomew Rd ST4 ..73 C1
Barthomley Rd
  Audley ST7 ....39 A4
  Barthomley CW2 .....38 A4

Barthomley Rd continued
  Betley ST7 ....38 C2
  Hanley ST1 ....57 B3
Bartic Ave DY6 .....275 C2
Bartlem St ST3 ......283 D5
Bartlett Cl ST19 .....207 C4
Barton Cottage Hospl
  DE13 ....183 B1
Barton Cres ST6 ......41 C1
Barton Gate DE13 ...183 A1
Barton La Bradley ST18 ..191 A4
  Kingswinford DY6 ..275 B4
Barton Lodge DE13 ..183 B1
Barton Rd WV4 .....266 C2
Barton St DE14 .....185 B4
Barton Turn DE13 ...184 A1
Barton's La TF9 .....112 A4
Barton's Rd TF9 ....112 A4
Barwood Ave ST7 ....25 A3
Basford La ST13 ....45 C4
Basford Lane Ind Est
  ST13 ....45 C4
Basford Park Rd ST5 ..56 B2
Basford Villas ST5 ...56 B1
Basfordbridge La ST13 ..45 B2
Basfordbridge Terr ST13 ..45 C3
Basil Cl ST17 ......174 C3
Basildon Gr ST3 ....283 C2
Basin La B77 ....250 B2
Baskerville Rd ST1 ..282 C3
Baskeyfield Cl WS14 ..231 B4
Baskeyfield Pl ST6 ....42 A3
Baslow Cl WS3 .....243 B2
Baslow Gn DE11 ....186 C3
Baslow Rd WS3 ....243 A2
Basnett's Wood Rd ST9 ..43 C3
Bass Cotts DE14 ....166 C2
Bass Mus The* DE14 ..166 B2
Bass's Bldgs DE14 ..166 C2
Bassenthwaite Ct WV6 ..275 B3
Bassett Cl Cheadle ST10 ..76 B2
  Wolv WV4 ....265 B3
Bassilow Rd ST4 ....283 C3
Baswich Bsns Pk ST17 ..156 B1
  Stafford ST17 ......156 B1
Baswich House Dr [10]
  ST17 ....175 B4
Baswich House Way [11]
  ST17 ....175 B4
Baswich La ST17 ....175 B4
Batch La DE6 ....127 A4
Batchelor Cl DY8 ...279 C4
Bateman Ave ST8 ....27 A3
Batesmans Way ST5 ..126 B4
Bateson Way WS9 ...197 B2
Batfield La DY7 .....272 B1
Bath Ct ST17 ......155 C1
Bath La DY7 ....277 B3
Bath Mews DY8 ....279 C3
Bath Rd Cannock WS11 ..209 C3
  Newcastle-u-L ST5 ....54 C1
  Stourbridge DY8 ...279 C3
Bath St Leek ST13 ....30 C3
  Meir ST3 ....74 A3
  Sedgley DY3 ....266 C1
  Stoke-on-T ST4 .....72 A4
Bath Terr ST4 ....72 A4
Bath Vale Cotts CW12 ...6 A2
Batholoi Way ST17 ...175 A4
Baths La ST18 ......158 B4
Baths Pas ST3 ......283 B4
Baths Rd ST3 ....283 B4
Bathurst St ST3 ....283 C4
Batkin Cl ST6 ....42 A3
Batten Cl ST3 ....90 B4
Batten House Way ST7 ..25 A3
Battison Cres ST3 ..283 C2
Battle Ridge ST18 ...156 B4
Battlefield Hill WV5 ..270 A4
Battlefield La WV5 ..270 A3
Battlefield Terr WV5 ..270 A3
Battlesteads ST17 ....78 B1
Baulk La ST11 ......106 C4
Baxter Gn ST16 ....155 A2
Bayham Wlk ST2 .....58 A2
Bayley Hills TF10 ...168 A2
Bayley Ho WS8 .....245 A3
Baylie Ct DY8 ......279 C2
Baylie St DY8 ......279 C1
Bayliss Ct WV3 .....255 C1
Bayston Ave WV3 ...265 C4
Bayswater Rd
  Rugeley WS15 .....178 B1
  Sedgley DY3 ....271 B1
Baytree Cl Hanley ST1 ..57 C2
  Walsall WS3 ....243 A1
Baytree Rd WS3 ....243 A1
Baywood Cl ST17 ...156 B4
Beach Ave WV4,WV14 ..266 C2
Beachcroft Rd DY6 ..270 B1
Beachwood Ave DY6 ..270 B1
Beacon Ctr for the Blind
  WV4 ....266 B3
Beacon Dr ST10 .....147 A2
Beacon Gdns WS13 ..214 A1
Beacon Hill WS9 ....256 B4
Beacon La Kinver DY7 ..277 A1
  Romsley WS15,DY7,DY12 ..276 C2
  Sedgley DY3 ....266 C1
Beacon Pas DY3 ....266 B1
Beacon Rd Aldridge WS9 ..256 A1
  Rolleston DE13 .....147 C2
  Stone ST15 ....120 A3
Beacon Rise
  Aldridge WS9 ......256 A2
  Sedgley DY3 ....266 C1
  Stone ST15 ....120 A3

Beacon St Lichfield WS13 ..213 C1
  Wolv WV14 ....266 C1
Beacon Trad Est WS9 ..256 A3
Beacon Way
  Brownhills WS9 ....245 A2
  Cannock WS12 ......210 C2
Beaconfields WS13 ..231 B4
Beaconsfield ST5 .....56 B4
Beaconsfield Ave WV4 ..266 B3
Beaconsfield Dr
  Longton ST3 ....72 C1
  Wolv WV4 ....266 B3
Beaconsfield Rd DE13 ..166 A4
Beaconside ST16 ....156 A3
Beaconside ST16 ....156 A3
Beaconside Cl ST16 ..156 A3
Beaconside Sports Ctr
  ST18 ....156 B2
Beadnell Gr ST3 ......73 B1
Beale St DY8 ....279 C3
Bealeys La WS3 .....243 A1
Beam Cl DE13 ......166 A4
Beamhill Rd DE13 ...165 C4
Beamish La WV7,WV8 ..237 C3
Beard Gr ST2 ....58 A4
Bearnett Dr WV4 ....265 B1
Bearnett La WV4 ....265 A1
Bearstone Rd TF9 ....82 C2
Bearwood Hill Rd DE15 ..167 A2
Beasley Ave ST5 .....55 C4
Beasley Pl ST5 ....55 C4
Beat La SK11 ....17 C4
Beata Rd ST5 ....40 C1
Beaton Rd B74 .....258 A2
Beatric Cl ST4 ....72 A1
Beatrice Cl ST4 .....166 A2
Beatrice Wlk ST8 ....27 A1
Beattie Ave ST5 ....284 B4
Beatty Dr CW12 ......6 A2
Beatty Rd ST13 ......31 A3
Beau Ct WS11 ....209 C1
Beaubrook Gdns DY6 ..275 C2
Beaubrook Gns DY6 ..275 C2
Beauchamp Pk B77 ..261 B4
Beauchamp Rd B77 ..261 C3
Beaudesert WS7 ....212 A1
Beaudesert View WS12 ..211 A3
Beaufort Ave ST9 ....59 A2
Beaufort Ct ST3 ......73 C1
Beaufort Rd
  Burton u T DE15 ...167 A1
  Stafford ST17 ......73 B1
Beaufort Way WS9 ..256 A2
Beaulieu Ave DY6 ..275 C2
Beaulieu Ct ST9 .....59 A2
Beaumaris Cl
  Sedgley DY3 ....271 C2
  Stoke-on-T ST4 .....71 B4
Beaumaris Ct ST4 ..284 B2
Beaumaris Rd TF10 ..168 C2
Beaumont Cl Biddulph ST8 ..16 B2
  Great Wyrley WS6 ..226 C1
  Newcastle-u-L ST5 ...70 C2
Beaumont Gdns ST17 ..174 A4
Beaumont Rd
  Great Wyrley WS6 ..226 C1
  Tunstall ST6 ....41 C2
Beaumont Way ST3 ..228 A2
Beauty Bank Cres DY3 ..279 C3
Beauty Bank Prim Sch
  DY8 ....279 C3
Beaver Cl ST4 ....71 C2
Beaver Dr ST10 ......76 A1
Bebington Cl WV8 ..255 C4
Beck Dr WS3 ....68 C4
Beck The DY9 ......216 C1
Beck's La DE13 .....162 C1
Beckbury Ave WV4 ..265 B3
Beckdale St14 ......126 A4
Beckenham Cl ST13 ..90 B4
Becket Cl
  Burton u T DE13 ...166 A3
  Sutton Coldfield B74 ..257 C3
Beckett Ave ST3 .....74 A1
Beckfields Cl ST8 ....17 A1
Beckford St ST1 ....282 C4
Beckminster Rd WV3 ..265 C4
Beckton Ave ST5 .....41 C2
Bedale Pl ST13 ......72 C1
Bedcroft ST12 ....88 C1
Beddow Way ST4 ....41 C3
Bedford Ave ST5 .....56 A2
Bedford Cres ST5 ....71 B2
Bedford Ho
  Burton u T DE13 ...185 B4
  Hanley ST1 ....282 A1
  Kidsgrove ST7 ......26 A2
Bedford St ST1 ....57 A1
Bedford Way WS15 ..196 B3
Bedford Terr ST1 ...208 A4
Bednall Cl ST17 ....193 C4
Bednall Rd ST17 ....175 B1
Bee La WV10 ....240 B2
Beech Ave
  Burton u T DE13 ...166 C4
  Cheddleton ST13 ....45 B2
  King's Bromley DE13 ..199 B3
  Tamworth B77 .....250 C2
Beech Cl Armitage WS15 ..198 B2
  Biddulph ST8 ....16 C2
  Cheadle ST10 ....76 C1
  Haughton ST18 .....172 C3
  Kinver DY7 ....278 A2
  Leek ST13 ....30 B1
  Newport TF10 .....168 C1
  Pattingham WV6 ...253 B1

Beech Cl continued
Sedgley DY3 .... 266 C1
Sutton Coldfield B75 .... 258 A2
Tamworth B79 .... 250 A4
Uttoxeter ST14 .... 126 A4
Wheaton Aston St19 .... 205 B3
Beech Cres WS7 .... 228 C3
Beech Croft Madeley CW3 .68 C4
Pattingham WV6 .... 253 B1
Beech Ct Cannock WS12 ..210 A4
Great Wyrley WS6 ...... 122 C2
Stone ST15 .... 120 A4
Beech Dale La ST12 ..... 103 C4
Beech Dr
Burton u T DE13 .... 166 C4
Talke ST7 .... 40 C4
Beech Gate B74 .... 257 B3
Beech Gdns Codsall WV8 238 C1
Lichfield WS14 .... 231 B3
Beech Gr Ashley TF9 .... 99 C3
Fenton ST4 .... 72 B2
Huntington WS12 ...... 209 B4
Leek ST13 .... 30 B3
Newcastle-u-L ST5 ..... 56 B2
Swadlincote DE11 ...... 186 C4
Beech Hurst Gdns WV5 264 A1
Beech La
Burton u T DE13 .... 166 C4
Coppenhall ST18 ...... 174 B2
Beech Pine Cl WS12 .... 210 A4
Beech Rd
Barton-u-N DE13 ...... 183 B1
Ecclesall ST21 .... 133 C3
Kingswinford DY6 ...... 275 C3
Longton ST3 .... 72 C1
Stourbridge DY8 ...... 279 C2
Tamworth B79 .... 250 A4
Wolv WV10 .... 240 A1
Beech St Burton u T DE14 166 A1
Longton ST3 .... 283 C3
Beech Tree Cl DY6 ..... 275 C4
Beech Tree La WS11 .... 226 B4
Beech Wlk WS5 .... 198 A1
Beecham Cl WS9 ...... 256 A4
Beechcliff La ST4,ST12 ..87 B1
Beechcroft ST12 .... 88 C1
Beechcroft Ave ST17 ...155 B1
Beechcroft Cres B74 ... 256 B1
Beechcroft Ct B74 ..... 258 A1
Beechdale Rd ST4,ST12 ..87 B1
Beecher Gr WS7 .... 228 C4
Beeches Cl DY6 .... 275 B3
Beeches Croft WS13 ... 215 B4
Beeches Mews DY6 .... 281 C2
Beeches Rd WS15 ..... 197 A3
Beeches The
Newcastle-u-L ST5 ..... 56 B4
Rugeley WS15 .... 178 B2
Sutton Coldfield B74 .... 257 B2
Beeches, Forsbrook Jun Sch
The ST11 .... 91 A4
Beechfield Dr ST17 .... 175 C3
Beechfield Rd ST4 ..... 88 A3
Beechfield Rise WS14 ..231 B4
Beechfields ST12 ...... 88 C1
Beechfields Way TF10 ..168 C3
Beechhouse La WV5 ...264 A1
Beechlawn Dr ST7 ..... 278 C4
Beechmere Rise WS15 ..178 A1
Beechmont Gr ST1 ..... 57 C3
Beechmount Rise 🖸
ST17 .... 175 B4
Beechtree La DY10 .... 280 C3
Beechtree Rd WS9 .... 244 C2
Beechway ST16 .... 155 B3
Beechwood WS14 ..... 232 C3
Beechwood Bsns Pk
WS11 .... 210 A2
Beechwood Dr
Stone ST15 .... 120 A3
Wolv WV6 .... 255 A1
Beecroft Ave WS13 .... 214 A1
Beecroft Cl WS11 ..... 209 C1
Beecroft Hill Sch WS11 209 C1
Beecroft Rd WS11 ..... 209 C1
Beelow La ST10 .... 78 B3
Bees La WS15 .... 178 C1
Beeston Rd DY10 ..... 280 A3
Beeston Ridge ST17 .. 174 A4
Beeston St ST3 .... 73 B3
Beeston View ST7 ..... 41 A4
Beffcote La ST20 ..... 171 C4
Beggars Bush La WV5 ..270 A3
Beggars La ST13 ...... 30 B3
Beighton Cl B74 ...... 257 C3
Belbroughton Rd
Blakedown DY10 ...... 281 B1
Stourbridge DY8 ...... 279 C2
Belfast Cl ST6 .... 42 A1
Belfield Ave ST5 ...... 56 B2
Belfield Pl ST4 .... 56 C1
Belfort Way ST17 ..... 175 A4
Belfry Cl WS3 .... 243 A2
Belfry Dr DY8 .... 279 C3
Belfry The
Burton u T DE13 ...... 147 B1
Perton WV6 .... 254 B2

Belgrave Rd WV10 .... 240 A1
Belgrave Ave ST3 .... 283 B2
Belgrave Cres St3 .... 283 C1
Belgrave Ct DY6 ..... 275 C2
Belgrave High Sch B77 250 C1
Belgrave Rd Longton ST3 283 C1
Newcastle-u-L ST5 .... 284 C2
Tamworth B77 .... 261 C4
Bell Ave ST3 .... 73 B1
Bell Cl Lichfield WS13 ..213 C1
Stafford ST16 .... 155 C3
Bell Cotts DE6 .... 127 B4
Bell Dr WS12 .... 210 B4
Bell Heather Rd WS8 ..244 B3
Bell La Barlaston ST12 ...88 C2
Barton-u-N DE13 ...... 183 B1
Doveridge DE6 .... 127 B4
Walsall WS3 .... 243 A1
Bell Orch TF9 .... 100 B3
Bell Rd WV5 .... 264 B1
Bell St DY8 .... 279 C3
Bell Vue ST6 .... 30 B3
Bell Vue St14 .... 30 B3
Bell's Hollow ST5 .... 42 C2
Bellamour La ST17,
  WS15 .... 178 B3
Bellamour Way WS15 ..178 C3
Bellaport Rd TF9 ..... 82 A2
Bellasis St ST16 ...... 155 C3
Bellbrook ST19 .... 192 C1
Belle Vue DY8 .... 275 B1
Belle Vue Prim Sch
DY8 .... 275 B2
Belfield View ST5 .... 56 B2
Bellen Croft Gdns WV3 265 B4
Bellerton La ST6 ..... 42 C1
Bellevue St WV4 ..... 266 C1
Bellflower Cl WV10 ...241 A4
Bellhouse La DE13 ...164 C3
Bellhurst La ST19 .... 205 A3
Bellingham B77 ...... 251 B1
Bellringer Cl ST18 .... 27 B4
Bellringer Rd ST14 ... 88 B4
Bells End Rd DE12 ....184 B1
Bells La Burntwood WS7 211 C1
Kingswinford DY8 ..... 275 B1
Bellsize Cl WS11 ..... 227 C3
Bellwood Cl ST3 ...... 90 A3
Belmont Ave WS11 ... 209 B1
Belmont Cl Aldridge WS9 256 A4
Great Wyrley WS11 .... 227 A2
Belmont Inf Sch ST1 ...57 A2
Belmont Rd Hanley ST1 ..57 A2
Ipstones ST10 .... 61 A4
Tamworth B77 .... 261 C4
Wolv WV4 .... 266 A3
Belmot Rd Anslow DE13 164 C4
Tutbury DE13 .... 145 C1
Belper Rd WS3 ...... 243 B2
Belsay Cl ST3 .... 283 C4
Belsize B77 .... 250 C1
Belt Rd WS11,WS12 ...210 A3
Belton Ave WV11 .... 241 A1
Belvedere Ave WV4 .. 266 A3
Belvedere Cl
Burntwood WS7 ...... 228 C3
Kingswinford DY6 ..... 275 C2
Stafford ST16 .... 175 B4
Tamworth B79 .... 250 B4
Belvedere Gdns WV6 ..255 C4
Belvedere Jun Sch
DE14 .... 166 A3
Belvedere Rd
Burton u T DE13 ...... 166 A3
Sedgley DY1 .... 271 C1
Belvoir Rd DE13 ...... 166 A3
Belwell Dr B74 .... 258 A1
Belwell La B74 .... 258 A1
Bemersley Rd
Chell Heath ST6 ...... 27 B1
Norton-on-t-M ST6 .... 42 C3
Ben Jones Ave TF10 ..169 A2
Benches Cl WS7 ..... 228 B3
Bencroft WS14 ...... 239 A2
Bend Oak Dr DE15 ...167 B2
Bend Oak Jun Sch DE15 167 B2
Benedict Pl ST2 ..... 58 A3
Benenden Cl ST17 ....156 A1
Benfleet Pl ST3 ...... 283 A3
Bengal Gr ST4 .... 283 B2
Bengry Rd ST3 .... 73 C1
Benion Rd WS11 ..... 209 C3
Benjamins Way ST7 ...39 C1
Bennett Pl ST5 ...... 56 A4
Bennett Rd B74 ..... 257 B2
Bennett St ST6 ...... 56 C4
Bennetts La Bosley SK11 ...7 C3
Perton WV6 .... 263 C4
Uttoxeter ST14 ...... 125 B3
Bennick Trad Est WS11 226 C3
Bennion Gr ST14 .... 95 C3
Bennion St ST3 ...... 283 C3
Benson Ave WV4 .... 266 B3
Benson Cl Lichfield WS13 214 B1
Benson Rd ST6 ...... 254 C3
Benson St ST6 ...... 41 C3
Benson View B79 .... 250 B4
Bent La Astbury CW12 ..15 A4
Whitmore ST5 .... 86 A2
Bentilee Prim Sch ST2 ..58 A2
Bentley Ave ST5 .... 56 A2

Bentley Brook La WS12 211 A3
Bentley Cl ST15 ..... 104 C1
Bentley Dr WV8 ..... 238 C2
Bentley Rd
Chell Heath ST6 ...... 42 B3
Uttoxeter ST14 ...... 110 C1
Wolv WV10 .... 240 C1
Bentley Way B79 .... 249 C4
Bentleys Rd TF9 .... 112 A4
Benton Cres WS3 ... 243 B1
Benton's La WS6 .... 227 A1
Bents La ST10 ...... 109 A2
Bentygrange La ST13 ...48 B2
Beowulf Covert DE13 ..147 A1
Berdmore St ST4 .... 283 A5
Beresford Cres ST5 ...71 A3
Beresford Dale DE11 ..186 C1
Beresford Dell CW3 .. 68 B3
Beresford La SK17 ... 24 B1
Beresford Meml CE Fst Sch
ST13 .... 31 A4
Beresford St ST4 .... 57 A1
Bergamot Dr ST3 .... 90 B3
Berkeley Cl Gonsall ST20 ..105 C4
Perton WV6 .... 254 C2
Berkeley Dr DY6 .... 275 B4
Berkeley St Hanley ST1 ..282 C2
Stone ST15 .... 104 C1
Berkeley Way WS15 ...196 A1
Berkshire Gr ST5 .... 71 B3
Berkshire The WS3 .. 243 A2
Berkswell Cl
Sedgley DY1 .... 271 C2
Sutton Coldfield B74 .. 257 C2
Berkswich CE Prim Sch
ST17 .... 175 C3
Bernard Cheadle La
ST15 .... 103 B2
Bernard Gr ST3 ...... 89 C2
Bernard St ST1 ...... 282 C2
Berne Ave ST5 ...... 70 C3
Bernwall Cl DY8 ..... 279 C2
Berrisford Cl TF9 .... 97 C1
Berrisford Rd TF9 ... 97 C1
Berry Hedge La DE15 167 B2
Berry Hill WS12 ...... 210 B2
Berry Hill High Sch ST2 58 A1
Berry Hill Rd ST4 ... 57 C1
Berry La ST3 .... 283 B3
Berry Rd ST16 ...... 155 A4
Berry St ST4 .... 72 A4
Berrybush Gdns DY3 ..271 C4
Berryfield Gr ST3 ... 73 C2
Berryfields WS9 .... 245 C3
Bert Smith Way TF9 ..97 B1
Bertlein Rd ST16 .... 155 C4
Berwick Dr WS11 ... 226 A4
Berwick Rd ST1 ..... 57 C4
Berwick Wlks ST5 ... 70 C4
Berwyn Gr WS6 .... 226 C2
Besom Way WS6 ... 226 B1
Best Ave DE15 ...... 167 A1
Best St ST4 .... 72 C3
Beswick Cl ST10 .... 76 B1
Beswick Rd ST16 ... 41 C3
Beswicks La TF9 .... 82 B4
Bethany Mews WS11 209 C2
Bethell Rd ST1 ...... 57 B4
Bethesda Rd ST1 ... 282 C1
Bethesda St ST1 ... 282 B2
Betjeman Pl WV10 ...241 A1
Betjeman Wlk ST17 ..174 B4
Betley CE Prim Sch CW3 53 A3
Betley Hall Gdns CW3 ..53 A3
Betley Pl ST5 .... 71 B3
Battlingspring La DE6 ..81 B2
Beton Way ST16 .... 155 B4
Bettany Glade WV10 ..240 C2
Bettany Rd ST6 ..... 57 A4
Betton Rd TF9 ...... 97 B2
Betty Hatch La ST16 ..155 B3
Betty's La WS11 .... 228 A2
Bevan Ave Talke ST7 ...40 C3
Bevan Lee Rd WS11 ..209 B2
Bevan Pl CW3 ...... 68 C4
Bevandean Cl ST4 ... 88 B3
Beveridge Cl ST3 ... 74 A1
Beverley Cl ST19 ... 207 C4
Beverley Cres
Forsbrook ST11 ...... 91 A4
Wolv WV4 .... 266 C2
Beverley Dr Blackpool ST2 58 B1
Stafford ST16 .... 155 B4
Beverley Hill WS12 ...210 B4
Beverley Rd DE14 ...185 A4
Beverly Dr DY6 ..... 275 B4
Beverston Rd WV6 ..255 A2
Beville St ST4 ...... 72 C3
Bevin Rd WS2 ...... 243 A4
Bew St ST6 .... 42 C3
Bewcastle Gr ST3 .. 90 A4
Bexhill Gr ST1 ...... 57 A3
Bexley St ST1 ...... 282 A4
Beyer Cl B77 .... 251 A1
Bhylls Acre Prim Sch
WV3 .... 265 B4
Bhylls Cres WV3 .... 265 B4
Bhylls La WV3 ...... 265 A4
Bibby's La WV10 ... 240 C2
Bickford Cl ST19 ... 192 A2
Bickford Rd ST19 ... 206 A4
Bickley Ave B74 .... 257 C4
Bickley Ho ST4 ..... 72 A4
Bida La CW12 ...... 16 A4

Biddles La ST21 ..... 102 B2
Biddulph Common Rd
ST8 .... 17 A3
Biddulph Grange Ctry Pk*
ST8 .... 16 C2
Biddulph Grange Gdn*
ST8 .... 16 C2
Biddulph High Sch ST8 ..17 A4
Biddulph Park Rd ST8 ...17 A3
Chell Heath ST6 ...... 42 A2
Congleton CW12 ...... 16 A4
Biddulph St CW12 ... 16 B4
Bideford Ave ST3 ... 73 C2
Bideford Way WV11 ...226 A4
Bideford Way WS12 ...210 B3
Biggin Cl WV11 ..... 226 A4
Bignall End Rd ST7 .. 40 A2
Bigsbury Wlk 🖸 ST6 ..56 C4
Bigwood La
Bradley ST18 .... 173 C2
Coppenhall ST18 .... 173 C2
Bilberry Bank WS11 ..209 C3
Bilberry Cl WS15 .... 178 B1
Bilberry Cres WS12 ..209 B3
Bilbrook CE Mid Sch
WV8 .... 239 A2
Bilbrook Gr WV8 ... 239 A2
Bilbrook Rd WV8 ... 239 A2
Bilbrook St WV8 .... 239 A2
Bilbrook Sta WV8 .. 239 A1
Billinge St ST6 ..... 56 C4
Billington Ave ST18 ..158 B1
Billington Bank ST18 ..173 B3
Billington La ST18 ... 173 B3
Billy Buns La WV5 .. 270 A4
Billy Wright Cl WV4 ..265 C3
Bilston Dr ST3 ...... 90 A3
Bilston St DY3 ...... 271 C4
Bilton St ST4 .... 72 A3
Bingley Ent Ctr WV3 266 A4
Bingley Prim Sch WV3 266 A4
Bingley St WV3 .... 266 A4
Birch Ave Biddulph St8 ..27 A2
Brownhills WS8 ...... 244 C4
Burntwood WS7 ..... 228 C3
Cannock WS11 .... 226 B4
Birch Brook La WS14 246 C3
Birch Bsns Pk WS11 226 B4
Birch Cl Burton u T DE14 185 A4
Colwich ST18 .... 158 B1
Denstone ST14 .... 95 B3
Stafford ST17 .... 175 C3
Birch Coppice WS9 .. 269 C3
Birch Croft WS9 .... 256 B4
Birch Dale ST3 ..... 68 C3
Birch Dr Little Aston B24 257 B3
Stourbridge DY8 ..... 279 C3
Birch Gr Blythe Bridge ST3 90 A3
Forsbrook ST11 ...... 91 A4
Lichfield WS14 .... 231 B4
Rosliston DE12 ...... 184 C1
Birch Green Gr ST1 ...57 C4
Birch Hill Ave WV5 .. 269 C3
Birch Ho B74 .... 257 A3
Birch House La WS11,
  ST21 .... 117 C4
Birch House Rd ST5 .. 55 B4
Birch La Aldridge WS9 245 B1
Rugeley WS15 ...... 197 A3
Walsall WS9 .... 244 B1
Birch Rd Audley ST7 .. 39 C1
Essington WV11 ..... 241 C1
Sedgley DY3 .... 266 C1
Stone ST15 .... 120 A4
Birch Rise TF9 ..... 99 C2
Birch St ST16 ...... 155 C3
Birch Terr
Burntwood WS7 ..... 212 A1
Hanley ST1 .... 282 B2
Birch Tree Gdns WS9 256 A3
Birch Tree La
The Bank ST7 .... 26 A4
Whitmore ST5 .... 85 B4
Birch Wlk ST3 ...... 73 A1
Birchall Ave ST6 .... 41 B3
Birchall Cl ST13 .... 30 C1
Birchall La ST13 .... 30 C1
Birchall Park Ave ST13 30 C2
Bircham Wlk ST5 ... 71 A1
Birchbrook Ind Pk
WS14 .... 246 C3
Birchcroft WV9 .... 240 A3
Birchdown Ave ST6 .. 42 A2
Birchendale Cl ST10 ..92 C1
Birchenfields La ST10 ..75 C3
Birchenwood Rd ST6,ST7 26 C1
Birches Ave ST18 ... 157 B4
Birches Barn Ave WV3 265 C4
Birches Barn Rd WV3 ..265 C4
Birches Cl DE13 .... 163 C1
Birches Farm Mews CW3 68 C3
Birches Head High Sch
ST1 .... 57 C4
Birches Head Rd ST1 ..57 C4
Birches Park Rd WV8 238 C1
Birches Rd WV8 .... 239 A1
Birches The ST10 .. 76 B4
Birches Valley WS15 ..195 B3
Birches Valley Forest Ctr*
WS15 .... 195 C4
Birchfield Ave WV6 ..255 A2
Birchfield Cl WV9 .. 240 A3
Birchfield Ct B74 ... 262 B1
Birchfield Rd Bucknall ST2 58 B3
Burton u T DE15 ..... 185 C3
Birchfield Sch WV7 ..237 B3
Birchfields Cl ST15 ..119 C3

Birchfields Dr WS12 ..210 B1
Birchgate ST2 ...... 58 B2
Birchgate Gr ST2 ... 58 B2
Birchglade WV3 .... 255 B1
Birchlands Rd ST1 .. 57 C3
Birchmoor La ST20 ..189 B1
Birchmoor Rd B78 .. 262 C4
Birchover Way ST6 .. 42 A4
Birchtree La WS15 ..196 C3
Birchwood Ave B78 ..262 C4
Birchwood Cl WV11 ..242 A2
Birchwood Prim Sch
B78 .... 262 C4
Birchwood Rd
Lichfield WS14 ...... 231 C4
Wolv WV4 .... 265 C4
Birchwood Rise WS15 ..161 A3
Bird End WS3 ...... 74 A1
Bird Cage Wlk ST17 ..282 B2
Bird Rd WS3 .... 74 A1
Bird St Lichfield WS13 ..231 A4
Sedgley DY3 .... 271 B2
Bird's Barn La DY11 ..277 B1
Birdhope B77 ...... 251 B1
Birds Bush Prim Sch
B77 .... 261 C4
Birds Bush Rd B77 .. 261 C4
Birdsgrove La DE6 ... 66 B2
Birkdale Ave DE14 .. 185 A3
Birkdale Cl DY8 .... 279 C1
Birkdale Dr Kidsgrove ST7 26 B2
Stafford ST16 .... 156 B2
Birkdale Rd WS3 ... 243 A2
Birkholme Dr ST3 .. 90 A3
Birks Dr TF9 .... 99 C3
Birks St ST4 .... 72 A3
Birmingham New Rd
WV4 .... 266 C2
Birmingham Rd
Aldridge WS9 .... 256 A2
Blakedown DY10 ..... 281 B1
Lichfield WS14 ...... 231 A2
Shenstone WS14 .... 247 A2
Birmingham St WV2 ..266 B4
Birrell St ST4 ...... 72 C3
Biscay Gr ST4 ..... 88 B4
Bishop Cl WS11 .... 209 B1
Bishop Ct ST2 ..... 58 A3
Bishop Rawle CE Prim Sch
ST10 .... 76 B2
Bishop Rd ST4 ..... 42 A3
Bishop St ST4 ..... 73 A3
Bishop Stamer CE Prim Sch
ST4 .... 72 A3
Bishop's Cl ST17 ... 40 B4
Bishops Cl ST21 ... 133 C4
Bishops Dr ST19 ... 223 B4
Bishops Grange WS15 ..178 C1
Bishops La TF9 .... 97 A1
Bishops Mdw B75 .. 258 C2
Bishops Way B74 .. 258 C2
Bishton La WS15 ... 178 A3
Bitham Cl ST19 .... 207 C4
Bitham Ct DE13 .... 147 B1
Bitham La DE13 .... 147 B1
Bittell Cl WV10 .... 240 C2
Bittern La ST10 .... 92 C1
Bitterne Pl ST2 ..... 73 B4
Bitterscote La B78 .. 250 A1
Black Bank Rd ST9,ST13 ..44 B3
Black Dr ST10 ..... 77 B3
Black Horse La ST1 ..282 B3
Black La Forton TF10 ..150 C1
Kingsley ST10 .... 62 B2
Blackbank Rd ST5 .. 55 B2
Blackberry La
Brownhills WS9 ..... 245 A2
Stafford ST16 .... 155 B2
Sutton Coldfield B74 .. 257 C2
Blackberry Way ST20 ..151 B4
Blackbird Cl ST14 .. 126 B3
Blackbrook CE Prim Sch
ST5 .... 54 C4
Blackbrook Ave ST5 .. 55 B4
Blackbrook Way WV10 240 C2
Blackbrook World of Birds &
  Animals* ST13 ..... 48 A2
Blackburn Ave WV6 .. 255 C4
Blackdown B77 .... 251 B1
Blackfriar's Rd ST5 .. 284 B2
Blackfriars Cl B79 .. 249 C3
Blackfriars F Ed Unit
ST2 .... 58 A3
Blackhalve La WV11 ..241 B1
Blackheath Cl ST13 .. 73 B2
Blackheath La ST18 ..156 C2
Blackhole La ST18 .. 154 B1
Blackies La ST15 .. 120 B4
Blacklake Dr ST3 .. 90 A2
Blackmere Ct TF10 .. 168 B1
Blackpit La
Doveridge DE6 ...... 127 A4
Wombourne WV4 .... 264 C2
Blackpool St DE14 .. 185 B4
Blackroot Cl WV2 .. 229 B2
Blackshaw CW12 .. 6 A1
Blackshaw Moor CE Fst Sch
ST13 .... 20 C3
Blacksmith La WS14 ..232 C3
Blacksmith's La
Eggington DE65 ..... 148 A3
Newton Solney DE15 ..167 C4
Blackthorn Ave WS12 ..210 B3
Blackthorn Cl WS12 ..210 B3
Blackthorn Cres ST12 ..211 A3
Blackthorn Pl ST5 .. 55 C4
Blackthorn Rd
Brierley Hill DY8 ..... 275 C1
Burton u T DE15 ..... 185 C3

Blackthorne Cl DY1 .....271 C2
Blackthorne Rd
  Dudley DY1 ....271 C3
  Lichfield WS14 ....231 B4
Blackwell's Row ST6 .....57 A3
Blackwood Pl ST3 ....73 C2
Blackwood Rd
  Aldridge B74 ....256 C1
  Tamworth B77 ....261 B4
Blackwood Sch B74 ......256 C1
Bladon Ave ST5 ....71 A2
Bladon Cl ST6 ....42 A4
Bladon House Sch
  DE15 ....167 A3
Bladon St DE15 ....167 B2
Bladon View DE13 ....148 A1
Bladon's Yd DE13 ....147 A2
Blaizefield Cl CW3 ....67 B1
Blake Cl WV11 ....210 A3
Blake High Sch WS12 ...209 C3
Blake St Burslem ST6 .....56 C4
  Sutton Coldfield B74 ...257 C3
Blake Street Sta B74 ....257 C3
Blakedown CE Prim Sch
  DY10 ....281 B1
Blakedown Sta DY10 ....281 B1
Blakeley Ave WV6 ....255 C4
Blakeley Heath Dr WV5 .270 A3
Blakeley Heath Prim Sch
  WV5 ....270 A3
Blakeley La ST10 ....63 A1
Blakeley Rise WV6 ......255 C4
Blakelow La DE6 ....65 A1
Blakelow Rd ST2 ....58 A3
Blakemore Rd WV9 .....245 A2
Blakenall Heath WS3 ...243 B1
Blakeney Ave
  Newcastle-u-L ST5 .....71 A2
  Stourbridge DY8 ....279 B3
Blakeney Cl DY3 ....271 B4
Blakenhall Ind Est WV2 266 A4
Blakeways Cl B79 ....217 B3
Blakiston St ST16 ....155 C2
Blanchard Cl ST3 ....90 B4
Blandford Dr DY8 ....275 C2
Blanefield WV8 ....239 C1
Blanford Gdns WS7 .....229 B3
Blanford Mere Prim Sch
  DY6 ....275 C4
Blantyre St ST3 ....283 C2
Blantyre Wlk ST3 ....283 C2
Blatchford Cl ST3 ....74 A1
Blaydon Ave B75 ....258 C1
Blaydon Rd WV9,WV10 .240 A1
Blaze Hill Rd DY6 ....275 A4
Blaze Pk DY6 ....275 A4
Bleak House Dr WS7 ....228 B4
Bleak Pl 10 ST6 ....57 A4
Bleak St ST5 ....56 C4
Bleakridge Ave ST5 ......56 A4
Bleeding Wolf La ST7 ...25 C3
Blencarn Gr ST19 ....43 B2
Blenheim Cl
  Burton u T DE15 ....167 B2
  Tamworth B77 ....250 B2
Blenheim Dr WS13 .....215 B3
Blenheim Rd
  Burntwood WS7 ....229 A4
  Kingswinford DY6 .....275 C3
  Norton Canes WS11 ...228 A2
Blenheim St ST4 ....72 B3
Blenheim Way DY1 .....271 C1
Bleriot Cl ST3 ....90 B4
Blessed William Howard RC
  High Sch ST17 ....155 B1
Bletchley Dr B77 ....261 B4
Blewitt St WS12 ....210 A4
Blithbury Rd
  Colton WS15 ....179 A2
  Hamstall Ridware WS15 .180 C2
Blithe View ST11 ....90 C3
Blithfield Cl ST9 ....59 A1
Blithfield Ho ST17 ....154 C1
Blithfield Pl WS11 ......210 A1
Blithfield Rd WS8 ......228 A1
Bloomfield Cl WV5 .....269 B3
Bloomfield Cres WS13 ..214 A1
Bloomfield Dr WV12 ...242 B1
Bloomfield Way B79 ....249 C4
Bloomsbury St 2 WV2 .266 B4
Bloomsbury Way WS14 .231 C4
Blore Rd TF9 ....98 C1
Blossomfield Cl DY6 ....275 C4
Blount Cl ST19 ....207 C4
Blounts Dr ST14 ....126 A3
Bloxwich CE Prim Sch
  WS3 ....243 A1
Bloxwich North Sta
  WS3 ....242 C1
Bloxwich Sta WS3 ......243 A1
Blue Cedars DY8 ....279 B3
Blue House Barns TF10 168 C2
Blue House La WV7 .....237 A4
Bluebell Cl Biddulph ST8 27 C4
  Cannock WS12 ....210 B3
  Kingswinford DY8 .....275 B1
Bluebell Dr ST5 ....71 A2
Bluebell La WS6 ....227 A1
Bluebell Rd WS9 ....245 A2
Bluebird Cl WS14 ......231 B4
Bluemeadow La WV5 ...270 A4
Bluestone Ave ST6 ....42 A1
Bluestone La DE15 .....186 A4
Bluestones Cl ST13 .....20 C2
Blundies La DY7 ....273 B2
Blunt St ST5 ....56 B2
Blunt's Hollow WS15,
  DE13 ....162 A2

Blurton High Sch ST3 ....88 C4
Blurton Prim Sch ST3 ....72 C1
Blurton Rd Barlaston ST12 89 A2
  Fenton ST3 ....72 C2
Blurton Waste Cotts ST3 .72 C1
Blythe Ave ST3 ....90 A3
Blythe Bridge High Sch
  ST11 ....90 C4
Blythe Bridge Rd ST11 ..74 C1
Blythe Bridge Sta ST11 ..90 C4
Blythe Cl
  Blythe Bridge ST11 .....90 B4
  Wolverhampton WS7 ...229 B3
Blythe Gdns WV8 ......238 C2
Blythe Mount Pk ST11 ...91 A4
Blythe Rd Forsbrook ST11 .91 A4
  Stafford ST17 ....174 C3
Blythe St B77 ....250 B2
Blythe View
  Blythe Bridge ST11 .....91 A1
  Hamstall Ridware WS15 .180 C1
Blythebridge Bank
  ST14,ST18 ....140 C3
Blythfield DE14 ....166 C2
Board School Gdns DY3 271 C3
Boardman Cres ST16 ...155 B2
Boardman Ind Est DE11 186 C2
Boardman Rd DE11 ....186 C1
Boardmans Bank ST6 ...28 A1
Boat House La WS13 ...198 A3
Boat La Wall WS14 .....229 C1
  Weston ST18 ....138 B2
Boathorse Rd
  Kidsgrove ST7 ....41 A4
  Tunstall ST6 ....41 A3
Boatman's La WS9 .....244 C1
Boatyard Cotts ST7 ......88 B1
Bodiam Ct WV6 ....255 A2
Bodicote Gr B75 ....258 C1
Bodington Gr WS7 .....229 C4
Bodington Rd B75 .....258 B2
Bodmin Ave ST17 ......175 B4
Bodmin Wlk ST6 ....42 B1
Bognop Rd WV11 ......241 B2
Bogs Cotts ST5 ....70 A4
Bogs La ST11 ....90 C3
Bolberry Cl ST3 ....73 C1
Bold St ST1 ....57 C3
Bolebridge Mews B79 ..250 A3
Bolebridge St B79 ......250 B2
Boley Cl WS14 ....231 B4
Boley Cottage La WS14 231 C4
Boley La WS14 ....231 C4
Boley Park Ctr WS14 ...231 C4
Boleyn Cl WS6 ....226 B1
Bolina Gr ST4 ....73 A3
Bollin Gr ST6 ....16 C1
Bolney Gr ST1 ....57 C3
Bolsover Cl ST6 ....42 A4
Bolton Pl ST3 ....89 C4
Bolton Way WS14 .....242 C2
Boma Rd ST4 ....87 C4
Bond End DE13 ....182 A1
Bond St Burton u T DE14 .166 B1
  Tunstall ST6 ....41 B2
Bondfield La DE13 .....181 C1
Bondfield Way ST3 ......74 A1
Bondway WS12 ....209 A1
Bonehill Ind Est B78 ...249 C1
Bonehill Rd B78 ....249 C2
Boney Hay Prim Sch
  WS7 ....211 C1
Boney Hay Rd WS7 ....174 A4
Boningdale Way WS17 .174 A4
Bonnard Cl ST3 ....90 B3
Bonner Cl ST4 ....71 C2
Bonnington Cres ST16 .155 B1
Bonville Gdns WV10 ...240 C2
Boon Ave ST4 ....72 A4
Boon Gr ST17 ....174 C3
Boon Hill Rd ST7 ....39 C1
Boons Ind Est ST18 ....154 C1
Booth Cl WS13 ....140 C2
Booth La ST18 ....140 C2
Booth St Audley ST7 .....39 B1
  Cannock WS12 ....210 A3
  Stoke-on-T ST4 ....72 A3
Boothen CE Prim Sch
  ST4 ....72 A3
Boothen Ct ST4 ....72 A3
Boothen Gn ST4 ....72 A3
Boothen Old Rd ST4 ....72 A3
Boothen Rd ST4 ....72 A3
Boothenwood Terr ST4 ..72 A3
Boothroyd St ST1 ......282 B2
Borden Cl DY10 ....280 A1
Bordeaux Cl DY1 ......271 C2
Bordeaux Rd ST3 ....90 A4
Bordeaux Wlk ST5 ......70 C2
Borden Cl
  Wheaton Aston ST19 ..205 B4
  Wolverhampton WV6 ..255 A3
Border Way ST17 ......174 C3
Bore St WS13 ....231 A4
Borman B79 ....249 C3
Borough Cres DY8 .....279 C3
Borough La WS15 ......162 C2
Borough Mus & Art Gal The*
  ST5 ....284 C4
Borough Rd
  Burton u T DE14 ......166 B2
  Newcastle-u-L ST5 ....284 C3
  Tamworth B77 ....250 B4
Borrowcop La WS14 ...231 B3
Borrowdale Rd ST6 .....42 C2
Boscobel Cl DY1 ......271 C2
Boscobel Gr ST19 .....223 B4

Boscobel Ho* ST19 ....221 C3
Boscombe Gr ST4 ....88 B3
Boscombe Cl ST19 ....207 C4
Boscomoor Cl ST19 ...207 C4
Boscomoor Ind Est
  ST19 ....207 C4
Boscomoor La ST19 ...207 C4
Boscomoor Sh Ctr ST19 207 C4
Bosinney Cl ST4 ....73 A3
Bosley Brook CW12 .....16 B3
Bosley Gr ST6 ....41 B3
Boss Gate Cl WV5 .....270 A3
Bostock Cl 5 ST15 ....120 B3
Boston Cl Cannock WS12 210 C1
  Tunstall ST6 ....41 B2
Boston Ind Est WS15 ..178 C1
Bosty La WS5 ....256 A2
Boswell Rd WS11 ......229 B3
Boswell St ST4 ....56 C1
Bosworth Cl DY3 ......271 C3
Bosworth Dr DE13 ....166 A4
Botany Bay Rd ST11 ....57 C3
Botany Dr DY3 ....271 B3
Botesworth Gdns ST6 ..41 B1
Botfield Cl WV7 ....237 A3
Botham Dr ST1 ....45 B3
Botterham La DY3 .....269 C2
Botteslow St ST1 ......282 C2
Bottom La
  Ipstones ST10,ST13 ....47 B3
  Market Drayton TF9 ...112 A4
  Swynnerton ST15 .....103 A4
Boucher Rd ST13 ....45 B2
Boughey Rd Audley ST7 .39 C1
  Newport TF10 ....168 C1
  Stoke-on-T ST4 ....72 B4
Boughey St ST4 ....72 A3
Boulevard The ST6 .....41 C2
Boulters La CW9 ......262 B1
Boulton Cl WS7 ....229 B4
Boulton St Hanley ST1 .282 C4
  Newcastle-u-L ST5 .....56 B3
Boundary Cl Leek ST13 .30 C2
  Stone ST15 ....119 C3
Boundary Cres DY3 ...271 B2
Boundary Ct ST1 ......282 B4
Boundary Hill DY3 .....271 B2
Boundary Ind Est WV10 240 B3
Boundary Rd
  Brownhills WS9 ......244 C2
  Eggington SE15 ......148 B4
  Hednesford WS12 ....211 B3
  Newcastle-u-L ST5 .....56 B1
Boundary View ST10 ...70 A1
Boundary Way
  Wolv WV6 ....254 C1
  Wolv, Springhill WV4 .265 B3
  Wolv & Penn ST18 ...153 B3
Bourne Av ST4 ....249 C1
Bourne Cl Cannock WS12 210 C1
  Tutbury DE13 ....146 A3
Bourne Dr ST3 ....30 B3
Bourne Rd ST7 ....25 C1
Bourne St Fenton ST4 ..72 C2
  Mow Cop ST7 ....28 A3
Bourne Vale WS9 .....256 B2
Bournes Bank ST6 ......56 C4
Bournes Bank S 9 ST6 .57 A4
Bouverie Par ST1 ....57 C4
Bow St WS15 ....178 C1
Bowden St ST6 ....42 A1
Bowdler Rd WV2 .....266 B4
Bowen St WV4 ....266 C3
Bowen-cooke Ave WV6 254 C3
Bower Cl WS13 ....214 B1
Bower End La CW3 .....68 B3
Bower La WS15 ....178 B2
Bower Norris RC Prim Sch
  ST17 ....174 B4
Bower St ST1 ....282 B1
Bower St DE15 ....120 B4
Bowers La Standon ST21 .102 A2
  Stone ST15 ....120 B2
Bowes Dr WS11 ....209 C4
Bowfell Gr ST4 ....73 A3
Bowhill La CW3 ....53 A3
Bowland Ave ST5 ....55 C1
Bowlers Cl ST6 ....42 A4
Bowling Green Ave ST17 44 B1
Bowling Green Rd DY9 279 C3
Bowman Gr ST6 ....42 A4
Bowmead Cl ST4 ....88 B3
Bowmere Cl ST8 ....16 B1
Bowness St ST1 ....282 A4
Bowness Dr WV6 .....255 B3
Bowran Ho ST 89 C4
Bowsey Wood Rd CW3 ..68 C4
Bowstead St ST4 ....72 A4
Bowyer Ave ST6 ....42 C3
Box La ST3 ....73 B1
Boxer Cl WS15 ....198 B2
Boxwood Pl ST5 ....56 B3
Boyce Cl Cannock WS12 210 A1
Boyden Cl Cannock WS11 209 A1
Boyes Gr ST19 ....208 A4
Boyles Hall Rd ST7 .....39 C1
Brabazon Cl ST3 ....90 B4
Brabazon Ave TF9 ....99 C3
Bracken Cl
  Blythe Bridge ST3 ......89 C3
  Cannock WS12 ....209 B4
  Lichfield WS14 ....231 C3

Bracken Cl continued
  Stafford ST16 ....155 A4
  Tittensor ST12 ....88 A1
Bracken Ct ST19 ......239 C1
Wolv WV8 ....239 C1
Bracken Dale ST13 ......30 A3
Bracken Park Gdns DY8 275 C1
Bracken Rd WS12 .....209 B3
Bracken St ST14 ....72 C2
Bracken View ST17 ...176 B2
Bracken Way
  Newport TF10 ....168 C2
  Rugeley WS15 ....178 B1
Brackenberry ST5 ......56 A2
Brackenfield Ave ST2 ...58 B1
Brackenfield Way ST5 .155 B4
Brackenhill Rd WS7 ...229 A4
Brackens The ST5 ......71 B1
Brackenwood Rd DE15 185 C3
Bracklesham Way B77 .251 A3
Brackley Ave ST5 ....42 A1
Bradbury Cl
  Brownhills WS8 ......244 C3
  Norton-in-t M ST6 .....42 C2
Bradbury La WS12 ....210 A4
Bradbury La
  Cannock WS12 ....210 A4
  Enville DY7 ....272 C2
  King's Bromley DE13 ..199 B3
Bradbury Rise ST16 ...185 C2
Braden Rd WV4 ....265 B2
Bradford Rd WS8 .....244 C4
Bradford St
  Cannock WS11 ......210 A3
  Tamworth B79 ......249 C3
Bradford Terr ST1 ......57 C3
Bradgate Dr B74 ......257 C3
Bradley Dr ST21 ....117 C2
Bradley La Bradley ST18 .173 A2
  Haughton ST18 ......173 A2
  Stafford ST18 ....174 B3
Bradley Lakes WS15 ..197 C1
Bradley Rd
  Stourbridge DY8 .....279 C3
  Wolv WV2 ....266 C4
Bradley St
  Burton u T DE15 ......185 C4
  Uttoxeter ST14 ....126 B4
Bradmore Rd
  Burton u T DE13 ......166 A3
  Wolv WV3 ....265 C4
Bradshaw Way ST16 ...155 B4
Bradwell Croft B75 ...258 C2
Bradwell Grange ST5 ...56 A4
Bradwell Hospl ST5 ....56 A4
Bradwell La
  Cannock WS15 ....211 C3
  Newcastle-u-L ST5 .....56 A4
Bradwell Prim Sch ST5 ..56 A4
Bradwell St ST6 ....56 A4
Braeburn Cl WS13 ....214 B1
Braeburn Ct ST3 ....90 B4
Braemar Ave DY8 .....275 B1
Braemar Cl Bucknall ST2 ..58 B2
  Sedgley DY3 ....266 B1
Braemar Gdns WS12 ..209 C4
Braemar Rd
  Norton Canes WS11 ..228 A2
  Pattingham WV6 .....253 B1
Braemore Rd ST12 ......58 A3
Braeside Way WS3 ....243 C2
Braham B79 ....249 C3
Brailsford Ave DE11 ..186 C3
Brain St B77 ....251 A1
Braithwaite Cl DY6 ...275 B3
Braithwell Dr ST2 ....43 A1
Brake La DY8 ....281 C2
Brake The Hagley DY8 .281 C3
  The Bank ST7 ....26 A4
Brake Village ST7 ......26 A4
Brakespeare St ST6 ....41 B4
Bramall Cl ST6 ....155 B3
Bramber B77 ....250 B1
Bramber Way DY8 .....279 C1
Bramble Cl WS8 ......244 C3
Bramble Cl W10 ......240 C2
Bramble Dr DE15 .....185 C3
Bramble Dr WS12 ....210 B4
Bramble Dr WV21 .....84 C2
Bramble La ST7 ....229 A4
Bramble Lea CW3 ......68 C3
Bramble Way WS15 ...178 B1
Brambles Ct ST8 ....27 B4
Brambles The
  Lichfield WS14 ....231 B3
  Newcastle-u-L ST5 .....71 B1
  Norton Canes WS11 ..228 A3
Bramblewode DY8 ....275 C1
Bramblewood Dr WV3 .265 C4
Bramblings ST19 ......192 A4
Brambling Cl ST13 ....126 B3
Bramblings The ST17 ..175 B3
Bramdean Dr ST19 ...192 C1
Bramdene Ave WV4 ..265 B3
Bramfield Cl DE14 ....184 C4
Bramford Dr ST5 .....284 C4
Bramhall Cl ST16 .....155 B3
Bramhall La ST16 .....155 B3
Bramley Cl ST10 ....76 C1
Bramley Dale ST11 ....90 C4
Bramley Rd WS11 ....209 A1
Bramley Way WS14 ..232 B3
Bramsall Dr ST11 ......90 C4
Bramwell Cl WS14 ....242 B1
Brampton Dr DY10 ...280 A2
Brampton Gdns ST5 ...209 A4
Brampton Dr WS12 ...210 C1
Brampton Ind Est ST5 .284 C4
Brampton Rd ST5 .....284 C4

Brampton Sidings ST5 .284 B4
Brampton Sidings Ind Est
  ST5 ....284 B4
Brampton Wlk ST3 ....283 C1
Bramshall Ind Est ST14 .125 C4
Bramshall Rd ST14 ...125 C4
Bramshaws The ST10 ...76 C1
Bramstead Ave WV6 ..255 A1
Bramwell Dr WS6 .....226 B1
Brancaster Cl B77 ....251 A3
Brandon Cl Aldridge WV9 256 C2
  Sedgley DY3 ....271 C4
Brandon Gr ST4 ....87 C4
Brandon Pk WV3 .....265 C4
Brandons The ST17 ...174 C3
Bransdale Rd WS8 ....244 C3
Branson Ave ST3 ....73 C2
Branston Rd
  Branston DE13,DE14 ..184 B4
  Burton u T DE14 ......185 B4
Branston Water Pk
  DE14 ....184 B3
Bransty Gr ST4 ....88 B3
Brant Ave ST5 ....56 A2
Brantley Ave WV3 ....255 B1
Brantley Cres DY7 ....267 C1
Brantley La
  Bobbington DY7 .....267 C1
  Seisdon WV5 ....263 A2
Branton Hill La WS9 ..256 B3
Brantwood Ave WS7 .229 A3
Brassington St CW3 ...53 A3
Brassington Way ST2 ..58 B1
Bratch Common Rd
  WV5 ....269 C4
Bratch Hollow WV5 ..269 C4
Bratch La WV5 ....269 C4
Bratch Pk WV5 ......269 C4
Brattswood Dr ST7 ....25 A3
Braunton Ave ST17 ...175 C4
Braystones Cl ST7 ......41 C4
Brazenhill La ST18 ....172 C4
Breach La Cheadle ST10 ..92 B3
  Draycott in t M ST50 ...92 B3
  Foston DE6 ....129 B3
Breach Rd ST16 ....43 A4
Breadmarket St WS13 231 A4
Bream B77 ....261 B4
Bream Way ST6 ....42 A2
Breamore Cres DY1 ...271 C2
Brean Rd ST17 ....175 C3
Brecon Way ST2 ....58 B1
Bredon Cl WV11 ......237 A3
Bredon Ct B75 ....258 A2
Bredon Ct ST3 ....73 C2
Bredon Rd WV4 ......265 C2
Breech Cl ST10 ....48 C1
Breedon Ct ST5 ....55 C2
Breedon Rd ST4 ......244 B1
Breeze Ave
  Norton Canes WS11 ..228 A3
  Tunstall ST6 ....41 C3
Brelades Cl DY1 ......271 C1
Brereton Croft ST15 ..106 B1
Brendale Cl ST4 ....72 A1
Brendon B77 ....251 A1
Brendon Cl ST17 .....175 B4
Brent B77 ....261 C4
Brentmill Cl WV10 ...240 C2
Brentnall Dr B75 .....258 A2
Brentnor Cl ST3 ....73 C2
Brenton Rd WV4 .....265 C2
Brentwood Dr ST9 ....59 A2
Brentwood Gr
  Caverswall ST9 ....59 A2
  Norton-in-t M ST9 .....43 B2
Brenwood Cl DY6 ....275 A4
Brereton Hill WS15 ...197 A3
Brereton Lodge WS15 .197 A3
Brereton Manor Ct 5
  WS15 ....197 A3
Brereton Pl ST6 ....41 C1
Brereton Rd WS15 ...196 C4
Brereton Ind Est ST16 .197 B1
Bretby Bsns Pk DE15 .186 C4
Bretby Hollow DE15 ..186 C4
Bretby La Bretby DE15 .167 C2
  Burton u T DE15 ......186 A4
Bretby Rd DE11 ....186 C4
Bretherton Pl ST6 ......42 A3
Bretlands Way DE15 ..186 A3
Brett La CW8 ....83 C1
Brevitt Rd WV2 ....266 B3
Brewers Dr WS3 ......244 A1
Brewers Terr WS3 ....244 A1
Brewery La ST18 ......156 C3
Brewery St Hanley ST1 .282 B3
Rugeley WS15 ....196 C1
Brewster Rd ST2 ......57 C2
Brewhouse Ct WS13 .213 C1
Brewood CE Mid Sch
  4
Brewood Rd WV8 .....224 A2
Brewster Cl B78 ......261 B3
Brianson Ave ST6 ......57 B4
Briar B77 ....261 C4
Briar Ave ST4 ....73 A2
Briar Cl Cannock WS12 210 A4
  Rugeley WS15 ....178 B1
  Stafford ST17 ....175 C3
Briar Way ST21 ....102 C1
Briarbank Cl ST4 ......33 B1
Briar Way ST13 ....118 C3
Briars The Hagley DY9 .281 C2
Briars Way WS12 .....211 B3

Briarsleigh ST17 ....175 B4
Briarswood ST7 ....26 A1
Briarwood DY3 ....74 A1
Brick House St 3 ST6 ...56 C4
Brick Kiln La
  Brocton ST17 ....175 C2
  Rolleston DE13 ....147 A2
  Salt ST18 ....137 C1
  Sedgley DY3 ....271 A2
  Stoke-on-T ST4 ....56 C1
  Wheaton Aston ST19 ....205 A3
Brick Kiln Way WS15 ....196 C3
Brick St DY3 ....271 B4
Brick-kiln La ST5 ....55 C4
Brickbridge La WV5 ......269 C3
Brickfield Cl ST18 ....139 B1
Brickfield Pl ST17 ....73 B3
Brickhill La DE13 ....163 A3
Brickhouse La B79 ....216 B1
Brickiln St WS8 ....244 C4
Brickworks Rd WS12 .....210 C1
Brickyard Rd
  Aldridge WS9 ....256 A4
  Brownhills WS9 ....244 C1
Bridal Path ST5 ....59 A2
Bridestone Cl ST3 ....90 A4
Bridge Ave WS6 ....226 C2
Bridge Cl Audley ST7 .....39 C1
  Brownhills WS8 ....244 C3
  Weston ST18 ....138 B2
Bridge Cres ST15 ....120 A4
Bridge Croft ST6 ....42 A3
Bridge Cross Rd WS7 ...229 A4
Bridge Ct Stoke-on-T ST4 .71 C2
  Uttoxeter ST14 ....126 B4
Bridge Farm DE13 ....147 C1
Bridge Ho ST5 ....55 B1
Bridge Ind Est ST6 ....57 A4
Bridge La ST18 ....139 A2
Bridge Rd
  Armitage WS15 ....198 B2
  Coxley DY10 ....280 A3
  Market Drayton TF9 ......97 A1
  Stoke-on-T ST14 ....71 C2
  Uttoxeter ST14 ....126 B4
  Walsall WS4 ....244 A1
Bridge St
  Brierley Hill DY8 ....275 C1
  Brownhills WS8 ....244 C3
  Burton u T, Stretton DE14 ..147 C1
  Burton u T, Winshill DE14 .166 C2
  Cannock WS11 ....226 C3
  Chell Heath ST8 ....27 A1
  Newcastle-u-L ST5 .....284 B3
  Newcastle-u-L, Silverdale
    ST5 ....55 B1
  Stafford ST16 ....155 C1
  Tamworth B77 ....250 C3
  Tutbury DE13 ....146 B4
  Uttoxeter ST14 ....126 B4
Bridge Street Ind Units
  ST14 ....126 B4
Bridge Terr
  Newport TF10 ....168 C2
  Thorncliffe ST13 ....20 C3
Bridge Way WS8 ....244 C3
Bridgefoot Wlk WV8 ....239 C1
Bridgeman Ct TF11 .....203 C1
Bridgemary Cl WV10 ....240 C2
Bridgemere Garden World*
  CW5 ....67 A2
Bridges Cres WS11 .....227 C3
Bridges Rd WS11 ....227 C3
Bridgeside DE13 ....147 C1
Bridgeside Trad Est
  B77 ....250 B2
Bridgett Cl ST4 ....71 C3
Bridgewater Cl
  Congleton CW12 ....6 A1
  Penkridge ST19 ....207 C4
Bridgewater Dr WV5 ....269 C4
Bridgewater Rd WS15 ..196 C4
Bridgewater St
  Burslem ST6 ....56 B4
  Tamworth B77 ....250 B3
Bridgewood St ST3 .....283 C4
Bridgford Ave DE14 ....166 B3
Bridgnorth Ave WV5 ...269 C3
Bridgnorth Gr WV5 ......40 C1
Bridgnorth Rd
  Enville DY7 ....273 B1
  Kinver DY7,DY8 ....270 A2
  Kinver DY7,DY8 ....278 A4
  Perton WV6 ....264 B4
  Seisdon WV6 ....263 C3
  Stourbridge DY7,DY8 ...279 B3
  Wolv WV6 ....255 A1
  Wombourne WV5 ......269 B3
Bridgtown Bsns Ctr
  WS11 ....227 A4
Bridgtown Prim Sch
  WS11 ....226 C3
Bridgewater Cl WS9 ...244 C2
Bridgwood Rd ST11 .....91 A4
Bridle La Ellenhall ST20 .153 B4
  Swadlincote DE15 .....186 A3
Bridle Path ST3 ....283 C1
Bridle Path The
  Madeley CW3 ....68 B4
  Newcastle-u-L ST5 ......70 C2
Bridle Rd Stafford ST17 .175 B3
  Stourbridge DY8 ....279 B3
Bridle Wlk WS15 ....178 A1
Bridleway The TF9 ....97 A1
Brierley Hill Rd DY8 ....275 C1

Brierley Rd CW12 ....6 A1
Brierley St ST16 ....42 B1
Brierlow Bar SK17 ....5 A4
Briertey Hill La WS15 ...212 A2
Brieryhurst Cl ST2 ....58 B3
Brieryhurst Rd ST7 ....26 A2
Bright Cres B77 ....250 B1
Bright St Mer ST3 ....71 A2
  Stourbridge DY8 ....279 B3
Brightgreen St ST3 ....73 B3
Brighton St ST4 ....72 A4
Brighton The ST5 ....55 A1
Brights Ave 2 ST7 ....26 A1
Brightstone Cl WV10 ...240 C2
Brimfield Pl 6 WV6 .....255 C2
Brindiwell Gr ST4 ....88 B3
Brindley Ave WV11 .....242 A1
Brindley Bank Rd WS15 178 C2
Brindley Brae DY7 ......278 B3
Brindley Cl
  Albrighton WV7 ....237 A3
  2 Brierley Hill DY8 ....275 C1
  Kidsgrove ST7 ....25 C1
  Penkridge ST19 ....208 A4
  Stafford ST16 ....155 C4
  Stone ST15 ....104 C1
  Talke ST7 ....40 B4
  Wombourne WV5 ......269 B3
Brindley Cres
  Cannock WS12 ....210 B4
  Cheddleton ST13 ....45 B2
Brindley Heath Jun Sch
  DY7 ....278 A3
Brindley Heath Rd
  Cannock WS12 ....210 B4
  Rugeley WS12 ....195 B1
Brindley La ST12,ST9 ...43 B2
Brindley Mill Mus The*
  ST13 ....43 B3
Brindley Pl ST6 ....42 B3
Brindley Rd
  Cannock WS12 ....194 C1
  Rugeley WS12 ....194 C1
Brindley St ST5 ....284 B3
Brindley Way CW12 ....6 A1
Brindleys Bsns Pk
  WS11 ....210 A2
Brindleys Way ST7 ....39 C1
Brindon Cl ST3 ....73 C4
Brinkburn Cl WS15 .....178 A1
Brinley Way ST6 ....275 B3
Brinscall Gn ST6 ....42 A4
Brinsford La WV10 .....240 B4
Brinsford Rd WV10 .....240 B2
Brinsley Ave ST4 ....88 A3
Brisbane Rd ST16 ......155 A4
Brisbane Way WS12 ...210 C2
Brisley Hill ST4 ....71 C3
Bristol Cl WS11 ....210 A1
Bristol St
  Newcastle-u-L ST5 ......56 B3
  Wolv WV3 ....266 A4
Britania Dr DE13 ....166 B4
Britannia Gn DY3 ......271 C3
Britannia Park Ind Est
  ST6 ....57 A4
Britannia St 6 ST13 .....30 C3
Britannia Way WS13 ...231 C4
Brittain Ave ST5 ....55 C4
Brittain Rd ST13 ....45 B3
Britannia Stadium (Stoke City
  FC) ST4 ....72 B2
Brittle Pl ST6 ....42 B1
Britton St ST4 ....56 C1
Brixham Cl ST2 ....57 C1
Brizlincote La DE15 ....167 B1
Brizlincote St DE15 ....166 C1
Broad Eye ST16 ....155 B2
Broad La
  Church Eaton ST20 ....171 C1
  Endon ST6 ....43 B4
  Great Wyrley WS3 .....242 C2
  Lichfield WS14 ....231 B3
  Walsall WS4 ....244 B1
  Whittington WS13 ......25 C1
  Wolv WV3 ....265 C4
Broad Lane Gdns WS3 .243 A1
Broad Mdw WS9 ....256 A4
Broad Mdw Croft ST6 ..155 A2
Broad Meadow Ct ST5 ...57 C1
Broad Meadow La WS6 .227 C2
Broad Oaks ST17 ......174 C3
Broad St Cannock WS11 .226 C3
  Hanley ST1 ....282 A1
  Kingswinford DY6 ......275 B3
  Leek ST13 ....30 C3
  Newcastle-u-L ST5 .....284 B3
  Stafford ST16 ....155 B2
Broad Way WS4 ....244 B1
Broadacres WV9 ....224 A2
Broadfield Cl DY6 ......275 B3
Broadfield House Glass
  Mus* DY6 ....235 B3
Broadfield Rd ST6 ....41 B4
Broadholes La ST19 ...205 A3
Broadhurst Cl WS12 ...194 C1
Broadhurst Gn WS12 ...194 C1
Broadhurst Green Rd
  ST19,WS12 ....194 B1
Broadhurst St ST6 ....42 A1
Broadlands
  Burton u T DE13 ....166 B4
  Wolv WV10 ....240 B3
Broadlands Rise WS14 .231 B4
Broadlawns Dr ST4 ......73 A3
Broadlee B77 ....251 B1
Broadmeadow DY6 ....275 C4
Broadmine St ST4 ....72 C3

Broadoak Way ST3 ....72 C1
Broadoaks Cl WS11 ....227 C3
Broadsmeath B77 ......250 B1
Broadstone Cl WV4 ....266 B3
Broadway Cannock WS12 209 C3
  Codsall WV8 ....238 C2
  Meir ST3 ....72 C1
  Newport TF10 ....169 A2
  Wolv, Bushbury WV10 ..240 C1
  Wolv, Compton WV3 ...255 B1
Broadway Ct 3 ST3 .....72 C1
Broadway Gdns WV10 ..240 C1
Broadway Gn ST4 ....49 A2
Broadway Pl 5 ST13 ....73 C1
Broadway St DE14 .....166 B1
Broadway The
  Dudley DY1 ....271 C2
  Stourbridge DY8 ....279 B3
  Wombourne WV5 ......270 A3
Broadwell La WV6 .....253 A1
Broc ST13 ....208 A4
Brockbank Pl ST6 ....42 A3
Brockeridge Cl WV12 ..242 B1
Brockhill TF9 ....99 B3
Brockhurst La B75 .....259 A4
Brockhurst Rd B75 .....258 B1
Brocklehurst Way ST1 ...57 C4
Brockley Sq ST1 ....282 B3
Brockley's Wlk DY7 ....278 A2
Brocksford Ct DE6 .....127 C2
Brocksford Hall Sch
  DE6 ....127 C4
Brocksford St ST4 ......283 B5
Brockton La ST21 .....117 B2
Brocton Cres ST17 ....175 C2
Brocton Hts ST17 ......176 B2
Brocton La ST17 ......175 C3
Brocton Rd ST17 ......176 B3
Brogan St ST4 ....72 C3
Bromfield Ct WV6 .....255 A2
Bromford Dale 2 WV6 .255 C2
Bromford Pl ST1 ....282 A1
Bromford Rise WV3 ....266 A4
Bromley Cl WS12 ......210 B4
Bromley Ct ST1 ....282 A4
Bromley Gdns WV8 ....239 A2
Bromley Hills Prim Sch
  DY6 ....275 C3
Bromley Ho WV4 ......266 A3
Bromley Hough ST4 .....71 C3
Bromley La DY6 ....275 C2
Bromley Lodge WV4 ...266 A3
Bromley Pl WV4 ....266 A3
Bromley St Hanley ST1 .282 A4
  Wolv WV2 ....266 B3
Bromleyhedge La ST13 .48 B2
Brompton Dr ST2 ....43 A2
Brompton Lawns WV6 .255 A2
Bromsberrow Way ST3 ..90 A4
Bromsgrove Pl ST13 ...283 A3
Bromwich Dr WS13 ....215 B4
Bromwynd Cl WV2 ....266 A3
Bronant Wlk 14 ST6 .....57 A4
Bronte Cl DE14 ....166 B4
Bronte Ct B79 ....250 A3
Bronte Dr ST1 ....210 B1
Bronte Gr ST2 ....43 A1
Bronte Rd WV2 ....266 C3
Brook Ave B77 ....250 B2
Brook Cl Brewood WV9 .224 A2
  Brownhills WS9 ....245 A2
  Doveridge DE6 ....127 B4
  Endon ST9 ....44 A4
  Forsbrook ST11 ....91 A4
  Lichfield WS13 ....214 A1
  Penkridge ST19 ....207 C4
Brook Cres DY6 ....275 B4
Brook End
  Burntwood WS7 ......229 A2
  Fazeley B78 ....261 A4
  Haughton ST18 ....172 C3
  Longdon WS15 ....197 C1
Brook Gdns ST6 ....16 B1
Brook Glen Rd ST17 ...174 C4
Brook Gr WV8 ....239 A1
Brook Ho TF10 ....168 C2
Brook House La WV10 .241 A4
Brook House Rd ST5 ....55 C4
Brook Houses Ind Est
  ST10 ....76 A1
Brook La Brocton ST17 .176 B2
  Brownhills WS9 ....244 C2
  Church Leigh ST10 ....108 C3
  Endon ST9 ....43 C4
  Great Wyrley WS6 ....242 C2
  Newcastle-u-L ST5 ....284 B2
  Ranton ST18 ....153 B2
Brook Mdws WV8 .....239 A2
Brook Meadow Rd WS4 .244 B1
Brook Pl
  Newcastle-u-L ST5 ......71 B3
  Stoke-on-T ST4 ....56 C1
Brook Prim Sch The
  DY8 ....275 C1
Brook Rd
  Cheslyn Hay WS6 .....226 C2
  Trentham ST4 ....88 A4
  Wombourne WV5 .....269 C3
Brook Sq 1 WS15 .....196 C4
Brook St Biddulph ST8 ..27 A3
  Burton u T DE14 ....166 C2
  Burton u T DE14 ....166 B2
  Kingswinford DY6 .....270 A1
  Leek ST13 ....30 C3
  Newcastle-u-L ST5 ......55 B1
  Sedgley DY3 ....271 B2
  Stoke-on-T ST4 ....72 A4

Brook St continued
  Stourbridge DY8 ....279 C3
  Swadlincote DE11 ....186 C3
Brook Vale WS11 ......226 C4
Brookbank Gdns ST3 ..271 A1
Brookbank Rd DY3 ....271 A1
Brookdale ST3 ....271 B2
Brookdale Dr WV4 ....265 C3
Brooke Rd WS12 ......209 C3
Brookers Ct ST4 ....72 C3
Brookfield TF9 ....99 B3
Brookfield Ave ST9 .....43 C4
Brookfield Cl ST10 ......62 A2
Brookfield Ct Hanley ST1 .282 B4
  Haughton ST18 ....172 C3
  Stone ST15 ....120 B3
Brookfield Dr WS11 ...226 C4
Brookfield Rd
  Aldridge WS9 ....245 A1
  Codsall WV8 ....239 A2
  Norton-in-I-M ST20 ....43 B2
  Stoke-on-T ST4 ....71 C3
Brookfields Rd ST10 ....62 A4
Brookfields Way ST10 ...62 A4
Brookglade ST3 ....91 A4
Brookhay La WS13 ....215 C2
Brookhill Cl WV12 .....242 B1
Brookhill Way WV12 ..242 B1
Brookhouse Cl WV10 ..241 A3
Brookhouse Ct ST14 ..126 C1
Brookhouse Dr ST12 ...88 B1
Brookhouse Green Prim Sch
  ST2 ....58 B1
Brookhouse La
  Bucknall ST2 ....58 C2
  Cheddleton ST13 ....45 A2
  Congleton CW12 ....6 B1
  Featherstone WV10 ...241 A3
Brookhouse Rd
  Cheadle ST10 ....76 A2
  Gnosall ST20 ....171 B4
  Meir ST3 ....74 A1
Brookhouse Way
  Cheadle ST10 ....76 A1
  Gnosall ST20 ....171 B3
Brookland Ave ST13 ...283 A1
Brookland Rd
  Brownhills WS9 ....244 C2
  Chell Heath ST6 ....41 C3
Brooklands DY8 ....275 C1
Brooklands Ave WS6 ..226 C2
Brooklands Cl ST14 ...126 A3
Brooklands Gr WS9 ...244 C2
Brooklands Rd
  Albrighton WV7 ....237 A3
  Cannock WS11 ....210 A2
Brooklands Sch ST16 ..155 B3
Brooklands The DY3 ...269 C1
Brooklands Way ST13 ...45 C4
Brooklime Gdns
  Featherstone WV10 ...241 A4
  Stafford ST16 ....155 A3
Brooklyn Gr DY6 ......275 A4
Brooklyn Rd
  Burntwood WS7 ......229 A2
  Cannock WS12 ....210 B1
Brookmead Gr ST4 ......73 A1
Brookmead Ind Est
  ST16 ....155 C4
Brookside Burslem ST6 ..56 B4
  Burton u T DE15 ......167 A2
  Enville DY7 ....273 B2
  Kingsley ST10 ....62 A2
  Ranton ST18 ....153 B3
  Rolleston DE13 ....147 A2
  Sedgley DY3 ....271 B1
Brookside Ave TF10 ...168 C1
Brookside Bsns Ctr
  ST15 ....118 A3
Brookside Bsns Pk
  ST14 ....126 B4
Brookside Cl
  Newcastle-u-L ST5 ....284 A1
  Wombourne WV5 .....269 C3
Brookside Ct ST10 ......76 A2
Brookside Dr Endon ST9 .44 A4
  Fenton ST3 ....72 C1
Brookside Gdns ST19 .221 C4
Brookside Ind Est ST6 ..56 B4
Brookside La ST15 ....119 C4
Brookside Rd
  Barton-u-N DE13 ......183 B1
  Tamworth B78 ....249 B1
  Uttoxeter ST14 ....126 B4
Brookside Way
  Blakedown DY10 ......281 A1
  Kingswinford DY6 .....275 B3
  Norton-in-I-M ST20 ....43 B2
Brookvale Dr ST3 ....73 C2
Brookweed B77 ....251 A2
Brookwillows 5 ST7 ...175 B4
Brookwood Cl ST5 ......71 A2
Brookwood Rd DY3 ....74 A1
Broom Hollow TF9 .....99 C3
Broom Leam TF9 ....99 B2
Broom St ST1 ....282 C4
Broom's La DE6 ....129 A1
Broome Cl DE13 ....199 A3
Broome Hill ST5 ....71 B1
Broome La ST7 ....281 C1
Broome Wlk WS10 ....198 B2
Broomfield Ave B78 ...261 A4
Broomfield Cl
  Newport TF10 ....168 B2
  Stone ST15 ....120 A3
Broomfield La DE6,ST10 .79 C1
Broomfield Pl TF10 ....168 B2
Broomfield Pl N ST1 ....57 A2

Broomfield Pl S ST1 ....57 A2
Broomfield Rd
  Newport TF10 ....168 B2
  Norton-in-I-M ST6 .....42 B3
Broomfields ST8 ....17 A1
Broomhill Bank WS11 .209 C2
Broomhill Cl WS11 ....209 C2
Broomhill St ST6 ....41 B2
Brooms Rd ST15 ....120 A3
Broomstead Cres ST18 .155 A3
Broomyclose La ST14 ..111 A2
Brough Cl Leek ST13 ....30 C3
Brough Rd WV4,WV14 .266 C2
Brough La ST14 ....88 A4
Brough Rd DE15 ......167 B2
Broughton Cl ST16 ....155 B4
Broughton Cres ST12 ...88 C1
Broughton Ct WV6 ....255 A2
Brow Hill ST13 ....30 C3
Brown Ave
  Lawton-gate ST7 ....25 A3
  Tamworth B77 ....261 B4
Brown La SK17 ....3 A2
Brown Lees Ind Est ST8 .27 A2
Brown Lees Rd
  Biddulph ST8 ....27 A2
  Kidsgrove ST7 ....26 C2
Brown St Burslem ST6 ..57 A4
  Wolv WV2 ....266 B4
Brown's La Dordon B78 ..262 B3
  Tamworth B79 ....250 B4
  Yoxall DE13 ....182 A1
Brown's Lake DY7 .....273 B2
Brownfield Rd ST3 ......74 A1
Brownhill Rd ST6 ....43 A4
Brownhills Bsns Pk ST6 .41 A1
Brownhills Com Sch
  WS8 ....228 C1
Brownhills High Sch WS6 .41 C1
Brownhills Rd
  Brownhills WS9 ....245 A2
  Norton Canes WS11 ..228 A2
  Tunstall ST6 ....41 B1
Brownhills West Prim Sch
  WS8 ....228 B1
Brownhills West Sta*
  WS7 ....228 B2
Browning Cl Cheadle ST10 .76 B1
  Tamworth B79 ....249 C4
Browning Cres WV10 ..240 B1
Browning Gr
  Perton WV6 ....254 C2
  Talke ST7 ....40 B4
Browning Rd
  Burntwood WS7 ......229 B4
  Longton ST3 ....72 C1
  Sedgley DY3 ....271 A2
Browning St ST16 .....155 B2
Brownley Rd ST6 ....42 B1
Browns Wlk WS15 ....178 B1
Brownsea Pl ST3 ....72 C2
Brownsfield Rd WS13 .214 B1
Brownshill Bsns Pk
  WS8 ....244 C3
Brownsholme B79 ....249 B3
Brownshore La WV11 .242 A2
Brownswall Rd DY3 ...255 A2
Broxwood Pk WV6 ....255 A2
Bruford Rd WV3 ....266 A4
Brunda La ST13 ....45 A2
Brundall Oval ST7 ......58 B1
Brundle Ave ST16 .....155 A2
Brunel Cl
  Burntwood WS7 ......229 A4
  Stafford ST16 ....155 C4
  Tamworth B79 ....250 A3
Brunel Ct Brewood WV10 .224 B3
  Wombourne WV5 .....270 A4
Brunel Gr WV6 ....254 C3
Brunel Wlk ST3 ....283 C4
Brunslow Cl WV10 ....240 B1
Brunswick Mill 3 ST13 .30 C3
Brunswick Pl ST1 .....282 B2
Brunswick Rd WS11 ..209 C1
Brunswick St Hanley ST1 .282 B3
  22 Leek ST13 ....30 C3
  Newcastle-u-L ST5 ....155 B1
Brunswick Terr ST13 ..30 C3
Brunt St ST6 ....56 A4
Brutus Rd ST7 ....55 B3
Bryan Ave WV4 ....265 B2
Bryan St ST1 ....282 B3
Bryans La WS15 ......178 C1
Bryans Way WS12 ....210 C2
Bryant Rd ST2 ....58 A3
Brymbo Rd ST5 ....55 C3
Brynmarw Rd WV14,
  WV14 ....266 C2
Bryony DE14 ....185 A4
Buccleuch Rd ST1 ......73 B1
Buckden B77 ....251 B1
Buckingham Cl
  Burton u T DE13 ......166 B4
  Stafford ST17 ....156 B1
Buckingham Cres ST14 .72 A1
Buckingham Ct ST16 ..167 B2
Buckingham Gdns
  WS14 ....231 A3
Buckingham Gr DY6 ...275 B4
Buckingham Pl 9
  WS11 ....210 B1
Buckingham Rd
  Tamworth B79 ....249 C4
  Wolv WV4 ....266 A3

Buckingham Rise DY1 ... 271 C1
Buckland Cl WS12 ... 210 B1
Buckland Gr ST4 ... 88 B3
Buckland Rd ST4 ... 136 B1
Buckland Wlk TF10 ... 168 C3
Buckley Cl ST14 ... 125 B4
Buckley Rd
Chell Heath ST6 ... 42 B3
Wolv WV4 ... 265 B3
Buckley's Row ST5 ... 284 B2
Buckmaster Ave ST5 ... 71 B3
Bucknall Hospl ST2 ... 58 B2
Bucknall New Rd ST1 ... 287 C4
Bucknall Old Rd ST1 ... 282 C3
Bucknall Rd Hanley ST1 ... 57 C2
Wolv WV11 ... 242 A1
Buckpool Sch DY8 ... 275 C2
Buckthorn Cl WV12 ... 209 C4
Buckton Cl B75 ... 258 C1
Buds Rd WS15 ... 211 C3
Buglawton Hall Speci Sch
CW12 ... 6 B3
Buglawton Prim Sch
CW12 ... 6 B3
Buildwas Cl WS3 ... 242 C1
Bull Hill ST16 ... 155 C2
Bull La Chell Heath ST6 ... 27 A1
Wombourne WV5 ... 265 A4
Bull Ring Claverley WV5 ... 271 B4
Sedgley DY3 ... 271 B4
Bull Ring The ST18 ... 138 B1
Bull St DY3 ... 271 B1
Bulldog La WS13 ... 214 A1
Buller St Hanley ST1 ... 282 C1
Wolv WV4 ... 266 C3
Bullgap La DE6 ... 65 B2
Bullmoor La WS14 ... 230 A1
Bullocks House Rd ST7 ... 26 C2
Bullows Rd WS8 ... 244 B3
Bulstrode St 6 ST6 ... 56 C4
Bumblehole Mdws WV5 ... 269 C4
Bun La Blymhill TF10 ... 188 B1
Great Chatwell TF10 ... 203 A4
Bungalows The ST20 ... 131 B2
Bungay La Sturton ST19 ... 207 B4
Bunny Hill ST5 ... 71 B3
Bunt's La WV9 ... 43 B2
Bunting Cl ST14 ... 126 A3
Bunting The
Cheddleton ST9 ... 60 A4
Kingsley ST10 ... 61 B2
Buntingdale Rd TF9 ... 112 A4
Bunyan Pl WS11 ... 209 C2
Burcham Cl ST16 ... 155 A4
Burdock Cl WS11 ... 210 A2
Burford Rd Stafford ST17 ... 156 B1
Wheaton Aston ST19 ... 205 A3
Burford Way ST2 ... 58 A1
Burgage Cl TF9 ... 97 B1
Burgage Ct TF10 ... 168 C1
Burgage The
Eccleshall ST21 ... 133 C4
Market Drayton TF9 ... 97 B1
Burgess St ST6 ... 56 C4
Burgesses The DY7 ... 278 A2
Burgis Cl ST13 ... 45 B2
Burgoyne St WS11 ... 210 A3
Burgundy Gr 6 ST3 ... 90 A4
Burland Ave WV6 ... 255 C3
Burland Rd ST5 ... 40 B1
Burleigh Cl WS12 ... 210 A4
Burleigh Croft WS7 ... 229 A2
Burleigh Gr ST5 ... 56 B2
Burleigh Rd WV3 ... 266 A4
Burlidge Rd ST6 ... 42 A3
Burlington Ave ST5 ... 56 B2
Burlington Ct B78 ... 261 A4
Burlington Dr ST17 ... 174 A4
Burmarsh Wlk
16 Burslem ST6 ... 56 C4
Wolv WV4 ... 255 C4
Burnaby Rd ST6 ... 41 B3
Burnell Gdns WV3 ... 265 C4
Burnet Gr WV10 ... 241 A4
Burnett Ct ST16 ... 155 A3
Burnett Pl ST6 ... 42 B2
Burnett Rd B74 ... 257 A1
Burnfield Dr WS15 ... 178 B1
Burnfields Cl WS9 ... 256 A4
Burnham Ave ST17 ... 175 B3
Burnham Cl DY6 ... 275 C2
Burnham Gn WS11 ... 226 A4
Burnside DE13 ... 147 A2
Burnside Ct ST3 ... 90 A4
Burnthill La WS15 ... 196 C4
Burntwood Rd
Burntwood WS7 ... 229 B2
Norton Canes WS11 ... 228 A4
Burntwood Recn Ctr
WS7 ... 228 C3
Burntwood Town Sh Ctr
WS7 ... 228 C4
Burntwood Com Prim Sch
ST6 ... 42 A3

Burnwood Ct ST6 ... 42 B1
Burnwood Gr ST7 ... 26 A1
Burnwood Pl ST6 ... 42 A3
Burrington Dr ST4 ... 88 B1
Burrows Rd ST6 ... 275 C2
Burrows The DE11 ... 186 C3
Burslem Cl WS3 ... 243 A2
Burslem Enm Ctr ST6 ... 57 A4
Burslem Cl ST17 ... 174 B3
Bursley Prim Sch ST6 ... 56 A4
Bursley Rd ST6 ... 57 A4
Bursley Way ST5 ... 56 A4
Bursnips Rd WV11 ... 242 B2
Burt St ST3 ... 74 A2
Burton Bank La
Stafford ST17,ST18 ... 174 B3
Stafford,Mosspit ST17 ... 174 C3
Burton Borough Sch The
DE14 ... 250 B4
Burton Coll (Town Campus)
DE14 ... 166 C1
Burton Cres Hanley ST1 ... 57 C4
Kingsley ST10 ... 76 C4
Burton Cl ST17 ... 174 C4
Burton Ent Pk DE14 ... 166 C3
Burton House Gdns
ST17 ... 174 B3
Burton Manor Prim Sch
ST17 ... 174 B3
Burton Manor Rd ST17,
ST18 ... 174 B3
Burton Mews ST14 ... 110 C1
Burton Old Rd
Lichfield WS14 ... 231 C4
Streethay WS13 ... 231 C4
Burton Old Rd E WS14 ... 231 C4
Burton Old Rd W WS14 ... 231 B4
Burton Pl ST1 ... 282 C3
Burton Rd Alrewas DE13 ... 201 A2
Burton u t DE14 ... 166 B1
Dudley DY1 ... 271 C2
Elford B79 ... 216 C1
Linton DE11 ... 186 B1
Repton DE15,DE65 ... 148 C1
Streethay WS13 ... 214 C1
Tutbury DE13 ... 146 B2
Whittington WS14 ... 232 C4
Willington DE65 ... 148 C4
Burton Sq ST17 ... 174 C4
Burton St Leek ST13 ... 36 B3
Tutbury DE13 ... 146 B3
Burton Tech Coll (Rolleston
Campus) DE13 ... 147 B2
Burton upon Trent Sta
DE14 ... 166 B1
Burway Mdw DE11 ... 201 A1
Bury Ring ST18 ... 173 B3
Bush Cl WV7 ... 237 A3
Bush Dr WS15 ... 178 C1
Bush Gr WS3 ... 243 A2
Bushberry Ct ST15 ... 119 C3
Bushbury Hall Jun & Inf Schs
WV10 ... 240 C1
Bushbury La WV10 ... 240 C1
Bushey Cl B74 ... 256 C1
Bushfield Rd WV7 ... 237 A3
Bushton La DE13 ... 146 A1
Bustomley La ST10 ... 108 A3
Bute St ST4 ... 283 A4
Butler Cl DE14 ... 166 A2
Butler St ST4 ... 72 A3
Butlers Lane Sta B74 ... 258 A2
Butt La ST18 ... 154 A1
Butler St B78 ... 258 A2
Butterbank La ST18 ... 154 A1
Butterfield Ct WV6 ... 254 B2
Butterfield Pl ST16 ... 41 C2
Butterhill Bank ST18 ... 121 A1
Butterhill La ST15,ST18 ... 121 C3
Butterhill Rd WS12 ... 262 A4
Buttermere Cl
Burslem ST6 ... 56 C4
Cannock WS11 ... 210 A2
Wolv WV6 ... 255 B4
Buttermere Dr WV6 ... 254 C2
Buttermere Dr WV11 ... 242 A2
Buttermere Gr WV11 ... 242 A1
Butthouse La ST5,ST21 ... 102 B3
Buttons Farm Rd WV4 ... 265 B2
Butts Cl WS11 ... 227 C2
Butts Croft DE13 ... 200 C2
Butts Gn ST2 ... 58 B3
Butts La
Norton Canes WS11 ... 227 C2
Warslow SK17 ... 23 B1
Butts Rd
Market Drayton TF9 ... 97 A1
Wolv WV4 ... 265 C2
Butts The Betley CW3 ... 53 A3
Burston ST18 ... 130 B1
Butts Way ST13 ... 63 C4
Buxton Ave Fazeley B78 ... 261 A4
Newcastle-u-L ST5 ... 55 A1
Buxton Cl WS3 ... 243 B2
Buxton Old Rd CW12 ... 6 A2
Buxton Rd
Alstonefield DE6 ... 35 A3
Congleton CW12 ... 6 B3
Leek ST13 ... 31 A4
Longnor SK17 ... 13 A4
Walsall WS3 ... 243 B2
Byatt's Gr ST3 ... 283 A2

Bycars Farm Croft
WS13 ... 215 C4
Bycars La ST6 ... 42 C1
Bycars Rd ST6 ... 41 C1
Byland B77 ... 250 B2
Byland Pl ST5 ... 71 A3
Byland Way WS3 ... 242 C1
Byrd's Cl ST14 ... 125 C4
Byrd's La ST14 ... 125 C4
Byrkley Park Ctr*
DE13 ... 164 A2
Byrkley St DE14 ... 166 A2
Byrne Rd WV2 ... 266 B4
Byron Ave
Burton u T DE15 ... 185 C4
Lichfield WS14 ... 231 A3
Byron Cl Burntwood WS7 ... 211 C1
Cheadle ST10 ... 76 A1
Market Drayton TF9 ... 112 A4
Stafford ST15 ... 156 A3
Byron Cotts Sedgley DY3 ... 271 A3
Sutton Coldfield B74 ... 257 C3
Byron Ct Kidsgrove ST7 ... 41 A4
Sutton Coldfield B74 ... 258 A3
Byron Pl Cannock WS11 ... 209 C3
Rugeley WS15 ... 178 B1
Byron Rd
Essington WV10 ... 241 A1
Tamworth B79 ... 250 A4
Byron St 7 Leek ST13 ... 30 B3
Stoke-on-T ST4 ... 56 B1
Bywater Gr 3 ST3 ... 73 B3
Byways WS3 ... 243 B2

C

Cable St WV2 ... 266 C4
Cackleshill La DE6 ... 81 B1
Cadeby Gr ST2 ... 43 A1
Cadley Hill Ind Est
DE11 ... 186 C1
Cadley Hill Rd DE11 ... 186 C2
Cadman Cres ST6 ... 42 C2
Cadman's La WS3 ... 243 B3
Cadogan Rd B77 ... 261 A3
Caernarvon Ave ST15 ... 120 B3
Caernarvon Cl
Burton u T DE13 ... 166 C4
Market Drayton TF9 ... 97 C1
Caernarvon Way DY1 ... 271 C1
Cairn Cl ST2 ... 58 B2
Cairns Cl DE15 ... 167 B2
Cairns Dr ST16 ... 156 A3
Caister B77 ... 251 A3
Caistor Cl Fazeley B78 ... 260 A4
Norton-in-t-M ST22 ... 43 A1
Calais Rd DE14 ... 166 A3
Calcot Dr WV6 ... 255 C4
Caldbeck Pl ST11 ... 282 C3
Calder Dr B77 ... 251 A1
Calder Rise DY3 ... 271 C2
Caldercotts TF10 ... 168 C2
Caldervale Dr 7 ST17 ... 175 B3
Caldew Gr ST4 ... 88 B3
Cale Cl B77 ... 250 B1
Caledonia Rd Hanley ST4 ... 57 A1
Wolv WV2 ... 266 C4
Caledonian B77 ... 250 C1
Calgary Cres DE15 ... 167 B2
California St ST3 ... 283 A3
Californian Gr WV7 ... 228 C4
Callaghan Gr 3 WS11 ... 210 B1
Callender Pl ST4 ... 57 A4
Callingwood La DE13 ... 164 C2
Callis Wlk B77 ... 261 C3
Callow Hill La ST10 ... 75 B2
Calrofold Dr ST5 ... 40 B1
Calvary Cres ST2 ... 73 B4
Calveley Cl ST15 ... 118 C3
Calver St 8 ST9 ... 41 B2
Calverley St ST13 ... 283 D2
Calvert Gr ST5 ... 56 A4
Calvin Cl Wolv WV10 ... 240 B2
Wombourne WV5 ... 269 C3
Calving Hill WS11 ... 209 C1
Camberley Ave WV4 ... 266 C1
Camberley Dr WV4 ... 266 A2
Camberley Rd DY6 ... 275 C2
Camberwell Gr ST4 ... 88 B3
Camborne Cl ST17 ... 175 C4
Camborne Cres ST5 ... 71 A3
Camborne Cl CW12 ... 15 C4
Cambria St WS11 ... 209 B2
Cambrian B77 ... 251 A1
Cambrian La ST15 ... 178 B2
Cambrian Way ST22 ... 58 B2
Cambridge Cl
Aldridge WS9 ... 256 A4
Biddulph ST8 ... 16 B1
Cambridge Ct ST15 ... 71 B2
Cambridge Dr ST5 ... 55 C1
Cambridge Gr
Burton u T DE14 ... 166 A1
Hanley ST1 ... 282 A2
Stafford ST16 ... 156 A2
Cambridge Rd
Stoke-on-T ST4 ... 250 C2
Camden St
Brownhills WS9 ... 244 C2
Fenton ST4 ... 73 C3
Camden Way DY6 ... 270 B1
Camelford Ct ST17 ... 175 C4
Camellia Cl ST4 ... 56 C1
Camelia Gdns
Brierley Hill DY8 ... 275 C1
Codsall WV8 ... 239 C2
Camelot Cl
2 Burton u T DE13 ... 147 C1

Camelot continued
Cannock WS11 ... 209 C2
Trentham ST4 ... 88 B2
Cameo Dr DY6 ... 279 C4
Camco Way ST16 ... 155 A4
Cameron Cl DE15 ... 167 A1
Camhouses B77 ... 251 A1
Camillus Rd ST5 ... 55 C1
Camoys Cl 16 ST6 ... 57 A4
Camoys Rd ST6 ... 57 A4
Camp Hill
Brierley Hill DY8 ... 275 C1
Maer ST5 ... 84 A3
Camp Hill Rd DY7 ... 273 C4
Camp Rd Brocton WS12 ... 194 B3
Chell Heath ST6 ... 42 B1
Sutton Coldfield B75 ... 258 B3
Campbell Ave ST13 ... 30 B2
Campbell Cl
Congleton CW12 ... 6 A2
Rugeley WS15 ... 178 B1
Tamworth B79 ... 249 C4
Campbell Pl ST4 ... 72 A4
Campbell St
Market Drayton TF9 ... 97 B1
Stoke-on-T ST4 ... 72 A3
Campbell Terr ST1 ... 57 C3
Campian's Ave WS6 ... 226 B1
Campion Ave ST5 ... 56 B2
Campion Cl
Eccleshall ST21 ... 133 B3
Wombourne WV5 ... 269 C3
Campion Dr
Featherstone WV10 ... 241 A4
Tamworth B77 ... 250 B2
Camrose Gdns WV9 ... 240 A2
Camsey La WS7 ... 229 C4
Canal La ST6 ... 41 B1
Canal Mews The ST4 ... 88 B3
Canal Rd CW12 ... 15 C4
Canal Side ST12 ... 88 B3
Canal St Brierley Hill DY8 ... 279 C3
Burslem ST6 ... 56 B4
Burton u T DE14 ... 166 B1
Canal View Bsns Pk
WS15 ... 197 A3
Canalside Cl
Penkridge ST19 ... 207 C4
Walsall WS3 ... 243 C1
Canalside Rd ST15 ... 104 C1
Canary Rd ST2 ... 73 B4
Canaway Wlk WS15 ... 178 B1
Canberra Cres ST3 ... 90 B4
Canberra Dr ST16 ... 156 A2
Candle La CW3 ... 67 A1
Canford Cres WV8 ... 238 C2
Cannel Rd WV7 ... 228 B3
Canning Rd B77 ... 250 C2
Canning St ST4 ... 72 C3
Cannock Wood Rd
WS12 ... 211 A3
Cannock Chase Ctry Pk*
WS12 ... 176 B1
* Rugeley WS12 ... 195 A2
Cannock Chase Ent Ctr
WS12 ... 195 B1
Cannock Chase High Sch
WS11 ... 209 B1
Cannock Chase Tech Coll
Cannock WS11 ... 209 B1
Cannock, Bridgtown WS11 ... 209 A1
Cannock Com Hospl
WS11 ... 209 C1
Cannock Ind Ctr WS11 ... 226 B3
Cannock Rd
Brocton ST17 ... 176 A2
Burntwood, Chase Terrace
WS7 ... 229 A4
Burntwood, Gorstey Ley
WS7 ... 229 A4
Cannock, Heath Hayes
WS12 ... 227 B4
Cannock, High Town
WS11,WS12 ... 210 A3
Featherstone WV10 ... 241 A2
Huntington ST19 ... 208 A4
Penkridge ST19 ... 192 C1
Stafford ST17 ... 175 B3
Cannock Sh Ctr 16
WS11 ... 209 C1
Cannock Sta WS11 ... 226 C4
Cannock Wood Ind Est
WS12 ... 211 A3
Cannock Wood Rd
WS12 ... 211 A3
Cannock Wood St
WS12 ... 211 A3
Cannon Pl ST1 ... 282 B2
Cannon Rd WS11 ... 270 A3
Cannon St ST1 ... 282 C3
Canons Cl ST15 ... 120 A3
Canterbury Cl
Lichfield WS13 ... 214 B2
Tamworth B77 ... 250 B2
Walsall WS3 ... 244 A2
Canterbury Dr
Burntwood WS7 ... 229 C4
Chell Heath ST6 ... 42 A2
Perton WV6 ... 254 C2
Canterbury Rd
Burton u T DE15 ... 167 B2
Wolv WV4 ... 265 C3
Canterbury Way WS12 ... 210 C4
Canvey Gr ST3 ... 90 A4
Canwell Dr B75 ... 259 A3
Cape Ave ST17 ... 174 A4

Cape Cl WS8 ... 245 A3
Cape St ST1 ... 282 B4
Capesthorne Cl ST19 ... 59 A2
Capewell St ST3 ... 283 C4
Capper Cl ST17 ... 26 A1
Capper St ST6 ... 41 C2
Capper's La WS14 ... 232 A4
Cappers La WS13,WS14 ... 231 C4
Capricorn Way ST6 ... 41 C3
Cardiff Gr ST1 ... 282 B1
Cardiff St WS13 ... 283 B3
Cardiff St WV3 ... 266 A4
Cardigan Ave WS15 ... 196 B3
Cardigan Gr ST4 ... 88 B3
Cardigan Ho WS12 ... 210 B3
Cardigan Pl WS12 ... 210 B3
Cardinal Griffin RC High Sch
WS11 ... 209 B1
Cardinal Way WS11 ... 209 B1
Cardington Cl ST5 ... 71 A2
Cardoness Pl DY1 ... 271 C1
Cardway ST5 ... 56 A4
Cardwell St ST1 ... 57 C3
Carey B77 ... 262 A3
Carfax WS11 ... 226 C4
Carier Ave WV8 ... 239 A2
Carina Gdns ST6 ... 42 B1
Carisbrooke B77 ... 251 A1
Carisbrooke Dr
5 Burton u T DE13 ... 147 C1
Stafford ST17 ... 174 A4
Carisbrooke Gdns
WV10 ... 240 C2
Carisbrooke Rd
Perton WV6 ... 255 A2
Wolv WV10 ... 240 C2
Carisbrooke Way ST4 ... 88 B3
Carlcroft B77 ... 251 A1
Carling Cl ST16 ... 155 A1
Carling Gr ST4 ... 73 A3
Carlisle Rd WS11 ... 226 A4
Carlisle St ST13 ... 283 B1
Carlos Cl ST10 ... 76 B2
Carlos Pl ST5 ... 41 A1
Carlton Ave Aldridge B74 ... 257 A1
Chell Heath ST6 ... 42 A2
Endon ST6 ... 43 A3
Newcastle-u-L ST5 ... 71 A2
Carlton Cl Cannock WS12 ... 210 B3
Cheadle ST10 ... 76 B1
Endon ST6 ... 43 A3
Carlton Cres
Burntwood WS7 ... 229 A4
Tamworth B79 ... 249 C4
Carlton Croft B74 ... 257 A1
Carlton Ct DE14 ... 166 A2
Carlton Ho B75 ... 258 A1
Carlton Rd Stoke-on-T ST4 ... 72 B4
Wolv WV3 ... 266 A4
Carlton Sq ST17 ... 174 A4
Carlton St DE13 ... 166 A3
Carlyon Pl ST1 ... 57 B3
Carmel Cl WS12 ... 210 B3
Carmichael Cl WS14 ... 231 B4
Carmount Rd ST2 ... 58 B2
Carmountside Prim Sch
ST2 ... 58 A4
Carnation Cl ST3 ... 74 A4
Carnforth Cl DY6 ... 275 A4
Carnforth Gr ST7 ... 41 C4
Carnoustie B77 ... 251 B3
Carnoustie Cl WS3 ... 243 A2
Carol Gdns DY8 ... 279 C4
Caroline Cl ST19 ... 59 A2
Caroline Cres ST6 ... 41 A3
Caroline St ST13 ... 283 C4
Caroline Terr DE14 ... 166 B3
Carousels The DE14 ... 166 B3
Carpenter Cl DE15 ... 167 B1
Carpenter Rd ST13 ... 283 C2
Carr Bank ST10 ... 78 A4
Carr La Audley ST7 ... 39 A1
Wetton DE6,ST13 ... 34 C1
Carr St ST7 ... 26 C1
Carriage Dr ST8 ... 16 C3
Carrick Cl WS3 ... 244 A3
Carrick Pl ST14 ... 72 A1
Carriers Fold WV5 ... 270 B4
Carriers Rd DE6 ... 148 A3
Carroll Dr ST3 ... 90 A4
Carron St ST4 ... 283 B4
Carroway Head Hill B78 ... 259 B3
Carryer Pl ST5 ... 284 C4
Carshalton Gr WV2 ... 266 C4
Carson Cl ST4 ... 88 B2
Carson Way ST16 ... 155 B2
Carter St ST14 ... 110 B4
Carters Croft ST10 ... 92 C2
Cartersfield La WS14 ... 245 B3
Cartlich St ST6 ... 41 B3
Cartlidge St ST4 ... 56 B1
Cartmel Pl ST16 ... 155 A1
Cartway The WV6 ... 254 B2
Cartwright Dr ST20 ... 171 B4
Cartwright Ho WS3 ... 243 A1

Cartwright Ind Est The
ST3 ....283 B2
Cartwright Rd B75 ....258 B2
Cartwright St
Longton ST3 ....283 B3
Wolv WV2 ....266 B4
Carver Gdns DY8 .....279 C1
Carver Rd
Burton u T DE13 .....166 B3
Stafford ST16 ....155 C3
Casa Mia Ct WS12 ....210 B3
Caswell Rd Hanley ST6 ..57 B4
Kingswinford DY6 .....275 B4
Casey La Burton u T DE14 .166 A2
Weston CW2 ....37 A3
Casey The ST13 ....48 A1
Cash La ST01 ....132 C2
Caslon Cres DY8 ......279 B2
Caspian Gr ST4 ....88 A4
Caspian Way ST19 ....205 B3
Cassandra Cl DY5 ....271 B1
Castel Cl ST5 ....70 C2
Castle Acre ST17 .....174 A4
Castle Bank ST17 .....174 A4
Castle Cl Brownhills WS8 .228 C1
Tamworth B77 ....250 C2
Castle Ct Tutbury DE13 ..146 B4
⬛ ST15 ....120 B3
Castle Dyke WS13 ....231 A4
Castle Gr ST12 ....58 A3
Castle Hayes La DE13 .146 A3
Castle Hill DE13 ......146 A4
Castle Hill Rd Alton ST10 .78 C1
Newcastle-u-l ST5 ...284 A3
Castle House Sch TF10 .168 C2
Castle Inn Rd CW12 ....16 B4
Castle Keep Ct ST5 ...284 A2
Castle Keep Mews ST5 .284 A2
Castle La CW3 ....68 C3
Castle Mount ST5 .....55 C3
Castle Park Inf Sch
DE13 ....166 A4
Castle Park Rd DE13 ..166 A4
Castle Prim Sch ST7 ...26 B3
Castle Rd
Brownhills WS8 ....245 A1
Cookley DY10 ....280 A2
Kidsgrove ST7 ....26 B4
Swadlincote DE11 ....186 C1
Tamworth B77 ....261 C3
Castle Ridge ST5 ....70 C4
Castle Ring Fort *
WS15 ....211 C3
Castle St Brownhills WS8 .228 C1
Eccleshall ST21 ......133 C4
Kinver DY7 ....278 A2
Newcastle-u-l ST5 ...284 C3
Newcastle-u-l, Chesterton
ST5 ....55 C4
Sedgley DY3 ....271 B4
Stafford ST16 ....155 B2
Tutbury DE13 ....146 B3
Castle View Biddulph ST8 .27 B3
Hatton DE65 ....146 B4
Seighford ST18 ......154 C1
Stafford ST16 ....155 B2
Tamworth B77 ....250 B2
Castle View Est ST18 ..154 C1
Castle Way ST16 ....155 B1
Castle Way The DE65 ..148 C3
Castlechurch Prim Sch
ST17 ....174 A4
Castlecroft WS11 ......227 C3
Castlecroft Ave WV3 ..265 A4
Castlecroft Gdns WV3 .265 B4
Castlecroft La WV6 ...254 C1
Castlecroft Prim Sch
WV3 ....265 A4
Castlecroft Rd WV3 ...265 A4
Castledene Dr ST16 ...155 B1
Castledine Gr ST3 .....73 C2
Castlefield St ST4 .....88 B4
Castlefields ST16 .....155 B1
Castlefort Jun Mix Inf Sch
WS9 ....245 A2
Castlefort Rd WS9 ....245 A2
Castlehall B77 ....251 A1
Castlehill Rd WS9 ....245 B2
Castleton Rd Meir ST3 ..89 C4
Walsall WS3 ....243 B2
Castleview Gr ST7 .....41 C4
Castleview Rd ST7 .....26 A2
Caswell Rd DY3 ....271 B4
Cat & Kittens La WV10 .240 C3
Catalan Cl ⬛ ST17 ...175 A4
Catalina Pl ST3 ....90 B3
Caterham Dr DY6 ......275 C2
Caterham Pl ST3 ....90 A3
Catesby Dr DY6 ....275 C4
Catharine Rd ST6 ......42 B3
Cathcart Rd DY8 ......279 C3
Cathedral Cl WS13 ....231 A4
Cathedral Rise WS13 ..231 A4
Catherine St ST5 ......56 B2
Catholic La DY3 ....271 B4
Catholme La DE13 ....201 C3
Catisfield Cres WV8 ..239 C1
Catkin Wlk WS15 .....178 B1
Catmeadow La WS15 ..197 B1
Caton Cres ST6 ....42 C1
Catsbridge La WS11 ..225 C4
Catshill Rd WS8 ....245 A4
Cauldon Ave
Cheddleton ST13 .....45 B3
Newcastle-u-l ST5 ....56 A4

Cauldon Cl ST13 ......30 C2
Cauldon Pl ST4 ....57 A1
Cauldon Prim Sch ST4 .57 B1
Cauldon Rd ST4 ....57 B1
Cauiton St ST6 ....41 C1
Caunsall Rd DY11 .....280 A3
Causeley Gdns ST2 ....58 A2
Causeley Rd ST2 ......58 A2
Causeway Pl ST13 .....33 C3
Cavalier Cir WV10 ....240 C2
Cavan's Cl WS11 ......209 C2
Cavandish Rd ST10 ....92 C3
Cavans Wood Mobile Homes
WS11 ....209 B3
Cavell Rd WS7 ....229 C4
Cavendish B79 ....249 C4
Cavendish Cl DY6 .....275 B2
Cavendish Dr DY9 ....281 C2
Cavendish Gr ST5 .....71 A2
Cavendish Rd ST13 ....57 A2
Cavendish Way WS9 ..256 A3
Caverswall La ST3 .....90 B4
Caverswall Old Rd ST11 .90 C4
Caverswall Rd
Dilhorne ST10 ....75 A2
Forsbrook ST11 ....90 C4
Meir ST3 ....74 A2
Caverswall Road Sta *
ST11 ....74 C1
Cavour St ST1 ....56 C2
Cawdry Bldgs ⬛ ST13 ..30 C3
Caxton Ct ⬛ WS11 ...226 C4
Caxton St WS11 ......226 C4
Cayley Pl ST3 ....90 B3
Cecil Ave ST6 ....282 A4
Cecil Payton Cl WS15 .160 C3
Cecil Rd DE11 ....186 C3
Cecil St Cannock WS11 .209 C2
Stourbridge DY8 .....279 C3
Cecily St ST10 ....76 C2
Cecily Terr ST10 ......76 C2
Cedar Ave
Brownhills WS8 ......245 A4
Forsbrook ST11 ....91 A3
Kidsgrove ST7 ....25 B1
Cedar Cl Burntwood WS7 .229 A3
Cannock WS12 ....195 A1
Cheadle ST10 ....76 C1
Lichfield WS14 ......231 C4
Market Drayton TF9 ..97 A1
Stourbridge DY8 .....279 B1
Uttoxeter ST14 ......110 C1
Cedar Cres Audley ST7 .39 C1
Endon ST9 ....43 C3
Kingswinford WS6 ..197 A3
Cedar Ct CW12 ....13 C4
Cedar Dr Albrighton WV7 .237 A3
Aldridge B74 ....256 C1
Tamworth B79 ......250 A4
Cedar Gdns DY7 ......277 C3
Cedar Gr Biddulph ST8 ..27 B3
Codsall WV8 ....239 A2
Fenton ST3 ....72 C2
Great Wyrley WS6 ..227 A2
Wolv WV3 ....265 C4
Cedar Ho B74 ....257 A3
Cedar Park Rd WV12 ..242 B1
Cedar Pk ST15 ....120 A4
Cedar Rd
Barton-u-N DE13 ....183 B1
Burntwood WS7 .....229 A4
Newcastle-u-l ST5 ....40 B1
Cedar Way ST17 ......175 C3
Cedar Wood Rd DY3 ..271 B3
Cedarhill ST10 ....78 B1
Cedarhill Dr WS11 ....209 C2
Cedars Ave
Kingswinford DY6 ...275 B2
Wombourne WV5 ....270 A3
Cedars Bsns Ctr The
WS11 ....226 B4
Cedars Dr ST15 ....120 A3
Cedars Hort Unit The
WV3 ....255 B1
Cedars The
⬛ Wolv WV6 ....255 C2
Wolv, Tattenhall WV6 .255 B3
Cedartree Gr ST11 ....57 C4
Cedarwood B74 ......258 A1
Cedarwood Cl WV9 ..224 A2
Celandine B77 ....250 B1
Celandine Cl
Kingswinford DY6 ...275 B2
Norton-in-t-M ST2 ....43 A1
Celandines The WV5 ..269 C3
Celebration Ct ST6 ....42 B2
Cellarhead Rd ST9 ....59 C2
Celtic Ave ST7 ....41 C4
Celtic Rd WS11 ......209 C2
Cemetery Ave ST3 ....283 B2
Cemetery Rd
Cannock WS11 ......209 C2
Hanley ST4 ....57 A1
Market Drayton TF9 ..97 A1
Newcastle-u-l, Knutton ST5 ..55 C2
Newcastle-u-l, Silverdale
ST5 ....55 B1
Weston CW2 ....37 A3
Cemetery St WS6 ....226 B1
Cemetery View
Longton ST3 ....283 B2
Newcastle-u-l ST5 ....55 C2
Cemetery Way WS3 ..243 A1
Cemlyn Ave ST3 ....72 C2
Central Ave Bucknall ST2 .58 A2
Cannock WS11 ......209 C3
Wolv WV4 ....266 C2
Central Cl WS3 ....243 A1

Central Dr Fenton ST3 ..72 C2
Sedgley DY3 ....271 B1
Walsall WS3 ....243 A1
Central St ST7 ....26 A3
Central Trad Est WV2 ..266 C4
Central Way DE13 ....166 A4
Centre Rd ST15 ......104 C1
Centurion Pk B77 ....262 A3
Centurion Way B77 ..262 A3
Century Rd ST5 ....40 C1
Century St ST1 ....282 A3
Chadsfield Rd WS15 ..178 C1
Chadsmead Prim Sch
WS13 ....214 A1
Chadsmoor CE Jun Sch
WS11 ....210 A2
Chadsmoor Inf Sch
WS11 ....210 A2
Chadswell Hts WS13 ..214 B1
Chadwell Gdns WV8 ..238 C2
Chadwell La
Gnosall TF10 ....188 A1
Woodcote TF10 ......187 C2
Chadwell Way ST2 ....58 B1
Chadwick Cl WV4 ....265 B3
Chadwick Cres WS15 .198 A4
Chadwick Ct ST5 .....196 C4
Chadwick St ST3 ....283 C3
Chadwyn Dr ST2 ......43 A1
Chaff La DE6 ....65 B1
Chaffinch Cl
Cannock WS12 ....210 A2
Sedgley DY3 ....266 B1
Chaffinch Dr Biddulph ST8 .27 C4
Uttoxeter ST14 ......126 B3
Chain La ST17 ....174 C2
Chain St ST6 ....42 B1
Chalcot Dr WS12 ....210 A4
Chaldon Cl WV9 ......240 A1
Chalfont Cl ST8 ....27 B3
Chalfont Ave WS11 ..226 B4
Chalfont Cres CW2 ....37 A1
Chalfont Gn ST2 ......58 B1
Challenge Cl ST6 ......42 B2
Challinor Ave ST13 ....30 C3
Challinor St ST6 ......41 C2
Chamberlain Ave ST4 ..72 A3
Chamberlain St ST1 ..282 B1
Chamberlain Way ST8 ..27 A4
Chamberlain's La WV4 .265 C2
Chamberlin Way WV9 .224 A1
Chance Hall La ST7 ....25 A4
Chancel Dr TF9 ....97 A1
Chancel Ind Est DY6 ..270 C1
Chancel Inf Sch WS15 .178 C1
Chancery Dr WS12 ...210 B3
Chancery La ST3 .....283 C3
Chandler Ave DY7 ....277 C3
Chandler Dr WV4 ....265 B2
Chandlers Cl WV4 ....240 A1
Chandlers Dr B77 ....255 A3
Chandlers Keep WS8 .245 A3
Chanterelle Gdns WV4 .266 A2
Chantry Rd Kinver DY7 .279 B4
Newcastle-u-l ST5 ...284 B1
Chapel Ave WS8 ......228 C1
Chapel Bank
Kidsgrove ST7 ....26 B3
Wheaton Aston ST19 .205 B3
Chapel Cl
Mount Pleasant ST7 ..26 A3
Wombourne WV5 ....269 C3
Chapel Ct Gnosall ST20 ..171 B3
Kidderminster DY10 ..280 A1
Newcastle-u-l ST5 ....55 B1
Chapel Dr WS8 ......228 C1
Chapel Gn DE6 ....127 B4
Chapel Hill DY10 ....280 A1
Chapel La Anslow DE13 .165 A3
Ashley TF9 ....100 A3
Ashley,Hookgate TF9 ..99 C2
Audley ST7 ....39 B3
Biddulph ST8 ....17 A1
Bradley ST18 ....191 A4
Burslem ST6 ....57 A4
Cannock WS15 ......211 C3
Cheadle ST10 ....76 A1
Clifton DE6 ....81 C3
Codsall WV8 ....238 C2
Endon ST6 ....28 A1
Hanbury DE13 ......144 C1
Kidsgrove ST7 ....26 C2
Kingsley ST10 ....62 A1
Lichfield WS14 ......231 A3
Longdon WS15 ......212 A2
Mucklestone ST9 ....83 B3
Newborough DE13 ..162 C4
Norton in Hales TF9 ..82 B2
Rolleston DE13 .....147 A2
Rudyard ST9 ....29 A1
Tatenhill DE13 ......164 B2
Whittington WS14 ..232 C3

Chapel St continued
Kingswinford, Wall Heath
DY6 ....275 A4
Longnor SK13 ....13 A3
Mount Pleasant ST7 ..26 A3
Newcastle-u-l, Knutton ST5 .55 C2
Newcastle-u-l, May Bank
ST5 ....56 B2
Newcastle-u-l, Silverdale
ST5 ....55 B1
Norton Canes WS11 ..227 C3
Stafford ST16 ....155 C2
Swadlincote DE11 ...186 C3
Walsall WS3 ....244 A2
Wolv WV2 ....266 B4
Wombourne WV5 ....269 C3
Chapel Terr ST16 ....155 C2
Chapel Wlk DY3 ......271 B1
Chapelon B77 ....251 A1
Chapelside WS15 ....178 B1
Chaplain Rd WS12 ...210 C1
Chaplin Rd ST3 ......283 C1
Chapter Wlk ST2 .....58 A3
Charlecote Dr DY1 ...271 C2
Charlemonte Cl WS12 .210 B2
Charles Ave
Essington WV11 .....241 C2
Kidderminster DY10 .280 A1
Wolv WV4 ....266 A3
Charles Cl WS6 ....226 B1
Charles Cotton Dr DY8 ..68 B3
Charles Cotton St ST16 .155 B3
Charles Cres WS3 ....244 A3
Charles Hayward Bglws
WV4 ....266 B2
Charles Rd DY8 ......279 C2
Charles St Biddulph ST8 ..27 B4
Cheadle ST10 ....76 B2
Hanley ST1 ....282 C2
Newcastle-u-l ST5 ....55 C4
Walsall WS1 ....257 C2
Wolv WV1 ....266 A4
Charles Way WS13 ..214 A1
Charlesdale Dr WS9 ..256 A2
Charlestown Gr ST3 ...90 A4
Charlesway TF9 ......112 A4
Charlock Gr WS11 ....210 B2
Charlock Rd B77 .....255 A3
Charlotte Cl ST18 ....177 B4
Charlotte St ST6 ......41 B4
Charlton St ST4 ....72 A4
Charminster Rd ST3 ...90 A4
Charmouth Cl ST1 .....58 A3
Charnwood Cl WS12 .210 B2
Charnes Rd TF9 .....100 B3
Charnley Dr B75 .....258 C1
Charnley Rd ST16 ...155 C3
Charnock Pl ST6 ......42 A4
Charnsford La TF9 ...100 A2
Charnwood ⬛ ST7 ...26 A1
Charnwood Dr ST3 ...266 B1
Charnwood Cl Leek ST13 .30 B2
Lichfield WS13 .....214 B1
Rugeley WS15 ......178 B1
Charnwood Ho WS13 .214 A1
Charnwood Prim Sch
WS13 ....214 B1
Charnwood Rd
Burton u T DE13 ....166 A4
Meir ST3 ....73 C1
Charolais Cres ST4 ...89 B4
Charsley Pl ST3 ....72 C1
Charter Cl WS11 ....227 C2
Charter Gr TF9 ....97 B1
Charter Rd ST5 ....56 A2
Charterfield Dr
Cannock WS11 ......210 B1
Kingswinford DY6 ..275 B4
Charterfields Sh Ctr ⬛
DY6 ....275 B4
Charterhouse Dr ST17 .156 A1
Charters Ave WV8 ...239 A1
Charters The WS11 ..214 A1
Chartley Cl
Blythe Bridge ST11 ..90 C3
Perton WV6 ....254 C2
Stafford ST18 ....155 B4
Chartley Cotts ST18 ..139 B3
Chartley Gate ST14 ..126 A3
Chartway The WS3 ..244 A2
Chartwell B79 ....249 B4
Chartwell Cl ST9 ......59 A2
Chartwell Dr
Sutton Coldfield B74 ..257 B2
Wolv WV10 ....240 C1
Wombourne WV5 ...269 C3
Chartwell Rd ST17 ...175 B4
Chartwood TF9 ....99 B3
Chase Ave WS6 ......226 C2
Chase Cres ST17 ....176 A2
Chase Cl CW WS12 ..209 B1
Chase La ST12/S11 ..103 C3
Chase Park Ind Est
WS7 ....228 B4
Chase Rd Brocton ST17 .176 B1
Brownhills WS8 .....229 A1
Burntwood WS7 ....229 A3
Sedgley DY3,DY5 ...271 B1
Chase Side Rd WS15 .196 B4
Chase Terrace High Sch
WS7 ....229 A4
Chase Terrace Prim Sch
WS7 ....229 C4
Chase Vale WS7 .....228 C3
Chase View
Huntington WS12 ...198 A2
Wolv WV4 ....266 C1
Chase View La ST18 ..174 B2
Chase Wlk
Huntington WS12 ...209 B2

Chase Wlk continued
Meir ST3 ....89 C4
Chaselands WS7 ......228 B4
Chaseley Ave WS11 ..209 B1
Chaseley Cl WS15 ....178 A1
Chaseley Croft WS11 .209 B1
Chaseley Gdns WS7 ..229 B4
Chaseley Rd WS15 ...178 A1
Chasepool Rd DY3 ...274 B4
Chaseside Dr WS11 ..210 A2
Chaseside Ind Est
WS11 ....210 A2
Chasetown Com Sch
WS7 ....228 C3
Chasetown High Sch
WS7 ....228 C3
Chasetown Ind Est WS7 .228 C3
Chasetown Sta * WS7 .228 B3
Chaseview Rd DE13 ..200 C1
Chasewater Country Pk *
WS7 ....228 C2
Chasewater Dr ST10 ..76 C2
Chasewater Heaths Sta *
WS7 ....228 B3
Chasewater Light Rly *
WS11 ....228 A2
Chasewater Water Sports
Venue** * WS8 ......228 B2
Chasewater Way WS11 .227 C3
Chasewood Park Bsns Ctr
WS12 ....210 C1
Chatcull La ST21 .....101 C1
Chatfield Cl DE15 ...167 B1
Chatfield Pl ST3 ....73 B1
Chatham St ST1 ......282 A1
Chatsworth B79 .....249 B4
Chatsworth Dr
Cannock WS11 ......210 A2
Caverswall ST9 ....59 A2
Norton-in-t-M ST6 ....42 C3
Tutbury DE13 ......146 B3
Chatsworth Gdns WV6 .255 A4
Chatsworth Mews ST21 .133 C4
Chatsworth Park Ave
ST4 ....72 A1
Chatsworth Pl Meir ST3 ..73 C1
Newcastle-u-l ST5 ....55 C4
Chatteris Cl ST3 ......90 A3
Chatterley Cl ST3 .....56 A4
Chatterley Dr ST7 .....41 A4
Chatterley Rd ST6 .....41 C1
Chatterley St ST6 ......41 C1
Chatterton Ave WS13 .230 C3
Chatterton Pl ST3 .....73 B2
Chatwell La
Blymhill TF10 ....188 B1
Great Chatwell TF10,TF11 .203 A4
Chaucer Ave DY3 ....271 A3
Chaucer Cl
Burton u T DE14 ....166 B3
Lichfield WS14 .....231 A3
Tamworth B79 .....250 A3
Chaucer Dr WV7 ....212 A1
Chaucer Rd ST17 ....174 B4
Chaulden Rd ST16 ...136 B1
Chawner Cl WS7 .....211 C1
Cheadle Cl ST19 .....207 C2
Cheadle High Sch ST10 .76 B1
Cheadle Hospl ST10 ..76 B1
Cheadle Prim Sch ST10 .76 B1
Cheadle Rd Alton ST10 ..78 C1
Cheddleton ST13 .....45 B2
Draycott-i-t-M ST11 ...91 C3
Forsbrook ST11 ......91 A4
Leek ST13 ....45 C4
Upper Tean ST10 .....92 B3
Uttoxeter ST14 ......110 C1
Warslow SK17 ....23 A1
Cheam Gdns WV6 ....255 C4
Cheapside Hanley ST1 ..282 B2
Newcastle-u-l ST5 ...284 B3
Cheatle Cl B77 ......261 B3
Chebsey Cl ST2 ....58 B2
Chebsey Dr ST16 ....155 A3
Checkley Dr ST8 ......16 B1
Checkley Gr ⬛ ST13 ..73 B3
Checkley La CW3 ......52 C1
Checkley La CW5 ......40 B1
Chedale Rd ST10 ......61 B1
Cheddar Dr ST5 ....54 C1
Cheddleton Craft Ctr *
ST13 ....45 A3
Cheddleton Flint Mill Mus *
ST13 ....45 B3
Cheddleton Heath Rd
ST13 ....45 B3
Cheddleton Park Ave
ST13 ....45 B3
Cheddleton Rd ST13 ...30 C2
Cheddleton Sta ST13 ...45 C3
Cheedale Cl DE15 ...167 A3
Chelford Cl ST19 ....193 A1
Chell Cl ST19 ....207 C4
Chell Gr ST5 ....56 A4
Chell Green Ave ST6 ..42 A3
Chell Green Ct ST6 ....42 A3
Chell Heath Rd ST6 ...42 B2
Chell Rd ST16 ....155 B2
Chell St ST1 ....57 B3
Chelmarsh Ave WV3 .265 A4
Chelmorton Dr ST3 ...73 C1
Chelmsford Dr ST21 ..58 B1
Chelmsford Rd ST1 ...56 B3
Chelsea Cl ST3 ....16 B1
Chelsea Dr B74 ......257 C2
Chelsea Way
Kingswinford DY6 ...275 B3
Stafford ST16 ....155 B1

Chelson St ST3 . . . . .283 C3
Chelston Dr WV6 . . . . .255 C2
Cheltenham Ave ST10 . . . .76 C3
Cheltenham Dr
  Kingswinford DY6 . . . . .275 A3
  Stafford ST17 . . . . .175 B4
Cheltenham Gr
  Hanley ST1 . . . . .57 C3
  Newcastle-u-L ST5 . . . . .54 C1
Chelwood St ST1 . . . . .282 A4
Chemical La ST6 . . . . .41 B1
Chenet Way 🖪 WS11 . . . . .209 C1
Chepstow Cl Biddulph ST8 .16 B1
  Perton WV6 . . . . .254 C2
Chepstow Dr ST17 . . . . .175 B4
Chepstow Rd
  Walsall WS3 . . . . .242 C1
  Wolv WV10 . . . . .240 B3
Chepstow Way WS3 . . . . . .242 C1
Chequer St WV3 . . . . .266 A3
Chequerfield Dr WV4 . . . .266 A3
Chequers Ave WV5 . . . . . . .265 A1
Chequers Ct WS11 . . . . . . .228 A3
Chequers The 🖪 WS13 . . .231 B4
Cheriton Gn ST7 . . . . .58 B1
Cheriton Gr WV6 . . . . .254 C2
Cherrington Dr WS6 . . . . . .226 C2
Cherrington Gdns WV6 .255 A1
Cherry Bank WS12 . . . . . . .210 B3
Cherry Cl
  Blythe Bridge ST11 . . . . . . .106 C4
  Burntwood WS7 . . . . .228 C3
  Newcastle-u-L ST5 . . . . .40 B1
Cherry Ct DE14 . . . . .184 C4
Cherry Gn DY1 . . . . .271 C2
Cherry Gr Fenton ST3 . . . . . .72 C2
  Stourbridge DY8 . . . . .279 C2
Cherry Hill DY3 . . . . .66 A3
Cherry Hill Ave ST3 . . . . . . .74 A1
Cherry Hill La ST5 . . . . .55 C1
Cherry La Cheadle ST10 . . . .27 B3
  Congleton CW12 . . . . .16 C4
  Gayton ST18 . . . . .138 C3
  Himley DY3 . . . . .270 B2
  Seighford ST18 . . . . .135 B2
Cherry Leys DE15 . . . . .167 B2
Cherry Orch
  Lichfield WS14 . . . . .231 B4
  Newcastle-u-L ST5 . . . . . . .284 B3
  Stone ST15 . . . . .120 B4
Cherry St
  Stourbridge DY8 . . . . .279 C2
  Tamworth B79 . . . . .279 C3
Cherry Tree Ave ST7 . . . . . .25 A3
Cherry Tree Cl
  Eccleshall ST21 . . . . .133 C4
  Stone ST15 . . . . .119 C3
  Swadlincote DE11 . . . . . . .186 C3
  Trentham ST4 . . . . .88 A3
Cherry Tree Gdns WV8 . .239 A2
Cherry Tree La
  Biddulph ST8 . . . . .17 A1
  Codsall WV8 . . . . .239 A2
  Woore CW3 . . . . .67 B1
Cherry Tree Rd
  Audley ST7 . . . . .38 C1
  Huntington WS12 . . . . .209 B4
  Kingswinford DY6 . . . . . . .275 C4
  Newcastle-u-L ST5 . . . . .40 C1
  Norton Canes WS11 . . . . . .228 A3
  Rugeley WS15 . . . . .196 C3
Cherry Tree Wlk B79 . . . . .250 A4
Cherry Trees Sch WV5 . . .269 C3
Cherry Way TF9 . . . . .97 B1
Cherrybrook Dr ST19 . . . . .193 A1
Cherryl Ho B74 . . . . .257 C2
Cherrytree Cres ST18 . . . .135 A2
Cherrytree Rd DE15 . . . . . .185 C4
Cherrywood Cl 🗓 ST17 . . .175 B3
Cherrywood Gr ST3 . . . . . . .89 C3
Cherrywood Rd B74 . . . . . .256 B1
Cherrywood Way B74 . . . .257 B2
Chertsey Pl ST1 . . . . .57 B4
Chervil Cl ST3 . . . . .90 A3
Cherwell B77 . . . . .250 B1
Cherwell Dr WS8 . . . . .228 B1
Chesham Gr ST3 . . . . .90 A3
Chesham Rd ST16 . . . . .155 C3
Cheshire Cl DY8 . . . . .279 C2
Cheshire Dr ST19 . . . . .223 B3
Cheshire Gdns TF9 . . . . .97 B1
Cheshire Gr WV6 . . . . .254 C2
Cheshire St TF9 . . . . .97 B1
Cheslyn Dr WS6 . . . . .226 C2
Cheslyn Hay High Sch
  WS6 . . . . .226 B2
Cheslyn Hay Prim Sch
  WS6 . . . . .226 B2
Chessington Cres ST4 . . . . .88 B4
Chestall Rd WS15 . . . . .211 C3
Chester Ave WV6 . . . . .255 C4
Chester Cl
  Cannock WS11 . . . . .210 A1
  Lichfield WS13 . . . . .214 B2
  Talke ST7 . . . . .40 C4
Chester Cres ST5 . . . . .71 A3
Chester Rd Aldridge B74 . .256 C2
  Audley ST7 . . . . .39 B1
  Brownhills WS9 . . . . .245 B2
  Chetwynd TF10 . . . . .168 B4
  Enville DY7 . . . . .273 C1
  Kinver DY7 . . . . .277 C4
  Talke ST7 . . . . .40 B4
  Whittington WS14 . . . . . . .232 B2
Chester Rd N WS8 . . . . . . .228 B1
Chesterfield Ave DE11 . . .186 C3
Chesterfield Ct WS9 . . . . .244 C2
Chesterfield Rd WS14 . . . .231 A3

Chesterton High Sch
  ST5 . . . . .55 C4
Chesterton Prim Sch
  ST5 . . . . .55 C4
Chesterton Rd
  Burton u T DE14 . . . . .166 B4
  Pattingham WV6 . . . . .253 A1
Chesterton Stad ST5 . . . . . .55 B3
Chesterton Way B79 . . . . .250 A4
Chesterwood WS9 . . . . . . .256 C1
Chesterwood Rd ST6 . . . . . .42 A2
Chestnut Ave B79 . . . . .250 A4
Chestnut Cl Aldridge B74 . .257 A2
  Armitage WS15 . . . . .198 B2
  Cannock WS11 . . . . .210 B1
  Codsall WV8 . . . . .238 C1
  Gnosall ST20 . . . . .171 B4
  Seighford ST18 . . . . .154 C1
  Stourbridge DY8 . . . . .279 B1
  Upper Tean ST10 . . . . .92 C2
Chestnut Cres ST11 . . . . . . .91 A3
Chestnut Ct
  Millmeece ST21 . . . . .102 B1
  Rugeley WS15 . . . . .196 C4
  Stafford ST16 . . . . .104 C1
Chestnut Dr
  Cheslyn Hay WS6 . . . . . . .226 B2
  Great Wyrley WS6 . . . . . . .226 C2
  Millmeece ST15 . . . . .118 C3
  Shenstone WS14 . . . . .246 C3
  Stafford ST17 . . . . .174 C3
  Walsall WS4 . . . . .244 A1
  Wombourne WV5 . . . . . . .270 A3
Chestnut Gr
  Kingswinford DY6 . . . . . . .275 C3
  Kinver DY7 . . . . .277 C3
  Newcastle-u-L ST5 . . . . .40 C1
  Penkridge ST19 . . . . .207 C4
  Stone ST15 . . . . .104 C1
  Tamworth B77 . . . . .250 B2
Chestnut La B79 . . . . .228 C3
Chestnut Rd Ashley TF9 . . . .99 C3
  Burton u T DE15 . . . . .185 C4
  Endon ST6 . . . . .43 B4
  Market Drayton TF9 . . . . . .112 A4
Chestnut Way WV3 . . . . . .265 B4
Chestov Pl ST3 . . . . .73 B3
Cheswardine Prim Sch
  TF9 . . . . .130 A4
Cheswardine Rd ST5 . . . . . .56 A4
Cheswell Cl WV6 . . . . .255 A1
Chetney Cl ST10 . . . . .155 A2
Chetton Gn WV10 . . . . . . .240 A2
Chetwode Cl TF9 . . . . .83 B3
Chetwynd Ave
  Caverswall ST12 . . . . .59 A2
  Norton-in-t-M ST6 . . . . .42 C3
Chetwynd Cl
  Penkridge ST19 . . . . .207 C4
  Rugeley WS15 . . . . .196 C4
Chetwynd Ctr The ST17 . .155 C1
Chetwynd End TF10 . . . . . .168 C2
Chetwynd Gdns WS11 . . .209 B2
Chetwynd Gr TF10 . . . . . . .168 C2
Chetwynd Pk
  Cannock WS12 . . . . .211 A3
  Chetwynd TF10 . . . . .168 B4
Chetwynd Rd
  Chetwynd TF10 . . . . .168 B3
  Edgmond TF10 . . . . .168 B3
  Newcastle-u-L ST5 . . . . .56 A3
  Newport TF10 . . . . .168 C2
  Wolv WV7 . . . . .266 A3
Chetwynd St
  Chell Heath ST6 . . . . .42 B1
  Newcastle-u-L ST5 . . . . .56 B3
Chevening Cl DY3 . . . . .271 C4
Chevin The DE13 . . . . .147 B1
Cheviot B77 . . . . .251 B1
Cheviot Cl ST5 . . . . .55 C2
Cheviot Ct B75 . . . . .258 A2
Cheviot Dr Chell Heath ST6 .42 B2
  Burton-u-N DE13 . . . . .183 B1
Chichester Dr WS12 . . . . . .210 B1
Chichester Wlk ST1 . . . . . .282 C4
Chieveley Cl WS15 . . . . . . .178 B1
Childerplay Rd ST8 . . . . .27 B2
Chilgrove Cl ST1 . . . . .57 C3
Chilgrove Gdns WV6 . . . . .255 B3
Chillingham B77 . . . . .261 B4
Chillington Cl WS6 . . . . . . .226 C1
Chillington Dr
  Codsall WV8 . . . . .238 C2
  Sedgley DY1 . . . . .271 C2
Chillington Hall* WV8 . . .222 C1
Chillington Ho WV6 . . . . . .255 C3
Chillington La WV8 . . . . . . .222 B3
Chiltern Cl
  Cheslyn Hay WS6 . . . . . . .226 B1
  Chorlton CW2 . . . . .37 A1
  Sedgley DY3 . . . . .271 B2
Chiltern Ct B75 . . . . .258 A2
Chiltern La ST21 . . . . .133 C3
Chiltern Pl ST5 . . . . .55 C2
Chiltern Rd
  Swadlincote DE11 . . . . . . .186 C2
  Tamworth B77 . . . . .251 B1
Chilton Ave ST18 . . . . .177 C4
Chilworth Gr ST3 . . . . .72 C1
China St ST4 . . . . .272 C4
Chingford Old DY8 . . . . . . .275 B2
Chivelstone Gr ST4 . . . . .88 B3
Cholerton Cl ST14 . . . . .72 C3
Chorley Ave ST6 . . . . .42 A3
Chorley Rd WV7 . . . . .212 A1

Chorley St WS13 . . . . .30 C3
Chorlton La CW2 . . . . .37 A1
Chorlton Rd ST1 . . . . .57 B3
Chorlton Terr ST14 . . . . . . .111 B1
Christ Church CE Inf Sch
  WV6 . . . . .255 B2
Christ Church CE Jun Sch
  WV6 . . . . .255 B2
Christ Church CE Mid Sch
  ST15 . . . . .105 A1
Christ Church CE Prim Sch
  WS13 . . . . .230 C4
Christ Church Gdns
  WS13 . . . . .230 C4
Christ Church Inf Sch
  DE14 . . . . .166 B4
Christ Church La TF9 . . . . .112 A4
Christchurch CE Prim Sch
  ST4 . . . . .72 C3
Christchurch La WS13 . . . .230 C4
Christchurch St ST14 . . . . . .72 C3
Christchurch Way ST15 . . .105 A1
Christie Ave DE16 . . . . .155 B2
Christie Pl ST3 . . . . .73 C3
Christine St ST2 . . . . .58 A2
Christopher Rd WV2 . . . . . .266 C4
Christopher Sq ST4 . . . . .72 C3
Christopher Terr ST17 . . . .161 A3
Christopher Wlk WS13 . . .214 A2
Chub B77 . . . . .261 B4
Chubb Way ST14 . . . . .71 C2
Chumleigh Gr ST6 . . . . .42 A1
Church Ave Grindon ST13 . .34 A1
  Hatton DE65 . . . . .146 B4
  Norton-in-t-M ST2 . . . . .43 A1
Church Bank Audley ST7 . . .39 B1
  Keele ST5 . . . . .69 C4
  Oakamoor ST10 . . . . .78 A3
  Waterhouses ST10 . . . . .63 C4
Church Cl Alrewas WS13 . .215 B4
  Biddulph ST8 . . . . .27 A3
  Blythe Bridge ST3 . . . . .89 C3
  Burton u T DE13 . . . . .167 A2
  Coppenhall ST18 . . . . .192 C4
  Drayton Bassett B78 . . . . .260 C3
  Gnosall ST20 . . . . .171 A2
  Haughton ST18 . . . . .172 C3
  Kingstone ST14 . . . . .141 B4
  Marchington ST14 . . . . . . .127 C1
  Ranton ST18 . . . . .153 B3
  Rugeley WS15 . . . . .196 A4
  Shenstone WS14 . . . . .247 A3
  Stafford ST17 . . . . .174 C3
  🖪 Stone ST15 . . . . .120 A4
  Wood End CV9 . . . . .262 B1
Church Cres WV11 . . . . . . .241 C2
Church Croft ST14 . . . . . . .125 B4
Church Dr B78 . . . . .264 C4
Church Eaton Prim Sch
  ST20 . . . . .190 A4
Church Eaton Rd TF10 . . .188 C3
Church Farm TF9 . . . . .100 B3
Church Farm Cl ST19 . . . . .192 C1
Church Fields Keele ST5 . . .69 C4
  Norton in Hales TF9 . . . . . . .82 B1
Church Gdns ST3 . . . . .283 C4
Church Gr ST21 . . . . .133 B4
Church Hill
  Cannock WS11 . . . . .210 B3
  Codsall WV8 . . . . .238 C3
  Kinver DY7 . . . . .277 A3
  Wolv WV9 . . . . .265 C2
Church Hill Dr WV6 . . . . . .255 C3
Church Hill Rd WV6 . . . . . .255 B3
Church Hollow B77 . . . . . . .167 A2
Church La
  Abbots Bromley WS15 . . . .160 C3
  Albrighton WV7 . . . . .237 A1
  Alrewas WS13 . . . . .215 C4
  Armitage WS15 . . . . .197 C3
  Barton-u-N DE13 . . . . .183 B1
  Betley CW3 . . . . .53 B3
  Biddulph ST8 . . . . .17 A1
  Bobbington DY7 . . . . .268 A1
  Bradley ST18 . . . . .173 B1
  Burntwood WS7 . . . . .224 A1
  Burntwood WS7 . . . . .229 B2
  Cheslyn Hay WS11 . . . . . .225 C4
  Chilcote DE12 . . . . .219 C2
  Codsall WV8 . . . . .238 C3
  Draycott in t M ST11 . . . . . .91 C3
  Eccleshall ST21 . . . . .116 A3
  Edingale B79 . . . . .217 B3
  Ellastone DE6 . . . . .80 A2
  Endon ST6 . . . . .43 C4
  Gayton ST18 . . . . .138 B3
  Gnosall TF10 . . . . .188 B4
  Hanbury DE13 . . . . .145 A2
  Hill Ridware WS15 . . . . . . .198 A4
  Hixon ST18 . . . . .158 B4
  Ipstones ST10 . . . . .46 C1
  King's Bromley DE13 . . . . .199 B3
  Kingstone ST14 . . . . .141 B4
  Lawton-gate ST7 . . . . .25 B2
  Leek ST13 . . . . .30 C3
  Marchington ST14 . . . . . . .127 C1
  Mayfield DE6 . . . . .81 B3
  Maddison B78 . . . . .260 B1
  Mow Cop ST7 . . . . .26 C4
  Newcastle-u-L, Knutton ST5 .55 C1
  Newcastle-u-L, Wolstanton
  ST5 . . . . .56 B2
  Newton Solney DE15 . . . . .166 B4
  Rocester ST14 . . . . .96 A2
  Roston DE6 . . . . .80 B4
  Rugeley WS15 . . . . .178 B1

Church La continued
  Scholar Green ST7 . . . . .25 B4
  Seighford ST18 . . . . .154 C1
  Seisdon WV5 . . . . .264 A1
  Shenstone WS9 . . . . .245 C2
  Shuttington B79 . . . . .251 C4
  Stafford ST16 . . . . .155 C2
  Standon ST21 . . . . .102 A2
  Stone ST15 . . . . .105 B3
  Tamworth B79 . . . . .250 A3
  Thorpe DE6 . . . . .51 B1
  Trentham ST4 . . . . .71 C1
  Upper Tean ST10 . . . . .109 A4
  Uttoxeter ST14 . . . . .124 A1
  Waterhouses ST10 . . . . .63 C4
  Wheaton Aston ST19 . . . . .206 A3
Church Lawton Prim Sch
  ST7 . . . . .25 A3
Church Mdw
  Ipstones ST10 . . . . .46 C1
  Norton in Hales TF9 . . . . . . .82 B1
Church Mews DE65 . . . . . .146 B4
Church Moat Way WS3 . .243 A1
Church of the Ascension
  Prim Sch DY6 . . . . .275 B4
Church Plantation ST5 . . . .70 A4
Church Rd Alrewas DE13 . .200 C2
  Ashley TF9 . . . . .100 B3
  Biddulph ST8 . . . . .27 B4
  Branston DE14 . . . . .184 C4
  Brewood ST19 . . . . .223 B3
  Brownhills, Catshill WS8 . .244 C4
  Burntwood WS7 . . . . .229 B4
  Burton u T DE13 . . . . .147 C1
  Codsall WV8 . . . . .238 C2
  Egginton DE65 . . . . .148 A2
  Elford B79 . . . . .216 B1
  Endon ST6 . . . . .43 A4
  Hixon ST18 . . . . .139 B1
  Huntington WS11 . . . . .209 A4
  Kingswinford DY6 . . . . . . .275 C3
  Kinver DY7 . . . . .88 C4
  Longton ST3 . . . . .88 C4
  Norton Canes WS11 . . . . . .227 C2
  Penkridge ST19 . . . . .192 C1
  Perton WV6 . . . . .254 C2
  Rolleston DE13 . . . . .147 A2
  Shareshill WV10 . . . . .225 B1
  Shenstone WS14 . . . . .246 C3
  Shenstone, Thornes WS9 . .245 C2
  Snelston DE6 . . . . .81 A2
  Swindon DY3 . . . . .269 B1
  Tamworth B77 . . . . .261 B2
  Walsall WS3 . . . . .244 A2
  Wolv, Elston Hall WV10 . .240 B1
  Wolv, Penn Fields WV3 . . .265 C4
  Wolv, Stockwell End WV6 . .255 B3
  Wolv, Tettenhall Wood
  WV6 . . . . .255 A2
  Wombourne WV5 . . . . . . .270 A4
Church View Mid Sch
  WS13 . . . . .31 A4
Church View Rd ST10 . . . . . .78 B4
Churnetside Bsns Pk
  ST13 . . . . .45 B3
Churns Hill La DY3 . . . . . . .270 A2
Churston Cl
  Newcastle-u-L ST5 . . . . .71 A1
  Walsall WS3 . . . . .243 A2
Churston Pl ST1 . . . . .57 B4
Cicely Haughton Sch
  ST13 . . . . .44 C1
Cinder Hill WV9 . . . . .224 A2
Cinder Hill La ST7 . . . . .25 C4
Cinder Rd
  Burntwood WS7 . . . . .228 C4
  Sedgley DY3 . . . . .271 A1
Cinderhill Ind Est ST3 . . . .73 C2
Cinderhill La ST3 . . . . .73 B2
Circular Rd WV7 . . . . .220 C1
City Arc WS13 . . . . .231 A4
City Bank ST6 . . . . .16 B1
City General Hospl ST4 . . .71 B4
City La ST9 . . . . .30 A2
City of Stoke-on-Trent Sixth
  Form Coll ST4 . . . . .72 B3
City Rd ST4 . . . . .72 B3
Cl The WS13 . . . . .231 A4
Clamgoose La ST10 . . . . . . .76 B4
Clanbrook Rd DY7 . . . . . . .278 A4
Clandon Ave ST6 . . . . .41 C2
Clanford Cl ST17 . . . . .174 C3
Clanford La ST18 . . . . .154 A3
Clanford Rd ST18 . . . . .154 A4
Clanway St ST6 . . . . .41 C3
Clap Gate Gr WV5 . . . . . . .269 C3
Clap Gate Rd WV5 . . . . . . .269 C3
Clare Ave
  Essington WV11 . . . . .241 C1
  Newcastle-u-L ST5 . . . . .56 A3
Clare Cres WV14 . . . . .266 C1
Clare Rd DE16 . . . . .155 B4
Clare St Kidsgrove ST7 . . . .26 C2
  Mount Pleasant ST7 . . . . . . .26 B2
  Stoke-on-T ST4 . . . . .72 A4
Claregate Prim Sch
  WV6 . . . . .255 C4
Claremont Cl
  Newcastle-u-L ST5 . . . . .56 B4
  🖪 Stone ST15 . . . . .120 A4
Claremont Cotts DY3 . . . .271 C4
Claremont Gr ST17 . . . . . . .174 A4
Claremont Mews WV3 . . .266 A4
Claremont Rd
  Eccleshall ST21 . . . . .133 C3
  Sedgley DY3 . . . . .271 C4
  Wolv WV3 . . . . .266 A4

Clarence Gdns B74 .... 257 C1
Clarence Rd Longton ST3 .283 B4
Sutton Coldfield B74 ....257 C2
Clarence St
Burton u T DE14 ....166 B1
Fenton ST4 ....72 C3
Newcastle-u-L ST5 ....284 D3
Newcastle-u-L, Porthill ST5 ..56 A3
Clarendon Dr ST17 ....174 A4
Clarendon Rd WS3 ....243 C2
Clarendon Rd
Sutton Coldfield B75 ....258 B2
Walsall WS4 ....243 A1
Clarendon St Fenton ST4 ..72 B3
Walsall WS3 ....243 A1
Claridge Rd ST4 ....56 C1
Clarion Way WS11 ....209 C3
Clark Rd WV3 ....255 C1
Clark St Stafford ST16 ...155 C2
Stourbridge DY8 ....279 C2
Clark's Cres WS15 ....161 A3
Clarke Ho WS6 ....243 A1
Clarke Ind Est DE14 .....166 C2
Clarke St ST1 ....282 A1
Clarke's Ave WS12 ....195 A1
Clarkes Cl ST14 ....111 A1
Claud St ST4 ....72 B2
Claverdon Cl WS8 ....245 A4
Claverdon Dr B74 ....257 A2
Claverhouse Rd DE15 .....167 A1
Claverley CE Prim Sch
WV5 ....267 B4
Claverley Dr WV4 ....265 B3
Clay Gates Rd ST19 ......207 A1
Clay Hills ST6 ....41 B2
Clay La ST9 ....43 C4
Clay Pit La WS14 ....230 C2
Clay St Burton u T DE15 ..166 C1
Penkridge ST19 ....192 C1
Clay St E DE15 ....192 A1
Clayalders Bank ST21 .....101 B3
Claydon Cres ST5 ....71 A1
Claydon Rd DY6 ....270 B1
Clayfield Gr ST3 ....73 B3
Clayfield Gr W ST3 ......73 B3
Claygate Rd WS12 ....210 C2
Clayhanger Cl ST5 ....56 A4
Clayhanger La WS8 ....244 B3
Clayhanger Rd WS8 ....244 C3
Clayhanger St **9** ST6 ..56 C4
Claymills Rd DE13 ....148 A1
Claymore B77 ....261 C4
Clays La DE14 ....184 C4
Clayton Ave CW12 ....6 A3
Clayton Cl WV2 ....266 B4
Clayton High Sch ST5 ....71 B2
Clayton La
Newcastle-u-L ST5 ....71 B2
Stoke-on-T ST4,ST5 ......71 B3
Clayton Rd ST5 ....71 B2
Clayton St ST3 ....283 C3
Claytonwood Rd ST4 ......71 C2
Cleadon Pl ST2 ....56 A3
Clear View DY6 ....275 A3
Clearwell Gdns DY11 .....271 C2
Cleasby B77 ....251 B1
Cleckly Wlk **4** ST6 ...56 C4
Clee Hill Dr WV3 ....255 A1
Clee Hill Rd DY3 ....271 B2
Clee Rd DY10 ....280 A3
Clee View Mdw DY3 ....266 B1
Clee View Rd WV5 ....269 C3
Cleeton St WS12 ....210 B1
Cleeve B77 ....250 B2
Cleeve Dr B74 ....257 C3
Cleeve Rd WS3 ....242 C2
Cleeve Way WS3 ....242 C2
Clegg Rd WS7 ....229 C4
Clematis B77 ....250 C2
Clematis Ave ST11 ....90 C3
Clematis Cl ST18 ....135 A1
Clematis Cres DE15 ......186 A4
Clematis Dr WV9 ....239 C2
Clement Cl ST16 ....155 C3
Clement Pl ST6 ....42 C2
Clement Rd ST6 ....42 A3
Clench View Rd DY8 ......279 B1
Clerk Bank ST13 ....30 C3
Clermont Ave ST4 ....72 A1
Clevedon Ave ST17 ....175 C4
Cleveland Cl WV11 ....241 C1
Cleveland Ct DE15 ....167 A2
Cleveland Dr WS11 ....210 A2
Cleveland Rd Hanley ST1 ..282 B1
Newcastle-u-L ST5 ....55 C2
Cleveland St
1 Burslem ST6 ....56 C4
Stourbridge DY8 ....279 C2
Cleveland Wlk ST17 ......174 A4
Cleves Cres WS6 ....226 B1
Clewley Dr WV9 ....240 A2
Clewley Rd DE14 ....184 C4
Clewley St DY3 ....283 D5
Clewlows Bank ST9 ....43 C2
Clews St ST6 ....56 C4
Clews Wlk ST6 ....56 B3
Cley Gr ST5 ....71 A1
Cliff Hall La B78 ....261 A1
Cliff La ST13 ....31 B4
Cliff St ST6 ....42 B1
Cliff Vale Ct ST4 ....56 C1
Cliff Vale Pl ST4 ....56 C1
Cliffdon Ho DE65 ....146 B4
Cliffe Pl ST6 ....42 A2
Clifford Ave ST6 ....42 C3

Clifford Cl B77 ....250 C2
Clifford Rd TF9 ....112 A4
Clifford St Hanley ST1 ...282 C1
Tamworth B77 ....250 C2
Cliffs La TF10,ST20 .....150 C1
Clifton Ave Aldridge WS9 .245 B1
Brownhills WS8 ....244 B4
Cannock WS11 ....226 B4
Tamworth B79 ....250 A4
Clifton CE Prim Sch DE6 ..81 C3
Clifton Cl Fenton ST4 ....72 C3
Stafford ST16 ....156 A2
Swadlincote DE11 ....186 C1
Clifton Dr ST16 ....156 A2
Clifton Gdns WV8 ....239 B2
Clifton La B79 ....235 A2
Clifton Rd Clifton DE6 ...81 C3
Cookley DY10 ....280 B2
Netherseal DE12 ....219 B3
Wolv WV6 ....255 B3
Clifton St Fenton ST4 ....72 C3
Newcastle-u-L ST5 ....56 B2
Stourbridge DY8 ....279 C2
Clifton Way DE15 ....167 A1
Clinton Cres WS7 ....229 A4
Clinton Gdns **9** ST15 .120 A4
Clinton Sq ST15 ....282 A2
Clive Ave ST2 ....43 A2
Clive Cl B75 ....258 B1
Clive Ho DE15 ....167 B2
Clive Rd Burntwood WS7 ..229 A4
Market Drayton TF9 ......97 B1
Newcastle-u-L ST5 ....56 B3
Pattingham WV6 ....263 B4
Clive St ST6 ....41 C2
Cliveden Ave WS9 ....245 A1
Cliveden Coppice B74 ....257 C1
Cliveden Dr ST3 ....283 C2
Cliveden Rd ST2 ....58 A2
Clockmill Ave WS3 ....243 C2
Clockmill Pl WS3 ....243 C2
Clockmill Rd WS3 ....243 C2
Cloister Wlk Bucknall ST2 ..58 A3
Whittington WS14 ....232 C3
Cloisters The
Burton u T DE15 ....166 C1
Gnosall ST20 ....171 C3
Close Bank DE13 ....146 B3
Close Jun Sch The ST4 ...71 C4
Close La ST17 ....26 B4
Close The Endon ST9 .....43 C4
Enville DY7 ....273 B1
Madeley CW3 ....43 B2
Meir ST3 ....74 A3
Sedgley DY3 ....271 B2
Stafford, Moss Pit ST17 ..174 C3
Stafford, Rowley Park
ST16 ....155 B1
Swindon DY3 ....269 C1
Tutbury DE13 ....146 A3
Cloud The* CW12 ....7 A2
Cloud View CW12 ....6 A1
Clough Hall Dr ST7 ......40 C3
Clough Hall Rd ST7 ......40 C4
Clough Hall Tech Sch
ST7 ....25 C1
Clough La ST9 ....59 A1
Clough St ST1 ....282 A2
Clover Heath WV5 ....267 B4
Clover La DY6 ....275 A4
Clover Mdws WS12 ....210 B1
Clover Rd ST5 ....56 B3
Clover Ridge WS6 ....226 B2
Cloverdale Perton WV6 ...254 B2
B Stafford ST17 .....175 B4
Cloverdale Pl ST13 ......73 C2
Cloverdale Rd ST5 ....56 A2
Clowes Rd ST2 ....43 A2
Club Cotts WV10 ....240 B3
Club La WV10 ....240 B3
Club Row DY3 ....271 C3
Club St ST14 ....72 A3
Clumber Ave ST5 ....71 B3
Clumber Gr ST5 ....71 B3
Clumber Pl ST2 ....58 A3
Clyde Ave ST8 ....16 C1
Clyde Pl ST5 ....71 A2
Clyde Rd ST6 ....57 A4
Clyde St ST1 ....282 A2
Clyde Wlk ST1 ....282 A2
Clydesdale Rd WS8 ....244 C3
Clynes Way ST3 ....74 A2
Co-operative La ST17 ....54 B4
Co-operative St ST16 ....155 B4
Coach House La WS15 .....178 C1
Coach House Rise B77 ....261 C4
Coachman's Wlk WS15 .....178 C3
Coal Haulage Rd WS11 ....227 B4
Coalbourn La DY8 ....279 C4
Coalbarnhill Glassworks*
DY8 ....279 C4
Coalmeadow Cl WS3 ....242 C2
Coalpit Hill ST7 ....40 B4
Coalpit La WS15 ....197 A3
Coalpitford La ST13 .....44 C2
Coalport Cl ST10 ....76 B1
Coalport Dr ST15 ....119 C3
Coalville Pl ST14 ....74 A3
Coalway Ave WV3 ....266 A3
Coalway Gdns WV3 ....265 B4
Coalway Rd
Rugeley WS15 ....197 A3
Walsall WS3 ....243 A1
Wolv WV3 ....265 C3
Coates Pl ST6 ....42 A4
Coatsgate Wlk WV8 ....239 C1

Cob Moor Rd ST7 ....26 A2
Cobbett Rd WS7 ....228 B4
Cobbles The ST19 ....205 B3
Cobden Cl WS12 ....210 B4
Cobden Ho WV2 ....266 B4
Cobden St Longton ST3 ...283 B1
Newcastle-u-L ST5 ....56 B3
Cobham Cl ST15 ....118 C3
Cobham Pl **3** ST3 .....90 A4
Cobia B77 ....261 B4
Cobridge Rd ST1 ....57 A3
Coburn Dr B75 ....258 B1
Cock Hill DE6 ....81 C3
Cock La ST17 ....193 C4
Cocketts Nook WS15 ......178 B2
Cocknage Rd Longton ST3 ..73 A1
Meir ST3 ....89 B3
Cocks La Norton-in-t-M ST9 ..43 B2
Norton-in-t-M ST9 ....43 B2
Cockshutts La ST14 ......126 A4
Cocksparrow La WS12,
WS13 ....209 A3
Cockspur St B78 ....262 C4
Cockster Brook La ST13 ...72 C2
Cockster Rd ST13 ....72 C2
Cockstubbles ST14 ....126 A4
Cocton Cl WV6 ....254 C3
Codsall Com High Sch
WV8 ....239 A2
Codsall Ho WV8 ....238 C2
Codsall L Ctr WV8 ....239 A2
Codsall Mid Sch WV8 .....239 A2
Codsall Rd Codsall WV8 ...239 A1
Wolv WV6 ....255 B4
Codsall Sta WV8 ....238 C2
Coghlan Rd ST17 ....174 B4
Colbourne Rd B78 ....250 A1
Colbrook B77 ....250 B1
Colclough Ave ST5 ....56 C2
Colclough La ST6 ....41 B4
Colclough Rd ST2 ....74 A1
Cold Meece Ind Est
ST15 ....118 A3
Cold Norton Cotts ST15 ..119 B3
Coldridge Cl WV8 ....239 C1
Coldstream Dr DY8 ....275 C2
Cole Dr ST16 ....155 B1
Cole St ST8 ....27 B4
Coleford Cl DY8 ....279 B1
Colehill B79 ....250 A1
Coleman St WV6 ....255 C2
Colenso Way ST5 ....56 A4
Coleridge Cl
Market Drayton TF9 ......112 A4
Tamworth B79 ....250 A3
Walsall WS3 ....244 A3
Coleridge Ct DE14 ....166 B3
Coleridge Dr
Cheadle ST10 ....76 B1
Perton WV6 ....254 C2
Stafford ST17 ....174 B4
Coleridge Rd ST3 ....73 A1
Coleridge Rise DY3 ......271 A2
Colesden Wlk WV4 ....265 B3
Coleshill Rd B78 ....261 A4
Coleshill St ST18 ....261 A4
Coley Gr ST18 ....177 B4
Coley La ST18 ....158 B1
Colin Cres ST13 ....44 C2
Colindene Gr ST14 ....72 A3
Colinwood Cl WS6 ....226 C1
Collard Ave ST5 ....56 A2
College Cl CW3 ....68 C4
College Ct WV6 ....255 B2
College Farm Cl WV6 .....255 B2
College Fields ST15 .....118 C3
College La B79 ....250 A3
College Rd Denstone ST14 ..95 B3
Hanley ST1,ST14 ....57 B1
Stoke-on-T ST4 ....282 B3
Wolv WV6 ....255 B2
College View WS6 ....255 B2
Collet Rd WV6 ....254 C3
Colletts Brook B75 ......259 A1
Collett B77 ....251 A1
Colley Gate ST10 ....41 C3
Colley La ST10 ....41 C3
Collier Cl Brownhills WS8 ..244 B4
Cheslyn Hay WS6 ....226 B1
Colliery Dr WS1 ....242 C2
Colliery Rd WS15 ....196 C2
Collin Rd ST4 ....71 C3
Collin St ST14 ....126 A4
Collinbourne Cl ST14 ....88 A3
Collindale Ct DY6 ....275 A4
Collingwood Gr ST4 ......71 C4
Collingwood Jun & Inf Schs
WV10 ....240 C1
Collingwood Rd WV10 .....240 C1
Collins Hill WS13 ....214 A1
Collins Rd WS8 ....245 A3
Collinson Rd
Barton-u-N DE13 ....183 B1
Tunstall ST6 ....41 B4
Collis Ave ST4 ....56 B1
Collis St DY8 ....279 C4
Colne Mount ST14 ....126 A4
Colonnade The **14** ST16 ..155 C2
Colshaw Rd DY8 ....279 C2
Coltman Cl WS14 ....231 B4
Colton Hills Com Sch
WV4 ....266 A2
Colton Rd WS15 ....178 C2
Coltsfoot View WS6 ......226 C1
Columbian Cres WS7 ......228 C4
Columbian Way WS11 .....209 C2
Columbine Wlk **10** ST6 ..41 A4
Colville Cl DE12 ....218 B4

Colville St ST4 ....72 C3
Colwall Rd DY3 ....271 B2
Colwich CE Prim Sch
ST17 ....177 C4
Colwich Cres ST16 ....156 B2
Colwyn Dr ST6 ....27 B3
Combe Dr ST3 ....90 A3
Comber Gr DY7 ....278 A2
Comber Rd DY7 ....277 C2
Comberford La B79 ....234 A1
Comberford Rd B79 ....250 A4
Combermere Cl TF9 ....97 B1
Combine Ct B75 ....258 B2
Comfrey Cl ST13 ....44 C2
Commerce Dr ST19 ....207 C4
Commerce St ST3 ....283 C3
Commercial Rd ST11 .....282 C2
Commercial St ST4 ......56 C1
Common Barn La DY10 ....280 B3
Common La
Acton Trussell ST17 ......194 A4
Alrewas WS13 ....215 B3
Betley CW3 ....52 C3
Cannock WS11 ....210 A2
Kingstone ST14 ....124 B1
Meir ST3 ....89 C2
Stone ST15 ....119 C3
Tamworth B79 ....250 A2
Waterhouses ST10 ....44 C4
Whitmore ST5 ....85 B3
Whittington WS14 ....232 B2
Common Rd
Stafford ST16 ....155 C4
Wombourne WV5 ....270 A3
Common Road Ind Est
ST16 ....155 C4
Common Side WS8 ....245 A3
Common The ST10 ....75 B2
Common View
Burntwood WS7 ....212 A1
Cannock WS12 ....210 A4
Common Wlk WS12 ....209 B3
Commonside
Longdon WS15 ....212 A2
Walsall WS3 ....244 A1
Commonside Cl ST16 .....155 B3
Community Dr ST6 ....42 B1
Como Pl ST5 ....70 C3
Compa The DY7 ....278 A2
Compton ST13 ....30 C3
Compton Cl Kinver DY7 ...277 C2
Stafford ST17 ....156 A1
Compton Ct B74 ....257 C2
Compton Dr DY6 ....275 B3
Compton Flats ST13 .....30 C3
Compton Gdns DY7 ....277 C2
Compton Gr DY6 ....275 A4
Compton Hill Dr WV3 .....255 B1
Compton Mews ST13 ......30 C3
Compton Park Recn Ctr
WV6 ....255 C2
Compton Rd Kinver DY7 ...277 B2
Stafford ST17 ....156 B1
Tamworth B79 ....249 C4
Wolv WV3 ....255 C1
Compton Rd W WV3 ....255 A1
Compton St ST4 ....282 A2
Comptons The TF9 ....130 A4
Condlyffe Rd ST13 ......30 C2
Condor Gr WS12 ....210 B1
Condor Rd WS11 ....228 A2
Conduit St WS13 ....231 A4
Conewood Pl ST3 ....72 C1
Coney Gr ST3 ....74 A2
Coneybere Gdns ST19 ....223 B4
Coneygreave Cl ST10 .....76 B1
Coneygreave La ST5 .....56 A4
Conford Cl ST2 ....57 C1
Congleton Edge Rd
CW12 ....16 A3
Congleton Rd
Biddulph ST8 ....16 B1
Kidsgrove ST7 ....25 B1
Mow Cop ST7 ....15 C1
Talke ST7 ....40 B4
Congleton Rd N ST7 .....25 C2
Congleton Rd S ST7 .....25 C1
Congleton Sta CW12 .....6 A1
Congreve Cl ST17 ....175 C4
Congreve Rd ST13 ....72 C1
Conifer Cl WS12 ....210 A4
Conifer Gr ST13 ....72 C1
Conifer Gr
Cannock WS11 ....210 A2
Stafford ST17 ....174 A4
Coniston B77 ....262 A4
Coniston Cl ST15 ....120 B4
Coniston Dr Cheadle ST10 ..76 C2
Kingswinford DY6 ....275 A4
Coniston Gr ST5 ....71 A2
Coniston Ho ST16 ....155 C2
Coniston Pl ST4 ....87 C4
Coniston Rd
Perton WV6 ....254 C2
Wolv WV6 ....255 B4
Coniston Way WS11 ......209 C1
Connaught Dr WV5 ....265 A1
Connaught St ST6 ....41 B1
Conners La TF10 ....146 B4
Conrad Cl ST3 ....73 B3
Consall Gr ST4 ....88 B3
Consall La ST9 ....60 B3
Consall Nature Pk* ST9 ..61 A3
Consall Sta ST9 ....60 B3
Consett Rd ST13 ....68 C4
Consort St ST4 ....72 A4
Constable Ave ST5 ......55 C3
Constable Cl ST3 ....90 A4
Constance Ave ST4 ......56 B1

Convent Cl
Burton u T DE15 ....185 C4
Cannock WS11 ....226 B4
Colwich ST18 ....177 B4
Stoke-on-T ST4 ....72 A4
Convent Ct ST4 ....72 A4
Convent La ST15 ....105 A2
Conway Cl
Burton u T DE13 ....166 B4
Kingswinford DY6 ....275 C2
Conway Gr ST10 ....76 C1
Conway Rd Biddulph ST8 ..27 B3
Cannock WS11 ....226 A4
Perton WV6 ....254 C2
Stafford ST16 ....155 A2
Conway St ST4 ....72 B4
Conygree La DE6 ....81 B4
Cook Gr WV6 ....254 C2
Cook Rd WS3 ....243 A1
Cook's Bank ST17 ....173 B1
Cook's Hollow ST13 .....47 A4
Cook's La ST15 ....32 A1
Cooke Cl ST19 ....192 C1
Cookley La DY7 ....278 A1
Cookley Sebright Fst Sch
DY10 ....280 A3
Cooknell Dr DY8 ....275 C1
Cookson Ave ST13 ....73 C4
Coombe Croft WV9 ....240 A2
Coombe Park Rd WS15 ....119 C3
Coombes Valley Nature
Reserve* ST10 ....46 B3
Coombesdale ST5 ....85 C1
Cooper & Jordan CE Prim
Sch WS9 ....256 B3
Cooper Ave ST5 ....56 C1
Cooper Cl ST15 ....120 B4
Cooper Perry Prim Sch
ST18 ....154 C2
Cooper St Hanley ST1 ....282 A1
Newcastle-u-L ST5 ......55 C3
Wolv WV2 ....266 C4
Cooper's Bank Rd DY5 ...271 B1
Cooper's Sq DE14 ....166 B1
Cooper's Cl ST13 ....30 B3
Coopers Way ST18 ......27 A4
Cope St Norton-in-t-M ST2 ..43 A1
Stafford ST16 ....155 C2
Cope's Dr B79 ....250 A4
Copeland Ave
Newcastle-u-L ST5 ......71 A2
Tittensor ST12 ....88 A1
Copeland Cl ST10 ......76 B1
Copeland Dr ST15 ......120 B3
Copeland St ST14 ......72 A4
Copelands The DY7 ......278 A2
Copes Ave ST6 ....41 C2
Copes Way ST14 ....111 A1
Copley La WV6 ....253 A1
Coplow Ave ST10 ....92 B2
Coplow La DE65 ....129 B3
Copp La ST6 ....41 B1
Copper Beech Dr
Kingswinford DY6 ....270 B1
Wombourne WV5 ....270 A3
Copper Glade ST16 .....156 A2
Copperas Rd DE13 ......186 B3
Copperfields WS14 .....231 B4
Copperhill Rd CW12 ....16 A4
Copperkins Rd WS12 ....210 C2
Coppermill Cl WS12 ....209 C4
Coppice Ave ST5 ....55 A1
Coppice Brook ST17 ....176 B2
Coppice Cl Biddulph ST8 ..27 B3
Burntwood WS7 ....228 C4
Cheslyn Hay WS6 ....226 B2
Sedgley DY3 ....271 B4
Stone ST15 ....105 A1
Wolv WV11 ....242 A1
Coppice Cres WS8 ......244 B4
Coppice Cres WS11 .....226 A4
Coppice Dr
Newport TF10 ....168 C3
Polesworth B78 ....262 C4
Coppice Farm Way
WV11 ....242 A1
Coppice Gdns ST15 .....105 A1
Coppice Gr
Lichfield WS14 ....231 C4
Meir ST3 ....74 A2
Coppice Ho ST7 ....40 B4
Coppice La Aldridge WS9 ..244 C1
Brownhills WS8 ....244 B4
Burntwood WS7,WS14 .....230 A2
Cheslyn Hay WS6 ....226 B2
Clifton Campville B79 ...218 C1
Middleton B75,B78 ......259 B1
Wolv WV6 ....255 A3
Coppice Rd
Brownhills WS8,WS9 .....244 C2
Rugeley WS15 ....196 C3
Stone ST15 ....105 A1
Talke ST7 ....40 B4
Wolv WV3 ....265 B4
Coppice Sch B75 ....258 A1
Coppice Sch The ST18 ...58 A1
Coppice Side Ind Est
WS8 ....244 B4
Coppice The
Cannock WS11 ....210 C1
Biddulph ST8 ....281 C3
Hanley ST6 ....42 B1
Market Drayton TF9 .....97 A1
Coppice View ST5 ......36 A3
Coppins The **11** Leek ST13 ..30 B3
2 Stafford ST17 ....175 B4
Copplestone Gr ST3 ....73 C2

Coppull Pl ST6 .....42 A4
Coppy Hall Gr WS9 .....245 A1
Coppy Nook La WS7 .....229 B3
Copse Cres WS13 .....244 A2
Copse Dr WS15 .....198 A2
Copse The B74 .....257 C1
Copsy Dale ST1 .....115 B3
Copthorne Ave WS7 .....228 C2
Copthorne Rd WV3 .....266 A4
Coracle Gr ST8 .....27 C3
Coral Gr ST4 .....88 A4
Corbet Ct TF9 .....97 B1
Corbett Ho 6 DY8 .....279 C4
Corbett Hospl DY8 .....279 C4
Corbett Prim Sch DY7 .....268 A1
Corbett Wlk 12 ST6 .....41 B2
Corbin Rd B78 .....262 C3
Corby Pl ST3 .....283 A3
Corden Ave DE13 .....166 C4
Cordy La WV7 .....237 A4
Corfe Cl WV6 .....254 C2
Corfe Gn ST3 .....73 B3
Corfield Pl ST6 .....42 B3
Corfton Dr WV6 .....255 B2
Corina Cl ST3 .....73 B2
Corina Way ST3 .....73 A3
Corinth Way 14 ST6 .....41 B2
Cormie Cl ST6 .....45 A4
Corncrake Rd DY1,DY3 .....271 C2
Cornel B77 .....250 C2
Cornelious St 3 ST3 .....74 A1
Cornes St ST1 .....57 B1
Corneville Rd ST12 .....58 B2
Cornfield WV8 .....239 C1
Cornfield Cl DY6 .....275 A4
Cornfield Dr WS14 .....231 C4
Cornfield Rd ST8 .....27 C4
Cornflower Cl WV10 .....241 A4
Cornflower Rd WS8 .....244 A3
Cornhill WS11 .....209 C3
Cornhill Cl ST5 .....40 B1
Cornhill Gdns ST13 .....30 C2
Cornhill Rd ST6 .....42 B3
Cornhill St 15 ST13 .....30 C3
Cornmill WV10 .....168 C2
Cornmill Gr WV6 .....254 B2
Cornmill La DE13 .....146 C3
Coronvian Cl WV4 .....254 C3
Corns Gr WV5 .....269 C3
Cornwall Ave
  Newcastle-u-L ST5 .....71 B2
  Tamworth B78 .....250 A1
Cornwall Cl
  Aldridge WS9 .....245 A1
  3 Congleton CW12 .....6 A1
  Kingswinford DY6 .....275 B4
Cornwall Ct WS15 .....196 B3
Cornwall Dr ST17 .....156 A1
Cornwall Rd
  Burton u-T DE15 .....185 C3
  Cannock WS12 .....210 A3
  Stourbridge DY8 .....279 B4
  Wolv WV6 .....255 B2
Cornwall St ST3 .....283 C4
Cornwallis St ST4 .....72 A3
Cornwood Gr ST3 .....89 C4
Coronation Ave
  Biddulph ST8 .....27 A3
  Longton ST3 .....283 B3
  Tamworth B78 .....249 B1
Coronation Cotts DE13 .....184 A4
Coronation Cres
  Kidsgrove ST7 .....25 C1
  Rocester ST14 .....96 A2
  Shuttington B79 .....251 C4
Coronation Rd
  Brownhills WS9 .....245 A2
  Newcastle-u-L ST5 .....284 C2
  Stafford ST16 .....156 A3
  Stoke-on-T, Hartshill ST4 .....71 C4
  Walsall WS4 .....244 A1
Coronation St
  Cheadle ST10 .....76 B2
  Tamworth B79 .....250 A3
  Tunstall ST6 .....41 C2
Corporation St
  Newcastle-u-L ST5 .....284 B3
  Stafford ST16 .....155 C2
  Stoke-on-T ST4 .....72 A3
  Tamworth B79 .....250 A3
Corran Rd ST17 .....174 B3
Correen B77 .....251 B1
Corrin Gr 4 DY6 .....275 B4
Corser St ST1 .....271 C1
Corsham Pl ST14 .....143 C4
Corsican Cl WS7 .....229 A4
Corsican Dr WS12 .....210 A4
Corsty La ST18 .....154 A2
Cort Dr WS7 .....229 A4
Corve Gdns WV6 .....255 C3
Corve View DY3 .....266 B1
Coseley St ST6 .....42 B3
Cosford Ct WV6 .....255 A3
Cosgrove Wlk WV8 .....239 C1
Cot La DY6,DY8 .....275 B3
Cote La DY7 .....273 C1
Cotehill Rd ST9 .....59 B1
Cotes La Millmeece ST21 .....102 C1
  Swynnerton ST12 .....103 A1
Coteshheath St ST1 .....57 B1
Coton Ave ST16 .....156 A2
Coton Green Prec B79 .....249 C4
Coton Green Prim Sch
  B79 .....249 C4
Coton La Ranton ST18 .....153 C2
  Seighford ST18 .....154 A2
  Tamworth B79 .....249 C4
Coton Pk DE12 .....186 B1

Coton Rd DE12 .....202 C3
Coton Rise ST12 .....88 C1
Cotsdale Rd WV4 .....265 C2
Cotswold Ave
  Great Wyrley WS6 .....226 C2
  Newcastle-u-L ST5 .....55 C2
Cotswold Cl
  Aldridge WS9 .....245 B1
  Cannock WS12 .....210 A4
Cotswold Cres ST2 .....43 A1
Cotswold Ct
  Sutton Coldfield B75 .....258 A2
  Wolv WV3 .....266 A3
Cotswold Dr WV7 .....237 A3
Cotswold Gr WV12 .....242 A1
Cotswold Rd
  Branston DE14 .....184 C4
  Cannock WS12 .....210 A4
  Wolv WV2 .....266 C4
Cottage Cl
  Burntwood WS7 .....228 C3
  Cannock WS12 .....210 B3
  Meir ST3 .....73 C1
Cottage Ct WS7 .....228 C3
Cottage Farm Rd B77 .....261 B4
Cottage La Biddulph ST8 .....28 A4
  Burntwood WS7 .....228 C3
  Wolv WV10 .....240 B2
Cottage Mews WS9 .....256 C2
Cottage St DY6 .....275 B4
Cottage The TF10 .....168 C2
Cottage View WV8 .....239 A2
Cottage Wlk B77 .....261 C3
Cotterill Dr ST5 .....56 A4
Cotterill Gr ST6 .....56 C4
Cotters Hill Cl ST18 .....147 A4
Cottesmore Rd DE15 .....167 A1
Cotton Cl DE13 .....200 C2
Cotton Colt ST10 .....63 B1
Cotton Gr WS12 .....195 A1
Cotton La ST10 .....63 A1
Cotton Rd Tunstall ST6 .....41 B3
  Wolv WV4 .....266 A3
Cotton Way WS7 .....211 C1
Cottonwood Dr ST7 .....26 C2
Cottonwood Gr ST3 .....283 C4
Cotts The 74 A4
Cotwall End Ho DY3 .....271 B3
Cotwall End Nature Ctr*
DY3 .....271 B3
Cotwall End Prim Sch
DY3 .....271 B4
Cotwall End Rd DY3 .....271 A3
Coulson Cl WS7 .....211 B1
Coulter Gr WV6 .....254 B2
Coulter La WV7 .....229 C4
Coulthwaite Way WS6 .....196 C3
Council Hos
  Chetwynd Aston TF10 .....187 A4
  Church Leigh ST10 .....109 A2
  Kingstone ST14 .....125 B1
  Kingstone, The Blythe
  ST18 .....140 C3
  Uttoxeter ST14 .....125 B4
Council Hos The ST21 .....116 A2
Country Park View ST7 .....58 A4
County Dr B78 .....250 A1
County La
  Codsall WV7,WV8 .....237 C2
  Stourbridge DY7 .....281 B4
County Rd ST16 .....155 C3
Coupe Dr ST9 .....74 A3
Court Cres DY6 .....275 B3
Court Dr WS14 .....246 C2
Court Farm La DE14 .....184 C4
Court La ST5 .....56 A2
Court No 1 ST3 .....73 C1
Court Par WS9 .....256 A3
Court Rd WV6 .....255 C2
Court Wlk CW3 .....53 A3
Courtland Mews ST16 .....155 C2
Courtland Rd DY6 .....275 C4
Courtlands The WV6 .....255 C3
Courtney Pl ST17 .....89 C4
Courtway Dr ST1 .....57 B4
Cousins St WV2 .....266 B4
Coven Cl WS3 .....244 A3
Coven Mill Cl WV9 .....224 B1
Coven St ST19 .....223 B2
Coventry Ct ST16 .....155 A3
Coverdale Cl ST13 .....90 A4
Coverley Pl ST14 .....71 C3
Covers La DY7 .....274 C1
Covert Cl ST18 .....158 A1
Covert Gdns ST17 .....40 B4
Covert La DY7 .....279 B4
Covert The Keele ST5 .....70 A4
  Newcastle-u-L ST5 .....71 B1
  Wolv WV7 .....239 C1
Covey Cl WS13 .....214 B3
Cow La Waterhouses ST10 .....63 C4
  Wood End B78 .....262 C2
Cowallmoor La ST13 .....28 A3
Cowan Dr ST16 .....156 A2
Cowen St ST6 .....42 C3
Cowhill La WS13 .....200 C1
Cowhouse La ST18 .....127 B1
Cowley B77 .....250 C1
Cowley Cl ST6 .....42 C3
Cowley Dr DY1 .....271 C1
Cowley Gn WS12 .....195 A1
Cowley La ST20 .....171 B3
Cowley Way ST12 .....73 C4
Cowlishaw Cl ST18 .....171 C1
Cowlishaw Rd ST6 .....42 B3
Cowlishaw Way WS15 .....196 C3

Cowlow La SK17 .....23 B2
Cowper St ST4 .....72 C3
Coxmoor Cl WS12 .....210 C4
Crab La Robbington DY7 .....268 B1
  Cannock WS11 .....210 A2
  Stafford ST16 .....155 A4
  Walsall WV12 .....242 B1
Crabbery St ST16 .....155 C2
Crabtree Ave ST8 .....27 B4
Crabtree Cl ST14 .....72 C4
Crabtree Ways WS15 .....178 B1
Crackley Bank ST5 .....40 C1
Crackley Bank CE Prim Sch
ST5 .....40 C1
Crackley Bank Prim Sch
ST5 .....55 C4
Crackley La ST5 .....54 C2
Cracow Moss CW3 .....53 A2
Craddock Rd DE16 .....155 B4
Craftdown Cl ST17 .....174 C2
Craigside ST8 .....27 B4
Cramer St ST17 .....155 C1
Cranberry Ave WV10 .....93 A1
Cranberry Cl ST16 .....155 B2
Cranberry Dr ST5 .....40 B1
Cranberry Marsh ST21 .....102 B2
Cranbourne Ave
  Norton-in-t-M ST2 .....43 A1
  Wolv WV4 .....266 C2
Cranbrook Cl ST14 .....88 A4
Cranbrook Gr WV6 .....254 C2
Cranbrook Wlk ST14 .....174 A4
Cranbrooks ST19 .....205 B4
Crane Dr WS7 .....229 A4
Crane Field WS13 .....214 A1
Crane Hollow WV5 .....269 C3
Crane St ST1 .....57 A3
Crane Terr WV6 .....255 C3
Cranebrook Hill B78 .....259 C3
Cranebrook La
  Shenstone WS14 .....245 C4
  Wall WS14 .....246 A4
Cranesbill Cl WV10 .....241 B4
Cranfield Pl ST2 .....58 A1
Cranfield Rd WS7 .....229 A4
Cranford Pl 8 WS11 .....209 C1
Cranford Rd WV3 .....265 B4
Cranford Way ST17 .....58 B2
Cranham Dr DY6 .....275 C3
Cranleigh Ave ST5 .....57 B4
Cranleigh Cl
  Aldridge WS9 .....256 A3
  Walsall WV12 .....242 B1
Cranleigh Way WS14 .....231 C4
Cranley Dr WV8 .....238 C2
Cranmer Gr ST4 .....257 C3
Cranmer St ST4 .....72 A4
Cranmere Ave WV6 .....255 A3
Cranmere Cl WV6 .....226 B1
Cranmore Gr ST15 .....210 B2
Cranmore Rd WV3 .....255 C2
Cranswick Gr ST2 .....58 B1
Crantock Cl WV11 .....242 B1
Cranwell Gn WV5 .....269 C3
Cranwell Pl ST13 .....89 C4
Cranwell Rise B78 .....249 B1
Cranwood Rd ST12 .....88 A1
Cranworth Gr ST3 .....89 C4
Crateford La ST19 .....224 A4
Crathorne Ave WV10 .....240 B1
Craufurd Rd CW12 .....6 A4
Crediton Ave ST16 .....42 B2
Creighton La ST14 .....111 A3
Cremorne Dr ST17 .....175 B4
Cremorne Rd B75 .....258 A1
Cremorne Wlk B75 .....258 A1
Crescent Gr ST4 .....56 C1
Crescent Rd ST17 .....174 C2
Crescent The Ashley TF9 .....100 B3
  Brownhall WS7 .....211 C1
  Cookley DY10 .....280 A2
  Eccleshall ST21 .....133 B3
  Great Wyrley WS6 .....227 A1
  Hagley DY8 .....281 C3
  Leek ST13 .....30 B3
  Mayfield DE6 .....81 B4
  Newcastle-u-L, Silverdale
    ST5 .....55 A1
  Newcastle-u-L, Westlands
    ST5 .....71 A3
  Rudyard ST13 .....13 B4
  Stafford ST17 .....175 C4
  Stafford, Doxey ST16 .....155 A2
  Stoke-on-T ST4 .....71 C2
  Stone ST15 .....105 A1
  Swadlincote DE11 .....186 A4
  Wolv WV5 .....255 A2
Cressington Dr B78 .....251 A4
Cresswell Ave ST5 .....40 B1
Cresswell Ct WV10 .....240 A2
Cresswell La
  Brewood ST19 .....223 B3
  Lichfield WS13 .....91 B2
Cresswell Old Rd ST11 .....91 C2
Cresswell Rd Hanley ST1 .....57 C2
  Hiderstone ST15 .....106 C2
Crest Cl ST13 .....30 C3
Crestbrook Rd ST2 .....58 B3

Crestfield Rd ST3 .....89 C4
Crestway Rd ST2 .....43 B1
Creswood B77 .....251 A3
Crestwood Cl DE13 .....166 B4
Crestwood Dr ST15 .....119 C3
Crestwood Glen WV6 .....255 C4
Crestwood Pk ST19 .....223 B4
Crestwood Rise WS15 .....178 B1
Crestwood Sch The
  DY6 .....275 C3
Creswell Cres WS13 .....242 C1
Creswell Dr ST18 .....154 C4
Creswell Gr ST18 .....154 B4
Creswell Gr ST18 .....155 A4
Crewe Gates Ind Est
  CW1 .....37 B4
Crewe Hall Ent Pk CW1 .....37 B4
Crewe La DE13 .....186 C3
Crichton Ave DE13 .....166 B4
Crick Rd ST1 .....57 C1
Cricket Cl DE15 .....167 C4
Cricket La WS14 .....231 B3
Cricket Mdw
  Sedgley DY3 .....271 C2
  Wolv WV10 .....240 B2
Cricketers Cl DE15 .....185 C4
Cricketers Mews ST5 .....56 B3
Cricketers The DE13 .....200 C1
Crigdon B77 .....251 B2
Crinan Gr ST17 .....174 B3
Cringlebrook B77 .....250 B1
Crispin Cl ST16 .....155 B4
Critchlow Gr ST13 .....74 A3
Crockford Dr B75 .....258 A2
Crockington Cl WV5 .....263 C1
Crockington La WV5 .....264 A1
Crocus Cres WV9 .....240 A2
Croft Ave Cannock WS12 .....195 A1
  Newcastle-u-L ST5 .....56 A3
Croft Cl Elford B79 .....216 C1
  Nethersaal DE12 .....219 C4
  Rolleston DE13 .....147 A2
Croft Cres
  Brownhills WS8 .....244 B4
  Stoke-on-T ST4 .....72 A3
Croft Ct ST6 .....42 B1
Croft Cty Sch WS15 .....197 C3
Croft Gdns WS7 .....229 A4
Croft Gr ST14 .....111 B3
Croft La ST19 .....207 B1
Croft Leys The WS15 .....198 B2
Croft Par WS9 .....256 A3
Croft Rd Cheadle ST10 .....76 B2
  Newcastle-u-L ST5 .....284 B4
  Stone ST15 .....119 C3
Croft Road Ind Est ST5 .....284 B4
Croft St Burslem ST6 .....56 C4
  Tamworth B79 .....250 A3
Croft The
  Blakedown DY10 .....281 B1
  Burton u-T DE15 .....166 C1
  Cheadle ST10 .....76 C3
  Cheddleton ST13 .....45 B2
  Cheslyn Hay WS6 .....226 C1
  Hixon ST18 .....158 B4
  King's Bromley DE13 .....199 B3
  Longdon WS15 .....197 C1
  Maer ST5 .....84 B1
  Norton in Hales TF9 .....82 A2
  Stafford ST5 .....71 C3
  Swadlincote DE11 .....186 C3
  Wombourne WV5 .....269 B3
Croft Way TF9 .....97 A1
Crofter Cl ST18 .....227 A3
Crofters Cl ST5 .....40 B2
Crofters Ct WS9 .....239 C1
Crofters Wlk WV8 .....239 C1
Croftlield St ST7 .....24 C3
Croftstead Ave ST14 .....95 B3
Cromartie St ST3 .....283 C2
Cromer Cres ST17 .....158 C3
Cromer Gdns WV6 .....255 C3
Cromer Rd ST1 .....57 C2
Cromer St ST15 .....56 B2
Crompton Cl ST18 .....177 C4
Crompton Gr WV8 .....239 C2
Crompton Gr ST4 .....88 B3
Crompton Rd ST15 .....120 A4
Cromwell Cl
  Hopton ST18 .....137 B1
  Lichfield WS13 .....146 B3
Cromwell Ct WS6 .....227 A1
Cromwell Rd
  Cannock WS12 .....210 C1
  Tamworth B79 .....249 C4
  Wolv WV10 .....240 C2
Cromwell St 5 Biddulph ST8 .....27 B4
  Hanley ST1 .....57 B3
Cromwell Terr 17 ST13 .....30 C3
Cromwells Mdw WS14 .....231 B3
Crony Cl ST13 .....45 B2
Crook La WS9 .....256 A3
Crooked Bridge Rd
  ST16 .....155 C2
Crosby Cl WV6 .....255 C2
Crosby Rd ST4 .....72 C4
Cross Butts ST17 .....133 B3
Cross Edge ST6 .....43 A4
Cross Hill ST6 .....56 C4
Cross Ho WV2 .....266 B3
Cross In Hand La
  Hanley West 1 .....213 B2
  Lichfield WS13 .....146 B4
Cross Keys WS13 .....231 A4
Cross St 1 .....39 C3
  Congleton CW12 .....6 A1
Lichfield WS13 .....231 B3
Rolleston DE13 .....147 A1

Cross La continued
Sedgley DY3 .....266 C1
Stone ST15 .....105 B3
Waterhouses ST10,ST13 .....48 C2
Cross May St ST5 .....284 A2
Cross of the Hand
  WS15 .....161 A1
Cross Pl DY3 .....266 C1
Cross Rd Albrighton WV7 .....237 A2
Rugeley WS15 .....196 A4
Uttoxeter ST14 .....111 A1
Cross Side DE6 .....81 C4
Cross St Biddulph ST8 .....27 B4
  Burntwood WS7 .....228 C4
  Burton u-T DE14 .....166 B2
  Cannock, Bridgtown WS11 .....226 C3
  Cannock, Hayes Heath
    WS12 .....210 C1
  Cheadle ST10 .....76 B2
  Cheslyn Hay WS6 .....226 B1
  Gnosall ST20 .....171 B3
  Kingsley ST10 .....61 B2
  8 Kingswinford DY6 .....275 B4
  Kingswinford, Wall Heath
    DY6 .....275 A4
Kingswinford, Wordsley
  DY6 .....275 B3
20 Leek ST13 .....30 C3
Market Drayton TF9 .....97 B1
Meir ST3 .....74 A3
Newcastle-u-L ST5 .....55 C4
Stafford ST16 .....155 B3
Stourbridge DY8 .....279 C3
Tamworth, Kettlebrook
  B77 .....250 B2
Tamworth, The Leys B79 .....250 A3
Tunstall ST6 .....56 B4
Walsall WS3 .....244 A1
Cross St S WV2 .....266 B4
Crossdale Ave ST2 .....43 A1
Crossfell B77 .....251 A1
Crossfield Ave
  Biddulph ST8 .....27 B3
  Forsbrook ST11 .....90 C3
Crossfield Rd WS13 .....231 A1
Crosshill Bank ST18 .....122 C3
Crossing La ST18 .....154 B1
Crossings The WS14 .....231 C4
Crossland Cres WV6 .....255 C4
Crossland Pl E 13 ST13 .....90 A4
Crossland Pl W 13 ST13 .....6 A1
Crosslands CW12 .....6 A1
Crossley Rd ST6 .....42 C2
Crossley Stone WS15 .....178 C1
Crosslow La DE6 .....36 C3
Crossman St DE14 .....166 A2
Crossmead Gr ST1 .....57 C3
Crossway ST13 .....156 A2
Crossway Rd ST6 .....57 B4
Crossway The ST5 .....56 B2
Crossways ST8 .....16 C1
Crossway ST17 .....25 A2
Croston St ST1 .....282 A1
Crotia Ave CW2 .....37 A3
Crouch Ave ST16 .....42 A2
Crouch La CW12 .....6 B2
Crowberry St WS8 .....248 B3
Crowberry Cl WS8 .....248 B3
Crowberry La
  Barton-u-N DE13 .....183 B1
  Middleton B78 .....260 B1
Crowborough Rd ST18,
  ST13 .....28 A3
Crowcrofts Rd ST4 .....88 C4
Crowden Rd B77 .....251 A1
Crowfoot La DE65 .....129 C4
Crowland Ave WV6 .....254 C2
Crown Bank
  Abbots Bromley WS15 .....161 A3
  Hanley ST1 .....282 B3
  Talke ST7 .....40 B3
Crown Bank Cres ST7 .....40 B3
Crown Bridge ST19 .....192 C1
Crown Cl DY3 .....266 B1
Crown Gdns ST7 .....40 B3
Crown Ind Est DE14 .....166 A1
Crown La Kinver DY10 .....281 B4
  Stourbridge DY8 .....279 C3
  Sutton Coldfield B74 .....257 C2
Crown Speci Sch DE13 .....147 B1
Crown St Hanley ST1 .....282 B2
  Newcastle-u-L ST5 .....55 B1
  Stone ST5 .....120 A4
Crowndale Pl ST17 .....41 C4
Crowther Gr WV6 .....255 C2
Crowther Rd WV6 .....255 C3
Crowther St ST4 .....72 B4
Crowtrees Farm Ind Est
  ST18 .....48 C1
Croxall Rd B79,WS13 .....217 A3
Croxden Abbey* ST14 .....94 B2
Croxden Rd ST22 .....58 A3
Croxdene Ave WS3 .....244 A3
Croxhall Rd DE13 .....201 A1
Croxley Dr WS12 .....210 C4
Croxstalls Cl WS3 .....243 A1
Croxstalls Rd WS3 .....243 A1
Croyde Pl ST3 .....90 A3
Croydon Dr ST19 .....207 C4
Cruso St ST13 .....30 C3
Crutchley Ave B78 .....250 A1
Crystal Ave DY8 .....275 C1
Crystal St ST6 .....42 C3
Cubley La DE6 .....96 C1
Cuckoo Cage La DE13 .....148 C1
Cuckoo Cl WS11 .....210 B3

Cull Ave ST16 .... 156 A2
Cullamore La ST14 ...... 126 A2
Culland Rd DE14 .... 185 A4
Cumberland Cl
 Kingswinford DY6 ...... 275 C2
 Talke ST7 .... 40 C4
Cumberland Cres WS7 ... 229 A4
Cumberland Dr B78 ..... 250 A1
Cumberland Rd
 Burton u T DE15 .... 185 B3
 Cannock WS11 .... 210 A2
Cumberland St
 Fenton ST4 .... 72 C3
 Newcastle-u-L ST5 ..... 284 C3
Cumberledge Hill WS15 . 211 C3
Cumberpatch Ave ST6 ... 42 A4
Cumbers The ST18 ...... 154 A3
Cumbria Ho ST5 .... 71 B3
Cumming St ST4 .... 71 C4
Cunningham Rd WV6 .... 254 C2
Curborough Rd WS13 ... 214 A1
Curland Pl ST3 .... 73 C1
Curlew B77 .... 262 A4
Curlew Cl Lichfield WS14 231 C4
Curlew Hill WS11 ...... 210 A2
Curtis Ct DE13 .... 166 B4
Curtis Way DE14 .... 166 A2
Curtiss Pl ST3 .... 90 B3
Curzon Cl WS15 .... 196 C4
Curzon Rd ST6 .... 42 A1
Curzon Rise ST3 .... 30 A3
Curzon St
 Burton u T DE14 ...... 166 B2
 Wolverhampton WV1 ... 90 A1
 Wolv WV2 .... 266 B4
Curzon St W DE14 ..... 166 A2
Cutts St ST1 .... 282 A1
Cwerne Ct DY3 .... 271 B2
Cyclamen Cl DE14 ..... 185 A4
Cygnet Cl Cannock WS12 210 B4
 Keele CW3 .... 69 A4
 Wolv WV6 .... 255 B1
Cynthia Gr ST6 .... 42 A1
Cypress Ave DY3 ...... 271 B3
Cypress Cl
 Market Drayton TF9 ... 97 A1
 Stafford ST17 .... 156 B1
Cypress Gdns [1] DY6 . 275 B2
Cypress Gr
 Forsbrook ST11 ...... 91 A3
 Newcastle-u-L ST5 ... 55 B4
Cypress Rise WS12 .... 211 A3
Cyprus St WV2 .... 266 B3

D

D'Urberville Cl WV2 .... 266 C3
D'Urberville Rd WV2 .... 266 C3
D'Urberville Wlk [1]
 WS11 .... 210 A1
Dace B77 .... 261 B4
Dace Gr ST6 .... 42 A2
Daffodil Cl DY3 .... 271 C4
Daffodil Wlk ST5 ...... 178 B1
Dag La DE12 .... 218 C4
Dahlia Cl ST3 .... 74 A3
Daimler Cl [3] ST17 ... 175 A4
Dain Pl ST5 .... 56 A3
Dain St ST6 .... 56 C4
Daintry Cl ST13 ...... 30 C3
Daintry Dr B79 .... 249 A4
Daintry St Leek ST13 .. 30 C3
 Stoke-on-T ST4 ...... 71 C2
Dairy Cl ST13 .... 31 A3
Dairyfields Way ST1 ... 57 B4
Dairyhouse La
 Cheadle ST10 .... 60 C1
 Dilhorne ST10 .... 60 A1
Dairylands Rd ST7 .... 25 A2
Daisy Ave ST10 .... 62 A4
Daisy Bank
 Cannock WS12 .... 209 C4
 Leek ST13 .... 30 C3
Daisy Bank Cl WS3 .... 244 A1
Daisy La DE13 .... 200 B1
Daisy Pl ST4 .... 72 C2
Daisy Wlk WV9 .... 240 A2
Dalbeg Cl WV8 .... 255 C4
Dale Ave ST6 .... 42 C3
Dale Cl Cheadle ST10 .. 76 C1
 Whitmore ST5 .... 85 B3
Dale Cres CW12 ...... 6 A1
Dale Dr WS7 .... 229 A4
Dale Gr CW12 .... 6 A1
Dale La Haughton ST18 173 A4
 Seighford ST18 ...... 144 C1
 Stanton DE6 .... 64 C2
Dale Rd DY8 .... 279 C1
Dale St Burslem ST6 .. 56 C4
 Burton u T DE14 ..... 166 B1
Dale The Ashley TF9 ... 100 A3
 Warslow SK17 .... 23 B1
Dale View
 Earl Sterndale SK17 .. 5 A2
 Kidsgrove ST7 .... 26 B3
 Meir ST3 .... 90 C1
Dale View Ct ST11 .... 90 C1
Dale View Dr ST5 .... 55 B1
Dalebrook Rd DE15 ... 167 A3
Dalecot Gn ST2 ...... 73 B4
Dalegarth Gr [1] ST3 . 89 C4
Dalehall Gdns [2] ST6 . 56 C4
Dalehead Ct ST17 .... 89 C4

Dalehouse Rd ST13 ... 45 B2
Daleian Ct ST5 .... 55 B1
Dalelands Est TF9 .... 112 A4
Dalelands W TF9 ..... 112 A4
Dales Cl Biddulph ST8 . 28 A4
 Swadlincote DE11 .... 186 C3
Dales Green Rd B77 .. 262 A4
Dales in E Sch The B77 262 A4
Dales Jun Sch B77 ... 262 A4
Daleside DE15 .... 167 A1
Dalesman Cl DY6 .... 275 A4
Dalewood Rd ST5 .... 55 C3
Dallow Cl DE14 ..... 166 B3
Dallow Cres DE14 ... 166 B3
Dallow St DE14 ..... 166 B3
Dalton Ave DE15 .... 167 A1
Dalton Ct WV5 ...... 269 C4
Dalton Gr ST3 ...... 89 A3
Dalton St WV3 ...... 266 A4
Daltry Way CW3 .... 68 C4
Daly Cres ST5 ...... 55 A3
Dam La Alsop en le D DE6 36 C2
 Biddulph ST8 ...... 17 A1
Dam St WS13 .... 231 A4
Dama Rd B78 .... 260 C4
Dame Paulet Wlk DE14 166 B3
Dampier St ST13 .... 30 C3
Dams The ST11 .... 74 B1
Damson Pk WV6 .... 253 B2
Danby Crest ST17 .. 174 A4
Danby Dr WS12 .... 211 B2
Dandillion Ave ST10 . 92 B4
Dane Dr ST8 .... 16 C1
Dane Gdns ST7 .... 26 B1
Dane Gr ST10 ..... 76 C1
Dane Wlk ST11 .... 282 C3
Danebower Rd ST4 . 88 A3
Danebridge Gr ST11 . 57 C3
Danehill Gr ST14 ... 71 C4
Danehill Wlk WV8 .. 255 C4
Danelagh Cl B79 ... 249 C4
Danemead Cl ST3 .. 90 A4
Danes Cl WV11 .... 241 C2
Danes Croft ST4 ... 88 A4
Danesbrook WV5 .. 267 B4
Danescourt Rd WV6 255 B3
Danesmore Park Jun & Inf
 Sch WV11 .... 242 A1
Daneswood Dr ST4 226 A3
Danford La WV5 ... 267 B4
Daniels Cross TF10 169 A2
Daniels La WS9 .... 256 B3
Danilo Rd WS11 .... 209 B1
Danta Way ST17 ... 156 B1
Darby Ave WS14 ... 232 C3
Darges La WS6 .... 226 C2
Darius Cl ST5 ..... 56 A4
Dark La Alrewas DE13 201 A2
 Farewell WS13 ..... 213 A1
 Deans Slade Dr WS14 231 A3
 Featherstone, Brinsford
 WV10 .... 240 B4
 Featherstone, Hilton Park
 WV10,WV11 ...... 241 B4
 Great Wyrley WS6 .. 227 B1
 Kinver DY7 .... 278 A2
 Longdon WS15 .... 212 B4
 Newborough DE13 .. 162 B4
 Newport TF10 ..... 168 C1
 Polesworth B78 .... 262 C4
Darley Cl DE15 ..... 167 A1
Darley Dale DE13 .. 186 C1
Darley Gr ST10 ..... 76 C1
Darlings La WS15 .. 212 A3
Darnbrook B77 .... 251 B1
Darnel Hurst Rd B75 258 B2
Darnford Cl ST16 ... 155 B4
Darnford La
 Lichfield WS14 ..... 231 C3
 Whittington WS14 .. 232 A3
Darnford Moors WS14 231 C3
Darnford View WS13 214 C1
Darnley St ST4 .... 72 A2
Darrall Gdns ST14 . 71 C2
Darsham Gdns ST5 . 71 B1
Dart Ave ST16 .... 156 B1
Dart Cl ST8 .... 16 B1
Dart Gr ST10 ...... 76 C1
Dart Pl ST5 .... 71 A2
Dartford Pl ST6 ... 42 B2
Dartford Rd WS3 . 242 C1
Dartmouth Ave
 Cannock WS11 .... 226 A4
 Kingswinford DY8 . 275 B2
 Newcastle-u-L ST5 . 71 A3
 Pattingham WV6 ... 253 B1
Dartmouth Pl ST13 . 89 C4
Dartmouth Rd WS11 209 B1
Dartmouth St
 Chell Heath ST6 ... 42 A1
 Stafford ST16 ..... 156 A4
 Wolv WV2 .... 266 B4
Darwell Pk B77 .... 251 A4
Darwin Cl
 Burntwood WS7 ... 229 A4
 Burton u T DE15 ... 167 A1
 Cannock WS12 .... 210 C1
 Lichfield WS13 .... 231 A4
 Stafford ST16 ..... 156 B2
 2 Stone ST15 .... 104 C1
Darwin Ct WV6 .... 254 C2
Darwin Gr ST6 .... 42 A3
Dash Gr ST6 ...... 42 B1
Datteln Rd WS11 .. 210 A2
Daurada Dr ST17 .. 175 A4
Davenport Cl ST13 . 30 A2
Davenport Rd WV6 . 254 B2
Davenport St Burslem ST6 56 B4

Davenport St continued
 Tunstall ST6 .... 41 C1
Davenport Way ST5 . 70 C2
Daventry Cl ST2 ... 57 C1
David Garrick Gdns
 WS13 .... 214 A1
David Rd ST3 ...... 73 C1
Davidson Ave CW12 . 6 A3
Davidson Rd WS14 . 231 A4
Davies Dr ST14 .... 110 C1
Davies Ho WS3 .... 243 A1
Davis Cl ST16 ..... 156 A2
Davis Rd B77 ...... 250 C2
Davis St ST4 ...... 57 A1
Davison St ST6 .... 57 A4
Davy Cl ST2 .... 58 A2
Davy Pl WS15 ..... 196 B3
Daw St WS3 .... 243 C1
Dawes La WS8 .... 229 A1
Dawley Brook Prim Sch
 DY6 .... 275 B4
Dawley Brook Rd DY6 275 B4
Dawley Rd DY6 .... 275 B4
Dawley Trad Est DY6 275 B4
Dawlish Ave ST17 . 175 B4
Dawlish Dr ST2 ... 58 B1
Dawn Ave ST6 .... 42 A2
Dawn View ST3 ... 74 A2
Dawney Dr B75 .. 258 A2
Dawson Ave WV14 . 266 C1
Dayson Pl ST5 .... 56 A4
Dayton Dr WS15 .. 178 B1
Daywell Rise WS15 . 178 B1
De Ferrers Croft DE13 166 B4
De Ferrers High Sch (Dove
 Campus) DE13 ... 166 A4
De Ferrers High Sch (Trent
 Campus) DE13 .. 166 B4
De Havilland Dr ST10 . 118 B3
De-Wint Rd ST15 . 120 A4
Deacon Way WS15 178 C1
Deakin Av ST6 .... 71 B3
Deakin Cl ST6 .... 71 B3
Deakin Rd ST16 .. 42 A3
Deal Ave WS7 ... 229 A4
Dean Cl TF9 ..... 97 A1
Dean Ct WV6 .... 254 C3
Dean Hollow ST7 . 39 B1
Dean Pl ST1 .... 282 C1
Dean Rd WV5 ... 269 C3
Dean St Brewood SP10 223 B3
 Bucknall SJ2 ..... 58 B2
 Sedgley DY3 ..... 271 B4
Dean's La ST5 .... 40 B1
Deanery Cl
 Rugeley WS15 .... 178 C1
 Shareshill WV10 .. 225 B1
Deans Coll ST14 .. 231 B4
Deans La CW2 .... 38 B2
Deansberry Ct ST14 88 A4
Deanscroft Way ST3 73 C2
Deansfield Cl ST19 . 223 B3
Deansfield Ho ST19 . 223 B4
Deansfield Rd ST19 223 B3
Deansgate [1] DE13 . 30 C3
Deanshill Cl ST16 . 155 B1
Deansway ST4 ... 88 A3
Dearnsdale Cl ST16 . 155 A4
Deavall Way WS11 . 210 C1
Deaville Rd ST7 ... 58 B2
Debenham Cres ST1 58 A1
Deborah Cl WV4 . 266 B3
Decade Cl ST16 .. 40 C1
De Burgh DE WS10 . 75 C1
Dee Gr WS11 .... 226 B4
Dee La ST5 ...... 71 A2
Dee Rd WS3 .... 243 C1
Deebank Ave ST13 31 A3
Deeley St ST7 ... 251 A1
Deep Cut Rd DE6 . 144 A4
Deep Hayes Ctry Pk*
 ST13 .... 45 A4
Deepdale Cl
 Burton u T DE15 . 167 A3
 Norton-in-t-M ST6 . 42 C1
Deepdale La
 Sedgley DY3 .... 271 C2
 Snelston DE6 .... 65 A1
Deepdales Stafford ST17 175 B3
 Wombourne WV5 . 269 C3
Deepmore Cl
 Alrewas DE13 .... 201 A1
 Featherstone WV10 . 224 B3
Deer Cl Huntington WV12 209 B3
 Norton Canes WS11 . 228 A4
 Walsall WS3 .... 243 B1
Deer Hill ST17 ... 176 B2
Deer Park Dr TF10 . 168 B3
Deer Pk ST20 .... 171 C4
Deer Wlk WV8 ... 239 C1
Deerfold Cres WS7 229 A4
Deerhill B77 ...... 251 A4
Deerhurst Rise WS12 210 C3
Deerleap Way WS15 178 B1
Defford Ave WS4 . 244 B1
Defoe Dr ST3 ... 73 C2
Delafield Way WS15 178 B1
Delamere Gr
 Newcastle-u-L ST5 . 284 C4
 Trentham ST4 .... 88 A4
Delamere La ST17 . 174 A4
Delaney Dr ST3 ... 73 C2
Delhi Cl ST5 ..... 71 A2
Delhurst Ave WV4 . 266 C2

Delius Gr ST1 ..... 57 C3
Dell Cl ST16 ..... 155 A4
Dell The Cannock WS12 . 210 C2
 Lichfield WS13 ... 230 C4
 Newcastle-u-L ST5 . 55 B1
Stourbridge DY8 .. 279 C3
Tamworth B79 ... 250 A3
Delius Cl DY8 .... 279 C3
Dellwood Gr **2** ST3 . 89 B3
Delph Wlk ST4 ... 72 C3
Delphouse Rd
 Cheadle ST10 ... 76 A1
 Forsbrook ST10 .. 75 C1
Delphside ST7 ... 39 C1
Delta Way WS11 . 226 C4
Delta Way Bsns Ctr
 WS11 .... 226 B3
Deltic B77 .... 251 A1
Delves Cres CV9 . 262 B1
Delves Pl ST5 ... 71 A3
Demontfort Way ST14 126 B3
Den La CW3,CW5 . 52 B2
Denbigh Cl Biddulph ST8 27 B3
 Burton u T DE13 .. 166 B4
Denbigh Cl DY6 .. 271 C1
Newcastle-u-L ST5 . 71 B2
Denbigh St ST1 .. 282 A4
Denbury Cl WS12 . 210 B1
Denby Ave ST3 ... 283 C5
Dency Gr ST6 .... 42 B2
Dene Ave DY6 ... 275 B2
Dene Cl ST19 .... 207 C4
Dene Rd
 Lower Penn WV4 . 264 C2
Stourbridge DY8 . 279 C2
Dene Side ST5 ... 284 A2
Denefield ST19 .. 207 C4
Denehurst Cl ST18 74 A1
Denewood Pl ST3 74 B4
Denford Rd ST9 . 44 C4
Denham Gdns WV3 265 A4
Denham Sq ST2 . 72 C1
Denleigh Rd DY6 275 C2
Denmark Rise WS12 210 B4
Denmark Villa WS13 230 B3
Dennfield Dr WS6 226 B1
Dennington Cres ST2 72 C1
Dennis B77 ...... 250 C1
Denns Barsby Cl ST14 186 C2
Dennis St
 Brierley Hill DY8 . 279 C4
 Fenton ST4 .... 72 C3
Dennis Viollet Ave ST4 72 B2
Denry Cres ST5 .. 56 A4
Denshaw Wlk ST3 . 283 C5
Denston Ct B74 . 257 C1
Denstone Ave ST17 156 A1
Denstone Coll ST14 95 A3
Denstone Cres ST3 72 C1
Denstone Gdns WV10 240 C2
Denstone La ST14 . 95 B4
Dent St B79 .... 250 B3
Dentdale Cl ST3 . 90 A4
Denton Cl ST3 .. 71 B2
Denton Dr DE13 . 166 A3
Denver Fold ST17 174 A4
Denzil Gn ST17 . 174 A4
Derby Ave WV6 . 255 C4
Derby Mews ST14 110 C1
Derby Pl ST5 ... 71 B2
Derby Rd
 Burton u T DE13,DE14 166 C4
 Doveridge DE6 .. 127 B4
 Egginton DE65 .. 148 B2
 Talke ST7 .... 40 B4
 Uttoxeter ST14 . 111 B1
 Whittington WS14 232 B2
Derby St Burton u T DE14 166 B2
 Hanley ST1 .... 282 C2
 Leek ST13 .... 30 C3
 Stafford ST16 . 155 B2
Derby Turn DE14 . 166 B3
Dereham Way ST7 . 58 B1
Derek Dr ST1 ... 57 C3
Derrington La
 Bradley ST18 ... 173 C4
 Seighford ST18 . 154 C1
Derry St Fenton ST4 . 72 C2
Derwent Ave ST15 120 B4
Derwent Cl Aldridge WS9 256 C2
 Burton u T DE14 . 166 C2
Derwent Cres ST7 . 26 B1
Derwent Dr Ashley TF9 99 C3
 Biddulph ST8 ... 16 C1
 Cheadle ST10 .. 76 C1
Derwent Gr
 Burntwood WS7 . 229 B3
 Cannock WS11 .. 226 B4
Derwent Ho ST17 . 174 C3
Derwent Pk DE14 . 166 C2
Derwent Pl ST5 .. 56 A2
Derwent Rd
 Burton u T DE15 . 167 A1
 Wolv WV6 .... 255 A4
Derwent St ST5 . 282 A4
Desborough Rd ST5 196 C4
Deva Wlk ST3 ... 74 B4
Devereux Rd B79 . 250 A2
Devereux Rd B75 . 258 B1
Deveron Cl DE11 . 147 B1
Devil's La ST9,ST13 29 C3
Devon Cl Burton u T DE15 185 C3
 Newcastle-u-L ST5 . 71 B2

Devon Cres WS9 ... 245 A1
Devon Ct WS11 ... 226 B4
Devon Gn WS11 ... 226 C4
Devon Gr ST8 ... 16 B1
Devon Ho **5** DE6 . 279 C4
Devon Rd Cannock WS11 226 C4
 Stourbridge DY8 . 279 C4
Devon St B79 .... 73 B1
 Stafford ST17 ... 174 B3
Devonshire Ct B74 258 A1
Devonshire Dr
 Rugeley WS15 ... 196 B3
 Tamworth B79 ... 250 A3
Devonshire Sq ST2 . 58 B1
Dewberry Rd DY8 **2** 275 C1
Dewick Ind Est ST17 175 C2
Dewsbury Cl DY8 . 275 C2
Dewsbury Dr
 Burntwood WS7 . 229 B3
 Wolv WV4 .... 266 A2
Dewsbury Rd ST14 . 72 C4
Dexter Way B78 . 262 C4
Dexter Gr ST4 ... 174 A4
Deykin Rd WS13 . 231 A3
Dial La Biddulph CW12 7 A1
 Brierley Hill DY8 . 279 C4
Diamond Ave [12] ST7 26 A1
Diamond Cl
 Barlaston ST12 ... 104 B4
 Biddulph ST8 .... 27 B4
 Blythe Bridge ST3 . 90 A2
Diamond Gr WS11 . 210 B1
Diamond Jubilee Cotts
 B86 .... 81 C4
Diamond Park Dr **4**
 DY8 .... 275 C1
Diamond Ridge ST12 104 B4
Diamond Way ST15 . 120 A3
Diana Cl WS9 ... 245 A2
Diana Rd ST11 ... 57 C3
Diarmid Rd ST4 . 71 C1
Dibble Rd DE14 . 185 A4
Dibdale Cl DY3 . 271 B2
Dibdale Rd DY1 . 271 C2
Dibdale Rd W DY1 . 271 C1
Dickens Cl
 Burton u T DE14 . 166 B3
 Sedgley DY3 .. 271 A3
 Stourbridge DY8 . 279 C4
Dickens St ST2 . 58 B2
Dickenson Rd E ST6 57 B4
Dickenson Rd W ST6 57 B4
Dickinson Rd WV5 270 A3
Dickinson Cl WS10 . 282 C1
Dickson Rd ST16 . 156 A3
Dicky's La ST20 . 151 C4
Didcot Dr ST14 . 143 C4
Dig St SK17 .... 24 B3
Digbeth La WV5 . 267 A4
Dighy Rd DY6 ... 275 B4
Diglake Cl ST7 .. 40 B3
Diglake St ST7 .. 39 C2
Digmire La DE6 . 51 B1
Dilhorne Endowed Prim Sch
 ST10 .... 75 B3
Dilhorne Gr ST3 . 283 C1
Dilhorne La
 Caverswall ST11 . 74 C2
 Dilhorne ST11 . 75 A1
Dilhorne Rd Cheadle ST10 76 A2
 Forsbrook ST10,ST11 . 75 A1
Dilke St ST1 .... 282 C4
Dill Gr ST3 .... 90 A3
Dimble La WS13 . 214 A4
Dimbles La WS13 . 214 A1
Dimmelow St ST4 . 74 A3
Dimmingsdale Rd WV4 . 264 C3
Dimmingsdale YH*
 ST10 .... 78 A2
Dimmock St WV4 . 266 C3
Dimsdale Par E ST5 . 56 B3
Dimsdale Par W ST5 . 56 A3
Dimsdale St ST6 . 56 C4
Dimsdale View E ST5 . 56 A3
Dimsdale View W ST5 . 56 A3
Dingle Dr DE13 . 165 C2
Dingle La Bridgemere CW5 67 A3
 Hilderstone ST15 . 106 B1
 Woodhouse Green SK11 . 17 C4
Dingle Rd
 Brownhills WS8 . 244 C3
 Wombourne WV5 . 269 C3
Dingle The
 Burton u T DE15 . 185 C4
 Endon ST9 ... 43 A4
 Wolv WV3 .... 255 B1
Dingle View DY3 . 271 B4
Dinham Gdns DY1 . 271 C2
Dippons Ho WV6 . 255 A2
Dippons Mill Cl WV6 . 255 A2
Dirty La ST19 ... 223 B3
Dirtyfoot La WV4 . 265 A3
District Ctr WS11 . 210 B1
Ditch Cotts SK17 . 5 C4
Ditch The SK17 .. 5 C4
Dividy Rd ST2 ... 58 A1
Dixon Cl **3** DE14 . 104 C1
Dixon St WV2 ... 266 C4
Dixon St WV2 .. 266 C4
Dixon's Row ST5 . 55 B4
Dobbinhorse La DE6 . 81 C3
Dobbs St WV2 .. 266 B4
Dobell Gr ST3 .. 283 D4
Dobree Cl ST17 . 177 C4

Dobson St ST6 ....57 B4
Dock Rd DY8 ....275 C1
Doctor's Bank TF9 ....100 B3
Doctors Cl ST8 ....27 B4
Doctors La Kinver DY6 ....274 C3
 Shenstone WS14 ....247 A3
Doddington Pl ST5 ....71 A3
Doddlespool Barns CW3 ....52 C4
Dodds La Astbury CW12 ....15 B3
 Farewell WS13 ....212 B2
Dodslow Ave DE13 ....147 A2
Dog Kennel La TF9 ....112 B4
Dog La Burlston ST13 ....33 C4
 Leek ST13 ....30 C3
 Netherseal DE12 ....219 C3
 Ranton ST18 ....153 B2
 Swynnerton ST4,ST5 ....86 B2
 Tamworth B77 ....251 A3
 Waterhouses ST10 ....50 A1
 Weeford WS14 ....248 A2
Dogcroft Rd ST6 ....42 B3
Doglands Rd ST18 ....123 A1
Dogmoor La ST10 ....64 C4
Dogshead La DE13 ....201 B4
Dolefoot La DE13 ....163 A2
Doles La DE6 ....81 C4
Dolespring Cl ST11 ....91 A4
Doley Cl ST20 ....171 B3
Dolly's La ST6 ....42 A1
Dolphin Cl Stafford ST17 ....156 B1
 Walsall WS3 ....243 C1
Dominic St Stoke-on-T ST4 ....72 A4
 ⬛ Stone ST15 ....104 C1
Don Gr WS11 ....226 B4
Donald Bates Ho ST4 ....71 C3
Donald Rd ST1 ....71 C3
Doncaster La ST4 ....71 C4
Donington La
 Albrighton WV7 ....237 A4
 Boscobel WV8 ....221 B1
Donithorne Cl DE13 ....166 B4
Donkey La ST10 ....76 C3
Dorado B77 ....261 B4
Dorcas Dr ST3 ....72 C2
Dorchester Cl
 Kidsgrove ST7 ....26 A2
 Walsall WV12 ....242 B1
Dorchester Rd
 Cannock WS11 ....209 A1
 Walsall WV12 ....242 B1
Dorchester Wlk ST2 ....58 B1
Dordon Rd B78 ....262 C4
Doreen Ave CW12 ....16 A4
Dorian Way ST9 ....43 C4
Dorking Cl ST2 ....57 C1
Dorlan Cl ST9 ....43 B2
Dormer Ave B77 ....250 B3
Dormston Dr ST3 ....271 C4
Dormston Sch The DY3 ....271 C4
Dormston Trad Est DY1 ....271 C2
Dorothy Clive Garden The*
 TF9 ....84 A2
Dorridge Gr ST5 ....56 C2
Dorrington Cl ST2 ....44 C1
Dorrington Dr ST16 ....155 C3
Dorrington Gr ST5 ....56 B4
Dorrington Ind Pk ST16 ....155 C3
Dorset Cl Bucknall ST2 ....58 B2
 Burton u T DE15 ....185 C3
 Tamworth B78 ....250 A1
Dorset Dr Aldridge WS9 ....245 A1
 Biddulph ST8 ....27 A4
Dorset Pl Kidsgrove ST7 ....26 A1
 Newcastle-u-L ST5 ....71 B2
Dorset Rd Cannock WS12 ....210 C1
 Stourbridge DY8 ....279 B4
Dosthill Prim Sch B77 ....261 B3
Dosthill Rd (Two Gates)
 B77 ....261 B4
Double Gates TF9 ....112 A4
Douglas Ave Biddulph ST8 ....27 B4
 Stoke-on-T ST4 ....271 C1
Douglas Pl ST1 ....57 C1
Douglas Rd
 Newcastle-u-L ST5 ....56 A2
 Stafford ST16 ....156 A3
Douglas Rd W ST16 ....156 A3
Douglas St ST1 ....57 A3
Doulton Cl Cheadle ST10 ....76 B1
 Stafford ST15 ....119 C3
Doulton Dr ST5 ....56 A2
Doulton Rd ST18 ....156 A4
Doulton St ⬛ ST6 ....57 A4
Douse La ST13 ....32 B1
Dove Bank Prim Sch ST4 ....126 B4
Dove Bank Prim Sch ST9 ....26 A1
Dove Cl Burntwood WS7 ....229 B3
 Stafford ST17 ....174 C3
Dove Fields ST14 ....126 B4
Dove Fst Sch ST14 ....96 A2
Dove Gr Biddulph ST8 ....16 B1
 Egginton DE65 ....148 A3
Dove Hollow
 Cannock WS12 ....210 C2
 Great Wyrley WS6 ....226 C1
Dove La ST14 ....96 A2
Dove Lea DE13 ....147 A2
Dove Rd ST11 ....91 A4
Dove Ridge SK17 ....13 B3
Dove Side DE65 ....146 B4
Dove St DE6 ....80 A1
Dove View DE13 ....146 B3
Dove Way The ST14 ....111 B1
Dove Wlk ST14 ....126 B4
Dovebank Gr ST3 ....90 A3
Dovecliff Cres DE13 ....147 C1
Dovecliff Rd DE13 ....147 C2

Dovecote Cl WV6 ....255 B2
Dovecote Pl ST3 ....89 C4
Dovecotes Prim Sch
 WV8 ....239 C1
Dovecotes The B75 ....258 A2
Dovedale WS11 ....210 A3
Dovedale Ave WS3 ....244 A3
Dovedale Cl
 Burton u T DE15 ....167 A3
 Cheadle ST10 ....76 C3
 Congleton CW12 ....6 A2
 Tunstall ST6 ....41 A4
Dovedale Ct WV4 ....266 C1
Dovedale Pl ST5 ....55 A1
Dovedale Rd
 Kingsley ST10 ....61 C1
 Kingswinford DY6 ....275 C4
 Wolv WV4 ....266 C2
Dovefields ST14 ....95 C2
Dovehouse Fields
 WS14 ....231 A3
Dover Cl DE13 ....166 B4
Dover Rd DE13 ....166 A4
Dover St ST1 ....282 C4
Doveridge Prim Sch
 DE6 ....127 B4
Doveridge Rd DE15 ....167 A1
Doveside DE6 ....81 B4
Dovestone B77 ....251 B1
Dowells Gdns DY8 ....275 B2
Dower Rd B75 ....258 A1
Downderry Cl ST17 ....174 A4
Downend Cl WV10 ....240 C2
Downesway WS11 ....209 B1
Downey St ST1 ....282 B2
Downfield Cl WS3 ....243 A2
Downfield Dr DY3 ....271 C3
Downfield Gr ST16 ....155 B4
Downfield Pl ST2 ....42 C1
Downford Cl ST19 ....205 B3
Downham Pl WV3 ....265 C4
Downham Rd ST5 ....55 C1
Downie Rd WV8 ....239 B2
Downing Ave ST5 ....56 C2
Downing Dr B79 ....249 C3
Downing Gdns ⬛ ST15 ....120 A4
Downs The Aldridge WS9 ....256 C1
 Stafford ST17 ....175 B4
Downsview Gr ST3 ....72 C2
Dowty Way WV9 ....240 A2
Doxey ST16 ....155 A2
Doxey Fields ST16 ....154 C2
Doxey Prim Sch ST16 ....155 A2
Dragon Sq ST5 ....55 C4
Drake Ave ST19 ....207 C3
Drake Cl Bucknall ST2 ....57 C1
 Walsall WS3 ....243 A1
Drake Croft ⬛ WS13 ....231 B4
Drake Ct WS3 ....243 A1
Drake Rd WS3 ....243 B1
Drakeford Cl ST6 ....42 C2
Drakeford Gr ST6 ....42 C2
Drakes Hill Cl DY8 ....279 B2
Draw-well La ST9 ....59 B2
Dray Ct DE14 ....166 B1
Draycott Cl WV4 ....265 B3
Draycott Cliff DE6 ....144 B3
Draycott Cres B77 ....250 B1
Draycott Cross Rd
 Cheadle ST10 ....76 A1
 Draycott in t M ST11 ....91 B4
Draycott Dr Cheadle ST10 ....76 B1
 Newcastle-u-L ST5 ....40 B1
Draycott Manor Prim Sch
 ST11 ....91 B4
Draycott Old Rd
 Draycott in t M ST11 ....91 B4
 Forsbrook ST11 ....91 B4
Draycott Rd ST10 ....92 B2
Drayton Gn ST2 ....58 A1
Drayton Gr ST9 ....97 B1
Drayton La B78 ....260 B3
Drayton Manor Dr
 Drayton Bassett B78 ....260 C4
 Fazeley B78 ....260 C4
Drayton Manor Pk*
 B78 ....260 C4
Drayton Rd Longton ST3 ....283 A4
 Swynnerton ST4 ....87 A3
Drayton St
 Newcastle-u-L ST5 ....284 A2
 Wolv WV2 ....266 B4
Dreieich Cl ST14 ....155 C3
Drenfell Rd ST7 ....25 C4
Dresden CE Prim Sch
 ST3 ....283 B1
Dresden St ST1 ....282 C2
Dreys The ST4 ....88 A4
Driffield Cl ST7 ....58 C1
Drive Fields WV4 ....265 A3
Drive The Audley ST7 ....54 C2
 Codsall WV8 ....238 C2
 Rudyard ST13 ....29 C4
Druid Park Rd WV12 ....242 B1
Druids Ave WS9 ....256 B4
Druids Way WS19 ....200 C4
Druids Wlk WS9 ....245 A2
Drumart Ho DY10 ....280 A3

Drumber La ST7 ....26 A4
Drumburn Cl ST7 ....41 C4
Drummond Cl WV11 ....242 A1
Drummond Rd ST16 ....155 C3
Drummond St ST6 ....41 B4
Drury La WV8 ....238 C2
Dryburg Wlk ST2 ....58 A2
Dryburgh Cl ST17 ....174 A4
Dryden Cres ST17 ....155 B1
Dryden Rd Burslem ST6 ....57 A3
 Tamworth B79 ....250 A3
 Wolv WV10 ....240 C1
Dryden Way ST10 ....76 B1
Dual Way WS12 ....209 B4
Dubarry Ave DY6 ....275 B4
Duchy Cl DE13 ....166 C4
Duchy Rd CW1 ....37 A4
Duck La WV8 ....239 A2
Duck St DE65 ....148 A3
Duddell St ST6 ....42 B1
Dudding Rd WV4 ....266 B1
Dudley Innovation Ctr
 DY6 ....275 C4
Dudley Pl ⬛ ST3 ....90 A4
Dudley Rd Himley DY3 ....270 B2
 Kingswinford DY6 ....275 C4
 Kingswinford, Wall Heath
 DY6 ....275 B4
 Sedgley DY3 ....271 C3
 Wolv WV2 ....266 B4
Dudley St ST3 ....271 B4
Dudley Wlk WV4 ....266 B2
Dudmaston Way DY1 ....271 C2
Duesbury Gn ST3 ....283 A3
Duffield Cl WV4 ....239 C1
Duffield La DE13 ....162 C4
Dugdale Cl WS12 ....210 C2
Dugdale Cres B75 ....258 B2
Duke Bank Terr ST6 ....42 C2
Duke Pl ST5 ....55 B1
Duke Rd WS7 ....211 C1
Duke St Biddulph ST8 ....27 B4
 Burton u T DE14 ....166 B1
 Fenton ST4 ....72 C3
 Leek ST13 ....30 C3
 Newcastle-u-L ST5 ....284 C1
 Sedgley DY3 ....271 B3
 Wolv WV1 ....266 A4
Dukes La ST13,ST10 ....63 B4
Dukes Rd B78 ....262 C3
Dulverton Ave WS5 ....71 A3
Dumbill Ho ST7 ....40 B4
Dumbleberry Ave DY3 ....271 B4
Dumolo's La B77 ....250 C2
Dumore Hay La WS13 ....215 C4
Duncalf Gr ST5 ....56 A4
Duncalf St ST6 ....56 A4
Duncalfe Dr B75 ....258 A2
Duncan St Fenton ST4 ....72 C3
 Wolv WV2 ....266 B4
Duncombe St DY8 ....279 B3
Dundalk La B77 ....226 B1
Dundas St ST1 ....282 B4
Dundee Rd ST1 ....57 A2
Dundee St ST3 ....283 B2
Dunedin B77 ....251 A1
Dunedin Cres DE15 ....167 B1
Dungarven Dr TF10 ....168 B1
Dunhampton Dr WV10 ....280 A1
Dunkirk ST5 ....284 A3
Dunkirk Ct ST5 ....284 A3
Dunlin Dr WV10 ....241 A4
Dunnerdale Rd WS8 ....244 B4
Dunning St ST6 ....41 B2
Dunnington Ave DY10 ....280 A1
Dunnock Cl ST14 ....126 B3
Dunnock Way ST8 ....27 C4
Dunrobin St ST3 ....283 C2
Dunsany Gr ST1 ....57 C3
Dunsford Ave ST2 ....43 A1
Dunsley Dr
 Kingswinford DY9 ....275 C2
 Kinver DY7 ....278 B2
Dunsley Gr WV4 ....266 A2
Dunsley Rd Kinver DY7 ....278 B2
 Stourbridge DY9 ....279 B2
Dunstall Brook DE15 ....167 A1
Dunstall Cross DE13 ....183 A3
Dunstall Hill DE13 ....183 B3
Dunstall La B78 ....260 C2
Dunstall Park Race Course
 WV6 ....255 C3
Dunstall Rd DE13 ....183 C2
 Burton u T B77 ....266 A3
Dunster Cl ST17 ....174 A4
Dunster Gr WV6 ....254 C2
Dunster Rd ST3 ....89 C4
Dunston Cl
 Kingswinford DY6 ....275 B4
Dunston Dr WS7 ....229 A4
Dunston Pl ST17 ....174 A4
Dunstone Rd ST14 ....125 B4
Dursley Dr WS11 ....209 A1
Dursley Rd WS7 ....229 A4

Durston Pl ST3 ....73 C2
Dutton Way ST15 ....119 C3
Duttons La B75 ....258 C2
Dyke Rd WS15 ....198 A2
Dyke St ST1 ....282 C3
Dykes La ST10 ....188 B4
Dylan Rd Biddulph ST8 ....27 C3
 Longton ST3 ....73 B2
Dyott Ave WS14 ....232 C3
Dyott Cl WS13 ....215 A1

E

Eagle Cl
 Cheslyn Hay WS6 ....226 B1
 Dudley DY1 ....271 C1
 Uttoxeter ST14 ....126 A3
Eagle Cres ST21 ....133 B3
Eagle Ct WV3 ....266 A4
Eagle Dr B77 ....251 B2
Eagle Gr WV7 ....210 B1
Eagle Hts DE15 ....167 B2
Eagle St Hanley ST1 ....57 C2
 Wolv WV2 ....266 C4
Eagley Brook Prim WS3 ....266 A4
Ealingham B77 ....251 A1
Eamont Ave ST6 ....42 A2
Eardley St ST4 ....71 C3
Eardleyend Rd ST7 ....39 C4
Earl Dr WS7 ....211 C1
Earl St Kingswinford DY6 ....275 B2
 Leek ST13 ....30 C3
 Newcastle-u-L ST5 ....284 D3
 Newcastle-u-L, Silverdale
 ST5 ....55 B1
 Stafford ST16 ....155 C2
Earl Sterndale CE Prim Sch
 SK17 ....2 C4
Earl's Dr ST5 ....71 A3
Earls Ct Burton u T DE13 ....166 B4
 Newcastle-u-L ST5 ....284 D3
Earlsfield La ST5 ....88 B4
Earls Way ST18 ....158 B1
Earlsbrook Dr ST4 ....88 B4
Earlsway ST10 ....64 A4
Earlswood Cres WV9 ....240 A2
Earlswood Dr ST1 ....58 A3
Earlswood Rd DY6 ....275 C4
Early La ST15 ....103 B2
Easby Cl ST17 ....174 A4
Easby Way WS3 ....242 C1
Easdale Pl ST5 ....71 A3
Easedale Cl ST12 ....43 A1
Easing La ST13 ....31 C4
East Ave CW2 ....7 B3
East Bank Ride ST11 ....91 A4
East Beeches WV9 ....240 A2
East Butts Rd WS15 ....178 A1
East Cannock Ind Est
 WS12 ....210 A2
East Cannock Rd WS12 ....210 A2
East Cl ST15 ....119 C4
East Cres Hanley ST1 ....57 C4
 Newcastle-u-L ST5 ....56 B2
East Croft Rd WV4 ....265 B3
East Dr Biddulph ST8 ....27 B4
 Cheddleton ST13 ....45 B4
East Gn ST13 ....31 C4
East Gr ST3 ....74 A1
East Prec ST1 ....282 C3
East Rd
 Featherstone WV10 ....241 A4
 Wolv WV4 ....266 C2
East St Burton u T DE15 ....167 B2
 Cannock WS11 ....226 C3
 Leek ST13 ....31 A3
 Meir ST3 ....74 A3
 Sedgley DY3 ....271 B2
 Tamworth B77 ....261 B3
East View Burslem ST6 ....56 C4
 Mayfield DE6 ....81 B4
 Tamworth B77 ....282 A4
Eastbank Rd ST1 ....282 A4
Eastbourne Cl ST13 ....30 B3
Eastbourne Rd ST1 ....57 C2
Eastbridge Ave ST1 ....167 B4
Eastcote Cres WS7 ....229 A3
Eastdean Ave ST22 ....58 A1
Eastern Ave
 Burton u T DE13 ....166 C4
 Lichfield WS13 ....214 B1
Eastern Way WS11 ....210 A1
Easters Gr ST2 ....43 A1
Eastfield WS9 ....256 A3
Eastfield Cl ST13 ....88 C4
Eastfields Rd ST14 ....126 B4
Eastgate Brewood ST19 ....223 B4
 Cannock WS12 ....211 A3
Eastgate St
 Burntwood WS7 ....228 C4
 Newcastle-u-L ST5 ....71 A3
 Trentham ST4 ....88 A4
Easthall Cl ST19 ....223 B3
Easthead Wlk ST11 ....282 A4
Eastlands WS11 ....106 B1
Eastlands Cl ST17 ....174 C4
Eastlands Gr ST17 ....174 C4
Eastlands Rd ST10 ....271 B4
Eastmoor Cl ST14 ....257 A1
Eastney Cres WV8 ....255 C4
Eastridge Croft WS14 ....247 A3
Eastward Glen WV8 ....239 B1
Eastwick Cres ST14 ....88 A4
Eastwood Ave
 Burntwood WS7 ....229 A4
 Chell Heath ST6 ....42 A2

Eastwood Pl ST1 ....282 B2
Eastwood Rd ST1 ....282 C1
Eastwood Rise ST5 ....85 A4
Easy Lawns CW3 ....53 A3
Eaton Cres DY3 ....271 A2
Eaton Park Prim Sch
 ST2 ....58 A1
Eaton Pk DY6 ....275 C3
Eaton Rd ST14 ....95 C2
Eaton St ST1 ....282 C3
Eaves Court Dr DY3 ....266 B1
Eaves La Bucknall ST2 ....58 B3
 Cheadle ST10 ....76 C1
 Oakamoor ST10 ....78 A4
Eaveswood Rd ST12 ....58 B3
Ebenezer St WS12 ....210 A4
Ebstree Mdw WV5 ....264 A1
Ebstree Rd WV5 ....264 A2
Ebury Gr ST3 ....73 C1
Eccleshall Ave WV10 ....240 B1
Eccleshall Bsns Pk
 DE14 ....166 C2
Eccleshall Rd Ashley TF9 ....99 C2
 Mucklestone TF9 ....99 A3
 Seighford ST18 ....135 B1
 Stafford ST16 ....155 B3
 Stone ST15 ....119 C3
Eccleston Pl ST6 ....42 A3
Edale B77 ....251 A1
Edale Cl
 Kingswinford DY6 ....275 A4
 Newcastle-u-L ST5 ....55 A1
 Tunstall ST6 ....41 A4
 Wolv WV4 ....266 C2
Eddens Wood Cl B78 ....260 C3
Eddies La B79 ....216 C1
Eddisbury Dr ST5 ....40 B1
Eden Cl Biddulph ST8 ....16 C1
 Cannock WS12 ....210 C1
 Kidsgrove ST7 ....26 A1
Eden Gr Ashley TF9 ....99 C3
 Cheadle ST10 ....76 C1
 Meir ST3 ....73 C1
Edenbridge View DY1 ....271 C2
Edenhurst Ave ST3 ....74 A1
Edenhurst Prep Sch ST5 ....70 C4
Edensor CE Prim Sch
 ST3 ....283 A2
Edensor Ct ST5 ....55 C4
Edensor High Sch ST3 ....283 B3
Edensor Rd ST3 ....283 B3
Edensor St ST5 ....55 C4
Edensor Terr ST13 ....283 A3
Edes Farm Dr ST14 ....95 C2
Edgar Cl B79 ....249 C4
Edgar Pl ST3 ....73 B3
Edge Ave ST6 ....42 A3
Edge Hill Inf Sch DY7 ....277 C2
 Wood End CV9 ....262 A1
Edge Hill Ave WV10 ....241 A1
Edge Hill Dr Perton WV6 ....254 C2
 Sedgley DY3 ....266 B1
Edge Hill Jun Sch DE15 ....185 C4
Edge Hill Rd B74 ....257 C2
Edge La ST9 ....43 B4
Edge St ST6 ....41 C1
Edge View Cl Kinver DY7 ....277 C3
 Norton-in-t-M ST7 ....43 B1
Edge View St ST8 ....27 B4
Edge View Rd ST12 ....58 B3
Edge View Wlk DY7 ....277 C3
Edgecliff High Sch DY7 ....278 A2
Edgefield La ST9 ....43 B3
Edgefield Rd ST3 ....73 B3
Edgehill Rd DE13 ....30 B3
Edgemoor Mdw WS12 ....210 B1
Edgemoor Rd WV12 ....242 B1
Edgeware St ST5 ....281 C2
Edgeware St1 ....282 A4
Edgmond Rd TF10 ....168 C2
Edgworth Ho WS13 ....214 A1
Edinbridge Cl CW2 ....37 A1
Edinburgh Cres DY8 ....275 B1
Edinburgh Rd CW2 ....6 A1
Edinburgh Way DE13 ....166 B4
Edison St ST4 ....72 B3
Edison Ct WS12 ....210 B4
Edison Rd ST16 ....155 C3
Edmonton Cl WS11 ....210 A1
Edmonton Gr ST22 ....42 C1
Edmonton Pl DE15 ....167 B1
Edmund Ave ST17 ....174 A4
Edmund Rd WV3 ....271 C3
Ednam Gr WV5 ....265 A1
Ednam Rd ST3 ....74 A1
Ednam Pl ST3 ....266 B3
Ednam Rd WV4 ....266 B3
Edward Ave
 Aldridge WS9 ....256 A4
 Newcastle-u-L ST5 ....71 A3
 Trentham ST4 ....88 A4
Edward Ct B77 ....250 C2
Edward Davies Rd ST10 ....42 B1
Edward Rd WV6 ....254 C3
Edward St Audley ST7 ....39 C2
 Burton u T DE13 ....166 B2
 Cannock WS11 ....209 C2
 Fenton ST4 ....72 C4
 Newcastle-u-L ST5 ....71 B3
 ⬛ Stone ST15 ....105 A1
 Tamworth B79 ....250 A3
 Wolv WV4 ....266 C4
Edwards Dr ST16 ....155 B2
Edwards Farm Rd WS13 ....215 C4

Edwards Rd
Burntwood WS7 ....228 C3
Sutton Coldfield B75 .....258 B2
Edwin Cl Penkridge ST19 .207 C4
Stafford ST17 ....155 A1
Effinch La DE13 ....201 C4
Egelwin Cl WV6 ....254 C3
Egerton Rd Aldridge B74 .256 C1
Stoke-on-T ST4 ....71 C4
Wolv WV10 ....240 C2
Egerton St ST1 ....57 B1
Egg La ST18 ....158 C4
Eggington Dr ST19 .....207 C4
Eggington Rd DV8 ......279 B3
Egginton Prim Sch
DE65 ....148 A3
Egginton Rd
Egginton DE65 ....148 A4
Hilton DE55 ....147 C4
Eighth Ave DE14 ....184 C4
Eights Croft WS2 ....228 B4
Elaine Ave ST6 ....42 A1
Elan Cl Cookley DY10 ...280 A2
Sedgley DY3 ....271 B2
Elan Dr ST4 ....271 B4
Elburton Rd ST4 ....73 A3
Elder Cl Cannock WS11 .210 B1
Uttoxeter ST14 ....126 A3
Elder Gr WV5 ....269 C3
Elder La WS2 ....229 B4
Elder Pl ST6 ....57 A3
Elder Rd ST6 ....57 A3
Elderberry Cl DV8 ......279 B2
Elderside Cl WS8 ....244 C4
Eldertree La TF9 ....100 B1
Eldon St Burton u T DE15 .167 A2
Hanley ST1 ....57 B3
Eldridge Cl WV9 ....239 C1
Eleanor Cres ST5 ....71 A3
Eleanor Harrison Dr
DY10 ....280 A3
Eleanor Pl ST5 ....71 A3
Eleanor View ST5 ....71 A3
Electric Ind Est DE14 ...166 C3
Electric St DE14 ....166 C3
Elenora St ST4 ....72 A4
Elford Cl ST16 ....155 B4
Elgar Cl Cannock WS11 ..209 C3
Lichfield WS13 ....214 A1
Elgar Cres ST1 ....58 A3
Elgin Cl DY3 ....266 C1
Elgin Ct WV6 ....254 C2
Elgin Rd WS3 ....243 A2
Elgin St ST4 ....57 A1
Elgood La ST6 ....41 A4
Elias Cl WS14 ....231 C3
Eliases La ST6 ....17 A1
Eliot Cl Armitage WS15 ..198 A2
Tamworth B79 ....250 A4
Eliot Way ST17 ....155 B1
Elizabeth Ave
Rolleston DE13 ....147 A2
Wolv WV4 ....266 A3
Elizabeth Ct
Market Drayton TF9 ....112 B4
Stoke-on-T ST4 ....71 C4
Talke ST7 ....40 B3
Elizabeth Dr
Newcastle-u-L ST5 ....55 C4
Tamworth B79 ....250 A3
Elizabeth Rd WS11 .....209 C3
Elizabeth St ST1 ....57 C2
Elkes Gr ST14 ....110 C1
Elkington Cl TF10 ....168 C1
Elkington Rise CW3 .....68 C4
Elkstone Cl ST16 ....41 C2
Elliman's Pl ST5 ....55 C1
Ellastone Gr ST4 ....73 C1
Ellastone Rd ST10,ST13 ..63 B3
Elldawn Ave ST6 ....42 C1
Ellerbeck B77 ....251 A1
Ellers Gr ST6 ....56 C4
Ellesmere Ct TF10 ......168 C1
Ellesmere Gr TF9 ....112 A4
Ellesmere Rd WS3 ......226 A4
Elligreave St ST6 ....56 C4
Ellington Ave ST16 .....156 A3
Ellington Cl ST2 ....58 A1
Elliot Dr ST9 ....59 A2
Elliot Rd ST4 ....72 C3
Elliot Cl WS11 ....209 C3
Elliott St ST5 ....56 B1
Elliotts La WV8 ....239 A2
Ellis St ST6 ....57 B4
Ellis Wlk WS11 ....226 C4
Ellison Points Ct ST5 ...56 B3
Ellison St ST5 ....56 B3
Ellowes Hall Sch The
DY3 ....271 B3
Ellowes Rd DY3 ....271 B2
Elm Ave ST17 ....175 C3
Elm Cl Branston DE14 ....184 C4
Colwich ST18 ....158 A1
Cookley DY10 ....280 A2
Doveridge DE6 ....127 B4
Kidsgrove ST7 ....41 A4
Leek ST13 ....30 B3
Newport TF10 ....168 C1
Sedgley DY3 ....271 A1
Stourbridge DY8 ....279 B1
Elm Cres ST18 ....158 B4
Elm Ct ST18 ....174 B3
Elm Dale Rd WV4 ....266 A3
Elm Dr Blakedown DY10 ..281 A1

Elm Dr continued
Bradley ST18 ....191 B4
Cheadle ST10 ....76 C1
Market Drayton TF9 ....112 A4
Elm Farm Rd WV2 ....266 B4
Elm Gdns WS14 ....231 B4
Elm Gr Codsall WV8 .....239 A2
Huntington WS12 ....209 B4
Kinver DY7 ....278 B2
Elm Pl Cookley DY10 ....280 A2
Longton ST3 ....72 C1
Elm Rd Kingswinford DY6 .275 C3
Norton Canes WS11 ....228 A3
Stone ST15 ....120 A4
Elm St Burslem ST6 ......57 A4
Newcastle-u-L ST5 ....56 B2
Elm Tree Cl WV5 ....269 C3
Elm Tree Dr ST7 ....39 C1
Elm Tree Wlk B79 ....249 C4
Elm View ST14 ....95 C3
Elm Wlk ST19 ....207 C4
Elmbridge Way DY3 .....251 A1
Elmbrook Cl ST13 ....89 C4
Elmcroft Gdns WV10 ....240 C2
Elmcroft Rd ST2 ....58 A3
Elmdale Dr WV9 ....256 B4
Elmdon Cl
Penkridge ST19 ....208 A4
Wolv WV10 ....240 A1
Elmdon Pl ST3 ....90 A4
Elmdon Rd WV10 ....240 A1
Elmhurst Eggington DE65 .148 A3
Walsall WS3 ....70 C2
Elmhurst Cl
Brewood WV9 ....224 A2
Bucknall ST2 ....57 C1
Stafford ST16 ....155 B4
Elmhurst Dr
Burntwood WS7 ....229 A2
Kingswinford DY6 ....275 C2
Elmley Gr WV6 ....254 C2
Elmore Green Prim Sch
WS3 ....243 A1
Elmore Green Rd WS3 ...243 A1
Elmore Ho WS15 ....178 C1
Elmore La WS15 ....178 C1
Elmore Row WS3 ....243 A1
Elms Cl WV10 ....225 B1
Elms Dr WS11 ....209 B3
Elms La WV10 ....225 B1
Elms Paddock The WV6 .253 B1
Elms Rd DE15 ....166 C1
Elms The ST5 ....56 B4
Elms Way ST3 ....74 A1
Elmsdale WV6 ....255 A1
Elmsmere Rd ST2 ....58 A3
Elmstead Cl ST4 ....71 C1
Elmstone Cl 10 ST17 ....175 B3
Elmtree Rd B74 ....256 B1
Elmwood Ave WV11 .....242 A2
Elmwood Cl
Cannock WS11 ....210 A2
Forsbrook ST11 ....91 A3
Gnosall ST20 ....69 A4
Lawton-gate ST7 ....25 A2
Elmwood Dr ST11 ....91 A3
Elmwood Gr ST14 ....110 C1
Elmwood Rd DV8 ....275 B1
Elmwood Rise DY3 ......266 A1
Elphinstone Rd ST14 ....71 C2
Elsby Pl ST6 ....42 A3
Elsdon Rd ST17 ....174 B3
Elsing St ST4 ....72 B3
Elsmere Ave ST3 ....73 A1
Elston Hall La WV10 .....240 B1
Elston Hall Prim Sch
WV10 ....240 B1
Elstree Cl ST3 ....73 C1
Elstree Gr ST1 ....58 A3
Elswick Rd ST4 ....72 C4
Eltham Gdns ST5 ....56 B2
Elton Cl
Newborough DE13 ....162 C4
Wolv WV10 ....240 C2
Elton La DE13 ....162 C4
Elton Terr ST6 ....41 B4
Elton Way ST20 ....171 B4
Elunda Gr WS7 ....228 C3
Elviron Dr WV6 ....255 A3
Elwell Cres DY1 ....279 C4
Elworthy Cl ST16 ....156 A3
Elwyn Cl DE13 ....147 B1
Ely Cl WS11 ....210 A1
Ely Wlk ST3 ....283 C4
Embers Way ST14 ....44 A4
Emberton St
Newcastle-u-L, Chesterton
ST5 ....55 C3
Newcastle-u-L, Wolstanton
ST5 ....56 B3
Embleton Wlk 1 ST6 ....56 C4
Embry Ave ST16 ....156 A3
Emerald Way ST3 ....120 A2
Emerson Cl DY3 ....271 A2
Emerson Rd Burslem ST6 .57 C4
Wolv WV10 ....240 C1
Emery Ave Hanley ST1 ...57 C4
Newcastle-u-L ST5 ....71 A4
Emery St ST6 ....57 A3
Emmanuel Rd WS7 ......228 C2
Empire Ind Est WS9 .....244 C1
Empire Pas ST4 ....72 A3
Empire Rd DE15 ....167 B2
Empire St ST4 ....72 A3
Emstone Cl ST3 ....88 C4
Emsworth Cres WV4 ....240 A1
Emsworth Rd ST3 ....88 C4

Encounter Pl ST1 ....57 C3
End Hall Rd WV6 ....255 A2
End The DE15 ....167 C4
Enderby Dr WV4 ....266 A3
Enderby Rise DE13 ......166 A4
Enderley Cl WS3 ....243 A2
Enderley Dr WS3 ....243 A2
Enderley St ST5 ....55 C4
Endon Dr ST8 ....27 A3
Endon Hall Prim Sch
ST9 ....43 C4
Endon High Sch ST9 ....43 C3
Endon Rd
Norton-in-t-M, Duke Bank
ST6 ....42 C2
Norton-in-t-M, Norton Green
ST6 ....42 C2
Endwood Dr B74 ....257 B2
Engelsea Brook La CW2 ..38 A2
Engine La
Brownhills WS8 ....244 B4
Tamworth B77 ....251 A1
Englesea Ave ST3 ....74 A3
Englesea Brook Mus of
Primitive Methodism*
CW2 ....38 A2
Engleton La ST19 ....223 B4
Engleton Mill La ST19 ...223 B4
English Martyrs RC Prim Sch
ST8 ....27 B4
Ennerdale Cl
Brownhills WS8 ....244 C4
2 Burslem ST6 ....56 C4
Ennerdale Dr WV6 ......254 C2
Ennerdale Rd WV6 ......255 B4
Enoch St ST6 ....56 C4
Ensall Dr DY8 ....275 C1
Ensford Cl B74 ....257 C3
Enson La Marston ST18 ..137 A4
Stone ST15,ST18 ....120 B1
Ensor Dr R78 ....251 C1
Enstone Ct ST5 ....71 A2
Enterprise Dr WV10 .....224 B3
Enterprise Gr WS3 ......244 A3
Enterprise Ind Pk WS13 .231 C4
Enville Cl WS3 ....243 A2
Enville Common Rd
DY7 ....273 C2
Enville Pl DY8 ....279 C3
Enville Rd
Kingswinford DY6 ....275 A4
Kinver DY7 ....278 A2
Sedgley DY3 ....271 B2
Wolv WV4 ....265 B3
Ephraim St ST1 ....282 C1
Epping Rd ST4 ....71 C2
Epsley's Yd ST16 ....155 C1
Epsom Cl Branston DE14 .184 C4
Kingsley ST10 ....76 C3
Lichfield WS14 ....231 B4
Perton WV6 ....254 C2
Epworth Dr ST17 ....175 B2
Epworth Ho DE15 ....167 B2
Epworth St ST4 ....72 A4
Erasmus Way WS13 .....231 A4
Erdington Rd WS9 ......256 B2
Eremon Cl WS15 ....196 C3
Erdington B77 ....251 A1
Ermington Rd WV4 ......266 B2
Ernald Gdns 8 ST15 ...120 A4
Eros Cres ST1 ....57 C3
Errill Cl ST4 ....72 B3
Erskine St ST1 ....283 C1
Esk Way ST5 ....71 A2
Eskdale Pl
Newcastle-u-L ST5 ....71 A3
Trentham ST4 ....88 A4
Essex Cl ST18 ....202 C1
Esperanto Way ST6 .....57 B4
Esselie Ave TF9 ....100 B3
Essex Ave DY6 ....275 A3
Essex Dr Biddulph ST8 ...16 B1
Cannock WS12 ....210 A2
Colwich ST18 ....158 A2
Kidsgrove ST7 ....25 C1
Rugeley WS15 ....196 B3
Stone ST15 ....119 C3
Essex Gdns DY8 ....279 B4
Essex Gr ST19 ....207 C4
Essex Pl ST5 ....71 A1
Essex Rd Burton u T DE15 .185 B3
Sutton Coldfield B75 .....258 B1
Essington Cl
Alrewas DE13 ....201 A2
Brierley Hill DY8 ....275 C1
Lichfield WS14 ....231 A3
Shenstone WS14 ....231 A3
Essington Ind Est WV11 .241 C2
Essington Rd WV12 .....242 A1
Estridge La WS6 ....227 A1
Etchell Rd R78 ....250 C2
Etching Hill CE Prim Sch
WS15 ....178 B1
Etching Hill Rd WS15 ...178 A1
Ethelfleda Rd B77 ......250 C3
Ethelred Cl B74 ....258 A2
Eton Ave ST5 ....70 C2
Eton Cl Burton u T DE14 .166 C3
Sedgley DY3 ....271 C3
Stafford ST17 ....156 A1
Eton Ct Lichfield WS14 ...231 A3
Sutton Coldfield B74 .....258 B1
Eton Park Jun Sch
DE14 ....166 B4
Eton Pk DE14 ....166 C3
Eton Rd DE14 ....166 B3
Etruria Old Rd ST1 ......56 C2

Etruria Rd Hanley ST1 ...282 A3
Newcastle-u-L ST5 ....56 C2
Etruria Sta ST4 ....56 C1
Etruria Vale Rd ST1 .....57 A2
Etruria Way ST5 ....56 C1
Etruscan St ST1 ....56 C1
Etruscan Wlk ST12 ......88 C2
Ettingshall Park Farm La
WV4 ....266 C2
Ettmore Cl DY3 ....271 B4
Ettmore Rd DY3 ....271 B4
Ettymore Rd W DY3 .....271 B4
Etwall Rd DE65 ....148 A4
Europa Way WS13 ......231 C4
Eva Gr ST5 ....87 B4
Evans Croft B78 ....250 A1
Evans St Burslem ST6 ....41 C1
Wolv WV4,WV14 ....266 C1
Eve La DY1 ....271 C3
Evelyn St ST4 ....72 B3
Everest Rd ST7 ....26 B2
Everglade Rd CV9 ....262 B1
Evergreen Hts WS12 ....210 A4
Evergreens The DE13 ...166 C4
Evershed Way DE14 .....166 B1
Eversley Ave ST13 ....30 C3
Eversley Gr ST13 ....266 B1
Eversley Rd ST13 ....73 C1
Evesham Cres WS3 ......242 C2
Evesham Way ST3 ....73 C2
Eveson Rd DY8 ....279 C1
Ewe Dale La DE6 ....35 A2
Exbury Cl WV9 ....239 C1
Excelsior Gr WS3 ....244 A3
Exchange Ind Est The
WS11 ....226 C3
Exchange Rd DE13 ......201 A2
Exchange The WS3 ......243 A1
Exeter Dr B79 ....249 C3
Exeter Grn ST2 ....58 B1
Exeter Rd WS11 ....226 A4
Exeter St ST17 ....174 C4
Exley B77 ....250 B1
Exmouth Gr ST6 ....57 A4
Exonbury Wlk 5 WS11 ..209 C1
Eyam Cl DE15 ....167 A1
Eynsham Ct WV6 ....255 C3
Eyre St ST6 ....56 C4
Eyrie The DE15 ....167 B2

F

Faber RC Prim Sch The
ST10 ....78 B4
Faceby Gr ST13 ....90 B4
Fair Lady Dr WS7 ....211 B1
Fair Lawn WV7 ....237 A3
Fair Mdws WS15 ....179 A4
Fair Oak TF10 ....168 C2
Fair Oak High Sch
WS15 ....196 B4
Fair Oak Rd ST5 ....40 B1
Fair Oaks Dr WS6 ....243 A4
Fair View WS15 ....198 B2
Fair View Rd ST13 ....31 A2
Fairbank Ave ST4 ....72 A3
Fairbanks Wlk ST15 .....103 A2
Fairburn Cres WS3 ......244 A3
Fairclough Pl ST16 ......42 A2
Fairfax Rd WV10 ....240 C2
Fairfax St ST1 ....57 B3
Fairfield Ave Endon ST6 ..43 A4
Longton ST3 ....89 B4
Newcastle-u-L ST5 ....56 B2
Rolleston DE13 ....147 B2
Fairfield Cl WS12 ....210 B1
Fairfield Cres DE11 .....186 C3
Fairfield Ct ST16 ....155 C3
Fairfield Dr Codsall WV8 .238 C2
Kinver DY7 ....278 A2
Penkridge ST19 ....207 C3
Walsall WS3 ....244 A2
Fairfield Rd
Cannock WS12 ....210 A2
Colwich ST18 ....158 A2
Uttoxeter ST14 ....126 A4
Fairfield Rise DV8 ....279 B3
Fairfields ST7 ....39 C1
Fairfields Hill B78 ......262 C4
Fairfields Rd Biddulph ST8 ..17 A1
Market Drayton TF9 ....97 B1
Fairford Gdns
Burntwood WS7 ....229 B3
Kingswinford DY8 ....275 C2
Fairgreen Rd ST5 ....85 B3
Fairgreen Way B74 .....257 A2
Fairham Rd DE13 ....147 C1
Fairhaven CW2 ....37 A1
Fairhaven Gr ST1 ....57 C3
Fairhaven Prim Sch
DY8 ....275 B2
Fairhills DY3 ....271 B4
Fairlady Dr WS7 ....228 B4
Fairlawn Cl Meir ST3 ....89 C4
Walsall WV12 ....242 B1
Fairlawn Dr DY6 ....275 B2
Fairlawn Way WV12 .....242 B1
Fairlawns ST3 ....284 B4
Fairlight Gr ST3 ....90 A4
Fairmead Cl ST17 ....175 B3
Fairmeadows Prim Sch
DE11 ....186 C3
Fairmount Way WS15 ...178 B1
Fairoak Cl ST15 ....70 C2
Fairoak Ave ST16 ....155 B4
Fairoak Bank ST21 ......115 B3
Fairoak Gr WV11 ....242 A1

Fairview Ave CW2 ....37 A3
Fairview Cl
Cheslyn Hay WS6 ....226 B1
Tamworth B77 ....250 C3
Fairview Cres DY6 ....275 C3
Fairview Rd WV4 ....265 B2
Fairview Villas ST5 ......85 B3
Fairview Way ST17 ......156 B1
Fairway Burton u T DE14 .185 A3
Cannock WS11 ....226 B3
Stafford ST16,ST17 ....156 A1
Tamworth B77 ....261 C3
Trentham ST4 ....87 C4
Walsall WS4 ....244 B1
Fairway Ct B77 ....251 A2
Fairway Rd ST6 ....56 C4
Fairway The Clifton DE6 ..81 C3
Swadlincote DE11 ....186 C3
Fairways Ave DY8 ....279 C1
Fairways Cl DY8 ....279 C1
Falcon B77 ....262 A3
Falcon Bsns Ctr DE14 ...166 C3
Falcon Cl
Burton u T DE14 ....166 C3
Cannock WS11 ....209 B1
Cheslyn Hay WS6 ....226 B1
Falcon Cres WV14 ......266 C1
Falcon Rd ST3 ....90 A3
Falcon Rise DV8 ....279 B3
Falcon Way DY1 ....271 C1
Falcondale Rd WV12 ....242 B1
Falconry Ctr * DY9 ......282 C1
Faldo Cl DE14 ....185 A3
Falkirk Grange ST5 ......70 C4
Falklands Cl DY3 ....266 A1
Fallow Deer Lawn TF10 .168 C3
Fallow Field
Cannock WS11 ....209 C2
Lichfield WS13 ....214 A2
Little Aston B74 ....257 A2
Fallow Rd B78 ....249 C1
Fallowfield Longton ST3 ..88 C4
Perton WV6 ....254 B2
Stafford ST17 ....175 B3
Wolv WV9 ....239 C1
Fallowfield Cl ST19 .....207 C4
Fallowfields Dr DE13 ....183 B1
Falmouth Ave ST17 .....175 C4
Falmouth Cl ST17 ....175 C4
Falmouth Cres ST5 ......71 B3
Falmouth Dr B77 ....250 C3
Falmouth Rd DE12 ......15 C4
Falna Cres B79 ....249 C4
Fancourt Ave WV4 ......265 B2
Fancy Wlk ST16 ....155 B3
Fane Rd WV11 ....242 A1
Fanlizard La ST20 ......171 B2
Far Green Ind Est ST1 ....57 B3
Far Lane Ind Est ST10 ...62 A4
Far Ridding ST20 ....171 B3
Far View WS9 ....245 A1
Faraday Pl ST14 ....71 C4
Faraday Rd ST16 ....155 C3
Farcroft Ave ST5 ....55 A4
Farcroft Dr TF9 ....97 A1
Fareham Cres WV4 ......265 B3
Fareham Gr 18 ST3 ......89 C4
Farewell La WS7 ....229 C3
Faringdon B77 ....250 C2
Farington Pl ST6 ....42 A3
Farland Gr ST6 ....42 A4
Farleigh Dr WV3 ....265 A4
Farleigh Gr ST2 ....58 B1
Farleigh Rd WV6 ....255 B2
Farley La ST10 ....78 B2
Farley Rd ST10 ....78 A3
Farm Cl Burton u T DE13 .166 A4
Cannock WS12 ....210 B2
Codsall WV8 ....239 A4
Market Drayton TF9 ....97 A1
Rugeley WS15 ....178 B1
Sedgley DY3 ....271 A4
Tamworth B79 ....250 B4
Farm Ct DE13 ....166 B4
Farm Gr DE13 ....168 B2
Farm La DE15 ....167 C4
Farm Lea
Hilderstone ST15 ....106 B1
Norton-in-t-M ST6 ....42 C3
Farm Rd Albrighton WV6 .252 B4
Burton u T DE13 ....166 B4
Wolv WV3 ....265 B4
Farm Side DE11 ....186 C3
Farm View ST15 ....106 B1
Farmadine ST4 ....88 A4
Farman Ct ST13 ....90 B4
Farmbrook Ave WV10 ...240 B2
Farmdown Rd ST17 .....156 B1
Farmer St ST3 ....283 C2
Farmers Bank ST5 ....55 B1
Farmfields Rise CW3 .....67 B1
Farmoor Way WV10 .....240 C2
Farmount Dr 5 WS11 ....226 C4
Farmside Gn WV9 ....239 C1
Farmside La ST18 ....74 A1
Farmstead Cl ST15 ....96 B2
Farnborough Ct B75 .....258 B1
Farnborough Dr ST13 ....90 B4
Farncote Dr B74 ....257 C2
Farndale Ave WV6 ......255 C3
Farndale Cl 8 ST6 ....41 B2
Farnell St ST16 ....42 A2
Farnham Dr ST8 ....17 B1
Farnham Dr ST18 ....27 A3
Farnworth Rd ST3 ....73 C2
Farrier Cl ST15 ....120 B4
Farrier Way DY6 ....275 A4

Fernleigh Gdns
Kingswinford DY8 ....275 B2
Stafford ST16 ....155 A3
Fernwood ST16 ....155 B4
Fernwood Croft ST13 ....30 B2
Fernwood Dr Leek ST13 ....30 B2
Rugeley WS15 ....178 C4
Fernwood Gn ST4 ....88 B4
Ferrand Cl ST4 ....72 A1
Ferrers Ave DE13 ....146 A3

Fircroft Cl [4] WS11 ....210 A2
Firecrest Cl WS12 ....210 B1
Firmstone Ct DY8 ....279 C4
Firmstone St DY8 ....279 C4
Firs Cl The ST17 ....175 B4
Firs Dr DY5 ....279 C3
Firs Rd The Cannock WS15 ....211 C3
Cannock, Hawks Green WS11 ....210 A1

Foley Ave WV6 ....255 B2
Foley Church Cl B74 ....255 C4
Foley Ct B74 ....256 C4
Foley Dr WV6 ....255 B2
Foley Gr WV5 ....269 C3

Foster Ave WS12 ....209 C3
Foster Cres DY7 ....278 A2

Foxton Cl DE13 ....201 A1
Foxwood Cl ST15 ....119 C3
Foxwood Rd B78 ....262 C4
Fradley Cl ST14 ....110 C3
Fradley Gr ST14 ....110 C3
Fradley La WS13 ....215 C4
Fradswell La ST18 ....123 A1

Framlingham Gr WV6 .....255 A2
Frampton Gr ST6 ....41 C3
Frances Dr WS3 ....243 A1
Francis Cl
2 Kingswinford DY6 .....275 B4
Penkridge ST19 ....208 A4
Francis Green La ST19 .207 C4
Francis Rd
Lichfield WS13 ....214 A1
Stourbridge DY8 ....279 B3
Francis St ST6 ....41 C3
Frank Foley Way ST16 ..155 B2
Frank Rogers Wlk
WS15 ....178 B1
Frank St ST4 ....72 A3
Franklin Cl
Burton u T DE15 ....167 A1
Perton WV6 ....254 C3
Franklin Dr WS7 ....229 A4
Franklin Rd ST4 ....71 C4
Franklyn St ST1 ....282 C1
Fraser Cl ST15 ....137 C3
Fraser St ST6 ....57 A4
Frayne Ave DY6 ....275 B4
Frazier Ho **3** ST3 ....89 C4
Freckleton Pl ST3 ....90 B4
Fred Brewer Way DE13 .165 C2
Frederick Ave ST4 ....72 A4
Frederick Ct B77 ....250 C2
Frederick Rd ST19 .....192 C1
Frederick St
Burton u T DE15 ....185 C4
Fenton ST4 ....72 C3
Wolv WV2 ....266 B4
Fredericks Cl DY8 ......279 C2
Free Trade St ST1 ......282 C4
Freebridge Cl ST3 ....73 C2
Freedom Dr ST7 ....26 C2
Freedom Wlk ST6 ....42 B2
Freeford Gdns WS14 ...231 C3
Freehold St ST5 ....284 C2
Freeland Gr **3** DY6 ....275 C2
Freemantle Dr WS22 ...210 C1
Freemen St ST16 ....155 C3
Freer Dr WS7 ....229 C4
Freeth Rd WS8 ....229 A1
Fremantle Rd ST4 ....71 C2
Fremont Dr DY1 ....271 C2
French Ave B78 ....249 B1
Frenchmore Gr ST3 ......73 C1
Frensham Cl WS6 ......226 C2
Freshwater Gr ST2 ......57 C2
Freville Gdns B79 ......250 A3
Frew Cl ST16 ....156 A2
Friar St Longton ST3 ...283 C4
Stafford ST16 ....155 B3
Friar's Alley WS13 .....231 A4
Friar's Ct ST5 ....284 B2
Friar's La ST11 ....220 B2
Friar's St ST5 ....284 B2
Friars Ave ST15 ....120 A4
Friars Cl Cheadle ST10 ..76 B2
Kingswinford DY8 .....275 B2
Friars Gorse DY7 ......279 B4
Friars Pl ST2 ....58 A4
Friars Rd ST2 ....58 A4
Friars Wlk B77 ....250 B2
Friars' Rd ST17 ....155 C1
Friars' Terr ST17 ......155 C1
Friars' Wlk
Newcastle-u-L ST5 .....71 A3
Stafford ST17 ....155 C1
Friarswood Prim Sch
ST5 ....284 B1
Friarswood Rd ST5 ....284 B2
Friary Ave
Abbots Bromley WS15 ..160 C3
Lichfield WS13 ....231 A3
Friary Dr ST17 ....257 C2
Friary Gdns WS13 .....231 A4
Friezland Way WS8 ....245 A3
Frinton Cl ST16 ....155 C3
Frith St ST13 ....30 B3
Frobisher Dr ST15 .....103 A2
Frobisher St ST6 ....43 A3
Frodingham Rd ST2 .....58 B1
Frog La Lichfield WS13 .231 A4
Market Drayton TF9 .....97 B1
Wheaton Aston ST19 ...205 B3
Froghall ST5 ....284 B3
Froghall Rd Cheadle ST10 .76 C3
Ipstones ST10 ....62 A2
Froghall Wharf* ST10 ..62 A2
Frogmore Rd TF9 ....97 B1
Frome Cl DY3 ....271 A3
Frome Wlk ST6 ....42 A2
Froyle Cl WV6 ....255 B3
Fuchsia Dr WV9 ....239 C2
Fulfen Prim Sch WS7 ..229 B4
Fulfen Prim Sch ST11 ..126 C3
Fulford Rd ST11 ....106 C4
Fullbrook Ave DE13 ...201 C4
Fullelove Rd WS8 .....245 A4
Fuller St ST6 ....42 C2

Fullerton Cl WV8 ......239 C1
Fullmore Cl ST19 .....207 C4
Fullwood Wlk ST2 ......58 B1
Fulmer Pl ST3 ....90 A4
Furber Pl DY6 ....275 C3
Ferguson St WV11 ....242 A1
Furlong Ave ST10 ....92 C2
Furlong Cl Alrewas DE13 .201 A1
Upper Tean ST10 ....92 C2
Weston ST18 ....138 C1
Furlong Dr ST10 ....92 C2
Furlong La Alrewas DE13 .201 A1
Alstonefield DE6 ....35 B2
Bradley ST18 ....173 B1
Burslem ST6 ....56 C4
Furlong Par **6** ST6 .....56 C4
Furlong Pas **6** ST6 ....56 C4
Furlong Rd ST6 ....41 C2
Furlong The ST15 .....118 C3
Furlong Rd DY3 ....271 B3
Furlongs Rd DY3 ......271 B3
Furmston PT ST13 ......31 A4
Furnace Cl WV5 ....269 C3
Furnace La CW3 ....68 C4
Furnace Rd ST3 ....73 B1
Furness B77 ....250 C2
Furness Cl WS3 ....242 C2
Furness Gr ST17 .....174 A4
Furnival St ST6 ....57 A3
Furnivall Cres WS13 ...214 B1
Furst St WS8 ....245 A4
Fyfield Rd DE15 ....185 C3
Fynney Fields ST13 .....45 C4
Fynney St ST13 ....30 C3

G

Gable Cotts ST11 ....74 C1
Gable Croft WS14 .....231 C3
Gable St ST4 ....72 A3
Gables The
Kingswinford DY6 ....275 A4
Swadlincote DE11 ....186 C3
Gaelic Rd WS11 ....209 B2
Gag La DE6 ....51 B3
Gagarin B79 ....249 C3
Gaia La WS13 ....231 A4
Gaia Stowe WS13 ......214 A1
Gaiafields Rd WS13 ...214 A1
Gaialands Cres WS13 .214 A1
Gail Cl WS9 ....245 C2
Gail Pk WV3 ....265 B4
Gailey Lea La ST19 ...208 A1
Gailey Pottery* ST19 ..207 B1
Gainford Cl WV8 ......239 C1
Gains La WS3 ....227 B1
Gainsborough Dr
Fazeley B78 ....260 A4
Perton WV6 ....255 A2
Gainsborough Pl DY1 .271 C1
Gainsborough Rd
Longton ST3 ....88 C4
Newcastle-u-L ST5 .....55 C3
Gainsborough Way
DE15 ....167 A2
Gainsbrook Cres WS11 .227 C3
Gairloch Rd WV11 ....242 A1
Galahad Dr DE13 .....147 C1
Galena Cl B77 ....251 A1
Galleys Bank ST7 ....26 A2
Galliers Cl B77 ....261 C3
Gallimore Cl ST6 ....41 C1
Gallimore Ho ST7 ......40 B4
Galloway Rd ST2 ......73 C4
Gallowstree La
Mayfield DE6 ....81 B4
Newcastle-u-L ST5 .....70 C4
Galsworthy Rd ST4 .....73 A3
Galway Rd WS7 ....229 A4
Gamesfield Gn WV3 ...255 C1
Ganton Rd WS3 ......243 A2
Ganton Wlk WV8 .....255 C4
Gaol Butts ST11 ....133 B3
Gaol Rd ST16 ....155 C2
Gaol Sq ST16 ....155 C2
Gaolgate St **8** ST16 ..155 C2
Garage Cl B77 ....261 B3
Garbett St ST6 ....41 B4
Garden Cotts ST20 ...171 B3
Garden Cres WS3 .....243 C2
Garden Croft WS9 ....256 A4
Garden Dr WS15 ......197 A4
Garden La ST19 ....206 B2
Garden Pl Stafford ST17 ..155 C1
Stoke-on-T ST4 ....71 C4
Garden St Leek ST13 ....30 B3
Newcastle-u-L ST5 ....284 C2
Stafford ST17 ....155 C1
Stoke-on-T ST4 ....71 C3
Garden View WS15 ...178 B1
Garden Village*
Pattingham WV6 ......263 C3
Upper Tean ST10 ....92 B2
Garden Wlk DY3 ......271 B1
Gardeners Cl ST8 ......27 A3
Gardeners Way WV5 ..269 C2
Gardenholm Cl ST3 ....89 C4
Gardens The B79 .....216 B1
Gardiner Dr ST3 ......283 A2
Gardner Pl ST14 ......111 A1
Garfield Ave ST4 ....71 C1
Garfield Cres ST14 .....71 C1
Garfield St ST1 ....282 A1
Garibaldi St ST1 ....56 C2
Garlick St ST6 ....42 A1

Garner St Burslem ST5 ..56 C2
Stoke-on-T ST4 ....56 C1
Garners Wlk CW3 ....68 C4
Garnet Cl WS9 ....245 C2
Garnet St ST1 ....57 A2
Garnett Rd E ST5 ......56 A3
Garnett Rd W ST5 ......56 A3
Garret Cl DY3 ....275 B4
Garrick Cl Dudley DY1 .271 C2
Lichfield WS13 ....213 C1
Garrick Cl 213 C1
Garrick Rd
Cannock WS11 ....209 B2
Lichfield WS13 ....213 C1
Garrick Rise
Burntwood WS7 ......229 A4
Rugeley WS15 ....197 A3
Garridge Cl WV7 .....237 A2
Garrigill B77 ....251 A1
Garrod Sq ST16 ......156 A3
Garsdale Cres ST3 .....88 C4
Gartan Rd DE14 ......185 A4
Garth Cl ST17 ....174 C3
Garth Rd ST17 ....174 C3
Garth St ST1 ....282 C3
Garth The WS13 .....214 A1
Gas St ST14 ....111 B1
Gaskell Rd ST2 ....58 B2
Gatacre St DY3 ....271 B2
Gatcombe Cl
Burton u T DE13 .....147 B1
Wolv WV10 ....240 C2
Gatcombe Rd DY1 ....271 C1
Gate St Meir ST3 ....74 A3
Sedgley DY3 ....271 C4
Gatehouse Trad Est
WS8 ....229 A1
Gateway ST5 ....40 B1
Gateway Ave ST5 ......85 B3
Gatherwynd La TF11 ..203 C3
Gatley Gr ST3 ....90 A3
Gauledge La SK17 .....13 A3
Gaunt St **8** ST1 ......282 B4
Gawain Gr DE13 .....147 C1
Gawsworth B79 ......249 B4
Gawsworth Cl ST3 .....73 B3
Gay La ST20 ....204 C4
Gaydon Cl WV6 ......254 C3
Gaydon Rd WS9 .....256 A2
Gayle B77 ....251 A1
Gaymore Rd DY10 ...280 A3
Gayton Ave ST2 ....42 A3
Geary La ST5 ....167 C1
Gedney Gr ST5 ....71 A1
Geen St ST4 ....72 A4
Gemini Dr WS11 .....226 C3
Gemini Gr ST6 ....41 C2
Geneshall Cl ST20 ...171 B4
Geneva Dr Hanley ST1 ..57 C3
Newcastle-u-L ST5 .....70 C3
Genge Ave WV4 .....266 C2
Genista Cl ST5 ......186 A4
Genthorne Cl WV4 ...266 C2
Gentian B77 ....257 C2
Gentleshaw Prim Sch
WS15 ....212 A3
Geoffrey Ave ST13 .....30 B3
Geoffrey Cl WS11 ....209 A2
George Ave Meir ST3 ...74 A1
Tamworth B78 ....249 A1
George Baily Ct ST17 .155 C1
George Brealey Cl
WS15 ....196 C4
George Eardley Cl ST6 ..41 B3
George Eastham Ave ST4 .72 B2
George Elliott Cl ST17 .126 B3
George La Lichfield WS13 ..231 B4
Stone ST15 ....120 B4
George St Audley ST7 ..39 B1
Brierley Hill DY8 .....275 C1
Burton u T DE12 .....166 B2
Cannock WS11 ......210 B2
Fenton ST4 ....72 C4
Newcastle-u-L ST5 ..284 C3
Newcastle-u-L, Chesterton
ST5 ....55 C4
Newcastle-u-L, Porthill ST5 .56 B3
Newcastle-u-L, Silverdale
ST5 ....55 A1
Stafford ST16 ....155 B3
Tamworth B79 ....250 A1
George Walker Ct DE14 .166 B3
Georges Ct ST3 ......283 B3
Georges Way ST7 ......39 C1
Georgian Pl **8** WS11 .209 C1
Gerald Rd DY8 ....279 C4
Gerard B79 ....249 C4
Gerards Way TF9 .....100 B3
Gerrard St ST14 ......72 A4
Gettings Cl WV7 .....229 C4
Gibb La ST6 ....128 C3
Gibbet La DY7 ....279 A2
Gibbins St ST1 ....282 C4
Gibbons Gr WV6 ....255 C2
Gibbons Hill Rd DY3 .266 B1
Gibbons Rd
Sutton Coldfield B75 .258 A2
Wolv WV6 ....255 C2
Gibraltar DY7 ....278 B2
Gibson Cl ST15 ....120 B3
Gibson Gr ST5 ....55 B4
Gibson Pl ST3 ....74 A1
Gibson Rd WV6 .....254 C2
Gibson St ST6 ....41 C1
Giddyhall La WS15 ...197 C1
Gideons Cl DY3 ......271 B3
Giffard RC Prim Sch
WV6 ....255 C3

Giffard Rd WV10 .....240 C1
Gifford Cl ST19 ......223 B3
Gifford Pl ST3 ....71 C3
Giffords Croft WS13 ..214 A1
Gig Mill Prim Sch DY8 .279 C2
Giggetty La WV5 ....269 C3
Gigmill Way DY8 ....279 C2
Gilbanks Rd DY8 ....279 B3
Gilbern Dr ST8 ....27 A3
Gilbert Cl
5 Kidsgrove ST7 .....26 A1
Newport TF10 ....168 B1
Gilbert La WV5 ......270 A4
Gilbert Rd WS13 ....214 B1
Gilbert St ST16 ....41 B4
Gilbert Wlk WS13 ...214 A1
Gilbeys Cl DY8 ....275 C1
Gilchrist Ct ST6 ....57 A3
Giles Cl ST10 ....76 B2
Giles Rd WS13 ......214 A2
Gilkes Wlk ST4 ....57 C3
Gill Bank Rd ST6 .....41 A4
Gill Wlk ST1 ....282 A2
Gilliard's Croft DE13 .199 B3
Gilliat Wlk ST17 ....58 B1
Gillingham Cres ST16 ..155 A1
Gillway B79 ....250 A4
Gilman Ave ST2 ....43 A1
Gilman Pl ST1 ....282 C3
Gilman St ST1 ......282 C2
Gilmour La DE13 ....183 C1
Gilpin Cres WS3 ....244 A2
Gilpins Croft WS6 ...226 B1
Gilwell Rd WS3 .....211 C3
Gimson St ST4 ....72 C3
Ginger Hill ST20 ....171 B3
Ginger La ST21 ......116 A2
Gipsy La Anslefield QG6 .226 C1
Cookley DY11 ....280 A4
Girsby Cl ST4 ....88 B3
Girton Rd WS11 .....226 C4
Gisborne Cl DE13 ...182 A2
Gitana St ST1 ....282 C3
Glade Ave WS7 ......229 A4
Glade The Cannock WS11 .209 B1
Newcastle-u-L ST5 .....71 A1
Stafford ST17 ....175 A4
Wolv WV8 ....239 C1
Glades The
Aldridge, Hardwick B74 .256 C1
Aldridge, Leighswood
WS9 ....256 A4
Gladman Bsns Quarter
WV9 ....239 C2
Gladstone Dr DY8 ...279 B3
Gladstone Gr
Biddulph ST8 ....27 C4
Kingswinford DY6 ....275 B4
Gladstone Pl ST3 ......71 C3
Gladstone Pottery Mus*
ST3 ....283 C3
Gladstone Rd
Cannock WS12 ....210 C1
Stourbridge DY8 .....279 B3
Gladstone St Leek ST13 ..30 B3
Stoke-on-T ST4 ....56 C1
Gladstone Way ST16 .156 A3
Glaisdale Gr ST3 ......73 B3
Glaisher Dr ST3 ....90 B4
Glamis Cl DE13 ......166 B4
Glamis Dr **7** ST15 ..120 B3
Glandore Rd ST3 ......73 C2
Glanville Cl B75 .....258 A2
Glascote Ct B77 ......250 C3
Glascote Heath Prim Sch
B77 ....251 A1
Glascote La B77 .....261 C4
Glascote Rd B77 ....250 C2
Glass La WS11 ....161 C1
Glass St ST1 ....282 B3
Glasscroft Cotts WS7 .229 C4
Glastonbury Cl
Norton-in-t-M ST19 ....43 B2
Stafford ST17 ....175 B3
Glastonbury Cres WS3 .242 C1
Glastonbury Way WS3 .242 C1
Glebe Ave ST15 ......155 B3
Glebe Cl
Cheswardine TF9 ....130 A4
Doveridge DE6 ....127 A4
Forsbrook ST11 ....91 A3
Rolleston DE13 .....147 A2
Glebe Ct Cheadle ST10 ..76 A1
Glebe La Gnosall ST20 ..171 C4
Newcastle-u-L ST5 .....70 C3
Glebe Prim Sch ST3 ...72 C3
Glebe Rd Armitage WS15 .198 B3
Stoke-on-T ST4 ....76 B1
Glebe St Kidsgrove ST7 ..25 B1
Stoke-on-T ST4 ....72 A4
Glebe The
Albrighton WV7 .....237 A3
Chebsey ST15 ....135 A4
Coven WV9 ....239 A3
Glebe Cl Cheadle ST10 ..76 A1
Glebedale Ct ST4 ......72 C3
Glebedale Rd ST4 .....72 C3
Glebefields ST20 .....151 B4
Glebelands
Bobbington DY7 .....267 C1
Stafford ST17 ......174 C3
Glebeville ST13 ....30 C2
Gledhill Pk WS14 ....231 B3
Glen Cl WS11 ....209 C3
Glen Ct Codsall WV8 .239 A2
Glen Dale ST15 ....85 A2
Glen Dr ST10 ....94 C4
Glen Park Rd DY3 ...271 B1
Glen Rd Sedgley DY3 .271 C3

Glen End continued
Stourbridge DY8 ....279 C2
Glen Rise ST13 ....166 A4
Glen The **7** ST15 ...120 A4
Glencastle Way ST4 ...88 B3
Glencoe Rd WS11 ...210 A2
Glencoe St ST13 .....283 B2
Glencroft Cl DE14 ...185 A4
Glendale Cl WV3 ....265 B4
Glendale Ct
Newcastle-u-L ST5 ....71 B1
Tamworth B77 ......262 A3
Glendale Dr WV5 ...270 A3
Glendale Gdns WS11 .210 A2
Glendale Rd ST16 .....57 A4
Glendene Cl ST19 ....210 B3
Glendon Cl TF9 ......112 A4
Glendower Cl ST20 ..171 B3
Glendower Rd WS9 ..245 A1
Glenduie Gr ST14 .....88 B3
Gleneagles B77 ......251 A3
Gleneagles Cres ST1 ..57 C3
Gleneagles Rd
Burton u T DE13 .....147 B1
Stafford ST16 ......156 B2
Gleneagles Rd
Perton WV6 ....254 B3
Walsall WS3 ....243 C2
Glenfield Cheadle ST10 .250 B1
Glenfield Rise DE13 ..166 A4
Glenfield Way ST2 .....73 C4
Glengarry Gdns WV3 .255 C1
Glenhaven WS5 ......178 B1
Glenmore Ave WV7 ..229 A3
Glenmore Cl WV3 ...266 C2
Glenmsyl Way DE14 .166 C2
Glenroyd Ave ST7 .....58 A1
Glenroyd Wlk ST2 .....58 B1
Glenthorne Cl ST17 ..175 B3
Glenthorne Ho WS6 ..226 C2
Glenthorne Prim Sch
WS6 ....226 C1
Glenville Ave CV9 ....262 B1
Glenwood Cl
Longton ST3 ....283 B4
Newcastle-u-L ST5 .....55 B1
Glenwood Rise WS9 ..245 B2
Globe Ave ST17 ......174 C3
Globe St ST6 ....56 C4
Gloucester Cl WS13 ..214 A2
Gloucester Grange ST5 ..71 B3
Gloucester Rd ST2 .....25 C1
Gloucester Way
Burton u T DE15 .....167 A1
Cannock WS11 ......210 A1
Glover St Cannock WS12 .210 C2
Hanley ST1 ....282 C4
Stafford ST16 ......155 B2
Glovers Cl WS12 ....211 A3
Glyme Dr WV6 ....255 C2
Glyn Pl ST16 ....41 C2
Glyndebourne B79 ..249 B4
Glynne Ave DY6 ....275 B3
Glynne Prim Sch DY6 .275 B2
Gnosall La TF10 ......188 B3
Gnosall Rd
Gnosall, Beffcote TF10 .170 B1
Gnosall, Knightley Dale
ST20 ....152 A2
Goddard St ST3 ......283 D4
Godfrey Rd ST2 ....58 B2
Godley La ST10 ....75 B3
Godleybarn La ST10 ...75 C3
Godolphin B79 ......249 B4
Godsall Gdns WV8 ..238 C2
Gofton B77 ....251 A1
Golborn Ave ST3 ......90 A2
Golborn Cl ST13 ......90 A2
Gold St ST3 ....283 B3
Goldcrest B77 ....262 A3
Goldcrest Way ST18 ...27 C4
Goldenhill Prim Sch ST6 .41 B4
Goldenhill Rd ST4 ...283 B5
Goldenhill St Joseph's RC
Prim Sch ST6 ....41 B4
Goldfinch View TF9 ....99 B2
Goldhurst Dr ST10 .....92 C1
Goldsborough B77 ...251 A1
Goldsmith Pl
Longton ST3 ....283 C4
Tamworth B79 .....250 A4
Goldthorn Ave WV4 ..266 A3
Goldthorn Cres WV4 ..266 A3
Goldthorn Hill WV2,WV4 .266 B3
Goldthorn Park Jun & Inf Sch
WV4 ....266 B3
Goldthorn Rd WV2,WV3 .266 A4
Golf Links Cl ST16 .....41 B4
Goms Mill Ct ST3 ....283 B2
Goms Mill Rd ST3 ...283 A2
Goodfellow St ST16 ....42 A2
Goodi Cl ST15 ....119 C3
Goodman St DE14 ...166 B3
Goodrich Ave WV6 ...250 A4
Goodthorn Cres WV4 ..266 A3
Goods Station La ST19 .192 C1
Goodson Cl ST20 .....55 C4
Goodwick Cl ST4 ......88 B3
Goodwin Ave ST3 ....284 B4
Goodwin Rd ST3 ......74 A1
Goodwood Ave ST10 ..76 C2
Goodwood Cl
Burton u T DE13 .....147 B1
Cannock WS12 ......211 A3
Lichfield WS14 .....231 B4

Goodwood Pl ST4 . . . . .88 A4
Goose La WS10 . . . . .160 C3
Goose St ST5 . . . . .284 B2
Goosefield Cl TF9 . . . . .97 A1
Goosemoor Gr 15 ST3 . . . . . .90 A4
Goostry Cl B77 . . . . .250 B3
Goostry Rd B77 . . . . .250 B3
Gordale Cl CW12 . . . . .6 A3
Gordon Ave Cheadle ST10 . .76 A2
  Hanley ST6 . . . . .57 B4
  Stafford ST16 . . . . .155 B4
  Wolv WV4 . . . . .266 C2
Gordon Banks Dr ST4 . . . . .72 B2
Gordon Cl ST13 . . . . .30 B2
Gordon Cres ST1 . . . . .57 C2
Gordon Ct ST5 . . . . .55 C2
Gordon Rd ST6 . . . . .41 B3
Gordon St
  Burton u T DE14 . . . . .166 B2
  Chell Heath ST6 . . . . .42 A1
  Newcastle-u-L ST5 . . . . . . .55 C2
  4 Wolv WV2 . . . . .266 B4
Gorse Cres TF9 . . . . .99 C3
Gorse Dr WS12 . . . . .209 B3
Gorse La Alrewas WS13 . . .215 A4
  Astbury CW12 . . . . .15 B3
  Gnosall ST20 . . . . .132 C4
  Lichfield WS14 . . . . .231 C3
  Rugeley WS15 . . . . .196 C3
  Seisdon WV5 . . . . .269 A3
Gorse Rd Rugeley WS15 . . .196 C3
  Sedgley DY3 . . . . .271 C4
Gorse St ST4 . . . . .72 C2
Gorse Way WS12 . . . . .210 B4
Gorsebrook Leys ST16 . . . . .155 A3
Gorseburn Way WS15 . . . . .178 B1
Gorsemoor Prim Sch
  WS12 . . . . .210 B1
Gorsemoor Rd WS12 . . . . . .210 B1
Gorsemoor Way WV11 . . . .242 A2
Gorseway WS7 . . . . .209 A3
Gorsey Bank ST6 . . . . .42 C3
Gorsey La Cannock WS11 . .209 B1
  Great Wyrley WS6 . . . . . . .226 C1
  Millmeece ST21 . . . . .102 C3
  Netherseal DE12 . . . . .219 C4
  Norton Canes WS3 . . . . . . .227 C1
Gorsey Dale ST17 . . . . .175 B3
Gorstey Lea WS7 . . . . .229 B4
Gorsty Bank WS14 . . . . . . .231 C4
Gorsty Hayes WV8 . . . . . . .238 C2
Gorsty Hill Cl CW2 . . . . .37 C1
Gorsty Hill Rd ST10 . . . . . . .92 C3
Gorsy Bank Rd B77 . . . . . . .261 C3
Gorsy La TF10 . . . . .150 A2
Gort Rd ST5 . . . . .55 C2
Gosberryhole La CW12 . . . . .7 A1
Goscote Ind Est WS3 . . . . .243 C1
Goscote La WS3 . . . . .243 C1
Goscote Rd WS3 . . . . .244 A1
Gosforth Gr ST3 . . . . .90 B4
Gospel Ash Rd DY7 . . . . . . .268 B1
Gospel End Rd DY3 . . . . . . .271 A4
Gospel End St DY3 . . . . . . .271 A4
Gottersley La DY7 . . . . .274 B1
Gough Cl ST16 . . . . .155 B4
Gough Side DE14 . . . . .166 B1
Gould Firm La WS9 . . . . . . .256 C2
Govan Rd ST4 . . . . .72 C4
Gowan Ave ST6 . . . . .42 A2
Gower Ave DY6 . . . . .275 C2
Gower Rd Sedgley DY3 . . . .266 A1
  Stone ST15 . . . . .120 A4
Gower St Longton ST3 . . . . .57 B4
  Newcastle-u-L ST5 . . . . . . .284 C3
  Wolv WV2 . . . . .266 B4
Gowland Dr WS11 . . . . .209 A1
Goya Cl WS11 . . . . .210 B1
Grace St ST13 . . . . .30 B3
Gradbach Mill* SK17 . . . . . . .2 A1
Graffam Gr ST10 . . . . .76 C2
Grafton Ave ST6 . . . . .42 A1
Grafton Ct 9 WV6 . . . . . . .255 C2
Grafton Gdns DY3 . . . . .271 A2
Grafton Ho WV4 . . . . .266 C2
Grafton Inf Sch ST3 . . . . . .283 C4
Grafton Rd
  Burton u T DE15 . . . . .167 A1
  Longton ST3 . . . . .283 C4
  Trentham ST4 . . . . .282 C3
Graham Cl DE14 . . . . .185 B4
Graham Ho B74 . . . . .256 C1
Graham Rd DY6 . . . . .275 B2
Graham St ST12 . . . . .58 A2
Grainger Cl WS11 . . . . .209 B1
Graiseley Hill WV2 . . . . . . .266 B4
Graiseley Prim Sch
  WV2 . . . . .266 B4
Graiseley Row WV2 . . . . . . .266 B4
Graisley Cl
  Cannock WS12 . . . . .210 A3
  Kingswinford DY6 . . . . . . .275 A4
Granary Rd WV8 . . . . .239 C1
Granary The WS9 . . . . .256 A3
Granby Wlk ST14 . . . . .146 C4
Granchester Cl ST13 . . . . . . .90 A3
Grange Ave
  Aldridge WS9 . . . . .245 A1
  Burntwood WS7 . . . . .229 A4
  Penkridge ST19 . . . . .207 C4
  Sutton Coldfield B75 . . . . .258 B2
Grange Cl
  Burton u T DE14 . . . . .166 A2
  Ellenhall ST21 . . . . .134 A1
  Tamworth B77 . . . . .261 B4
Grange Cres ST19 . . . . .207 C4
Grange Croft ST18 . . . . .158 B4
Grange Ct Biddulph ST8 . . . .16 B1

Grange Ct continued
  Egginton DE65 . . . . .148 A3
Grange Dr WS11 . . . . .209 C1
Grange Gdns ST13 . . . . .30 B2
Grange Hill WS15 . . . . .197 B1
Grange Ind Sch DE14 . . . . .166 A2
Grange La
  4 Kingswinford DY6 . . . . .275 C2
  Lichfield WS13 . . . . .213 C1
  Newcastle-u-L ST5 . . . . . . .56 B3
  Sutton Coldfield B75 . . . . .258 B2
Grange Pk Dr ST8 . . . . .16 C2
Grange Prim Sch ST13 . . . . .90 A4
Grange Rd Biddulph ST8 . . . .16 C2
  Burntwood WS7 . . . . .229 A3
  Cheddleton ST13 . . . . .45 B2
  Gnosall ST20 . . . . .151 C3
  Meir ST3 . . . . .90 A3
  Norton Canes WS11 . . . . .228 A3
  Penkridge ST19 . . . . .207 C4
  Stone ST15 . . . . .120 B4
  Swadlincote DE11 . . . . . . .186 C3
  Uttoxeter ST14 . . . . .111 A1
  Wolv, Blakenhall WV2 . . . .266 A3
  Wolv, Tettenhall WV6 . . . .255 B2
Grange St Burslem ST6 . . . . .57 A3
  Burton u T DE14 . . . . .166 A2
Grange The
  Burton u T DE14 . . . . .166 A2
  King's Bromley DE13 . . . . .199 B3
  Longdon WS15 . . . . .197 B1
  Meir ST3 . . . . .74 A1
  Stafford ST18 . . . . .174 B3
  Wall WS14 . . . . .230 B1
  Wombourne WV5 . . . . . . .270 A4
Grangefield Cl
  Cheddleton ST13 . . . . .45 B2
  Wolv WV8 . . . . .239 C1
Grangefield ST8 . . . . .16 C2
Grangewood Ave ST3 . . . . . .89 C3
Grangewood Rd ST3 . . . . . . .74 A1
Granstone Cl ST16 . . . . .42 A4
Grant Cl DY6 . . . . .275 B4
Grant St ST4 . . . . .72 B4
Grantham Pl ST12 . . . . .58 A3
Grantley Cl ST3 . . . . .73 A1
Grantley Cres DY6 . . . . .275 B4
Grantown Gr WS3 . . . . .243 A2
Granville B77 . . . . .250 C1
Granville Ave Hanley ST1 . . .57 B4
  Newcastle-u-L ST5 . . . . . . .284 C3
  Newport TF10 . . . . .168 C1
Granville Cl
  Newport TF10 . . . . .168 C1
  3 Wolv WV2 . . . . .266 B4
Granville Dr DY6 . . . . .275 C3
Granville Rd Bucknall ST2 . .58 A3
  Newport TF10 . . . . .168 C1
Granville Sq 3 ST15 . . . . . .105 A1
Granville St WV2 . . . . .266 B4
Granville Terr ST15 . . . . . . .105 A1
Granville Vilas TF10 . . . . . .168 C1
Grasmere Ave
  Little Aston B74 . . . . .257 A1
  Newcastle-u-L ST5 . . . . . . .71 A2
  Perton WV6 . . . . .254 C2
Grasmere Cl
  Burton u T DE15 . . . . .167 A1
  Kingswinford DY6 . . . . . . .275 A4
  Wolv WV6 . . . . .255 C4
Grasmere Dr DY8 . . . . .279 C2
Grasmere Pl WS11 . . . . . . .209 C3
Grasmere Terr ST6 . . . . .42 A2
Grassholme B77 . . . . .262 A4
Grassmere Ct WS6 . . . . . . .226 B2
Grassmere Hollow ST16 . . .154 C3
Grassy La WV11 . . . . .241 A1
Grassygreen La ST7 . . . . . . .39 C1
Gratley Croft WS12 . . . . . . .209 B2
Gratton La ST19 . . . . .59 B2
Gratton Rd ST2 . . . . .58 B2
Gravel Hill WV5 . . . . .270 A3
Gravel La
  Huntington WS12 . . . . . . .209 B3
  Stafford ST17 . . . . .155 B1
Gravelly Bank ST3 . . . . .89 C4
Gravelly Dr TF10 . . . . .168 C1
Gravelly Hill TF9 . . . . .100 A3
Gray La WS13 . . . . .245 C2
Gray Rd WS12 . . . . .209 C3
Gray Wlk ST17 . . . . .174 B4
Gray's Cl ST7 . . . . .26 A4
Graycar Bsns Pk DE13 . . . .184 A1
Grayling B77 . . . . .261 B3
Grayling Gr ST6 . . . . .42 A2
Grayling Willows CW3 . . . . .68 C3
Grayshott Rd ST6 . . . . .41 C3
Grayston Ave B77 . . . . .250 C2
Grazier Ave B77 . . . . .261 B4
Grazings The DY7 . . . . .278 B2
Greasely St ST2 . . . . .58 A3
Great Charles St WS8 . . . . .244 C4
Great Checkhill Rd DY7 . . . .274 B2
Great Fenton Bsns Pk
  ST4 . . . . .72 B2
Great Furlong DE13 . . . . . . .201 A1
Great Hales St TF9 . . . . .97 B1
Great Moor Rd WV6 . . . . . .253 C1
Great Wood Prim Sch
  ST10 . . . . .92 C2
Great Wood Rd ST10 . . . . . .92 C2
Great Wyrley High Sch
  WS6 . . . . .226 C2
Greatbatch Ave ST4 . . . . . . .71 C4
Greatmead B77 . . . . .250 B1
Greaves Cl WS14 . . . . .244 C3
Greaves La DE6,DE13 . . . . .144 C2
Green Acres WV5 . . . . .269 C3
Green Barn St ST18 . . . . . . .138 B1

Green Barns La WS14 . . . . .258 B4
Green Brook St ST5 . . . . .56 A2
Green Cl Barlaston ST12 . . . .88 B1
  Blythe Bridge ST11 . . . . . . .90 B4
  Pattingham WV6 . . . . .253 B1
Green Cres ST5 . . . . .119 C4
Green Gore La ST17 . . . . . .175 C4
Green Heath Rd WS12 . . . . .210 A4
Green La Aldridge WS9 . . . .256 C3
  Alsop en le D DE6 . . . . .36 B1
  Ashley TF9 . . . . .100 B3
  Brownhills WS8 . . . . .229 A1
  Brownhills, High Heath
  WS9 . . . . .244 B2
  Burntwood WS7 . . . . .212 B1
  Burton u T DE13 . . . . .166 A4
  Cannock WS11 . . . . .226 C3
  Clifton DE6 . . . . .81 C4
  Eccleshall ST21 . . . . .133 C3
  Farewell WS13 . . . . .212 B2
  Forsbrook ST11 . . . . .91 A3
  Forton TF10 . . . . .150 C1
  Hamstall Ridware WS15 . . .181 A2
  Heaton ST13 . . . . .18 C1
  Kingswinford DY6 . . . . . . .275 B4
  Marchington ST14 . . . . . . .128 A1
  Newport TF10 . . . . .168 C2
  Polesworth B77,B78 . . . . .262 B4
  Roston DE6 . . . . .96 C4
  Rugeley WS15 . . . . .178 B1
  Sedgley DY3 . . . . .271 C3
  Stafford ST18 . . . . .174 B2
  Tutbury DE13 . . . . .146 B3
  Wall WS14 . . . . .230 B1
  Walsall WS4,WS9 . . . . . . .244 A2
  Waterhouses DE6,ST10 . . .65 A4
  Whitgreave ST18 . . . . .135 C4
  Wolv WV6 . . . . .255 C4
Green Lane Venture Ctr
  WS11 . . . . .226 C3
Green Lea Fst Sch ST18 . . .122 B2
Green Mdws 7 WS11 . . . . .210 B1
Green Meadow Cl WV5 . . . .269 C3
Green Oak Rd WV8 . . . . . . .239 A1
Green Pk
  Blythe Bridge ST11 . . . . . . .90 C1
  Eccleshall ST21 . . . . .133 C3
  Upper Tean ST10 . . . . .109 A4
Green Rd Stoke-on-T ST4 . . .71 C2
  Weston ST18 . . . . .138 B1
Green Rock La WS3 . . . . . . .243 B1
Green Rock Prim Sch
  WS3 . . . . .243 C1
Green Slade Gr WS12 . . . . .210 B4
Green St Burton u T DE14 . .166 B1
  Stourbridge DY8 . . . . .279 C2
Green The Aldridge WS9 . . .256 B3
  Armitage WS15 . . . . .198 B3
  Newcastle-u-L DE13 . . . . .183 B1
  Blythe Bridge ST11 . . . . . . .90 C1
  Brocton ST17 . . . . .176 B4
  Brocton, Old Acre ST17 . . .176 A2
  Caverswall ST11 . . . . .147 C1
  Cheadle ST10 . . . . .76 A1
  Chebsey ST21 . . . . .134 C3
  Dordon B78 . . . . .262 B2
  Endon ST6 . . . . .43 A4
  Kingsley ST10 . . . . .61 B1
  Kingswinford DY8 . . . . . . .275 B1
  Lawton-gate ST7 . . . . .25 A2
  Newcastle-u-L, Clayton ST5 .71 B2
  Rugeley WS15 . . . . .177 B2
  Seckington B79 . . . . .236 A2
  Stoke-on-T ST4 . . . . .71 C4
  Tamworth B77 . . . . .251 A3
  Tamworth, Bonehill B78 . . .249 C1
  Walsall WS3 . . . . .243 A1
  Weston ST18 . . . . .138 B1
  Whittington WS14 . . . . . . .232 C3
  Woodseaves ST20 . . . . . . .151 B4
Green Valley Dr DE13 . . . . .166 A4
Green View TF11 . . . . .203 C4
Green Way Aldridge WS9 . . .245 A1
  Uttoxeter ST14 . . . . .126 A4
Green's La ST2 . . . . .58 C2
Greenacre ST18 . . . . .139 B1
Greenacre Cl B77 . . . . .251 A3
Greenacre Dr WV8 . . . . . . .239 A1
Greenacre The DE6 . . . . .81 C4
Greenacres
  Brewood WV9 . . . . .224 A2
  Rugeley WS15 . . . . .196 C4
  Sedgley DY3 . . . . .266 A1
  Wolv WV6 . . . . .255 A3
Greenacres Ave
  Blythe Bridge ST11 . . . . . . .90 B4
  Essington WV10 . . . . .241 A1
Greenacres Cl ST15 . . . . . . .256 C1
Greenacres Dr ST14 . . . . . .111 A1
Greenacres Prim Sch
  B77 . . . . .251 A3
Greenacres Way TF10 . . . . .168 B2
Greenbank Ave WV10 . . . . .241 B4
Greenbank Gdns DY8 . . . . .275 C1
Greenbank Rd
  Chell Heath ST6 . . . . .42 A2
  Newcastle-u-L ST5 . . . . . . .56 B2
Greenbirches Ind Est
  ST6 . . . . .41 B2
Greencroft
  Kingswinford DY6 . . . . . . .275 B2
  Lichfield WS13 . . . . .214 A1
Greendale Dr ST5 . . . . .40 B1
Greendale La ST10 . . . . .77 B2
Greendock St ST3 . . . . .283 B3
Greenfield ST8 . . . . .27 B3

Greenfield Ave
  Armitage WS15 . . . . .198 A2
  Endon ST6 . . . . .43 B4
  Stourbridge DY8 . . . . .279 C3
Greenfield Bldgs WS9 . . . . .270 A4
Greenfield Cl ST6 . . . . .43 B4
Greenfield Cres ST10 . . . . . .76 C2
Greenfield Dr ST14 . . . . . . .126 A4
Greenfield La WV10 . . . . . . .240 C3
Greenfield Pl ST6 . . . . .43 B4
Greenfield Prim Sch
  DY8 . . . . .279 C3
Greenfield Rd
  Stafford ST17 . . . . .175 B3
  Tunstall ST6 . . . . .41 C3
Greenfield View DY3 . . . . . .271 A4
Greenfields
  Aldridge WS9 . . . . .256 A4
  Cannock WS11 . . . . .209 C1
  Denstone ST14 . . . . .95 B3
  Gnosall ST20 . . . . .171 C4
Greenfields Dr WS15 . . . . . .178 B1
Greenfields La TF9 . . . . .97 A1
Greenfields Rd Endon ST9 . .43 C4
  Hixon ST18 . . . . .139 B1
  Kingswinford DY6 . . . . . . .275 C3
Greenfinch Cl ST14 . . . . . . .126 B3
Greengate St ST16 . . . . . . .155 C2
Greengates St ST16 . . . . . . .41 C2
Greenhall* Com Specl Sch
  ST16 . . . . .155 B2
Greenhead St ST6 . . . . .56 C4
Greenheart B77 . . . . .251 A2
Greenhill Lichfield WS13 . . .231 A4
  Wombourne WV5 . . . . . . .270 A3
Greenhill Cl B77 . . . . .261 B3
Greenhill Gdns WV5 . . . . . .270 A3
Greenhill La ST19 . . . . .205 B4
Greenhill Mews WS13 . . . . .231 B4
Greenhill Rd
  Norton-in-t-M ST6 . . . . .42 C3
  Sedgley DY3 . . . . .271 C3
Greenhill Way WS9 . . . . . . .245 A1
Greenhough Rd WS13 . . . . .231 A4
Greenland Cl DY6 . . . . .275 C4
Greenlands WV5 . . . . .269 C4
Greenlea B77 . . . . .262 A4
Greenlea Cl ST14 . . . . .88 B3
Greenleighs DY3 . . . . .266 B2
Greenly Rd WV4 . . . . .266 C2
Greenmeadow Gr ST9 . . . . .43 C3
Greenmeadows Rd CW3 . . .68 C4
Greenmoor Ave ST6 . . . . . . .42 A4
Greenoak Cl ST5 . . . . .70 C4
Greens Ind Est WS12 . . . . .210 B4
Greensforge La DY6,DY7 . .274 C2
Greenside
  Newcastle-u-L ST5 . . . . . . .284 A3
  Swynnerton ST15 . . . . . . .118 C3
Greenside Ave ST9 . . . . .43 C3
Greenside Cl ST17 . . . . .41 A4
Greenside Dr ST5 . . . . .70 C4
Greensmith Cl DE15 . . . . . .167 B2
Greensome Cl ST14 . . . . . . .155 A2
Greensome Cres ST16 . . . . .155 A3
Greensome La ST16 . . . . . .155 A3
Greensway Dr ST10 . . . . . . .76 C2
Greenvale ST15 . . . . .105 C4
Greenway
  Burton u T DE15 . . . . .167 A2
  Eccleshall ST21 . . . . .133 C3
  Fenton ST4 . . . . .72 C2
  Sedgley DY3 . . . . .266 C1
  Stafford ST16 . . . . .155 B4
  Trentham ST4 . . . . .87 C4
Greenway Ave
  3 Brierley Hill DY8 . . . . . .275 C1
  Chell Heath ST6 . . . . .42 A1
  Stone ST15 . . . . .120 A3
Greenway Bank
  Biddulph ST8 . . . . .27 B2
  Norton-in-t-M ST2 . . . . . . .42 A3
Greenway Bank Ctry Pk*
  ST8 . . . . .27 C2
Greenway Gdns
  Pattingham WV6 . . . . .253 B1
  Sedgley DY3 . . . . .266 C1
Greenway Hall Rd ST2,
  ST9 . . . . .43 B2
Greenway Pl ST12 . . . . .58 A4
Greenway Rd ST8 . . . . .16 C1
Greenway The
  Hagley DY9 . . . . .281 C3
  Newcastle-u-L ST5 . . . . . . .55 B3
  Pattingham WV6 . . . . .253 B1
Greenways Audley ST7 . . . . .39 C1
  Farewell WS13 . . . . .212 C2
  Kingswinford DY8 . . . . . . .275 B1
  Penkridge ST19 . . . . .208 A4
  Stafford ST18 . . . . .174 B3
Greenways Dr ST10 . . . . . . .76 C2
Greenways Prim Sch ST9 . .43 B2
Greenwood Ave ST4 . . . . . . .71 C1
Greenwood Gr ST17 . . . . . .174 B4
Greenwood Pk
  Aldridge WS9 . . . . .245 B1
  Cannock WS12 . . . . .210 A4
Greenwood Rd
  Aldridge WS9 . . . . .245 A1
  Burton u T DE15 . . . . .185 C4
  Forsbrook ST11 . . . . .91 A3
Greenwoods The DY8 . . . . .279 C3
Gregory La ST20 . . . . .150 B3

Gregory Rd
  Burntwood WS7 . . . . .229 C4
  Stourbridge DY8 . . . . .279 B3
Gregory St ST3 . . . . .283 B3
Gregorys Gn WV9 . . . . .224 A2
Gregson Cl 8 ST3 . . . . .73 A2
Greig Ct WS11 . . . . .210 B1
Grenadier Cl ST4 . . . . .88 B2
Grendon Gdns WV3 . . . . . . .265 B3
Grendon Gr ST2 . . . . .58 B1
Grenfell Rd WS3 . . . . .243 B2
Grenville Cl ST14 . . . . .110 C1
Grenville Rd DY1 . . . . .271 C1
Gresham Rd WS11 . . . . . . .209 C2
Gresley B77 . . . . .250 C1
Gresley Cl B74 . . . . .258 A2
Gresley Row WS13 . . . . . . .231 B4
Gresley Way ST7 . . . . .39 C1
Gresley Wood Rd DE11 . . . .186 C1
Gresty St ST7 . . . . .72 A4
Gretton Ave DE13 . . . . .147 C1
Greville Cl ST19 . . . . .207 C4
Greville St ST1 . . . . .282 C4
Grey Friars ST16 . . . . .155 B3
Grey Friars Way ST16 . . . . .155 B3
Grey Friars' Pl ST16 . . . . . .155 B3
Greyfriars Bsns Pk ST16 . .155 B2
Greyfriars Cl DY1 . . . . .271 C2
Greyfriars Ct ST16 . . . . .155 B3
Greyfriars Dr B79 . . . . .249 C3
Greyfriars Rd ST2 . . . . .58 A3
Greyhound Ct CW3 . . . . .68 C3
Greyhound La
  Lower Penn WV4 . . . . .264 C3
  Stourbridge DY8 . . . . .279 B1
Greyhound Way ST1,ST6 . . .57 A2
Greylarch La ST17 . . . . .175 B4
Greysan Ave ST7 . . . . .41 C4
Greysbrooke WS14 . . . . . . .247 A3
Greysbrooke Prim Sch
  WS14 . . . . .247 A3
Greystoke Dr DY6 . . . . .275 B3
Greyswood Rd ST4 . . . . .71 C2
Grice Rd ST4 . . . . .71 C4
Griffin Cl Burntwood WS7 . .228 C4
  Norton in Hales TF9 . . . . . .82 B1
Griffin St ST3 . . . . .283 B3
Griffithgreen WV5 . . . . .267 B4
Griffiths Dr Wolv WV11 . . . .242 A1
  Wombourne WV5 . . . . . . .270 A3
Griffiths Rd WV12 . . . . .242 B1
Griffiths Way ST15 . . . . . . .120 B3
Grimley Way WS11 . . . . . . .209 C2
Grindcobble Gr WS15 . . . . .178 B2
Grindley Bank ST18 . . . . . . .140 C3
Grindley Hill Ct ST14 . . . . . .71 C3
Grindley La ST3,ST11 . . . . . .90 A3
Grindley Pl ST14 . . . . .71 C3
Grindsbrook B77 . . . . .262 A4
Grisedale Cl 7 WS3 . . . . . . .90 A4
Grissom Cl ST16 . . . . .155 A3
Gristhorpe Way ST2 . . . . . . .58 B1
Gritton St ST6 . . . . .56 A3
Grizedale Cl DE15 . . . . .167 A1
Grocott Cl ST19 . . . . .192 C1
Grosvenor Ave
  Aldridge B74 . . . . .256 C1
  Stoke-on-T ST4 . . . . .72 C4
Grosvenor Cl Endon ST9 . . .43 C4
  Lichfield WS14 . . . . .231 B3
  Penkridge ST19 . . . . .192 C1
  Sutton Coldfield B75 . . . . .258 B1
  Wolv WV10 . . . . .240 B1
Grosvenor Cres WV10 . . . . .240 B1
Grosvenor Ct
  Sedgley DY3 . . . .
  Shenstone WS14 . . . . .246 C3
  Wolv WV6 . . . . .255 A2
Grosvenor Gdns ST5 . . . . . .284 C2
Grosvenor Pk WV4 . . . . . . .266 C3
Grosvenor Pl
  Newcastle-u-L ST5 . . . . . . .56 B3
  Tunstall ST6 . . . . .41 C3
Grosvenor Rd
  Market Drayton TF9 . . . . . . .97 B1
  Meir ST3 . . . . .73 C1
  Newcastle-u-L ST5 . . . . . . .284 C2
  Sedgley DY3 . . . . .271 C1
  Wolv, Bushbury WV10 . . . .240 B1
  Wolv, Ettingshall Park
  WV4 . . . . .266 C2
Grosvenor Road S ST3 . . . .271 B1
Grosvenor St Leek ST13 . . .30 C3
  Longton ST3 . . . . .283 B3
Grosvenor Way ST17 . . . . . .175 C3
Grotto La WV6 . . . . .255 C3
Grotto Rd TF9 . . . . .112 A4
Grounds Dr B74 . . . . .257 C2
Grounds Rd B74 . . . . .257 C2
Groundslow Hospl ST12 . .103 C4
Grove Ave Fenton ST4 . . . . .72 C2
  Kidsgrove ST7 . . . . .25 A2
  Lawton-gate ST7 . . . . .25 A2
Grove Cl WS11 . . . . .227 C3
Grove Cres Walsall WS3 . . .243 C2
  Woore CW3 . . . . .97 B1
Grove Gdns DY8 . . . . .279 B2
Grove Jun Sch ST1 . . . . . . .282 C4
Grove La Doveridge DE6 . . .127 C4
  Norton Canes WS3 . . . . . . .227 C1
  Wolv WV6 . . . . .255 A1
Grove Park Ave ST7 . . . . . . .25 A2
Grove Pk DY6 . . . . .275 B4
Grove Pl ST1 . . . . .282 A1
Grove Prim Sch WV2 . . . . . .266 C4

Grove Prim Sch The
ST17 . . . . 174 B4
Grove Rd Fenton ST4 . . . . 72 B2
  Stone ST15 . . . . 119 C4
Grove Road Ind Est ST4 . . 72 B2
Grove Sch The TF9 . . . . . . 97 B1
Grove St Burslem ST6 . . . . 57 A3
  Leek ST13 . . . . 30 B3
  Newcastle-u-L ST5 . . . . . 55 C2
  Wolv WV2 . . . . 266 B4
Grove The
  Blythe Bridge ST11 . . . . . 90 C3
  Burntwood WS7 . . . . . . 228 B4
  Chell Heath ST6 . . . . 42 A1
  Lawton-gate ST7 . . . . . . 25 A2
  Little Aston B74 . . . . . . 257 B3
  Newcastle-u-L ST5 . . . . . 71 A3
  Stone ST15 . . . . 120 B2
  Tatenhill DE13 . . . . 184 A4
  Wolv WV4 . . . . 266 C3
Grovebank Rd ST4 . . . . . . 71 C2
Grovelands Cres WV10 . . . 240 B2
Groveside La Perton WV6 . . 97 B1
Groveside Way WS3 . . . . 244 A3
Grub St ST20 . . . . 151 A3
Grunmore Dr DE13 . . . . 147 C1
Guernsey Cl CW12 . . . . 6 A1
Guernsey Dr ST3 . . . . 70 C2
Guernsey Wlk **2** ST3 . . . 73 C2
Guild La TF10 . . . . 169 C4
Guild St DE14 . . . . 166 B2
Guildford St ST4 . . . . 72 B4
Guinevere Ave DE13 . . . . 147 C1
Gullet The B78 . . . . 251 C1
Gullick Way WS7 . . . . . . 228 B4
Gun Battery La ST8 . . . . . 28 A4
Gunby Hill DE12 . . . . . . 219 C4
Gungate B79 . . . . 250 A3
Gunn St ST8 . . . . 27 B4
Gunnel Cl ST16 . . . . 155 B1
Gunstone La WV8 . . . . . . 238 C3
Gurnard B77 . . . . 261 B3
Guthrum Cl Perton WV6 . . 254 C3
  Wolv WV6 . . . . 254 C3
Guy St ST7 . . . . 58 A2
Guy's Almshouses B79 . . . 250 A3
Guy's La DY3 . . . . 271 A1
Guys Cl B79 . . . . 249 C4
Gwendoline Way WS9 . . . 245 A2
Gwenys Cres ST3 . . . . . . 72 C2
Gwyn Ave ST8 . . . . 27 B3
Gypsum Way DE6 . . . . . . 144 B3

H

Hackett Cl Longton ST3 . . . 283 D4
  Wolv WV14 . . . . 266 C1
Hackford Rd WV4 . . . . . . 266 C2
Hackwood Cl ST12 . . . . . . 88 C2
Hadden Ct ST9 . . . . 59 A1
Haddon Gr ST5 . . . . 55 C3
Haddon La ST5 . . . . 85 C1
Haddon Pl Bucknall ST2 . . . 58 B3
  Stone ST15 . . . . 120 B4
Haden Cl DY8 . . . . 275 B1
Hadfield Gn ST6 . . . . 42 B1
Hadleigh Cl ST5 . . . . 71 A1
Hadleigh Rd ST2 . . . . 58 A3
Hadley Park Gdns WS15 . . 196 B4
Hadley St DE13 . . . . 181 C2
Hadrian Way ST5 . . . . 55 B3
Hadrians Cl B77 . . . . 261 B4
Haggar St WV2 . . . . 266 B3
Hagley Ct DY3 . . . . 271 B2
Hagley Dr WS15 . . . . 178 B1
Hagley Park High Sch
  WS15 . . . . 196 B4
Hagley RC High Sch
  DY8 . . . . 281 C3
Hagley Rd WS15 . . . . 178 B1
Haig Cl WS11 . . . . 210 A3
Haig Rd ST13 . . . . 31 A4
Haig St ST3 . . . . 73 B1
Haigh Cl ST13 . . . . 45 B3
Hailes Park Cl WV2 . . . . . 266 C3
Hailsham Cl ST6 . . . . 41 C3
Hainult Cl DY8 . . . . 275 B2
Halcyon Ct DE14 . . . . . . 166 A2
Halcyon Way DE14 . . . . . 166 A2
Haldale B77 . . . . 261 B1
Hales Hall Rd ST10 . . . . . 76 C2
Hales Pl ST3 . . . . 283 C1
Halesworth Cres ST5 . . . . 71 A1
Halesworth Rd WV9 . . . . 239 C1
Halford Ave ST7 . . . . 57 B4
Halford St B79 . . . . 250 A3
Halfshire La DY10 . . . . . . 281 A1
Halfway Pl ST5 . . . . 55 C1
Halifax Cl ST3 . . . . 90 B4
Halifax Rd WV7 . . . . 220 C1
Haling Cl ST19 . . . . 207 C4
Haling Rd ST19 . . . . 192 C1
Hall Ave ST13 . . . . 31 A4
Hall Bank SK17 . . . . 24 C3
Hall Cl Pattingham WV6 . . 253 B1
Hall Ct ST17 . . . . 175 A4
Hall Dr Enville DY7 . . . . . 273 B1
  Meir ST3 . . . . 74 A2
Hall End ST11 . . . . 105 C3
Hall End Cl WV6 . . . . 253 B1
Hall End La WV6 . . . . 253 B1
Hall Farm Cl ST18 . . . . . . 139 B1
Hall Farm Cres ST18 . . . . 137 C2
Hall Gdns ST14 . . . . 127 C1

Hall Green Ave DE13 . . . . 147 C1
Hall Hill Dr ST7 . . . . 73 B4
Hall La Brownhills WS9 . . . 244 C2
  Burntwood WS7 . . . . . . 229 C2
  Doveridge DE6 . . . . 127 A4
  Great Wyrley WS6 . . . . . 222 B1
  Hilderstone ST15 . . . . . 106 C2
  Standon ST21 . . . . 102 B2
  Swynnerton ST15 . . . . . 103 B2
  Walsall WS3 . . . . 243 C2
  Wolv WV14 . . . . 266 C4
  Wootton DE6 . . . . 79 C4
Hall Mdw WS11 . . . . 226 A3
Hall Orch Cheadle ST10 . . . 76 B2
  Uttoxeter ST14 . . . . 125 B4
Hall Pl ST5 . . . . 56 B3
Hall Rd Armitage WS15 . . 198 B3
  Marchington ST14 . . . . . 127 C1
  Rolleston DE13 . . . . 146 C2
  Uttoxeter ST14 . . . . 126 A4
Hall St Audley ST7 . . . . . . 39 B1
  Burslem ST6 . . . . 56 C4
  Newcastle-u-L ST5 . . . . . 284 B3
  Sedgley DY3 . . . . 271 B4
Hall Yd ST10 . . . . 92 C2
Hallahan Cl ST15 . . . . . . 120 B3
Hallahan Gr ST4 . . . . 72 A4
Hallam Rd ST14 . . . . 110 C1
Hallam St ST4 . . . . 72 B3
Hallams Row DE14 . . . . . 166 B2
Hallbridge Cl WS3 . . . . . . 243 C1
Hallcourt Cl **3** WS11 . . . 226 C4
Hallcourt Cres **4** WS11 . 226 C4
Hallcourt La WS11 . . . . . 226 C4
Hallcroft Cl TF10 . . . . . . 168 C2
Hallcroft Gdns TF10 . . . . 168 C2
Hallcroft Way WS9 . . . . . 256 B3
Halldearn Ave ST10 . . . . . 74 B2
Hallfarm Cl ST19 . . . . . . 223 B3
Hallfarm Rd ST19 . . . . . . 223 B3
Hallfield Gr ST6 . . . . 41 C3
Hallfields Rd DE15 . . . . . 186 B2
Hallhill La WS15 . . . . . . 161 A3
Halls Rd Biddulph ST8 . . . 16 B1
  Mow Cop ST7 . . . . 26 B4
Halston Rd **5** WS7 . . . . 229 A4
Halton Gn ST3 . . . . 88 C4
Haltonlea B77 . . . . 262 A4
Ham La DY6 . . . . 270 C1
Hamble B77 . . . . 250 B1
Hamble Gr WV6 . . . . 254 C2
Hamble Rd WV4 . . . . 265 B3
Hamble Way WV10 . . . . . 240 A1
Hambleton Pl ST8 . . . . . . 27 A3
Hambledge Cl ST17 . . . . . 174 B4
Hambro Pl ST16 . . . . 42 A4
Hamble St WS11 . . . . 209 C2
Hames La B79 . . . . 236 B2
Hamil Dr ST13 . . . . 30 B3
Hamil Rd ST6 . . . . 42 A1
Hamilton Ave DY8 . . . . . 279 B3
Hamilton Cl
  Cannock WS12 . . . . 210 C2
  Kingswinford DY8 . . . . . 275 B1
  Sedgley DY3 . . . . 271 B4
Hamilton Ct ST5 . . . . 71 B1
Hamilton Dr DY8 . . . . . . 275 B1
Hamilton Fields DE15 . . . 167 A1
Hamilton Gdns WV10 . . . 240 C2
Hamilton Ho WS3 . . . . . . 243 B1
Hamilton Inf Sch ST1 . . . . 57 B3
Hamilton Lea WS11 . . . . . 228 A3
Hamilton Rd
  Burton u T DE15 . . . . . . 167 A1
  Longton ST3 . . . . 283 D2
Hamilton Rise ST2 . . . . . . 43 A1
Hamilton St Fenton ST4 . . . 72 B3
  Walsall WS3 . . . . 243 B1
Hamlet The WS11 . . . . . . 227 C3
Hamlett Pl ST5 . . . . 71 A1
Hammersley Hayes Rd
  ST10 . . . . 76 C3
Hammerton Av ST1 . . . . . 57 C3
Hammerton Ave ST2 . . . . 57 C1
Hammerwich Hospl
  WS7 . . . . 229 A3
Hammerwich La WV2 . . . . 229 C2
Hammerwich Rd WS7 . . . . 229 B3
Hammond Ave ST6 . . . . . 43 A4
Hammond Ho ST1 . . . . . . 282 C1
Hammond Rd ST5 . . . . . . 55 C4
Hammonds Croft ST18 . . . 158 B4
Hamner Gn ST2 . . . . 73 B4
Hampden Ho DE15 . . . . . 185 C3
Hamps Cl WS7 . . . . 229 B4
Hamps Valley Rd ST10 . . . 48 C1
Hampshire Cl Endon ST9 . . 43 C4
Hampshire Dr ST17 . . . . . 174 A4
Hampshire Cres ST3 . . . . 89 B4
Hampstead Gr ST14 . . . . . 88 B4
Hampton Cl
  Newport TF10 . . . . 169 A2
  Newport TF10 . . . . 250 B4
Hampton Ct
  Essington WV10 . . . . . . 241 A1
  Leek ST13 . . . . 30 B3
Hampton Dr
  Market Drayton TF9 . . . . 97 B1
  Newport TF10 . . . . 169 A2
Hampton Gn WS11 . . . . . 226 C4
Hampton Gr Kinver DY7 . . 278 B2
  Walsall WS3 . . . . 244 A2
Hampton Rd WV10 . . . . . 240 A1
Hampton St
  Cannock WS11 . . . . 226 B4
  Hanley ST1 . . . . 282 C1

Hams Cl ST8 . . . . 27 B4
Hanbridge Ave ST5 . . . . . 56 A4
Hanbury Cres WV4 . . . . . 265 C3
Hanbury Hill DE13 . . . . . 145 A3
Hanbury Rd
  Brownhills WS8 . . . . 228 C1
  Norton Canes WS11 . . . . 227 C3
  Tamworth B77 . . . . 250 C2
Hanbury's Farm Prim Sch
  B77 . . . . 250 B1
Hanch Hall* WS15 . . . . . 213 C4
Hanchurch Cl DE15 . . . . . 167 A2
Hanchurch Hills Circular
  Wlks* ST4 . . . . 86 C3
Hanchurch La ST4 . . . . . . 87 A4
Hancock St ST4 . . . . 54 C1
Hand La TF11 . . . . 187 B1
Hand St ST6 . . . . 41 C1
Handel Ct WS11 . . . . 210 B1
Handel Gr ST1 . . . . 58 A3
Handel Wlk WS13 . . . . . . 214 B1
Handley Banks ST11 . . . . 74 C2
Handley Dr ST8 . . . . 27 A1
Handley St ST8 . . . . 27 A1
Handsacre Cl DE11 . . . . . 186 C2
Handsacre Cres WS15 . . . 198 B2
Handsacre Rd ST13 . . . . . 223 B4
Hangmans La B79 . . . . . . 236 A1
Hanley Rd ST6,ST1 . . . . . 57 B4
Hanlith B77 . . . . 262 A4
Hannaford Way WS11 . . . 209 C1
Hanney Hay Rd WS7,
  WS8 . . . . 229 A2
Hanover Ct
  Newcastle-u-L ST5 . . . . . 284 C3
  Tamworth B79 . . . . 249 C4
  Wolv WV6 . . . . 255 B2
Hanover Ho DY8 . . . . 279 C4
Hanover Pl **14** WS11 . . . 209 C1
Hanover St Hanley ST1 . . . 282 B3
  Newcastle-u-L ST5 . . . . . 284 C3
Hanyards La ST18 . . . . . . 157 A3
Harald Cl WV6 . . . . 254 C3
Harber St ST3 . . . . 283 C3
Harbin Rd DE12 . . . . 184 B1
Harborough Ct B74 . . . . . 258 A1
Harborough Dr WS9 . . . . 256 A3
Harbourne Cres ST10 . . . . 76 C2
Harbourne Rd DE13 . . . . 146 C2
Harbury St DE13 . . . . . . 166 A3
Harcourt Ave ST3 . . . . . . 73 C1
Harcourt Dr
  Newport TF10 . . . . 169 A2
  Sedgley DY3 . . . . 271 B1
  Sutton Coldfield B74 . . . 257 C2
Harcourt Ho B79 . . . . 250 A2
Harcourt Rd DE14 . . . . . . 184 C4
Harcourt St ST4 . . . . 282 A1
Harcourt Way ST16 . . . . . 155 A4
Hardewick Cl ST14 . . . . . 59 A2
Hardie Ave WS15 . . . . . . 196 C4
Hardie Gn WS11 . . . . 209 C2
Harding Ct ST4 . . . . 282 A1
Harding Rd ST1 . . . . 282 B1
Harding Terr ST4 . . . . 72 A3
Hardings Mdw ST7 . . . . . 25 C1
Hardingswood Rd ST7 . . . 25 C1
Hardington Way ST17 . . . 175 B4
Hardmann St ST4 . . . . . . 43 A1
Hardon Rd WV4 . . . . 266 C3
Hardwick Cl
  Aldridge B74 . . . . 256 C1
  Tamworth B79 . . . . 250 B3
Hardwick Rd B74 . . . . . . 257 A1
Hardy Cl Barton-u-N DE13 . 201 C4
  Cheadle ST10 . . . . 76 B1
Hardy Rd ST17 . . . . 174 A4
Hardy Sq WV2 . . . . 266 C3
Hardy St ST6 . . . . 41 B2
Harebell Cl
  Cannock WS11 . . . . 210 B1
  Featherstone WV10 . . . . 241 A4
Harebell Gr ST17 . . . . 26 C1
Harecastle Ave ST7 . . . . . 25 C1
Haregate Rd ST13 . . . . . . 31 A4
Haregate Terr ST13 . . . . . 31 A4
Harehedge La DE13 . . . . . 166 A4
Hareshaw Gr ST6 . . . . . . 42 A4
Harewell Dr B75 . . . . 258 B1
Harewood Cl ST10 . . . . . . 76 B2
Harewood Est ST10 . . . . . 76 A3
Harewood St ST6 . . . . . . 41 B1
Hargate Rd DE15 . . . . . . 167 C4
Hargreave Cl ST13 . . . . . 90 B4
Hargreaves La ST17 . . . . . 155 B1
Harington Dr ST3 . . . . . . 73 C3
Harland Cl ST18 . . . . 177 B4
Harland Rd B74 . . . . 258 A2
Harlaxton St DE13 . . . . . 166 A4
Harlech Ave ST13 . . . . . . 73 C1
Harlech Dr ST18 . . . . 27 B3
Harlech Way
  Burton u T DE14 . . . . . . 166 B4
  Congleton CW12 . . . . 6 A1
Harlequin Dr ST6 . . . . . . 42 B1
Harlestones Ho DY8 . . . . 279 C4
Harley Cl Brownhills WS8 . 245 A3
  Rugeley WS15 . . . . 196 C3
Harley St ST1 . . . . 282 C2
Harley Thorn La ST4 . . . . 87 A2
Harlow Gdns WV4 . . . . . . 265 A3
Harmer Gn ST17 . . . . 174 A4
Harmon St WS15 . . . . . . 199 C2
Harmony Gn ST17 . . . . . . 174 A4
Harney Ct WS15 . . . . 178 B2
Harold St ST6 . . . . 42 B1

Harper Ave
  Burton u T DE13 . . . . . . 166 B4
  Newcastle-u-L ST5 . . . . . 56 A2
Harper Ct DE13 . . . . 166 B4
Harper St ST6 . . . . 56 C4
Harpfield Prim Sch ST4 . . . 71 B4
Harpfield Rd ST4 . . . . 71 C3
Harplands Hospl ST4 . . . . 71 B3
Harplow La ST10 . . . . 76 A1
Harptree Wlk ST4 . . . . . . 71 C1
Harpur-Crewe Cotts DE6 . 35 B2
Harriers Dr ST3 . . . . 90 A3
Harrietts Hayes Rd
  WV8 . . . . 237 C3
Harringay Dr DY8 . . . . . . 279 C2
Harrington Wlk WS13 . . . 213 C1
Harris Rd ST16 . . . . 156 A2
Harris St ST4 . . . . 72 A4
Harriseahead La ST7 . . . . 26 B2
Harrison & Woodburn Cotts
  ST5 . . . . 54 B2
Harrison Cl Audley ST7 . . . 54 B4
  Burton u T DE14 . . . . . . 185 A4
  Great Wyrley WS6 . . . . . 226 B1
  Walsall WS3 . . . . 243 B1
Harrison Ct ST5 . . . . 284 C1
Harrison Rd
  Cannock WS11 . . . . 226 C4
  Norton-in-t-M ST6 . . . . . 42 C2
  Sutton Coldfield B74 . . . 257 C3
  Walsall WS3 . . . . 244 B1
Harrison St
  Newcastle-u-L ST5 . . . . . 284 C2
  Walsall WS3 . . . . 243 B1
Harrison Way ST13 . . . . . 45 B3
Harrisons La ST19 . . . . . . 207 C1
Harrogate Gr ST5 . . . . . . 54 C1
Harrop St ST1 . . . . 57 B3
Harrop Way DY9 . . . . 279 C4
Harrots La SK17 . . . . 24 B3
Harrow Dr DE14 . . . . 185 B4
Harrow Dr ST4 . . . . 257 C1
Harrow Rd DY6 . . . . 270 B1
Harrowby Dr ST5 . . . . . . 70 C2
Harrowby Rd Meir ST3 . . . 90 A4
  Wolv WV10 . . . . 240 B1
Harrowby St ST16 . . . . . . 156 A2
Hart Cl ST5 . . . . 284 B3
Harthill Rd WV4 . . . . 265 B2
Hartill St ST4 . . . . 72 B4
Hartington CE Prim Sch
  SK17 . . . . 24 C3
Hartington St Leek ST13 . . 30 C3
  Newcastle-u-L ST5 . . . . . 56 A3
Hartland Ave
  Chell Heath ST6 . . . . . . 42 B2
  Stafford ST17 . . . . 175 C4
Hartlands Rd ST21 . . . . . 133 C4
Hartlebury Cl WS11 . . . . . 210 B1
Hartlebury Rd WV9 . . . . . 256 A2
Hartley Cl ST15 . . . . 120 C4
Hartley Gdns CW12 . . . . . 16 A4
Hartleyburn B77 . . . . 262 A4
Hartopp Rd B74 . . . . 257 C1
Hartsbourne Way ST17 . . . 175 B4
Hartshill Rd ST4 . . . . 54 C1
Hartslade WS14 . . . . 231 C3
Hartwell ST5 . . . . 70 C2
Hartwell Gr ST16 . . . . . . 155 A3
Hartwell La
  Barlaston ST3,ST15 . . . . 89 B1
  Great Wyrley WS6 . . . . . 227 A2
Hartwell Rd ST3 . . . . 90 A4
Hartwood Cl TF10 . . . . . . 168 C3
Harvard Cl DY1 . . . . 271 C2
Harvest Cl DY3 . . . . 271 C2
Harvest Fields Way B75 . . 258 C2
Harvester Way DY6 . . . . . 275 A4
Harvesters Cl WS9 . . . . . 256 C1
Harvesters Wlk WV8 . . . . 239 C1
Harvey Dr B75 . . . . 258 B1
Harvey Pl ST14 . . . . 111 A1
Harvey Rd
  Armitage WS15 . . . . 198 B2
  Burton u T DE14 . . . . . . 185 A4
Harwarden Cl WV12 . . . . . 7 A1
Harwell Cl B79 . . . . 250 B4
Harwin Cl WV6 . . . . 255 C4
Harwood Ave DE14 . . . . . 184 C4
Harwood Dr B77 . . . . 261 B2
Harwood Rd WS13 . . . . . 214 A2
Haslemere Ave ST2 . . . . . 43 A1
Haslington Cl ST5 . . . . . . 40 B1
Hassall St ST1 . . . . 282 C2
Hassam Ave ST5 . . . . 284 A4
Hassam Par ST5 . . . . 56 A3
Hassell St ST5 . . . . 284 C3
Haste Hill La ST10 . . . . . . 61 C1
Hastings Cl B77 . . . . 261 C3
Hastings Rd ST16 . . . . . . 42 C4
Hatch Heath Cl WV5 . . . . 269 C4
Hatch La TF11 . . . . 203 B2
Hatchett La B77 . . . . 217 B3
Hateley Dr WV4 . . . . 266 C2
Hatfield Cres ST3 . . . . . . 88 C4
Hathaway Rd B74 . . . . . . 258 B3
Hathersage Cl ST3 . . . . . . 73 B3
Hatherton Cl ST5 . . . . 40 B1
Hatherton Croft WS11 . . . 209 B1
Hatherton Gdns WV10 . . . 240 C1
Hatherton Rd WV9 . . . . . 256 A4
Hatherton Rd
  Cannock WS11 . . . . 209 B1

Hatherton Rd continued
  Penkridge ST19 . . . . 192 C1
Hatherton St
  Cheslyn Hay WS6 . . . . . 226 B1
  Stafford ST16 . . . . 156 A2
Hatrell St ST5 . . . . 284 C2
Hatton Rd Cannock WS11 . 209 A1
  Wolv WV6 . . . . 255 C2
Hatton Waterworks Cotts
  ST21 . . . . 109 A4
Hattons Gr WV8 . . . . 239 A1
Haughton St Giles CE Prim
  Sch ST18 . . . . 172 C3
Haunton Rd B79 . . . . 217 B2
Havannah Prim Sch CW12 . 6 A3
Havefield Ave WS14 . . . . . 231 C4
Havelet Dr ST5 . . . . 70 C2
Havelock Ave WV3 . . . . . 265 C4
Havelock Gr ST8 . . . . 27 B4
Havelock Pl ST11 . . . . . . 282 A1
Haven Ave ST6 . . . . 57 B4
Haven Cres ST9 . . . . 59 A2
Haven Gr ST5 . . . . 56 B4
Haven The
  Kingswinford DY8 . . . . . 275 B1
  Wolv WV2 . . . . 266 B4
Havergal CE Prim Sch
  WV10 . . . . 225 B1
Havergal Wlk ST13 . . . . . 283 C5
Haverhill Cl Chorlton CW2 . 37 A2
  Walsall WS3 . . . . 243 A2
Havisham Ct TF10 . . . . . . 168 C2
Hawcroft WS15 . . . . 197 C1
Hawes St ST6 . . . . 41 B2
Haweswater Dr DY6 . . . . . 275 B3
Hawfield La
  Burton u T DE15 . . . . . . 167 B2
  Newton Solney DE15 . . . 167 C2
Hawfinch B77 . . . . 262 A3
Hawfinch Rd ST10 . . . . . . 76 C2
Hawk Cl ST3 . . . . 90 A4
Hawk's Dr DE15 . . . . 167 B2
Hawke Rd ST15 . . . . 155 B4
Hawkesford Cl DE14 . . . . 258 A1
Hawkesmoor Dr
  Lichfield WS14 . . . . 231 B4
  Perton WV6 . . . . 254 B2
Hawkesmore Dr ST18 . . . 177 B4
Hawkestone Cl ST5 . . . . . 284 C2
Hawkesville Dr **7**
  WS11 . . . . 209 C1
Hawkeswell Dr DY6 . . . . . 270 B1
Hawkhurst Dr WS15 . . . . 197 C1
Hawkins Cl WS13 . . . . . . 214 A1
Hawkins Dr WS11 . . . . . . 226 B2
Hawkins La
  Burton u T DE14 . . . . . . 166 C3
  Fradswell ST18 . . . . 122 C1
Hawkins Lane Ind Est
  DE14 . . . . 166 C3
Hawkins St ST14 . . . . 72 B3
Hawks Cl WS6 . . . . 226 B1
Hawks Green La WS11 . . . 210 A1
Hawksdale Cl ST13 . . . . . 90 A4
Hawkside B77 . . . . 262 A4
Hawksley Dr DE13 . . . . . 147 A2
Hawksmoor Cl ST14 . . . . . 89 C4
Hawksmoor Rd ST17 . . . . 174 C4
Hawkstone Ave TF10 . . . . 168 C1
Hawkstone Ct WV6 . . . . . 254 B3
Hawkswell Ave WV5 . . . . 270 A3
Hawkswell Dr DY6 . . . . . . 275 B4
Hawksworth B77 . . . . 250 C1
Hawksworth Cl WS13 . . . . 30 B2
Hawksworth Ct ST13 . . . . 30 B2
Hawkyard Cl WS11 . . . . . 210 A2
Hawley Cl **2** ST15 . . . . . 120 B3
Haworth Ave CW12 . . . . . 6 A3
Hawthorn Ave
  Great Wyrley WS6 . . . . . 227 A1
  Nethersole DE14 . . . . . . 219 C4
  Stone ST15 . . . . 119 C3
Hawthorn Cl
  Denstone ST14 . . . . 95 C3
  Gnosall ST20 . . . . 171 C4
  Haughton ST18 . . . . 172 C3
  Lichfield WS14 . . . . 231 B4
  Seighford ST18 . . . . 135 A1
Hawthorn Cres DE15 . . . . 185 C4
Hawthorn Gdns ST7 . . . . . 40 B4
Hawthorn Gr ST18 . . . . . . 27 C4
Hawthorn Pl **8** ST3 . . . . 89 C4
Hawthorn Rd
  Aldridge B74 . . . . 257 A1
  Newcastle-u-L ST5 . . . . . 40 A1
  Walsall WS8 . . . . 244 A1
Hawthorn Rise DE11 . . . . 186 C4
Hawthorn St ST16 . . . . . . 57 A3
Hawthorn Way
  Market Drayton TF9 . . . . 97 B1
  Rugeley WS15 . . . . 178 B1
  Stafford ST17 . . . . 156 A1
Hawthornden Ave ST14 . . 126 A4
Hawthornden Cl ST14 . . . 126 A4
Hawthornden Gdns
  ST14 . . . . 125 C4
Hawthornden Manor Mews
  ST14 . . . . 126 A4
Hawthorne Ave
  Audley ST7 . . . . 39 C1
  Stoke-on-T ST4 . . . . 71 C3
  Tamworth B79 . . . . 250 A4
Hawthorne Cl ST10 . . . . . 92 C2
Hawthorne Cres WS7 . . . . 229 A3
Hawthorne Gr ST19 . . . . . 205 B3
Hawthorne Gr DY3 . . . . . 271 B1
Hawthorne La WV8 . . . . . 238 C1

Hawthorne Rd
Cannock WS12 . . . . 210 C2
Cheslyn Hay WS6 . . . . 226 C2
Essington WV11 . . . . 242 A2
Huntington WS12 . . . . 209 B4
Wheaton Aston ST19 . . . . . . 205 B3
Wolv WV2 . . . . 266 B3
Hawthorne Terr ST13 . . . . . 30 C3
Hawthorne Way DY7 . . . . 278 B2
Hawthorns The
Hagley DY9 . . . . 281 C2
Keele ST5 . . . . 69 C4
Hay Barns The ST15 . . . . 103 A2
Hay End La WS13 . . . . 111 C2
Hay La Elastone DE6 . . . . . . 79 C2
Foston DE65 . . . . 129 C3
Longdon WS15 . . . . 213 A4
Haybarn The ST16 . . . . . . 155 C4
Haybridge Ave DY8 . . . . . 281 C3
Haybridge High Sch
DY8 . . . . 281 C3
Haycock Dr B74 . . . . 258 A2
Haydock Cl
Burton u T DE14 . . . . 185 A4
Kingsley ST10 . . . . 76 C3
Tamworth B77 . . . . 261 B2
Haydock Ct ST5 . . . . 55 B1
Haydon Cl ST14 . . . . 56 C1
Haydon St ST14 . . . . 56 C1
Hayes Cl ST13 . . . . 30 C4
Hayes Meadow Prim Sch
WS15 . . . . 198 B2
Hayes St ST6 . . . . 42 B1
Hayes The TF9 . . . . 112 A4
Hayes View WS13 . . . . . . 213 C1
Hayes View Dr WS6 . . . . . 226 C2
Hayes Way WS11,WS12 . . . 210 B1
Hayeswood La ST7 . . . . 54 C3
Hayfield Cres ST4 . . . . 72 C4
Hayfield Hill WS15 . . . . . . 211 C2
Hayfield Rd ST5 . . . . 55 A1
Hayhead Cl ST7 . . . . 26 A1
Hayle B77 . . . . 250 B1
Hayley Ct DY6 . . . . 275 B3
Hayling Dr WV2 . . . . 266 A3
Hayling Pl ST3 . . . . 72 C2
Haymarket St6 . . . . 41 B2
Haymarket The WV8 . . . . 239 C1
Haymoor WS14 . . . . 231 C4
Hayner Gr ST3 . . . . 74 A2
Hayrick Dr DY6 . . . . 275 A4
Hays La ST10 . . . . 48 C2
Haywain Cl WV9 . . . . 239 C1
Haywards Cl WS3 . . . . 243 C2
Haywood Dr WV6 . . . . 255 B2
Haywood Grange ST18 . . . 177 B4
Haywood High Sch ST6 . . . 42 A1
Haywood Hts ST18 . . . . . . 177 B4
Haywood La TF9 . . . . 113 B1
Haywood Rd ST6 . . . . 42 A1
Haywood St Leek ST13 . . . . 30 C3
Stoke-on-T ST4 . . . . 57 A1
Hayworth Cl B79 . . . . 249 C4
Hayworth Rd WS13 . . . . . . 214 B1
Hazel Cl Kidsgrove ST7 . . . . 26 A2
Stoke-on-T ST4 . . . . 57 A2
Uttoxeter ST14 . . . . 126 A3
Hazel Dr Armitage WS15 . . 198 A2
Uttoxeter ST14 . . . . 211 A3
Hazel Gdns WV8 . . . . 239 A2
Hazel Gr Biddulph ST8 . . . . 17 A1
Lawton-gate ST7 . . . . 25 A2
Leek ST13 . . . . 31 B4
Lichfield WS14 . . . . 231 B4
2 Meir ST3 . . . . 73 C1
Stafford ST16 . . . . 155 B4
Stourbridge DY8 . . . . 279 B2
Wombourne WV5 . . . . 270 A4
Hazel La WS6 . . . . 227 A1
Hazel Rd
Kingswinford DY6 . . . . 275 C2
Newcastle-u-L ST5 . . . . 55 B4
Wolv WV3 . . . . 265 C4
Hazel Slade Com Prim Sch
WS12 . . . . 211 A3
Hazeldene ST18 . . . . 158 B1
Hazeldene Rd ST4 . . . . 88 B4
Hazelgarth B77 . . . . 250 A2
Hazelhurst Dr ST13 . . . . . . 45 B2
Hazelhurst Rd ST6 . . . . 41 C3
Hazelhurst St ST11 . . . . . . 282 C1
Hazelmere Dr
Burntwood WS7 . . . . 228 C2
Wolv WV3 . . . . 255 A1
Hazels The DY9 . . . . 265 C4
Hazelside Ho WS12 . . . . . . 211 A3
Hazelslade Nature Reserve*
WS12 . . . . 211 A3
Hazelton Gn ST17 . . . . 174 B3
Hazelwood Cl
Cheslyn Hay WS6 . . . . 226 B1
Hanley ST6 . . . . 56 C3
Hazelwood Gr WS11 . . . . . 226 B4
Hazelwood Rd
Aldridge B74 . . . . 256 B1
Burton u T DE15 . . . . 185 C2
Endon ST19 . . . . 43 C3
Hazlemere Dr B74 . . . . 258 A1
Hazlemere Gr WS11 . . . . . 226 A4
Hazlescross Rd ST10 . . . . . . 61 B2
Hazlestrine La ST17 . . . . . 175 B3
Hazlewood Gr WS11 . . . . . 226 B4
Hazlewood Rd DY1 . . . . 73 C3
Hazlitt Way ST19 . . . . 73 C1
HCM Ind Est DE14 . . . . . . 166 C2
Headborough Wlk WS9 . . . 245 A1
Headingley Dr DY7 . . . . . . 274 C1
Headland Dr WV3 . . . . 255 A1

Headland Way ST10 . . . . 78 C1
Headlands The B74 . . . . . . 257 B2
Headway Rd WV10 . . . . . . 240 B2
Heakley Ave ST6 . . . . 42 C2
Healey B77 . . . . 250 C1
Healey Ave ST8 . . . . 27 A3
Heanor Pl ST3 . . . . 283 A2
Heantun Row WV11 . . . . . 242 A1
Hearn Ct ST17 . . . . 174 B4
Heart Of The Country Ctr*
WS14 . . . . 247 C4
Hearthcote Rd DE11 . . . . . 186 C2
Heathcote Ave Cheddleton ST9 . . 59 C2
Newcastle-u-L ST5 . . . . 56 B2
Whittington WS14 . . . . 232 B2
Heath Cl WV10 . . . . 240 C3
Heath Croft Rd B75 . . . . . . 258 B1
Heath Cross ST14 . . . . 126 A4
Heath Dr
Kidderminster DY10 . . . . . . 280 A1
Stafford ST16 . . . . 155 A4
Heath Farm Rd
Codsall WV8 . . . . 239 A1
Stourbridge DY8 . . . . 279 C2
Heath Gap WS13 . . . . 215 B4
Heath Gap Rd WS11 . . . . . 209 C2
Heath Gdns ST15 . . . . 119 C3
Heath Gn DY1 . . . . 271 C3
Heath Gr Ashley TF9 . . . . . . 99 B2
Blythe Bridge ST3 . . . . 90 A3
Codsall WV8 . . . . 239 A2
Heath Hayes Prim Sch
WS12 . . . . 210 C1
Heath Hill TF11 . . . . 187 B1
Heath Hill Rd WV6 . . . . . . 254 C1
Heath House Dr WV5 . . . . 269 B3
Heath House La
Bucknall ST2 . . . . 58 A2
Codsall WV8 . . . . 238 C1
Rudyard ST13 . . . . 18 B1
Upper Tean ST10 . . . . 93 A2
Heath La Admaston WS15 . . 140 B1
Stafford ST17 . . . . 179 A4
Heath Mill Cl WV5 . . . . . . 269 B2
Heath Mill Rd WV5 . . . . . . 269 B2
Heath Rd
Burton u T DE15 . . . . 185 C4
Gnosall TF10 . . . . 188 C4
Uttoxeter ST14 . . . . 111 A1
Walsall WV12 . . . . 242 B1
Whitmore ST5 . . . . 85 B4
Heath Row CW3 . . . . 69 A4
Heath St Biddulph ST8 . . . . 27 A4
Cannock WS12 . . . . 210 A4
Newcastle-u-L ST5 . . . . 284 B3
Newcastle-u-L, Broad Meadow
ST5 . . . . 55 C3
Stourbridge DY8 . . . . 279 C2
Tamworth B79 . . . . 250 B3
Tunstall ST6 . . . . 41 B4
Heath Top TF9 . . . . 99 C2
Heath View
Burntwood WS7 . . . . 212 A1
Cannock WS12 . . . . 227 C4
Weston CW2 . . . . 37 A3
Heath Way
Cannock WS11 . . . . 210 A1
Hatton DE65 . . . . 146 B4
Heath's Pas ST3 . . . . 283 D3
Heathbank Dr WS12 . . . . . 209 B3
Heathbrook Ave DY6 . . . . . 275 A4
Heathcote Ave TF9 . . . . 99 C2
Heathcote Cl B77 . . . . 262 A4
Heathcote Rd Audley ST7 . . 54 C4
Longton ST3 . . . . 283 B3
Heathcote Rise ST3 . . . . . . 74 A3
Heathcote St
Kidsgrove ST7 . . . . 26 A1
Longton ST3 . . . . 73 B3
Newcastle-u-L ST5 . . . . 55 C3
Heathdene Cl ST13 . . . . . . 283 B4
Heather Cl Brocton ST17 . . 176 B2
Burton u T DE14 . . . . 185 A4
Caverswall ST9 . . . . 59 A2
Rugeley WS15 . . . . 196 C3
Seighford ST18 . . . . 135 B1
Heather Cres ST13 . . . . 90 A2
Heather Dr
Huntington WS12 . . . . 209 B3
Kinver DY7 . . . . 277 C2
Heather Glade CW3 . . . . . . 68 B4
Heather Hill ST17 . . . . 176 B2
Heather Hills ST9 . . . . 43 B3
Heather Mews WS12 . . . . . 210 A4
Heather Valley WS12 . . . . . 210 B3
Heather View ST6 . . . . 42 C3
Heatherlands Cl ST13 . . . . . 89 C3
Heatherleigh Gr ST13 . . . . . 88 C4
Heatherside ST7 . . . . 27 A4
Heathfield Ave ST15 . . . . . 120 A4
Heathfield Cl ST16 . . . . 41 B4
Heathfield Dr
Newcastle-u-L ST5 . . . . 40 B1
Walsall WS3 . . . . 243 A3
Heathfield Gdns DY8 . . . . . 279 C2
Heathfield La ST17 . . . . . . 176 B3
Heathfield Rd
Chell Heath ST6 . . . . 42 B3
Sutton Coldfield B74 . . . . . 257 C2
Uttoxeter ST14 . . . . 126 A4
Heathfield Specl Sch
Burton u T DE15 . . . . 167 A2
Fenton ST4 . . . . 72 B3
Heathfields Inf Sch B77 . . 261 C3
Heathlan Cl WS12 . . . . 210 B1

Heathlands Cl DY6 . . . . 275 C4
Heathlands The ST14 . . . . . 111 A1
Heathlands The WV5 . . . . . 269 B3
Heathley La B78 . . . . 260 B3
Heathley Mews DE14 . . . . . 185 B4
Heathmill Ent Ctr DY3 . . . 269 B2
Heathside Dr WS3 . . . . 244 A2
Heathside La ST6 . . . . 41 B4
Heathview ST13 . . . . 45 C4
Heathway Colton WS15 . . . 179 A4
Gnosall ST20 . . . . 171 B3
Heathwood Rd TF10 . . . . . 168 C1
Heatley Back La WS15 . . . . 141 B2
Heatley La WS15 . . . . 141 B1
Heaton Cl WV10 . . . . 240 C3
Heaton Terr Endon ST9 . . . . 29 A1
Newcastle-u-L ST5 . . . . 56 A3
Heaton Villas ST6 . . . . 43 B4
Hebden B77 . . . . 262 A4
Hebden Gr WV11 . . . . 242 A1
Heber St ST3 . . . . 283 C4
Hedgerow Cl WS12 . . . . . . 209 C4
Hedgerow Dr DY6 . . . . 270 B1
Hedgerow Wlk WV8 . . . . . 239 C1
Hedgerows The B77 . . . . . . 261 C4
Hedges The WV5 . . . . 269 C3
Hedging La ST7 . . . . 261 C3
Hedging Lane Ind Est
B77 . . . . 261 C4
Hedley Pl ST5 . . . . 70 C4
Hednesford Rd
Brownhills WS8 . . . . 228 B1
Cannock, Blackfords
WS11 . . . . 209 C1
Cannock, Little Hayes
WS12 . . . . 210 C1
Norton Canes WS11 . . . . . 227 C1
Rugeley WS15 . . . . 196 B4
Hednesford St WS11 . . . . . 209 C1
Hednesford Sta ST18 . . . . 210 A3
Heenan Gr
Lichfield WS13 . . . . 213 C1
Stafford ST17 . . . . 174 C3
Heighley Castle Way
CW3 . . . . 68 C4
Heighley Ct CW3 . . . . 53 A3
Heighley La CW3 . . . . 53 C2
Heights The ST13 . . . . 30 A1
Helen Sharman Dr
ST16 . . . . 156 A3
Helford St ST17 . . . . 174 A4
Heligan Pl WS12 . . . . 210 C1
Hellier Dr WV5 . . . . 269 C4
Hellier Rd WV10 . . . . 240 C1
Helmingham B79 . . . . 249 B4
Helston Ave ST3 . . . . 73 C2
Helston Cl
Kingswinford DY8 . . . . 275 B1
Stafford ST17 . . . . 156 B1
Tamworth B79 . . . . 250 B4
Heming Pl ST2 . . . . 58 B3
Hemingway Rd ST3 . . . . 73 B2
Hemlock Pk WS11 . . . . 210 A1
Hemlock Rd ST3 . . . . 283 B4
Hemlock Way WS11 . . . . . . 210 A2
Hemmings Cl DY8 . . . . 279 C2
Hempbutts The ST15 . . . . . 120 A4
Hempits Gr ST17 . . . . 175 A1
Hemplands Rd DY8 . . . . . . 279 C3
Hempstalls Ct ST5 . . . . 284 B4
Hempstalls Gr ST5 . . . . 56 A2
Hempstalls La ST5 . . . . 284 C4
Hempstalls Prim Sch
ST5 . . . . 56 A2
Hemsby Way ST5 . . . . 71 A1
Hen La ST10 . . . . 108 B3
Hencroft ST13 . . . . 30 C3
Henderson Cl WS14 . . . . . 231 B4
Henderson Gr ST3 . . . . 74 A1
Hendon Cl DY3 . . . . 271 B1
Henhurst Farm DE13 . . . . . 165 B3
Henhurst Hill DE13 . . . . . . 165 B2
Henhurst Ridge DE13 . . . . 165 B2
Henley Ave ST8 . . . . 27 A3
Henley Cl Barlaston ST12 . . . 88 C2
Tamworth B79 . . . . 250 A3
Walsall WS3 . . . . 243 C1
Henley Ct WS14 . . . . 231 C3
Henley Dr Newport TF10 . . 169 A2
Sutton Coldfield B74 . . . . . 258 A2
Henley Grange WS15 . . . . . 178 A1
Henley Rd Chorlton CW2 . . . 37 A1
Wolv WV10 . . . . 240 A1
Henney Cl ST19 . . . . 207 C2
Henry Chadwick Prim Sch
WS15 . . . . 198 A4
Henry Prince CE Fst Sch The
DE6 . . . . 81 B4
Henry St Stafford ST16 . . . 155 C3
Tunstall ST6 . . . . 41 B2
Hensel Dr WV3 . . . . 265 B4
Henshall Hall Dr CW12 . . . . 6 A1
Henshall Pl ST6 . . . . 41 B3
Henshall Rd ST5 . . . . 55 C4
Henshaw Way ST15 . . . . . . 119 A3
Henwood Cl WV6 . . . . 255 B2
Henwood Rd WV6 . . . . 255 B2
Hepburn Cl WS9 . . . . 256 A2
Hepworth Cl WV6 . . . . 254 C2
Herbert Rd Aldridge WS9 . . 245 A1
■ Longton ST3 . . . . 73 B1
Stafford ST17 . . . . 156 C1
Herbert St
Burton u T DE14 . . . . 167 A2
Fenton ST4 . . . . 72 B4
Herbhill Cl WV4 . . . . 266 B2
Herd St ST6 . . . . 41 C1

Hereford Ave ST5 . . . . 71 B2
Hereford Cl WS9 . . . . 256 A4
Hereford Gr ST2 . . . . 58 B1
Hereford Rd WS12 . . . . 210 A2
Hereford Way B78 . . . . 250 A1
Heritage Ct WS14 . . . . 231 B3
Heritage Way DE15 . . . . . . 167 A1
Herm Cl ST5 . . . . 70 C2
Hermes Cl ST3 . . . . 90 B4
Hermes Ct B74 . . . . 257 C2
Hermes Rd WS13 . . . . 214 B1
Hermit St DY3 . . . . 271 B3
Hermitage Gdns 1
ST14 . . . . 111 A1
Hermitage La DE6 . . . . 81 A3
Heron Cl CW3 . . . . 68 B4
Heron Cross Prim Sch
ST4 . . . . 72 B2
Heron Dr Brewood WV9 . . . 224 A1
Penkridge ST19 . . . . 208 A3
Heron Mill WS3 . . . . 243 C2
Heron Pool Dr ST5 . . . . 85 B2
Heron St Fenton ST4 . . . . . . 72 C3
Rugeley WS15 . . . . 196 C4
Heron Way TF10 . . . . 168 C3
Herondale WS12 . . . . 210 A2
Herondale Cres DY8 . . . . . 279 B2
Herondale Rd DY8 . . . . 279 B2
Heronry The WV6 . . . . 254 C1
Herons Cl ST17 . . . . 175 B4
Herons Gate Rd DY7 . . . . . 277 A2
Heronswood ST17 . . . . 175 B4
Hertford Gr ST5 . . . . 71 B2
Hertford St ST14 . . . . 72 C2
Hesketh Ave ST6 . . . . 42 B3
Hesketh Rd ST17 . . . . 174 C3
Heskin Way ST6 . . . . 42 A3
Hesleden B77 . . . . 262 A4
Hester Cl ST3 . . . . 73 B3
Hethersett Wlk ST17 . . . . . . 58 B1
Hever Cl DY1 . . . . 271 C2
Hewell Cl DY6 . . . . 270 B1
Hewitt Cl WS13 . . . . 214 A1
Hewitt Cres ST9 . . . . 59 A2
Hewitt St ST4 . . . . 41 C3
Hewston Croft WS12 . . . . . 210 B2
Hexham Way DY1 . . . . 271 C1
Hextall La ST18 . . . . 153 B3
Heybridge Cl ST10 . . . . 92 C1
Heyburn Cres ST6 . . . . 56 C4
Heyfields Cotts ST12 . . . . . 104 A4
Heygate Way WS9 . . . . 245 A1
Heysham Cl ST3 . . . . 74 A2
Hick St ST5 . . . . 284 B2
Hickman St ST5 . . . . 284 B3
Hickmerelands La DY3 . . . 266 B1
Hickory Ct WS11 . . . . 210 B1
Hidden Hills CW3 . . . . 68 C4
Hide La SK17 . . . . 24 C4
Hide Pl ST4 . . . . 72 A4
Hide St ST4 . . . . 72 A4
Higgins Rd DE11 . . . . 186 C3
Higginson Cl CW12 . . . . 16 B4
Higgott Cl DE14 . . . . 185 A4
Higgs Rd WV11 . . . . 242 A1
High Arcal Dr DY3 . . . . 271 C4
High Arcal Rd DY3 . . . . 270 C2
High Arcal Sch The
DY3 . . . . 271 C4
High Bank WS11 . . . . 226 C4
High Bank Pl ST6 . . . . 42 A1
High Bank Rd DE15 . . . . . . 167 A2
High Broome Ct B78 . . . . . 250 A2
High Carr Bsns Pk ST5 . . . . 40 C2
High Chase Rise ST18 . . . . 177 B4
High Croft WS9 . . . . 245 A1
High Croft Cres WS14 . . . . 231 B4
High Cross SK17 . . . . 24 C3
High Gn Brewood ST19 . . . 223 B3
Cannock WS11 . . . . 209 B1
High Grange
Cannock WS11 . . . . 210 A3
Lichfield WS13 . . . . 213 C1
High Green Ct WS11 . . . . . 209 B1
High Hill WV11 . . . . 242 A1
High Holborn DY3 . . . . 271 B3
High House La WV7 . . . . . . 237 B2
High La Audley ST7 . . . . 55 A3
Chell Heath ST6 . . . . 42 B2
Endon ST6 . . . . 43 A3
Leek ST13 . . . . 45 C4
High Land Rd WS9 . . . . 245 A2
High Lowe Ave CW12 . . . . . . 6 A2
High Lows La ST15 . . . . 118 C3
High Mdw Cannock WS15 . . 211 C2
Norbury ST20 . . . . 151 A2
High Mdws
Newport TF10 . . . . 169 A2
Wolv WV6 . . . . 255 B2
Wombourne WV5 . . . . 270 A3
High Mount St WS12 . . . . . 210 B4
High Offley Rd ST20 . . . . . 151 B4
High Park Ave DY8 . . . . 279 A2
High Park Cl DY3 . . . . 271 B4
High Park Cres DY3 . . . . . . 266 B2
High Pk Cl ST13 . . . . 30 A3
High Pk St13 . . . . 155 B1
High St
Abbots Bromley WS15 . . . . 161 A3
Alrewas WS13 . . . . 237 A3
Alsop en le Dale DE6 . . . . . 64 B1
Aldridge WS9 . . . . 256 A3
Alton ST10 . . . . 78 C1
Audley ST7 . . . . 40 A3
Audley, Alsagers Bank ST7 . . 54 C3
Biddulph ST8 . . . . 27 B4
Brierley Hill DY8 . . . . 279 C4
Brownhills, Catshill WS8 . . 244 C4

High St continued
Brownhills, Clayhanger
WS8 . . . . 244 C3
Brownhills, Walsall Wood
WS9 . . . . 244 C3
Burntwood WS7 . . . . 211 C1
Burton u T DE14 . . . . 166 C1
Caverswall ST11 . . . . 74 C2
Cheadle ST10 . . . . 76 B2
Cheslyn Hay WS6 . . . . 226 B1
Cheswardine TF9 . . . . 130 A4
Church Eaton ST20 . . . . . . 190 A4
Claverley WV5 . . . . 267 B4
Colton WS15 . . . . 179 A3
Dilhorne ST10 . . . . 75 B2
Eccleshall ST21 . . . . 133 C4
Edgmond TF10 . . . . 168 A2
Gnosall ST20 . . . . 171 B3
Hixon ST18 . . . . 158 B4
Ipstones ST10 . . . . 47 A1
Kidsgrove, Harriseahead
ST7 . . . . 26 C3
Kidsgrove, Newchapel ST7 . . 26 C1
Kidsgrove, The Rookery ST7 . . 26 B2
Kingsley ST10 . . . . 61 C1
Kingswinford DY6 . . . . 275 C3
Kingswinford, Wall Heath
DY6 . . . . 275 C4
Kingswinford, Wordsley
DY8 . . . . 275 C1
Kinver DY7 . . . . 278 A2
Leek ST13 . . . . 30 C3
Longdon WS15 . . . . 197 C1
Longnor SK17 . . . . 13 B3
Marchington ST14 . . . . 127 C1
Market Drayton TF9 . . . . . . 97 B1
Mow Cop ST7 . . . . 26 B4
Newcastle-u-L ST5 . . . . 55 C4
Newcastle-u-L, Chesterton
ST5 . . . . 55 C4
Newcastle-u-L, Knutton ST5 . . 55 C4
Newcastle-u-L, Silverdale
ST5 . . . . 55 B1
Newcastle-u-L, Wolstanton
ST5 . . . . 56 B3
Newport TF10 . . . . 168 C2
Norton Canes WS11 . . . . . 228 A3
Pattingham WV6 . . . . 253 B2
Rocester ST14 . . . . 95 C2
Sedgley DY3 . . . . 271 B4
Stone ST15 . . . . 120 A4
Stourbridge DY8 . . . . 279 C4
Swadlincote DE11 . . . . 186 C3
Swindon DY3 . . . . 269 C1
Talke ST7 . . . . 40 B3
Tamworth B77 . . . . 261 B2
Tunstall ST6 . . . . 41 B2
Tunstall, Goldenhill ST6 . . . . 41 B2
Tutbury DE13 . . . . 146 B3
Upper Tean ST10 . . . . 92 C2
Uttoxeter ST14 . . . . 126 B4
Walsall WS3 . . . . 243 A1
Walsall, Pelsall WS3 . . . . . 244 A3
Wheaton Aston ST19 . . . . . 205 A3
Wolv WV6 . . . . 255 B2
Wombourne WV5 . . . . 270 A4
High St (May Bank) ST5 . . . 56 B2
High St (Sandyford) ST6 . . . 41 B3
High View
Blythe Bridge ST3 . . . . 90 A3
Mount Pleasant ST7 . . . . . . 26 A3
Wolv WV14 . . . . 266 C1
High View Rd Endon ST9 . . 43 C4
Leek ST13 . . . . 31 A3
High Wood Cl DY6 . . . . 275 B3
Highbrook Cl WV9 . . . . 240 A1
Highbury Rd
Caverswall ST9 . . . . 59 B2
Sutton Coldfield B74 . . . . . 257 B2
Highcliffe Rd B77 . . . . 261 B4
Highcroft WS3 . . . . 244 A3
Highcroft Ave DY8 . . . . 275 C2
Highcroft Dr
Burton u T DE14 . . . . 165 C2
Sutton Coldfield B74 . . . . . 257 B2
Highcroft Wlk ST6 . . . . 42 A1
Higher Ash Rd ST7 . . . . 40 B4
Higher Woodcroft ST13 . . . 30 B2
Higherland ST5 . . . . 284 C2
Higherland Ct 2 ST7 . . . . . 26 A1
Highfied Dr DE11 . . . . 166 C2
Highfield TF10 . . . . 168 A2
Highfield Ave
Burntwood WS7 . . . . 229 A4
Cheadle ST10 . . . . 76 B2
Essington WV10 . . . . 241 A1
Meir ST3 . . . . 73 C1
Newcastle-u-L ST5 . . . . 56 B2
Tamworth B77 . . . . 251 A3
Highfield Cl
Acton Trussell ST17 . . . . . . 193 A4
Blythe Bridge ST11 . . . . 90 B4
Burntwood WS7 . . . . 229 A4
Highfield Cres ST10 . . . . 76 B2
Highfield Ct
Cannock WS11 . . . . 71 B3
Highfield Dr
Colwich ST18 . . . . 177 B4
Fenton ST4 . . . . 72 C3
Highfield Gdns WS14 . . . . 231 C3
Highfield Gr ST17 . . . . 174 B4
Highfield Grange ST5 . . . . . 56 C2

Highfield La SK17 . . . . 24 C3
Highfield Rd
Burntwood WS7 . . . . 229 B4
Cannock WS12 . . . . 210 C1
Coxkley DY10 . . . . 280 A3
Hixon ST18 . . . . 158 B4
Sedgley DY3 . . . . 266 B1
Walsall WS3 . . . . 244 A2
Highfield Rd E ST8 . . . . 27 B4
Highfield Rd N WS3 . . . . . . 243 C3
Highfield Rd W ST8 . . . . . . 27 B4
Highfield Rise ST4 . . . . 87 C4
Highfield Way WS9 . . . . . . 245 A1
Highfields
Burntwood WS7 . . . . 229 A4
Market Drayton TF9 . . . . . . 112 A4
Highfields Ave WS15 . . . . . 198 B2
Highfields Ct WV4 . . . . 265 B3
Highfields Dr WV5 . . . . 270 A3
Highfields Grange WS6 . . 226 B1
Highfields Pk WS6 . . . . 226 B1
Highfields Prim Sch
WS7 . . . . 229 B4
Highfields Rd WS7 . . . . 228 C2
Highfields Sch WV4 . . . . . . 265 B3
Highfields The
Eccleshall ST21 . . . . 116 A3
Wolv WV6 . . . . 255 A2
Highgate Aldridge B74 . . . . 257 A3
Highgate Cl DY3 . . . . 271 C3
Highgate Ave WV4 . . . . 265 B3
Highgate Cl ST6 . . . . 42 C2
Highgate Country Pk*
DY3 . . . . 269 A1
Highgate Rd DY7 . . . . 273 C4
Highgrove Stone ST15 . . . . . 120 B3
Wolv WV6 . . . . 255 B2
Highgrove Cl
Burton u T DE13 . . . . 147 B1
Tamworth B79 . . . . 250 A4
Highgrove Pl DY1 . . . . 271 C1
Highland Cl Biddulph ST8 . . 28 A4
Blythe Bridge ST11 . . . . 90 C4
Highland Dr ST3 . . . . 73 B1
Highland Rd
Huntington WS12 . . . . 209 B2
Newport TF10 . . . . 168 C1
Highland Way WS15 . . . . . 178 B2
Highlands Stafford ST17 . . . 174 B4
Stone ST15 . . . . 119 C3
Highlands Dr DE15 . . . . 167 A2
Highlands Rd WV3 . . . . 265 B4
Highlanes ST21 . . . . 116 C3
Highover Dr B75 . . . . 258 A2
Highton St ST22 . . . . 43 B1
Highup Rd ST13 . . . . 19 B1
Highview Dr DY6 . . . . 275 C2
Highview Rd ST11 . . . . 106 C4
Highway La ST5 . . . . 69 C4
Highwood Rd ST14 . . . . . . 126 B3
Higson Ave ST4 . . . . 72 A4
Hilary Dr Aldridge WS9 . . . 256 A3
Wolv WV3 . . . . 265 B3
Hilcote Hollow ST16 . . . . . 155 A3
Hilderstone Rd ST15 . . . . . 106 B3
Hill Ave WV4 . . . . 266 C2
Hill Avenue Jun & Inf Sch
WV4 . . . . 266 C2
Hill Cl Sedgley DY3 . . . . . . 266 C1
Uttoxeter ST14 . . . . 110 C1
Hill Cres Audley ST7 . . . . . . 54 C3
Stone ST15 . . . . 120 A3
Hill Crest Sedgley DY3 . . . . 271 B2
Stafford ST17 . . . . 174 B4
Hill Crest Dr WS13 . . . . . . 214 A1
Hill Croft ST18 . . . . 158 B4
Hill Dr Hanbury DE13 . . . . . 145 A2
Stone ST15 . . . . 120 A3
Hill Hook Rd B74 . . . . 257 C3
Hill Hook Rd B74 . . . . 257 C3
Hill La Burntwood WS7 . . . 211 C1
Cheslyn Hay WS6 . . . . 226 C1
Sutton Coldfield B75 . . . . . . 259 A1
Hill Pk WS9 . . . . 245 A2
Hill Pl WV11 . . . . 242 A1
Hill Rise ST18 . . . . 137 C2
Hill Side DY3 . . . . 271 B2
Hill St Brierley Hill DY8 . . . 279 C4
Burntwood WS7 . . . . 228 C3
Burton u T DE15 . . . . 185 C4
Cannock WS12 . . . . 210 B2
Essington WV11 . . . . 241 C2
Newcastle-u-L ST5 . . . . 284 B4
Norton Canes WS11 . . . . . . 227 C3
Rugeley WS15 . . . . 196 C4
Sedgley DY3 . . . . 271 B3
Stoke-on-T ST4 . . . . 72 A4
Stourbridge DY8 . . . . 279 C2
Swadlincote DE11 . . . . 186 C3
Hill Terr ST7 . . . . 39 B1
Hill Top Ave B79 . . . . 250 A4
Hill Top Cl ST6 . . . . 41 B4
Hill Top Cres ST3 . . . . 90 A3
Hill Top View WS15 . . . . . 198 B2
Hill Top Wlk WS9 . . . . 245 B1
Hill View Aldridge WS9 . . . 245 A1
Leek ST13 . . . . 31 A3
Norton-on-t-M ST22 . . . . 43 A3
Hill Village Rd B75 . . . . . . 258 A2
Hill West Inf Sch B74 . . . . 257 C2
Hill West Jun Sch B74 . . . 257 C2
Hill Wood WS3 . . . . 243 C1
Hill Wood Rd B75 . . . . 258 A3
Hillary Ave CW12 . . . . 6 A1

Hillary Crest
Rugeley WS15 . . . . 196 C3
Sedgley DY3 . . . . 271 C3
Hillary Rd ST7 . . . . 26 A2
Hillary St ST6 . . . . 57 A3
Hillberry Cl ST12 . . . . 58 C1
Hillboro Rise DY7 . . . . 278 A3
Hillchurch St ST1 . . . . 282 B3
Hillcott Wlk ST3 . . . . 283 D3
Hillcrest Brewood ST19 . . . 223 B4
Hixon WS15 . . . . 140 A1
Leek ST13 . . . . 30 B3
Tutbury DE13 . . . . 146 A3
Hillcrest Ave
Burton u T DE15 . . . . 167 A2
Kingsley ST10 . . . . 62 A3
Hillcrest Cl Kingsley ST10 . . 62 A3
Tamworth B79 . . . . 250 A3
Hillcrest Rise WS7 . . . . . . 229 A2
Hillcrest St ST1 . . . . 282 C3
Hillcroft Ave ST17 . . . . 175 C4
Hillcroft Rd DY6 . . . . 275 C4
Hilldene Rd DY6 . . . . 275 B2
Hillfarm Cl ST17 . . . . 174 C3
Hillfield Ave ST4 . . . . 71 C2
Hillfield La DE13 . . . . 147 C1
Hillgreen Rd ST3 . . . . 73 B3
Hillman B77 . . . . 250 C1
Hillman St ST3 . . . . 43 A1
Hillmorton Rd B74 . . . . . . 257 C2
Hillport Ave ST5 . . . . 56 A4
Hillrise ST10 . . . . 94 C4
Hillsdale La S113 . . . . 33 C2
Hillsdale Rd DE15 . . . . 167 A3
Hillside
Abbots Bromley WS15 . . . . . 161 A3
Brownhills WS8 . . . . 245 A3
Eccleshall ST21 . . . . 133 C3
Lichfield WS14 . . . . 231 B3
Market Drayton TF9 . . . . . . 112 C2
Newcastle-u-L ST5 . . . . 284 A2
Tutbury DE13 . . . . 146 B3
Wombourne WV5 . . . . 269 C4
Wombourne, Brickbridge
WV5 . . . . 269 C3
Hillside Ave Endon ST9 . . . . 43 C4
Forsbrook ST11 . . . . 91 A4
Kidsgrove ST7 . . . . 41 A4
Meir ST3 . . . . 73 C1
Hillside Cl Biddulph ST8 . . . . 17 A1
Blythe Bridge ST11 . . . . 106 C4
Brownhills WS8 . . . . 245 A3
Cannock WS12 . . . . 210 A4
Kidsgrove ST7 . . . . 26 B4
Norton-on-t-M ST22 . . . . 43 B2
Rugeley WS15 . . . . 197 A3
Hillside Cres WS3 . . . . 243 C2
Hillside Dr Colwich ST18 . . . 177 B4
Leek ST13 . . . . 30 B2
Hillside Gdns DE11 . . . . . . 186 C1
Hillside Gr DY10 . . . . 280 B2
Hillside Prim Sch ST1 . . . . . 43 A1
Hillside Rd Caverswall ST9 . . 59 A2
Cheddleton ST13 . . . . 45 B2
Norton-on-t-M ST22 . . . . 43 A2
Sutton Coldfield B74 . . . . . . 258 A2
Hillside Wlk ST4 . . . . 71 B4
Hillside Cl WS7 . . . . 228 C3
Hillswood Ave ST13 . . . . . . 43 C4
Hillswood Cl ST9 . . . . 43 C4
Hillswood Dr ST9 . . . . 43 C4
Hilltop WS15 . . . . 196 C4
Hilltop Ave ST5 . . . . 56 C1
Hilltop Ct DY2 . . . . 271 C2
Hilltop Prim Sch ST7 . . . . . . 40 B4
Hillview Cres ST5 . . . . 83 B3
Hillway Cl WS15 . . . . 178 B1
Hillwood Cl DY6 . . . . 275 B2

Hinckley Gr ST4 . . . . 88 A3
Hinde St ST1 . . . . 282 B1
Hines St ST4 . . . . 72 C3
Hingley Croft WS9 . . . . . . 256 C2
Hinksford Gdns DY3 . . . . . 269 C1
Hinksford La DY6 . . . . 269 C1
Hinsford Cl DY6 . . . . 269 C1
Hinsley Mill La TF9 . . . . 97 C1
Hinstock Cl WV4 . . . . 266 A2
Hinton Cl ST3 . . . . 88 C4
Hints Ct B78 . . . . 248 B1
Hints La Hints B78 . . . . 248 C2
Hopwas B78 . . . . 249 A3
Hints Rd Hopwas B78 . . . . 249 A3
Tamworth B78 . . . . 249 B1
Hislop Rd WS15 . . . . 196 C3
Histons Dr WV8 . . . . 238 C3
Histons Hill WV8 . . . . 238 C1
Hitchman St ST14 . . . . 126 B3
Hixon Airfield Est (Ind Est)
ST18 . . . . 139 A1
Hixon Ind Est ST18 . . . . . . 158 A4
**HM Young Offender Inst
(Swinfen Hall)** WS14 . . . . 231 C1
Hoarstone DY8 . . . . 281 C3
**Hob Hill CE Methodist Prim
Sch** WS15 . . . . 197 A3
Hob's Rd WS13 . . . . 214 C1
Hobart Cl DE15 . . . . 167 B1
Hobart St B74 . . . . 258 A2
Hobart Rd WS12 . . . . 210 C1
Hobble St ST6 . . . . 57 A4
Hobb La ST14 . . . . 142 A4
Hobble End La WS6 . . . . . . 243 A4
Hobbs View WS15 . . . . 197 A3
Hobby Cl 9 ST3 . . . . 90 A4
Hobfield La WS15 . . . . 161 A4
Hobnock Rd WV11 . . . . . . 242 A3
Hobs Hole La WS9 . . . . . . 256 B4
Hobson St ST6 . . . . 57 A4
Hobstone Hill La WS7,
WS13 . . . . 212 C1
Hockley Rd
Tamworth B77 . . . . 261 C3
Uttoxeter ST14 . . . . 126 A4
Hodge La B77 . . . . 251 A3
Hodgkins Cl WS8 . . . . 245 A3
Hodgkinson St ST5 . . . . 55 C3
Hodnet Gr ST1 . . . . 282 A4
Hodnet Pl WS11 . . . . 210 A1
Hodson Way WS11 . . . . . . 210 A1
Hogan Way ST16 . . . . 156 B2
Hogarth Pl ST5 . . . . 55 C3
Holbeach Ave ST2 . . . . 58 B4
Holbeach Way ST16 . . . . . 155 A2
Holbeache La DY6 . . . . . . 270 B1
Holbeache Rd DY6 . . . . . . 275 B4
Holborn St ST5 . . . . 284 B3
Holborn Row ST10 . . . . 92 C2
Holborn Sh Ctr The
DY3 . . . . 271 B4
Holborn The CW3 . . . . 68 C3
Holbrook Vlle ST2 . . . . 58 A1
Holbury Cl WV9 . . . . 240 A1
Holcroft Rd DY6 . . . . 270 B1
Holdcroft Rd ST2 . . . . 58 B3
Holden Ave ST5 . . . . 56 B4
Holden Ave N ST6 . . . . 57 B4
Holden Ave S ST6 . . . . 57 B4
Holden Lane High Sch
ST1 . . . . 57 C4
Holden Lane Prim Sch
ST1 . . . . 57 C4
Holden Rd WV4 . . . . 265 B2
Holder Dr WS11 . . . . 209 A1
Holder St ST11 . . . . 57 A3
Holdiford Rd
Brocton ST17,ST18 . . . . 176 B4
Tixall ST18 . . . . 157 B1
Holding Cres ST17 . . . . 54 B4
Holditch Rd ST5 . . . . 55 C3
Holecroft St 7 ST6 . . . . 57 A4
Holehouse La
Endon ST6,ST9 . . . . 28 B1
Scholar Green ST7 . . . . 25 B4
Holehouse Rd ST7 . . . . 58 B3
Holland Cl WS13 . . . . 215 A1
Holland Ct B79 . . . . 217 B3
Holland Pk DE13 . . . . 183 C1
Holland St 2 ST16 . . . . 41 B2
Holland's Way WS3 . . . . . . 243 C2
Hollands Pl WS3 . . . . 243 B1
Hollands Rd WS3 . . . . 243 B1
Hollands The ST8 . . . . 17 B2
Hollies Ave ST18 . . . . 159 C3
Hollies Brook Cl ST20 . . . 171 B4
Hollies Cl Clifton DE6 . . . . . 81 C3
Newton Solney DE15 . . . . . . 167 C4
Hollies Ct WS11 . . . . 209 C1
Hollies Dr ST17 . . . . 156 C4
Hollies Ind Est WV2 . . . . . 266 B4
Hollies La Enville DY7 . . . . 276 C4
Pattingham WV6 . . . . 253 C3
Hollies Park Rd WS11 . . . . 209 C1
Hollies The
Newcastle-u-L ST5 . . . . 284 C4
Wolv WV4 . . . . 266 B4
Hollings St ST4 . . . . 283 A5
Hollington Dr ST6 . . . . 42 A4
Hollington La ST14 . . . . . . 110 C3
Hollington Rd ST10 . . . . 93 B4
Hollins Bsns Ctr ST16 . . . . 155 B3
Hollins Grange ST7 . . . . 40 B4
Hollins La ST10 . . . . 60 C1
Hollinsclough CE Prim Sch
SK17 . . . . 4 C3
Hollinsclough Rake SK17 . . 4 A1

Hollinscroft Ct ST10 . . . . . . 92 C2
Hollinshead Ave ST5 . . . . . . 56 A2
Hollinshead Cl ST7 . . . . 25 C4
Hollinwell Cl WS3 . . . . 243 A2
Hollinwood Cl ST7 . . . . 40 C4
Hollinwood Rd ST7 . . . . 40 C4
Hollis La ST14 . . . . 95 A3
Hollow Cres DE15 . . . . 167 B2
Hollow La
Burton u T DE15 . . . . 167 B2
Cheddleton ST13 . . . . 45 B3
Colton WS15 . . . . 179 A3
Draycott-in-t C DE6 . . . . . . 144 B3
Mayfield DE6 . . . . 66 B1
Hollow The
Caverswall ST11 . . . . 74 C2
Mount Pleasant ST7 . . . . 26 A3
Roston DE6 . . . . 96 C3
Uttoxeter ST14 . . . . 126 B3
Holloway B79 . . . . 250 A2
Holloway Dr WV5 . . . . 269 C3
Holloway La ST5,TF9 . . . . . 84 B3
Holloway St ST3 . . . . 271 B2
Holloway St W DY3 . . . . . . 271 B2
Holloway The
Brierley Hill DY8 . . . . 279 C4
Seisdon WV5 . . . . 264 A2
Stone ST15 . . . . 120 B3
Wolv WV9 . . . . 255 B1
Hollowood Pl ST6 . . . . 42 C3
Hollowood Wlk ST6 . . . . . . 42 B3
Holly Ave ST13 . . . . 45 B2
Holly Bank ST4 . . . . 87 C4
Holly Bank View WS15 . . . 197 A3
Holly Bush Cotts ST13 . . . . 44 C4
Holly Bush La ST5 . . . . 85 A2
Holly Bush Rd DE6,DE13 . . 143 C1
Holly Cl Kinver DY7 . . . . . . 277 A4
Market Drayton TF9 . . . . . . 112 A4
Tamworth B79 . . . . 250 A4
Holly Ct ST2 . . . . 73 C4
Holly Dr Alrewas WS13 . . . 215 B4
Caverswall ST12 . . . . 77 A1
Stafford ST17 . . . . 175 C3
Holly Fields ST15 . . . . 118 C3
Holly Gn DE15 . . . . 185 C4
Holly Gr Stone ST15 . . . . . . 120 A4
Stourbridge DY8 . . . . 279 C3
Wolv WV3 . . . . 265 C4
Holly Grove La WS7 . . . . . 211 C1
Holly Grove Prim Sch
WS7 . . . . 211 C1
Holly Hill WS6 . . . . 242 C4
Holly Hill Rd
Cannock WS11 . . . . 211 C3
Shenstone WS14 . . . . 246 C3
Holly La Aldridge WS9 . . . . 256 C4
Bradley ST18 . . . . 173 B1
Brownhills WS9 . . . . 245 B2
Great Wyrley WS6 . . . . 242 C4
Huntington WS12 . . . . 209 B4
Kidsgrove ST7 . . . . 26 C3
Seighford ST18 . . . . 153 C1
Sutton Coldfield B74 . . . . . . 258 B4
Uttoxeter ST14 . . . . 125 B1
Holly Mdw ST10 . . . . 109 B2
Holly Mews ST10 . . . . 69 C4
Holly Pl ST4 . . . . 72 C2
Holly Rd Barton-u-N DE13 . 183 B1
Newcastle-u-L ST5 . . . . 40 C1
Holly St Burton u T DE15 . . 185 C4
Cannock WS12 . . . . 209 C3
Holly Tree Dr ST8 . . . . 16 B1
Holly View WV11 . . . . 242 A2
Hollybank Ave WV11 . . . . . 242 A2
Hollybank Cl WS3 . . . . 243 A1
Hollybank Cres ST4 . . . . . . 72 A3
Hollybush Cl DE12 . . . . . . 219 C4
Hollybush Cres ST3 . . . . . . 72 C2
Hollybush La
Brierley Hill DY8 . . . . 279 C4
Codsall WV8 . . . . 238 C1
Wolv WV4 . . . . 265 B2
Hollybush Rd ST3 . . . . 72 C2
Hollycroft Gdns WV6 . . . . 255 A3
Hollyhill La WS14 . . . . 246 C3
Hollyhock Way DE14 . . . . 184 C3
Hollyhurst ST7 . . . . 175 B3
Hollyhurst Dr DY6 . . . . 275 C2
Hollyhurst La ST18 . . . . . . 140 C2
Hollyoak Way WS11 . . . . . 209 C1
Hollys Rd DE13 . . . . 182 A1
Hollywall La ST6 . . . . 41 B3
Hollywood Gr ST16 . . . . . . 54 B1
Holm Oak Dr CW3 . . . . 68 B3
Holm Rd ST10 . . . . 78 B1
Holm View ST14 . . . . 126 A4
Holmbridge Gr WS4 . . . . . 244 B1
Holmcroft Gdns WV9 . . . . 224 B1
Holmcroft Rd ST16 . . . . . . 155 B3
Holme Bank DE6 . . . . 81 B4
Holme Farm Ave DE6 . . . . 185 C4
Holme Mill WV10 . . . . 240 B2
Holme Rise ST19 . . . . 193 A1
Holmes Cl DE15 . . . . 86 A3
Holmes The WV10 . . . . . . 240 B2
Holmes Way ST6 . . . . 42 A4
Holmesfield Wlk ST3 . . . . . 283 D3
Holst Dr ST1 . . . . 56 A4
Holston Cl WS12 . . . . 210 C1
Holsworth Cl B77 . . . . 250 B1
Holt Cres WS11 . . . . 210 A1
Holt La ST10 . . . . 61 C1
Holt's La DE13 . . . . 146 A3
Holte Dr B75 . . . . 258 B4
Holwich B77 . . . . 262 A4
Holy Austin Rock* DY7 . . . 277 C2

Holy Rosary RC Prim Sch
DE15 . . . . 167 A2
Holy Trinity CE Prim Sch
Brownhills WS8 . . . . 244 C3
Burton u T DE14 . . . . 166 C2
Holyhead Cres ST3 . . . . 74 A2
Holyhead Rd
Albrighton WV7 . . . . 237 B1
Codsall WV8 . . . . 238 B1
Holyoake Pl WS15 . . . . 178 B2
Holyrood Cl ST15 . . . . 120 B3
Holywell Cl ST8 . . . . 27 C3
Holywell Rise WS14 . . . . . 231 B3
Home Farm Ct DE11 . . . . . 186 B1
Home Farm Rd WV6 . . . . . 252 B4
Homefield Rd WV8 . . . . . . 239 B2
Homer Pl ST6 . . . . 42 B3
Homer Rd B75 . . . . 258 B1
Homer St ST1 . . . . 57 C2
Homestead Cl DY3 . . . . . . 271 C3
Homestead Ct ST16 . . . . . 155 C4
Homestead Dr B75 . . . . . . 258 B2
Homestead Rd ST3 . . . . 73 B4
Homestead The ST22 . . . . . 43 B2
Honesty Cl WS8 . . . . 244 B3
Honeybourne B77 . . . . 250 B1
Honeybourne Cres WV5 . . 269 C3
Honeysuckle Ave
Forsbrook ST11 . . . . 90 C3
Kingswinford DY6 . . . . 275 C4
Honeysuckle Cl ST10 . . . . . 92 C2
Honeysuckle Dr WV10 . . . 241 B4
Honeysuckle La ST9 . . . . . . 29 C1
Honeysuckle View
DE15 . . . . 186 A4
Honeysuckle Way WS6 . . . 227 A2
Honeytree Cl DY6 . . . . 275 C2
Honeywall ST4 . . . . 72 A4
Honeywall La Keele CW3 . . 69 A4
Stanton DE6 . . . . 80 C4
Honeywood ST5 . . . . 284 B4
Honiton Cl ST17 . . . . 175 B4
Honiton Wlk ST3 . . . . 283 D3
Honor Ave WV4 . . . . 266 B3
Hoo La DY7 . . . . 273 C2
Hood La Armitage WS15 . . . 198 A2
Longdon WS15 . . . . 197 C1
Hook Dr B74 . . . . 257 C2
Hook La Shenstone WS14 . . 246 B2
Stramshall ST14 . . . . 111 A3
Hook La The WV7 . . . . 237 A1
Hoomill La S118 . . . . 158 A3
Hoon Ave ST5 . . . . 56 A2
Hoor Rd DE65 . . . . 146 B4
Hoover St ST6 . . . . 41 B2
Hope St Audley ST7 . . . . 39 C2
Hanley ST1 . . . . 282 B3
Kidsgrove ST7 . . . . 26 B4
Hopedale Cl Fenton ST4 . . . . 73 A3
Newcastle-u-L ST5 . . . . 71 A2
Hopley Rd DE13 . . . . 165 A3
Hopleys Cl B77 . . . . 250 C2
Hopstone Gdns WV4 . . . . . 265 C2
Hopton Bank ST18 . . . . . . 137 B1
Hopton Cl WV4 . . . . 254 C2
Hopton Ct ST16 . . . . 155 B3
Hopton La ST18 . . . . 137 B1
Hopton Mdw WS12 . . . . . . 210 B1
Hopton St ST16 . . . . 155 C3
Hopton Way ST16 . . . . 42 A4
Hoptonhall La ST18 . . . . . . 137 B1
Hopwas Hill B78 . . . . 249 A3
Hopwood Pl ST2 . . . . 58 A2
Hopyard Cl DY3 . . . . 271 A2
Hopyard La DY3 . . . . 271 A2
Horatius Rd ST5 . . . . 55 B3
Hordern Cl WV6 . . . . 255 C3
Hordern Gr WV6 . . . . 255 C3
Hordern Rd WV6 . . . . 255 C3
Hordley St ST1 . . . . 282 C3
Hornbeam B77 . . . . 251 A2
Hornbeam Cres WS12 . . . 211 A3
Hornbeams The 2
ST14 . . . . 111 A1
Hornbrook Cl DE13 . . . . . . 166 A4
Hornbrook Rd DE13 . . . . . 166 A4
Hornby Rd WV4 . . . . 266 B3
Hornby Row ST14 . . . . 72 A4
Horninglow Croft DE13 . . . 166 B3
Horninglow Inf Sch
DE13 . . . . 166 B3
Horninglow Rd DE14 . . . . . 166 B3
Horninglow Rd N DE13 . . . 166 B4
Horninglow St DE14 . . . . . 166 C3
Horns Croft WS15 . . . . 196 A4
Hornton Cl B74 . . . . 257 B3
Hornton Rd DE13 . . . . 166 A4
Horse Bridge La DY7 . . . . 278 B1
Horse Fair
Eccleshall ST21 . . . . 133 C4
Rugeley WS15 . . . . 196 C4
Horse Rd ST10 . . . . 78 C1
Horsebrook La ST19 . . . . . 223 B4
Horsecroft Cres ST13 . . . . . 31 A4
Horsecroft Gr ST13 . . . . 31 A4
Horsehills Dr WV3 . . . . 255 C1
Horseshoe Dr WS15 . . . . . 178 B2
Horsey La WS15 . . . . 212 B4
Horsham Ave DY8 . . . . 275 B2
Horsley Gr ST13 . . . . 88 C4
Horsley La
Eccleshall ST21 . . . . 132 C3
Wall WS14 . . . . 246 B4
Horsley Rd B74 . . . . 257 A1
Horton Ave DE13 . . . . 166 C4
Horton Cl DY3 . . . . 271 B4

Horton Dr ST3 .....74 A3
Horton Lodge Sch ST13 .18 B1
Horton Rd DY7 .....277 C3
Horton St Leek ST13 .....30 C3
  Newcastle-u-L ST5 .....284 D3
Horwood ST5 .....70 B3
Horwood Gdns ST6 .....62 A5
Hose St ST6 .....41 B2
Hoskins Cl ST15 .....120 B4
Hoskins Rd ST6 .....41 C3
Hospital La
  Cheslyn Hay WS6 .....226 A1
  Market Drayton TF9 .....112 A4
Hospital Rd WS7 .....229 A3
Hospital St B79 .....250 A3
Hot La Biddulph ST8 .....17 B1
  Burslem ST6 .....57 A4
Hot Lane Ind Est ST6 .....57 A4
Hotel Bldgs WS14 .....230 A1
Hothill La ST10 .....109 B1
Hough Hill ST6 .....43 A4
Hougher Wall Rd ST7 .....39 B1
Houghton St ST1 .....282 B1
Houghwood La ST9 .....43 B2
Houlbrooke Ho
  WS14 .....231 B4
Houldsworth Dr ST6 .....42 A4
Housefield Rd ST2 .....73 B4
Houseman Dr ST3 .....72 C1
Houting B77 .....261 B3
Houx The DY8 .....279 C4
Hoveringham Dr ST2 .....57 C1
Howard Cl Caverswall ST9 .....73 A3
  WS12 .....30 B2
Howard Dr ST5 .....71 A3
Howard Pl Hanley ST1 .....282 A1
  Newcastle-u-L ST5 .....71 A3
Howard Prim Sch B79 .....216 B1
Howard Rd ST17 .....174 C4
Howard St Longton ST3 .....283 C2
  Wolv WV2 .....266 B4
Howard Wlk ST4 .....283 C2
Howdle's La WS8 .....228 C1
Howe Gr ST5 .....55 C1
Howell Rd WV2 .....266 C4
Howitt Cres ST14 .....111 A1
Howitt House Sch DE13 .....144 C2
Howland Cl WV9 .....239 C1
Howson St ST1 .....282 C2
Hoylake B77 .....251 A2
Hoylake Cl WS3 .....243 A2
Hoylake Rd WV6 .....254 B3
Hubbal La TF11 .....220 B2
Huddlesford La WS14 .....232 B4
Huddlestone Cl WV10 .....241 A3
Huddock's View ST5 .....243 C3
Hudson Cl
  Cannock WS12 .....210 A1
  Gnosall ST20 .....171 C4
Hudson Dr WS7 .....229 B3
Hudson Gr WV6 .....254 C3
Hudson Wlk ST3 .....283 C4
Hugh Bourne Pl ST8 .....27 A1
Hugh Porter Way WV6 .....255 C3
Hughes Ave
  Newcastle-u-L ST5 .....284 B4
  WS10 .....265 C4
Hughes St ST6 .....57 A4
Hughson Gr ST6 .....42 C2
Hugo Meynell CE Prim Sch
  TF9 .....99 C2
Hugo St ST13 .....30 C3
Hulland Cl ST5 .....55 A1
Hullock's Pool Rd ST7 .....39 C3
Hulme Cl ST5 .....55 A1
Hulme La ST9 .....59 A3
Hulme Rd ST13 .....73 A3
Hulme St ST14 .....71 C4
Hulse St ST4 .....73 A3
Hulton Rd ST2 .....58 A3
Hulton St ST1 .....282 C4
Humber Way ST15 .....71 A2
Humbert St ST1 .....56 C2
Humphrey St DY3 .....271 B2
Humphries Ho WS8 .....244 C4
Hungerford La CW3 .....69 A3
Hungerford Pl CW2 .....38 B3
Hungerford Rd DY8 .....279 C1
Hungry La WS14 .....247 C3
Hunsford Cl ST3 .....283 C4
Hunstan Way WS7 .....229 A4
Hunt St ST6 .....41 C2
Huntbach St ST1 .....282 B3
Hunter Ave WS7 .....229 A4
Hunter Cl WS14 .....231 B3
Hunter Rd WS11 .....226 C4
Hunter St DE14 .....166 B3
Hunter's Point TF9 .....99 B3
Hunter's Ride DY7 .....275 A1
Hunters Cl ST8 .....27 B4
Hunters Ct ST18 .....137 C2
Hunters Dr ST14 .....71 C3
Hunters Rise ST17 .....174 C2
Hunters Way ST14 .....72 A3
Huntilee Rd ST6 .....41 C2
Huntingdon Cl B78 .....249 C1
Huntingdon Pl ST5 .....57 C3
Huntingdon Rd DE15 .....185 B4
Huntington Ind Est
  WS12 .....209 A3
Huntington Prim Sch
  WS12 .....209 B4
Huntington Terrace Rd
  WS11 .....209 C2

Huntley Ave ST4 .....72 A3
Huntley Cl ST10 .....76 B1
Huntley La ST10 .....92 B4
Huntley Rd ST13 .....44 C4
Hunts La DE12 .....219 C4
Hunts Mill Dr DY5 .....271 B1
Huntsbank Dr ST5 .....40 B1
Huntsman's Hall WS15 .....197 B1
Huntsmans Dr DY7 .....277 C3
Huntsmans Gate WS7 .....229 A4
Huntsmans Rise WS12 .....209 B4
Huntsmans Wlk
  Kinver DY7 .....277 C3
  Rugeley WS15 .....197 B1
Hurlingham Rd ST16 .....155 B4
Huron Cl WS11 .....210 A1
Huron Gr ST14 .....88 A4
Hurst Cl ST7 .....40 B3
Hurst Dr DE13 .....147 C1
Hurst Rd Biddulph ST8 .....17 A2
  Sedgley WV14 .....266 C1
Hurst St ST3 .....283 A2
Hurstbourne Cl WS15 .....178 B1
Hurstmead Dr ST17 .....175 B3
Hurstons La ST10 .....78 C1
Hurstons The ST10 .....78 C1
Husphins La WV8 .....238 A3
Hussey Cl ST19 .....207 C4
Hussey Rd
  Brownhills WS8 .....244 C4
  Norton Canes WS11 .....227 C3
Huston Ave ST9 .....43 C4
Hut Hill La WS6 .....227 A2
Hutchinson Cl WS15 .....178 A1
Hutchinson Meml CE First Sch
  ST10 .....109 A4
Hutchinson Wlk ST13 .....73 A2
Hutton Cl CW12 .....6 A1
Hutton Dr CW12 .....6 A1
Hutton Way ST12 .....58 B1
Huxley Cl WV9 .....240 A2
Huxley Pl ST2 .....73 A3
Hyacinth Ct ST5 .....284 C4
Hyacinth Rd ST4 .....56 C1
Hyde Cl DY7 .....278 A3
Hyde Ct ST17 .....174 B4
Hyde La DY7 .....278 A3
Hyde Lea Bank ST18 .....174 B3
Hyde Mill Croft ST19 .....223 B3
Hyde Mill La ST19 .....223 B3
Hylton Cl DE14 .....185 A4
Hyndley Cl ST2 .....58 A2
Hyperion Dr WV4 .....266 A2
Hyperion Rd DY7 .....279 B4
Hyssop Cl ST11 .....210 A2

I-Mex Bsns Pk ST4 .....72 C3
Ian Rd ST7 .....26 B1
Ibsen Rd ST3 .....74 A2
Ibstock St DE13 .....166 A3
Ickenfield Cl B74 .....257 A1
Idonia Rd WV6 .....254 C3
Ikins Dr ST7 .....39 C1
Ilam CE Prim Sch DE6 .....50 C1
Ilam Cl ST5 .....56 A1
Ilam Ctry Pk DE6 .....50 C3
Ilam-moor La DE6 .....50 C3
Ilford Side ST13 .....44 B1
Ilkley Pl ST5 .....54 C1
Illshaw WV9 .....240 A2
Imandra Ct ST14 .....88 A4
Imex Bsns Pk
  Burton u T DE14 .....166 A2
  Wolv WV2 .....266 B4
Imex Tech Pk ST4 .....88 B4
Imogen Cl ST14 .....73 A3
Imperial Ct ST11 .....282 C1
Impstones ST20 .....188 B3
Imsigine Dr DY8 .....275 B2
Inge Dr DE13 .....201 A1
Ingelow Cl ST13 .....73 A1
Ingestre Cl
  Cannock WS11 .....210 A1
  Newport TF10 .....168 B1
  Walsall WS3 .....242 C2
Ingestre Ho WV6 .....255 C3
Ingestre Rd
  Stafford ST17 .....155 C1
  Wolv WV10 .....240 B1
Ingestre Sq ST3 .....74 B3
Ingewood Ave WV3 .....265 C4
Ingleborough Pl ST2 .....43 B1
Ingleby Gdns WV6 .....255 C3
Ingleby Rd ST3 .....283 A1
Inglefield Ave ST6 .....42 A1
Inglemere Dr ST17 .....175 B3
Ingleside WS15 .....178 B1
Inglenook Gr ST3 .....90 A4
Inglewood ST17 .....155 B3
Inglewood Cl DY6 .....265 B3
Inglewood Dr ST5 .....56 B3
Inglewood Gr
  Aldridge B74 .....256 C1
  Newcastle-u-L ST5 .....56 B3
Inglis St ST4 .....72 B4
Ingram Pit La ST4 .....251 A3
Ingram Pl WS3 .....243 B1
Ingram Rd WS3 .....243 B1
Inhedge St DY3 .....271 C3
Intake La ST20 .....190 A4
Intake Rd ST6 .....42 B2
Intakes La ST10 .....108 C2
Inworth WV9 .....240 A2
Iona Pl ST3 .....72 C2
Irene Ave Cheli Heath ST6 .....41 C2

Irene Ave continued
  Newcastle-u-L ST5 .....56 B1
Ireton Rd WV10 .....240 C2
Iris Cl Meir ST3 .....74 B3
  Tamworth B79 .....250 B3
Irnham Rd B74 .....258 A1
Ironbridge Dr ST5 .....55 C1
Ironmarket ST5 .....284 B3
Ironstone La WS13 .....215 C3
Ironstone Rd WS12 .....211 B2
Ironwalls La ST10 .....146 B3
Irvine Rd ST9 .....59 B2
Irving Cl Lichfield WS13 .....213 C1
  Sedgley DY3 .....271 A2
Irwell B77 .....250 C1
Isabel Cl ST17 .....175 A3
Isherwood Pl ST13 .....283 D4
Island Gn ST17 .....174 B3
Island The Oakamoor ST10 .....78 A3
  Tamworth B78 .....249 B1
  Upper Tean ST10 .....92 B2
Islay Wlk B35 .....184 B1
Islington Cl TF10 .....168 C2
Islington Cres CV9 .....262 B1
Ismere Way WS14 .....280 A1
Itchen Gr WV6 .....254 C2
Ivanhoe Rd WS14 .....214 B1
Ivatt B77 .....250 C1
Iverley La DY10 .....276 C3
Ivetsey Bank Rd ST19 .....221 C4
Ivetsey Cl ST19 .....221 C4
Ivetsey Rd ST19 .....221 C4
Ivy Cl Acton Trussell ST17 .....175 A1
  Cannock WS11 .....226 B4
  Forsbrook ST11 .....90 C3
  Uttoxeter ST14 .....126 A4
Ivy Cotts ST13 .....20 A3
Ivy Croft WV9 .....239 C2
Ivy Ct Acton Trussell ST17 .....175 A1
  Egginton DE65 .....148 A3
  Hixon ST18 .....158 A4
Ivy Gdns WS11 .....228 A3
Ivy Gr ST Brownhills WS8 .....245 A2
  Burton u T DE13 .....166 B4
  Trentham ST4 .....87 C4
Ivy House La ST19 .....206 C1
Ivy House Rd Biddulph ST8 .....16 B1
  Hanley ST1 .....57 C2
Ivy La WS15 .....211 C3
Ivy Lodge Cl DE15 .....185 C4
Ivyhouse Dr ST12 .....58 B1
Ivyhouse Wlk B77 .....261 C3
Izaak Walton Ave CW3 .....68 C3
Izaak Walton Cl ST16 .....155 B3
Izaak Walton St ST16 .....155 B3
Izaak Walton's Cottage &
  Mus* ST15 .....135 A4

J

Jack Ashley Ct ST4 .....72 B3
Jack Haye La Bagnall ST2 .....58 C4
  Norton-in-H M ST2 .....43 B1
Jack La CW2 .....37 B3
Jack's La ST14 .....127 C1
Jackdaw Cl DY3 .....266 B1
Jackfield Inf Sch ST4 .....42 A1
Jackfield St ST6 .....42 A1
Jacklin Cl DE14 .....185 A3
Jackman Cl WS13 .....215 B3
Jackman Rd WS13 .....215 B3
Jackson Ave DE13 .....166 C4
Jackson Cl
  Featherstone WV10 .....241 A3
  Norton Canes WS11 .....227 C2
Jackson Rd WS13 .....214 A2
Jackson St ST6 .....57 A4
Jacob's Hall La WS6 .....227 A1
Jacobean Ct DE15 .....167 B2
Jacobs Croft ST16 .....155 B4
Jacqueline St ST6 .....41 B2
Jade Ct ST3 .....73 B2
Jade Gr WS11 .....210 B1
Jaguar B77 .....250 C1
Jamage Rd ST7 .....40 B3
James Beattie Ho WV6 .....255 B2
James Brindley Cl ST17 .....57 B3
James Brindley High Sch ST6 .....41 C3
James Brindley Way
  DE13 .....166 C4
James Cres ST3 .....74 A2
James Ct DE14 .....166 B1
James Greenway WS13 .....214 A1
James Hutchens Ct
  WS7 .....228 C3
James St Burton u T DE14 .....166 B1
  Cannock WS11 .....209 C3
  Kinver DY7 .....278 A2
  Leek ST13 .....30 B3
  Newcastle-u-L ST5 .....55 B3
  Stoke-on-T ST4 .....283 D1
  Uttoxeter ST14 .....126 A4
James Warner CE WS15 .....178 B1
James Way ST18 .....27 A3
Janet Pl ST1 .....57 C3
Janson St ST4 .....72 B4
Jardines La ST14 .....95 B2
Jasmine Way ST7 .....26 C1
Jasmine Cl
  Burton u T DE15 .....186 A4
  Wolv WV9 .....240 A2
Jasmine Cl ST11 .....90 C3
Jasmine Gr WV8 .....239 A2
Jasmine Rd
  Seighford ST18 .....135 B1
  Tamworth B77 .....251 A2

Jason Cl B77 .....250 B3
Jason St ST5 .....284 A4
Jasper Cl Barlaston ST12 .....88 C2
  Newcastle-u-L ST5 .....56 A4
Jasper St ST1 .....282 B2
Java Cres ST4 .....88 A4
Jay Rd DY6 .....275 B4
Jaycean Ave ST5 .....41 C2
Jean Cl ST6 .....42 A1
Jedburgh Ave WV6 .....256 C2
Jeddo St WV2 .....266 B4
Jeffcock Rd WV3 .....266 A4
Jefferson St ST6 .....41 B2
Jeffrey Ave WV4 .....266 C3
Jeffrey Cl WS15 .....178 B2
Jeffs Ave WV2 .....266 B4
Jenkins St B11 ST6 .....56 C4
Jenkinson Cl ST5 .....70 C4
Jenkinstown Rd WS12 .....211 A4
Jenks Ave DY7 .....277 C3
Jenks Rd WV5 .....269 C3
Jennings Way DE14 .....166 A2
Jenny Walkers La WV6 .....254 B1
Jensen B77 .....250 C1
Jephson Rd DE14 .....185 A4
Jerbourg Cl ST5 .....70 C4
Jeremy Cl ST4 .....71 C3
Jeremy Rd WV4 .....266 B3
Jerningham St ST16 .....155 B2
Jerome Ct B74 .....256 C1
Jerome Dr WS11 .....228 A3
Jerome Prim Sch WS11 .....227 C3
Jerome Rd WS11 .....228 A3
Jerome Way WS7 .....229 B4
Jerry's La WS14 .....248 A4
Jersey Cl Congleton CW12 .....6 A1
  Newcastle-u-L ST5 .....70 C4
Jersey Cres ST3 .....73 B1
Jervis Cres B74 .....257 B2
Jervis La ST15 .....104 B2
Jervis Rd Stone ST15 .....120 A4
  Tamworth B77 .....261 A3
Jervis St ST1 .....282 C4
Jervison St ST3 .....73 B3
Jesmond Dr WS12 .....211 A3
Jesmond Gr ST3 .....88 C4
Jessie Rd WS9 .....245 A1
Jessop Dr B77 .....250 C3
Jew's La DY3 .....271 C2
Jinny Cl DE65 .....146 B4
Joan Eaton's Cross
  ST20 .....189 C4
John Amery Dr WV2 .....266 C3
Joanhurst Cres ST1 .....282 A1
Jockey Field DY3 .....271 C3
Jodrell View ST7 .....41 A4
Joeys La WV8 .....239 B2
John Bamford Prim Sch
  WS15 .....178 B2
John Baskeyfield CE Prim Sch
  ST6 .....56 C4
John Bright St ST1 .....282 C4
John Donne St ST6 .....155 B3
John O' Gaunt's Rd ST15 .....104 C3
John of Rolleston Prim Sch
  DE13 .....147 B2
John Offley Rd CW3 .....68 B3
John Pershall Ct ST21 .....133 B4
John Rhodes Way ST6 .....41 B3
John St Biddulph ST8 .....27 B4
  Brierley Hill DY8 .....275 C1
  Cannock, High Town
    WS11 .....210 A2
  Cannock, Wimblebury
    WS12 .....211 A4
  Hanley ST1 .....282 B2
  Leek ST13 .....30 C3
  Newcastle-u-L ST5 .....284 D3
  Newcastle-u-L, Knutton ST5 .....56 B3
  Stafford ST16 .....156 A2
  Swadlincote DE11 .....186 C3
  Tamworth B77 .....250 C2
  Uttoxeter ST14 .....126 A4
John Taylor High Sch
  DE13 .....183 C1
John Till Cl WS15 .....178 B2
John Wheeldon Prim Sch
  ST16 .....155 C3
John Wood CE Inf Sch
  WS11 .....226 C4
Johndory B77 .....261 B3
Johns Ave WS15 .....198 B3
Johns La WS5 .....227 A2
Johnsgate ST19 .....223 B4
Johnson Ave ST5 .....56 A2
Johnson Cl Congleton CW12 .....6 A1
  Lichfield WS13 .....214 B1
  Rugeley WS15 .....197 C4
Johnson Cres ST10 .....61 B1
Johnson Dr ST15 .....120 B4
Johnson Rd ST16 .....42 A3
Johnson Rd
  Burntwood WS7 .....228 C4
  Cannock WS11 .....209 B2
  Uttoxeter ST14 .....111 A1
Johnson St
  Newcastle-u-L ST5 .....55 B4
  Wolv, Blakenhall WV2 .....266 C4
  Wolv, Cinder Hill WV14 .....266 C1
  Wood End CV9 .....262 B2
Johnstone Ave ST19 .....59 B2
Joiner's Square Ind Est
  ST1 .....282 C1
Joiner's Square Prim Sch
  ST1 .....282 C1

K

Kara Pl ST4 .....88 A4
Kay Dr DE11 .....186 C3
Kaydor Cl ST9 .....59 A2
Kayne Cl DY6 .....275 B4
Kean Cl WS13 .....213 C1
Kearsley Way ST3 .....88 C4
Kearyn St ST14 .....72 A3
Keates St 7 ST6 .....56 C4
Keating Gdns B75 .....258 A2
Keats Ave Cannock WS11 .....209 C3
  Stafford ST17 .....174 B4
Keats Cl Sedgley DY3 .....271 A3
  Sutton Coldfield B74 .....257 C3
  Tamworth B79 .....249 C4
Keats Gdns ST7 .....41 A4
Keats Rd WV10 .....265 B2
Keble Cl Burntwood WS7 .....229 B4
  Burton u T DE15 .....167 B1
  Cannock WS11 .....226 C4
Keble Way ST3 .....73 A1
Keble Wlk B79 .....250 A3
Kedleston Cl
  Burton u T DE13 .....147 B1
  Walsall WS3 .....243 A2
Kedleston Rd ST6 .....42 A1
Keele Rd ST5 .....70 B4
Keele Service Area ST5 .....69 C2
Keele St ST6 .....41 B2
Keele Univ ST5 .....70 A4
Keeling Dr WS11 .....209 A1
Keeling Rd ST10 .....76 C2
Keeling St ST5 .....56 B3
Keelings Dr ST4 .....71 C3
Keelings Rd ST1 .....57 C3
Keene Cl ST6 .....42 A2
Keep The ST17 .....174 B4
Keeper's Cl WS7 .....229 A3
Keepers Cl Brownhills WS9 .....244 C2
  Kingswinford DY6 .....275 A4
  Lichfield WS14 .....231 C4
Keepers La Codsall WV8 .....239 A1
  Wolv WV6 .....255 A4
Keepers Rd B74 .....257 B3
Keir Pl DY8 .....279 C4

Keld Ave ST17 . . . . .174 A4
Keldy Cl WV6 . . . . .255 C3
Kelham Rd ST4 . . . . .73 A3
Kelly Ave WS15 . . . . .196 C3
Kelly Gn ST6 . . . . .42 A3
Kelmore Cl ST3 . . . . .283 B4
Kelsall St ST6 . . . . .42 A1
Kelsall Way ST7 . . . . .39 B1
Kelso Gdns WV6 . . . . .254 B2
Kelvedon Way WS15 . . . . . .178 B1
Kelvestone Ho WS11 . . . . . .209 B1
Kelvin Ave ST1 . . . . .57 B4
Kelvin St ST11 . . . . .210 A2
Kelvin St ST5 . . . . .56 B2
Kemball Ave ST4 . . . . .72 B2
Kemball Specl Sch ST4 . . . .72 C3
Kemberton Cl WV3 . . . . . . .255 B3
Kemberton Rd WV3 . . . . . .255 B1
Kemnay Ave ST6 . . . . .42 A4
Kempson Rd ST19 . . . . . . .192 C1
Kempthorne Ave WV10 . . .240 C1
Kempthorne Gdns WV3 . . .243 A1
Kempthorne Rd ST1 . . . . . .282 C1
Kempton Cl WS12 . . . . .211 A3
Kempton Dr
  Great Wyrley WS6 . . . . .226 C1
  Tamworth B77 . . . . .261 B2
Kempton Gr ST10 . . . . .76 C3
Kempton Rd DE15 . . . . .167 A2
Kempton Way DY8 . . . . . . .279 C2
Kendal Cl Stafford ST17 . . .174 A4
  Wolv WV6 . . . . .255 C3
Kendal Ct
  Brownhills WS9 . . . . .244 C2
  Cannock WS11 . . . . .226 A4
Kendal Gr ST2 . . . . .58 B1
Kendal Pl ST5 . . . . .71 A3
Kendal Rise WV6 . . . . .255 C3
Kendall Rise WV6 . . . . .275 C3
Kenderdine Cl ST17 . . . . . .193 C4
Kendlewood Rd DY10 . . . . .280 A1
Kendrick St ST3 . . . . .283 D3
Kenelyn Cres ST3 . . . . .72 C2
Kenilworth Ave DE13 . . . . .166 B4
Kenilworth Cl
  Kingswinford DY8 . . . . .275 B1
  Market Drayton TF9 . . . . . . .97 C1
  Penkridge ST19 . . . . .208 A4
Kenilworth Cres WV4 . . . .266 C2
Kenilworth Ct ▆ WS11 . . . .209 C1
Kenilworth Dr WS11 . . . . . .209 B2
Kenilworth Gr
  ▆ Meir ST3 . . . . .73 C1
  Newcastle-u-L ST5 . . . . .56 C2
Kenilworth Rd
  Perton WV6 . . . . .254 C2
  Tamworth B77 . . . . .250 C2
Kenilworth Wlk ST10 . . . . . .76 A1
Kenley Ave ST9 . . . . .43 C4
Kenmoor Ave WS12 . . . . . .209 C4
Kennedy Cl B77 . . . . .250 B1
Kennedy Cres DY3 . . . . . . .271 B2
Kennedy Ct DY8 . . . . .279 C3
Kennedy Rd ST4 . . . . .88 A4
Kennedy Way ST16 . . . . . . .155 A4
Kennedy Wlk ST9 . . . . .59 A2
Kennermont Rd ST2 . . . . . . .58 B3
Kennet B77 . . . . .250 B1
Kennet Cl
  Brownhills WS8 . . . . .228 B1
  Newcastle-u-L ST5 . . . . .71 A2
Kenrick Cl CW3 . . . . .67 B1
Kensington Cl ST15 . . . . . .120 B3
Kensington Ct
  Stoke-on-T ST4 . . . . .71 C2
  Tunstall ST6 . . . . .41 C2
Kensington Dr
  Sutton Coldfield B74 . . . . .257 C3
  Tamworth B79 . . . . .250 A4
Kensington Gdns DY8 . . . . .275 B1
Kensington Pl WS12 . . . . . .227 B4
Kensington Rd
  Burton u T DE15 . . . . .167 A2
  Stoke-on-T ST5 . . . . .71 A2
Kent Ave B78 . . . . .249 C1
Kent Cl WS9 . . . . .245 A1
Kent Dr ST9 . . . . .43 C3
Kent Gr Newcastle-u-L ST5 .55 C4
  Stone ST15 . . . . .104 C1
Kent Ho ST7 . . . . .40 B3
Kent Pl Cannock WS12 . . . .210 C1
  Fenton ST4 . . . . .72 C3
Kent Rd Burton u T DE15 . .185 C3
  Stafford ST17 . . . . .175 A4
  Stourbridge DY8 . . . . .279 B4
  Wolv WV2 . . . . .266 C4
Kent St DY3 . . . . .271 C3
Kentish Cl ST17 . . . . .174 A4
Kentmere Cl Longton ST4 . . .73 A3
  Penkridge ST19 . . . . .193 A1
  Stafford ST17 . . . . .174 A4
Kentmere Pl ST5 . . . . .71 A4
Kenton Ave WV6 . . . . .255 C2
Kents Row ST12 . . . . .88 C1
Kentwell B79 . . . . .249 B4
Kenworthy Rd ST16 . . . . . .155 C3
Kenworthy St ST6 . . . . .41 C2
Kepler B79 . . . . .249 C4
Kerria Ctr B77 . . . . .251 A2
Kerria Rd B77 . . . . .251 A2
Kerridge Cl WV9 . . . . .240 A1
Kerry La ST21 . . . . .133 B3
Kersbrook Cl ST4 . . . . .88 B3
Kervis Gr ST3 . . . . .90 A3

Kesterton Rd B74 . . . . .257 C3
Kesteven Wlk ST2 . . . . .58 A2
Kestrel B77 . . . . .262 A3
Kestrel Ave ST3 . . . . .90 B4
Kestrel Cl Biddulph ST8 . . . .27 A3
  Newport TF10 . . . . .169 A3
  Stafford ST17 . . . . .156 B1
  Uttoxeter ST14 . . . . .126 A3
  Whittington WS14 . . . . .232 C3
Kestrel Dr TF9 . . . . .99 B2
Kestrel Gr WS12 . . . . .210 B1
Kestrel La ST10 . . . . .76 C2
Kestrel Rd B74 . . . . .257 C3
Kestrel Rise WV6 . . . . .255 C4
Kestrel Way
  Burton u T DE15 . . . . .167 B2
  Cheslyn Hay WS6 . . . . .226 B1
Keswick Dr DY6 . . . . .275 B3
Keswick Gr Aldridge B74 . .256 C1
  Stafford ST17 . . . . .174 A4
Keswick Pl ST5 . . . . .71 A3
Ketley Rd DY6 . . . . .275 C4
Kettering Dr ST2 . . . . .57 C1
Kettlebank Rd DY3 . . . . . . .271 A1
Kettlebrook Rd B77 . . . . . . .250 B2
Ketton Cl ST6 . . . . .42 A4
Kewstoke Cl WV12 . . . . . . .242 B1
Kewstoke Rd WV12 . . . . . .242 B1
Key Cl WS12 . . . . .210 B2
Keyes Dr DY6 . . . . .270 B1
Keynsham Wlk ST6 . . . . . . .42 B1
Keyspark Rd WS12 . . . . . . .210 C2
Keystone La WS15 . . . . . . .196 C4
Keystone Mews ▆
  WS15 . . . . .196 C4
Keystone Rd WS15 . . . . . . .196 C4
Keyworth Wlk ST2 . . . . .58 A1
Kibblestone Rd ST15 . . . . .105 B2
Kibworth Gr ST1 . . . . .282 B4
Kidbrooke Pl ST4 . . . . .88 B4
Kiddemore Green Rd
  ST19 . . . . .222 B3
Kidderminster Rd
  Kingswinford DY6 . . . . .275 A4
  Kinver DY7,DY10 . . . . .281 B4
Kidderminster Rd S
  DY9 . . . . .281 C2
Kidsgrove Bank ST7 . . . . . . .41 A4
Kidsgrove Rd ST6 . . . . .41 B4
Kidsgrove Sta ST7 . . . . .25 C1
Kielder Cl WS12 . . . . .210 C1
Kilburn Dr DY6 . . . . .270 C1
Kilburn Pl ST2 . . . . .42 C1
Kilburn Way DE11 . . . . .186 C3
Kilbye Cl B77 . . . . .261 C3
Kildare St ST3 . . . . .283 C2
Kilmorie Rd WS11 . . . . .209 B1
Kiln Croft ST10 . . . . .92 B2
Kiln La ST13 . . . . .30 B3
Kiln Way B78 . . . . .251 C1
Kilnbank Cres TF9 . . . . . . .112 B4
Kilnbank Rd TF9 . . . . .112 B4
Kilndown Cl ST1 . . . . .57 A2
Kilsby Gr ST2 . . . . .43 A1
Kimberlee Ave DY10 . . . . . .280 A2
Kimberley Cl B77 . . . . .261 C4
Kimberley Ct B74 . . . . .257 A1
Kimberley Dr
  Burton u T DE15 . . . . .167 B2
  Uttoxeter ST14 . . . . .110 C1
Kimberley Grange ST5 . . . .284 B4
Kimberley Rd Hanley ST1 . . .57 A2
  Newcastle-u-L ST5 . . . . . . .284 B4
Kimberley St
  Longton ST3 . . . . .283 B2
  Wolv WV3 . . . . .266 A4
Kimberley Way
  Rugeley WS15 . . . . .196 C3
  Stafford ST17 . . . . .174 A4
Kinder Pl ST5 . . . . .55 A1
Kineton Rise DY3 . . . . .266 B1
Kinfare Dr WV6 . . . . .255 A2
Kinfare Rise DY3 . . . . .271 C2
King Charles Cl ST3 . . . . . . .90 A4
King Edward Pl DE14 . . . . .166 A2
King Edward St ST10 . . . . . .76 C2
King Edward VI High Sch
  ST17 . . . . .155 B1
King Edward VI Sch
  WS14 . . . . .231 B3
King Edward's Row ▇
  WV2 . . . . .266 B4
King George St ST1 . . . . . . .282 C4
King St Audley ST7 . . . . .39 B1
  Biddulph ST8 . . . . .27 B4
  Blymhill TF10,TF11 . . . . . . .189 A1
  Brownhills WS9 . . . . .244 C1
  Burntwood WS7 . . . . .228 C3
  Burton u T DE14 . . . . .166 B1
  Fenton ST4 . . . . .72 C3
  Kidsgrove ST7 . . . . .26 A1
  Leek ST13 . . . . .30 C3
  Longton ST3,ST4 . . . . .283 B4
  Newcastle-u-L ST5 . . . . . . .284 C3
  Newcastle-u-L, Chesterton
   ST5 . . . . .55 C4
  Newcastle-u-L, Cross Heath
   ST5 . . . . .56 A2
  Rugeley WS15 . . . . .196 C4
  Stone ST15 . . . . .104 C3
  Talke ST7 . . . . .40 B3
  Tamworth B79 . . . . .250 A3
  Yoxall DE13 . . . . .182 A2
King William St
  Stoke-on-T ST4 . . . . .279 C4
  Tunstall ST6 . . . . .41 C2
King's Ave
  Newcastle-u-L ST5 . . . . . . .56 B3

King's Ave continued
  Stone ST15 . . . . .105 A1
King's Bromley La
  WS15 . . . . .198 B3
King's CE Sch The
  WV6 . . . . .255 A3
King's Croft ST14 . . . . .56 B1
King's Hill Rd WS14 . . . . . .231 B3
King's La B79 . . . . .236 B3
Kingcross St ST3 . . . . .283 C3
Kingcup Rd ST17 . . . . .174 C3
Kingfisher B77 . . . . .262 A3
Kingfisher Cl
  Madeley CW3 . . . . .68 C4
  Newport TF10 . . . . .168 C3
Kingfisher Dr Sedgley DY3 .266 B1
Kingfisher Cres
  Blythe Bridge ST11 . . . . . .106 C4
  Cheadle ST10 . . . . .76 C2
Kingfisher Dr
  Newcastle-u-L ST5 . . . . . .210 B3
  Colwich ST18 . . . . .177 C4
  Stourbridge DY8 . . . . .279 B2
Kingfisher Gr ST6 . . . . .42 B2
Kingfisher War ST14 . . . . . .126 A3
Kingfisher Wlk ST19 . . . . . .207 C4
Kingham Ct DY3 . . . . .271 B3
Kings Ave Cannock WS12 . .210 B2
  Market Drayton TF9 . . . . . .112 A4
Kings Bridge WV9 . . . . .224 A2
Kings Bromley Rd DE13 . . .200 C1
Kings Croft WS12 . . . . .210 C2
Kings Ct Stourbridge DY8 . .279 C3
  Sutton Coldfield B75 . . . . .258 A2
Kings Pl ST4 . . . . .56 B1
Kings Rd Hopton ST18 . . . .156 B4
  Sedgley DY3 . . . . .271 C4
  Shareshill WV10 . . . . .225 A3
  Trentham ST4 . . . . .72 A2
Kings Terr ST4 . . . . .56 B1
Kings Wlk DE13 . . . . .199 A3
Kingsbridge Ave ST5 . . . . . .71 A3
Kingsbury Cl DE15 . . . . . . .167 A2
Kingsbury Gr ST1 . . . . .57 C3
Kingsclere Gr ST1 . . . . .57 C4
Kingsclere Wlk WV4 . . . . . .265 B3
Kingscroft ST18 . . . . .158 B1
Kingsdale Cl ST3 . . . . .90 A4
Kingsdale Croft DE13 . . . . .166 B4
Kingsdene Ave DY6 . . . . . . .275 B2
Kingsdown Mews ST5 . . . . .71 B2
Kingsdown Rd WS7 . . . . . .211 C1
Kingsfield La ST4 . . . . .71 C3
Kingsfield Fst Sch ST8 . . . . .27 B4
Kingsfield Oval ST4 . . . . . . .56 B1
Kingsfield Rd
  Biddulph ST8 . . . . .27 B4
  Stoke-on-T ST4 . . . . .56 B1
Kingsford Ctry Pk*
  DY11 . . . . .277 B1
Kingsford La DY7,DY11 . . . .277 B1
Kingsford Pl ▇ ST3 . . . . . . .90 A4
Kingshayes Rd WS9 . . . . . .245 A1
Kingside Gr ST4 . . . . .88 B3
Kingsland Ave ST4 . . . . .71 C3
Kingsland Cl ST15 . . . . . . .120 B4
Kingsland Ct ST15 . . . . . . .120 B4
Kingsland Rd ST15 . . . . . . .120 B4
Kingsleigh Croft B75 . . . . .258 A1
Kingsley Ave
  Cannock WS12 . . . . .210 B4
  Wolv WV6 . . . . .255 A2
Kingsley Cl Stafford ST17 . .174 C4
  Talke ST7 . . . . .40 B3
  Tamworth B79 . . . . .250 A3
Kingsley Gdns WV8 . . . . . .238 C2
Kingsley Gr DY3 . . . . .271 A3
Kingsley Rd
  Burton u T DE14 . . . . .166 B3
  Cheddleton ST9,ST10 . . . . .60 A2
  Congleton CW12 . . . . .6 A2
  Kingswinford DY6 . . . . .275 A3
  Stafford ST17 . . . . .174 C4
  Talke ST7 . . . . .40 B3
Kingsley St ST13 . . . . .74 A1
Kingsley View ST13 . . . . . . .45 B3
Kingsley Wood Rd
  WS15 . . . . .195 B4
Kingslow Ave WV4 . . . . . . .265 B3
Kingsmead DE13 . . . . .166 C4
Kingsmead High Sch
  WS12 . . . . .210 B2
Kingsmead Hospl ST16 . . .155 C2
Kingsmead Rd ST11 . . . . . .89 C4
Kingsnorth Pl ST13 . . . . . . .30 A3
Kingston Ave Hanley ST1 . . .57 C4
  Stafford ST16 . . . . .156 A2
Kingston Dr B79 . . . . .250 B4
Kingston Dr ST15 . . . . .120 A3
Kingston Hill Ct ST16 . . . . .156 B2
Kingston Pl Biddulph ST8 . . .11 C2
  Norton-in-t-M ST6 . . . . .42 C2
Kingston Rd DE15 . . . . .167 B1
Kingston Row ST16 . . . . . . .156 A2
Kingston Row DY6 . . . . . . .275 B4
Kingsway
  Burton u T DE14 . . . . .185 A4
  Cannock WS11 . . . . .210 A2
  Essington WV11 . . . . .242 A2
  Stafford ST16 . . . . .156 A3
  Stoke-on-T ST4 . . . . .72 A4
  Stourbridge DY8 . . . . .279 B4
Kingsway E ST5 . . . . .71 A3
Kingsway W ST5 . . . . .71 A3
Kingswear Ave WV6 . . . . . .254 C2
Kingswell Rd ST4 . . . . .56 B1
Kingswinford Pl ST4 . . . . . . .57 B4

Kingswinford Sch The
  DY6 . . . . .275 B3
Kingswood ST7 . . . . .26 A1
Kingswood Ave
  Cannock WS11 . . . . .226 B4
  Chorlton CW2 . . . . .37 A2
Kingswood Bsns Pk
  WV7 . . . . .237 C1
Kingswood Ctr WV7 . . . . . .237 C1
Kingswood Dr
  Great Wyrley WS6 . . . . .227 A2
  Norton Canes WS11 . . . . . .227 A3
Kingswood Gdns WV4 . . . .265 C3
Kingswood Mobil Homes
  WV7 . . . . .237 C1
Kingswood Rd
  Albrighton WV7 . . . . .237 B2
  Kingswinford DY6 . . . . .275 B2
Kinlet Cl WV3 . . . . .265 A4
Kinloch Dr DY1 . . . . .271 C2
Kinnersley Ave ST7 . . . . . . .40 C4
Kinnersley St ▆ ST3 . . . . . .283 D3
Kinross Ave WS12 . . . . . . .209 C4
Kinsall Gn B77 . . . . .262 B3
Kinsey St ST5 . . . . .55 A1
Kinver Cl DE6 . . . . .81 B4
Kinver Cres WS9 . . . . .245 B1
Kinver Dr WV4 . . . . .265 B3
Kinver Edge* DY7 . . . . .277 C2
Kinver La DY11 . . . . .280 A4
Kinver Rd
  Burton u T DE15 . . . . .167 A2
  Kinver DY7 . . . . .277 C4
Kinver St Chell Heath ST6 . .42 B1
  Kingswinford DY8 . . . . .275 C1
Kiplass La ST18 . . . . .121 B2
Kipling Ave WS7 . . . . .212 A1
Kipling Rd Sedgley DY3 . . .271 A3
  Wolv WV10 . . . . .240 B1
Kipling Rise B79 . . . . .249 C4
Kipling Way ST2 . . . . .58 B1
Kirby Dr DY1 . . . . .271 C2
Kirby St ST6 . . . . .42 B1
Kirk St ST6 . . . . .42 B1
Kirkbride Cl ST3 . . . . .73 B2
Kirkham St ST14 . . . . .72 A3
Kirkland La ST4 . . . . .72 A3
Kirkland Way B78 . . . . .260 A4
Kirkside Gr WS8 . . . . .244 C4
Kirkstall Ave ST17 . . . . .174 A4
Kirkstall Cl WS3 . . . . .242 C1
Kirkstall Cres WS3 . . . . . . .242 C1
Kirkstone Cres WV5 . . . . . .269 C3
Kirkup Wlk ST3 . . . . .283 A3
Kirkwall Gr ST2 . . . . .43 A1
Kirstead Gdns WV6 . . . . . .255 A2
Kirtley B77 . . . . .250 C1
Kirton Gr WV6 . . . . .255 B2
Kitchen La WV11 . . . . .241 C1
Kite Gr Kidsgrove ST7 . . . . .26 B2
  Meir ST3 . . . . .90 A3
Kitling Greaves La
  DE13 . . . . .166 A4
Kitlings La ST17 . . . . .175 C4
Kittoe Rd B74 . . . . .258 A2
Kitwood Ave B78 . . . . .262 C3
Knarsdale Cl ▆ ST3 . . . . . . .73 B3
Knaves Castle Ave WS8 . . .228 C1
Knebworth Ct CW2 . . . . .16 A4
Knenhall ST15 . . . . .105 C4
Knenhall La ST15 . . . . .89 C1
Knight Ave ST16 . . . . .156 A2
Knight La ST10 . . . . .78 A2
Knight Rd WS7 . . . . .211 C1
Knight St ST16 . . . . .41 B2
Knightley Ct ST20 . . . . .171 B3
Knightley Way ST20 . . . . . .171 B4
Knighton Cl B74 . . . . .257 C2
Knighton Dr B74 . . . . .257 C2
Knighton Rd
  Cannock WS12 . . . . .210 C2
  Sutton Coldfield B74 . . . . .257 B2
Knights Ave WV6 . . . . .255 C3
Knights Cl ST19 . . . . .207 C4
Knights Cres WV6 . . . . .255 C4
Knights Croft ST5 . . . . .69 C4
Knights Ct
  ▆ Burton u T DE13 . . . . . .147 C1
  Norton Canes WS11 . . . . . .228 A2
Knights Hill WS9 . . . . .256 A2
Knightsbridge Cl B74 . . . . .257 C2
Knightsbridge Way
  Burton u T DE13 . . . . .166 B4
  ▆ Tunstall ST6 . . . . .41 B2
Knightsfield Rd DE13 . . . . .144 C1
Kniveden La ST13 . . . . .31 A3
Knoll Cl WS7 . . . . .229 A1
Knoll Croft WS9 . . . . .245 B1
Knoll The DY6 . . . . .275 C3
Knotty La CW12 . . . . .6 A1
Knowlbank Rd ST7 . . . . .53 C4
Knowle La WS14 . . . . .231 A1
Knowle Rd Biddulph ST8 . . .27 B4
  Stafford ST17 . . . . .175 B4
Knowle St ST4 . . . . .72 A4
Knowle Wood View ST3 . . . .72 C2
Knowles Hill DE13 . . . . . . .147 A2
Knowsley La ST7 . . . . .25 C2
Knowsley Rd ST9 . . . . .44 B2
Knox Rd WV2 . . . . .266 B3
Knox's Grave La WS14,
  B78 . . . . .248 B4
Knutton La ST5 . . . . .55 C1
Knutton Inf Sch ST5 . . . . . . .55 C1
Knutton La ST5 . . . . .55 C1

Knutton Rd ST5 . . . . .56 B3
Knutton St Mary's CE Jun Sch
  ST5 . . . . .55 C1
Knypc Cl ST5 . . . . .56 A4
Knype Way Biddulph ST8 . . .27 A3
Newcastle-u-L ST5 . . . . .56 A4
Knypersley Fst Sch ST8 . . . .27 A3
Kohima Dr DY8 . . . . .279 C3
Kurtus B77 . . . . .261 B3
Kyffin Rd ST2 . . . . .58 A3
Kyle Cl WV10 . . . . .240 A1
Kynaston Cres WV8 . . . . . .239 A1
Kynnersley Croft ST14 . . . .111 A1

L

Laburnam Cl ST7 . . . . .40 C3
Laburnham Ct WS14 . . . . .231 B3
Laburnham Rd DY6 . . . . . . .275 C3
Laburnum Ave
  Cannock WS11 . . . . .226 C4
  Newcastle-u-L ST5 . . . . . . .250 A4
Laburnum Cl
  Cannock WS11 . . . . .226 C4
  Forsbrook ST11 . . . . .91 A3
  Kinver DY7 . . . . .277 C3
  Market Drayton TF9 . . . . . . .97 B2
  Seighford ST18 . . . . .135 A1
  Stourbridge DY8 . . . . .279 C4
  Walsall WS3 . . . . .244 A1
Laburnum Gr
  Burntwood WS7 . . . . .228 C3
  Fenton ST3 . . . . .72 C2
Laburnum Ho WS4 . . . . . . .244 B1
Laburnum Pl ▉ Meir ST3 . .89 C4
  Newcastle-u-L ST5 . . . . .40 B1
Laburnum Rd
  Brownhills WS9 . . . . .245 A2
  Burton u T DE15 . . . . .185 C3
  Swadlincote DE11 . . . . . . .186 C3
  Wolv WV4 . . . . .266 C2
Laburnum St ST3 . . . . .279 C4
Laches Cl WV10 . . . . .224 B3
Laches La WV10 . . . . .224 C1
Lad La ST5 . . . . .284 B3
Ladbrook Gr DY3 . . . . .271 A2
Ladderedge ST13 . . . . .30 B1
Ladderedge Ctry Pk*
  ST13 . . . . .30 A2
Ladford Covert Ind Pk
  ST18 . . . . .134 C1
Ladford Trad Pk ST18 . . . . .134 C1
Ladfordfields Ind Est
  ST18 . . . . .134 B1
Ladfordfields Ind Pk
  ST18 . . . . .153 C3
Ladies Wlk DY3 . . . . .271 B4
Ladle End La DE12 . . . . . . .146 B4
Lady Grey's Wlk DY8 . . . . .279 B3
Lady Hill Terr WS15 . . . . . .196 A4
Lady Meadow Cl ST14 . . . . .95 C3
Ladybank Gr ST3 . . . . .88 C4
Ladydale Cl ST13 . . . . .30 C2
Ladyfields Way DE11 . . . . .186 C3
Ladygates ST3 . . . . .53 A3
Ladymoor La ST6 . . . . .28 A2
Ladysmith Rd ST11 . . . . . . .57 A2
Ladysmith St ST3 . . . . .283 B2
Ladywell Cl
  Burton u T DE13 . . . . .147 C1
  Wombourne WV5 . . . . .270 A4
Ladywell Rd ST6 . . . . .41 B2
Ladywood Rd B74 . . . . .258 A1
Lagonda B77 . . . . .250 C2
Lagonda Cl ST8 . . . . .27 A3
Lagrange B79 . . . . .249 C3
Lair The B79 . . . . .262 C4
Lake Rd ST13 . . . . .18 B1
Lake St DY3 . . . . .271 B2
Lakeland Dr B77 . . . . .262 A4
Lakenheath B79 . . . . .250 B4
Lakeside Bellevy CW3 . . . . .53 A3
  Bosley SK11 . . . . .7 B4
  Little Aston B74 . . . . .257 B3
Lakeside Cl ST5 . . . . .85 B2
Lakeside Dr WS11 . . . . . . .228 A3
Lakeside Pk B74 . . . . .257 B3
Lakeside Prim Sch B77 . . . .250 C1
Lakeside View WS15 . . . . .198 A2
Lakewood Dr ST12 . . . . .88 C2
Lakewood Gr ST1 . . . . .57 A2
Lally Pl ST18 . . . . .27 A1
Lamb Cres WV5 . . . . .269 C3
Lamb La ST5 . . . . .119 C4
Lamb St Hanley ST1 . . . . . .282 B3
Kidsgrove ST7 . . . . .26 A1
Lambert Ct DY6 . . . . .275 B4
Lambert Dr WS7 . . . . .229 A4
Lambert Rd ST14 . . . . .110 C1
Lambert St ST4 . . . . .41 C2
Lambert's La CW12 . . . . .11 C4
Lambourn Cl WS3 . . . . .243 B1
Lambourn Pl ST3 . . . . .88 C4
Lambourne Cl
  Great Wyrley WS6 . . . . .226 C2
  Lichfield WS14 . . . . .231 C4
Lambourne Dr ST2 . . . . .43 B1
Lambourne Way WS11 . . . .228 A3
Lamerton Gr ST3 . . . . .73 C1
Lammas Rd DY8 . . . . .275 B3
Lammascote Rd ST16 . . . .155 C2
Lamorna Cl WV3 . . . . .265 A4
Lamotte Cl ST14 . . . . .73 A3
Lamprey B77 . . . . .261 B3
Lanark Wlks B77 . . . . .70 C4
Lancaster Ave
  Aldridge WS9 . . . . .256 A4

Lancaster Ave continued
Blythe Bridge ST11 .... 90 C1
Leek ST13 .... 30 C4
Newcastle-u-L ST5 .... 284 D2
Lancaster Cres ST4 .... 71 B4
Lancaster Dr
Norton-in-I-M ST6 .... 42 C2
Tutbury DE13 .... 146 A3
Lancaster Gdns WV4 ..... 265 C1
Lancaster Ho
6 Brierley Hill DY8 ...... 279 C4
Cannock WS12 .... 210 B1
Lancaster Pl WS3 .... 243 B1
Lancaster Rd
Alrewas WS13 .... 215 B3
Newcastle-u-L ST5 .... 284 D2
Stafford ST17 .... 175 A4
Lance Dr WS7 .... 211 C1
Lancelot Dr DE13 .... 147 C1
Lanchester Cl
Biddulph ST8 .... 27 A3
Tamworth B79 .... 249 C4
Lancia Cl ST17 .... 27 A3
Lancing Ave ST17 .... 175 A4
Lander Cl ST15 .... 120 B4
Lander Pl ST6 .... 42 A3
Landon St ST3 .... 283 C3
Landor Cres WS15 .... 196 C4
Landport Rd WV2 .... 266 C4
Landrake Gr ST7 .... 41 C4
Landsberg Dr ST7 .... 249 C3
Landseer Pl ST5 .... 56 C3
Landstone Rd 4 ST17 ... 175 A4
Landywood Ent Pk WS6 . 242 C4
Landywood Gn WS6 ...... 226 C1
Landywood La WS6 ...... 226 C1
Landywood Prim Sch
WS6 .... 242 C4
Lane End SK17 .... 23 B4
Lane Farm Gr ST1 .... 57 C4
Lane Green Ave WV8 ..... 239 B1
Lane Green Ct WV8 ...... 239 A2
Lane Green Fst Sch
WV8 .... 239 A2
Lane Green Rd WV8 ...... 239 A1
Lane Green Rd Masionettes
WV8 .... 239 A2
Lane Green Sh Par
WV8 .... 239 A2
Lane Head SK17 .... 13 A4
Lane The ST18 .... 174 A2
Lane's Cl DE11 .... 199 B3
Lanehead Rd ST1 .... 56 C2
Lanehead Wlk WS15 ..... 178 B1
Lanes Cl WV5 .... 269 C3
Langdale Cl WS8 .... 244 C3
Langdale Cres ST1 .... 57 B4
Langdale Dr B77 .... 251 A3
Langdale Dr WS11 .... 226 B4
Langdale Gn WS11 .... 226 B4
Langdale Jun & Inf Schs
ST5 .... 71 A3
Langdale Rd ST5 .... 71 A3
Langer Cl DE14 .... 185 A3
Langford Rd Bucknall ST2 . 58 B2
Newcastle-u-L ST5 .... 71 A2
Langford St ST13 .... 30 B3
Langham Gn B74 .... 256 C1
Langham Rd ST2 .... 43 A1
Langholm Dr WS12 ...... 210 C1
Langland Dr Longton ST3 . 73 A1
Sedgley DY3 .... 271 B4
Langley Cl ST5 .... 40 B1
Langley Gdns WV3 ...... 265 B4
Langley Rd
Lower Penn WV3 .... 265 A4
Wolv WV3,WV4 .... 265 A4
Langley St ST4 .... 56 B1
Langton Cl ST12 .... 115 B2
Langstone Rd DY1 .... 271 C1
Langton Cres WS14 ...... 232 C3
Langton Ct Caverswall ST9 . 92 B4
Lichfield WS13 .... 214 A1
Langtree Cl WS12 .... 210 B1
Lanrick Gdns WS15 ...... 178 C1
Lansbury Cl ST17 .... 174 C4
Lansbury Dr WS11 .... 209 C2
Lansbury Gr ST1 .... 74 A2
Lansbury Rd WS15 ...... 196 C3
Lansdell Ave ST5 .... 56 A3
Lansdowne Ave WV8 .... 238 C1
Lansdowne Cl Leek ST13 . 30 B3
Stone ST15 .... 119 C3
Lansdowne Cres
Caverswall ST9 .... 59 A2
Tamworth B77 .... 261 B4
Lansdowne Inf Sch
DE14 .... 166 B3
Lansdowne Rd
Branston DE14 .... 184 C4
Stoke-on-T ST4 .... 56 C1
Lansdowne St ST13 ...... 73 A1
Lansdowne Terr DE14 .. 166 B3
Lansdowne Way
Rugeley WS15 .... 178 B1
Stafford ST17 .... 175 B3
Lant Cl DE13 .... 199 B3
Lapley Ave ST16 .... 155 A4
Lapley Hall Mews ST19 . 206 A3
Lapley La ST19 .... 206 B2
Lapley Rd ST19 .... 205 B4
Lapper Ave WS14 ...... 266 C1
Lapwing B77 .... 262 A3
Lapwing Cl WS6 .... 226 B1
Lapwing Rd ST7 .... 26 B2
Lapworth Ave DY6 ..... 275 C3
Lapworth Way TF10 .... 169 A2

Lara Cl ST16 .... 155 A2
Larch Cl Kidsgrove ST7 . 41 A4
Kinver DY7 .... 278 B2
Lichfield WS14 .... 231 C4
Larch Ct 1 ST6 .... 57 A4
Larch Gr Fenton ST3 .... 72 C1
Sedgley DY3 .... 271 C4
Larch Pl ST5 .... 55 C4
Larch Rd
Kingswinford DY6 ...... 275 C4
Rugeley WS15 .... 196 C3
Swadlincote DE11 ..... 186 C3
Larches The TF10 ...... 168 C1
Larchfields ST15 .... 120 A3
Larchmere Dr WV11 ... 242 A2
Larchmount Cl ST4 .... 88 A4
Larchwood Keele ST5 .. 70 A3
Stafford ST17 .... 175 B3
Larchwood Dr WS11 .. 210 A2
Larcombe Dr WV4 ..... 266 B3
Lark Ave ST7 .... 26 B2
Lark Hall Inf Sch B79 . 250 A4
Lark Rise ST14 .... 126 C4
Larkfield ST7 .... 26 A1
Larkhill La TF9 .... 100 A2
Larkhill Rd DY8 .... 279 B2
Larkholme Cl WS15 .... 178 A1
Larkin Ave ST3 .... 73 B2
Larkin Cl Essington WV10 241 A1
Stafford ST17 .... 174 B4
Larks WS11 .... 243 C2
Larksfield Rd ST6 ...... 42 B1
Larksmeadow Vale
ST17 .... 175 B3
Larkspur B77 .... 261 B2
Larkspur Ave WS7 .... 229 A3
Larkspur Dr WV10 .... 241 A4
Larkspur Gr ST17 ..... 174 C4
Larkspur Way WS8 ... 244 B3
Larkstone La DE6,ST13 . 34 C1
Larkswood Dr
Sedgley DY3 .... 271 B4
Wolv WV4 .... 265 B2
Lascelles St ST6 .... 41 B1
Lask Edge Rd ST9,ST13 . 28 B4
Laski Cres ST3 .... 74 A1
Latebrook Cl ST6 ...... 41 B4
Latham Cl DE15 .... 167 B1
Latham Gr ST6 .... 42 A4
Latherford Cl WV10 ... 224 C3
Latherford La WV10 ... 225 A2
Lathkill Dale DE11 ..... 186 C1
Latimer Way ST2 ...... 58 B1
Lauder Cl DY3 .... 266 B1
Lauder Pl N ST2 ...... 73 C4
Lauder Pl S ST2 ...... 73 C4
Lauderdale Cl WS8 .... 244 C3
Lauderdale Gdns WV10 240 C2
Launceston Cl B77 ..... 250 B1
Laurel Bank B79 ...... 250 A3
Laurel Cl WS14 .... 231 B4
Laurel Cres ST9 .... 59 A2
Laurel Dr
Burntwood WS7 ...... 229 B4
Cannock WS12 .... 210 C2
Kidsgrove ST7 .... 26 C2
Newport TF10 .... 168 C2
Laurel Gr
Burton u T DE15 ..... 185 C3
Fenton ST3 .... 72 B1
Stafford ST17 .... 174 C4
Wolv WV4 .... 265 C3
Laurel Rd DY1 .... 271 C2
Laurels The ST15 .... 196 C4
Lauren Cl ST14 ..... 72 C3
Laurence Gr WV6 ... 255 C4
Lauriston Cl DY1 ... 271 C2
Lavender Ave ST11 . 90 C3
Lavender Cl
Burton u T DE14 ... 185 A4
Codsall WV9 .... 239 C2
Meir ST3 .... 74 B3
Seighford ST18 ... 135 B1
Lavender La ST14 ... 279 B2
Lavender Lodge ST17 174 C4
Lavender Rd B77 ... 250 C2
Laverock Gr CW3 ... 68 C3
Lawford Ave WS14 . 231 C4
Lawford Cotts ST17 174 C2
Lawley Cl WS4 ..... 244 C3
Lawley St ST3 ..... 73 B2
Lawn Ave DY8 ..... 279 C2
Lawn Farm Cres ST2 73 B4
Lawn La Brewood WV9 240 A4
Cheswardine TF9 ... 113 C1
Lawn Rd Stafford ST17 155 B1
Wolv WV2 .... 266 C3
Lawn St DY8 .... 279 C2
Lawn The ST17 .... 174 C3
Lawnoaks Cl WS8 . 228 B1
Lawns The
Market Drayton TF9 . 97 B1
Rolleston DE13 .... 147 A2
Uttoxeter ST14 .... 111 A1
Lawnsfield Wlk ST16 136 B4
Lawnswood DY7,DY6 275 A2
Lawnswood Ave
Burntwood WS7 ... 228 C3
Kingswinford DY8 . 275 B2
Wolv, Blakeley Green
WV6 .... 255 C4
Wolv, Parkfield WV4 266 C2
Lawnswood Cl 6 WS11 210 B1
Lawnswood Dr
Brownhills WS9 ... 245 A4
Kinver DY7 .... 275 A1
Lawnswood Rd
Kingswinford DY8 . 275 B2

Lawnswood Rd continued
Sedgley DY3 .... 271 B3
Lawnswood Rise WV6 255 C4
Lawrence Ct B79 .. 250 A3
Lawrence Dr ST15 . 103 A2
Lawrence St Hanley ST1 282 A1
Stafford ST17 ..... 155 B1
Lawson Cl WS9 ... 256 A2
Lawson Terr ST5 ... 56 B4
Lawton Ave ST7 ... 25 B2
Lawton Coppice ST7 25 C2
Lawton Cres ST8 .. 24 B4
Lawton St Biddulph ST8 27 B4
Chell Heath ST6 ... 42 A1
Kidsgrove ST7 ..... 26 B2
Lawtongate Est ST7 25 A2
Laxey Rd ST5 ..... 56 A4
Laxton Gr ST4 .... 88 B2
Lazar La ST17 .... 176 A3
Lazy Hill WS9 .... 245 B1
Le More B74 ..... 258 A1
Lea Castle Dr DY10 280 B2
Lea Castle Hospl DY10 280 B2
Lea Cl ST5 .... 85 B3
Lea Cres ST17 ... 174 B4
Lea Gn ST16 ..... 155 B4
Lea Hall Dr WS7 . 211 B1
Lea Hall Ent Pk WS15 197 A3
Lea Hall La WS15 . 197 A3
Lea La Colton WS15 159 C1
Cookley DY10 .... 280 A3
Great Wyrley WS6 227 A2
Lea Manor Dr WV4 265 C2
Lea Pl ST3 ...... 74 A1
Lea Rd Hixon ST18 139 C1
Stone ST15 ...... 119 C3
Wolv WV3 .... 266 A4
Lea The ST4 ..... 88 A4
Lea Vale Rd DY8 . 279 C1
Lea Wlk WS11 ... 210 A2
Leacliffe Way WS9 256 C2
Leacote Dr WV6 . 255 B2
Leacroft ST15 ... 120 B4
Leacroft Ave WV10 240 C1
Leacroft Cl WS9 . 245 A1
Leacroft La WS11 226 C3
Leacroft Rd
Kingswinford DY6 275 C4
Meir ST3 ...... 90 A4
Penkridge ST19 . 193 A1
Leadbeater Ave ST4 71 C3
Leadendale La ST3 89 C2
Leadendale Mews ST3 89 C4
Leafdown Cl WS12 210 B2
Leafenden Ave WS7 229 A3
Leaford Way DY6 275 C3
Leaford Wlk ST1 . 57 C1
Leafy Glade B74 . 257 A2
Leafy Rise DY1 . 271 C3
Leahurst Cl 8 ST17 175 B3
Leaks Alley ST3 . 283 B2
Leam Dr WS7 .. 229 B4
Leamington Cl WS11 226 C4
Leamington Gdns ST5 56 C2
Leamington Rd DE14 184 C4
Leamonsley Cl WS13 230 C4
Leander Cl
Burntwood WS7 . 211 C1
Great Wyrley WS6 226 C1
Leander Rise DE15 186 A4
Lear Rd WV5 .... 270 A4
Leas The WV10 . 241 B4
Leasawe Cl ST18 158 B1
Leaside Ave WS15 198 B3
Leaside Rd ST4 . 72 C3
Leason Rd ST3 . 74 A1
Leason St ST4 .. 72 A4
Leasowe Rd WS15 197 A3
Leasowe The WS13 214 A1
Leasowes Dr
Perton WV6 .... 254 B2
Wolv WV4 ...... 265 B3
Leasowes Jun & Inf Schs
ST17 .... 175 B4
Leasowes La ST5 71 B1
Leaswood Pl ST5 71 B2
Leathermill La WS15 178 C1
Leathersley La DE6,DE65 129 B1
Leawood Rd ST4 71 C2
Lebanon Gr WS7 228 C4
Ledbury Cl WS9 245 A2
Ledbury Cres ST1 57 C3
Ledstone Way ST3 73 C2
Lee Ct WS9 .... 244 C2
Lee Gr ST5 .... 71 A2
Leech Ave ST5 55 C3
Leech St ST5 .. 284 C1
Leedham Ave B77 250 B2
Leedhams Croft DE12 202 B4
Leefield Cl ST5 72 C3
Leek Coll of F Ed ST13 30 C3
Leek Fst Sch ST13 31 A1
Leek High Sch ST13 31 A3
Leek La ST8,ST13 28 A4
Leek Morlands Hospl
ST13 .... 31 A3
Leek New Rd
Chell Heath ST6,ST1 57 B4
Norton-in-I-M ST6 42 C1
Leek Rd Bucknall ST2 58 A3
Cheadle ST10 .. 76 B3
Cheddleton ST9,ST10 60 B2
Cheddleton, Cellarhead ST9 59 C2
Cheddleton, Cheddleton Heath
ST13 .... 45 B1
Congleton CW12 .. 10 A4
Endon ST9 ...... 43 C3
Endon, Brown Edge ST9 43 B4

Leek Rd continued
Hanley ST1 ...... 57 C1
Longnor SK17 ... 13 A3
Norton-in-I-M ST6 42 C2
Stoke-on-T ST4 . 72 B4
Warslow SK17 ... 23 A1
Wetton DE6 .... 34 B2
Leekbrook Ind Est ST13 45 C4
Leekbrook Way ST13 30 C1
Lees Cl WS15 ... 197 A3
Lees La ST10 ... 108 C1
Leese La
Acton Trussell ST17 175 A1
Stone ST15 ..... 105 C3
Leese St ST4 ... 72 A4
Leet Ct WS15 .. 198 A2
Legge La ST18 . 139 B1
Legge St
Newcastle-u-L ST5 284 C2
Wolv WV2 ..... 266 C3
Legion Cl WS11 228 A3
Legs La WV10 . 240 C2
Leicester Cl ST5 71 B3
Leicester Ct ST14 110 C1
Leicester Pl ST2 58 B1
Leicester St DE14 185 B4
Leigh Ave WS7 229 A4
Leigh Bank ST10 108 C4
Leigh Cl ST17 . 174 C3
Leigh La
Church Leigh ST10 108 B3
Tunstall ST6 ... 41 B1
Upper Tean ST10 92 C1
Uttoxeter ST14 . 125 A4
Leigh Rd Congleton CW12 9 A2
Newport TF10 . 168 C1
Leigh St ST6 ... 42 A1
Leighs Cl WS4 244 B1
Leighs Rd WS4 244 A1
Leighswood 1 ST7 175 B4
Leighswood Ave WS9 256 A4
Leighswood Cl WS11 227 C3
Leighswood Ct WS9 256 A3
Leighswood Gr WS9 256 A4
Leighswood Ind Est
WS9 .... 256 A4
Leighswood Rd WS9 256 A3
Leighton Cl
Norton-in-I-M ST9 43 B2
Sedgley DY3 ... 271 C1
Uttoxeter ST14 126 B3
Leighton Rd
Uttoxeter ST14 126 B3
Wolv WV4 .... 265 C3
Leisure La SK17 . 24 C3
Leisure Wlk B77 261 C3
Lema Way ST16 156 B2
Lennox Gdns WV3 266 A4
Lennox Rd ST3 283 D1
Lenpark Ind Est ST3 283 C3
Lenthall Ave CW12 15 C4
Leofric Cl DE13 199 B3
Leomansley Cl WS13 230 C4
Leomansley Rd WS13 230 C4
Leomansley View WS13 230 C4
Leonard Ave
Kidderminster DY10 280 A1
Norton-in-I-M ST2 43 A2
Leonard Dr ST6 42 A3
Leonard Rd DY8 279 B3
Leonard St
Chell Heath ST6 42 A1
Leek ST13 .... 30 C3
Leonora St ST6 56 C4
Leopold St ST4 72 A4
Lerridge La ST20,ST21 131 C3
Lerryn Cl DY6 275 C3
Lerwick Cl DY6 275 C3
Lesley Dr DY6 275 C2
Leslie Rd B74 257 A1
Lesscroft Cl WV9 240 A2
Lessways Cl ST5 56 A4
Lessways Wlk 12 ST5 56 A4
Lester Gr WS9 256 C1
Letchmere Cl WV6 253 B1
Letchmere La WV6 253 B1
Lethbridge Gdns ST17 174 A4
Levedale Cl ST16 155 A4
Levedale Rd
Bradley ST18 191 B4
Penkridge ST19 192 B2
Levels The WS15 196 C3
Leven Dr WV11 242 A1
Leveson Ave WS6 226 C1
Leveson Rd
Essington WV11 241 C1
Trentham ST4 72 C1
Levett Rd Hopwas WS14 232 B1
Levetts Fields WS14 231 B4
Levetts Hollow WS11 210 B2
Levetts Sq WS13 231 A4
Levington Cl WV10 254 C3
Levita Rd ST4 71 C2
Lewis Cl WS14 231 C3
Lewis Dr DE13 166 A4
Lewis St ST14 72 A4
Lewis's La DE13 199 B3
Lewisham Dr ST6 41 A4
Lewisham Rd WV10 240 A1
Lewthorne Rise WV4 266 B2
Lexham St ST17 73 C1
Lexington Gn ST17 174 A4
Ley Gdns ST3 283 A2
Ley Hill Rd B75 258 B3
Ley Rise DY3 266 B1
Leybourne Cres WV9 239 C1

Leycett La ST5 ... 54 B1
Leycett Rd ST5 .. 54 C2
Leyfield Rd ST4 . 88 A3
Leyfields WS13 .. 214 A1
Leyfields Farm Mews
DE13 ...... 165 B4
Leyland Ave WV3 255 C1
Leyland Croft WS3 243 C2
Leyland Dr WS15 178 C1
Leyland Gn ST6 42 A3
Leyland Rd B77 250 C2
Leys Dr ST5 ... 70 C2
Leys La ST2 ... 43 B2
Leys The DE11 186 C3
Liberty La ST6 42 B2
Liberty Pk ST17 174 A4
Liberty Rd B77 261 C3
Libra Cl B79 .. 249 C4
Libra Pl ST6 ... 41 C3
Lichen Cl WS12 200 B3
Lichfield (Trent Valley) Sta
WS13 ..... 231 C4
Lichfield Bsns Ctr WS13 214 B1
Lichfield Cathedral Sch
WS13 ..... 231 A4
Lichfield City Sta WS14 231 A4
Lichfield Cl ST5 55 B1
Lichfield Ct ST17 155 C1
Lichfield Dr
Colwich ST18 158 A1
Hopwas B78 249 A4
Lichfield Rd
Abbots Bromley WS15 161 A2
Armitage WS15 198 B2
Branston DE13,DE14 184 B2
Brownhills, Gatehouse Trad Est
WS8 ..... 245 A4
Burntwood, Burntwood Green
WS7 ..... 229 B3
Burntwood, New Town
WS8,WS14 ... 229 B1
Cannock WS11 226 C4
Hamstall Ridware WS15 180 C1
King's Bromley DE13 199 A3
Sandon ST18 137 B4
Stafford ST17 155 C1
Stone ST15 120 B4
Sutton Coldfield B74 258 A2
Talke ST7 ... 40 B4
Tamworth B78,B79 249 C3
Walsall WS4 244 B1
Walsall, New Invention
WS3,WS4,WS8,WS9 242 C1
Walsall, Pelsall WS3 244 A3
Wolv WV3 .. 243 B1
Lichfield Road Ind Est
B79 ..... 249 C3
Lichfield St
Burton u T DE14 166 B1
Hanley ST1 ... 282 C1
Rugeley WS15 196 C4
Stone ST15 120 A4
Tamworth B78 249 C1
Lid La Cheadle ST10 76 B2
Roston DE6 96 C4
Liddiard Ct DY8 279 C3
Liddle St ST4 72 A3
Lidgate Gr ST3 72 C1
Lidgate Wlk ST5 71 A1
Liffs Rd DE6,SK17 36 B4
Lifton Croft DY6 275 C3
Light Ash WV9 224 B2
Light Ash Cl WV9 224 B2
Light Ash La WV9 224 B2
Light Oaks Ave ST2 43 B1
Lightfoot Rd ST14 110 C1
Lightwater Gr ST2 42 C1
Lightwood Rd
Longton ST3 283 C2
Meir ST3 ... 89 C3
Newcastle-u-L ST5 40 B1
Yoxall DE13 181 C1
Lilac Ave WS11 226 B4
Lilac Cl Meir ST3 74 B3
Newcastle-u-L ST5 40 B1
Seighford ST18 135 B1
Uttoxeter ST14 126 A3
Lilac Dr WV5 269 C3
Lilac Gr Burntwood WS7 228 C4
Burton u T DE15 185 C3
Fenton ST3 72 C1
Stafford ST17 174 C4
Lilac Ho WS4 244 B1
Lilac La WS6 243 A4
Lilac Rd B79 250 A4
Lilian Cres WV2 266 B4
Lilleshall Hall National
Sports Ctr TF10 187 A1
Lilleshall Rd ST5 71 B3
Lilleshall St ST3 283 C2
Lilleshall Way ST17 174 B4
Lilington Cl WS13 231 A4
Lillydale Rd ST2 58 A2
Lily St ST5 56 B3
Limbrick Rd ST7 39 A4
Lime Cl
Church Leigh ST10 109 A3
Doveridge DE6 127 A4
Great Wyrley WS6 226 C2
Meir ST3 ... 74 B3
Lime Gr Barlaston ST12 88 C4
Burntwood WS7 229 B3
Burton u T DE15 185 C3
Kinver DY7 278 B2

Lime Gr *continued*
Lichfield WS14 ....231 B4
Waterhouses ST10 ....48 C2
Lime Kiln La Alton ST10 ....78 C1
Kidsgrove ST7 ....25 C1
Lime La WS3 ....244 A4
Lime Rd Huntington WS12 209 B4
Sedgley DY3 ....266 C1
Lime St Stoke-on-T ST4 ....72 A3
Wolv WV3 ....266 A4
Lime Tree Ave WV6 ....255 A2
Lime Tree Gdns WV8 ......239 A2
Lime Tree Rd WV8 ....239 A2
Lime Wlk ST19 ....207 C4
Limeheath Pl S16 ....41 C3
Limehurst Ave WV3 ....255 B1
Limepit La WS11,WS12 ....209 B3
Limes Ave ST9 ....30 A1
Limes Rd WV6 ....255 B2
Limes The
Albrighton WV7 ....237 A2
Newcastle-u-L ST5 ....56 B4
Limes View DY3 ....271 B4
Limetree Ave ST16 ....155 B3
Limetree Rd B74 ....256 B1
Limewood Cl ST11 ....91 A3
Linacre Rd ST21 ....133 C3
Linacre Way ST3 ....73 C3
Lincoln Ave
Newcastle-u-L ST5 ....71 B3
Tamworth B79 ....249 C3
Lincoln Cl WS13 ....214 B2
Lincoln Croft WS14 ....247 A3
Lincoln Ct ST14 ....110 C1
Lincoln Dr WS11 ....226 C4
Lincoln Gn WV10 ....240 B1
Lincoln Gr ST5 ....71 B3
Lincoln Mdw ST17 ....174 A4
Lincoln Rd Burslem ST6 ....57 A4
Burton u T DE15 ....185 B4
Kidsgrove ST7 ....25 C1
Lincoln St ST1 ....282 C2
Linda Rd ST6 ....41 C3
Lindale Cl CW12 ....6 A3
Lindale Dr WV5 ....269 C3
Lindale Gr 10 ST13 ....90 A4
Linden Ave WS7 ....229 A4
Linden Cl Congleton CW12 .16 A4
Newcastle-u-L ST5 ....56 A2
Stafford ST17 ....174 A4
Tamworth B77 ....250 C2
Linden Dr ST8 ....16 B1
Linden Gr ST5 ....56 A2
Linden Lea WV3 ....255 B1
Linden Pl ST13 ....72 C1
Linden Rd DE13 ....183 B1
Linden View WS12 ....210 A2
Linden Way TF9 ....97 A1
Lindenbrook Vale ST17 ....175 B4
Lindens The Stone ST15 ....120 A3
Wolv WV6 ....255 C2
Lindera B77 ....251 A2
Lindisfarne B77 ....250 B2
Lindley Pl ST3 ....90 A2
Lindley St ST6 ....57 A4
Lindon Dr WS8 ....245 A3
Lindon Rd WS8 ....244 C3
Lindon View WS8 ....245 A3
Lindop Ct ST1 ....282 C3
Lindop St ST1 ....282 C3
Lindops La CW3 ....68 C4
Lindrick Cl WS13 ....242 C2
Lindrosa Rd B74 ....256 C2
Lindsay St ST1 ....282 A2
Lindum Ave ST4 ....88 B4
Line Cl DE15 ....185 C4
Lineker Cl ST16 ....155 A2
Linfield Gdns DY3 ....266 B1
Linfield St ST1 ....282 C3
Linford Cl WS15 ....198 B2
Ling Rd WS12 ....209 B3
Lingard St ST6 ....57 A4
Lingfield Ave Endon ST6 ...43 A4
Wolv WV10 ....240 B3
Lingfield Cl WS6 ....226 C1
Lingfield Dr WV6 ....254 C2
Lingfield Rd DE14 ....184 C4
Linhope Gr 10 ST3 ....90 A4
Link Rd Brownhills WS9 ...245 A2
Wombourne WV5 ....270 A4
Linkend Cl ST11 ....57 C3
Links Ave
Newcastle-u-L ST5 ....56 A2
Wolv WV6 ....255 B4
Links Dr DY8 ....279 C1
Links Rd WV4 ....266 A2
Links Side Way WS3 ....256 B4
Links View B74 ....257 A1
Linksfield Cl ST16 ....155 B4
Linksway WV6 ....15 C4
Linkway CW12 ....15 C4
Linkway Ret Pk WS11 ....226 B3
Linkwood Ind Est DY8 ....279 C3
Linley Dr WV10 ....240 C1
Linley Gr Lawton-gate ST7 .25 A2
Sedgley DY3 ....271 A1
Linley La ST7 ....25 A1
Linley Rd Stoke-on-T ST4 ..71 C4
Talke ST7 ....40 B4
Linley Trad Est ST7 ....25 B1
Linnburn Rd ST13 ....73 C2
Linnet Cl WV12 ....209 B4
Linnet Way ST18 ....207 C4
Linslade Cl WV4 ....266 B2

Lintake Dr WS15 ....160 C3
Linthouse Wlk B77 ....261 C3
Lintly B77 ....262 A4
Linton Rd WV4 ....265 C3
Linwood Dr WS12 ....209 C4
Linwood Way ST6 ....41 C3
Lion La ST5 ....55 C4
Lion Ind Est WS9 ....256 A4
Lion Pas DY8 ....279 C3
Lion St Rugeley WS15 .....178 C1
Stourbridge DY8 ....279 C3
Lion Way ST17 ....175 A4
Lion's Den WS7,WS14 ....229 C1
Lionel Gr ST4 ....71 C3
Lionfields Cl DY10 ....280 A3
Lionfields Rd DY10 ......280 A3
Lisbon Pl ST5 ....70 C4
Liskeard Cl ST17 ....58 A1
Lister Rd ST14 ....155 C3
Litchfield Cath* WS13 ....231 A4
Litley Dr ST10 ....92 B4
Little Aston Hall Dr B74 ..257 A3
Little Aston Hospl B74 ....257 A3
Little Aston La B74 ....257 B3
Little Aston Park Rd
B74 ....257 A2
Little Aston Prim Sch
B74 ....257 A3
Little Aston Rd WS9 ......256 B3
Little Barrow Wlk WS13 ..214 A1
Little Birches WV3 ....265 C4
Little Bloxwich CE Prim Sch
WS3 ....243 B1
Little Burton E DE14 ......166 B2
Little Burton W DE14 .....166 B2
Little Checkhill La DY6,
DY7 ....274 A2
Little Chell La ST6 ....41 C3
Little Church La B79 ......250 A3
Little Cliffe Rd ST3 ....72 C2
Little Comm WS3 ....244 A2
Little Eaves La ST7 ....58 B3
Little Field ST4 ....71 C2
Little Grange WS13 ....213 C1
Little Hardwick Rd WS9 ..256 B1
Little Hay La WS14 ....247 B2
Little Johnson's La
WS9 ....256 A1
Little La ST3 ....89 C2
Little Lawns Cl WS9 ......245 A2
Little Marsh Gr ST19 .....192 C1
Little Moss Cl ST7 ....25 C3
Little Moss La ST7 ....25 C3
Little Oaks Dr ST7 ....275 A1
Little Onn Rd ST20 ......190 A4
Little Orch WS15 ....178 C1
Little Pipe La WS13 ......213 A1
Little Pountney St 6
WV2 ....266 B4
Little Rd ST10 ....75 C1
Little Row
14 Kidsgrove ST7 ....26 A1
Stoke-on-T ST4 ....58 C3
Little Sutton La B75 ......258 B1
Little Sutton Prim Sch
B75 ....258 B2
Little Sutton Rd B75 .....258 B1
Little Tixall La ST18 ......158 B1
Littlecote B79 ....249 B4
Littlefield La
Ellastone DE6 ....80 A1
Snelston DE6 ....81 A2
Littlehales Rd TF10 ......187 A3
Littleton Bsns Pk WS12 ..209 B4
Littleton Cl ST16 ....156 A2
Littleton Cres ST19 ......192 C1
Littleton Dr WS12 ....209 B4
Littleton Way WS7 ....211 B1
Littlewood La WS6 ....226 C2
Littlewood Rd WS6 ....226 C2
Littleworth Hill WS12 ...210 B2
Littleworth Rd WS12 ....210 C2
Litton B77 ....251 B1
Liverpool Rd
Kidsgrove ST7 ....26 A1
Newcastle-u-L ST5 ....284 B3
Newcastle-u-L, Cross Heath
ST5 ....56 A2
Newcastle-u-L, Red Street
ST5 ....40 B1
Stoke-on-T ST4 ....72 A4
Liverpool Rd E ST7 ....25 C1
Liverpool Rd W ST7 ......25 A2
Livingstone Dr WV6 .....254 C3
Livingstone Rd WS3 .....243 C1
Livingstone St
Chell Heath ST6 ....42 B1
Leek ST13 ....30 C3
Lizard La ST11 ....220 A3
Llewellyn Roberts Way
TF9 ....97 B1
Lloyd Dr WV4 ....265 B1
Lloyd George Gr WS11 ..210 B1
Lloyd Hill WV4 ....265 B2
Lloyd Rd WV6 ....255 B3
Lloyd Roberts Bldgs
WV4 ....265 C1
Lloyd St Cannock WS11 ..209 B1
Longton ST3 ....283 C2
Stafford ST16 ....155 C2
Wolv WV6 ....255 C2
Lochalsh Gr WV11 ....242 A1
Lochsong Ct B77 ....261 B2
Lock Keepers Ct WS11 ...227 C2
Lock Rd ST19 ....207 C4

Locke Way ST16 ....156 A2
Lockerbie Cl ST13 ....31 A3
Lockett St ST1 ....57 B3
Locketts La ST3 ....283 D2
Lockfield Cl DY8 ....275 C1
Lockhart Dr B75 ....258 B1
Lockington Ave ST2 ......58 B1
Lockley St ST1 ....57 C3
Locks View DY8 ....275 C1
Lockside WS5 ....269 C4
Lockside View WS15 .....196 C4
Lockwood Cl ST10 ....62 A1
Lockwood Rd ST10 ....77 A3
Lockwood St
Newcastle-u-L ST5 ....284 D3
Norton-in-t-M ST2 ....43 A2
Lode La DE6 ....35 C2
Lodge Barn Rd ST8 ......27 C3
Lodge Gr Aldridge WS9 ..256 A3
Lodge Hill DE13 ....146 C2
Lodge La Alstonefield DE6 .35 A2
Cheslyn Hay WS11 ....226 B3
Eccleshall ST21 ....115 C3
Ilam DE6 ....50 B2
Kingswinford DY6 ....275 A3
Longdon WS15 ....212 B2
Woodseaves ST20 ....151 C2
Yoxall DE13 ....182 A4
Lodge Pk WV5 ....267 B4
Lodge Rd
Burntwood WS7 ....211 C1
Netherseal DE12 ....219 C4
Rugeley WS15 ....197 A3
Stoke-on-T ST4 ....71 C4
Walsall WS4 ....244 A4
Lodge View WS6 ....226 B2
Loftus Ct WS7 ....229 A3
Loftus St ST1 ....282 A4
Loganbeck Gr ST3 ....73 C3
Lohengrin Ct 11 DE13 ..147 C1
Lomas St ST4 ....57 A1
Lomax Cl WS13 ....214 A1
Lomax Rd WS12 ....210 A4
Lombard Gdns WS13 ....231 A4
Lombard St WS13 ....231 A4
Lombardy Gr
Burntwood WS7 ....228 C4
Meir ST3 ....74 A1
Lomita Cres B77 ....261 B4
Lomond Cl B79 ....249 C4
Lomond Gr WS12 ....210 A4
Lomond Rd DY3 ....266 B1
Lomond Wlk ST14 ....88 C4
London Rd
Bridgemere CW5 ....67 A3
Lichfield WS14 ....231 B3
Newcastle-u-L, Chesterton
ST5 ....55 C3
Newcastle-u-L, City General Hospl
ST5 ....284 C1
Sutton Coldfield B75 .....259 A2
Sutton Coldfield B75 .....259 B1
Weeford WS14 ....247 C2
Weston ST18 ....138 B1
Woore, Dorrington CW3,
TF9 ....83 B3
London St ST13 ....30 C3
Long Acre WV8 ....238 C1
Long Bridge Rd WS14 ....231 B3
Long Cl DY9 ....281 C2
Long Croft WS12 ....209 B2
Long Furrow WV8 ....239 C1
Long La Alrewas DE13 ...200 C1
Alstonefield DE6 ....35 A3
Great Wyrley WS6 ....242 C3
Haughton ST18 ....154 B1
Kidsgrove ST7 ....26 C2
Long Mdw
Newcastle-u-L ST5 ....71 B2
Stafford ST17 ....174 C3
Long Meadow Dr DY8 ...281 C2
Long Mynd Cl WV11 ....242 A1
Long Row Alrewas DE13 ..200 C1
Alstonefield DE6 ....35 A3
Great Wyrley WS6 ....242 C3
Wheaton Aston ST19 ....205 B3
Long Valley Rd ST18 ......16 B1
Longacres
Cannock WS12 ....210 C3
Little Aston B74 ....257 B2
Longboat La DY8 ....275 C1
Longbow Cl DE13 ....147 B1
Longbow Gr DE13 ....147 B1
Longbridge Hayes Rd
ST5 ....56 B4
Longbrook Ave ST3 ......72 C1
Longclough Rd ST5 ......56 B4
Longcroft La DE13 ....182 A2
Longdon Ave WV4 ....266 B3
Longdon Dr B74 ....257 C2
Longdon Gn DE14 ....166 B4
Longdon Hall Sch
Longdon WS15 ....209 C2
Longfellow Rd
Burntwood WS7 ....212 A1
Sedgley DY3 ....271 A3
Longfellow Wlk ST9 ......249 C4
Longfield Ave ST15 ....119 C4
Longfield Cl B77 ....250 C2
Longfield Dr ST4 ....71 C4
Longfield Gn WV5 ......269 B3
Longford Cl WS11 ....226 A4
Longford Gn WS11 ......226 A3
Longford Ind Est WS11 ..226 B3

Longford Prim Sch
WS11 ....226 B4
Longford Rd
Cannock WS11 ....226 B4
Newport TF10 ....168 B1
Longford Wlk ST2 ....58 A1
Longhedge La DE13 .....146 C1
Longhope Dr ST15 ......119 C3
Longhurst Dr ST16 ......156 B2
Longlake Ave WV6 ....255 A2
Longlands Dr B77 ......250 C2
Longlands La TF9 ....97 B1
Longlands Pl WS15 ......160 C3
Longlands Prim Sch TF9 ..97 B1
Longlands The WV5 .....270 A3
Longleat Dr DY1 ....271 C1
Longleat Rd WS9 ....245 B4
Longley Rd ST3 ....73 B3
Longmead Rd DE13 .....166 B3
Longnor Craft Ctr* SK17 .13 B3
Longnor Pl ST2 ....58 A1
Longport Rd ST6 ....56 B4
Longport Sta ST6 ....56 B4
Longsdon Cl ST5 ....40 B1
Longsdon Gr ST3 ....73 C2
Longshaw Ave ST5 ....56 A4
Longshaw La ST10 ....78 C4
Longslow Cl TF9 ....97 A1
Longslow Cl ST17 ....174 B3
Longslow Dr TF9 ....97 A1
Longslow Rd TF9 ....97 A1
Longstaff Ave WS12 .....211 B2
Longton Craft WS13 ....213 C1
Longton Exchange ST3 ..283 C3
Longton Hall Rd ST3 ....72 C1
Longton High Sch ST3 ..73 C1
Longton Hospl ST3 ......73 B1
Longton Rd
Barlaston ST12 ....88 C1
Stone ST15 ....105 B2
Trentham ST4 ....88 A3
Longton Sta ST3 ....283 B4
Longus Ind Est ST6 ......56 B4
Longview Cl ST3 ....73 B3
Longwood Path B78 ....249 B1
Longwood Prim Sch
B78 ....249 B1
Longwood Rd WS9 .....256 A1
Lonsdale CE Prim Sch
ST21 ....133 B3
Lonsdale Ct
Eccleshall ST21 ....133 B4
Market Drayton TF9 ......97 B1
Lonsdale Rd
Burton u T DE14 ....185 A4
Wolv WV3 ....266 A4
Lonsdale St ST4 ....72 A3
Loomer Rd ST5 ....55 C3
Loomer Road Ind Est
ST5 ....55 C3
Lord Cromwell Ct WS11 .210 A3
Lord St Biddulph ST8 ....27 B4
Chell Heath ST6 ....42 B1
Lords La DY7 ....274 C1
Lordship La ST4 ....73 B4
Lordshire Pl ST7 ....26 C1
Lordsley Rd TF9 ....100 A4
Lordswell Rd DE14 .....165 C2
Lorien Cl ST13 ....30 B2
Lorien Ct ST4 ....72 A4
Loring Rd ST5 ....56 A3
Loring Terr S ST5 ....56 B3
Lorne St Burntwood WS7 228 C4
Chell Heath ST6 ....26 C1
Lorraine St ST17 ....26 C1
Lorton B70 ....249 B4
Lothersdale B77 ....262 B4
Lothians Rd Walsall WS3 .244 A3
Wolv WV6 ....255 C3
Lotus Ct ST7 ....250 C2
Lotus Ave ST8 ....27 A3
Lotus Ct ST15 ....105 A1
Lotus Dr WS11 ....209 C3
Lotus Way ST16 ....155 C3
Loughborough Wlk ST3 .283 C4
Loughshaw B77 ....251 B1
Louise Dr ST3 ....72 C2
Louise St Chell Heath ST6 .42 A1
Sedgley DY3 ....271 B2
Lount La DE13 ....146 C1
Louvain Ave ST1 ....57 B4
Lovage Gr ST2 ....58 A2
Lovatt Ave ST5 ....56 A2
Lovatt Cl DE13 ....147 C1
Lovatt Dr ST5 ....209 C3
Lovatt St Stafford ST16 ..155 B3
Stoke-on-T ST4 ....72 A4
Love La
Great Wyrley WS6 ....227 A2
Rugeley WS15 ....178 C1
Wolv WV6 ....255 B3
Lovelace Cl ST17 ....174 B4
Lovell B79 ....249 C3
Lovell Dr ST16 ....156 A3
Lovell Rd DE13 ....182 A1
Loveridge Cl WV8 ....238 C2
Lovers La TF9 ....97 C2
Loveston Gr ST3 ....283 D4
Lovett Ct WS15 ....178 B1
Low Farm WS9 ....245 C2
Low St WS6 ....226 B2
Lowdham B77 ....251 B1
Lowe Dr DY6 ....275 C4
Lowe St ST4 ....72 A4
Lowell Dr ST3 ....209 C2
Lower Ash Rd ST7 ....25 C1
Lower Bedford St ST4 ...57 A1

Lower Bethesda St ST1 .282 B2
Lower Bromstead La
TF10 ....188 B4
Lower Brook St WS15 ...178 C1
Lower Bryan St ST1 .....282 B4
Lower Cres ST4 ....71 C4
Lower Cross St ST3 .....283 C4
Lower Farm Prim Sch
WS3 ....243 B2
Lower Foundry St ST1 ...282 B3
Lower Hadderidge 3
ST6 ....56 C4
Lower High St
Mow Cop ST7 ....26 B4
Stourbridge DY8 ....279 C3
Tutbury DE13 ....146 B4
Lower House La CV9 ....262 C1
Lower La WS13 ....212 B2
Lower Mayer St ST1 ....282 C4
Lower Milehouse La ST5 .55 C2
Lower Outwoods Rd
DE13 ....165 C3
Lower Oxford Rd ST5 ...56 A3
Lower Penkridge Rd
ST17 ....175 B1
Lower Rd Ashley TF9 ....100 A2
Cannock WS12 ....210 B2
Gnosall ST20 ....152 A3
Lower Sandford St
WS13 ....231 A4
Lower Spring Rd 3 ST13 .73 B1
Lower St 1 Burslem ST6 ..57 A4
Doveridge DE6 ....127 A4
Newcastle-u-L ST5 ....284 B3
Wolv WV6 ....255 C3
Lower Villiers St WV2 ....266 B4
Lower Way WS15 ....197 B1
Lower Wood La WS13 ...210 C1
Loweport B77 ....250 B1
Loweswater Dr DY3 .....271 B2
Lowfield Dr ST5 ....56 C3
Lowfield La ST20 ....171 C3
Lowforce B77 ....261 B3
Lowhurst Dr ST6 ....42 A4
Lowland Rd WS12 ......209 B3
Lowlands Ave WV6 .....255 C3
Lowlands Ct WV6 ......255 C3
Lowlands Rd ST16 ......41 A4
Lowndes Cl ST14 ....71 C3
Lowndes Rd DY8 ....279 C3
Lowry Cl WV6 ....254 C2
Lowther Pl ST13 ....31 A3
Lowther St ST1 ....282 A4
Lowthorpe Way ST2 ....58 C1
Loxley Hall Sch ST14 ...125 B3
Loxley La ST14 ....125 B3
Loxley Pl ST3 ....89 C4
Loxley Rd B75 ....258 B2
Loynton Cl ST16 ....155 A4
Loynton Sands ST20 ....155 C3
Lucas St ST6 ....56 C4
Lucepool La DE13 ......182 B2
Lucerne Pl ST15 ....70 C4
Lud La B79 ....250 A3
Ludbrook Rd ST14 .....71 C3
Ludford Cl ST5 ....40 B1
Ludgate B79 ....250 A3
Ludgate St DE13 ....146 B3
Ludgrove Way 2 ST17 ..175 A4
Ludlow Cl WS11 ....210 B1
Ludlow St ST1 ....282 C3
Ludlow Way DY1 ....271 C1
Ludstone Ave WV4 .....265 B3
Ludwall Rd ST3 ....73 C1
Lugano Cl ST5 ....72 C3
Luke St ST6 ....56 C4
Lukes Wlk WS13 ....214 A1
Lukesland Ave ST4 .....71 C3
Lullington Rd
Clifton Campville B79 ....218 C2
Edingale B79 ....217 B3
Lunns Croft WS13 ......231 B4
Lutley Cl WV3 ....265 C4
Lutley La DY7 ....273 A4
Luttrell Rd B74 ....257 B3
Luxton Cl B74 ....257 B3
Lydford Pl ST3 ....73 C2
Lydford Rd WS3 ....243 A2
Lydgate Rd DY6 ....275 C3
Lydia Croft B74 ....57 C3
Lydia Dr ST1 ....57 C3
Lydiates Cl DY3 ....271 A4
Lyme Brook Pl ST4 .....71 C2
Lyme Ct ST5 ....284 C1
Lyme Dr ST14 ....71 B3
Lyme Gr ST5 ....56 A2
Lyme Rd ST3 ....74 A1
Lyme Valley Rd ST5 ....284 C1
Lyme Wood Gr ST5 ....284 B1
Lymedale Small Firms Ctr
ST5 ....55 C3
Lymer Rd WV10 ....240 B1
Lymer's La ST18 ....123 A1
Lymes Rd ST5 ....70 A2
Lymevale Rd ST4 ....71 C2
Lymewood Cl ST5 .....284 B2
Lymington Rd
Burntwood WS7 ....211 C1
Stafford ST16 ....156 B2
Lyminster Gr ST22 ......43 A1
Lymsey Croft DY8 ......275 B2
Lyn Ave WS13 ....213 C1
Lynam St ST4 ....72 A4

Lynam Way CW3 .... 68 C4
Lynch The B78 .... 251 C1
Lyncroft WV7 .... 237 A3
Lyncroft House Sch
 WS11 .... 226 C4
Lyndale B77 .... 261 C3
Lyndale Rd DY3 .... 266 A1
Lyndham Ave DE15 .... 166 C1
Lyndhurst Dr Biddulph ST8 .87 A3
 Brierley Hill B79 .... 275 C1
Lyndhurst Gr ST15 .... 120 B3
Lyndhurst Rd
 Cannock WS12 .... 210 C1
 Wolv WV3 .... 266 A4
Lyndhurst St ST6 .... 56 C4
Lyndon Cl DY3 .... 266 C1
Lyndon Gr DY6 .... 275 A4
Lyne Ct DE14 .... 166 A2
Lyne Hill Ind Est ST19 .207 C4
Lyneham Cl B79 .... 250 B4
Lynehill La ST19 .... 207 C3
Lyneside Rd ST8 .... 27 A2
Lynfield Rd WS13 .... 213 C1
Lynmouth Cl ST18 .... 27 B3
Lynmouth Gr ST6 .... 41 C4
Lynn Ave ST7 .... 40 B4
Lynn La WS14 .... 246 B3
Lyn St ST3 .... 74 A3
Lynsey Cl ST7 .... 54 C4
Lynton Ave Stafford ST17 .175 B4
 Wolv WV6 .... 255 C3
Lynton Gr ST3 .... 89 C4
Lynwood Ave DY6 .... 275 A4
Lynwood Cl DE14 .... 184 C4
Lynwood Dr DY10 .... 281 B1
Lynwood Rd DE14 .... 184 C4
Lyric Cl ST17 .... 174 C3
Lysander Rd ST3 .... 90 A4
Lysander Way WS11 .... 209 C2
Lysways La WS15 .... 213 A4
Lytham B77 .... 251 B3
Lytham Cl ST7 .... 279 C1
Lytham Dr ST16 .... 156 B2
Lytham Gr WS3 .... 243 A2
Lytham Rd WV6 .... 254 B2
Lyttelton Rd DY8 .... 279 B3
Lytton Ave ST4 .... 265 C2
Lytton St ST4 .... 72 B4

M

Macadam Cl WS7 .... 229 A4
Macbeth Ho ST7 .... 40 B4
Macclesfield Rd
 Congleton CW12 .... 6 A4
 Leek ST13 .... 30 B4
Macclesfield St ST16 .... 42 A1
Macdonald Cres ST3 .... 74 A2
Mace St ST14 .... 71 C2
Macgregor Cres B77 .... 250 C2
Macgregor Tithe B79 .... 250 A3
Machin Cres ST5 .... 56 A4
Machin St ST6 .... 41 C2
Macintyre St ST6 .... 57 A4
Mackay Rd WS3 .... 243 B1
Mackenzie Cres ST10 .... 76 C1
Maclagan St ST4 .... 72 A3
Macrome Rd WV6 .... 255 C4
Madden Cl WS15 .... 196 C3
Maddock St Audley ST7 .... 39 B1
 Burslem ST6 .... 56 C4
Madeira Ave WV8 .... 239 A1
Madeley La ST6 .... 41 B2
Madeley High Sch CW3 .68 C3
Madeley **5** DY6 .... 275 C2
Madeley St
 Newcastle-u-L ST5 .... 55 A1
 Tunstall ST6 .... 41 B2
Madeley St N ST5 .... 55 A1
Madford Ret Pk ST16 .155 B2
Madison St ST6 .... 41 B2
Madox Cl ST9 .... 249 C4
Madras Rd DE15 .... 167 B2
Madrona B77 .... 251 A2
Maer La
 Market Drayton TF9 .... 97 B1
 Standon ST21 .... 101 C1
Maerway La ST5,TF9 .... 84 B3
Maesfield Dr ST17 .... 155 B1
Mafeking St ST3 .... 283 B2
Magdalen Rd ST3 .... 88 C4
Magdalen Wlk ST3 .... 88 C4
Magenta Dr ST5 .... 55 C1
Magna Cl WS6 .... 226 C2
Magnolia B77 .... 251 A2
Magnolia Cl ST18 .... 135 A1
Magnolia Dr ST6 .... 42 C1
Magnolia Gr WV8 .... 239 A2
Magnolia Way **6** DY8 .275 C1
Magnus B77 .... 261 C3
Magnus St ST6 .... 56 C4
Magpie Cres **11** ST7 .... 26 A1
Maidendale Rd DY6 .... 275 A4
Maidensbridge Dr DY6 275 B4
Maidensbridge Gdns
 DY6 .... 275 A4
Maidensbridge Prim Sch
 DY6 .... 270 A1
Maidensbridge Rd DY6 .270 A1
Maidstone Dr
 Burntwood WS7 .... 229 B3
 Kingswinford DY8 .... 275 C2
Maer St ST4 .... 58 B1
Main Rd Adbaston ST20 .131 B3
 Armitage WS15 .... 197 B2
 Betley CW2,CW3 .... 53 A3

Main Rd continued
 Cheddleton ST9 .... 60 A4
 Colwich ST18 .... 177 B4
 Cotton ST10 .... 63 C2
 Draycott in t C DE6 .... 144 B4
 Edingale B79 .... 217 B3
 Harlaston B79 .... 217 B1
 Newton Regis B79 .... 236 B1
 Norton in Hales TF9 .... 82 B1
 Stafford ST17 .... 176 A4
 Weston DE6 .... 128 C3
 Sudbury, Aston DE6 .... 129 A2
 Weston CW2 .... 37 B3
 Wigginton B79 .... 234 A1
Main Rd Brereton
 WS15 .... 197 A3
Main St Alrewas DE13 .201 A1
 Anslow DE13 .... 165 B4
 Barton-u-N DE13 .... 183 B1
 Branston DE14 .... 184 C4
 Burton u T, Stapenhill
 DE15 .... 185 C4
 Burton u T, Stretton DE13 .147 C1
 Clifton Campville B79 .218 C1
 Egginton DE65 .... 148 A3
 Meir ST3 .... 74 A3
 Nethersteal DE12 .... 219 C4
 Newton Solney DE15 .167 C4
 Shenstone WS14 .... 246 C3
 Shenstone, Stonnall WS9 .245 B2
 Swadlincote DE11 .... 186 C3
 Tatenhill DE13 .... 165 A4
 Walton-on-T DE12 .... 184 B1
 Whittington WS14 .... 232 C3
 Yoxall DE13 .... 182 A1
Mainvaring Dr B79 .258 C1
Maitland B77 .... 250 C1
Maitland Gr ST4 .... 88 A3
Maitland Rd DY1 .... 271 C1
Major St WV2 .... 266 C4
Majors Barn ST10 .... 76 B1
Maker La DE13 .... 162 B1
Malam St ST1 .... 282 B4
Malcolm Cl ST2 .... 43 A1
Malcolm Cr ST2 .... 58 B3
Malcolm Dr ST2 .... 58 B3
Malcolm Rd ST17 .... 174 B3
Malham Rd
 Newcastle-u-L ST5 .... 55 C1
 Tamworth B77 .... 251 B1
Malhamdale Rd CW12 ....6 A3
Malins Rd WV4 .... 266 C3
Mallard Ave ST17 .... 175 A4
Mallard Cl
 Uttoxeter ST14 .... 126 B3
 Walsall WS3 .... 244 A3
Mallard Croft **6** WS13 .231 A4
Mallard Way
 Chell Heath ST6 .... 42 B2
 Penkridge ST19 .... 208 A3
Mallens Croft ST14 .125 B4
Mallicot Cl WS13 .... 214 B1
Mallorie Rd ST6 .... 42 B2
Mallory Cl ST15 .... 120 A3
Mallory Cres WS13 .243 B1
Mallory Rd WV6 .... 254 C2
Mallory Way ST10 .... 76 C2
Mallow Cl ST21 .... 133 C3
Mallowdale Cl ST14 .... 88 B3
Malpas Wlk ST6 .... 41 B4
Malpass Gdns WV6 .238 C2
Malt House Rd WS15 .212 A3
Malt La ST3 .... 283 C2
Malt Mill La ST16 .... 155 C2
Malthouse La
 Barlaston ST12 .... 88 C1
 Bradley ST18 .... 173 B1
 Caverswall ST3 .... 74 B4
 Church Eaton ST20 .... 190 A4
 Wheaton Aston ST19 .205 B3
 Wolv WV6 .... 255 C3
Malthouse Rd ST2 .... 58 A2
Maltings Ind Est DE14 .166 C3
Maltings The
 Aldridge WS9 .... 256 B3
 Brewood WV9 .... 224 A1
 Burton u T DE15 .... 167 A1
 Uttoxeter ST14 .... 126 B4
Malton Gr ST6 .... 41 B3
Malvern Ave
 Burton u T DE15 .... 167 A1
 Swadlincote DE11 .... 54 C1
Malvern Cl Stafford ST11 .156 C1
 Trentham ST4 .... 88 A4
Malvern Ct B77 .... 251 A3
Malvern Dr Aldridge WS9 .256 B4
 Rugeley WS15 .... 178 B1
Malvern St DE15 .... 166 C1
Malvern View Rd DY3 .271 B2
Mamble Rd DY8 .... 279 B3
Manchester St ST14 .... 110 C1
Mancroft Cl DY6 .... 275 A4
Mancroft Gdns WV6 .255 B3
Mancroft Rd WV6 .255 B3
Mandela Way ST3 .... 283 D2
Manderley Cl DY3 .... 266 B1
Manderville Gdns DY6 .275 B3
Mandeville Cl ST6 .... 42 B2
Manifold CE Prim Sch
 SK17 .... 23 A1
Manifold Cl
 Burntwood WS7 .... 229 B3
 Newcastle-u-L ST5 .... 55 A1
 Waterhouses ST10 .... 48 C1
Manifold Dr ST10 .... 48 C1
Manifold Rd ST11 .... 90 C4
Manifold Wlk ST2 .... 58 B1

Manley Rd WS13 .... 214 B1
Manlove St WV3 .... 266 A4
Mann St ST3 .... 74 B2
Mannin Cl ST3 .... 74 A2
Manor Ave
 Cannock WS11 .... 209 B1
 Great Wyrley WS6 .... 227 A2
Manor Cl Codsall WV8 .239 A2
 Colwich ST18 .... 158 A1
 Congleton CW12 .... 6 A1
 Draycott in t M ST11 .... 91 B3
 Harlaston B79 .... 217 B1
 Market Drayton TF9 .... 97 B1
 Swadlincote DE15 .186 A3
 Uttoxeter ST14 .... 126 A4
Manor Cres ST18 .... 138 B1
 Wolv WV4 .... 265 C2
Manor Court Dr WS15 .198 A2
Manor Cres DE15 .... 186 A3
Manor Croft
 Burton u T DE14 .... 166 C1
 Tatenhill DE13 .... 184 A4
Manor Ct DE13 .... 183 B1
Manor Ct St ST4 .... 71 C3
Manor Dr
 Burton u T DE14 .... 166 C1
 Nethersteal DE12 .... 219 C3
 Sedgley DY3 .... 271 A2
 Shareshill WV10 .... 225 B1
 Swindon DY3 .... 269 C1
Manor Farm Cres ST17 .174 C3
Manor Farm Rd ST18 .177 B4
Manor Fields DE13 .... 200 C2
Manor Fold WV8 .... 238 B1
Manor Gdns
 Albrighton WV7 .... 237 A3
 Market Drayton TF9 .... 97 B1
 Wombourne WV5 .... 270 A4
Manor Glade ST5 .... 85 A4
Manor Gn ST17 .... 174 B4
Manor Hill Fst Sch
 ST5 .... 119 C4
Manor Ho WV6 .... 255 B3
Manor House Pk WV8 .239 A2
Manor La Harlaston B79 .217 B1
 Stourbridge DY8 .... 279 B2
 Wigginton B79 .... 223 A2
Manor Pk DY6 .... 275 B3
Manor Prim Sch
 Aldridge B78 .... 257 A1
 Drayton Bassett B78 .260 C2
Manor Rd Aldridge B74 .257 A1
 Edgmond TF10 .... 168 A2
 Gnosall ST20 .... 171 C4
 King's Bromley DE13 .199 B3
 Kingswinford DY8 .... 275 C1
 Madeley CW3 .... 68 C2
 Mow Cop ST7 .... 26 B4
 Swadlincote DE15 .186 A3
 Tamworth B77 .... 250 B2
 Tamworth, Mile Oak B78 .249 B1
 Uttoxeter ST14 .... 126 A4
 Whitmore ST5 .... 85 A4
 Wolv WV4 .... 265 C2
Manor Rise
 Burntwood WS7 .... 229 A3
 Lichfield WS14 .... 231 B4
 Stone ST15 .... 119 C4
Manor Sq ST17 .... 174 B4
Manor St Fenton ST4 .... 72 C4
 Wolv WV6 .... 255 B3
Manor Trad Est DE14 .166 C2
Manor Way WS15 .... 179 A3
Manor Wlk DE13 .... 199 A3
Manorfield Cl ST19 .207 C4
Manorial Rd B75 .... 258 C2
Mansard Cl WV4 .... 265 C4
Manse Cl ST13 .... 283 C4
Mansell Cl ST16 .... 155 B1
Mansfield Cl
 Newcastle-u-L ST5 .... 71 B1
 Tamworth B79 .... 249 C3
Mansfield Dr ST18 .... 27 A3
Mansion Cl ST10 .... 76 C1
Mansion Ct WV5 .... 269 B3
Manston Dr WS7 .... 229 B2
Manston Dr WV6 .... 254 C3
Manston Hill ST19 .207 C4
Manston View B79 .250 B4
Manta Rd B77 .... 261 B3
Manton Cl
 7 Burton u T DE13 .... 147 C1
 Swadlincote DE11 .... 186 C3
Maple Ave
 Newcastle-u-L ST5 .... 40 C1
 Talke ST7 .... 40 A3
Maple Cl Burntwood WS7 .228 C4
 Cheadle ST10 .... 76 C1
 Kinver DY7 .... 281 B3
 Norton-in-t-M ST6 .... 43 A3
 Stourbridge DY8 .... 279 B1
 Swynnerton ST15 .... 118 C3
Maple Cres
 Cannock WS11 .... 209 B1
 Forsbrook ST11 .... 91 A3
Maple Ct Lichfield WS14 .231 B3
 Stafford ST17 .... 155 B1
Maple Dr Ashley TF9 .... 99 B3
 Huntington WS12 .... 209 A3
 Sedgley DY3 .... 271 A1
 Seighford ST18 .... 154 B1
Maple Gdns ST15 .... 120 A3
Maple Gr
 Burton u T DE13 .... 185 C3
 Kingswinford DY6 .... 275 C3
 Lichfield WS14 .... 231 C4
 Stafford ST17 .... 174 C4
 Wolv WV3 .... 255 B1

Maple Hayes Sch for
 Dyslexics WS13 .... 230 B4
Maple Ho B74 .... 257 A3
Maple Pl ST3 .... 74 A1
Maple Rd Walsall WS3 .243 C1
 Wolv WV3 .... 265 C4
Maple Rise B77 .... 251 A2
Maple St WS3 .... 243 B1
Maple Way
 Branston DE14 .... 184 C4
 Burton u T DE14 .... 185 A4
Maple Wood ST17 .... 175 B3
Mapledene Cl **8** ST17 .175 B3
Maplehurst Cl ST6 .... 57 A4
Marcel Cl ST4 .... 72 A1
March Banks WS15 .178 B1
March Gr WS6 .... 226 B1
March La Dilhorne ST10 .... 60 A2
 Whitgreave ST18 .... 135 C3
March Rd ST3 .... 283 B4
March Way WS9 .... 245 B1
Marchant Rd WV6 .255 C1
Marchington Ind Est
 ST14 .... 143 C4
Marchwood Ct ST4 .... 71 C3
Marcia Rice Ct WS15 .161 A3
Marconi Gate ST18 .156 B3
Marconi Pl WS12 .... 210 B4
Marcus Ind Est ST1 .... 57 C2
Mardale Cl CW12 .... 6 A3
Mare Gr WV11 .... 242 A1
Margam Cres WS3 .242 C1
Margam Terr WS3 .... 242 C1
Margam Way WS3 .... 242 C1
Margaret Ave ST4 .... 87 C4
Margaret Dr WS11 .209 C3
Margaret St Hanley ST1 .57 C2
 10 Stone ST15 .... 104 C1
Margery Ave ST7 .... 25 C4
Margill Cl ST1 .... 282 A2
Marholm Cl WV9 .... 239 C1
Maries Way ST5 .... 55 B1
Marigold Cl WS11 .210 B2
Marina Cres WS12 .210 A3
Marina Rd ST4 .... 71 C2
Marina Way Burslem ST1 .57 A2
 Newcastle-u-L ST1 .... 56 C2
Marine Cres DY8 .... 275 C1
Marine Gdns DY8 .... 275 C1
Mariner B79 .... 249 C3
Market Drayton Cottage
 Hospl TF9 .... 112 B4
Market Drayton Inf Sch
 TF9 .... 112 A4
Market Drayton Jun Sch
 TF9 .... 112 B4
Market Hall DE14 .... 166 C1
Market Hall St WS11 .209 C1
Market La Hanley ST1 .282 B3
 Lower Penn WV4 .... 264 C3
 Newcastle-u-L ST5 .... 284 B1
 Wall WS14 .... 230 C2
Market Mews TF10 .168 C2
Market Pl
 Abbots Bromley WS15 .161 A3
 Brewood ST19 .... 223 B3
 Burslem ST6 .... 56 C4
 Burton u T DE14 .... 166 C1
 12 Cannock WS11 .209 C1
 Cheadle ST10 .... 76 B2
 Hartington SK17 .... 24 B3
 8 Leek ST13 .... 30 C3
 Longnor SK17 .... 12 A2
 Tamworth B79 .... 250 A2
 Uttoxeter ST14 .... 126 B4
Market Sq Arc ST1 .282 B3
Market St Cannock WS12 .210 B3
 Kidsgrove ST7 .... 26 A1
 Kingswinford DY6 .... 275 B3
 Leek ST13 .... 30 C3
 Lichfield WS13 .... 231 A4
 Longton ST3 .... 283 C3
 Penkridge ST19 .... 192 C1
 Rugeley WS15 .... 178 C1
 Stafford ST16 .... 155 C2
Marketfields ST21 .133 C4
Markham Croft WV9 .260 A4
Markham Dr DY6 .... 275 C2
Marklew Cl WS8 .... 245 A3
Marklin Ave WV10 .... 240 B1
Marks Wlk WS13 .... 214 A1
Marlborough Ave ST16 .156 B2
Marlborough Cl
 Colwich ST18 .... 158 B1
 Endon ST9 .... 43 C4
 Sutton Coldfield B74 .257 C3
Marlborough Cres DE15 .186 A4
Marlborough Croft
 Lichfield WS13 .... 231 A4
 Sutton Coldfield B74 .257 C1
Marlborough Gdns
 Kingswinford DY6 .... 275 C2
 Wolv WV6 .... 255 C2
Marlborough Ind Est
 WV2 .... 266 B4
Marlborough Rd
 Longton ST3 .... 283 C3
 Sedgley DY3 .... 271 C3
 Stone ST15 .... 119 C2
Marlborough St
 Fenton ST4 .... 72 B3

Marlborough St continued
 Walsall WS3 .... 243 A1
Marlborough Way
 Tamworth B77 .... 250 C1
 Uttoxeter ST14 .... 110 C1
Marlbrook Dr WV4 .266 A3
Marlbrook La WV6 .253 A1
Marlburn Way WV5 .269 C3
Marldon Pl ST6 .... 41 B3
Marley Mount Cres TF9 .97 B1
Marlin B77 .... 261 B3
Marlow Cl ST3 .... 73 B3
Marlow Dr ST4 .... 185 A4
Marlow Rd Longton ST3 .73 B3
 Tamworth B77 .... 250 B3
Marlowe Rd ST17 .... 174 A4
Marlpit La Denstone ST14 .95 B3
 Ellastone DE6 .... 80 A2
 Stone ST15 .... 105 C3
 Sutton Coldfield B75 .258 B2
Marlpool Dr WS3 .... 244 A1
Marmion St B79 .... 250 A3
Marnel Dr WV3 .... 265 C4
Marney Wlk ST6 .... 42 A1
Marquis Dr WS12,WS15 .195 B2
Marquis Drive Visitor Ctr*
 WS15 .... 195 B2
Marriatt B77 .... 251 B1
Marriott St ST4 .... 73 A3
Mars St ST6 .... 42 B1
Marsden St ST1 .... 282 C3
Marsett B77 .... 262 B4
Marsh Ave Chell Heath ST6 .42 A1
 Kidsgrove ST7 .... 26 C1
 Newcastle-u-L ST5 .... 56 B3
Marsh Cl ST9 .... 59 A2
Marsh Cres DY8 .... 275 B2
Marsh Ct ST16 .... 155 B3
Marsh Gr Riddulph ST8 .16 B2
 Swindon DY3 .... 269 C1
Marsh Green Cl ST8 .... 16 B1
Marsh Green Rd ST8 .... 16 B1
Marsh La
 Cheswardine TF9 .... 130 A4
 Ellenhall ST21 .... 134 A1
 Lichfield WS14 .... 231 B3
 Penkridge ST19 .... 192 C1
 Stanton DE6 .... 80 A4
 Whittington WS14 .... 232 A3
 Wolv WV10 .... 240 A1
Marsh Lane Par WV10 .240 B1
Marsh Par ST5 .... 284 C3
Marsh Prim Sch ST11 .91 A3
Marsh St N ST1 .... 282 B3
Marsh St ST1 .... 282 B2
Marsh View ST3 .... 90 A3
Marsh Way ST5 .... 56 B3
Marshall Ave ST16 .... 43 A4
Marshall Cl WS9 .... 256 A2
Marshall Gr CW12 .... 16 A4
Marshall St Burslem ST6 .41 C1
 Tamworth B77 .... 250 C3
Marshalls Ind Est ST19 .266 B4
Marshbrook Fst Sch
 ST19 .... 192 C1
Marshfield La ST8 .... 16 B1
Marshland Gr ST16 .... 42 A4
Marshlands Sch ST17 .175 B3
Marshwood Cl **2** WS11 .210 A1
Marsland Cl ST16 .... 155 A2
Marsland Rd ST16 .... 155 A2
Marston Cl
 Stourbridge DY8 .... 279 B2
 Wheaton Aston ST19 .205 B3
Marston Croft ST19 .205 B3
Marston Ct ST16 .... 155 B3
Marston Gr ST1 .... 57 B4
Marston Inst Ind Est WV2 .266 B4
Marston La Hatton DE65 .146 B4
 Marston ST19 .... 136 C1
 Rolleston DE13 .... 147 C4
Marston Old La DE65 .146 B4
Marston Rd
 Cannock WS12 .... 209 C3
 Marston on D DE65 .147 A4
 Stafford ST16 .... 155 C2
 Wheaton Aston ST19 .205 A4
Marston Rise B77 .... 185 C4
Marston Road Trad Pk
 ST16 .... 155 C2
Marsworth Way ST16 .136 B1
 Wolv WV6 .... 255 A1
Martin Croft WS13 .214 A1
Martin Dale TF9 .... 99 B3
Martin Dr B79 .... 250 B4
Martin St Hanley ST1 .... 57 A4
Stafford ST16 .... 155 C2
 Wolv WV4 .... 266 B1
Martin's La DE13 .... 145 A2
Martindale
 Cannock WS11 .... 210 A1
 Stafford ST17 .... 175 B3
Martindale Cl B79 .... 89 C4
Martindale Trad Est
 WS11 .... 210 A1
Martins Hill CW12 .... 6 A1
Martins Way ST18 .... 156 A4
Martinslow La ST10,ST13 .48 C2
Martley Rd WS3 .... 244 B1
Martlin La WS15 .... 179 A3
Marton Ave WS7 .... 229 A4
Marwood Croft B74 .... 257 A1

Mary Howard CE Prim Sch
B79 ...217 B3
Mary Rand CI ST17 ...174 B4
Mary Rose CI ST2 ...58 A2
Mary St ST1 ...210 A4
Marychurch CE Prim Sch
ST2 ...58 A2
Marychurch Rd ST2 ...58 A2
Maryfield Wlk ST4 ...71 C4
Maryhill CI ST7 ...26 A2
Maryhill High Sch ST7 ...26 A2
Maryhill Prim Sch ST7 ...26 A2
Marysgate ST19 ...223 B4
Maryvale CI WS14 ...231 B4
Masefield CI
　Burntwood WS7 ...212 A1
　Cheadle ST10 ...76 B3
　Lichfield WS14 ...231 A3
Masefield Cres DE14 ...166 B4
Masefield Dr B79 ...250 A4
Masefield Gr WS11 ...209 C2
Masefield Rd
　Essington WV10 ...241 A1
　Longton ST3 ...73 A1
　Sedgley DY3 ...271 A2
Mason Cres WV4 ...265 C3
Mason Ct ST4 ...24 A3
Mason St Fenton ST4 ...72 C3
　Wolv WV2 ...266 B4
Mason's PI TF10 ...168 C3
Masons Lawn ST20 ...171 B3
Masterson St ST4 ...72 B3
Matthews Wlk ST1 ...282 C3
Matlock CI WS3 ...243 B2
Matlock Dr WS11 ...210 A2
Matlock PI ST5 ...55 A1
Matlock Rd WS3 ...243 B2
Matlock St ST1 ...282 B1
Matthews PI CV12 ...6 A1
Matthews Rd ST17 ...174 B4
Matthews Wlk WS13 ...214 A1
Maud St ST4 ...72 C4
Maunders Rd ST2 ...43 A1
Maureen Ave ST6 ...41 B3
Maureen Gr ST5 ...56 B2
Mavesyn CI WS15 ...198 A4
Mavis Rd WS12 ...210 A4
Mavor Ave WS7 ...211 B1
Mawdesley St ST6 ...57 A3
Mawgan Dr WS14 ...231 B3
Mawson Gr ST4 ...57 B1
Maxstoke CI
　Tamworth B77 ...261 B2
　Walsall WS3 ...243 A2
Maxtock Ave WS13 ...231 A3
Maxton Way ST3 ...74 A1
Maxwell CI ST4 ...231 B4
Maxwell PI ST4 ...71 C4
Maxwell Rd
　Congleton CW12 ...16 A4
　Wolv WV7 ...266 B4
May Ave Newcastle-u-L ST5 ...56 B2
　Tunstall ST6 ...41 C2
May Bank Inf Sch ST5 ...56 A2
May CI WS7 ...211 C1
May PI Longton ST4 ...283 B5
　Newcastle-u-L ST5 ...56 B2
May St Chell Heath ST6 ...42 A1
　Newcastle-u-L ST5 ...55 B1
Mayall Dr B75 ...258 B2
Mayama Rd B74 ...260 C4
Maybank WS15 ...196 C4
Maybank CI WS14 ...231 C4
Maybrook Ind Est WS8 ...244 C3
Maybrook Rd WS8 ...244 C3
Maybury CI WV8 ...238 C2
Maybury Way ST2 ...43 A1
Maybush Gdns WV10 ...240 B1
Maycroft CI WS12 ...209 C4
Mayer Ave ST5 ...284 B4
Mayer Bank 6 ST6 ...57 A4
Mayer St ST1 ...282 C3
Mayfair DE11 ...186 C3
Mayfair Ave ST10 ...62 A4
Mayfair CI WV7 ...237 A3
Mayfair Dr
　Drayton Bassett B78 ...261 A4
　Kingswinford DY6 ...275 B4
Mayfair Gdns
　18 Tunstall ST6 ...41 B2
　Wolv WV3 ...255 B1
Mayfield B77 ...262 B4
Mayfield Ave Hanley ST1 ...57 C3
　Mayfield DE6 ...81 B4
　Newcastle-u-L ST5 ...284 A2
　Penkridge ST19 ...207 C4
Mayfield CI ST13 ...30 A3
Mayfield Cres ST1 ...57 C2
Mayfield Dr
　Blythe Bridge ST11 ...90 B4
　Burton u T DE15 ...186 A4
Mayfield PI ST5 ...56 B2
Mayfield PI E ST4 ...71 C3
Mayfield PI W ST4 ...71 C3
Mayfield Rd
　Albrighton WV7 ...237 A3
　Biddulph ST8 ...27 B3
　Burton u T DE15 ...167 A2
　Burton u T ST17 ...156 B1
Mayfield Terr DE6 ...81 B3
Mayfields Dr WS8 ...228 A1
Mayflower Dr WS15 ...178 B1
Maygrove Rd DY6 ...275 B4
Maylea Cres ST6 ...57 B4

Maynard Ave DY8 ...279 B2
Maynards Croft TF10 ...169 A2
Mayne St ST4 ...71 C1
Mayneford PI ST4 ...71 C1
Mayock Cres ST16 ...155 A1
Mayou CI WS3 ...244 A2
Maypole CI WV5 ...270 A3
Maypole Dr DY8 ...279 C3
Maypole St WV5 ...270 A4
Mays Wlk DE13 ...200 C2
Mayswood Dr WV6 ...254 C1
Maythorn Gdns
　Codsall WV8 ...239 A2
　Wolv WV6 ...255 B2
Maythorne Rd ST13 ...73 A1
Maywood CI DY6 ...275 A3
McAdam CI DE15 ...167 A1
McBean Rd WV6 ...255 C2
McGeough Wlk WS11 ...210 A3
McGough St ST13 ...210 A3
McGough St 7 ST6 ...41 B2
McGowan Ho ST7 ...40 B4
McKellin CI ST11 ...39 C1
McKie Way WS15 ...196 C3
McKinley St ST6 ...41 B2
Mclean Rd WV10 ...240 B1
Mead Ave ST7 ...25 C4
Mead CI WS9 ...256 A3
Mead Cres DE15 ...186 A3
Mead The Sedgley DY3 ...271 A4
　Trentham ST4 ...88 A4
Mead Wlk DE15 ...186 A3
Meadfoot Dr DY6 ...275 A4
Meadlands The WV5 ...269 C3
Meadow Ave
　Cheddleton ST9 ...60 A3
　13 Longton ST3 ...73 B1
　Newcastle-u-L ST5 ...56 A2
　Weston CW2 ...37 A3
Meadow Bank Wlk
　ST16 ...155 B4
Meadow CI Aldridge B74 ...256 C1
　Blythe Bridge ST11 ...90 C3
　Eccleshall ST21 ...133 C4
　Forsbrook ST11 ...91 A4
　Gnosall ST20 ...171 C4
　Leek ST13 ...31 A3
　Market Drayton TF9 ...97 A1
　Penkridge ST19 ...207 C4
　Wheaton Aston ST19 ...205 A3
Meadow Croft
　Hagley DY9 ...281 C2
　Huntington WS12 ...209 B2
　Perton WV6 ...254 B2
　Streethay WS13 ...215 A1
Meadow Ct Barlaston ST12 ...88 B1
　Burton u T DE14 ...166 B2
　Packmoor ST7 ...26 C1
　Stafford ST17 ...174 B4
Meadow Dr Cheadle ST10 ...76 B2
　Haughton ST18 ...172 C3
　Longton ST3 ...89 A4
Meadow Glade DE18 ...158 B4
Meadow Gr WS6 ...227 A1
Meadow Hill Dr 6
　WS11 ...210 A2
Meadow La
　Acton Trussell ST17 ...193 A4
　Blythe Bridge ST11 ...106 C4
　Brewood WV10 ...240 B3
　Burton u T DE13 ...167 A4
　Colwich ST18 ...167 A4
　Millmeece ST21 ...117 C4
　Newcastle-u-L ST5 ...56 A2
　Roston DE6 ...96 B4
　Seighford ST18 ...154 C1
　Swadlincote DE11 ...186 C3
　Trentham ST4 ...88 B4
　Wombourne WV5 ...270 A4
　Yoxall DE13 ...200 A4
Meadow Lark CI WS12 ...210 A2
Meadow Pk ST9 ...249 C3
Meadow PI ST3 ...74 A1
Meadow Rd
　Albrighton WV7 ...237 A3
　Aldridge WS9 ...256 A2
　Barlaston ST12 ...88 B1
　Burton u T DE14 ...166 C2
　Chell Heath ST6 ...42 B3
　Endon ST9 ...43 A3
　Newport TF10 ...169 A2
　Stafford ST17 ...174 C4
　Tamworth B77 ...249 C2
　Wolv WV3 ...265 B4
Meadow Ridge ST17 ...175 B4
Meadow Rise DE13 ...183 C1
Meadow Side ST8 ...27 A3
Meadow St
　Newcastle-u-L ST5 ...55 C3
　Norton-in-t-M ST2 ...43 A1
　Tamworth B77 ...250 B2
Meadow The ST9 ...43 C4
Meadow Vale WV8 ...239 A1
Meadow View
　Burntwood WS7 ...229 B3
　Doveridge DE6 ...127 B4
　Rolleston DE13 ...147 B2
　Sedgley DY3 ...266 B1
Meadow View CI TF10 ...169 A2
Meadow View Rd
　Newport TF10 ...169 A2
　Swadlincote DE11 ...186 C3
Meadow View Terr
　WS11 ...255 C2
Meadow Way
　Armitage WS15 ...198 A2
　Cannock WS12 ...210 B3
　Codsall WV8 ...238 C1

Meadow Way continued
　Kingswinford DY6 ...275 B1
　Lawton-gate ST7 ...25 A3
　Stone ST15 ...119 C3
　Upper Tean ST10 ...92 B2
　Whitmore ST5 ...85 B3
Meadowbank Ave ST18 ...138 C1
Meadowbank Grange
　WS6 ...226 C2
Meadowbrook Ct 4
　ST15 ...120 B3
Meadowbrook Gdns
　WV8 ...239 A2
Meadowcroft Rd WS13 ...214 A2
Meadowcroft Ave ST5 ...90 B4
Meadowcroft Gdns
　ST19 ...205 A3
Meadowfields CI DY8 ...275 C1
Meadowhill Dr 1 DY8 ...275 C1
Meadowlands Dr WS4 ...244 B1
Meadowpark Rd DY8 ...279 B4
Meadows Gr WV8 ...239 A2
Meadows Prim Sch CW3 ...69 A4
Meadows Rd ST7 ...25 C1
Meadows St ST8 ...27 B3
Meadows The
　Brewood ST19 ...223 B3
　Hilderstone ST15 ...106 B1
　Kingstone ST14 ...141 B4
　Rugeley WS15 ...197 A3
　Salt ST18 ...137 C2
　Uttoxeter ST14 ...111 A1
Meadowside Ashley TF9 ...99 C3
　Blythe Bridge ST11 ...91 A1
　Mayfield DE6 ...81 B3
　Trentham ST4 ...88 A4
Meadowside Ave ST7 ...25 B4
Meadowside Dr DE14 ...166 C2
Meadowside La ST7 ...26 A4
Meadowside Rd B74 ...257 C2
Meadowsweet Way
　WS12 ...210 C2
Meadowview
　Norton-in-t-M ST6 ...42 C2
　Swynnerton ST15 ...118 C3
Medway CI WS12 ...210 B2
Medway CI DE7 ...175 B3
Medway St WS7 ...229 A3
Medway The WV6 ...255 A3
Meaford Ave ST5 ...104 C1
Meaford Dr ST3 ...72 C2
Meaford Rd ST12,ST15 ...104 B3
Meakin Ave ST5 ...71 A2
Meakin CI Cheadle ST10 ...76 B1
　Congleton CW12 ...16 B3
　Stone ST15 ...120 B3
Meakin Gr ST16 ...155 A3
Meakin Ho ST15 ...104 C1
Mear Greaves La DE15 ...167 A2
Mear's La WS15 ...198 C4
Mease Ave WV7 ...229 B3
Mease La B79 ...218 A1
Mease The DE65 ...147 C4
Meddins CI DY7 ...278 A2
Meddins La DY7 ...277 C2
Meddins Rise DY7 ...277 C2
Medina CI WV10 ...240 C2
Medina CI ST4 ...88 A4
Meerbrook CI ST14 ...88 A3
Meerbrook Rd ST13 ...19 C1
Meerbrook YH* ST13 ...19 B1
Meere CI ST5 ...42 C2
Meeson CI WV7 ...237 A3
Meg La WS7 ...229 A2
Megacre ST7 ...40 A1
Meigh Rd ST9 ...59 A2
Meigh St ST1 ...282 C3
Meiklejohn PI ST6 ...42 A3
Meir Heath Prim Sch
　ST3 ...90 A2
Meir Prim Sch ST3 ...74 A1
Meir Rd ST3 ...73 C1
Meir St ST6 ...41 C2
Meir View ST3 ...74 A1
Meirhay Rd ST3 ...73 B1
Melbourne Ave DE15 ...167 B2
Melbourne CI DY6 ...275 C2
Melbourne Cres
　Cannock WS12 ...210 C1
　Stafford ST16 ...156 A3
Melbourne Rd WS12 ...210 C1
Melbourne St ST13 ...73 C1
Melbury Way 1 WS11 ...209 C1
Melchester Gr ST3 ...73 C1
Melchester Wlk 2
　WS11 ...209 C1
Melfont St ST6 ...42 A1
Melford B79 ...249 C3
Melford CI DY3 ...266 B1
Melford Grange WS12 ...210 C1
Melford Rise WS7 ...211 C1
Meliden Way ST4 ...71 C4
Mellard St Audley ST7 ...39 B1
Mellbreak CI ST5 ...284 A4

Mellor Dr
　Sutton Coldfield B74 ...257 C2
　Uttoxeter ST14 ...111 A1
Mellor Rd DE14 ...185 A4
Mellor St ST14 ...111 A1
Mellors Bank ST7 ...26 B3
Mellow La ST10,ST13 ...47 C2
Mellowdew Rd DY8 ...275 B2
Mellwaters B77 ...262 B4
Melmerby B77 ...262 B4
Melrose Ave
　Blythe Bridge ST3 ...90 A2
　Hanley ST1 ...57 B4
　Newcastle-u-L ST5 ...71 A3
　Stafford ST17 ...174 C4
　Stone ST15 ...120 B3
　Stourbridge DY8 ...279 C1
Melrose Cres TF9 ...112 A4
Melrose Dr
　Cannock WS12 ...209 C4
　Wolv WV6 ...254 C2
Melrose PI ST11 ...30 A3
Melstone Ave ST6 ...41 C2
Melville CI ST5 ...71 B1
Melville Rd ST5 ...73 C1
Melville St ST1 ...57 C3
Melvyn Cres ST6 ...56 B4
Menai Dr ST8 ...27 B3
Menai Gr ST3 ...283 C5
Mendip Ave ST17 ...175 C3
Mendip CI Sedgley DY3 ...271 B2
　Wolv WV2 ...266 C4
Mendip Gn ST2 ...43 A1
Mendip PI ST5 ...55 C2
Mendip Rd WS12 ...195 A1
Mendip Way B77 ...249 B1
Mentone Cres TF10 ...168 A2
Menzies Ho 6 ST3 ...89 C4
Meole Ho WS6 ...244 B1
Meon Gr WV6 ...254 C2
Mercer Ave ST15 ...120 B4
Mercer St ST5 ...73 A1
Merchant CI WV6 ...253 B2
Merchants Way WS14 ...231 B4
Mercia CI Hatton DE65 ...146 B4
　Tamworth B79 ...249 C4
Mercia Cres ST4 ...57 A3
Mercia Dr WV6 ...254 C3
Mercian CI
　6 Lichfield WS14 ...231 B4
　Market Drayton TF9 ...97 B1
Mercian Rd B77 ...251 A2
Mercian Way
　Tamworth B77 ...251 A2
　Wheaton Aston ST19 ...206 A4
Mercury CI B77 ...251 A2
Mercury PI ST6 ...42 A2
Mercury Rd WS11 ...210 A3
Mere CI TF10 ...168 C2
Mere Croft WS11 ...227 C2
Mere Green B75 ...258 B1
Mere Green Comb Sch
　B75 ...258 B2
Mere Green Rd B75 ...258 B1
Mere La DY7 ...273 B3
Mere Oak Rd WV6 ...254 C3
Mere Pool Rd B75 ...258 C1
Mere Rd Stourbridge DY8 ...279 C2
　Weston CW2 ...37 A3
Mere Rise ST21 ...132 B4
Meredith CI DE14 ...166 B3
Meredith Rd WV2 ...266 C4
Merelake Rd ST7 ...40 A4
Meremore Dr ST5 ...40 B1
Merevale Ave ST7 ...58 A1
Merganser B77 ...262 A3
Meriden Ave B79 ...249 B3
Meriden CI
　Cannock WS11 ...226 A4
　Stourbridge DY8 ...279 B3
Meriden Rd
　Newcastle-u-L ST5 ...71 B1
　Wolv WV10 ...240 A1
Merino CI ST3 ...89 A4
Merlin CI Cannock WS11 ...209 C1
　Chell Heath ST6 ...42 A4
　Tamworth B77 ...262 A2
　Uttoxeter ST14 ...126 B3
Merlin Cres DE14 ...184 C4
Merlin Gn CW3 ...68 C3
Merlin Way Kidsgrove ST7 ...25 A4
　Whittington WS14 ...232 C3
Merrial St ST5 ...284 B3
Merrick St ST1 ...282 C4
Merridale Ave WV3 ...255 C1
Merridale Ct WV3 ...255 C1
Merridale La WV3 ...255 C1
Merridale Rd WV3 ...255 C1
Merridale St WV3 ...266 A4
Merrill CI WS6 ...226 C1
Merrion Dr ST6 ...42 A2
Merrivale Rd ST17 ...174 C4
Merry Rd ST17 ...156 B1
Merrydale Rd DE15 ...186 A4
Merryfield Rd DY1 ...271 C1
Merryfields Sch ST5 ...56 A2
Mersey CI WS15 ...178 C2
Mersey Rd
　Newcastle-u-L ST5 ...71 A2
　Walsall WS3 ...243 C1
Mersey St ST1 ...282 A2
Merthyr Gr B77 ...27 C3
Merton Ct WV7 ...228 C3
Merton St ST3 ...73 A2
Mervyn Rd DE15 ...167 A2
Mesnes Gn WS14 ...231 B4
Metcalf CI WS7 ...229 B4

Metcalfe CI WS12 ...210 B3
Metcalfe Rd ST6 ...42 A2
Metfield CI B79 ...250 B4
Metfield Croft DY6 ...275 C3
Mewies CI DE12 ...184 B1
Mews CI ST3 ...58 A1
Mews The Cannock WS11 ...209 B1
　Newcastle-u-L ST5 ...56 B2
Meynell CI DE15 ...167 A1
Meyrick Rd ST17 ...155 C1
Mica CI B77 ...251 A1
Michael CI ST3 ...89 A4
Michael's La DE6 ...80 B3
Michaels CI ST5 ...56 B4
Michigan CI WS11 ...210 A1
Michigan Gr ST4 ...58 A1
Micklea La ST9 ...29 C1
Micklebly Way ST3 ...90 B4
Micklegate ST19 ...223 B4
Micklehome Dr DE11 ...201 A2
Mickleholme Dr DE11 ...201 A2
Micklewood CI LA T19 ...207 C4
Micklewood La ST19 ...208 A2
Middle Cross St ST3 ...283 C4
Middle Entry B79 ...250 A2
Middle Friars ST17 ...155 C1
Middle La Brewood WV9 ...240 A3
　Codsall WV8 ...238 B1
　Codsall, Coven Heath WV9 ...240 A3
　Congleton CW12 ...6 B2
　Gnosall TF10 ...188 B4
Middlefield Gnosall ST20 ...171 C4
　Wolv WV8 ...239 C1
Middlefield Rd ST2 ...73 B4
Middlefurlong Gdns
　ST7 ...41 C4
Middlehurst Specl Sch
　ST7 ...41 C4
Middlemore La West WS9 ...256 A3
Middlepark Rd WS9 ...271 C1
Middlesmoor B77 ...262 B4
Middleton CI ST16 ...42 C2
Middleton Hall* B78 ...260 C1
Middleton Rd
　Aldridge B74 ...257 A1
　Brownhills WS8 ...229 A1
　Whittington WS14 ...232 C3
Middleway WS12 ...211 A3
Middleway Ave DY8 ...275 B2
Midfield CI ST8 ...16 B1
Midge La ST5 ...258 A1
Midhurst CI ST7 ...41 C4
Midhurst Dr WS12 ...210 B4
Midhurst Gr WV6 ...255 B3
Midland Rd WS12 ...209 B4
Midway Dr ST11 ...90 C3
Midway The ST15 ...284 B2
Midwinter CI ST6 ...56 C3
Milan Dr ST5 ...70 B3
Milborne CI ST4 ...58 A1
Milburn B77 ...262 B4
Milburn Rd ST6 ...57 A3
Milcote Way DY6 ...275 A4
Mildenhall B79 ...250 B4
Mile Ct ST5 ...56 C2
Mile Flat DY6 ...274 C4
Mile Oak Cross Roads
　B78 ...249 B1
Milehouse La ST5 ...56 A2
Miles Bank ST1 ...282 B3
Miles Green Rd ST7 ...54 C4
Milestone Dr WV6 ...255 A2
Milestone Dr DY9 ...281 C2
Milford Ave ST3 ...59 A2
Milford CI DY8 ...275 C2
Milford Rd
　Newcastle-u-L ST5 ...284 A1
　Stafford ST17 ...175 C4
Milford St ST4 ...72 C3
Milgreen Ave ST1 ...57 B4
Milk St ST13 ...30 C3
Milking Bank DY1 ...271 C1
Milking Bank Prim Sch
　DY1 ...271 C1
Mill Bank DY3 ...271 B4
Mill CI Blakedown DY10 ...281 A1
　Caverswall ST11 ...74 B2
　Newton Solney DE15 ...167 C4
　Sedgley DY3 ...271 B3
Mill Cotts ST18 ...139 B3
Mill Cres
　Barton-u-N DE13 ...201 C4
　Cannock WS11 ...210 A1
Mill End La DE13 ...158 A1
Mill End La DE13 ...200 C2
Mill Farm Ct ST11 ...134 B3
Mill Fields DY7 ...278 A2
Mill Gn WV10 ...240 B2
Mill Gr Cheadle ST10 ...76 C1
　Codsall WV8 ...239 B2
Kidsgrove ST7 ...25 B4
Mill Green Nature Pk*
　WS11 ...209 C1
Mill Hayes Rd
　Biddulph ST8 ...27 B2
　Burslem ST6 ...41 C1
Mill Hill Cres DE15 ...167 A2
Mill Hill La DE15 ...167 A2
Mill Hill Prim Sch ST6 ...41 C2
Mill Ho DY7 ...278 A2
Mill La
　Acton Trussell ST17 ...175 A1
　Albrighton WV7 ...220 C1
　Aldridge WS9 ...256 C4
　Barthomley CW2 ...38 B4
　Barton-u-N DE13 ...201 C4
　Blakedown DY10 ...281 A1
　Blakenhall CW5 ...52 A2

Mill La *continued*
Burntwood WS7 229 B2
Cheddleton ST9 59 C4
Cheslyn Hay WS11 226 B3
Codsall WV8 238 C3
Colwich ST18 158 A1
Congleton CW12 16 B4
Doveridge DE6 127 A4
Edingale B79 217 B2
Ellastone DE6 80 A1
Fazeley B78 261 A4
Foston DE65 129 B4
Gnosall ST20 171 B3
Hartington SK17 24 B3
Kingstone ST14 124 C2
Kinver DY7 278 A2
Kinver, Blundies DY7 274 A2
Little Aston WS9 257 A4
Madeley CW3 68 C4
Milwich ST18 122 B2
Oakamoor ST10 78 A3
Roston DE6 96 B4
Rugeley WS15 178 C1
Scropton DE65 129 C1
Shenstone WS14 247 A3
Shenstone, Lower Stonnall WS9,WS14 246 A2
Standon ST21 102 B2
Stone ST15 105 C3
Tamworth B79 250 B3
The Bank ST7 26 A4
Upper Tean ST10 92 C1
Weston CW2 37 A3
Weston-u-L TF11 220 B4
Wheaton Aston ST19 205 B3
Wolv WV6 255 A2
Wombourne WV5 270 A3
Mill Meece Marsh ST21 102 B1
Mill Meece Pumping Sta* ST21 117 C4
Mill Park Ind Est WS11 210 A1
Mill Pk WS11 210 A1
Mill Pond The WS13 214 B1
Mill Pool Rd WS12 210 A3
Mill Rd
Brownhills, Catshill WS8 245 A4
Cheadle ST10 76 C1
Walsall WS4 244 B1
Mill Rise ST7 26 A1
Mill St Cannock WS11 209 C1
Kingswinford DY8 275 C1
Leek ST13 30 B3
Newcastle-u-L ST5 55 B1
Penkridge ST19 192 C1
Rocester ST14 96 A2
Stafford ST16 155 C2
Stone ST15 120 A4
Mill Stream Cl WV8 239 A2
Mill View ST6 42 B3
Mill Waters ST10 76 C1
Mill Way WS15 198 A1
Mill Way The ST15 103 A2
Millbank ST16 155 C2
Millbank Dr ST14 96 A2
Millbank Pl ST5 55 C1
Millbank St
Essington WV11 241 C1
Longton ST3 283 C3
Millbeck Cl CW2 37 A3
Millbridge Cl ST3 90 A3
Millbrook Cl 4 WS11 209 C1
Millbrook Dr WS14 246 C3
Millbrook Gr ST2 43 A1
Millbrook Way ST10 76 C1
Millcourt ST4 87 C4
Millcroft Way WS15 198 B2
Milldale Cres WV10 240 B2
Milldale Rd WV10 240 B2
Millend La ST7 39 B3
Millenium Cl WS3 244 A2
Millenium Way
Newcastle-u-L ST5 40 C1
Stone ST15 104 C1
Millennium Way WV8 239 A2
Miller St ST5 284 C3
Millers Gate 2 ST15 120 A4
Millers Gn WV7 237 A2
Millers Green Dr DY6 275 A4
Millers La
Burton u T DE14 166 B2
Norton-in-t-M ST2 43 A1
Millers Vale
Cannock WS12 210 B1
Wombourne WV5 269 B3
Millers View Cheadle ST10 76 C1
Kidsgrove ST7 26 A1
Millers Wlk WS3 243 C2
Millersdale Cl DE15 167 A3
Millett Rd ST2 58 A2
Millfield Ave
Walsall WS3 243 B2
Walsall, Shelfield WS4 244 A1
Millfield Cres ST2 43 A1
Millfield Dr TF9 97 C1
Millfield Prim Sch
Brownhills WS8 245 A4
Fazeley B78 261 A4
Millfield Rd WS8 245 A4
Millfields Way WV5 269 C3
Millhouse Dr ST10 76 C1
Millhouse Gdns ST19 192 C1
Millicent Cl WS12 210 A3
Millicent St ST4 72 C3
Millington St WS15 178 C1
Millmoor Ave WS15 198 A2
Millpool The WV5 263 C1
Millrise Rd ST2 43 A1
Mills Cres WV2 266 C4
Mills Rd WV2 266 C4
Millside WS15 196 A4
Millstone Ave ST7 25 C1
Millstone Edge ST13 45 A1
Millstream Cl ST10 76 C1
Milltown Way ST13 31 A2
Millwalk Ave ST15 120 B4
Millwalk Dr WV9 240 A2
Millward Rd ST2 58 B2
Millway La DE6 35 C2
Milne Ave WS13 215 B3
Milner Dr B79 251 C4
Milner Terr ST13 31 A4
Milnes Cl ST3 73 A1
Milo Cres B78 250 A1
Milton Ave B79 250 A4
Milton Cres Sedgley DY3 271 A3
Talke ST7 40 B4
Milton Ct WV6 254 C2
Milton Dr TF9 97 B1
Milton Gr ST17 174 A4
Milton Ho DE14 166 B2
Milton Prim Sch ST2 43 A1
Milton Rd Cannock WS11 209 C2
Hanley ST1 57 C4
Milton St Burton u T DE14 166 B2
Hanley ST1 282 A1
Milvale St ST6 56 C4
Milverton Dr ST14 110 C1
Milverton Pl 4 ST3 73 A2
Milward Gr ST3 89 C3
Mimosa Wlk DY6 275 C4
Minard Gr ST3 74 A2
Minden Gr ST6 57 B4
Mineal Rd ST2 73 B4
Minehead Rd
Dudley DY1 271 C1
Wolv WV10 240 A1
Miners Wlk B78 251 C1
Minerva Cl Biddulph ST8 27 A3
Tamworth B77 250 B3
Minerva Rd ST4 72 C3
Minewood Cl WS3 242 C2
Minfield Cl ST7 41 A4
Minn-End-La SK11 8 A3
Minors Hill WS14 231 B3
Minshall Ct ST4 72 B3
Minshall St ST4 72 B3
Minster St ST6 42 A1
Minster The WV3 266 A4
Minsterley Cl WV3 265 C4
Minsterpool Wlk WS13 231 A4
Minton Cl Cheadle ST10 76 B1
Congleton CW12 6 A1
Minton Pl ST5 56 B3
Minton St
Newcastle-u-L ST5 56 B3
Stoke-on-T ST4 71 C4
Miranda Gr ST6 42 B1
Miras Bsns Est WS12 210 B2
Mires Brook La WS15 160 C3
Mires The DE6 35 A2
Mirfield Cl WV9 240 A2
Miss Pickerings Field ST17 175 A1
Mistley Wlk ST6 41 B4
Mitcham Cl WS12 209 C4
Mitchel Rd DY6 275 C2
Mitchell Ave ST7 25 B1
Mitchell Dr ST7 25 B1
Mitchell High Sch ST2 58 B2
Mitchell Rise ST15 118 C3
Mitchell St ST6 41 C1
Mitchell's Ct B79 250 A3
Mitre Cl WV11 242 A2
Mitre Rd WS6 226 B1
Mitton Rd ST18 191 B4
Moat Bank DE15 167 B1
Moat Brook Ave WV8 238 C2
Moat Dr B78 260 C3
Moat Farm Way WS3 244 A3
Moat Hall Prim Sch WS6 226 C2
Moat House Dr ST18 172 C3
Moat La Audley ST7 39 A2
Great Wyrley WS6 227 A1
Newborough DE13 162 C3
Moat The ST3 74 A2
Moat Way WS15 198 A2
Moatbrook La WV8 238 B2
Moathouse Cl ST17 193 A4
Moatside Cl WS3 244 A3
Mob La WS4 244 B2
Mobberley Rd ST6 41 B4
Moccasin Way ST16 155 C3
Moden Cl DY3 271 B3
Moden Hill DY3 271 B3
Modular Ct WV10 224 B3
Moffat Gr ST2 73 C4
Moffat Way ST5 55 A1
Moises Hall Rd WV5 270 A4
Moisty La
Marchington ST14 127 B2
Uttoxeter ST14 126 C2
Mollatts Cl ST13 30 A1
Mollatts Wood Rd ST13 30 A1
Mollison Rd ST3 90 A4
Mona Rd DE13 166 A3
Monaco Pl ST5 70 C4
Monarch Cl DE13 166 B4
Moncreiff Dr DE13 148 A1
Monk St DE13 146 B4
Monkhouse ST10 76 B2
Monkleigh Cl ST4 88 A3
Monks Cl
Newcastle-u-L ST5 71 B3
Wombourne WV5 269 C3
Monks Way
Swynnerton ST15 103 A2
Tamworth B77 250 C3
Monks Wlk ST20 171 B3
Monksfield TF9 97 A1
Monkton Cl ST3 73 A1
Monmore Bsns Pk WV2 266 C4
Monmouth Pl ST5 71 B2
Monpelier Cl DE14 185 A4
Monsal Gr ST1 57 C3
Monsaldale Cl
Brownhills WS8 244 B4
Burton u T DE15 167 A2
Monteagle Dr DY6 270 B1
Montford Gr DY3 271 B4
Montfort Pl ST5 71 A3
Montgomery Ct ST5 284 A3
Montgomery Pl ST3 74 A1
Montley B77 262 B4
Montpellier Gdns DY1 271 C1
Montrose Cl WS11 209 C3
Montrose St ST4 72 C3
Montville Dr ST17 155 A1
Monty Pl ST4 73 A3
Monument Cl ST12 88 A1
Monument Dr WV10 241 B4
Monument La
Sedgley DY3 266 C1
Tittensor ST12 88 A1
Monument Rd ST7 40 B3
Monument View ST7 39 C1
Monyash Cl ST3 90 B4
Monyash Dr ST13 31 A3
Moon's La WS6 226 B1
Moor Cl
Acton Trussell ST17 175 A1
Biddulph ST8 16 C1
Burntwood WS7 229 A4
Moor Croft WS15 179 A3
Moor Fst Sch ST8 17 A1
Moor Furlong DE13 147 C1
Moor Gr ST14 126 A4
Moor Hall Dr B75 258 B1
Moor Hall La ST19 208 A4
Moor Hall Prim Sch B75 258 B1
Moor La Cheadle ST10 76 C2
Church Leigh ST10 108 C3
Colton WS15 179 A4
Gayton ST18 138 C3
Pattingham WV6 253 B1
Seighford ST18 154 B4
Shenstone WS14 246 C1
Tamworth, Amington B79 251 A3
Tamworth, Bolehall B77 250 B3
Moor Pk Perton WV6 254 B3
Walsall WS3 243 A2
Moor St Burton u T DE14 166 B1
Tamworth B79 250 A3
Moor St S WV2 266 B4
Moor The WS13 215 B4
Moor View WS7 212 A1
Moorcroft (Mus)* ST6 57 A4
Moorcroft Ave ST5 71 A2
Moorcroft Cl ST10 76 B1
Moore Cl Perton WV6 254 C2
Sutton Coldfield B74 257 C3
Moore St Burslem ST6 57 A4
Cannock WS12 210 B4
Moores Cl DE13 166 A3
Moores Croft B79 217 B3
Moorfield Ave ST8 27 B4
Moorfield Ct TF10 168 C1
Moorfield La TF10 168 B1
Moorfield Prim Sch TF10 168 C1
Moorfield Rd WV2 266 B4
Moorfields Leek ST13 30 C3
Stafford ST16 155 B4
Moorfields Cl Cotton ST10 63 C2
Millmeece ST21 102 C1
Moorfields Ind Est ST21 102 C2
Moorgate B79 250 A3
Moorgate Prim Sch B79 250 A3
Moorhead Dr ST9 43 C2
Moorhill Prim Sch WS11 209 C2
Moorhouse Ct ST15 119 A3
Moorhouse St ST13 30 C3
Moorings The
Alrewas DE13 200 C2
Colwich ST17 177 C4
Wolv WV9 239 C1
Moorland Ave ST9 59 B2
Moorland Cl
Caverswall ST9 59 A2
Rugeley WS15 178 B1
Moorland Rd Biddulph ST8 27 B4
Burslem ST6 57 A4
Cannock WS11 209 C3
Cheddleton ST13 45 B3
Chell Heath ST6 42 A1
Kidsgrove ST7 26 B4
Leek ST13 31 A3
Newport TF10 168 C1
Moorland View ST6 42 B2
Moorland Wlk ST10 76 B2
Moorlands Dr DE6 81 B4
Moorlands Farm Pk The* ST10 47 B2
Moorlands Sixth Form Ctr ST10 76 B1
Moorleys La ST18 139 A3
Moorpark Jun Sch ST6 42 A1
Moors Dr WV9 224 A1
Moorside High Sch ST9 59 C2
Moorside Rd ST9 59 B2
Moorson Ave ST7 25 C4
Moorsyde Rd ST4 71 C3
Moorthorne Cres ST5 56 A3
Moorview Gdns ST7 26 C3
Moran Gr ST6 56 C4
Moran Rd ST5 55 C1
Mordaunt Dr B75 258 C1
Moresby Cl ST2 43 A1
Moreton Ave
Kingsley ST10 61 B1
Tittensor ST5 87 B4
Wolv WV4 266 C2
Moreton Cl
Caverswall ST9 59 A1
Kidsgrove ST7 41 A4
Moreton Com Sch WV10 240 C1
Moreton La Colwich ST18 158 C2
Draycott in t C DE6 144 B4
Moreton Par ST5 56 B2
Moreton Rd WV10 240 B1
Moreton St WS11 209 C2
Morfe La DY7 273 B2
Morford Rd WS9 256 A4
Morgan Rd B78 250 A1
Morgan Way ST6 42 A3
Morland Cl ST15 120 A3
Morley Dr CW12 6 A1
Morley Rd WS7 229 A4
Morley Road Sh Ctr WS7 229 A4
Morley St Hanley ST1 282 A2
Leek ST13 30 B3
Morley's Hill DE13 166 A4
Morlings Dr WS7 229 A4
Morning Pines DY8 279 C2
Morningside CW3 68 C3
Mornington Rd ST1 57 C4
Morpeth B77 261 B4
Morpeth St ST3 283 C3
Morridge View ST13 45 B2
Morris Dr ST16 156 B2
Morris Sq ST5 56 B3
Morston B77 261 B2
Morston Dr ST5 71 A1
Mortimer Pl ST3 73 C2
Morton Rd ST17 174 B3
Morton St ST6 56 C4
Morville Cl ST4 72 C4
Mosedale Ave ST3 89 C4
Moseley Ct WV11 241 C2
Moseley Old Hall* WV10 241 A3
Moseley Old Hall La WV10 241 A3
Moseley Rd WV10 241 A2
Moseley Row ST18 137 B1
Mosley Dr ST14 111 A1
Mosley Prim Sch DE13 165 B4
Mosley St DE14 166 B2
Moss Cl Aldridge WS9 256 A3
Caverswall ST9 59 A2
Huntington WS12 209 B3
Moss Gn WS15 178 B1
Moss Gr
Kingswinford DY6 275 B4
Newcastle-u-L ST5 40 B2
Moss Green Rd ST2 73 B4
Moss Hill ST9 43 B3
Moss La
Blythe Bridge ST15 106 C3
Cheadle ST10 77 A1
Cheswardine TF9 114 B2
Gnosall ST20 151 C4
Lawton-gate ST7 25 C2
Madeley CW3 68 B3
Maer ST5 84 C1
Norton in H TF9 97 C3
Stone ST15 119 A4
Whitmore ST5 85 B3
Moss Park Ave ST9 59 A2
Moss Pl ST7 26 A2
Moss Rd Cannock WS11 210 A2
Congleton CW12 15 C4
Moss Rise ST5 71 B1
Moss Side ST1 57 C4
Moss St Cannock WS11 210 A2
Norton-in-t-M ST6 42 C3
Mossbank Ave WS7 229 A3
Mossdale B77 262 B4
Mossdale Way DY3 271 C4
Mossfield TF9 130 A3
Mossfield Cres 13 ST7 26 A1
Mossfield Dr ST8 27 C4
Mossfield Rd ST3 73 B3
Mossland Rd ST3 73 B3
Mossley CE Prim Sch CW12 16 A4
Mossley Cl WS3 242 C1
Mossley Ct CW12 15 C4
Mossley La WS3 242 C1
Mossley Prim Sch WS3 242 C1
Mosspit ST17 174 C3
Mossvale Gr ST16 155 A3
Mosswood St WS11 226 B4
Moston St ST1 57 B3
Mostyn Cl ST8 27 C3
Mott Pl ST6 56 B4
Moulton Rd ST3 283 B4
Mount Ave
Cannock WS12 210 A4
Stoke-on-T ST4 71 C4
Stone ST15 104 C1
Mount Cl Caverswall ST9 59 B2
Cheslyn Hay WS6 226 C1
Sedgley DY3 271 B1
Wombourne WV5 270 A4
Mount Cres ST15 104 C1
Mount Ct WV6 255 A1
Mount Dr WV5 270 A4
Mount Edge ST18 137 A1
Mount Fields ST10 94 A1
Mount Gdns WV8 238 C2
Mount Ind Est ST15 104 C1
Mount La
Market Drayton TF9 112 B4
Sedgley DY3 271 B1
Mount Pl ST11 91 A4
Mount Pleasant
Ashley TF9 99 C3
Cheslyn Hay WS6 226 C1
Hanley ST1 282 A2
Ipstones ST10 62 A4
Kidsgrove ST7 26 A1
Kingswinford DY6 275 B2
Leek ST13 30 C3
Newcastle-u-L ST5 284 C2
Newcastle-u-L, Chesterton ST5 55 C3
Seighford ST18 154 C1
Tamworth B77 261 B4
Mount Pleasant Ave WV5 269 C4
Mount Pleasant CE Prim Sch ST4 72 B3
Mount Pleasant Cl 1 ST15 120 B3
Mount Pleasant Rd ST7 26 A4
Mount Rd
Burntwood WS7 229 A3
Forsbrook ST11 91 A4
Kidsgrove ST7 26 A1
Kingswinford DY8 275 C1
Leek ST13 31 A3
Linton DE11 186 B1
Rugeley WS15 178 A1
Stone ST15 104 C1
Walsall WS3 244 A2
Wolv, Cinder Hill WV4 266 C1
Wolv, Colton Hills WV4 266 A2
Wolv, Tettenhall Wood WV6 255 A2
Wombourne WV5 270 A4
Mount Road Ind Est WS7 229 A3
Mount Row ST16 155 C2
Mount Sch for Deaf The ST4 71 C4
Mount Side Rd WS12 210 B4
Mount St
Burton u T DE15 167 A2
Cannock WS12 210 A4
Hanley ST1 57 C3
Newcastle-u-L ST5 55 C3
3 Stafford ST16 155 C2
Stone ST15 105 A1
Mount The Kidsgrove ST7 26 A1
Newcastle-u-L ST5 55 C3
Scholar Green ST7 25 C4
Mountain Ash Rd WS8 244 C3
Mountain Pine Cl WS12 210 A4
Mountbatten Cl
Burntwood WS7 211 C1
Burton u T DE13 166 B4
Mountfield Pl ST4 72 B3
Mountford Cres WS9 256 B4
Mountford St ST6 41 C1
Mountside Gdns ST13 31 A3
Mountsorrel Cl ST4 88 B3
Mountwood Covert WV6 255 A2
Mouse Hill WS3 243 C2
Mousley St ST6 56 C4
Mow Cop Rd ST7 26 B3
Mow La Biddulph ST7,ST8 16 A1
Mount Pleasant ST7 26 A3
Mowbray Croft WS7 211 C1
Mowbray Wlk ST1 57 C4
Moxhull Cl WV12 242 B1
Moxhull Gdns WV12 242 B1
Moxley Ave ST1 57 B4
Mozart Ct WS11 210 B1
Muchal Rd WV4 266 A3
Mucklestone Rd TF9 99 B3
Mucklestone Wood La TF9 99 C3
Muirfield B77 251 B3
Muirfield Cl WS3 243 A2
Muirville Cl 5 DY8 275 B2
Mulberry Cl TF10 168 C1
Mulberry Gn DY1 271 C3
Mulberry Pl
Newcastle-u-L ST5 55 C4
Walsall WS3 242 C1
Mulberry Rd
Cannock WS11 209 C2
Walsall WS3 243 A1
Mulberry St ST1 282 C2
Mulberry Way ST13 31 A2
Muldoon Cl WS11 210 A2
Mulgrave St ST1 282 A4
Mulliner Cl ST2 58 B2
Munro St ST4 72 A3
Munster Terr ST4 71 C3
Murhall St ST6 56 C4
Murray St ST6 41 B4
Murton B77 262 B4
Mus of Cannock Chase* WS12 210 B3
Muse La DE6 129 A4
Musk La DY3 271 A2
Musk La W DY3 271 A2
Mustang Cl ST6 41 B2

Muxloe Cl WS3 .... 243 A2
Myatt Ave
  Burntwood WS7 .... 229 A4
  Wolv WV2 .... 266 C3
Myatt Cl WV2 .... 266 C3
Myatt St S11 .... 282 C4
Myatt Way WS15 .... 196 C3
Mynors St Hanley ST1 .. 282 C3
Stafford ST16 .... 156 A2
Myott Ave ST5 .... 284 A1
Myrtle Ave ST3 .... 74 A2
Myrtle Gr Brewood ST19 . 223 B3
  Wolv WV3 .... 265 C3
Myrtle St WV2 .... 266 C3

N

Nab Hill Ave ST13 .... 30 B3
Nab Hill Ct ST13 .... 30 B3
Nabb La Alton ST10 ...... 94 C4
  Denstone ST14 .... 95 A2
Nabbs Cl ST7 .... 26 A1
Nabbsword Rd ST17 ...... 26 A1
Naden Ho ST17 .... 209 B3
Naesby Rd WV4 .... 254 C2
Nagington Dr ST19 ...... 207 C4
Nailers Dr WS7 .... 229 B3
Nairn Rd WS3 .... 243 A2
Nankirk La DE13 .... 165 A3
Nanny Goat La ST15 .... 105 A1
Nantwich Rd Betley ST7 .. 38 C1
  Woore CW3 .... 67 A1
Naomi Way WS9 .... 245 A2
Napier B77 .... 250 C2
Napier Gdns [5] ST7 .... 26 A1
Napier Rd WV2 .... 266 B4
Napier St
  Burton u T DE14 ...... 166 B1
  Fenton ST4 .... 72 B3
Naples Cl ST13 .... 73 C2
Naples Dr ST5 .... 70 C3
Napley Dr TF9 .... 82 B1
Napley Rd TF9 .... 82 B1
Narlow La DE6 .... 51 C1
Narrow La
  Brownhills WS8 .... 244 C4
  Colton WS15 .... 179 A4
  Denstone ST14 .... 95 B3
  Milwich ST15 .... 121 C4
Narvik Cres ST6 .... 42 A1
Nash Ave Perton WV6 ... 254 C2
  Stafford ST16 .... 155 A3
Nash La
  Acton Trussell ST17 ... 193 A4
  Elmhurst WS13 .... 214 A3
Nash Peake St ST6 .... 41 B2
Nash St ST5 .... 55 C1
Nashe Dr ST13 .... 73 A1
Natham Cl ST11 .... 74 B2
Nathan Ct WS15 .... 196 C3
National Meml Arboretum
  The* DE13 .... 201 B1
Navigation Loop ST15 ... 104 C1
Navigation Rd ST6 ...... 56 C4
Navigation St ST6 ...... 56 C4
Navigation Way WS11 .. 210 A1
Naylor St ST5 .... 41 C3
Naylor Ho [1] ST13 ..... 30 C3
Naylors Gr DY3 .... 271 C2
Neachless Ave WV5 ..... 270 A3
Neachley La TF11 .... 220 A1
Neal Croft WS14 .... 232 C3
Neale Pl ST2 .... 58 A3
Neander B79 .... 249 C3
Near Ridding ST20 ..... 171 B3
Neath Cl ST13 .... 73 B2
Neath Pl WS3 .... 73 B3
Neath Rd WS3 .... 242 C1
Neath Way WS3 .... 242 C1
Needwood CE Prim Sch
  DE13 .... 162 C4
Needwood Cl WV2 ...... 266 A3
Needwood Ct DE13 ..... 146 B3
Needwood Dr WV4 ...... 266 C2
Needwood Grange
  WS15 .... 161 A3
Needwood Hill WS13 ... 214 A1
Needwood Pk DE13 .... 183 B1
Needwood St DE14 ..... 166 A2
Nellan Cres ST6 .... 42 B1
Nelson Bank ST7 ...... 41 A4
Nelson Bldgs ST7 .... 26 A1
Nelson Cres ST21 ...... 102 C1
Nelson Dr WS12 .... 210 C2
Nelson Ind Est ST7 ..... 25 B1
Nelson Pl Hanley ST1 .. 282 C2
  Newcastle-u-L ST5 .... 284 C3
Nelson St
  Burton u T DE15 ...... 167 B2
  Fenton ST4 .... 72 B3
  Leek ST13 .... 30 C4
  Newcastle-u-L ST5 ..... 56 B3
Nelson Way ST17 .... 174 C3
Nemesia B77 .... 251 A2
Nene Cl DE13 .... 147 B1
Nene Way DE65 .... 147 C4
Nephew St ST6 .... 56 C4
Neptune Gr ST1 .... 42 B1
Ness Gr ST10 .... 76 C3
Nest Comm WS4 .... 243 C3
Nether Beacon WS13 ... 214 A1
Nether La WS7 .... 229 B4

Nether Stowe High Sch
  WS13 .... 214 A1
Netherbridge Ave WS14 231 C4
Netherby Rd ST1 .... 271 B4
Nethercote Pl ST2 ...... 73 B4
Nethergate DY3 .... 271 C3
Netherseal Rd
  Chilcote DE12 .... 219 C2
  Clifton Campville B79 . 218 C1
Netherset Hey La CW3 .. 68 C2
Netherstone Gr B74 .... 257 C3
Netherstowe WS13 .... 214 B1
Netherstowe La WS13 .. 214 B1
Netherton Gr ST2 .... 43 B1
Netherway Dr WV6 ..... 255 A3
Netley Pl ST3 .... 88 C4
Netley Rd WS3 .... 242 C1
Netley Way WS3 .... 242 C1
Nevada La ST6 .... 57 A4
Neve Ave WV10 .... 240 C1
Nevill St B79 .... 250 A3
Neville Ave WV4 .... 266 B3
Neville Cl DE13 .... 147 A2
Neville St Stoke-on-T ST4 71 C2
  Tamworth B79 .... 250 C2
Nevin Ave ST8 .... 27 B3
Nevis Ct WV6 .... 255 C1
Nevis Gr WV12 .... 242 A1
New Ave ST11 .... 91 B3
New Barns La WS14 .... 246 A2
New Bldgs Barlaston ST12 88 B1
  Biddulph ST8 .... 27 A2
New Century St ST1 .... 282 A3
New Chapel Ct ST6 ..... 41 B2
New Close Ave ST11 .... 91 A4
New Cotts Ipstones ST10 . 62 B3
  Kinver DY7 .... 278 C4
New Council Hos TF9 ... 98 B1
New Dudley Rd DY6 .... 275 B4
New Ford Prim Sch ST6 . 42 B1
New Forest Ind Est ST7 . 282 C4
New Garden St ST12 ... 155 C1
New Haden Rd ST10 .... 76 A1
New Hall Rd ST3 .... 73 C1
New Hall St ST1 .... 282 B3
New Hampton Rd W
  WV6 .... 255 C2
New Hayes Rd
  Cannock WS11 .... 211 B2
  Tunstall ST6 .... 41 C2
New Homage Gdns
  WV9 .... 224 A1
New Horse Rd WS6 .... 226 C2
New Inn Bank ST21 ... 131 B4
New Inn La ST4 .... 88 A4
New Inn Row ST17 ..... 175 C2
New King St ST7 .... 39 B1
New Kingsway ST3 ...... 74 A2
New La ST6 .... 28 A1
New Landywood La
  WS6 .... 242 C4
New Mill La B78 .... 261 A4
New Park Gdns ST4 ..... 88 B3
New Penkridge Rd
  WS11 .... 209 B1
New Rd Aldridge WS9 . 256 A3
  Alton ST10 .... 78 C1
  Armitage WS15 .... 198 A3
  Astbury CW12 .... 15 A2
  Audley ST7 .... 39 C2
  Bobbington ST7 .... 268 C2
  Brownhills WS8 .... 244 C4
  Burntwood WS7 ...... 229 A4
  Caverswall ST3 .... 58 C2
  Cookley, Caunsall DY11 . 280 A4
  Cookley, Lea Castle Hospl
  DY10 .... 280 B2
  Dilhorne ST10 .... 75 B2
  Featherstone WV10 ... 224 C1
  Hixon ST18 .... 158 A4
  Madeley CW3 .... 68 C4
  Penkridge ST19 .... 192 C1
  Shenstone WS14 ...... 246 C3
  Shuttington B79 ...... 235 B1
  Swadlincote DE11 ... 186 C3
  Swindon DY3 .... 269 A2
  Tamworth B77 .... 261 C4
  Upper Tean ST10 ...... 92 B2
  Upper Tean, Checkley
  ST10 .... 109 A4
  Uttoxeter ST14 .... 111 A1
  Wolv WV6 .... 255 C2
New Rd Est (Ind Est)
  ST18 .... 139 A1
New Row
  Drayton Bassett B78 . 260 C3
  Keele CW3 .... 69 A4
  Stafford ST18 .... 174 B3
  Tatenhill DE13 .... 165 A1
New St Biddulph ST8 ... 28 A4
  Burntwood, Chase Terrace
  WS7 .... 228 C4
  Burntwood, Chasetown
  WS7 .... 228 C3
  Burslem ST6 .... 56 C4
  Burton u T DE14 ..... 166 B1
  Cannock, Bridgtown WS11 226 B3
  [6] Cannock, Hill Top WS12 210 B2
  [4] Cannock, Mill Green
  WS11 .... 226 C4
  Chebsey ST15 .... 135 A4
  Essington WV11 ...... 242 A2
  Fazeley B78 .... 261 A4
  Great Wyrley WS6 .... 227 A1
  Kingswinford DY6 .... 275 B4

New St continued
  Kingswinford, Wordsley
  DY8 .... 275 B1
  Leek ST13 .... 30 C3
  Newcastle-u-L ST5 .... 56 B3
  Newport TF10 .... 168 C2
  Polesworth B78 .... 262 C4
  Sedgley DY3 .... 271 B2
  Stafford ST16 .... 155 B3
  Stourbridge DY8 ...... 279 C3
  Tamworth, Glascote Heath
  B77 .... 250 C2
  Tamworth, Mount Pleasant
  B77 .... 250 B1
  Uttoxeter ST14 .... 126 A4
  Walsall WS3 .... 243 A1
  Walsall, Sheffield WS4 248 B1
  Wolv, Merry Hill WV3 . 265 B4
  Wolv, Parkfield WV4 .. 266 C3
New St Cotts CW12 ...... 6 A3
New Wood Cl DY7 ..... 279 B4
New Wood Gr WS9 .... 245 A2
Newall Ave ST16 ...... 156 A3
Newark Gr ST6 .... 41 B4
Newborough Cl ST1 .... 57 C3
Newbridge Ave WV6 ... 255 C2
Newbridge Cres WV6 .. 255 C2
Newbridge Dr WV6 .... 255 C2
Newbridge Gdns WV6 . 255 C2
Newbridge Mews [8]
  WV6 .... 255 C2
Newbridge Prep Sch
  WV6 .... 255 C2
Newbridge Rd DY6 .... 275 B4
Newbridge St WV6 .... 255 C2
Newburn Gr ST4 .... 88 A4
Newbury Cl
  Great Wyrley WS6 .... 226 C1
  Stafford ST17 .... 175 B4
Newbury Dr DE13 ..... 147 B1
Newbury Gr ST3 .... 88 C4
Newbury Rd
  Kingswinford DY8 .... 275 B1
  Norton Canes WS11 .. 228 A3
  Wolv WV10 .... 240 B1
Newby Cl DE15 .... 167 A1
Newcastle Com High Sch
  ST5 .... 70 C4
Newcastle Ent Ctr ST5 . 55 C1
Newcastle La ST4 .... 71 C3
Newcastle Rd
  Ashley TF9 .... 100 A4
  Astbury CW12 .... 15 A4
  Eccleshall ST21 ...... 133 C4
  Keele CW3 .... 69 A4
  Leek ST13 .... 30 B2
  Madeley CW3 .... 68 C4
  Market Drayton TF9 ... 97 C1
  Millmeece ST21 ...... 102 C2
  Stoke-on-T ST4 .... 71 C3
  Stone ST15 .... 104 C1
  Talke ST7 .... 40 C4
  Tittensor ST5 .... 87 B4
  Woore CW3 .... 67 C1
Newcastle St Burslem ST6 56 C4
  Newcastle-u-L ST5 .... 55 B1
  Stone ST15 .... 104 C1
Newcastle-under-Lyme Coll
  ST5 .... 284 A3
Newcastle-under-Lyme Sch
  ST5 .... 284 C2
Newchapel Obsy* ST7 .. 26 C1
Newchapel Rd ST7 ...... 26 B2
Newcomen Cl WS7 .... 229 B4
Newcomen Gr ST2 ...... 73 B4
Newcott Cl WV9 ...... 239 C1
Newcrofts Wlk ST6 ..... 42 B3
Newfield Dr DE15 ..... 167 A2
Newfield Rd DE15 .... 167 A2
Newfield St ST6 .... 41 B2
Newfold Cres ST6 ...... 43 A4
Newford Cres ST6 ...... 42 C1
Newgate St ST6 .... 57 A4
Newgate St WS3 .... 253 B2
Newland Ave ST14 .... 155 B4
Newland Ct ST16 ..... 244 B1
Newlands Cl
  Newcastle-u-L ST5 .... 71 A3
  Penkridge ST19 ...... 207 C3
  Stone ST15 .... 119 C3
Newlands Ct WS12 .... 227 C4
Newlands La
  Colton WS15 .... 179 B4
  Norton Canes WS12 .. 227 B4
Newlands St ST4 .... 57 A1
Newleigh St ST2 .... 43 A1
Newlyn Ave WV12 ...... 15 C4
Newlyn Cl WS14 ...... 231 B4
Newman Ave WV2 .... 266 C2
Newman Cl DE14 .... 146 A2
Newman Dr ST14 ..... 185 A4
Newman Gr WV15 .... 196 C4
Newman Rd WV10 .... 241 A1

Newmarket Rd WS11 .. 228 A2
Newmarket Way ST10 .. 76 C3
Newmill St ST2 .... 43 A1
Newnham Rd ST4 .... 73 A3
Newpool Cotts ST8 ...... 27 A3
Newpool Rd ST8 .... 27 A4
Newpool Terr ST8 .... 27 A3
Newport B77 .... 250 C3
Newport CE Jun Sch
  TF10 .... 168 C1
Newport Cl DE14 ..... 166 C4
Newport Croft ST19 ... 223 B3
Newport Cty Inf Sch
  TF10 .... 168 C1
Newport Girls High Sch
  TF10 .... 168 C1
Newport Gr ST5 .... 40 C1
Newport La ST6 .... 56 C4
Newport Rd
  Albrighton TF11 ...... 220 B1
  Chetwynd TF10 ...... 168 B2
  Codsall WV7 .... 237 C1
  Eccleshall ST21 ...... 133 C3
  Seighford ST18 ...... 135 B1
  Stafford ST16,ST17 .. 155 B1
  Sutton TF9 .... 112 C3
  Tong TF11 .... 220 B2
  Woodseaves ST20 .... 151 B4
Newrange Gr
  Brewood ST19 .... 223 B3
  Burslem ST6 .... 56 C4
Newquay Ave ST17 .... 175 B4
Newquay Ct CW12 ...... 15 C4
Newshaw Wlk ST1 ..... 282 C3
Newstead Prim Sch ST3 88 C3
Newstead Rd ST12 .... 155 B4
Newstead Trad Est ST4 . 88 B4
Newton ST10 .... 77 C1
Newton Cl ST16 .... 167 C4
Newton Cl ST9 .... 59 A2
Newton La
  Newton Regis B79,CW9 . 236 C1
  Newton Solney DE15 . 167 C4
  Seckington B79 ...... 236 A2
Newton Leys DE15 .... 167 B2
Newton Mews DE15 .. 166 C2
Newton Rd
  Burton u T DE15 ..... 167 A3
  Lichfield WS13 .... 213 C1
  Newcastle-u-L ST5 .... 56 A3
  Stafford ST16 .... 155 C3
Newton Regis CE Prim Sch
  B79 .... 236 C1
Newton's Coll WS13 .. 231 A4
Newtown Market Drayton
  TF9 .... 26 C1
  Market Drayton TF9 . 112 B4
Niall Rd ST4 .... 71 C1
Nicholas Gr ST13 .... 30 A3
Nicholas St [5] ST6 ..... 56 C4
Nicholl's La ST15 ...... 105 A2
Nicholls St ST4 .... 72 A3
Nicholls Way WS12 ... 210 C1
Nicholson Way
  Burton u T DE14 ..... 166 A1
  Leek ST13 .... 30 B3
Nicklaus Cl DE14 ..... 185 A4
Nidderdale Cl CW12 ..... 6 A3
Nightingale Cl
  Huntington WS12 .... 209 B4
  Upper Tean ST10 ...... 92 C1
Nightingale Wlk WS7 . 229 C4
Nile St ST6 .... 57 A4
Nimbus B77 .... 261 B2
Ninefoot La B77 ...... 261 C4
Ninian Pk B77 .... 261 B3
Ninian Way B77 ...... 261 C3
Nirvana Cl WS11 ...... 209 B1
No Man's Green La DY7 276 C3
No Man's Heath Rd
  DE12 .... 219 C2
No Name Rd WS7 .... 228 C3
Noblett Rd ST1 .... 57 C4
Nocke Rd WV11 ...... 241 C1
Noddington Ave WS14 . 232 C3
Noddington La WV14 . 232 C3
Noddy Park Rd WV9 .. 256 A4
Noddy Pk WS9 .... 256 A4
Nook The WS6 .... 226 B1
Noon Croft DE13 ..... 200 C1
Norbroom Ct TF10 .... 169 A2
Norbroom Dr TF10 ... 169 A2
Norbury Ave
  Norton-in-h M ST2 .... 43 A1
  Walsall WS3 .... 244 A2
Norbury CE Prim Sch
  DE6 .... 96 C4
Norbury Cl ST13 .... 171 B3
Norbury Cres WV4 .... 266 C2
Norbury Ct ST15 ...... 120 A4
Norbury Hollow DE6 .. 80 B1
Norbury Rd ST20 ..... 170 C4
Norcliffe Cl ST15 ..... 71 A1
Norfolk Cres WS9 .... 256 A4
Norfolk Dr B78 .... 250 A1
Norfolk Pl WS3 .... 243 A1
Norfolk Rd Biddulph ST8 16 B1
  Great Wyrley WS6 .... 226 C1
Norfolk Rd ST5 .... 40 B3
Norfolk Rd 185 B4
Kidsgrove ST7 .... 25 C1

Norfolk Rd continued
  Stourbridge DY8 ...... 279 B4
  Wolv WV3 .... 266 A3
Norfolk St ST1 .... 282 A1
Norfolk Way ST17 .... 174 B4
Normacot Grange Rd
  ST3 .... 90 A4
Normacot Rd ST3 ...... 283 C3
Norman Ave ST6 .... 41 C2
Norman Cl B79 .... 249 C4
Norman Gr ST5 .... 56 B1
Norman Keep DE13 ... 146 B3
Norman Rd
  Penkridge ST19 ...... 208 A4
  Tutbury DE13 .... 146 B3
Normanbrook Ct TF9 .. 97 B1
Normandy Gr ST7 ..... 43 B4
Normanton Gr ST3 ...... 73 B3
Norris Cl TF9 .... 100 B3
Norris Rd ST4 .... 41 C2
North Ave Leek ST13 ... 30 B3
  Stafford ST16 .... 155 B2
North Castle St ST16 .. 155 B2
North Cres WV10 ..... 241 B4
North Dr ST3 .... 171 B3
North Gn WV4 .... 265 B3
North Oval DY3 ...... 271 C3
North Pl Bucknall ST2 .. 58 A3
North Prim Sch ST6 ..... 57 A4
North Rd Burslem ST6 .. 57 A4
  Wolv WV4 .... 266 C1
North Springfield DY3 266 C1
North St Burntwood WS7 211 C1
  Burton u T DE15 ...... 167 A2
  Cannock WS11 .... 226 C3
  Leek ST13 .... 30 B3
  Mount Pleasant ST7 ... 26 A3
  Newcastle-u-L ST5 .... 284 C3
  Stoke-on-T ST4 .... 72 A4
North Staffordshire Hospl Ctr
  ST6 .... 42 A2
North Staffordshire Hospl Ctr
  (Outpatients Dept) ST4 71 C4
North Staffordshire
  Maternity Hospl ST4 71 B4
North Staffordshire Medical
  Inst ST4 .... 71 C4
North Staffordshire Nuffield
  Hospl The ST5 .... 71 B2
North Staffordshire Royal
  Infmy ST4 .... 71 C4
North Terr ST6 .... 56 A3
North Walls ST16 ..... 155 C2
North West Terr ST6 .... 42 B1
North Wlk ST3 .... 74 A1
Northam Rd ST1 .... 57 B3
Northcliffe [3] ST13 ... 30 B3
Northcote Ave ST4 ...... 72 A4
Northcote Cl ST18 .... 177 C4
Northcote Ct ST5 ..... 284 C3
Northcote Pl ST5 ..... 284 C3
Northcote St ST4 .... 57 A1
Northdale WV6 .... 255 A2
Northesk Pl ST5 .... 71 A3
Northesk St [4] ST5 ... 105 A1
Northfield Ave ST14 ... 96 A2
Northfield Cl ST14 .... 111 A1
Northfield Dr ST18 ..... 16 C1
Northfield Gr WV3 .... 265 B4
Northfield Rd DE13 ... 166 B4
Northfields Way WS8 . 244 B4
Northfleet St ST7 .... 58 A2
Northgate Aldridge WS9 256 A4
  Brownhills WS9 ...... 245 A1
Northgate Ct ST4 ...... 71 C1
Northgate Way WS9 .. 256 A4
Northicote Recn Ctr
  WV10 .... 240 C2
Northicote Sch The
  WV10 .... 240 C2
Northlands CW3 .... 67 B1
Northover Cl WV9 .... 240 C1
Northumberland Rd B78 250 A1
Northumberland Rd
  .... 185 B4
Northway DY3 .... 266 B1
Northwood Cl ST5 ..... 71 B1
Northwood Cl ST1 .... 282 C3
Northwood Gn ST1 .... 57 C2
Northwood Inf Sch ST1 57 C2
Northwood La
  Ellastone DE6 .... 80 B2
  Newcastle-u-L ST5 ..... 71 B1
Northwood Park Cl
  WV10 .... 240 C2
Northwood Park Rd
  Hanley ST1 .... 57 C2
  Wolv WV10 .... 240 C2
Northwoycte Farm & Ctry Pk*
  WV10 .... 240 C2
Northycote La WV10 .. 240 C2
Norton Ave ST6 .... 42 A2
Norton Bridge Sta ST15 135 A4
Norton Canes High Sch
  WS11 .... 228 A3
Norton Canes Prim Sch
  WS11 .... 228 A3
Norton Cl Tamworth B79 250 B4
Norton Cl ST5 .... 70 C4
Norton Cres ST6 .... 57 B4
Norton Dr ST6 .... 57 B4
Norton Grange WS11 . 227 C2
Norton Grange Cres
  WS11 .... 227 C2
Norton Green La ST6 .. 227 C2
Norton Hall Cl ST6 ..... 42 C2
Norton Hall La WS11 . 227 B2

Norton La
  Burntwood WS7 .... 229 B3
  Great Wyrley WS6 .... 227 A2
  Norton Canes WS11 .... 227 A4
  Norton-in-t-M St6 .... 42 C2
Norton Lakeside Sta*
  WS7 .... 228 B3
Norton Prim Sch St6 .... 42 C2
Norton Rd
  Burton u T DE13 .... 166 A3
  Norton Canes WS11,WS12 227 C4
  Stourbridge DY8 .... 279 C1
  Walsall WS3 .... 244 A3
Norton Springs WS11 .... 227 C3
Norton St St7 .... 43 A1
Norton Terr WS11 .... 227 C3
Norton-in-Hales CE Prim Sch
  TF9 .... 82 B1
Norwich Cl WS13 .... 214 B2
Norwich Pl St5 .... 71 B3
Norwich Rd St2 .... 58 B1
Norwood Ho WS15 .... 178 A1
Nottingham Ct ST14 .... 110 C1
Nottingham Rd WS14 .... 232 B2
Novi La ST13 .... 31 A4
Nuffield Hospl WV6 .... 255 B2
Nunn St ST13 .... 30 B3
Nunn's Cl St13 .... 74 B3
Nuns La WS15 .... 180 A3
Nurseries The WV9 .... 224 A1
Nursery Ave
  Aldridge WS9 .... 256 A3
  Norton-in-t-M St9 .... 43 B2
Nursery Cl Bradley ST18 . 191 B4
  Cheadle ST10 .... 76 B2
  Endon ST6 .... 43 A4
  Kidsgrove ST7 .... 25 B1
Nursery Croft WS13 .... 213 C1
Nursery Dr Biddulph ST8 . 16 A1
  Penkridge ST19 .... 192 C1
  Wombourne WV5 .... 269 C2
Nursery Fields Prim Sch
  WS15 .... 197 A3
Nursery Gdns
  Brierley Hill DY8 .... 275 C1
  Codsall WV8 .... 238 C2
Nursery La Hopwas B78 . 249 A3
  Norton-in-t-M St9 .... 43 B2
  Stafford ST16 .... 155 B3
  Sutton Coldfield B74 .... 258 A1
Nursery Rd
  Rugeley WS15 .... 197 A3
  Scholar Green St7 .... 25 C3
Nursery St St4 .... 72 A3
NurseryView Cl WS9 .... 256 C1
Nursery Way St18 .... 158 A2
Nursery Wlk WV6 .... 255 B2
Nurton Bk WV6 .... 254 A2
Nurton Hill Rd WV6 .... 253 C3
Nutbrook Ave St4 .... 72 B2
Nuthurst Dr WS11 .... 226 C2
Nyewood Ave St3 .... 73 B3
Nymet B77 .... 261 C4

O

O'Hare Pl ST13 .... 31 A4
Oadby Rise DE13 .... 166 A3
Oak Ave Cheddleton ST13 . 45 B2
  Great Wyrley WS6 .... 227 A2
  Huntington WS12 .... 209 B4
  Newport TF10 .... 168 C1
  Stafford ST17 .... 175 C3
Oak Cl Church Eaton ST20 190 A4
  Colwich ST18 .... 158 B1
  Kinver DY7 .... 278 B2
  Uttoxeter ST14 .... 110 C1
Oak Ct B74 .... 257 C3
Oak Dr Seisdon WV5 .... 263 C1
  Wheaton Aston ST19 .... 205 B3
Oak Farm Craft Ctr*
  B78 .... 260 A3
Oak Gdns ST18 .... 172 C3
Oak Gn WV6 .... 255 A2
Oak Hill WV3 .... 255 B1
Oak Ho
  Great Wyrley WS6 .... 227 A1
  Little Aston B74 .... 257 A3
Oak Ind Pk The DY6 .... 270 C1
Oak La Bradley ST18 .... 191 B4
  Burntwood WS7 .... 212 A1
  Cheslyn Hay WV10,WS11 . 225 B4
  Kingswinford DY6 .... 270 C1
Oak Lea ST13 .... 30 A2
Oak Leys WV3 .... 255 A3
Oak Mount Rd St19 .... 59 B2
Oak Park Rd DY9 .... 275 C1
Oak Pl ST3 .... 73 C1
Oak Rd Barton-u-N DE13 . 201 B4
  Brewood ST19 .... 223 B3
  Brownhills, Holly Bank
  WS9 .... 245 A2
  Denstone ST14 .... 95 B3
  Eccleshall ST21 .... 133 B3
  Newcastle-u-L ST5 .... 55 B1
  Stone ST15 .... 120 A4
  Walsall WS3 .... 243 C3
  Walsall, Shelfield WS4 .... 244 B1
Oak Rd Flats ST19 .... 223 B3
Oak Sq DE11 .... 186 C1
Oak St Burton u T DE14 . 166 B1
  Cheadle ST10 .... 76 B2
  Hanley ST1 .... 57 C3
  Kingswinford DY6 .... 275 B3
  Newcastle-u-L ST5 .... 56 B2
Oak Tree Cl ST17 .... 174 A4
Oak Tree La ST7 .... 40 B3

Oak Tree Wlk B79 .... 249 C4
Oakamoor Rd ST10 .... 77 B2
Oakapple Cl ST19 .... 221 C4
Oakdale St5 .... 71 B2
Oakdale Cl CW2 .... 37 A2
Oakdale Trad Est DY6 .... 270 C1
Oakden Cl ST14 .... 125 B4
Oakdene Ave St5 .... 56 A3
Oakdene Cl
  Cheslyn Hay WS6 .... 226 B1
  Forsbrook ST11 .... 91 A3
  Newcastle-u-L ST5 .... 56 A3
Oakdene Gr ST5 .... 56 A3
Oakdene Rd WS7 .... 229 A3
Oakdene Way ST8 .... 27 B4
Oaken Covert WV8 .... 238 C1
Oaken Dr WV8 .... 238 C2
Oaken Gdns WS7 .... 229 A4
Oaken Gr WV8 .... 238 C1
Oaken Grange WS6 .... 226 C1
Oaken La WV8 .... 238 B2
Oaken Lanes WV8 .... 238 C2
Oaken Pk WV6 .... 239 A1
Oakenfield WS13 .... 214 A1
Oakenhampers Cres WS8 228 C1
Oakenhayes Dr WS8 .... 228 C1
Oakfield Ave DY6 .... 275 C3
Oakfield Cl
  Brierley Hill DY8 .... 275 C1
  Rugeley WS15 .... 178 A1
Oakfield Dr WS3 .... 244 A3
Oakfield Gr ST8 .... 27 C4
Oakfield Rd
  Alrewas DE13 .... 201 A1
  Codsall WV8 .... 239 A1
  Market Drayton TF9 .... 97 A1
Oakfields DE13 .... 145 A2
Oakham Way ST2 .... 58 B1
Oakhill Ave ST4 .... 71 C2
Oakhill Prim Sch
  Stoke-on-t St4 .... 71 C2
  Tamworth B77 .... 250 C1
Oakhill Rd WS11 .... 209 C1
Oakhurst WS14 .... 231 B4
Oakhurst Cres ST3 .... 90 A3
Oakhurst Pk WS15 .... 196 C3
Oakland Dr DY3 .... 271 A1
Oakland Ho B74 .... 258 A2
Oakland Rd WS3 .... 266 A4
Oaklands Ave ST5 .... 56 B3
Oaklands Cl
  Alrewas WS13 .... 215 B3
  Cheddleton ST9 .... 44 B3
  Hill Ridware WS15 .... 198 A4
  Huntington WS12 .... 209 B3
Oaklands Dr ST17 .... 155 B1
Oaklands Ind Est WS12 . 210 A2
Oaklands Rd WV3 .... 266 A4
Oaklands The
  Church Eaton ST20 .... 190 A4
  Rugeley WS15 .... 178 B1
Oaklands Way WS3 .... 244 A2
Oakleigh Ave DE11 .... 186 C3
Oakleigh Ct ST15 .... 120 B3
Oakleigh Dr Codsall WV8 239 A2
  Rugeley WS15 .... 197 A3
  Sedgley DY3 .... 271 B4
Oakleigh Wlk DY6 .... 275 C4
Oakleighs (WV8) 225 B3
Oakley Ave WS9 .... 256 A3
Oakley Cl Lichfield WS13 . 214 A1
  Penkridge ST19 .... 193 A1
Oakley Copse WS15 .... 196 A4
Oakley Folly TF9 .... 99 A2
Oakley Gr WV4 .... 265 B3
Oakley Rd WV4 .... 42 A4
Oakley Rd WV4 .... 265 B3
Oakleys ST15 .... 223 B3
Oakmount Cl WS3 .... 243 C2
Oakover Cl ST14 .... 126 B3
Oakridge Cl ST17 .... 175 C3
Oakridge Dr WS6 .... 226 C1
Oakridge Prim Sch
  ST17 .... 175 C3
Oakridge Way ST17 .... 175 C3
Oaks Dr Cannock WS11 . 209 B1
  Featherstone WV10 .... 240 C4
  Wombourne WV5 .... 270 A3
Oakshaw Cl WV9 .... 224 A2
Oakshaw Gr ST4 .... 88 A4
Oaksmoor Cl ST19 .... 205 B3
Oaktree Rd
  Rugeley WS15 .... 196 C3
  Trentham ST4 .... 88 A3
Oakville Ave St6 .... 42 A1
Oakwell Cl ST3 .... 73 B1
Oakwell Gr ST13 .... 73 B1
Oakwood WS15 .... 178 A1
Oakwood Cl
  Brownhills WS9 .... 244 C2
  Essington WV11 .... 242 A2
  Hatton DE65 .... 146 B4
  Shenstone WS14 .... 247 A3
Oakwood Pl ST5 .... 55 C4
Oakwood Rd Leek ST13 . 30 B3
  ST15 .... 72 C1
Oakwood Sch WS9 .... 245 A2
Oakwoods WS11 .... 226 B4
Oasthouse Cl DY6 .... 275 A4
Oatfield Cl WV7 .... 237 C2
Oatlands Way WV6 .... 254 B2
Oban Cl ST5 .... 70 C4
Oberon Cl ST6 .... 42 B1
Occupation Rd WS9 .... 245 A2
Occupation St St1 .... 284 C2
Octagon Ctr The DE14 . 166 B1
Octagon Sh Pk The St1 . 57 A2

Odell Gr ST6 .... 41 C1
Odger Cl ST3 .... 74 A1
Odiam Cl B79 .... 250 B4
Odin Cl WS11 .... 210 A3
Offa St B79 .... 250 A3
Offa's Dr WV6 .... 254 C3
Offadrive B79 .... 250 A3
Offoxey Rd TF11 .... 221 B3
Ogden Rd ST1 .... 282 C2
Ogley Cres ST8 .... 245 A4
Ogley Hay Inf Sch WS8 . 244 C4
Ogley Hay Rd
  Burntwood WS7 .... 212 A1
  Burntwood, Triangle WS7,
  WS8 .... 229 A2
Ogley Rd WS8 .... 245 A4
Ogmore Gr ST3 .... 90 A4
Ohio Gr St6 .... 52 A4
Old Armoury The TF9 .... 112 B4
Old Bank DE6 .... 81 B4
Old Barn Cl ST20 .... 171 C4
Old Butt La ST7 .... 25 B1
Old Cannock Rd WV10 .. 225 B1
Old Castle Gr WS8 .... 228 C1
Old Chancel Rd WS15 ... 178 C1
Old Chapel Cl ST5 .... 69 C4
Old Coach La ST17 .... 176 A2
Old Coach Rd ST19 .... 221 C4
Old Coalpit La SK17 .... 5 C4
Old Colehurst Manor*
  TF9 .... 112 A2
Old Cottage Hospl The DE6
  ST13 .... 30 C3
Old Croft Rd ST17 .... 175 C3
Old Dalelands TF9 .... 112 A4
Old Eaton Rd WS15 .... 178 C2
Old Fallings La WV10 .... 240 C1
Old Fallow Ave WS11 .... 209 C2
Old Fallow Rd WS11 .... 209 C2
Old Falls Cl WS6 .... 226 B2
Old Farm Dr WV8 .... 239 A2
Old Farm Mdw WV4 .... 265 B4
Old Forge Cl DE65 .... 148 A3
Old Forge The ST18 .... 158 A1
Old Hall Ct B79 .... 236 B2
Old Hall Dr Elford B79 .. 216 B1
  Newcastle-u-L ST5 .... 56 A4
Old Hall La
  Alrewas WS13 .... 215 B4
  Millmeece ST21 .... 117 C4
  Norton Canes WS11,WS12 227 A4
Old Hall Rd WV10 .... 241 B4
Old Hall St ST1 .... 282 B3
Old Hampton La WV11 .. 241 B3
Old Hedging La B77 .... 261 B3
Old Hednesford Rd
  WS11,WS12 .... 210 A2
Old La WV10 .... 255 B3
Old Knotty Way ST14 ... 126 B4
Old Lā Endon ST6 .... 28 B1
  Featherstone WV10 .... 241 B4
  Swynnerton ST4 .... 87 A1
  Upper Tean ST10 .... 109 A4
  Wolv WV6 .... 254 C1
Old Landywood La WS6 . 242 B4
Old Lodge Hill Ctry Pk*
  WS15 .... 211 C2
Old London Rd WS14 ... 231 B1
Old Manor Cl B78 .... 260 C3
Old Manor Flats WV6 ... 255 B3
Old Mill Gdns WS4 .... 244 B1
Old Mill La Bagnall ST9 .. 44 A2
  Bagnall, Tompkin ST9 .... 44 B2
Old Oak Cl WV9 .... 256 A4
Old Park Rd
  Cannock WS12 .... 211 A3
  Dudley DY1 .... 271 C1
  Weston CW1 .... 37 B4
Old Penkridge Rd WS11 209 B1
Old Quarry Dr DY3 .... 271 B3
Old Rd Armitage WS15 .. 198 A3
  Audley ST7 .... 39 C2
  Betley CW3 .... 53 A2
  Branston DE14 .... 184 C4
  Stone ST15 .... 105 B3
  Trentham ST4,ST12 .... 88 B2
  Upper Tean ST10 .... 92 B2
  Weston ST18 .... 138 B1
Old Rd Cl St5 .... 105 A1
Old Rectory Gdns WS9 . 256 B3
Old Rectory Rd ST15 ... 120 A4
Old Rickerscote La
  ST17 .... 175 A3
Old School Cl ST18 .... 136 A3
Old School Dr ST15 .... 105 B3
Old School Yd The B77 . 251 A3
Old Shackerley La WV7 . 235 A3
Old Smithy Cl WV6 .... 253 B2
Old Stafford Rd WV10 .. 224 B1
Old Stoke Rd ST14 .... 54 B3
Old Town La WS3 .... 243 C2
Old Town Rd ST1 .... 282 B4
Old Tramway ST4 .... 72 C3
Old Vicarage Cl
  WS3 .... 244 A1
  Wombourne WV5 .... 270 A4
Old Weston Rd ST19 .... 221 C4
Old Wharf Pl ST1 .... 57 C1
Old Wharf Rd DY8 .... 279 C3
Old Wheldon Rd ST4 ... 73 B3
Oldacre La ST17 .... 176 A2
Oldacres Rd ST4 .... 88 B3
Oldbury Ct B79 .... 250 B4
Oldcastle Ave WS4 .... 56 A3
Oldcott Cres ST7 .... 41 B4
Oldcott Dr ST7 .... 41 B4

Oldcourt St ST6 .... 41 B2
Olde Hall La WS6 .... 226 C2
Oldershaws La ST20 .... 150 C4
Oldfield Ave St6 .... 42 B3
Oldfield Dr ST15 .... 120 B3
Oldfield La DE13 .... 164 C3
Oldfield Ind Est ST4 .... 72 C3
Oldfield La
  Egginton DE65 .... 148 A4
  Snelston DE6 .... 81 A2
Oldfield St St4 .... 283 A5
Oldfields Cres ST18 .... 158 B2
Oldfields Hall Mid Sch
  ST14 .... 126 A4
Oldfields Rd ST14 .... 126 A4
Oldford La ST18 .... 154 A2
Oldham Cotts WS15 .... 179 A3
Oldham St St1 .... 282 C1
Oldhill Cl St7 .... 40 C3
Oldhill La ST18 .... 157 B1
Oldicote La DE15 .... 167 C2
Oldmill St ST4 .... 72 B4
Oldway Pl ST3 .... 73 B3
Olive Ave WV4 .... 265 B3
Olive Gr ST5 .... 40 B1
Oliver Lodge Ho ST4 ... 72 A4
Oliver Rd ST4 .... 71 C4
Ollison Dr B74 .... 256 C1
Olof Palme Gr ST3 .... 249 B4
Omega Way St4 .... 88 A4
One Oak Rise ST17 .... 174 C3
Onneley La CW3 .... 67 C2
Onsetter Rd ST2 .... 73 B4
Ontario Cl St14 .... 88 A4
Opal Bsns Ctr ST15 .... 120 A3
Opal Rd ST4 .... 72 C3
Opal Way ST15 .... 120 A3
Oram's La WS13 .... 216 B1
Orange La WS15 .... 161 B1
Orb St ST1 .... 282 B2
Orbital Way WS11 .... 226 C3
Orchard Ave WS11 .... 209 B1
Orchard Cl Ashley TF9 . 100 B3
  Brewood WV9 .... 224 A1
  Cheslyn Hay WS6 .... 226 C2
  Claverley WV5 .... 267 B4
  Lichfield WS13 .... 213 C1
  Pattingham WV6 .... 253 B2
  Penkridge ST19 .... 192 C1
  Rugeley WS15 .... 178 C2
  Stone ST15 .... 119 C4
  Stone, Oulton ST15 .... 105 B2
  Sudbury DE6 .... 128 C3
  Tamworth B77 .... 261 B3
  Uttoxeter ST14 .... 111 A1
  Walton-on-t DE12 .... 184 B1
Orchard Cotts WV12 .... 198 A3
Orchard Cres
  Kidsgrove ST7 .... 25 B1
  Penkridge ST19 .... 192 C1
  Wolv WV3 .... 265 A4
Orchard Ct
  Kingswinford DY6 .... 275 B3
  Wolv WV3 .... 265 A4
Orchard Gdns
  Cannock WS12 .... 209 C3
  Leek ST13 .... 30 B3
Orchard Gr Aldridge WS9 256 A2
  Cookley DY11 .... 280 A1
  Kinver DY7 .... 278 A2
  Sedgley DY3 .... 271 A2
  Sutton Coldfield B74 .... 257 C2
  Wolv WV4 .... 266 A2
Orchard La Codsall WV8 239 A2
  Shareshill WV10 .... 225 C3
Orchard Pk DE14 .... 166 B1
Orchard Pl ST12 .... 88 B1
Orchard Rd DY10 .... 280 B2
Orchard Rise
  Blythe Bridge ST11 .... 90 C4
  Market Drayton TF9 .... 112 A4
Orchard St
  Burton u T DE14 .... 166 B1
  Newcastle-u-L ST5 .... 56 B3
  Stafford ST17 .... 155 C1
  Swadlincote DE11 .... 186 C3
  Tamworth B79 .... 250 C2
  Tamworth, Kettlebrook
  B77 .... 250 B2
Orchard The
  Albrighton WV7 .... 237 A3
  Brewood ST19 .... 223 B3
  Colwich ST18 .... 177 B4
  Endon ST6 .... 43 A4
  Stramshall ST14 .... 111 A2
  Swynnerton ST15 .... 103 A2
  Walsall WS3 .... 243 B1
  Wolv WV6 .... 255 C3
Orchards The
  Armitage WS15 .... 198 B2
  Fenton ST3 .... 72 C2
Orchid Cl DE15 .... 186 A4
Orchid Gr ST4 .... 56 C1
Ordish Ct DE14 .... 166 B1
Ordish St DE14 .... 166 B1
Ordley La DE6 .... 65 C1
Oregon Cl DY6 .... 275 A4
Oregon Gdns WS7 .... 228 C4
Orford Rd ST9 .... 43 C4
Orford St ST5 .... 56 B4
Orford Way ST13 .... 88 C4
Orgreave St St6 .... 56 A4
Orgreaves Cl ST19 .... 56 A4
Oriel Cl Cannock WS11 . 210 C1
  Sedgley DY3 .... 271 C1
Oriel Dr WV10 .... 240 B4
Oriel St St4 .... 72 A4

Nor – Ove 317

Oriole Cl ST14 .... 126 B3
Orion Cl WS6 .... 226 C1
Orion Ct ST5 .... 70 C4
Orion St St6 .... 42 B1
Orion Way WS11 .... 209 C3
Orkney Ave St7 .... 41 C4
Orkney Dr B77 .... 261 C4
Orlestone Pl ST6 .... 42 A4
Orme Rd Biddulph ST8 .. 27 B3
  Newcastle-u-L ST5 .... 284 A2
Orme St St6 .... 56 C4
Ormes La WV6 .... 255 B2
Ormonde St ST4 .... 72 C3
Ormonds Cl WS13 .... 230 B3
Oroxden Cl ST10 .... 92 B4
Orpheus Gr St1 .... 57 C3
Orton Gr WV4 .... 265 B2
Orton La WV4,WV5 .... 265 A1
Orton Rd St5 .... 260 B3
Orwell Cl DY8 .... 279 B2
Orwell Dr Longton St13 . 73 C3
  Stafford ST17 .... 174 A4
Orwell Pl ST5 .... 71 A2
Osberton Dr DY1 .... 271 C1
Osborn Rd B79 .... 249 B4
Osborne Cres St17 .... 175 B4
Osborne Ct DE13 .... 166 A3
Osborne Rd
  Stoke-on-T St4 .... 71 C4
  Wolv WV4 .... 265 C3
Osborne St
  Burton u T DE15 .... 167 A2
  Leek ST13 .... 31 A3
Oslo Gr ST1 .... 57 C3
Osmaston Rd DY8 .... 279 C1
Osprey B77 .... 262 A3
Osprey Ave ST3 .... 90 A4
Osprey Cl
  Burton u T DE15 .... 167 B2
  Wolverhampton WS14 ... 232 C3
Osprey Dr DY1 .... 271 C1
Osprey Gr WS12 .... 210 B1
Osprey Vale WS7 .... 229 A4
Osprey View St7 .... 26 B2
Ostend Pl ST5 .... 70 C4
Ostler Cl DY6 .... 275 A4
Ostlers La ST13 .... 45 A2
Oswald Ave St7 .... 74 A3
Otherton Cl ST19 .... 207 C3
Otherton La ST19 .... 207 C3
Otterburn Cl
  Cannock WS12 .... 210 C1
  [6] Stafford ST17 .... 175 B3
Otterstone Cl DY3 .... 266 B3
Ottery B77 .... 262 A3
Oulton CE Fst Sch ST15 105 B2
Oulton La TF10,ST20 .... 170 A4
Oulton Mews ST15 .... 105 A1
Oulton Rd Cheadle ST10 . 76 C2
  Chell Heath ST6 .... 42 A4
  Stone ST15 .... 105 A1
Oulton Way ST13 .... 155 A3
Oundle Ct St4 .... 257 C1
Ounsdale Cres WV5 .... 270 A4
Ounsdale High Sch
  WV5 .... 269 C4
Ounsdale Rd WV5 .... 269 C4
Ounty John La DY8 .... 278 B2
Our Lady & St Benedict RC
  Prim Sch ST2 .... 58 A3
Our Lady & St Werburgh's RC
  Prim Sch ST5 .... 71 A2
Our Lady's RC Prim Sch
  ST4 .... 72 B2
Our Lady's RC Prim Sch
  ST5 .... 103 A2
Dusley La DE6 .... 80 B3
Outclough Rd ST18 .... 27 A1
Outfield Rd DE15 .... 185 C4
Outlook The ST16 .... 42 B2
Outwards Gn ST18 .... 138 B1
Outwoods Cl
  Burton u T DE13 .... 166 A3
  Weston ST18 .... 138 B1
Outwoods La
  Anslow DE13 .... 165 B4
  Burton u T DE13 .... 165 C4
Outwoods St DE14 .... 166 A3
Oval Bglws The TF10 ... 169 A2
Oval The Cheddleton ST9 . 59 C2
  Longton ST3 .... 283 A2
  Market Drayton TF9 .... 112 B4
  Stafford ST17 .... 155 C1
Over The Mill St18 .... 17 A1
Overbrook Cl DY3 .... 271 B1
Overcroft ST14 .... 125 B4
Overdale Pl ST13 .... 30 A3
Overfield Rd DY1 .... 271 C1
Overhill Rd
  Burntwood WS7 .... 229 A3
  Stafford ST17 .... 175 B3
Overhouse St St6 .... 41 C1
Overland Ct WS15 .... 197 A3
Overland Dr ST6 .... 43 A4
Overpool Cl WS15 .... 196 B4
Oversetts Ct DE11 .... 186 C3
Oversetts Rd DE11 .... 186 C3
Oversley Rd St6 .... 42 A4
Overstrand WV9 .... 239 C2
Overton Bank [7] ST13 . 30 C3
Overton Cl ST5 .... 283 A2
Overton La WS7 .... 229 B2
Overton Rd St8 .... 16 C3
Overton Wlk WV4 .... 265 C4
Overwood Pl ST7 .... 41 C4

Overwoods Rd ST4 . . . . .262 A3
Owen Gr 3 ST4 . . . . .57 A4
Owen Rd WV3 . . . . .266 A4
Owen Wlk ST17 . . . . .174 B4
Owens Cl WS15 . . . . .178 C1
Ox Pasture ST13 . . . . .45 B3
Ox St DY3 . . . . .271 B3
Ox-Hey Cres ST8 . . . . .16 B1
Ox-Hey Dr ST8 . . . . .16 B1
Oxbarn Ave WS11 . . . . .265 C4
Oxbarn Rd ST17 . . . . .174 B3
Oxbridge Way B79 . . . . .249 C3
Oxclose La DE6 . . . . .36 B1
Oxford Ave ST4 . . . . .57 B4
Oxford Cl WV6 . . . . .226 C2
Oxford Cres ST14 . . . . .122 C4
Oxford Dr DY8 . . . . .279 C2
Oxford Gdns ST16 . . . . .155 C3
Oxford Gn WS11 . . . . .226 C4
Oxford Rd Cannock WS11 . . . . .226 C4
  Chell Heath ST6 . . . . .42 A4
  Newcastle-u-l ST5 . . . . .56 B2
Oxford St
  Burton u TDE14 . . . . .166 A1
  Stoke-on-T ST14 . . . . .72 A4
Oxhay Ct ST5 . . . . .56 B2
Oxhay View ST5 . . . . .56 B2
Oxhey Fst Sch ST8 . . . . .16 C1
Oxleathers Ct ST17 . . . . .174 A4
Oxley Cl WS6 . . . . .226 C1
Oxley Moor Rd
  Wolv, Blakeley Green
  WV9 . . . . .255 C4
  Wolv, Oxley WV9, WV10 . . . . . . .240 A1
Oxley Rd DE15 . . . . .167 A2
Oxmead DE6 . . . . .81 B4

P

Pacific Rd ST4 . . . . .88 A4
Pack Horse La ST6 . . . . .56 C4
Packett St ST14 . . . . .283 B4
Packington Ct B74 . . . . .257 C2
Packington La B78 . . . . .248 C3
Packmoor Prim Sch ST7 . . . . . .26 C1
Padarn Cl DY3 . . . . .266 B1
Padbury WV9 . . . . .240 A2
Padbury La WS7 . . . . .212 B1
Paddock Cl ST16 . . . . .155 B4
Paddock Cotts ST4 . . . . .88 A3
Paddock La
  Aldridge WS9 . . . . .256 A3
  Great Wyrley WS6 . . . . .227 A2
Paddock Rise ST4 . . . . .88 A3
Paddock The
  Brewood WV8 . . . . .224 A1
  Burton u T DE15 . . . . .167 A2
  Cheadle ST10 . . . . .76 B1
  Claverley WV5 . . . . .267 B4
  Codsall WV8 . . . . .238 C1
  Lichfield WS14 . . . . .231 B3
  Perton WV6 . . . . .254 B2
  Rolleston DE13 . . . . .147 A2
  Sedgley DY3 . . . . .271 C3
  Seighford ST18 . . . . .154 B3
  Wombourne WV5 . . . . .269 C3
Paddocks Cl B78 . . . . .251 C1
Paddocks Gn CW12 . . . . .6 C1
Paddocks The
  Market Drayton TF9 . . . . .97 A1
  Swynnerton ST15 . . . . .186 C3
Padget High Sch DE14 . . . . . . .185 A4
Padstow Rd ST4 . . . . .250 C3
Padstow Way ST4 . . . . .88 B3
Padworth St ST3 . . . . .74 A2
Paget Cl ST19 . . . . .208 A4
Paget Dr WS7 . . . . .211 C1
Paget Rd Wolv WV6 . . . . .255 C2
Paget Rise WS15 . . . . .160 C3
Paget St DE14 . . . . .166 B1
Pagham Cl WV9 . . . . .239 C1
Painsley RC High Sch
  ST10 .77 A3
Paisley Cl ST2 . . . . .73 C4
Paladin Ave ST3 . . . . .74 A2
Palatine Dr ST5 . . . . .55 B3
Pale St DY3 . . . . .271 C3
Palfrey Rd DY8 . . . . .279 B3
Pall Mall ST1 . . . . .282 B2
Palmbourne Ind Pk
  ST16 . . . . .155 B2
Palmer Cl
  Barton-u-N DE13 . . . . .183 B1
  Burton u T DE14 . . . . .185 A4
  Essington WV11 . . . . .241 C1
  Stafford ST16 . . . . .156 A2
Palmer St ST13 . . . . .283 A1
Palmers Cl WV8 . . . . .239 A1
Palmers Cross Prim Sch
  WV6 . . . . .255 B4
Palmers Gn ST4 . . . . .71 B4
Palmers Way
  Codsall WV8 . . . . .239 B1
  Newcastle-u-l ST5 . . . . .71 B4
Palmerston St
  Hanley ST1 . . . . .282 C1
  4 Newcastle-u-l ST5 . . . . .56 B3
Palmerston Way ST8 . . . . .16 B1
Palomino Cl ST3 . . . . .89 A4
Pandora Gr ST1 . . . . .57 C3
Panton Cl ST16 . . . . .156 A2
Pantuff Cl ST17 . . . . .155 A1
Panturner Rd ST2 . . . . .73 B4

Parade The
  Brownhills WS8 . . . . .228 C1
  Kingswinford DY6 . . . . .275 A4
  Newcastle-u-l ST5 . . . . .55 B1
Parade View WS8 . . . . .244 C4
Paradise Gr WS3 . . . . .243 C2
Paradise La
  Featherstone WV10 . . . . .224 C1
  Walsall WS3 . . . . .243 C2
Paradise St
  Newcastle-u-l ST5 . . . . .284 B2
  5 Tunstall ST6 . . . . .41 B2
Paragon Ave ST5 . . . . .71 A2
Paragon Cl ST10 . . . . .76 B1
Paragon Rd ST3 . . . . .283 D3
Paramount Bsns Pk ST6 . . . . . .57 A4
Parbury B77 . . . . .261 B3
Parchments The WS13 . . . . . . .214 A1
Pargeter St DY9 . . . . .279 C2
Paris Ave ST5 . . . . .70 C3
Park Ave Burntwood WS7 . . . . .209 B3
  Cheadle ST10 . . . . .76 C1
  Meir ST3 . . . . .74 A3
  Newcastle-u-l ST5 . . . . .56 B3
  Norton Canes WS11 . . . . .228 A3
  Stafford ST17 . . . . .174 B4
  Stone ST15 . . . . .119 C4
  Talke ST7 . . . . .40 C4
  Uttoxeter ST14 . . . . .111 A1
  Wolv WV4 . . . . .266 B3
  Wombourne WV5 . . . . .269 C3
Park Ave W ST5 . . . . .56 A3
Park Bldgs DY3 . . . . .271 B2
Park Cl Barton-u-N DE13 . . . . . .183 B1
  Brownhills WS8 . . . . .244 C4
  Cheslyn Hay WS6 . . . . .226 C2
  Madeley CW3 . . . . .68 C4
Park Cres ST17 . . . . .155 C1
Park Croft WS7 . . . . .228 B4
Park Ct ST5 . . . . .55 C4
Park Dr Barlaston ST12 . . . . . . .104 B4
  Caverswall ST9 . . . . .59 B2
  Cheadle ST10 . . . . .76 B2
  Little Aston B74 . . . . .257 B2
  Sutton Coldfield B74 . . . . .257 C1
  Trentham ST4 . . . . .87 C4
  Wolv WV4 . . . . .266 B3
Park End Lichfield WS14 . . . . . .231 C4
  Newport TF10 . . . . .168 C3
Park Farm Rd B77 . . . . .250 B1
Park Farm View ST4 . . . . .41 B4
Park Gate Rd
  Cannock WS11 . . . . .211 C3
  Kidderminster DY10 . . . . .280 A1
Park Hall Ave ST3 . . . . .74 A2
Park Hall Bsns Village
  ST3 . . . . .73 C3
Park Hall Cres ST3 . . . . .74 A2
Park Hall Inf Sch ST3 . . . . .74 A2
Park Hall Prim Sch ST3 . . . . . . .74 A2
Park Hall Rd Longton ST3 . . . . . .73 C3
  Wolv WV4 . . . . .266 B3
Park Hall St ST3 . . . . .283 C4
Park House Dr ST15 . . . . .120 B4
Park La Astbury TF9 . . . . .100 A4
  Audley ST7 . . . . .39 A2
  Biddulph ST8 . . . . .27 B3
  Blore TF9 . . . . .99 A1
  Brewood ST19 . . . . .223 B1
  Brocton ST17 . . . . .176 A2
  Cheadle ST10 . . . . .76 B2
  Cheddleton ST13 . . . . .45 A3
  Colton WS15 . . . . .179 A4
  Congleton CW12 . . . . .6 A1
  Endon ST9 . . . . .44 A4
  Fenton ST4 . . . . .72 C3
  Great Wyrley WS6 . . . . .227 A2
  Haughton ST18 . . . . .172 C3
  Ipstones ST10 . . . . .47 A1
  Kingswinford DY6 . . . . .275 C4
  Shenstone WS14 . . . . .247 A2
  Tamworth B78 . . . . .249 C1
  Tutbury DE13 . . . . .146 A3
  Wheaton Aston ST19 . . . . .206 A3
  Whittington WS13 . . . . .232 B4
  Woodseaves ST20 . . . . .132 A1
Park Lane Cl ST10 . . . . .76 B2
Park Mid Sch ST8 . . . . .27 B3
Park Pale The DE13 . . . . .146 B3
Park Pl Fenton ST4 . . . . .72 C3
  Uttoxeter ST14 . . . . .126 B4
Park Rd Alrewas DE13 . . . . .201 A2
  Barton-u-N DE13 . . . . .183 B1
  Burntwood, Chase Terrace
    WS7 . . . . .208 C4
  Burntwood, Triangle WS7 . . . . . .229 A3
  Cannock WS11 . . . . .209 B1
  Caverswall ST9 . . . . .59 B2
  Chell Heath ST6 . . . . .42 A1
  Featherstone WV10 . . . . .241 B4
  Leek ST13 . . . . .30 C4
  Newcastle-u-l, Butterton
    ST5 . . . . .70 C1
  Norton Canes WS11 . . . . .228 A3
  Sedgley DY3 . . . . .271 B2
  Stourbridge DY8 . . . . .279 B2
  Swadlincote DE11,DE15 . . . . . .186 B3
  Tamworth B77 . . . . .261 B3
  Walsall WS3 . . . . .243 A1
Park Rd N DY8 . . . . .279 B3
Park Rise WV3 . . . . .255 C1
Park Sch B79 . . . . .250 A4
Park St Brierley Hill DY8 . . . . . .279 A2
  Burton u T DE14 . . . . .166 B1
  Cheslyn Hay WS6 . . . . .226 C2

Park St continued
  Fenton ST4 . . . . .72 C3
  Kingswinford DY6 . . . . .275 B3
  Stafford ST17 . . . . .155 C1
  Tamworth B79 . . . . .250 A3
  Uttoxeter ST14 . . . . .111 B1
Park St S WV2 . . . . .266 B3
Park Terr ST6 . . . . .41 C2
Park The DE6 . . . . .81 B4
Park Venture Ctr WS11 . . . . . .226 C3
Park View
  Blythe Bridge ST11 . . . . .90 C3
  Swynnerton ST15 . . . . .103 A2
Park View Ct
  Cannock WS11 . . . . .209 B1
  Longton ST3 . . . . .73 A1
Park View Rd
  Kidsgrove ST7 . . . . .26 A2
  Sutton Coldfield B74 . . . . .257 B2
Park View Terr WS15 . . . . .178 B1
Park Way Forsbrook ST11 . . . . . .91 A4
  Wolv WV11 . . . . .242 A1
Park Wood Cl B74 . . . . .257 C1
Park Wood Dr ST5 . . . . .85 A4
Parkdale DY3 . . . . .271 B4
Parkend ST11 . . . . .91 A4
Parker Bowles Dr TF9 . . . . . . .112 A4
Parker Paul Ind Est
  ST4 . . . . .57 A4
Parker Rd WV11 . . . . .241 C1
Parker St
  Burton u T DE14 . . . . .166 B3
  Hanley ST1 . . . . .282 A3
  Leek ST13 . . . . .30 C4
  Walsall WS3 . . . . .243 A1
Parker's Croft Rd ST17 . . . . . . .155 C2
Parker-Jervis Rd ST3 . . . . .73 C2
Parkers Cl ST20 . . . . .190 A4
Parkers Ct WV9 . . . . .224 B1
Parkes Ave WV8 . . . . .239 A1
Parkes Hall Rd DY1 . . . . .271 A4
Parkfield Ave B77 . . . . .250 B1
Parkfield Cl
  Barlaston ST12 . . . . .88 B1
  Tamworth B77 . . . . .261 B4
Parkfield Colliery WV4 . . . . . . .266 C3
Parkfield Cres
  Tamworth B77 . . . . .261 B4
  Wolv WV2 . . . . .266 C3
Parkfield Gr WV2 . . . . .266 C3
Parkfield High Sch
  WV4 . . . . .266 C3
Parkfield Jun & Inf Sch
Parkfield La DE6 . . . . .81 B2
Parkfield Rd Longton ST3 . . . . . .73 A1
  Wolv WV2,WV4 . . . . .266 C3
Parkfields Endon ST9 . . . . .43 C4
  Stafford ST17 . . . . .174 B4
Parkfields Cl ST5 . . . . .56 A3
Parkgate La DE6 . . . . .79 C3
Parkhall Cty Pk ST3 . . . . .73 C3
Parkhall La ST10 . . . . .109 A3
Parkhead Cres ST3 . . . . .74 A2
Parkhead Dr ST3 . . . . .74 A2
Parkhead St ST3 . . . . .74 A2
Parkhill Rd WS7 . . . . .229 A4
Parkhouse Gdns DY3 . . . . .271 A4
Parkhouse Ind Est ST5 . . . . . . .40 C1
Parkhouse Ind Est E ST5 . . . . .56 A4
Parkhouse Ind Est W
  ST5 . . . . .55 C4
Parkhouse Rd E ST5 . . . . .40 C1
Parkhouse Rd W ST5 . . . . .40 C1
Parklands Stafford ST1 . . . . . . .282 A1
  4 Stafford ST1 . . . . .17 A1
Parklands Biddulph ST8 . . . . . . .17 A1
  Kidsgrove ST7 . . . . .26 A1
Parklands Rd ST10 . . . . .92 C2
Parklands The
  Congleton CW12 . . . . .6 A1
  Kingswinford DY6 . . . . .275 B3
  Wolv WV3 . . . . .255 B1
Parks Cres WV11 . . . . .242 A2
Parkside Tamworth B77 . . . . . . .250 C1
  Trentham ST4 . . . . .88 A4
Parkside Ave ST6 . . . . .155 B4
Parkside Cres ST9 . . . . .143 C4
Parkside Dr ST5 . . . . .56 B2
Parkside Gr ST5 . . . . .56 B2
Parkside Ind Est WV1 . . . . . . .266 C4
Parkside La Gayton ST18 . . . . . .139 A4
  Huntington WS11 . . . . .209 A1
Parkside Prim Sch
  ST16 . . . . .155 B4
Parkside Way B74 . . . . .257 A1
Parkstone Ave ST5 . . . . .284 A4
Parkstone Cl WS4 . . . . .244 B1
Parkview Ct WV6 . . . . .275 A4
Parkview Dr WS8 . . . . .228 C1
Parkway Branston DE14 . . . . . . .165 C1
  Stone ST15 . . . . .120 B4
  Trentham ST4 . . . . .88 A4
Parkway The Hanley ST1 . . . . . .282 B1
  Perton WV6 . . . . .254 C2
Parkwood Ave ST4 . . . . .87 A3
Parkwood Cl WS8 . . . . .245 A3
Parkyn St WV2 . . . . .266 C3
Parliament Row ST1 . . . . .282 B3
Parliament Sq ST1 . . . . .282 B3
Parliament St DE11 . . . . .186 C3
Parnell Sq CW12 . . . . .6 A1
Parr Cl ST15 . . . . .120 B4
Parson's Croft WV9 . . . . .224 A1
Parson's Wlk B79 . . . . .218 C1
Parsonage St ST6 . . . . .41 B2
Parsons Cl SK17 . . . . .24 A3
Parsons Dr ST20 . . . . .171 C3
Parsons Hollow B77 . . . . .261 C4

Parsons La ST13 . . . . .33 B2
Parton Gr ST3 . . . . .74 A2
Partridge Cl
  Huntington WS12 . . . . .209 B4
  10 Meir ST3 . . . . .90 A4
Partridge Croft WS13 . . . . . . .231 B4
Partridge Dr ST14 . . . . .126 B3
Partridge Mill WS3 . . . . .243 C2
Partridge Rd DY8 . . . . .279 B2
Partridge Ride TF9 . . . . .99 B2
Parva Ct ST14 . . . . .110 C1
Paskin Cl WS13 . . . . .215 B4
Pass Ave WS14 . . . . .232 C3
Passfield Ave WV12 . . . . .259 A4
Pastoral Cl CW3 . . . . .68 C3
Pasture Cl ST5 . . . . .85 B3
Pasture Gate WS11 . . . . .209 B1
Pasture La WS11 . . . . .243 C1
Pasturefields Ent Pk
  ST18 . . . . .158 A3
Pasturefields La ST18 . . . . . . .158 A3
Pastures The
  Perton WV6 . . . . .254 B2
  Swadlincote DE11 . . . . .186 C3
Patch Cl DE13 . . . . .166 A3
Patch Mdw Rd ST10 . . . . .76 A2
Paterson Ave ST21 . . . . .117 C2
Paterson Pl WS8 . . . . .245 A3
Patricia Ave WV4 . . . . .266 B3
Patrick Gr 3 WS11 . . . . .213 A2
Patrick Mews WS13 . . . . .213 C1
Patrick Pl ST18 . . . . .27 A1
Patshull Ave WV10 . . . . .240 A2
Patshull Gr WV10 . . . . .240 A2
Patshull Ho WV6 . . . . .255 C3
Patshull Rd WV6 . . . . .253 A2
Patterdale Rd WS11 . . . . .210 A2
Patterdale St ST6 . . . . .42 A2
Pattingham La WV7 . . . . .243 B1
Pattingham Rd WV6 . . . . .254 B1
Paul St 1 WV2 . . . . .266 B4
Paulet High Sch DE15 . . . . . . .185 C4
Pauls Coppice WS8 . . . . .245 A3
Pauls Wlk WS13 . . . . .215 B4
Pavement The ST19 . . . . .223 B3
Pavilion Cl WS9 . . . . .256 B4
Pavilion Dr ST1 . . . . .57 A3
Pavilion End DY7 . . . . .274 C1
Pavilion The B77 . . . . .251 A2
Pavior's Rd WS7 . . . . .227 A4
Paxton Ave WV6 . . . . .254 C2
Paxton St ST1 . . . . .282 C1
Paynter St ST4 . . . . .72 C3
Peace Cl WS6 . . . . .226 C2
Peachaven Gr ST18 . . . . .43 A1
Peach Ave ST17 . . . . .174 C4
Peacock Hay Rd ST7 . . . . .40 C2
Peacock La ST4,ST5 . . . . .87 A4
Peacock Rd ST5 . . . . .55 C3
Peak Dale Ave ST6 . . . . .41 B4
Peak Dr DY3 . . . . .271 C2
Peak View ST13 . . . . .31 A3
Peake Cres WS8 . . . . .244 C3
Peake Rd WS8 . . . . .245 A3
Peake St ST5 . . . . .55 C2
Peakes Rd WS15 . . . . .178 A1
Peaks L Ctr B79 . . . . .250 A2
Pear Cl ST7 . . . . .73 B4
Pear Tree Ave DE11 . . . . .186 C4
Pear Tree Cl
  Barlaston ST12 . . . . .88 B1
  Gnosall ST20 . . . . .171 C3
  Huntington WS12 . . . . .209 B4
  Shuttington B79 . . . . .251 C4
Pear Tree Com Prim Sch
  WS15 . . . . .196 C4
Pear Tree Cor CW3 . . . . .68 B4
Pear Tree La
  Brownhills WS8 . . . . .228 B1
  Essington WV11 . . . . .241 A1
  Wolv WV2,WV3,WV4 . . . . .266 A4
Pear Tree Rd ST7 . . . . .39 C1
Pearis Dr ST10 . . . . .94 C4
Pearl Gr ST18 . . . . .27 A1
Pearson Dr ST15 . . . . .120 B4
Pearson St WV2 . . . . .266 B4
Peartree La WS15 . . . . .180 A3
Peascroft Rd ST6 . . . . .42 A2
Pebble Cl B77 . . . . .251 A2
Pebble Mill Cl WS11 . . . . .209 C1
Pebble Mill Dr WS11 . . . . .210 A1
Pebble Mill St ST1 . . . . .56 C2
Peck Mill La ST10 . . . . .27 B1
Peckforton Mew ST17 . . . . . . .174 A4
Pedley Gr ST6 . . . . .42 B1
Pedley La CW12 . . . . .6 A1
Peebles Gn ST2 . . . . .58 B1
Peebles Rd ST5 . . . . .54 C1
Peel Ave WV12 . . . . .259 A4
Peel Cl Longton ST3 . . . . .283 C1
  Newcastle-u-l ST5 . . . . .56 B3
  Stafford ST16 . . . . .155 B2
  Tunstall ST6 . . . . .56 C4
Peel Teer ST6 . . . . .155 C3
Peelers Way ST14 . . . . .250 B1
Pegasus Gr ST6 . . . . .42 B1

Pegasus Wlk B79 . . . . .249 C4
Peggs La ST20 . . . . .150 C4
Peggy's Bank ST7 . . . . .54 C4
Pegroy Gr ST6 . . . . .42 B1
Pelham St ST1 . . . . .282 C1
Pellfield Ct ST18 . . . . .138 B1
Pelsall La Walsall WS4 . . . . . . .244 A1
  Walsall, Bloxwich WS3 . . . . . . .243 B2
Pelsall Rd WS8 . . . . .244 B4
Pelsall Village Sch ST3 . . . . . .243 C2
Pemberton Cres DY10 . . . . . . .280 B2
Pemberton Dr ST3 . . . . .90 A3
Pembridge Rd ST17 . . . . .188 A2
Pembroke Cl B79 . . . . .249 B3
Pembroke Ct ST5 . . . . .284 A1
Pembroke Dr
  Newcastle-u-l ST5 . . . . .284 A2
  Wolv WV4 . . . . .266 B3
Pembroke Gdns DY8 . . . . .275 B1
Pembroke Rd ST2 . . . . .43 A1
Pen-y-Bony Wlk ST8 . . . . .27 C3
Pen-y-bryn Way TF10 . . . . . . .168 C1
Penarth Rd ST1 . . . . .282 B4
Penarth Pl ST5 . . . . .284 A1
Pencombe Dr WV4 . . . . .266 B3
Penda Gr WV6 . . . . .254 C3
Pendeford Ave WV6 . . . . .255 C4
Pendeford Hall La WV9 . . . . . .239 B3
Pendeford High Sch
  WV10 . . . . .240 A1
Pendeford La WV9 . . . . .240 A2
Pendeford Mill La WV8 . . . . . .239 C2
Pendeford Mill Nature
  Reserve* WV9 . . . . .239 C2
Pendene Ct WV4 . . . . .266 A3
Penderel St WS3 . . . . .243 B1
Penderell Cl WV10 . . . . .241 A3
Pendinas Dr WV8 . . . . .239 A2
Pendine Gr ST4 . . . . .73 A3
Pendle Hill WS12 . . . . .210 B2
Pendrel Cl WS6 . . . . .240 C3
Pendrell Cl WV8 . . . . .239 A2
Pendrell Hall Coll WV8 . . . . . . .238 B3
Pendrill Rd WV10 . . . . .240 C2
Pendryl Cl ST19 . . . . .223 B4
Penfleet Ave ST3 . . . . .74 A1
Pengrove Cl ST7 . . . . .41 C4
Penhallow Dr WV4 . . . . .266 C3
Penk Dr WS7 . . . . .229 B3
Penk Dr N WS15 . . . . .178 B1
Penk Dr S WS15 . . . . .178 B1
Penk La ST19 . . . . .190 A4
Penk Rise WV6 . . . . .255 A2
Penkhull Inf Sch ST4 . . . . .72 A4
Penkhull New Rd ST4 . . . . .72 A3
Penkhull Terr ST4 . . . . .72 A3
Penkridge Bank WS15 . . . . . . .195 B3
Penkridge Ind Est ST19 . . . . . .207 C4
Penkridge L Ctr ST19 . . . . .208 A4
Penkridge Mid Sch
  ST19 . . . . .193 A1
Penkridge Sta ST19 . . . . .193 A1
Penkridge Wharf ST19 . . . . . . .207 C4
Penkside WV9 . . . . .224 A2
Penkvale Rd ST17 . . . . .174 C3
Penkville St ST4 . . . . .72 A3
Penleigh Gdns WV5 . . . . .269 C4
Penmark Gr ST3 . . . . .89 C4
Penmere Dr
  Caverswall ST9 . . . . .59 A2
  Newcastle-u-l ST5 . . . . .71 B4
Penn Cl WS3 . . . . .243 B1
Penn Croft ST18 . . . . .177 B4
Penn Croft La WV4 . . . . .266 A1
Penn Fields Sch WV3 . . . . .266 A4
Penn Hall Sch WV4 . . . . .265 C2
Penn Hospl WV4 . . . . .265 C2
Penn Rd Himley DY3 . . . . .270 C4
  Wolv WV2,WV3,WV4 . . . . .266 A4
Penn St WV3 . . . . .266 A4
Penncroft WV4 . . . . .265 C2
Pennel St ST1 . . . . .58 A2
Pennhouse Ave WV4 . . . . .265 C3
Pennine Dr
  Cannock WS11 . . . . .209 C1
  Sedgley DY3 . . . . .271 B2
Pennine Way
  Biddulph ST8 . . . . .16 C1
  Newcastle-u-l ST5 . . . . .55 C2
  Tamworth B77 . . . . .262 A4
Pennington Cl ST3 . . . . .74 B1
Penns Wood Cl DY3 . . . . .266 B1
Pennwood Cl WV4 . . . . .266 A3
Pennwood La WV4 . . . . .266 A3
Pennwood Ct WV4 . . . . .265 C2
Penny Cres Gn WS11 . . . . .227 C2
Penny Ct WS6 . . . . .242 C4
Penny Farthing Arc
  DY3 .271 B4
Penny La ST10 . . . . .76 B2
Penny Royal Cl DY3 . . . . .271 B1
Pennycress Gdns WV10 . . . . . .241 A4
Pennycroft La ST14 . . . . .111 B1
Pennycroft Rd ST14 . . . . .111 A1
Pennycrofts ST16 . . . . .155 C2
Pennycrofts Ct ST16 . . . . .155 C2
Pennyfields Ave ST4 . . . . .57 B3
Pennyfields Rd ST7 . . . . .26 B1
Pennymoor Rd B77 . . . . .262 A4
Pennymore Cl ST4 . . . . .88 A4
Penny Croft WS13 . . . . .214 C1
Penport Gr ST3 . . . . .283 A2
Penrhyn Ave ST6 . . . . .42 A1
Penrith Cl ST4 . . . . .88 B3
Penrith Ct ST5 . . . . .71 A3

Pens Meadow Sch DY8 . 275 C2
Pensett Trad Est The
  DY6 .... 271 A1
Pensford Gr ST1 ....57 C3
Pensgreave Rd DE13 ....166 A3
Penshaw Cl WV9 ....240 A1
Pensnett Trad Est The
  DY6 .... 275 C4
Penstone La WV4 ....264 C2
Pentire Rd WS14 ....231 B3
Pentland Gdns WV6 .....255 C1
Pentland Gr ST5 ....55 C2
Penton Pl ST3 ....88 C4
Penton Wlk ST3 ....88 C4
Penzer St DY6 ....275 B4
Peolsford Rd WS3 ....244 A2
Peover La CW12 ....6 C3
Pepper St Keele ST5 ....54 C1
  Newcastle-u-L ST5 .....284 B2
Perceval St ST1 ....57 C3
Percival Dr ST9 ....43 B2
Percy St ST1 ....282 B3
Peregrine Cl
  Burton u T DE15 ....167 B2
  Dudley DY1 ....271 C1
  Whittington WS14 ....232 C3
Peregrine Gr ST3 ....90 A3
Perivale Cl ST1 ....58 A3
Periwinkle Cl WS8 ....244 B3
Perkins St ST16 ....41 B4
Perks Rd WV11 ....242 A1
Perle Brook ST21 ....133 B4
Perott Dr B75 ....258 B1
Perrin Cl ST17 ....174 C1
Perry Cl ST1 ....282 C2
Perrycrofts Cres B79 ....250 B4
Perrymount Ct ST14 ....71 C3
Pershore Cl WS3 ....242 C1
Pershore Dr DE14 ....185 A4
Pershore Rd WS3 ....242 C1
Pershore Way WS3 ....242 C1
Persia Wlk [15] ST6 ....41 B2
Perth Cl DE15 ....167 B1
Perth St ST14 ....283 A5
Perton Cl ST7 ....87 C4
Perton Brook Vale WV6 .254 C3
Perton Fst Sch WV6 .....254 C3
Perton Gr WV6 ....254 C3
Perton Mid Sch WV6 ....255 A3
Perton Rd WV6 ....254 C3
Perton Sandown Fst Sch
  WV6 ....254 C2
Perton Wood View ST3 ...72 C2
Pessall La B79 ....217 B4
Petard Cl B77 ....261 B4
Peter James CE ST16 ....155 C3
Peter's La WS7 ....230 A3
Peterborough Dr WS12 .210 B1
Peterdale Dr WV4 ....265 C2
Peterhead B77 ....250 C3
Peters Wlk WS13 ....209 C2
Petersfield WS11 ....209 C2
Petersfield Rd ST6 ....42 A4
Petershouse Dr B74 ....57 C3
Peterson Ho [7] ST3 ....89 C4
Pethills La ST13 ....43 B4
Petrel Gr ST3 ....90 A4
Pettiford Cl WS13 ....215 B3
Pevensey Gr ST3 ....73 B3
Peverill Rd Perton WV6 .254 C2
  Wolv WV4 ....266 C2
Pezenas Dr ST9 ....97 A1
Pheasant Wlk TF9 ....99 B2
Philip Gr WS11 ....209 C3
Philip La ST9 ....59 A2
Philip St ST4 ....112 B4
Phillips Ave WV11 ....241 C1
Phillips Cl ST15 ....120 B4
Phillipson Way ST16 ....57 B4
Phoenix Cl Kidsgrove ST7 ..76 C1
  Rugeley WS15 ....196 C3
Phoenix Ctr WS11 ....226 C3
Phoenix Rd WS11 ....210 A1
Phoenix Rise WV2 ....266 B3
Phoenix St [3] Tunstall ST6 .41 B2
  Wolv WV3 ....266 B3
Picasso Cl WS11 ....210 B1
Picasso Rise ST3 ....90 A4
Piccadilly Hanley ST1 ...282 B2
  Tamworth B78 ....261 C1
Piccadilly Arc ST1 ....282 B3
Piccadilly Cres B78 .....261 C1
Piccadilly La DE6 ....66 B1
Piccadilly St [6] ST6 .....41 B2
Pickering Cl ST3 ....283 A1
Pickford Pl [8] ST3 ....74 A1
Pickleys La DE6 ....127 B4
Pickmere Cl ST12 ....42 C3
Picknall La ST14 ....126 A4
Picknalls Fst Sch ST14 ..126 A4
Pickwick Pl ST7 ....25 B1
Pickwood Ave ST13 ....31 A1
Pickwood Cl ST13 ....31 A3
Picton St Hanley ST1 ....282 C2
  Leek ST13 ....30 B3
Piddocks Rd DE15 ....186 A3
Pidduck St ST6 ....56 C4
Pier St ST6 ....244 C4
Pierce St ST6 ....41 A2
Pigeonhay La ST14 ....110 B1
Piggott Gr ST2 ....58 A2
Pike Cl ST16 ....156 A3
Pike La WS15 ....198 A2
Pikelow La ST10 ....49 A2
Pilgrim Pl ST16 ....155 C1
Pilgrim St ST16 ....155 C1
Pilkington Ave ST5 ....71 A3

Pillar Cl ST2 ....73 B4
Pillaton Cl ST19 ....207 C4
Pillaton Dr WS12 ....209 B3
Pilsbury St ST5 ....56 B3
Pilsden Pl ST3 ....90 B4
Pimlico Ct DY3 ....271 B2
Pinch The DE6 ....36 A1
Pine Cl Burton u T DE14 .185 A4
  Great Wyrley WS6 ....226 C2
  Kingswinford DY6 ....275 B3
  Kinver DY7 ....278 B2
  Market Drayton TF9 .....97 A1
  Talke ST7 ....84 A4
  Tamworth B79 ....250 A4
Pine Cres ST17 ....175 C3
Pine Ct Ashley TF9 ....99 C2
  Blythe Bridge ST11 ......90 B4
Pine Gr Burntwood WS7 .228 C3
  Swadlincote DE11 .....186 C3
Pine Leigh B74 ....258 A1
Pine Rd ST4 ....72 B2
Pine St WS3 ....243 B1
Pine Tree Cl WS12 ....195 A1
Pine View Rugeley WS15 .178 B2
  Swindon DY3 ....269 B2
Pine Wlk Codsall WV8 ...238 C1
  Uttoxeter ST14 ....125 C4
Pinehurst Cl ST5 ....71 A2
Pines Park Mobile Homes
  The WS12 ....209 B3
Pines The Lichfield WS14 .231 C4
  Wolv WV3 ....255 B1
Pineside Ave WS10 ....211 C3
Pinetree Dr Aldridge B74 .256 A1
  Blythe Bridge ST11 ......90 B4
Pinetrees La TF9 ....99 C3
Pineways
  Kingswinford DY6 ....275 B1
  Sutton Coldfield B74 ....257 B2
Pineways Dr WV6 ....255 C2
Pinewood Ave
  Cannock WS11 ....209 B2
  Wood End CV9 ....262 B1
Pinewood Cl
  Brownhills WS8 ....228 C1
  Wolv WV3 ....265 A4
  Wombourne WV5 ....270 A3
Pinewood Cres ST3 ....74 B1
Pinewood Dr ST18 ....177 B4
Pinewood Gr
  Forsbrook ST11 ....91 A3
  Newcastle-u-L ST5 ....40 C1
Pinewood Prim Sch ST4 .112 B4
Pinewood Rd Ashley TF9 ..99 C3
  Burton u T DE15 ....185 C3
Pinewoods TF10 ....168 C1
Pinewoods Ave DY9 .....281 C2
Pinewoods Cl DY9 ....281 C2
Pinewoods Ct DY9 ....281 C2
Pinfold Ave ST6 ....42 C2
Pinfold Cl Tutbury DE13 .146 B3
  Wheaton Aston ST19 ...205 A3
Pinfold Cres WV4 ....265 B3
Pinfold Dr WS15 ....198 B3
Pinfold Gr WV4 ....265 B3
Pinfold Hill WS14 ....246 C3
Pinfold La
  Abbots Bromley WS15 ..161 B2
  Blore TF9 ....98 B1
  Cheslyn Hay WS6 ....226 C2
  Norbury ST20 ....151 A2
  Norton Canes WS11 ....227 C2
  Penkridge ST19 ....192 B1
  Wheaton Aston ST19 ...205 A3
  Wolv WV4 ....265 A3
Pinfold Rd WS13 ....213 C1
Pinfold St ST14 ....126 B4
Pingle Farm Rd DE11 ...186 C3
Pingle La
  Burntwood WS7 ....229 B3
  Stone ST15 ....120 A4
Pingle The WS15 ....196 A4
Pinhoe Pl ST3 ....73 C2
Pinnox St ST6 ....41 C1
Pintail Cl ST17 ....175 A4
Pioneer Pl ST6 ....42 B2
Pipe Hall Farm Nature
  Reserve* WS13 ....230 A4
Pipe Hay La DE6 ....144 B3
Pipe La WS15 ....198 A4
Pipe Wood La WS15 .....180 A2
Piper Cl WV6 ....254 C2
Piper Pl DY9 ....279 C4
Piper's La TF10 ....168 A2
Piper's Lodge TF10 .....168 A2
Pipers Croft WS13 ....214 A1
Pippins The
  Newcastle-u-L ST5 ....71 B2
  Stafford ST17 ....174 C3
Pirefold Pl ST5 ....41 A1
Pirehill Fst Sch ST15 ...119 C3
Pirehill La ST15 ....119 C3
Pirehill Rd ST15 ....119 C3
Pirie Cl DY9 ....279 C4
Pirie Rd CW12 ....6 A2
Pit La ST7 ....40 B3
Pitcairn St ST1 ....74 B1
Pitchcroft La TF10 ......187 A3
Pitcher La WS13 ....31 A3
Pitfield Ave ST5 ....56 B3
Pitgreen La ST5 ....56 B3
Pitlea Pl [7] ST3 ....73 B3
Pitsford St ST3 ....283 A1
Pitstone Cl ST16 ....136 B1
Pitt St
  Kidderminster DY10 ....280 A1

Pitt St continued
  Stafford ST16 ....155 B3
Pitt St E ST6 ....57 A4
Pitt St W ST6 ....57 A4
Pitts Hill Bank ST6 ....41 C3
Plainfield Gr ST2 ....73 B4
Plainview Cl WS9 ....256 C1
Plaisaunce The ST5 ....71 A3
Plane Gr ST5 ....40 C1
Planks La WV5 ....269 C3
Plant Cres ST17 ....174 C4
Plant La WS7 ....228 C4
Plant St Cheadle ST10 ....76 C1
  Kingswinford DY8 ....275 C1
  Longton ST3 ....283 C4
Plant Way WS15 ....243 C2
Plantation La
  Hampton B78 ....249 A2
  Wombourne DY3 ....270 A2
Plantation Pk ST5 ....70 B3
Plantation Rd
  Cannock WS12 ....195 A1
  Longton ST4 ....88 B4
Plants Cl WS6 ....243 A4
Plardiwick Rd ST20 .....171 A3
Platt St WS11 ....210 A3
Platts Ave ST3 ....43 C3
Platts Cres DY8 ....279 C4
Platts Dr DY8 ....279 C4
Platts Rd DY8 ....279 C4
Playdale TF10 ....168 A2
Pleasant Cl DY6 ....275 B2
Pleasant St ST6 ....56 C4
Pleasant View DY3 ......271 B1
Plex St ST6 ....41 B2
Pleydell St ST1 ....57 C4
Plough Bank ST9 ....60 A4
Plough La TF10 ....168 C3
Plough Mews DY7 ......278 B2
Plough St ST1 ....282 C4
Ploughmans Croft TF10 .169 A2
Ploughmans Pl B75 .....258 B2
Ploughmans Wlk
  Kingswinford DY6 ......275 A4
  Lichfield WS13 ....214 B2
  Wolv WV8 ....239 C1
Plover Cl
  Featherstone WV10 ....241 A4
  Meir ST3 ....90 A4
Plover Dr ST8 ....27 C4
Plover Field DY3 ....68 B3
Plovers Rise WS15 ......178 B1
Plummer Rd DE11 ....186 C3
Plumtree Gr ST1 ....55 C4
Plymouth Gr ST5 ....54 C4
Pochard Cl ST6 ....42 B1
Podmore Ave ST7 ....54 C3
Podmore La ST7 ....57 A4
Podmore St ST6 ....57 A4
Polesworth High Sch
  B78 ....262 C4
Police Dr TF9 ....112 B4
Polperro Way [15] ST2 ....90 A4
Pomona Rise ST1 ....57 B4
Pond Cres WV7 ....266 C4
Pond Gr WV2 ....266 C4
Pond La WV4 ....266 B4
Ponesfield Rd WS13 .....214 A1
Ponesgreen WS13 ......214 A1
Pool Ave
  Norton Canes WS11 ....228 A3
  Norton-in-t-M ST7 ....43 A1
Pool Cl WV10 ....225 B1
Pool Cres WS8 ....228 B1
Pool Dam ST5 ....284 B2
Pool Gn WS9 ....256 A3
Pool Hall Cres WS3 .....265 A4
Pool Hall Rd WV3 ....265 A4
Pool House Rd WV5 .....269 B3
Pool La Brocton ST17 ....176 B2
  Burntwood WS7 ....228 C2
Pool Mdw WS6 ....226 B2
Pool Meadow Cl WS15 ..196 B4
Pool Rd Brownhills WS8 .228 C1
  Burntwood WS7 ....228 C2
Pool Side
  Newcastle-u-L ST5 .....284 A3
  Scholar Green ST7 ....25 A4
Pool St Fenton ST4 ....73 A3
  Newcastle-u-L ST5 .....284 A2
  Wolv WV2 ....266 B4
Pool View WS6 ....227 A2
Poole St DY8 ....279 C2
Poole's Way WS7 ....229 B4
Pooles Rd WS13 ....214 A2
Pooley La Gnosall TF10 .188 B4
  Polesworth B78 ....251 C1
Poolfield Ave ST5 ....70 C4
Poolfield Ave N ST5 ......71 A4
Poolfield Rd WS13 ......230 C3
Poolfields Ave ST16 ......43 B4
Poolfields Cl ST15 ....70 C4
Poolhill Cl ST3 ....283 A2
Poolside Longton ST3 .....88 C3
  Madeley CW3 ....6 B3
Pope Gdns ST17 ....174 B4
Pope Gr WS17 ....209 C3
Pope Rd WV10 ....241 A1
Poplar Ave
  Brownhills WS8 ....228 C3
  Burntwood WS7 ....228 C2
  Cannock WS11 ....209 C4
  Newcastle-u-L ST5 ....56 A2
Poplar Cl Ecclesahall ST21 .133 C3
  Forsbrook ST11 ....91 A3
  Haughton ST18 ....172 C3
  Newcastle-u-L ST5 ....56 A2

Poplar Cl continued
  Stone ST15 ....119 C4
  Uttoxeter ST14 ....110 C1
  Wombourne WV5 ....270 A3
Poplar Cres DY8 ....279 B2
Poplar Ct ST5 ....56 A2
Poplar Dr Kidsgrove ST7 ..26 A1
  Longton ST3 ....73 A1
Poplar Gr Longton ST3 ...73 A1
  Newcastle-u-L ST5 .....284 D3
  Wolv WV5 ....79 C3
Poplar Rd
  Brownhills WS8 ....245 A4
  Great Wyrley WS6 ....227 A1
  Kingswinford DY6 ....275 C2
  Stourbridge DY8 ....279 C2
  Wolv WV3 ....266 A3
Poplar Rise B74 ....257 B3
Poplar St
  Norton Canes WS11 ....228 A3
  Wolv WV2 ....266 B3
Poplar Way ST17 ....174 C3
Poplars Dr WV8 ....238 C1
Poplars Farm Way WV9 .224 A1
Poplars Rd
  Armitage WS15 ....198 B2
  Burton u T DE13 ....166 B4
Poplars The
  Cannock WS11 ....209 C2
  Kingswinford DY8 ......275 C1
Poppit's La ST14 ....110 C1
Poppy Gdns DE13 ....201 A1
Porchester Cl WS9 ......245 A1
Porlock Ave ST17 ....175 B4
Porlock Gr ST4 ....88 A3
Porthkerry Gr DY3 ......271 A4
Portland Ave
  Aldridge WS9 ....256 A3
  Burton u T DE14 ....185 A4
  Tamworth B79 ....249 C4
Portland Cl ST11 ....90 B4
Portland Ct WS9 ....256 A3
Portland Dr Biddulph ST8 .16 B1
  Forsbrook ST11 ....91 A4
  Market Drayton TF9 .....97 A1
  Stone ST15 ....119 C4
Portland Gr ST5 ....71 A2
Portland Mews ST5 ....56 A3
Portland Pl
  Barlaston ST12 ....88 C2
  Cannock WS11 ....226 B4
  Waterhouses ST10 ......48 C1
Portland Rd
  Aldridge WS9 ....256 A3
  Longton ST3 ....73 A1
Portland St Hanley ST1 .282 A4
  Leek ST13 ....30 C3
Portland St N ST13 ....30 C3
Portland St S ST13 ....30 C3
Portleven Cl ST17 ....175 C4
Portleys La B78 ....260 B2
Portobello WS15 ....178 C1
Portrush Rd WV6 ....254 B2
Portswood Cl WV9 ......239 C1
Portway Cl DY6 ....275 C3
Portway Dr DE13 ....166 B4
Portway La B79 ....234 B4
Portway Pl DY10 ....280 A3
Portway The DY6 ....275 C3
Post La ST9 ....43 C3
Post Office La Betley CW2 .37 C1
  Gnosall TF10 ....188 B4
  Rugeley WS15 ....196 A4
Post Office Rd
  Alrewas DE13 ....201 A2
  Seisdon WV5 ....263 C2
Post Office Sq CW3 ....68 C2
Postern Rd DE13 ....165 A2
Postmans La ST18 ......122 B4
Pothooks La ST13 ....33 C2
Potteries Sh Ctr ST1 ....282 B3
Potteries Way ST1 ......282 B4
Potters Ave ST15 ....118 C3
Potters Croft B79 ....218 C1
Potters End ST18 ....16 B1
Potts La ST14 ....141 A4
Pouk La WS14 ....246 C4
Poulson St ST4 ....72 A4
Pound Gdns ST6 ....42 C1
Pound St ST5 ....267 B4
Poundsgate Gr ST4 ......88 A4
Pountney St WV2 ....266 B4
Povey Pl ST5 ....41 A1
Powderham Cl ST7 ....41 C4
Powell Pl TF10 ....168 C2
Powell St ST1 ....282 A4
Power Gr ST3 ....283 A4
Power Station Rd WS15 .178 C1
Power Station Road Ind Est
  WS15 ....178 C1
Power Wash Ind Est ST8 .27 A2
Pown St SK17 ....23 C3
Powy Dr ST7 ....24 B4
Poxon Rd WS9 ....245 A2

Poplar Cl continued
Stone ST14 ....119 C4
Uttoxeter ST14 ....156 A2
Wombourne WV6 ....255 C3
Poynings The WV6 ......255 B3
Precinct The B79 ....250 A3
Preedys Cl WS15 ....160 C3
Prescott Ave ST16 ......156 A2
Prescott Dr ST19 ....193 A1
Prestbury Ave ST5 ....71 A1
Preston St ST6 ....57 B4
Preston Vale La ST19 ...192 B1
Prestwick Rd DY6 ....275 B3
Prestwood Cl ST17 .....155 C1
Prestwood Dr DY7 ......279 A4
Prestwood Rd ST14 ......79 C1
Prestwood Rd DY7 .....278 C3
Pretoria Rd ST1 ....57 A2
Priam Cl ST5 ....41 A1
Priam Gr WS3 ....244 A3
Price Ave B78 ....249 B1
Price Cl TF9 ....99 B3
Price St DE14 ....166 A2
Price St Burslem ST6 .....56 C4
  Cannock WS11 ....209 C1
Prices Rd DY3 ....271 B2
Priestley Dr ST3 ....283 D4
Prime St ST1 ....57 C3
Primethorpe La ST7 ......26 B4
Primley Ave B77 ....261 C3
Primrose Ave WV10 ....240 B2
Primrose Cl Walsall WS3 .244 A3
  Wheaton Aston ST19 ...205 B4
Primrose Dell CW3 ....68 B3
Primrose Dr
  Burton u T DE14 ....185 A4
  Newport TF10 ....168 C1
Primrose Gdns
  Codsall WV8 ....239 A2
  Featherstone WV10 ....241 A4
Primrose Gr ST5 ....284 C4
Primrose Hill
  Kingswinford DY8 ......275 C1
  Trentham ST4 ....72 A1
Primrose Mdw [1] WS11 .210 B1
Prince Albert Terr ST15 .135 A4
Prince Ave ST18 ....172 C3
Prince Charles Ave ST13 .31 A4
Prince George St ST10 ...76 B2
Prince Rupert Mews
  WS13 ....231 A4
Prince Rupert's Way
  WS13 ....231 A4
Prince St Brownhills WS9 .244 C1
  Cannock WS12 ....209 C3
  Leek ST13 ....31 A3
Prince's St ST15 ....105 A1
Princefield Ave ST19 ...207 C4
Princefield Fst Sch
  ST19 ....207 C4
Princes Dr WV8 ....239 A1
Princes Gdns WV8 ......239 A1
Princes Rd Stoke-on-T ST4 .71 C4
  Stourbridge DY8 ....279 B2
Princes Sq ST6 ....56 B4
Princes St [4] ST16 ......155 C2
Princess Ave Audley ST7 .39 B1
  Leek ST13 ....31 A4
Princess Ct ST17 ....228 C4
Princess Ct ST7 ....40 B3
Princess Dr ST3 ....74 A2
Princess Gdns TF10 ....168 C1
Princess Rd ST14 ....155 C3
Princess Rd ST16 ....111 A1
Princess St ST6 ....57 B4
  Burntwood WS7 ....228 C4
Princess Way DE13/DE14 .166 C4
Princeton Gdns WV9 ...239 C1
Princetown Cl ST3 ....90 A4
Priorfield Cl ST3 ....283 B4
Priory Cl ST9 ....97 A1
Priors Mill DY3 ....271 C2
Priory Ave ST13 ....31 A4
Priory CE Prim Sch ST4 .71 C4
Priory Cl Congleton CW12 .16 A4
  Tamworth B79 ....249 C4
  Tutbury DE13 ....146 A3
Priory Ct Brownhills WS9 .245 A2
  Market Drayton TF9 .....97 A1
  Newcastle-u-L ST5 .....284 B2
Priory Dr ST18 ....177 A4
Priory Field CV14 ......266 C1
Priory Green Prim Sch
  WV9 ....240 A1
Priory La DY3 ....271 B4
Priory Lands DE13 .....147 C1
Priory Rd ST17 ....26 A2
Priory Rd Bucknall ST2 ...58 A3
  Cannock WS11 ....210 B2
  Newcastle-u-L ST5 .....284 B1
  Rugeley WS15 ....197 A3
  Stone ST15 ....120 A4
Priory The ST16 ....44 A4
  Sedgley DY3 ....271 C1
Pritchett Ave WV4 .....266 C2
Probert Rd WV10 ....240 A1
Probyn Ct ST13 ....283 C2
Proctors Rd WS15 ......198 B2
Proffitt Cl WS8 ....245 A4
Progress Dr WS11 ....226 C4
Progress Ind Ctr WS13 .231 C4
Progress St ST3 ....231 C4
Prospect Manor Ct
  WS12 ....210 B2

Prospect Pk WS11 . . . . .226 B4
Prospect Pl 14 ST13 . . . . .30 C3
Prospect Rd
　Burntwood WS7 . . . . .229 A3
　Leek ST13 . . . . .31 A3
　Market Drayton TF9 . . . . .97 A1
　Sedgley DY3 . . . . .271 B1
　Stafford ST16 . . . . .155 C3
Prospect St Burslem ST6 . . . . .56 C3
　Tamworth B79 . . . . .250 A3
Prospect Terr ST5 . . . . .284 A3
Prosper Mdw DY6 . . . . .275 C4
Providence St ST1 . . . . .282 C4
Provost Pl ST13 . . . . .31 A4
Pruden Ave WV4 . . . . .266 C2
Puddle Hill ST18 . . . . .139 B1
Puddy La ST9 . . . . .44 A3
Pudsey Dr B75 . . . . .258 B2
Pugh Rd WV4,WV14 . . . . .266 C1
Pugin Cl WV6 . . . . .254 B2
Pullman Cl B27 . . . . .251 A1
Pullman Ct ST10 . . . . .76 B1
Pulteney Dr ST16 . . . . .155 A3
Pump Bank ST5 . . . . .69 C4
Pump La Doveridge DE6 . . . . .127 A4
　Rugeley WS15 . . . . .178 B2
Pump St Leek ST13 . . . . .31 A4
　Stoke-on-T ST4 . . . . .72 A4
Purbeck St ST6 . . . . .57 A4
Purbrook B77 . . . . .261 C4
Purbrook Rd WV1 . . . . .266 C4
Purcell Ave WS13 . . . . .214 B1
Pye Green Rd WS11 . . . . .209 C2
Pye Green Valley Prim Sch
　WS12 . . . . .210 A4
Pye Green Valley Primary
　Sch WS12 . . . . .210 A4
Pyebirch La ST21 . . . . .134 A3
Pyenest St ST1 . . . . .282 A1
Pyrus Gr WS15 . . . . .196 C3

Q

Quabbs La ST11 . . . . .91 B4
Quadrangle The ST9 . . . . .43 C4
Quadrant Rd ST1 . . . . .282 B3
Quadrant The
　Hanley ST1 . . . . .282 B3
　Sedgley DY3 . . . . .266 B1
Quadrille Lawns WV9 . . . . .259 C1
Quail Gn WV6 . . . . .254 C1
Quail Gr ST3 . . . . .90 A4
Quale Gr 6 DY8 . . . . .275 B2
Quantock Cl ST48 . . . . .245 A2
Quarry Ave ST4 . . . . .71 C4
Quarry Bank Keele ST5 . . . . . .69 C4
　Upper Tean ST10 . . . . .94 A2
Quarry Bank Rd
　Keele ST5 . . . . .69 C4
　Market Drayton TF9 . . . . .112 A4
Quarry Berry La DE12 . . . . . . .236 C4
Quarry Brow DY3 . . . . .271 C3
Quarry Cl Caverswall ST9 . . . . .59 A2
　Cheslyn Hay WS6 . . . . .226 C2
　Norton-in-t-M ST9 . . . . .43 B2
Quarry Hills La WS14 . . . . .231 B3
Quarry House La TF9 . . . . .112 A4
Quarry La ST20 . . . . .171 B2
Quarry Pl TF9 . . . . .112 A4
Quarry Rd Stoke-on-T ST4 . . . .71 C4
　Upper Tean ST10 . . . . .92 C2
Quarry Terr ST7 . . . . .26 A1
Quarter La SK17 . . . . .23 A1
Quee La ST14 . . . . .126 A1
Queen Anne St ST4 . . . . .72 A4
Queen Elizabeth's Mercian
　Sch B79 . . . . .250 B3
Queen Margaret's Rd
　TF9 .99 B3
Queen Mary Rd ST4 . . . . .99 B1
Queen Mary's Dr ST12 . . . . . . .88 C2
Queen St Audley ST7 . . . . .39 B1
　Brownhills WS9 . . . . .244 C1
　Burntwood WS7 . . . . .228 C3
　Burslem ST6 . . . . .56 C4
　Burton u T DE14 . . . . .166 B1
　Cannock WS11 . . . . .209 B1
　Cannock, High Town
　WS11 . . . . .210 A3
　Cheadle ST10 . . . . .76 C2
　Cheslyn Hay WS6 . . . . .226 B2
　Kidsgrove ST7 . . . . .26 A1
　Kingswinford, Moss Grove
　DY6 . . . . .275 B4
　Kingswinford, Wordsley
　DY8 . . . . .275 B2
　Leek ST13 . . . . .30 C3
　Lichfield WS13 . . . . .231 A4
　Longnor SK17 . . . . .13 A3
　Market Drayton TF9 . . . . .97 B1
　Newcastle-u-L ST5 . . . . .284 C3
　Newcastle-u-L, Chesterton
　ST5 .56 A4
　Newcastle-u-L, Porthill ST5 . .56 A3
　Rugeley WS15 . . . . .196 C4
　Stourbridge DY8 . . . . .279 C3
　Uttoxeter ST14 . . . . .126 C3
Queen Victoria Prim Sch
　DY3 . . . . .271 B4
Queen's Ave ST6 . . . . .41 C2
Queen's Croft Com Sch
　WS13 . . . . .231 A4
Queen's Dr ST8 . . . . .27 B3

Queen's Prim Sch ST4 . . . . . . .73 A3
Queen's Rd Stoke-on-T ST4 . . .71 C4
　Stourbridge DY8 . . . . .279 C3
Queen's Row ST12 . . . . .88 C3
Queen's Sq 9 ST15 . . . . .105 A1
Queens Cotts ST19 . . . . .206 A4
Queens Ct
　Burton u T DE14 . . . . .185 A4
　Stafford ST17 . . . . .73 A1
　Newcastle-u-L ST5 . . . . .284 C3
Queens Dr
　Burntwood WS7 . . . . .228 C3
　Leek ST13 . . . . .31 A4
　Newport TF10 . . . . .168 C1
Queens Gdns
　Codsall WV8 . . . . .238 C2
　Talke ST7 . . . . .40 B3
Queens Hospl DE11 . . . . .166 A3
Queens Par WS3 . . . . .243 A1
Queens Park Ave ST3 . . . . .73 A1
Queens Rd Sedgley DY3 . . . . . .271 C4
　Shareshill WV10 . . . . .225 A3
Queens Rise DE13 . . . . .146 B3
Queens Sq WS11 . . . . .210 A3
Queens Terr ST1 . . . . .57 C2
Queens Way B78 . . . . .262 C3
Queens Wlk ST1 . . . . .74 A2
Queensberry Rd ST13 . . . . .73 B3
Queensland Cres DE15 . . . . . .167 B1
Queensmead Rd ST13 . . . . .69 C4
Queensville ST17 . . . . .156 A1
Queensville Ave ST17 . . . . . . .156 A1
Queensville Bridge
　ST17 . . . . .156 A1
Queensway
　Newcastle-u-L ST5 . . . . .71 A3
　Rugeley WS15 . . . . .196 C4
　Stafford ST16 . . . . .155 C2
　Stoke-on-T ST4 . . . . .72 B3
　Tamworth B79 . . . . .250 A4
Queensway Ct 7 ST4 . . . . .74 A1
Queensway Ind Est ST6 . . . . . .56 B4
Queenswood Rd B75 . . . . .258 A1
Queenville ST17 . . . . .156 A1
Quendale WV5 . . . . .269 C3
Quillets Rd 3 DY8 . . . . .275 B2
Quince B77 . . . . .251 A2
Quince Tree Sch B77 . . . . .251 A2
Quinton Ave WS6 . . . . .226 C2
Quinton Gr ST5 . . . . .56 A2
Quinton Wlk ST6 . . . . .42 B1
Quixhill Bank ST14 . . . . .95 C4
Quixhill La ST14 . . . . .79 C1
Quorn Cl DE15 . . . . .167 A1
Quorn Cres 4 DY8 . . . . .275 B2

R

Rabbit La WV10 . . . . .241 A4
Rabone St ST6 . . . . .41 C2
Raby St WV2 . . . . .266 B4
Race Course ST5 . . . . .55 B1
Racecourse La DY8 . . . . .279 C1
Racecourse Rd ST14 . . . . .126 C2
Rachel Gr ST4 . . . . .73 A3
Raddle La B79 . . . . .217 C3
Radford Bk ST17 . . . . .175 B4
Radford Cl ST15 . . . . .105 A1
Radford Dr WS4 . . . . .244 B1
Radford La WV3,WV4 . . . . . . .264 A4
Radford Rd ST4 . . . . .56 C1
Radford Rise ST17 . . . . .175 B4
Radford St ST15 . . . . .105 A1
Radhurst Rise DE13 . . . . .183 B1
Radley Way ST4 . . . . .59 A2
Radmore Cl WS7 . . . . .228 B4
Radmore La
　Abbots Bromley WS15 . . . . . .161 B4
　Gnosall TF10,ST20 . . . . .170 B4
Radnor Cl WS9 . . . . .244 C2
Radnor Rd DY3 . . . . .271 B4
Radnor Rise WS12 . . . . .210 A2
Radstock Cl ST17 . . . . .175 C3
Radstock Rd WV12 . . . . .242 B1
Radstone Rise ST5 . . . . .71 A2
Radway Green Rd CW2 . . . . . .38 C4
Ragees Rd DY6 . . . . .275 C2
Raglan Ave WV6 . . . . .254 C2
Raglan Cl Aldridge WS9 . . . . . .256 C2
　Burton u T DE13 . . . . .166 B4
　Sedgley DY3 . . . . .271 A4
Raglan St ST4 . . . . .72 B3
Raglan Wlk ST4 . . . . .72 B3
Ragley Cl WS3 . . . . .243 A1
Raikes La
　Shenstone WS14 . . . . .246 B4
　Wall WS14 . . . . .246 B4
Railswood Dr WS3 . . . . .244 A2
Railton Ave ST3 . . . . .73 A1
Railway Cotts
　Chebsey ST15 . . . . .135 A4
　Congleton CW12 . . . . .6 A1
　Draycott in t M ST11 . . . . .91 B2
　Eggington DE65 . . . . .148 A4
　Leek ST13 . . . . .30 C1
　Rugeley WS15 . . . . .197 A3
Railway Ct ST9 . . . . .43 C4
Railway Ent Ctr ST4 . . . . .72 B3
Railway La WS7 . . . . .211 C1
Railway Pas ST4 . . . . .283 C4
Railway Rd ST3 . . . . .73 C1
Railway St
　Cannock WS11 . . . . .226 C4
　Norton Canes WS11 . . . . .228 A3
　Stafford ST16 . . . . .155 B2
　Tunstall ST6 . . . . .41 C1

Railway Terr
　Brocton ST17 . . . . .176 B4
　Kingsley ST10 . . . . .62 A2
　Longton ST3 . . . . .283 B3
Rainbow St 9 WV2 . . . . .266 B4
Rainford St ST17 . . . . .26 C1
Rainham Gr ST6 . . . . .42 A4
Rainscar B77 . . . . .262 A4
Rake End Ct WS15 . . . . .179 C1
Rake Hill WS7 . . . . .229 A4
Rakegate Jun & Inf Schs
　WV10 . . . . .240 A1
Rakes La DE6 . . . . .49 C4
Rakeway Rd ST10 . . . . .76 C1
Raleigh Hall Ind Est
　ST21 . . . . .117 C1
Ralph Ct ST17 . . . . .174 A4
Ralph Dr ST1 . . . . .57 C4
Ralston Cl WS3 . . . . .243 A2
Ramage Gr ST3 . . . . .73 B1
Rambleford Way ST16 . . . . . . .155 B4
Ramillies Cres WS6 . . . . .226 C1
Ramsey Cl ST12 . . . . .88 C2
Ramsey Rd ST5 . . . . .284 A1
Ramsey St ST4 . . . . .72 B3
Ramshaw Gr 8 ST3 . . . . .73 B3
Ramshaw View ST3 . . . . .31 A4
Ramshorn Rd ST10 . . . . .78 C4
Randall Cl DY6 . . . . .275 C2
Randle Dr B75 . . . . .258 B2
Randles La ST9 . . . . .60 A3
Ranelagh Ho WV2 . . . . .266 B4
Ranelagh Rd WV2 . . . . .266 B3
Ranelagh St ST1 . . . . .282 B2
Rangeley View 1 WS15 . . . . .104 C1
Rangemoor La DE6 . . . . .80 B3
Rangemoor Hill DE13 . . . . . . .183 A4
Rangemoor La DE6 . . . . .80 A3
Rangemore Terr ST5 . . . . .56 B2
Ranger's Wlk WS15 . . . . .178 A1
Rangeways Rd DY6 . . . . .275 C2
Rangifer Rd B78 . . . . .249 C1
Ranleigh Ave DY6 . . . . .275 C2
Ranscombe Dr DY3 . . . . .271 B1
Ransom Park Area 3
　WS11 . . . . .210 A1
Ranworth Cl ST5 . . . . .71 A1
Ranworth Rise WV4 . . . . .266 B2
Ratcliffe Ave DE14 . . . . .185 A4
Ratcliffe Cl WV4 . . . . .271 C3
Rathbone Ave ST5 . . . . .56 B2
Rathlin Cl WV9 . . . . .240 A2
Rathmore Cl DY8 . . . . .279 C1
Rattigan Dr ST3 . . . . .73 C2
Ratton St ST1 . . . . .282 C3
Raven Cl Cannock WS12 . . . . .210 C2
　Cheslyn Hay WS6 . . . . .226 B1
　Huntington WS12 . . . . .209 B4
Raven Ct TF9 . . . . .97 B1
Raven Rd DE13 . . . . .182 A1
Raven's La ST17 . . . . .39 C2
Ravenhill Cl WS15 . . . . .196 C3
Ravenhill Dr WV8 . . . . .239 A2
Ravenhill Prim Sch
　WS15 . . . . .196 C3
Ravenhill Terr WS15 . . . . .196 C4
Ravenna Way ST3 . . . . .73 C3
Ravens Cl ST7 . . . . .39 C2
Ravens Ct WS8 . . . . .244 C4
Ravens Way DE14 . . . . .166 A2
Ravenscliffe Rd ST7 . . . . .41 A4
Ravenscroft DY8 . . . . .279 B3
Ravensdale DE14 . . . . .167 A3
Ravenscourt St ST17 . . . . .156 B1
Ravenslea Rd WS15 . . . . .196 C3
Ravensmead Prim Sch
　ST7 .39 C2
Ravenstone B77 . . . . .262 A4
Ravenswood Cl ST5 . . . . .71 A2
Ravenswood Crest 4
　ST17 . . . . .175 B4
Rawle Cl ST17 . . . . .76 B2
Rawlett High Sch B79 . . . . . . .234 A1
Rawlett Sports Ctr B79 . . . . . .234 A1
Ray Cl B74 . . . . .258 A1
Raygill B77 . . . . .262 A4
Rayleigh Rd WV3 . . . . .266 A4
Rayleigh Way ST2 . . . . .58 B1
Raymond Ave ST1 . . . . .57 B4
Raymond St ST1 . . . . .57 C4
Reacliffe Rd SK11,ST13 . . . . . .18 A2
Read Ave ST16 . . . . .155 C3
Reades La CW12 . . . . .16 B4
Reading Way ST7 . . . . .58 B1
Reads Rd ST4 . . . . .72 C4
Reapers Wlk WV8 . . . . .239 C1
Reason Rd ST17 . . . . .174 C3
Rebecca Gdns WV4 . . . . .265 C2
Rebecca St ST4 . . . . .72 A4
Recorder Gr ST16 . . . . .42 A3
Recreation Rd ST3 . . . . .73 C1
Rectory Cl
　Church Leigh ST10 . . . . .109 A3
　Drayton Bassett B78 . . . . . . .260 C3
Rectory Dr TF11 . . . . .203 C1
Rectory Fields ST10 . . . . .275 C1
Rectory Gdns
　Armitage WS15 . . . . .198 A2
　Talke ST7 . . . . .40 B3
Rectory La
　Armitage WS15 . . . . .197 C2
　Haughton ST18 . . . . .172 C3
Rectory Mews
　Eggington DE65 . . . . .148 A2
　Mucklestone ST7 . . . . .99 A4
Rectory Rd Hanley ST1 . . . . . .282 A1

Rectory Rd continued
　Upper Tean ST10 . . . . .94 B1
Rectory St Hanley ST1 . . . . . . .282 A1
　Kingswinford DY6 . . . . .275 B3
Rectory View ST7 . . . . .40 B3
Red Bank Longton ST3 . . . . . .283 C1
　Market Drayton TF9 . . . . .112 A4
Red Bank La TF9 . . . . .112 A4
Red Hall Jun Sch DY3 . . . . . . .271 B2
Red Hall La ST7 . . . . .54 B3
Red Hill DY7 . . . . .277 C2
Red Ho The WV7 . . . . .237 A3
Red House Cres ST3 . . . . .283 A3
Red House Ind Est WS9 . . . . . .256 A3
Red La Himley DY3 . . . . .271 A4
　Madeley CW3 . . . . .68 C3
　Norton-in-t-M ST2 . . . . .43 B1
Red Lion Ave WS11 . . . . .228 A2
Red Lion Cl ST17 . . . . .40 B4
Red Lion Cres WS11 . . . . .228 A2
Red Lion La WS11 . . . . .228 A2
Red Lion Pas ST1 . . . . .282 A2
Red Lion St ST10 . . . . .155 C2
Red Rd ST10 . . . . .78 B2
Red Rock Dr WV8 . . . . .238 C1
Redacres WV6 . . . . .255 C3
Redbourn Rd WS3 . . . . .243 A2
Redbourne Dr CW2 . . . . .37 B1
Redbridge Cl ST4 . . . . .71 C1
Redbrook Cl WS12 . . . . .210 B1
Redbrook La WS15 . . . . .196 C3
Redcar Rd Trentham ST4 . . . . .88 A4
　Wolv WV10 . . . . .240 B2
Redcliff B77 . . . . .250 C3
Redcliffe Dr WV5 . . . . .270 A3
Redfern Dr WS7 . . . . .229 A3
Redfern Rd Stone ST15 . . . . . .119 C3
　Uttoxeter ST14 . . . . .111 A1
Redford Dr WV7 . . . . .237 A3
Redgrave Dr ST16 . . . . .155 B1
Redhall Rd DY3 . . . . .271 B1
Redheath Cl ST1 . . . . .55 A1
Redhill Ave WV5 . . . . .270 A3
Redhill Ct DY9 . . . . .250 A4
Redhill Dr ST10 . . . . .92 C3
Redhill Gdns 3 DE15 . . . . . . .120 A4
Redhill Gorse ST16 . . . . .155 B4
Redhill La DE13 . . . . .146 A3
Redhill Prim Sch WS11 . . . . . .209 C2
Redhill Rd
　Cannock WS11 . . . . .209 C2
　Stone ST15 . . . . .105 B1
Redhills Rd ST2 . . . . .57 C4
Redhouse Cone & Mus*
　DY8 . . . . .275 C1
Redhouse Rd WV6 . . . . .255 A3
Redhurst Dr WV10 . . . . .240 A2
Redlake B77 . . . . .261 C4
Redland Dr ST2 . . . . .58 C4
Redlands The ST15 . . . . .120 B4
Redlands Way B74 . . . . .257 A1
Redlock Field WS14 . . . . .231 A3
Redman Gr ST6 . . . . .41 C2
Redmine Cl ST5 . . . . .56 A2
Redmond Cl WS15 . . . . .178 B1
Redmoor Cl DE15 . . . . .167 A2
Redmoor Gdns WV4 . . . . .266 A3
Redmoor Way B76 . . . . .211 C2
Rednall Dr B75 . . . . .258 B2
Redruth Cl DY6 . . . . .275 B4
Redruth Dr ST17 . . . . .156 B1
Redwell Cl B77 . . . . .250 B4
Redwing B77 . . . . .262 A3
Redwing Cl WS7 . . . . .229 B3
Redwing Dr Biddulph ST8 . . . . .27 C4
　Huntington WS12 . . . . .209 B4
Redwood Ave
　Dudley DY1 . . . . .271 C3
　Stone ST15 . . . . .120 A3
Redwood Cl B74 . . . . .256 C1
Redwood Dr
　Burntwood WS7 . . . . .228 C4
　Burton u T DE15 . . . . .186 A4
　Cannock WS11 . . . . .210 A2
Redwood Pl ST13 . . . . .73 C1
Redwood Rd DY7 . . . . .278 B2
Reedbed Cl ST16 . . . . .42 B2
Reedham Gdns WV4 . . . . .265 B3
Reedham Way ST2 . . . . .58 B1
Reedly Rd WV12 . . . . .242 B1
Reedmace B77 . . . . .250 B1
Rees Dr WV5 . . . . .270 A4
Reeve Cl WS11 . . . . .198 A2
Reeve La WS13 . . . . .231 A4
Reeves Ave
　Chell Heath ST6 . . . . .42 A2
　Newcastle-u-L ST5 . . . . .56 A2
Reeves Gdns WV8 . . . . .239 A2
Refinery St ST4 . . . . .284 C2
Regal Cl B27 . . . . .261 B4
Regency Cl ST17 . . . . .40 B2
Regency Ct 1 WS15 . . . . .197 A3
Regency Dr ST9 . . . . .43 B2
Regency Way DE13 . . . . .166 B4
Regency Wlk B74 . . . . .257 B3
Regent Ave ST6 . . . . .41 C2
Regent Ct DY6 . . . . .275 B3
Regent Ct Ipstones ST10 . . . . .62 A4
　Newcastle-u-L ST5 . . . . .56 A3
Regent Rd Hanley ST1 . . . . . . .282 B1
　Wolv WV4 . . . . .265 C3
Regent St Leek ST13 . . . . .30 C3
　Stoke-on-T ST4 . . . . .72 A3
　Stone ST15 . . . . .104 C1
Regina Cres WV6 . . . . .255 A2
Regina St ST6 . . . . .42 B1

Reginald Mitchell Prim Sch
　ST7 .25 B1
Reginald Mitchell Way
　ST7 .41 B3
Reginald St 5 ST6 . . . . .57 A4
Regis Beeches WV6 . . . . .255 B3
Regis Rd WV6 . . . . .255 B3
Registry St ST4 . . . . .72 A4
Reid Cl WV7 . . . . .229 C4
Reid St ST6 . . . . .56 C4
Reindeer Rd B78 . . . . .260 C4
Relay Dr B77 . . . . .262 B4
Rembrandt Cl WS11 . . . . .210 B1
Rembrandt Way ST3 . . . . .90 A3
Rener St ST6 . . . . .57 A3
Remington Dr WS11 . . . . .226 C4
Renard Way ST2 . . . . .90 A4
Rendel Cl ST15 . . . . .104 C1
Rendermore Cl ST19 . . . . .207 C4
Rene Rd B77 . . . . .250 C3
Renfrew Cl
　Kingswinford DY8 . . . . .275 B2
　Newcastle-u-L ST5 . . . . .70 C4
Renfrew St ST4 . . . . .72 A1
Rennie Cres ST13 . . . . .45 B3
Rennison Dr WV5 . . . . .270 A3
Renown Cl ST2 . . . . .57 C1
Renshaw Dr DE11 . . . . .186 C3
Renshaw Wood La WV8 . . . . .221 C1
Renton Gr WV10 . . . . .240 A1
Renton Rd WV10 . . . . .240 A1
Repington Rd ST1 . . . . .57 C4
Repington Rd N B77 . . . . .251 A3
Repington Rd S B77 . . . . .251 A3
Repton Ave WV6 . . . . .254 C2
Repton Cl Cannock WS11 . . . .226 A4
　Stafford ST17 . . . . .156 A1
Repton Dr ST5 . . . . .70 C3
Repton Rd DE15 . . . . .167 C4
Reservoir Rd
　Burton u T DE14 . . . . .165 C2
　Cannock WS12 . . . . .210 B2
　Longton ST3 . . . . .73 C1
Retreat Gdns DY3 . . . . .271 C4
Retreat Gdns The WV6 . . . . . .253 B2
Retreat St WV3 . . . . .266 A4
Reva Rd ST17 . . . . .174 C4
Revival St WS3 . . . . .243 A1
Reynards La SK17 . . . . .24 C2
Reynards Rise TF9 . . . . .99 B3
Reynolds Ave ST5 . . . . .55 C3
Reynolds Cl
　Lichfield WS13 . . . . .214 A1
　Swindon DY3 . . . . .269 C1
Reynolds Gr WV6 . . . . .254 C3
Reynolds Rd ST6 . . . . .42 A2
Rhein Way 4 ST17 . . . . .175 A4
Rhodes Cl DY3 . . . . .271 A2
Rhodes Ct ST5 . . . . .56 B4
Rhodes Ho DE15 . . . . .167 B2
Rhodes St ST1 . . . . .57 B3
Rhondda Ave ST6 . . . . .57 B4
Rialto Pl ST6 . . . . .41 B2
Ribble Cl ST5 . . . . .71 A2
Ribble Dr ST8 . . . . .16 C1
Ribblesdale B77 . . . . .262 A4
Ribblesdale Ave CW12 . . . . . . .6 A3
Ricardo St ST3 . . . . .73 B1
Riceyman Rd ST5 . . . . .56 A4
Richard Clarke Fst Sch
　WS15 . . . . .161 A3
Richard Cooper Rd
　WS14 . . . . .246 C3
Richard Crosse CE Prim Sch
　DE13 . . . . .199 B3
Richard Wakefield CE Prim
　Sch DE13 . . . . .146 B3
Richards Ave
　Stafford ST16 . . . . .156 A2
　Tunstall ST6 . . . . .41 C2
Richards Ct WS11 . . . . .227 C3
Richardson Dr DY8 . . . . .279 C4
Richardson Pl ST16 . . . . .42 A3
Richborough Dr DY1 . . . . .271 C2
Riches St WV6 . . . . .255 C2
Richfield La ST17 . . . . .193 C4
Richmere Ct WV6 . . . . .255 A2
Richmond Ave Hanley ST1 . . . .57 B4
　Wolv WV3 . . . . .255 C1
Richmond Cl
　Cannock WS11 . . . . .210 A3
　Newport TF10 . . . . .168 C1
　Stafford ST17 . . . . .174 C4
　Tamworth B79 . . . . .250 A3
Richmond Dr
　Lichfield WS13 . . . . .231 B4
　Perton WV6 . . . . .254 C2
　Wolv WV3 . . . . .255 C1
Richmond Gdns
　Brierley Hill DY5 . . . . .279 C4
　Wombourne WV5 . . . . .270 A3
Richmond Gr DY8 . . . . .279 C4
Richmond Pk DY6 . . . . .275 B4
Richmond Rd
　Sedgley DY3 . . . . .271 C4
　Trentham ST4 . . . . .72 A1
　Wolv WV3 . . . . .255 C1
Richmond St
　Burton u T DE14 . . . . .166 B2
　Stoke-on-T ST4 . . . . .72 A4
Richmond Terr ST1 . . . . .282 A1
Rickerscote Ave ST17 . . . . . . .175 A3
Rickerscote Hall La
　ST17 . . . . .175 A3
Rickerscote Rd ST17 . . . . .174 C3
Ridding Bank B77 . . . . .87 A4
Ridding La Denstone ST14 . . . .79 C1
　Kingstone ST14 . . . . .124 B2

Riddings Cres WS3 .... 243 C2
Riddings La DE6 .... 144 C3
Riddings The
Brewood ST19 .... 223 B4
Tamworth B77 .... 250 C3
Rider's Way WS15 .... 178 A1
Ridge CI ST12 .... 104 B4
Ridge Cres ST3 .... 89 C3
Ridge Croft ST15 .... 120 B4
Ridge Hill Dr CW3 .... 69 A4
Ridge Ho ST1 .... 57 A2
Ridge Prim Sch The
DY8 .... 279 B3
Ridge Rd
Kingswinford DY6 .... 275 B3
Tunstall ST6 .... 41 B3
Ridge St DY8 .... 279 B3
Ridge Way WS9 .... 256 A2
Ridge Wlk ST3 .... 89 C4
Ridgefields ST8 .... 17 A1
Ridgehouse Dr ST1 .... 57 A2
Ridgemont CI ST15 .... 120 B4
Ridget La DE13,WS13 .... 231 A4
Ridgeway Hixon ST18 .... 158 B4
Sedgley DY3 .... 271 B4
Ridgeway CI
Hopton ST18 .... 156 A4
Stafford ST18 .... 174 B3
Ridgeway Dr WV4 .... 265 C2
Ridgeway Prim Sch
WS7 .... 229 A3
Ridgeway Rd
Brierley Hill DY8 .... 275 C1
Burton u T DE15 .... 185 C4
Ridgeway The
Burntwood WS7 .... 229 A2
Stafford ST18 .... 155 A3
Ridgewood Ave DY8 .... 279 B4
Ridgewood Dr B75 .... 258 A1
Ridgewood High Sch
DY8 .... 279 B3
Ridgewood Rise B77 .... 251 A3
Ridgmont Rd ST5 .... 70 C2
Ridgway Dr ST11 .... 90 B4
Ridgway Pl ST15 .... 56 B3
Ridings Brook Dr 🄴
WS11 .... 210 A1
Ridings CI TF9 .... 97 A1
Ridings Park Trad Est
WS11 .... 210 A2
Ridley St ST4 .... 72 B3
Ridley Wlk ST4 .... 72 B3
Ridware Ho WS13 .... 214 C1
Ridware Rd WS15 .... 198 A3
Rifle Range Cnr WS15 .... 195 A3
Rigby Dr WS11 .... 209 C2
Rigby Rd ST7 .... 24 B2
Righton Ho B77 .... 250 B1
Riley B77 .... 250 C2
Riley Ave ST6 .... 42 A1
Riley Cres WV4 .... 266 A3
Riley La ST20 .... 151 C4
Riley St N ST6 .... 56 C4
Riley St S ST6 .... 56 C4
Rileys Way ST7 .... 39 C1
Rill St ST4 .... 283 B4
Rimbach Dr ST18 .... 177 B4
Rimini CI ST3 .... 73 C3
Rindle The ST10 .... 76 A2
Rindleford Ave WV4 .... 265 B3
Ring Rd WS7 .... 228 C4
Ring The ST18 .... 158 B1
Ringhills Rd WV8 .... 239 A1
Ringland CI ST1 .... 282 C3
Ringway WS11 .... 209 C1
Ringway Ind Est WS13 .... 214 B2
Ringwood Ave WS9 .... 256 A3
Ringwood Rd WV4 .... 240 B1
Ripon Ave ST5 .... 55 C4
Ripon Dr ST17 .... 175 B4
Ripon Rd ST3 .... 72 A4
Rise The
Kingswinford DY6 .... 275 C3
Rugeley WS15 .... 196 C3
Stafford ST17 .... 175 C4
Swadlincote DE11 .... 186 C3
Riseley Rd ST14 .... 71 B4
Rishworth Ave WS15 .... 178 C1
Rising Brook
Stafford ST17 .... 174 C4
Wolv WV6 .... 255 A2
Rising Brook High Sch
ST17 .... 174 C3
Riskin CI ST3 .... 73 B3
Rivendell Gdns WV6 .... 255 B3
Rivendell La ST13 .... 30 C1
River Lea Mews CW3 .... 68 C3
River View SK17 .... 13 A3
River Way ST15 .... 120 A4
Rivercroft CI ST14 .... 96 A2
Riverdale CI DE15 .... 167 A3
Riverdale Dr ST7 .... 41 C4
Riverdrive B78,B79 .... 250 A2
Riverfield Gr B77 .... 250 B3
Riverhead CI ST4 .... 42 C3
Riversfield Dr ST14 .... 95 C2
Riverside Rugeley WS15 .... 178 C1
Walton-on-T DE12 .... 184 B1
Riverside Dr DE14 .... 184 C4
Riverside Gdns
Burton u T DE14 .... 166 C3
Codsall WV8 .... 239 A3
Riverside Ho ST19 .... 192 C1
Riverside Ind Est B78 .... 250 A1
Riverside L Ctr ST16 .... 155 C2
Riverside Rd
Stoke-on-T ST4 .... 71 C1

Riverside Rd continued
Upper Tean ST10 .... 92 B2
Riverside Way WV9 .... 224 A1
Riversleigh Dr DY8 .... 279 C4
Riversmead ST5 .... 71 A2
Riversmead Way ST16 .... 155 A3
Riverway ST16,ST17 .... 155 C1
Rivington CI DY8 .... 279 C2
Rivington Cres ST6 .... 42 A3
Rixdale CI ST1 .... 282 B4
Roach B77 .... 261 B3
Roaches The* ST13 .... 10 B1
Road One CW1 .... 37 B4
Road Two CW1 .... 37 B4
Robert CI B79 .... 249 C4
Robert Heath St ST6 .... 42 B1
Robert St Sedgley DY3 .... 271 B2
Tunstall ST6 .... 41 B2
Robert Sutton RC High Sch
DE15 .... 186 A4
Robert Wynd WV14 .... 266 C1
Roberts Ave ST5 .... 284 B4
Roberts CI Audley ST7 .... 54 C3
Brownhills WS9 .... 244 C1
Roberts Green Rd DY3 .... 271 C2
Roberts Prim Sch DY3 .... 271 B2
Robertson Dr ST5 .... 55 C2
Robertson Sq ST4 .... 71 C2
Robertville Rd ST2 .... 58 A2
Robey's La B78 .... 251 B2
Robin CI
Huntington WS12 .... 209 B4
Tamworth B77 .... 261 B4
Uttoxeter ST14 .... 126 A3
Robin Croft 🄴 ST6 .... 56 C4
Robin Hill ST8 .... 28 A4
Robin Hill Gr ST4 .... 72 C3
Robin La TF10 .... 168 A2
Robina Dr ST10 .... 76 C2
Robinia B77 .... 251 A2
Robins CI WS6 .... 226 B1
Robins La WS7 .... 228 C4
Robins The TF9 .... 99 B2
Robinson Ave ST6 .... 57 B4
Robinson CI B79 .... 249 C4
Robinson Rd
Burntwood WS7 .... 228 C4
Swadlincote DE11 .... 186 C3
Trentham ST4 .... 87 C4
Robinswood CI ST17 .... 175 B3
Robson CI SW58 .... 228 C3
Robson St ST1 .... 282 A2
Rocester La ST10 .... 49 A1
Roche Ave ST3 .... 31 A4
Roche Rd WS3 .... 242 C1
Roche The
Burntwood WS13 .... 230 A4
Cheddleton ST13 .... 45 B2
Rochester Ave WS7 .... 229 A4
Rochester Rd ST3 .... 73 B3
Rochester Way WS12 .... 210 B1
Rochford CI ST13 .... 30 A1
Rochford Gr WV4 .... 265 B3
Rochford Way ST7 .... 58 B1
Rock Cres ST15 .... 105 B2
Rock End Rd ST13 .... 45 A1
Rock Farm Rd WS14 .... 232 C3
Rock Hill B78,WS14 .... 248 B2
Rock House Dr ST12 .... 88 B1
Rock La Ashley TF9 .... 100 B4
Mucklestone TF9 .... 99 B4
Standon ST21 .... 102 A1
Rock Rd WV14 .... 271 C4
Rock St DY3 .... 271 C3
Rockeries The ST1 .... 175 A3
Rockfield Ave ST2 .... 43 B1
Rockhouse Dr ST18 .... 158 A1
Rockhouse La ST7 .... 40 B4
Rockingham CI
Sedgley DY3 .... 271 A2
Walsall WS3 .... 243 A1
Rockingham Dr
Cheadle ST10 .... 76 C2
Perton WV6 .... 254 C2
Rocklands ST5 .... 56 B4
Rocklands La WS15 .... 214 B1
Rocklands Sch WS13 .... 231 B4
Rockrose Gdns WV10 .... 241 A4
Rocks The Endon ST6 .... 43 A4
Stanton ST21 .... 102 B1
Rockside ST7 .... 26 B3
Rocky Wall DY7 .... 277 C2
Rodbaston Coll
Hopwas WS14 .... 248 A3
Penkridge ST19 .... 207 C2
Rodbaston Dr ST19 .... 207 C3
Roddam Ct TF10 .... 168 C1
Rodge La WS13 .... 216 A4
Rode Hall* ST7 .... 25 A4
Rodger Ave CW3 .... 53 A3
Rodgers St ST6 .... 41 B4
Rodway CI WV4 .... 266 B2
Roe Deer Gn TF10 .... 168 C3
Roe La ST5 .... 71 A2
Roe Pk CW12 .... 15 C1
Roebuck Ct ST15 .... 106 B1
Roebuck Sch Dr ST5 .... 284 B2
Roebuck St ST4 .... 72 B4
Roedean Ave ST17 .... 175 A4
Roford Ct DY7 .... 271 C3
Rogate CI ST4 .... 73 A3
Rogers Ave ST5 .... 55 C2
Rogers CI WV11 .... 242 A1
Rogerstone Ave ST4 .... 71 C3
Rokewood CI DY6 .... 270 B1
Rokholt Cres WS11 .... 209 B1
Rolfe CI ST14 .... 72 A1

Rolleston La DE13 .... 146 B3
Rolleston Rd DE13 .... 166 B4
Rolt CI ST12 .... 104 C2
Roma CI ST13 .... 89 B4
Roman CI WS8 .... 228 C1
Roman Ct Cannock WS11 .... 226 C3
Tamworth B77 .... 261 C4
Roman Dr ST5 .... 55 B3
Roman La B74 .... 257 A2
Roman Rd ST4 .... 257 A2
Roman Pl ST17 .... 43 A1
Roman Rd Brewood WV9 .... 224 A2
Little Aston B74 .... 257 A2
Roman Rd (Sandy La)
DY8 .... 279 B2
Roman View WS11 .... 226 C3
Roman Way
Lichfield WS14 .... 231 B4
Tamworth B79 .... 249 C4
Roman Wlk WS14 .... 230 B1
Romans Grange B74 .... 257 B3
Romany Way DY8 .... 279 B2
Romer Side ST2 .... 73 B4
Romford Mdw ST21 .... 133 B3
Romford Pl ST1 .... 90 A4
Romford Rd ST3 .... 73 B3
Romilly CI Lichfield WS14 .... 231 C4
Stourbridge DY8 .... 279 C3
Romney B77 .... 261 C4
Romney Ave ST5 .... 55 C3
Romney Dr ST3 .... 73 B3
Romsey CI ST2 .... 73 B4
Romsey Gr WV10 .... 240 B2
Romsey Rd WV10 .... 240 B2
Romsey Way WS5 .... 242 C4
Romsley CI WV4 .... 244 B1
Romsley La WV15,DY12 .... 276 A1
Ronald St ST3 .... 283 C2
Ronald Wlk ST3 .... 283 C2
Ronaldsay Dr ST5 .... 284 A4
Ronson Ave ST4 .... 71 C2
Rook The WV6 .... 255 B3
Rooker Ave WV2 .... 266 C3
Rooker Cres WV2 .... 266 C3
Rookery Ave ST3 .... 73 A1
Rookery C
Armitage WS15 .... 198 B3
Yoxall DE13 .... 182 A1
Rookery Cotts ST21 .... 115 C3
Rookery Cres ST11 .... 91 B1
Rookery Ct
Lichfield WS13 .... 230 C4
Stoke-on-T ST4 .... 71 C2
Rookery La Aldridge WS9 .... 256 A3
Hints B75,B78 .... 248 B1
Stoke-on-T ST4 .... 71 C2
Wolv WV2 .... 266 A3
Rookery Par WS9 .... 256 A3
Rookery La Kidsgrove ST7 .... 25 B2
Wombourne WV5 .... 270 A3
Rookery Rise WV5 .... 270 A3
Rookery The
Newcastle-u-L ST5 .... 55 A1
Stoke-on-T ST5 .... 71 C2
Rookswood Copse 🄴
Rookwood Dr WV6 .... 254 C1
Rooney St ST4 .... 72 B3
Roper Way DY3 .... 271 C3
Roper Wlk DY3 .... 271 C3
Ropewalk The DE14 .... 166 B1
Rose Ave
Burton u T DE13 .... 148 A1
Kingswinford DY6 .... 275 C3
Rose Bank Cres ST10 .... 78 A3
Rose Bank St ST13 .... 30 C3
Rose Bank Terr ST13 .... 30 C3
Rose Bay Mdw 🄴 WS11 .... 210 B1
Rose Cott Gdns DE14 .... 166 B1
Rose Cottage Dr 🄴 DY8 .... 275 B2
Rose Dr WS8 .... 244 C3
Rose La ST13 .... 44 A3
Rose La WV2 .... 229 B4
Rose Mill TF9 .... 99 C3
Rose St ST1 .... 57 C3
Rose Tree Ave ST4 .... 71 C1
Rose Tree La DE11 .... 186 C4
Rose Way WS15 .... 178 B1
Roseacre ST5 .... 89 C3
Roseacre La ST11 .... 90 C3
Rosebank Dr CW3 .... 68 C4
Roseberry Gdns DY10 .... 280 B2
Roseberry CI ST8 .... 27 C4
Rosebery Rd B77 .... 261 B2
Rosebery St ST6 .... 41 C3
Rosebery Way WV5 .... 269 C3
Rosedale Wlk DY6 .... 275 C4
Rosehill WS12 .... 209 C4
Rosehill CI ST2 .... 43 A1
Roseland Cres ST2 .... 43 A1
Roseleigh Cres DE11 .... 186 C3
Rosemary Ave
Cheslyn Hay WS6 .... 226 B2
Stafford ST17 .... 174 C3
Wolv WV4 .... 266 B3
Rosemary CI WS6 .... 226 B2
Rosemary Cres
Sedgley DY1 .... 271 C3
Wolv WV4 .... 266 B3
Rosemary Cres W WV4 .... 266 B3
Rosemary Dr
Huntington WS12 .... 209 B3
Uttoxeter ST14 .... 126 A3
Rosemary Hill Rd B74 .... 257 B2
Rosemary La DY8 .... 279 B2

Rosemary Nook B74 .... 257 B3
Rosemary Pl ST1 .... 57 C4
Rosemary Rd
Cheslyn Hay WS6 .... 226 B2
Tamworth B77 .... 250 C2
Rosemary St ST5 .... 55 C1
Rosemount Rd DE15 .... 166 C2
Rosendale Ave ST5 .... 55 C3
Rosendale Rd ST5 .... 56 A3
Rosenadth Pl ST2 .... 43 A1
Rosevale Ct ST5 .... 55 C4
Rosevale Rd ST5 .... 55 C4
Rosevale St ST2 .... 43 A1
Roseville Dr CW12 .... 16 A4
Roseville Gdns WV8 .... 239 A2
Rosewood Ave ST9 .... 43 B2
Rosewood CI B77 .... 250 B2
Rosewood Dr WS12 .... 242 A2
Rosewood Gdns WV11 .... 242 A1
Rosewood Pk WS6 .... 226 B1
Rosewood Rd DE15 .... 185 C3
Rosewood Specl Sch
DY1 .... 271 C1
Rosey Bk ST9 .... 43 B2
Rosliston Rd
Burton u T DE15 .... 185 C4
Swadlincote DE15 .... 185 B2
Walton-on-T DE12 .... 184 C2
Rosliston Rd S DE15 .... 185 C3
Rosomount WV6 .... 255 B3
Ross CI Longton ST3 .... 74 A2
Wolv WV6 .... 255 C1
Ross Dr DY6 .... 275 B4
Ross Rd ST10 .... 62 B3
Rossall Ave ST5 .... 55 C2
Rossett Gr ST7 .... 41 C4
Rosslyn Rd ST3 .... 283 C2
Rosvean CI ST1 .... 282 B4
Rosy Cross B79 .... 250 B2
Rothay B77 .... 261 C4
Rothbury Gn WS12 .... 210 C1
Rother Wlk ST6 .... 42 A2
Rotherwood Dr ST17 .... 175 B4
Rotherwood Gdns ST16 .... 155 B2
Rothesay Ave ST5 .... 70 C4
Rothesay Ct Longton ST3 .... 73 B1
Newcastle-u-L ST5 .... 70 C4
Rothesay Dr DY8 .... 275 B2
Rothesay Rd ST3 .... 73 B1
Rothley Gn ST3 .... 88 C4
Rothsay Ave ST1 .... 57 C4
Rothwell St ST4 .... 71 C3
Rotten Row WS14 .... 231 B4
Rotterdam ST5 .... 55 C1
Rotterdam Rd ST5 .... 55 C1
Rough Bank CW12 .... 16 C4
Rough Close CE Prim Sch
ST3 .... 89 C2
Rough Hills CI WV2 .... 266 C3
Rough Hills Rd WV2 .... 266 C3
Roughcote La ST11 .... 74 B3
Roughley Dr B75 .... 258 A3
Roughley Farm Rd B75 .... 258 C2
Round Hill DY3 .... 266 B1
Round House Rd DY3 .... 271 C2
Roundfield S ST7 .... 43 B2
Roundhill Way WS8 .... 229 A1
Roundway ST13 .... 162 B4
Roundway Down WV6 .... 254 C2
Roundwell St ST6 .... 41 B2
Rouse CI ST16 .... 155 B1
Row The ST18 .... 137 C2
Rowallan Rd B75 .... 258 B1
Rowan CI Biddulph ST8 .... 28 A4
Lichfield WS14 .... 231 C4
Stone ST15 .... 120 A3
Rowan Cres WV3 .... 265 C4
Rowan Dr
Armitage WS15 .... 198 B2
Essington WV11 .... 242 A2
Norton Pl ST10 .... 168 C1
Stafford ST16 .... 155 B3
Rowan Gr Brewood ST19 .... 223 B3
Burntwood WS7 .... 228 C4
Rowan Rise DY6 .... 275 C3
Rowanburn CI ST13 .... 73 B3
Rowbury Dr DE15 .... 167 A1
Rowena Gdns DY3 .... 271 C1
Rowhurst CI ST5 .... 55 B4
Rowhurst Pl ST5 .... 55 B4
Rowland St ST4 .... 42 B3
Rowley Ave
Newcastle-u-L ST5 .... 55 C1
Stafford ST17 .... 175 B1
Rowley Bank ST17 .... 174 C4
Rowley Bank Gdns
ST17 .... 174 C4
Rowley Bank Ho ST17 .... 174 C4
Rowley CI Cannock WS11 .... 210 A4
Edingale B79 .... 217 B3
Rugeley WS15 .... 197 A3
Rowley Gr ST17 .... 174 C4
Rowley Hall Dr ST17 .... 155 B1
Rowley Hall Hospl ST17 .... 174 B4
Rowley St WS1 .... 155 B3
Rowleyhill Dr ST10 .... 206 C2
Rowley Pl 🄴 ST4 .... 74 A1
Rownall Rd
Cheddleton ST9 .... 59 B3
Meir ST3 .... 72 A4

Rownall View ST13 .... 30 B2
Rowney CI TF9 .... 99 B2
Rowton Ave WV6 .... 254 C2
Rowton St DE13 .... 166 B3
Roxall CI DY10 .... 281 B1
Roxburghe Ave ST3 .... 283 D2
Royal CI B74 .... 256 C1
Royal Doulton Mus*
ST6 .... 57 A4
Royal Oak Dr ST19 .... 221 C4
Royal St ST4 .... 283 A5
Royal Wlk ST10 .... 76 B2
Royal Wolverhampton Jun
Sch The WV3 .... 266 A4
Royal Wolverhampton Sch
The WV3 .... 266 A4
Royce Ave ST8 .... 27 A3
Roycroft CI ST5 .... 56 A4
Royden Ave ST1 .... 57 C2
Royds CI ST18 .... 172 C3
Roylance St ST6 .... 41 B2
Royston Chase B74 .... 257 A2
Royston Way DY3 .... 271 B4
Royston Wlk ST3 .... 283 C3
Royville Pl ST6 .... 57 B4
Rozel Ave ON10 .... 280 A1
Ruabon CI ST8 .... 27 C3
Rubens CI DY3 .... 271 B3
Rubens Way ST3 .... 90 A4
Rubian St ST4 .... 72 C3
Ruby Dr ST3 .... 73 B1
Rudge Dale Rd TF9 .... 100 A2
Rudge Rd
Pattingham WV6 .... 253 A1
Rudge WV6 .... 263 A4
Rudyard CI Stone ST15 .... 104 C1
Wolv WV10 .... 240 C2
Rudyard Gr ST5 .... 56 B2
Rudyard Ho ST17 .... 174 C3
Rudyard Rd Biddulph ST8 .... 17 B1
Heaton ST13 .... 19 C4
Rudyard ST13 .... 29 C4
Rudyard Way ST10 .... 76 C2
Ruelow Mdw ST10 .... 62 A4
Ruffin Ct ST15 .... 120 B4
Rufford B79 .... 249 C3
Rufford CI Burton u T DE14 .... 185 B4
Newcastle-u-L ST5 .... 56 B2
Rugby Rd DY8 .... 279 B4
Rugeley Rd
Armitage WS15 .... 197 B3
Burntwood WS7 .... 229 B4
Cannock WS12 .... 211 A4
Cannock, Hednesford
WS12 .... 210 B4
King's Bromley DE13 .... 199 A3
Rugeley Sta
WS15 .... 196 C4
Rugeley Town Sta
WS15 .... 178 C2
Ruiton St DY3 .... 271 B2
Rumer Hill Bsns Est
WS11 .... 226 C4
Rumer Hill Rd WS11 .... 226 C4
Running Hills WS15 .... 197 C2
Runnymede ST15 .... 120 A3
Runnymede Dr ST5 .... 283 C2
Rupert St ST18 .... 27 B4
Rush La
Market Drayton TF9 .... 97 A1
Tamworth B77,B78 .... 261 B2
Rushall CI DY8 .... 279 C4
Rushall JMI Sch WS4 .... 244 A1
Rushall Rd WV10 .... 240 C1
Rushbrook CI WS8 .... 244 C3
Rushcliffe Dr ST3 .... 90 A4
Rushes Hall WS3 .... 243 C2
Rushey La WV7 .... 252 B4
Rushford Ave WV5 .... 270 A3
Rushton St ST6 .... 70 C2
Rushton CI ST10 .... 61 B1
Rushton CE Prim Sch
SK11 .... 8 A1
Rushton CI ST6 .... 43 A4
Rushton Gr 🄴 ST6 .... 57 A4
Rushton Mews WS12 .... 211 B2
Rushton Rd ST6 .... 57 A4
Rushton Way ST11 .... 91 A4
Rushwater CI WV15 .... 105 C3
Rushwater CI WV5 .... 269 C3
Ruskin Ave Sedgley DY3 .... 271 A3
Wolv WV4 .... 266 C3
Ruskin CI ST13 .... 283 C5
Ruskin Dr ST18 .... 154 C1
Ruskin Pl DE14 .... 166 B3
Ruskin Rd WV10 .... 241 A1
Rusper CI ST1 .... 57 C3
Russel St ST4 .... 155 B2
Russell Bank Rd B74 .... 257 C2
Russell Rd ST16 .... 81 B3
Russell St
Burton u T DE14 .... 166 B1
Leek ST13 .... 30 C3
Newcastle-u-L ST5 .... 56 B3
Russell's Hall Rd DY1 .... 271 C1
Russells Hall Prim Sch
DY1 .... 271 C1
Russet CI ST3 .... 90 A4

Russet Wlk WV8 .....239 C1
Russett Cl WS7 .....229 A3
Russetts The TF17 .....174 C3
Rustington Ave ST3 .....73 C2
Ruston Ave ST6 .....42 A3
Ruston Cl DE13 .....146 B3
Rutherford Ave ST5 .....71 A2
Rutherford Pl ST14 .....71 C4
Rutherglen Cl WS15 .....178 B1
Ruthin St ST9 .....27 C3
Ruthin Rd ST2 .....58 B1
Rutland Ave
  Rugeley WS15 .....196 B3
  Wolv WV4 .....265 B2
Rutland Cl DE15 .....185 B3
Rutland Cres WV9 .....256 A4
Rutland Dr B78 .....250 A1
Rutland Pl
  Newcastle-u-l ST5 .....71 B2
  Stourbridge DY8 .....279 B4
Rutland Rd
  Cannock WS12 .....210 C1
  Kidsgrove ST7 .....26 A1
  Longton ST3 .....283 C4
Rutland St ST1 .....282 A4
Ruxley Ct ST17 .....57 C2
Ruxley Rd ST7 .....58 A2
Ryburn Cl CW2 .....37 A2
Rycroft CE Mid Sch ST14 .....95 C2
Rydal B77 .....262 A4
Rydal Cl WS12 .....210 A4
Rydal Dr WV6 .....254 C2
Rydal Ho ST16 .....155 C2
Rydal Way ST5 .....71 A2
Ryder Cl DE11 .....186 C1
Ryder Rd ST3 .....90 A4
Ryders St DY8 .....275 B1
Ryders Hayes Com Sch
  WS3 .....244 A3
Ryders Hayes La WS3 .....244 A2
Rye Bank ST5 .....284 B3
Rye Bank Cres ST5 .....284 B3
Rye Ct ST16 .....155 A3
Ryebrook Dr ST6 .....41 C3
Ryecroft ST5 .....284 B3
Ryecroft Ave WV9 .....240 B4
Ryecroft Cl Sedgley DY3 .....271 B4
  Upper Tean ST10 .....92 C2
Ryecroft Cotts WV4 .....266 A3
Ryecroft Dr 3 WS7 .....229 A4
Ryecroft Rd ST6 .....42 C2
Ryecroft St ST7 .....229 A4
Ryedale Way CW12 .....16 B4
Ryefield WV8 .....239 C1
Ryehills ST7 .....39 C1
Ryhope Wlk WV9 .....240 A2
Rykneld Prim Sch DE14 .....184 C4
Rykneld St WS13 .....215 C4
Ryknild Cl B74 .....257 C3
Ryknild St Alrewas DE13 .....201 A1
  Lichfield WS14 .....231 C3
Rykneld Trad Est ST14 .....166 C3
Rylands Dr WV4 .....266 A2
Ryle St WS7 .....243 B1
Rylestone Cl ST13 .....90 A4
Ryton B77 .....261 C4
Ryton Way DE65 .....147 B4

S

Sabine St ST17 .....155 C1
Sabrina Rd WV6 .....254 C1
Sackville St ST4 .....56 C1
Saddler Ave ST15 .....120 B4
Saddlers Cl WS14 .....231 C4
Saddlestones The WV6 .....254 B2
Saddleworth Rd WS3 .....243 A2
Sadler Ctr WS8 .....245 A4
Sadler Rd WS8 .....245 A4
Sadlers Mill WS8 .....245 A4
Saffron B77 .....251 A2
Saffron Cl
  Burton-u-T DE13 .....183 B1
  Meir ST3 .....90 A3
Saffron Gdns WV4 .....266 A2
Sage Cl ST1 .....282 B1
Sainte Foy Ave WS13 .....231 A3
St Aidan's Cl DE13 .....166 B4
St Aidan's Ct WV4 .....266 A3
St Aidan's Rd WS11 .....209 C3
St Aidan's St ST6 .....41 B2
St Albans Cl WV11 .....242 A3
St Albans Ct DE13 .....166 B4
St Albans Rd WS14 .....155 C4
St Andrew Cl WS12 .....211 A3
St Andrew's CE Sch
  B79 .....218 C1
St Andrew's Cl
  Clifton Campville B79 .....218 C1
  Sedgley DY3 .....271 A2
St Andrew's Dr
  Burton-u-T DE13 .....166 B4
  Newcastle-u-l ST5 .....70 C4
St Andrews B77 .....251 A2
St Andrews Ave WS3 .....244 A3
St Andrews CE Prim Sch
  Weston ST18 .....138 B1
  Wolv WV6 .....255 C2
St Andrews Cl DY8 .....279 C1
St Andrews Cres ST17 .....57 B4
St Andrews Dr
  Kidsgrove ST7 .....26 B2
  Perton WV6 .....254 B3
St Andrews Rd ST17 .....174 B4

St Andrews Way TF10 .....168 C1
St Ann St ST1 .....282 C3
St Ann Wlk ST1 .....282 C3
St Anne's CE Prim Sch
  ST6 .....28 A1
St Anne's Cl WS7 .....228 C2
St Anne's RC Prim Sch
  ST17 .....175 B4
St Anne's Rd WV10 .....240 A1
St Anne's Vale ST6 .....43 A4
St Annes Rd WS13 .....214 A2
St Anthony's Dr ST5 .....71 A4
St Anthony's RC Prim Sch
  WV10 .....240 B2
St Anthonys Cl WS15 .....196 C4
St Anthonys Dr WS3 .....244 A3
St Augustine's Fst Sch
  DE6 .....144 B3
St Augustine's Rd WS15 .....196 C3
St Augustines RC Prim Sch
  ST3 .....89 C4
St Austell Cl
  Stafford ST17 .....175 B4
  Tamworth B79 .....250 A3
St Austin's RC Prim Sch
  ST17 .....155 C1
St Barbara's Rd WS15 .....198 B3
St Bartholomew's CE Prim
  Sch SK17 .....13 A4
St Bartholomew's CE Prim
  Sch WV4 .....265 C2
St Bartholomews Cl ST6 .....42 C2
St Bedes Sch WS15 .....178 A3
St Benedict Biscop CE Prim
  Sch WV5 .....270 A4
St Benedict's Dr ST18 .....127 B4
St Benedict's Rd WS7 .....229 A3
St Benedicts Rd WS7 .....270 A3
St Bernadette's RC Prim Sch
  WS8 .....244 C4
St Bernadettes RC Prim Sch
  WV5 .....269 C3
St Bernard Pl ST2 .....58 A3
St Bernard's Rd ST5 .....56 A3
St Bernards Cl WS12 .....211 B2
St Bertelin Ct ST16 .....155 B3
St Blaise Rd B75 .....258 B2
St Brides Cl Sedgley DY3 .....271 B4
  Wombourne WV5 .....269 C3
St Catherine's Cres
  WV4 .....265 C2
St Catherine's Rd DE11 .....186 C3
St Catherines Rd WS13 .....214 A2
St Chad's CE Prim Sch
  ST15 .....40 B1
St Chad's Cl
  Burton-u-T DE13 .....166 B4
  Cannock WS11 .....210 A2
  Denstone ST14 .....95 B3
  Lichfield WS13 .....214 A1
  Sedgley DY3 .....271 A2
  Stone ST15 .....120 B4
St Chad's Pl 12 ST16 .....155 C2
St Chad's Rd
  Burton-u-T DE13 .....166 B4
  Lichfield WS13 .....214 B1
St Chad's Stowe CE Prim Sch
  WS13 .....231 B4
St Chads CE Prim Sch
  WV6 .....253 B2
St Chads Cl
  Brewood ST19 .....223 B3
  Colwich ST18 .....177 B4
  Pattingham WV6 .....253 B1
St Chads Ct WS13 .....231 A4
St Chads RC Sch DY3 .....271 B4
St Chads Rd
  Ecclesshall ST21 .....133 B3
  Tunstall ST6 .....41 C2
St Chads Way TF9 .....71 C3
St Christopher Ave ST4 .....71 C3
St Christopher Cl WS12 .....211 A3
St Christopher's Dr B77 .....250 B1
St Christophers Ct
  WV8 .....239 A2
St Clair St ST3 .....283 C2
St David Cl WS12 .....211 A3
St David's Dr DE13 .....166 B4
St Davids Cl WS3 .....244 A3
St Davids Pl WS13 .....243 B1
St Davids Rd
  Clifton Campville B79 .....218 C1
  Stafford ST17 .....174 B4
St Davids St ST18 .....27 C3
St Dominic's Priory Sch
  ST15 .....104 C1
St Dominic's Sch ST19 .....223 B4
St Dominics Ind Jun Sch
  ST14 .....71 C4
St Editha's CE Prim Sch
  ST19 .....250 A3
St Editha's Ct
  Church Eaton ST20 .....190 A4
  Tamworth B79 .....250 A4
St Edmund's Ave ST5 .....56 B3
St Edmund's Cl WV6 .....255 C2
St Edmunds RC Sch
  WV3 .....255 C2
St Edward St ST13 .....30 C3
St Edward's CE Fst Sch
  ST13 .....45 A3
St Edward's Rd ST13 .....45 B2
St Edwards CE Mid Sch
  ST13 .....30 B3
St Edwards Ct DE11 .....186 C3
St Edwards Gn 7 WS15 .....196 C4

St Elizabeth's RC Prim Sch
  B79 .....249 C4
St Filumena's RC Prim Sch
  ST11 .....74 C1
St Francis Cl
  Burton u T DE13 .....166 B4
  Cannock WS12 .....211 A3
  Wolv WV3 .....244 A3
St Francis of Assisi RC Sch
  WS9 .....256 B3
St Francis RC Prim Sch
  WS4 .....244 B1
St Gabriel's RC Prim Sch
  B77 .....250 C1
St George & St Martin RC
  Prim Sch ST1 .....282 C4
St George Dr WS12 .....211 A3
St George's Ave N ST5 .....56 A3
St George's Ave S ST5 .....56 A3
St George's Ave W ST5 .....56 A3
St George's Cres ST4 .....72 A1
St George's Rd
  Burton u T DE13 .....165 C3
  Newcastle-u-l ST5 .....284 A2
  Stafford ST17 .....156 A1
  Stone ST15 .....120 A4
  Stourbridge DY8 .....279 B1
St George's Way 4 ST13 .....30 C3
St George's Way B77 .....250 C2
St Georges Ave
  Chell Heath ST6 .....42 A2
  Endon ST9 .....43 C3
St Georges Ct B74 .....257 B4
St Georges Hospl ST16 .....155 C2
St Gile's Rd ST5 .....56 A3
St Giles & St George's CE
  Prim Sch ST5 .....284 C2
St Giles Gr ST18 .....172 C3
St Giles Rd WS7 .....229 A3
St Giles' RC Prim Sch
  ST10 .....76 B2
St Gregory's RC Jun & Inf
  Schs ST3 .....283 B2
St Gregory's Rd ST3 .....283 A3
St Helens Rd WS13 .....214 B2
St Helier Cl ST5 .....70 C2
St Hilda's Ave ST13 .....45 B2
St Ives Cl Stafford ST17 .....175 B4
  Tamworth B79 .....250 A3
St James CE Prim Sch
  Longdon WS15 .....198 A1
  Stourbridge DY8 .....279 B4
St James Cl
  Longdon WS15 .....198 A1
  Walsall WS3 .....244 A3
St James Cres ST17 .....193 A4
St James Ct Audley ST7 .....39 B1
  Barton-u-N DE13 .....183 B1
St James Gn ST21 .....102 C2
St James Pl ST4 .....72 A1
St James Prim Sch
  WS8 .....244 C4
St James Rd
  Cannock WS11 .....209 B1
  Norton Canes WS11 .....228 A3
  Sutton Coldfield B75 .....258 B3
St James St ST1 .....282 A2
St James Wlk WS8 .....244 C4
St James' Cl ST8 .....16 C2
St James' Rd DE13 .....183 B1
St James' St DY3 .....271 B3
St John Cl B75 .....258 B2
St John Fisher RC High Sch
  ST5 .....284 A4
St John St Hanley ST1 .....282 C4
  Walsall WS3 .....231 A4
St John The Evangelist RC
  Prim Sch (Annexe) ST7 .....25 C1
St John's Ave
  Newcastle-u-l ST5 .....56 B2
  Stoke-on-T ST4 .....71 C2
  Stone ST15 .....105 B2
St John's CE Fst Sch
  ST19 .....221 C4
St John's CE Prim Sch
  Cheddleton ST9 .....60 A4
  Essington WV11 .....242 A2
  Keele ST5 .....69 C4
  Stafford ST16 .....156 A2
St John's Cl
  Brownhills WV9 .....244 C2
  Cannock WS11 .....226 B4
  Lichfield WS13 .....231 A3
  Swindon DY3 .....269 B1
St John's Ct
  Burton u T DE13 .....166 B4
  Cannock WS12 .....210 C1
  Walsall WS3 .....243 A1
St John's Dr
  Shenstone WS14 .....246 C3
  Swadlincote DE11 .....186 C3
  Wolv WV11 .....242 A3
St John's Hill WS14 .....246 C3
St John's Pl Biddulph ST8 .....27 B4
  Newcastle-u-l ST5 .....55 C1
St John's Prim Sch
  DY3 .....269 C1
St John's RC Prim Sch
  ST10 .....78 C1
St John's Rd Biddulph ST8 .....27 B4
  Burton-u-T DE13 .....166 B4
  Cannock WS11 .....226 C4
  Congleton CW12 .....6 A3
St John's Sq
  6 Burslem ST6 .....56 C4
  Uttoxeter ST14 .....110 C1
St John's St B79 .....250 A3

St John's Wlk ST16 .....156 A2
St John's Wood ST7 .....25 C1
St Johns CE Prim Sch
  WS9 .....256 B3
St Johns Cl Hixon ST18 .....139 B2
  Rugeley WS15 .....196 B4
St Johns Ho B74 .....257 C2
St Johns Rd Ashley TF9 .....100 B3
  Brownhills, Shire Oak
    WS9 .....245 A3
  Essington WV11 .....242 A2
  Stafford ST17 .....174 B4
  Walsall WS3 .....244 A3
St Johns Ret Pk 3 WV2 .....266 B4
St Johns Sch WS13 .....231 A4
St Johns Way TF9 .....100 B3
St Joseph & St Theresa RC
  Prim Sch WS7 .....228 C3
St Joseph St ST6 .....41 B4
St Joseph's Coll ST4 .....71 C2
St Joseph's Convent Prim
  Sch WV6 .....255 C3
St Joseph's RC Prim Sch
  Cannock WS12 .....210 B2
  Lichfield WS13 .....231 B4
  Rugeley WS15 .....196 C4
  Uttoxeter ST14 .....126 A4
St Josephs Cl WS3 .....244 A2
St Josephs Ct WV4 .....265 B3
St Jude's CE Inf Sch
  WV6 .....255 C2
St Jude's Cl 4 WV6 .....255 C2
St Jude's Ct WV6 .....255 C2
St Jude's Rd WV6 .....255 C2
St Jude's Rd W WV6 .....255 C2
St Jude's Way DE13 .....166 B4
St Lawrence CE Prim Sch
  ST20 .....171 C3
St Lawrence Dr WS11 .....210 A1
St Lawrence View SK17 .....2 A3
St Lawrence Way ST20 .....171 B4
St Leonard's Ave
  Ipstones ST10 .....62 A4
  Stafford ST17 .....156 A1
St Leonard's CE Fst Sch
  Copenhall ST18 .....192 C4
  Ipstones ST10 .....62 A4
St Leonard's CE Prim Sch
  B79 .....234 B1
St Leonards Cl
  ST17 .....156 A1
St Leonard's Way CW3 .....67 B1
St Leonards View B78 .....262 C4
St Lucy's Dr ST5 .....56 B4
St Luke St ST1 .....282 C2
St Luke's CE Prim Sch
  Hanley ST1 .....282 C2
  Newcastle-u-l ST5 .....55 A1
St Luke's Cl
  Cannock WS11 .....226 B4
  Newcastle-u-l ST5 .....55 A1
St Luke's Rd
  Barton-u-N DE13 .....183 B1
  Burntwood WS7 .....229 B3
  Burton u T DE13 .....166 B4
St Luke's Wlk WS15 .....198 B2
St Lukes CE Prim Sch
  ST9 .....43 C4
St Lukes Cl WS15 .....135 A4
St Lukes Ct ST1 .....282 C2
St Lukes Inf Sch WV2 .....266 B4
St Margaret Ward RC High
  Sch ST6 .....41 C3
St Margaret's B77 .....250 B2
St Margaret's CE Jun Sch
  ST5 .....56 B2
St Margaret's Ct
  Betley CW3 .....53 A3
  Draycott in t M ST11 .....91 C3
  Newcastle-u-l ST5 .....56 B3
St Margaret's Dr ST1 .....57 C4
St Margaret's Rd B79 .....250 A4
St Margarets Dr ST3 .....72 C2
St Margarets Rd
  Lichfield WS13 .....214 A2
  Walsall WS3 .....244 A3
St Maria Goreti RC Prim Sch
  ST2 .....58 B1
St Mark's CE Prim Sch
  ST1 .....282 A1
St Mark's Ct ST1 .....282 A2
St Mark's Rd
  Burntwood WS7 .....229 B3
  Burton u T DE13 .....166 B4
St Mark's St ST1 .....282 A1
St Marks Cl WS6 .....226 C2
St Marks Rd
  Brownhills, Shire Oak
    WS8 .....245 A3
  Walsall WS3 .....244 A2
St Martin's Cl
  Betley CW3 .....53 A3
  Wolv WV2 .....266 C3
St Martin's La ST13 .....283 C4
St Martin's Pl 11 ST16 .....155 C2
St Martin's Rd
  Newcastle-u-l ST5 .....70 C4
  Talke ST7 .....40 C3
St Mary & St Chad CE Fst Sch
  ST19 .....223 B3
St Mary of the Angels RC
  Prim Sch WS9 .....256 A3
St Mary's CE Fst Sch
  Uttoxeter ST14 .....111 A1

St Mary's CE Fst Sch continued
  Wheaton Aston ST19 .....205 B4
St Mary's CE Prim Sch
  CW12 .....15 A4
St Mary's CE Prim Sch
  Bosley SK11 .....7 B4
  Colton WS15 .....178 C3
St Mary's CE Prim Sch
  DE6 .....275 B4
St Mary's CE Prim Sch
  Mucklestone TF9 .....99 A4
  Tunstall ST6 .....41 B2
St Mary's Cl
  Albrighton WV7 .....237 A3
  Newton Solney DE15 .....167 C4
  Sedgley DY3 .....271 C4
  Upper Tean ST10 .....109 A4
St Mary's Cres ST14 .....111 A1
St Mary's Ct 11 ST13 .....30 C3
St Mary's Dr
  Burton u T, Clay Mills
    DE13 .....147 C3
  Burton u T, Horninglow
    DE13 .....166 B4
  Newcastle-u-l ST5 .....284 A2
St Mary's Gate 7 ST16 .....155 C2
St Mary's Pl 8 ST16 .....155 C2
St Mary's RC Prim Sch
  Cannock WS11 .....226 C4
  Leek ST13 .....30 C3
  Newcastle-u-l ST5 .....284 A3
  Norton-in-t-M ST6 .....42 C2
St Mary's Rd Ashley TF9 .....99 B3
  Colwich ST18 .....177 B4
  Lichfield WS13 .....214 A2
  Longton ST3 .....73 B3
  Newcastle-u-l ST5 .....56 B3
St Mary's St
  Market Drayton TF9 .....97 B1
  Newport TF10 .....168 C2
St Mary's Way
  Aldridge WS9 .....256 A3
  Tamworth B77 .....250 C2
St Marys & St Johns RC Jun
  & Inf Sch WV2 .....266 B4
St Marys CE Prim Sch
  WV7 .....237 A3
St Marys Cl Bradeley ST18 .....173 B1
  Shareshill WV10 .....225 B1
St Marys Gr B79 .....236 B2
St Marys RC Prim Sch
  ST19 .....223 A3
St Mathew Cl WS12 .....211 A3
St Matthew St ST4 .....72 C3
St Matthew's Ave ST17 .....175 B4
St Matthew's Rd WS7 .....229 C4
St Matthew's St DE14 .....185 B4
St Matthews Cl WS3 .....244 A3
St Matthews Ct ST14 .....72 C3
St Matthews Dr ST18 .....154 C1
St Mawes Cl WV10 .....175 B4
St Michael CE Jun & Inf Sch
  WV6 .....255 C3
St Michael Rd WS13 .....231 B4
St Michael's CE Fst Sch
  Rudyard ST13 .....18 B1
  Stone ST15 .....120 B4
St Michael's CE Prim Sch
  ST1 .....231 B4
St Michael's Cl
  Adbaston ST20 .....131 B2
  Penkridge ST19 .....207 C4
  Stafford ST17 .....175 C4
  Walsall WS3 .....244 A1
St Michael's Ct WV6 .....255 C3
St Michael's Dr WS15 .....197 A3
St Michael's Hospl
  WS13 .....231 B4
St Michael's RC Prim Sch
  WV3 .....265 B4
St Michael's Rd
  Chell Heath ST6 .....41 C3
  Newcastle-u-l ST5 .....56 A2
  Penkridge ST19 .....207 C4
  Rugeley WS15 .....197 A3
  Uttoxeter ST14 .....110 C2
St Michael's Sq ST19 .....192 C1
St Michaels CE Fst Sch
  ST19 .....192 C1
St Michaels Cl
  Stone ST15 .....120 A4
  Wood End CV9 .....262 B1
St Michaels Dr WS12 .....211 A3
St Michaels Mount
  WS13 .....120 B3
St Michaels Rd
  Burton u T DE13 .....166 B4
  Himley DY3 .....270 C3
St Mildred's CE Prim Sch
  ST10 .....62 B2
St Modwen's Cl DE13 .....166 B4
St Modwen's RC Prim Sch
  DE13 .....166 A3
St Modwen's Wlk DE14 .....166 B4
St Modwena Way ST19 .....207 C4
St Nicholas Ave ST6 .....42 C2
St Nicholas CE Fst Sch
  WV8 .....238 C2
St Nicholas Cl WS12 .....244 A2
St Nicholas Way WS15 .....160 B3
St Oswald's CE Fst Sch
  DY10 .....280 A1
St Patrick Cl WS12 .....211 A3
St Patrick's Dr ST5 .....70 C4

St Patrick's Pl **1** ST16 .....155 C2
St Patrick's RC Prim Sch
 ST16 ....155 C3
St Patrick's Sq **2** ST16 ...155 C2
St Patricks Rd DE13 ......166 B4
St Paul St ST6 ....155 C2
St Paul's CE Fst Sch
 WV9 ....224 B2
St Paul's CE Prim Sch
 ST17 ....155 C1
St Paul's Cl
 Brewood WV9 ....224 B1
 Cannock WS11 ....210 A1
St Paul's Ct
 Burton u T DE14 ....166 A2
 Longton ST3 ....72 C1
 Tamworth B77 ....261 B2
St Paul's Mews **4**
 WS15 ....196 C4
St Paul's Rd
 Burntwood WS7 ....229 B3
 Cannock WS11 ....210 C2
 Newcastle-u-L ST5 ....284 A2
St Paul's Sq DE14 ....166 A2
St Pauls CE Jun Sch ST6 ..41 C1
St Pauls CE Sch WV9 .....240 A1
St Pauls Cres WS3 ....244 A4
St Pauls Rd **3** WS15 ......196 C4
St Peter & St Paul RC Prim
 Sch
 Lichfield WS13 ....214 A1
 Newport TF10 ....168 C2
St Peter's Bridge DE14,
 DE15 ....166 C1
St Peter's CE Fst Sch
 Alton ST10 ....78 C1
 Marchington ST14 ....127 C1
St Peter's CE High Sch
 ST4 ....71 C4
St Peter's CE Prim Sch
 Caverswall ST11 ....74 B1
 Edgmond TF10 ....168 A2
 ST18 ....158 A4
St Peter's CE Prim Sch
 Netherseal DE12 ....219 C3
 Shenstone WS9 ....245 C2
 Yoxall DE13 ....182 A2
St Peter's Cl
 Shenstone WS9 ....245 C2
 Tamworth B77 ....250 B1
St Peter's Collegiate CE Sch
 WV3 ....255 C2
St Peter's Gdns ST17 .....174 C3
St Peter's RC Prim Sch
 Hanley ST6 ....57 A3
 Walsall WS3 ....243 A1
St Peter's Rd
 Burntwood WS7 ....229 B3
 Cannock WS11 ....210 B2
St Peter's St DE15 ....166 C1
St Peter's Wlk ST6 ....57 A3
St Peters Cl
 Stafford ST17 ....174 C3
 Stoke-on-T ST4 ....72 A4
St Peters Ct
 Burton u T DE15 ....166 C1
 Lichfield WS13 ....214 A1
 Walsall WS3 ....243 A1
St Peters Dr WS3 ....244 A2
St Phillip's Ave WV3 ....265 C4
St Phillip's Gr WV3 ....265 C4
St Saviour's CE Prim Sch
 ST7 ....25 B1
St Saviour's St ST7 ....25 B1
St Saviours Cl WV2 ....266 C3
St Stephen's Rd WS7 ......229 B3
St Stephens Cl
 Burton u T DE13 ....166 B4
 Cannock WS12 ....210 B2
St Stephens Prim Sch
 WS13 ....215 B4
St Teresa's RC Prim Sch
 ST4 ....71 C1
St Theresa's RC Prim Sch
 WV4 ....266 C3
St Thomas Aquinas RC Prim
 Sch ST4 ....56 C2
St Thomas CE Prim Sch
 ST7 ....26 A1
St Thomas Dr WS12 ....211 A3
St Thomas La ST18 ....156 B2
St Thomas More RC Coll
 ST3 ....73 A2
St Thomas More RC Prim Sch
 WS6 ....227 A2
St Thomas Pl ST4 ....71 C3
St Thomas RC Prim Sch
 ST10 ....92 C2
St Thomas St
 Kidsgrove ST7 ....26 C4
 Stafford ST16 ....156 A2
St Thomas' Cl WS9 ....245 A1
St Thomas's Rd ST10 ......92 C2
St Vincent Pl ST15 ....55 C1
St Vincent Rd DE15 ....119 C4
St Werburgh's CE Prim Sch
 Hanbury DE13 ....145 A2
 Kingsley ST10 ....61 C1
St Wilfrid's RC Prim Sch
 ST6 ....41 C2
St Wulstan's RC Prim Sch
 ST5 ....56 B4
Salcombe Ave ST17 ....175 B4

Salcombe Cl WS11 ....226 B4
Salcombe Pl ST1 ....57 B4
Sale La DE13 ....200 B1
Salem St ST11 ....56 C2
Sales La DE15 ....167 B2
Salisbury Ave
 Burton u T DE15 ....167 B2
 Hanley ST1 ....282 B1
Salisbury Cl
 Lichfield WS13 ....214 B2
 Madeley CW3 ....68 C4
 Sedgley DY1 ....271 C2
Salisbury Dr
 Cannock WS12 ....210 A1
 Stafford ST16 ....156 A2
Salisbury Hill View TF9 ...112 A4
Salisbury Rd
 Market Drayton TF9 .....112 A4
 Stafford ST16 ....156 A2
Salisbury St Leek ST13 ....30 C3
 Tunstall ST6 ....41 C2
Salkeld Pl ST6 ....42 A3
Sallow Gr WS8 ....229 A1
Sally Ward Dr WS9 ....245 C4
Sallyfield La DE6 ....65 C1
Salmond Ave ST16 ....156 A3
Salop Dr WS11 ....226 C4
Salop Gr ST5 ....71 B2
Salop Pl ST17 ....26 A2
Salt Ave ST17 ....155 C1
Salt Banks ST18 ....137 B2
Salt La ST18 ....137 B3
Salt Rd Salt ST18 ....137 C2
 Stafford ST17 ....155 C1
Salt Works La ST18 ....138 B1
Saltbrook La DE6 ....144 C4
Saltdean Cl ST13 ....73 C1
Salter St ST16 ....155 C2
Salter's Ct TF10 ....168 C2
Salter's La TF10 ....168 C2
Salter's Rd WS9 ....245 A2
Salters Cl ST19 ....59 A2
Salters Grange WS15 .....160 C3
Salters Green Way
 WS13 ....201 A2
Salters La Caverswall ST9 ..59 A1
 Tamworth B79 ....250 A3
Saltersford La ST10 ....94 C4
Salthealth La ST18 ....137 C2
Salts La B78 ....260 C3
Sam Barber Ct WS12 .....210 C1
Sambar Rd B78 ....249 C1
Sambrook Cres TF9 ....97 C1
Sampson St ST1 ....282 A3
Samuel Cl WS13 ....214 B1
Samuel Ho WS3 ....243 A1
Samuel Johnson's
 Birthplace Mus*
 WS13 ....231 A4
Samuel St Bumacor ST7 ..26 C1
 Walsall WS3 ....243 A1
Sancton Gn **24** ST6 ......56 C4
Sand Bank WS3 ....243 A1
Sand Rd DE13 ....164 B4
Sandalwood Dr ST16 .....155 C3
Sandalwood Gr ST3 ....88 C4
Sandalwood Rd DE15 ....185 C3
Sandbach Rd ST6 ....57 A4
Sandcrest Pl ST3 ....73 C1
Sandcrest Wlk ST3 ....73 C1
Sanderling Cl WV10 ......241 A4
Sandering Rise WS7 ....229 A4
Sandfield Bridge DY5 ....271 A1
Sandfield Gr DY3 ....271 A1
Sandfield Rd DY8 ....275 C1
Sandford Cl WS15 ....198 A4
Sandford Cres CW7 ....37 B1
Sandford Hill Prim Sch
 ST3 ....73 B3
Sandford Rd DY1 ....271 C1
Sandford Rise WV6 ....255 C3
Sandford St
 Lichfield WS13 ....231 A4
 5 Longton ST3 ....73 B3
 Newcastle-u-L ST5 ....55 C4
Sandgate St ST7 ....38 C3
Sandhill St WS3 ....243 A1
Sandhurst Ave **6** ST13 ....73 C1
Sandhurst Cl ST5 ....56 B2
Sandhurst Dr WV4 ....266 A2
Sandhurst Gr DY8 ....275 C2
Sandhurst Rd B74 ....257 C2
Sandiford Cres TF10 ......168 C1
Sandiway DE13 ....201 C4
Sandiway Pl ST1 ....57 C3
Sandmere Rise WV10 ....240 C1
Sandon Ave ST5 ....71 A1
Sandon Cl ST11 ....91 B1
Sandon High Sch ST3 ....89 C4
Sandon Ho WV6 ....255 C3
Sandon La ST18 ....122 B3
Sandon Mews ST15 ....155 C3
Sandon Old Rd ST3 ....89 C4
Sandon Rd
 Draycott in t M ST11 .....91 B2
 Hilderstone ST15 ....106 B1
 Meir ST18 ....143 B2
 Sandon ST18 ....89 C4
 Stafford ST16 ....155 C3
 Wolv WV10 ....240 A1
Sandon St Hanley ST1 .....57 A2
 Leek ST13 ....30 C2
Sandown B77 ....250 C3
Sandown Ave WS6 ....226 C2
Sandown Cl
 Burntwood WS7 ....211 C1
 Burton u T DE14 ....185 A4

Sandown Cl continued
 Cannock WS12 ....211 A3
 Kingsley ST10 ....56 C3
Sandown Dr WV6 ....254 C2
Sandown Pl ST17 ....43 B1
Sandpiper B77 ....262 A3
Sandpiper Cl WS12 ....210 B4
Sandpiper Ct ST17 ....26 B1
Sandpiper Dr ST14 ....126 A3
Sandra Cl Aldridge WS9 ..256 A3
 Chell Heath ST6 ....42 A1
Sandringham Ave DE15 ..167 A1
Sandringham Cl
 Burntwood WS7 ....211 C1
 Market Drayton TF9 .....97 C1
 Stafford ST17 ....175 B4
Sandringham Dr WS9 ....245 A1
Sandringham Pl DY8 .....275 B1
Sandringham Rd
 Kingswinford DY8 ....275 B1
 Pattingham WV6 ....253 B1
 Stafford ST17 ....175 B4
 Wolv WV4 ....266 A2
 Wombourne WV5 ....269 C3
Sands La ST6 ....28 A1
Sands Rd ST7 ....26 C3
Sandsdown Cl ST8 ....16 B1
Sandstone Cl
 Sedgley DY3 ....271 B2
 Walsall WS3 ....243 B2
Sandstone Rd WS3 ....243 B2
Sandwell Pl ST3 ....89 C4
Sandwell Rd WV10 ....240 A1
Sandwick Cres ST1 ....57 C3
Sandwood Cres ST13 .....73 B3
Sandy Bank ST21 ....102 B2
Sandy Cres WV11 ....242 A1
Sandy Gr WS8 ....228 C1
Sandy Hill ST9 ....59 B2
Sandy Hollow WV6 ....255 B1
Sandy La Ashley TF9 ......100 A4
 Blore TF9 ....98 B2
 Brewood ST19 ....223 B3
 Cannock WS11 ....209 A1
 Chapel Chorlton ST5 .....85 B2
 Codsall WV8 ....238 C2
 Eccleshall ST21 ....132 B4
 Endon ST6 ....43 A4
 Kinver DY7,DY11 ....277 C1
 Linton DE12 ....186 A1
 Longsdon ST9 ....44 C4
 Newcastle-u-L ST5 ....284 C4
 Newton Regis B79 ....236 B3
 Norton-in-t-M ST22 .....43 B1
 Rugeley WS15 ....196 C4
 Standon ST21 ....102 B2
 Stourbridge DY8 ....279 B2
 Sutton TF9 ....112 B3
 Upper Tean ST10 ....93 C4
 Weston ST18 ....174 A4
 Whittington WS14 ....232 B2
 Wolv, Claregate WV6 ....255 C3
 Wolv, Elston Hall WV10 ..240 C1
Sandy Mount WV5 ....270 A4
Sandy Rd Biddulph ST8 ...16 B1
 Stourbridge DY8 ....279 B1
 Tunstall ST6 ....41 B3
Sandy Way B77 ....251 A2
Sandybrook Cl ST13 ......30 C2
Sandybrook La ST13 ......30 C1
Sandycroft TF10 ....168 C2
Sandyfield Rd ST1 ....57 C3
Sandyfields St 85 A4
Sandyfields Rd DY3 ....271 A3
Sandyford Ct ST16 ....155 C2
Sandyford St ST16 ....155 C2
Sangster La ST6 ....42 B1
Sankey Cres WS15 ....196 C4
Sankey Rd WS11 ....209 C2
Sankey's Cnr WS7 ....228 C4
Sant St ST6 ....56 C4
Saplings Cl ST19 ....192 C1
Saplings The
 Newcastle-u-L ST5 ....71 B2
 Penkridge ST19 ....192 C1
Sapperton La DE65 ....129 C4
Sapphire Dr WS11 ....210 B2
Sara Cl B74 ....258 A2
Saracen Way **10** ST3 ......74 A1
Sarah Challinor Cl
 WS15 ....196 C4
Saredon Cl WS3 ....244 A1
Saredon Rd
 Cheslyn Hay WS6,WS11,
 WV10 ....225 B1
 Shareshill WV10 ....225 B3
Saredon St ST1 ....57 A2
Sark Cl ST5 ....70 C2
Sark Pl **1** ST3 ....73 B3
Sarraine Ind Pk ST10 .....76 A1
Sarver La ST10 ....75 B2
Satchmore Rd ST6 ....55 C2
Saturn Rd Cannock WS11 ..210 B3
 Chell Heath ST6 ....42 B1
Saul Ct ST14 ....126 A3
Saunders Cl WS12 ....211 A3
Saunders Rd ST5 ....56 A2
Saverley Green Rd
 ST11 ....106 C4
Savey La DE13 ....181 C1
Savoureuse Dr ST14 ......175 A4
Savoy Rd SW1 ....37 A4
Sawpit La ST17 ....176 B4
Sawyer Dr ST18 ....16 B1
Saxifrage Dr ST15 ....54 B3
Saxon Cl Burton u T DE15 ..185 C4
 Great Wyrley WS6 ....227 A1
 Polesworth B78 ....251 C1

Saxon Cl continued
 Tamworth B77 ....261 C3
Saxon Ct WS13 ....230 C4
Saxon Hill Sch WS14 .....231 B3
Saxon Mill La B79 ....250 B2
Saxon Rd ST19 ....207 C4
Saxon St DE15 ....185 C4
Saxon Wlk WS13 ....230 C3
Saxoncourt WV6 ....255 B3
Saxondrive B79 ....250 C3
Saxonfields WV6 ....255 B3
Saxton Dr B74 ....257 C3
Sayers Rd ST16 ....155 B4
Scalpcliffe Cl DE15 ....166 C2
Scalpcliffe Rd DE15 ......166 C2
Scammerton B77 ....262 A4
Scamnell La ST21 ....134 C4
Scampton Cl WV6 ....254 C3
Scampton Way B79 ......250 B4
Scarecrow La B75 ....258 C2
Scarlett St ST5 ....284 B2
Scarratt Cl ST11 ....91 A4
Scarratt Dr ST11 ....91 A4
Sceptre St ST1 ....282 B2
Schofield La B79 ....217 B3
Scholar Green Prim Sch
 ST7 ....25 C3
Scholars Gate
 Burntwood WS7 ....229 B4
 4 Rugeley WS15 ....197 A3
School Ave WS8 ....244 C4
School Bank ST10 ....94 A1
School Cl Audley ST7 .....40 A1
 Burntwood WS7 ....228 B4
 Codsall WV8 ....239 A2
 Dilhorne ST10 ....75 B2
 Leek ST13 ....30 B2
 Norton Canes WS11 .....228 A3
 Seisdon WV5 ....269 B4
 Wolv WV3 ....265 A4
School Cres WS11 ....228 A3
School Ct WS12 ....210 B3
School Dr
 Brierley Hill DY8 ....279 C4
 Norton Canes WS11 .....210 A4
School Ground La TF10 ...169 A2
School Ho The WS7 ....229 B4
School House La WS15 ...196 C4
School La
 Admaston WS15 ....159 C2
 Ashley TF9 ....100 A3
 Astbury CW12 ....15 A4
 Biddulph ST8 ....17 A1
 Blymhill TF11 ....203 C3
 Bradnop ST13 ....31 C2
 Brewood WV9 ....224 A2
 Burntwood WS7 ....228 B4
 Caverswall ST11 ....74 B1
 Colton WS15 ....178 C3
 Colwich ST18 ....158 A1
 Coppenhall ST18 ....192 B4
 Edingale B79 ....217 B3
 Hill Ridware WS15 ....198 A4
 Hints B78 ....248 B1
 Hopwas B78 ....249 A4
 Longdon WS15 ....212 A3
 Longsdon ST9 ....30 A1
 Longton ST3 ....89 A4
 Market Drayton TF9 .....112 A4
 Norton Canes WS3 ......227 C1
 Rolleston DE13 ....147 A2
 Sandon ST18 ....137 C4
 Shareshill WV10 ....225 B1
 Shuttington B79 ....217 B2
 Stafford, Hillcroft Park
 ST17 ....175 C4
 Stafford, Rickerscote ST17 ..174 C4
 Sudbury DE6 ....128 C2
 Tamworth B77 ....261 B3
 Walsall WS3 ....243 C2
 Warslow SK17 ....23 A1
 Wheaton Aston ST19 ....206 B2
 Wolv WV10 ....240 C1
School Lane CE Prim Sch
 WS15 ....161 A3
School Of St Mary & St Anne
 WS15 ....161 A3
School Pl ST16 ....155 C2
 Brewood ST19 ....223 B3
 Bucknall ST2 ....58 A4
 Ecclesall ST21 ....133 B3
 Egmond TF10 ....168 A2
 Himley DY3 ....270 A2
 Norton Canes WS11 .....228 A3
 Rugeley WS15 ....178 B1
 Seisdon WV5 ....269 B4
 Uttoxeter ST14 ....110 C1
 Wheaton Aston ST19 ....205 B3
 Wolv WV6 ....255 A2
 Wombourne WV5 ....269 B4
School St **18** Leek ST13 ...30 C3
 Newcastle-u-L ST5 ....284 C3
 Newcastle-u-L, Broad Meadow
 ST5 ....55 C3
 Sedgley DY3 ....71 C2
 Stoke-on-T ST4 ....71 C2
 Stourbridge DY8 ....279 C3
 Tamworth B77 ....250 C2
 Walsall WS4 ....244 B1
School View ST14 ....141 B4
School Wlk WV10 ....228 B4
Schoolacre Rise ST14 ....175 B3
Schoolfields Rd WS14 ....247 A3
Schoolgate Cl WV4 ....266 A2
Scimitar Cl B79 ....249 C4
Scot Hay Rd Audley ST7 ..54 C2
 Newcastle-u-L ST5 ....54 C2

Scotch Orch WS13 ....214 B1
Scotch Orchard Prim Sch
 WS13 ....214 B1
Scotia Bsns Pk ST6 ......41 C1
Scotia Rd Cannock WS11 ..209 B2
 Tunstall ST6 ....41 C1
Scott Ave WV4 ....265 C2
Scott Cl WS14 ....243 C2
Scott Lidgett Ind Est ST6 ..56 B4
Scott Lidgett Rd ST6 ......56 B4
Scott Rd Chell Heath ST6 ..41 C3
 Tamworth B77 ....250 C2
Scott St Cannock WS12 ..210 C2
 Newcastle-u-L ST5 ....284 C3
Scott Way WS7 ....211 C1
Scott's Rd DY8 ....279 C3
Scotts Ho ST16 ....155 B3
Scragg St ST7 ....41 C4
Scrimshaw Dr ST6 ....42 B2
Scrivener Rd ST4 ....56 C1
Scropton Old Rd DE65 ...146 B4
Scropton Rd
 Hatton DE65 ....146 A4
 Scropton DE65 ....129 C1
Seabridge Jun & Inf Schs
 ST5 ....71 A2
Seabridge La ST5 ....71 A2
Seabridge Rd ST5 ....284 A1
Seabrook Rd WS15 ....197 A3
Seafield B77 ....250 C3
Seafield Cl DY6 ....275 C2
Seaford St ST4 ....284 A4
Seaforth Gr WV11 ....242 A1
Seagrave Pl ST5 ....71 A3
Seagrave St ST5 ....284 C3
Searle Ave ST16 ....155 B1
Seaton B77 ....261 C4
Seaton Ave ST17 ....175 B4
Seaton Cl ST3 ....89 C4
Seaton Pl DY8 ....275 B1
Sebring Ave ST3 ....89 C4
Seckham Rd WS13 ....231 A4
Second Ave
 Branston DE14 ....165 C1
 Brownhills WS8 ....229 A1
 Bucknall ST2 ....58 B2
 Kidsgrove ST7 ....25 C1
 Kingswinford DY6 ....275 C4
 Newcastle-u-L ST5 ....56 B4
 Stafford ST16 ....155 B4
Sedbergh Ct ST5 ....70 C2
Seddon Ct ST11 ....282 C3
Seddon Rd ST3 ....89 C4
Sedgefield Cl DY1 ....271 C2
Sedgefield Gr WV6 ....254 C2
Sedgefield Rd
 Branston DE14 ....184 C4
 Burton u T DE14 ....185 A4
Sedgefield Way WS11 ....228 A2
Sedgeley Rd WV4 ....265 C1
Sedgemoor Ave WS7 ....229 A3
Sedgley Hall Ave DY3 ....271 B4
Sedgley St WV2 ....266 B4
Sedgley Wlk ST3 ....283 C4
Seedcroft La WS15 ....160 C2
Seedfields Rd ST3 ....72 C2
Seeds La WS8 ....244 C4
Seedymill La WS13 ....213 C4
Seesall The ST20 ....171 C4
Sefton Ave Congleton CW12 ..6 A1
 Hanley ST1 ....57 C4
Sefton Cl DE15 ....167 A1
Sefton Rd Longton ST3 ..73 C1
 Tamworth B77 ....261 B2
Sefton St ST1 ....57 A2
Segram Way ST14 ....126 B4
Seighford Rd ST18 ....154 B3
Seisdon Rd WV5 ....264 A1
Selborne Rd ST13 ....30 C2
Selbourne Dr ST6 ....41 C4
Selby Cl ST5 ....71 A3
Selby St ST13 ....84 A3
Selby Way WS3 ....242 C1
Selby Wlk ST3 ....88 C4
Selker Dr B77 ....250 C3
Sellman St ST20 ....171 C3
Selman's Hill WS3 ....243 B1
Selman's Par WS3 ....243 B1
Seisdon Rd WS3 ....242 C2
Selwood Cl ST13 ....84 A3
Selworthy Dr ST17 ....175 C3
Selworthy Rd ST6 ....43 A3
Selwyn Cl Alrewas DE13 ..201 A2
 Wolv WV2 ....266 B4
Selwyn Ct ST21 ....133 C4
Selwyn St ST4 ....72 A3
Selwyn Wlk B74 ....257 B2
Semper Cl WV12 ....6 A2
Senator Cl WV11 ....242 A2
Serin Cl ST14 ....126 B3
Seton Ho B74 ....257 C1
Setterfield Way WS15 ....196 C2
Settle Gr ST3 ....90 A4
Seven Acres DE14 ....165 A1
Seven Acres WS9 ....256 A3
Seven Arches Way ST4 ...72 B4
Seven Springs Nature Trail*
 ST17 ....177 B3
Sevenoaks Gr ST14 ....90 A3
Sevenoaks Dr ST14 ....90 A3
Sevens Rd WS12 ....211 B2
Severn Cl Biddulph ST8 ...16 C1
 Burton u T DE13 ....147 B1
 Congleton CW12 ....6 A1
 Uttoxeter ST14 ....126 B3

Severn Dr
Brownhills WS8 . . . . 228 B1
Burntwood WS7 . . . . 229 B3
Burton u T DE14 . . . . 166 C2
Newcastle-u-L ST5 . . . . 71 A2
Severn Ho DY3 . . . . 254 C2
Severn Ho DY3 . . . . 271 B2
Severn Rd
Stourbridge DY8 . . . . 279 C2
Walsall WS3 . . . . 243 C1
Severn St ST1 . . . . 282 A4
Sevard Cl WS14 . . . . 231 B3
Seymour Ave DE14 . . . . . . 166 C4
Seymour Cl WS6 . . . . 226 B1
Seymour Gdns BR4 . . . . . . 257 C2
Seymour St ST1 . . . . 57 C2
Shackerley La WV7 . . . . . . 221 A1
Shackleton Dr
Perton WV6 . . . . 254 C3
Tunstall ST6 . . . . 41 B2
Shackleton Rd WS3 . . . . . . 243 B1
Shackson Cl ST1 . . . . 282 B1
Shadwell Dr DY3 . . . . 271 B2
Shaffalong La ST13 . . . . . . 45 A3
Shaftesbury Ave ST6 . . . . . 42 A1
Shaftesbury Dr WS12 . . . . . 210 B4
Shaftsbury Rd WS15 . . . . . 196 C3
Shakespeare Ave WS14 . . . 231 A3
Shakespeare Cl
Kidsgrove ST7 . . . . 41 A4
Norton-in-t-M ST2 . . . . 43 A1
Tamworth B79 . . . . 250 A3
Shakespeare Cl ST8 . . . . . . 27 B4
Shakespeare Gr WS11 . . . . 209 B2
Shakespeare Rd
Burntwood WS7 . . . . 228 C4
Burton u T DE14 . . . . 166 B3
Sedgley DY3 . . . . 271 A2
Stafford ST17 . . . . 174 B4
Shaldon Ave ST9 . . . . 43 B2
Shales The WV5 . . . . 269 C3
Shallcross La DY3 . . . . 271 B2
Shallowford Cl ST1 . . . . 57 A2
Shallowford Mews
ST16 . . . . 155 B3
Shanklin Cl WS6 . . . . 227 A2
Shannon Dr B77 . . . . 261 C4
Shannon App DE14 . . . . . . 166 B1
Shannon Dr
Brownhills WS8 . . . . 228 B1
Tunstall ST6 . . . . 41 B4
Shannon Rd ST17 . . . . 174 B3
Shannon Wlk WS8 . . . . 228 B1
Shanti Niketan WV2 . . . . . . 266 B4
Shardlow Cl Fenton ST4 . . . 73 A3
Stone ST15 . . . . 120 B3
Sharman Cl ST14 . . . . 71 C4
Sharmon Way ST20 . . . . . . 171 C4
Sharnbrook Dr WS15 . . . . . 178 B1
Sharnbrook Gr ST17 . . . . . . 175 B3
Sharon Cl WV4 . . . . 266 C3
Sharon Way WS12 . . . . 210 B2
Sharpe St B77 . . . . 251 A3
Sharplands TF9 . . . . 99 B3
Sharrat Field B75 . . . . 258 B1
Sharron Dr ST13 . . . . 31 A3
Shaver's La WS11 . . . . 197 A1
Shaw La WS13 . . . . 215 B4
Shaw Dr WS7 . . . . 212 A1
Shaw Gdns ST17 . . . . 174 B4
Shaw Hall La WV9 . . . . 240 B4
Shaw La Albrighton WV7 . . . 237 A3
King's Bromley WS15 . . . . . . 198 C1
Lichfield WS13 . . . . 213 A2
Longdon WS15 . . . . 212 A2
Tong TF11 . . . . 220 B3
Wolv WV6 . . . . 255 A2
Shaw Pl ST13 . . . . 31 A3
Shaw Rd WV4 . . . . 266 B3
Shaw St Biddulph ST8 . . . . . 27 B4
Hanley ST1 . . . . 282 A4
Newcastle-u-L ST5 . . . . 284 B3
Shaw's La WS6 . . . . 227 A1
Shaw~wall La Cotton ST10 . 62 C4
Ipstones ST10 . . . . 62 C4
Shawbury Gr WV6 . . . . 254 C3
Shawe Park Rd ST10 . . . . . 76 C4
Shawmains La ST18 . . . . . . 172 C4
Shawms Crest ST17 . . . . . . 175 B3
Shawport Ave ST5 . . . . 56 A4
Shaws La ST21 . . . . 133 B3
Shay La Forton TF10 . . . . . . 150 A2
Ipstones ST10 . . . . 62 B3
Shayler Gr WV2 . . . . 266 B4
Sheaf Pas ST3 . . . . 283 C3
Sheaf St ST1 . . . . 282 A1
Shearer St ST1 . . . . 282 A1
Shebdon Cl ST16 . . . . 155 A4
Sheep Fair WS15 . . . . 178 C1
Sheep Market ST13 . . . . . . 30 C3
Sheepcote La B77 . . . . 250 C2
Sheepwalks La DY7 . . . . . . 277 A4
Sheepwash La DY11 . . . . . . 277 B1
Sheffield Ct ST14 . . . . 110 C1
Sheffield St DE14 . . . . 166 C3
Shefford Rd ST5 . . . . 70 C2
Shelburne St ST4 . . . . 72 A3
Sheldon Ave CW12 . . . . 6 A1
Sheldon Cl ST5 . . . . 55 B3
Sheldon Rd WV10 . . . . 240 A1
Sheldrake Gr ST14 . . . . 73 A3
Shelfield Com Sch WS4 . . . 244 B1
Shelford Rd ST6 . . . . 41 B3
Shelley Rd DE14 . . . . 166 B3

Shelley Cl
Armitage WS15 . . . . 198 A2
Burton u T DE14 . . . . 166 B3
Colwich ST18 . . . . 177 B4
Kidsgrove ST7 . . . . 41 A4
Sedgley DY3 . . . . 271 A3
Stafford ST16 . . . . 156 A3
Shelley Dr Cheadle ST10 . . . 76 B1
Sutton Coldfield B74 . . . . . . 257 C3
Shelley Rd Bucknall ST2 . . . 58 A3
Burntwood WS7 . . . . 212 A1
Cannock WS11 . . . . 209 C3
Tamworth B79 . . . . 250 A4
Wolv WV10 . . . . 240 B1
Shelmore Cl ST16 . . . . 155 A4
Shelmore Way ST20 . . . . . . 171 B4
Shelsey Rd ST10 . . . . 76 C2
Shelsley Cl ST19 . . . . 193 A1
Shelton Farm Rd ST1 . . . . . 282 A4
Shelton New Rd ST14 . . . . . 56 C1
Shelton Old Rd ST14 . . . . . 72 A4
Shelton St B77 . . . . 261 C4
Shemilt Cres ST6 . . . . 42 B2
Shendon Ct ST5 . . . . 56 B1
Shendon Gn ST2 . . . . 58 B1
Shenley Gr ST17 . . . . 174 B3
Shenstone Ave DY8 . . . . . . 279 B2
Shenstone Cl B74 . . . . 257 C3
Shenstone Ct WV3 . . . . 266 A3
Shenstone Dr WS9 . . . . 236 A4
Shenstone Ho WS11 . . . . . . 232 A4
Shenstone Lodge Specl Sch
WS14 . . . . 247 A2
Shenstone Sta WS14 . . . . . 246 C3
Shenton St ST3 . . . . 283 C5
Shephard Cl ST18 . . . . 158 B2
Shepherd Cl WS13 . . . . 214 B2
Shepherd St ST8 . . . . 27 B4
Shepherds Bush St
ST16 . . . . 155 C3
Shepherds Ct TF10 . . . . . . 169 A2
Shepherds Fold ST17 . . . . . 175 B3
Shepherds Pool Rd B75 . . . 258 C1
Shepherds Wlk WV8 . . . . . . 239 C1
Shepley Cl ST15 . . . . 120 B4
Shepley Gr ST13 . . . . 88 C4
Sheppard St ST4 . . . . 72 A3
Shepwell Gdns WV10 . . . . . 241 B4
Sheraton Cl
Aldridge WS9 . . . . 256 A3
Cannock WS12 . . . . 210 A4
Sheraton Grange DY8 . . . . . 279 C1
Sherborne Cl ST13 ST14 . . . 88 C4
Sherborne Ct WV10 . . . . . . 240 C1
Sherborne Dr ST5 . . . . 71 A3
Sherborne Gdns WV8 . . . . . 239 A2
Sherborne Rd WV10 . . . . . . 240 B1
Sherbourne Ave WS12 . . . . 210 C2
Sherbourne Dr DE14 . . . . . 185 A4
Sherbrook Cl ST17 . . . . 176 A2
Sherbrook Rd WS11 . . . . . . 209 B1
Sherbrooke Ave B77 . . . . . . 261 C3
Sheridan Gdns
Himley DY3 . . . . 270 C3
Longton ST3 . . . . 72 C1
Sheridan St ST16 . . . . 156 B2
Sheridan Way WS15 . . . . . 120 B4
Sheridan Way ST5 . . . . 55 C1
Sheriffs Cl WS14 . . . . 231 C3
Sheriffs Way ST21 . . . . 133 B4
Sheriboot La B75 . . . . 258 A2
Sheringham Covert
ST16 . . . . 156 B2
Sheringham Dr WS15 . . . . . 178 A1
Sheringham Pl ST5 . . . . 56 B2
Sherington Dr WV4 . . . . 266 B3
Sherracop La WS11 . . . . . . 232 A4
Sherrans Dell WV4 . . . . 266 B2
Sherratt St ST6 . . . . 42 B2
Sherringham Dr WV11 . . . . . 242 B1
Shervale Cl WV4 . . . . 266 A3
Sherwin Rd ST6 . . . . 41 C2
Sherwood Ave ST17 . . . . . . 174 C4
Sherwood Cl CV9 . . . . 262 B1
Sherwood Rd ST5 . . . . 210 A2
Sherwood Rd Meir ST3 . . . . 89 C4
Stourbridge DY8 . . . . 279 B2
Shetland Ave B77 . . . . 261 C4
Shetland Rd ST3 . . . . 72 C2
Shillingford Dr ST4 . . . . 88 A4
Shilton Cl ST14 . . . . 71 C3
Shinwell Gr ST3 . . . . 90 A4
Shipley Cl DE14 . . . . 185 A4
Shipley Pl ST6 . . . . 42 B1
Shippy La ST18 . . . . 172 B4
Shipston Rd ST17 . . . . 156 B1
Shipton Cl DY1 . . . . 271 C2
Shipton Dr ST14 . . . . 110 C1
Shirburn Rd ST13 . . . . 31 A3
Shire Lea WS8 . . . . 245 A3
Shire Oak Sch WS8 . . . . . . 245 A3
Shirebrook Cl ST3 . . . . 88 C4
Shirehall Pl WS11 . . . . 210 A1
Shirelea Cl WS7 . . . . 229 A4
Shireoaks Dr B77 . . . . 175 B3
Shireview Gdns WS3 . . . . . 244 A2
Shireview Rd WS3 . . . . 244 A2
Shirley Ave ST9 . . . . 43 A4
Shirley Dr ST10 . . . . 94 C4
Shirley Rd ST1 . . . . 282 B1
Shirley St Burslem ST6 . . . . 56 B4
Leek ST13 . . . . 30 B3
Shirley Wlk B79 . . . . 249 C4
Shirleywich ST18 . . . . 138 C1
Shirrall Dr ST8 . . . . 259 C2
Shoal Hill Cl WS11 . . . . 209 A1
Shobnall Cl DE14 . . . . 166 A2

Shobnall Ct DE14 . . . . 166 A2
Shobnall Prim Sch
DE14 . . . . 165 C2
Shobnall Rd DE14 . . . . 166 A2
Shobnall St DE14 . . . . 166 A2
Sholing Cl WV8 . . . . 239 C1
Shoobridge St ST13 . . . . . . 30 C3
Shooting Butts Rd
WS15 . . . . 196 A4
Shop La Brewood ST19 . . . . 223 B3
Codsall WV8 . . . . 238 B1
Perton WV6 . . . . 264 A4
Shops The 2 DY6 . . . . 263 B2
Short Bambury St ST3 . . . . 73 B3
Short La Barton-u-N DE13 . . 183 B1
Cheslyn Hay WS6 . . . . 226 C2
Kingstone ST14 . . . . 124 B1
Short Rd WV10 . . . . 240 C1
Short St Brownhills WS8 . . . 228 C1
Newcastle-u-L ST5 . . . . 185 C4
Cannock WS11 . . . . 209 C2
Longton ST3 . . . . 283 D3
Stourbridge DY8 . . . . 279 C3
Uttoxeter ST14 . . . . 126 A4
Short Street Com Inf Sch
DE15 . . . . 185 C4
Shortbutts La WS14 . . . . . . 231 A3
Shortlands La WS3 . . . . . . 243 C2
Shorwell Gr ST7 . . . . 41 C4
Shotsfield Pl ST7 . . . . 43 A3
Shotsfield St ST7 . . . . 43 A1
Shotwood Cl DE13 . . . . 147 A2
Shotwoodhill La DE13 . . . . 147 A2
Showan Ave ST5 . . . . 56 B2
Showell La WV4 . . . . 265 A2
Shraleybrook Rd ST7 . . . . . 54 A4
Shredicote La ST18 . . . . . . 191 A4
Shrewsbury Cl WS3 . . . . . . 242 C1
Shrewsbury Dr ST5 . . . . . . 40 C1
Shrewsbury Rd
Burton u T DE14 . . . . 147 C1
Edgmond TF10 . . . . 168 A2
Market Drayton TF9 . . . . . . 112 A4
Stafford ST17 . . . . 155 C1
Shrewsbury Way TF10 . . . . 168 C1
Shropshire Brook Rd
WS15 . . . . 198 A2
Shropshire St TF9 . . . . 97 B1
Shrubbery Cl DY10 . . . . . . 280 A3
Shrubbery The
Ilford B79 . . . . 216 C1
Rugeley WS15 . . . . 197 A3
Shruggs La ST18 . . . . 121 B1
Shugborough Cl WS3 . . . . . 243 A1
Shugborough Cotts
ST18 . . . . 177 B4
Shugborough Dr DY1 . . . . . 271 C1
Shugborough Farm Mus*
ST17 . . . . 177 A4
Shugborough Hall*
ST17 . . . . 177 A4
Shugborough Rd WS15 . . . . 157 A1
Shugborough Way
WS11 . . . . 210 B1
Shughborough Cl ST19 . . . . 59 A1
Shuker's Cl ST14 . . . . 169 A1
Shut La ST21 . . . . 163 A1
Shutt Green La ST19 . . . . . 223 A4
Shuttington Rd B79 . . . . . . 251 A3
Sich La DE15 . . . . 182 B2
Sidcot Pl ST1 . . . . 57 B4
Siddals Rd DE15 . . . . 167 A3
Siddons Cl WS13 . . . . 213 C1
Sides La DE6 . . . . 81 A2
Sideway Rd ST4 . . . . 72 A3
Sidings Ind Est DE14 . . . . . 166 C2
Sidings Pl WS13 ST15 . . . . 283 B4
Sidings Rd WS15 . . . . 104 C1
Sidings The
Cannock WS12 . . . . 210 B4
Cheadle ST10 . . . . 76 B1
Stone ST15 . . . . 120 A4
Sidmouth Ave
Newcastle-u-L ST5 . . . . 284 C3
Stafford ST17 . . . . 156 B1
Sidney Ave ST17 . . . . 174 C4
Sidney Dr ST10 . . . . 142 B1
Sidney St WV2 . . . . 266 B4
Sidon Hill Way WS11 . . . . . 210 B1
Siemens Rd ST17 . . . . 155 C1
Signal Gr WS3 . . . . 243 A1
Signal Wlk B77 . . . . 261 A3
Silica Rd B77 . . . . 251 A1
Silk Mill La DE13 . . . . 146 B3
Silk St ST13 . . . . 30 C3
Silkmore Cres ST17 . . . . . . 175 A4
Silkmore La ST17 . . . . 175 A4
Silkmore Prim Sch
ST17 . . . . 174 C4
Sill La B79 . . . . 234 B1
Sillitoe Pl ST14 . . . . 72 A3
Silsden Gr ST3 . . . . 74 B1
Silva Ave DY6 . . . . 275 C2
Silver Birch Coppice
B74 . . . . 257 B3
Silver Birch Dr
Kinver DY7 . . . . 277 C3
Uttoxeter ST14 . . . . 126 A3
Silver Birch Rd
Aldridge B74 . . . . 256 C4
Huntington WS12 . . . . 209 B4
Norton Canes WS11 . . . . . . 228 A3
Wolv WV2 . . . . 266 C4
Silver Cl ST8 . . . . 27 B4
Silver Ct WS8 . . . . 244 C4
Silver Ct Gdns WS8 . . . . . . 244 C4
Silver Fir Cl WS12 . . . . 210 A4
Silver La ST14 . . . . 127 C1

Silver Link Rd B77 . . . . 250 C1
Silver Poplars Mobil Homes
Pk WV7 . . . . 237 C1
Silver Ridge ST12 . . . . 104 B4
Silver St Brownhills WS8 . . . 244 C4
Cheadle ST10 . . . . 76 C3
Norton-in-t-M ST6 . . . . 42 C2
Tamworth B79 . . . . 250 A3
Uttoxeter ST14 . . . . 126 A4
Silverdale TF10 . . . . 168 A2
Silverdale Bsns Pk ST5 . . . 55 B1
Silverdale Cl TF10 . . . . 168 C1
Silverdale Gdns DY8 . . . . . 275 B2
Silverdale Prim Sch ST5 . . . 55 B1
Silverdale Rd ST5 . . . . 55 B2
Silverdale St ST5 . . . . 55 C2
Silvergate Ct CW12 . . . . . . 15 C4
Silverhill Cl DE13 . . . . 146 B4
Silvermine Cl 17 ST7 . . . . . 26 A1
Silvers Cl WS3 . . . . 243 C2
Silverstone Ave ST10 . . . . . 76 B2
Silverstone Cres ST7 . . . . . 41 C4
Silverthorn Way ST17 . . . . . 175 B4
Silverton Cl ST5 . . . . 56 A4
Silverwood ST7 . . . . 26 A1
Silvester Way ST17 . . . . . . 175 C3
Simcox St WS12 . . . . 210 B2
Simeon Way ST15 . . . . 120 B3
Simister Ct 9 ST6 . . . . 41 B2
Simmonds Cl WS3 . . . . 243 A3
Simmonds Rd WS3 . . . . 243 B2
Simmonds Way WS8 . . . . . 245 A3
Simmons Cl B78 . . . . 260 A1
Simmons Rd WV11 . . . . 242 A1
Simon Pl ST14 . . . . 71 C4
Simonburn Ave ST4 . . . . . . 71 B3
Simons Rd TF9 . . . . 112 A4
Simpkins Cl WS9 . . . . 245 A2
Simpson Cl ST16 . . . . 155 A4
Simpson Rd WS13 . . . . 214 A1
Simpson St Hanley ST1 . . . . 282 C1
Newcastle-u-L ST5 . . . . 284 B3
Sinai Cl DE14 . . . . 165 C2
Sion Ave DY10 . . . . 280 A1
Sion Hill Mid Sch DY10 . . . . 280 A1
Sir Graham Balfour High Sch
ST16 . . . . 155 B4
Sir John Offley CE Prim Sch
CW3 . . . . 68 C3
Sir Robert Peel Hospl
B78 . . . . 249 B1
Sir Thomas Boughey High
Sch ST7 . . . . 54 B4
Siskin Cl WS7 . . . . 229 B3
Siskin Pl ST3 . . . . 90 A4
Sister Dora Ave WS3 . . . . . 229 C4
Sitwell Gr ST3 . . . . 283 D4
Six Ashes Rd DY7 . . . . 272 B4
Six Roads End DE13 . . . . . 144 B2
Skeath La ST18 . . . . 137 B2
Skellern Ave ST6 . . . . 42 B2
Skellern St ST1 . . . . 25 B1
Skidmore Ave
Tamworth B79 . . . . 261 B3
Wolv WV3 . . . . 265 C4
Skipacre Ave ST6 . . . . 42 B1
Skippacks B77 . . . . 250 C3
Skipton Pl WS11 . . . . 226 A4
Skye Cl Longton ST3 . . . . . . 73 C2
Tamworth B79 . . . . 261 C4
Skylark Cl
Huntington WS12 . . . . 209 B4
Sedgley DY5 . . . . 271 B1
Uttoxeter ST14 . . . . 126 B3
Slab La ST9,ST20 . . . . 190 A1
Slack La DE6 . . . . 81 B4
Slacken La ST7 . . . . 25 B4
Slacky La WS3 . . . . 243 C1
Slade Ave WS7 . . . . 229 A4
Slade Fields ST14 . . . . 111 A1
Slade Gdns WV8 . . . . 239 A2
Slade Rd WS8 . . . . 255 C2
Slade La
Sutton Coldfield B75 . . . . . . 259 A2
Tamworth B77 . . . . 261 A2
Waterhouses ST10,ST13 . . . 49 A3
Slade Rd
Sutton Coldfield B75 . . . . . . 258 C2
Wolv WV10 . . . . 240 B2
Sladeview La DE6 . . . . 65 B1
Sladhollow La B79 . . . . 235 C1
Slaidburn Ave Hanley ST1 . . 57 C2
Stafford ST17 . . . . 175 B4
Slaney St ST5 . . . . 284 C1
Slang La WS13 . . . . 211 C3
Slapton Cl ST7 . . . . 57 C1
Slate La WV8 . . . . 238 B3
Slater St Biddulph ST8 . . . . 27 B4
Burslem ST6 . . . . 56 C3
Sleeve The ST13 . . . . 30 B2
Sleigh Gr ST13 . . . . 30 C3
Slessor Rd ST16 . . . . 156 A3
Slindon Cl ST5 . . . . 40 B1
Sling La ST19 . . . . 206 A2
Slingsby B77 . . . . 261 B4
Slippery La ST1 . . . . 282 A2
Slitting Mill Rd WS15 . . . . . 196 A4
Sloane Way ST4 . . . . 73 A3
Small La ST21 . . . . 133 C4
Small Meers DE13 . . . . 183 C1
Smallbrook La WV5 . . . . . . 270 A4
Smallcross Cl ST14 . . . . . . 126 B3
Smalldale Cl WS12 . . . . . . 210 A3
Smallman St ST16 . . . . 155 B4
Smalldridge WS3 . . . . 213 C1
Smallshire Way DY8 . . . . . . 279 B4
Smallthorne Prim Sch
ST6 . . . . 42 B1

Smallwood Cl ST5 . . . . 40 B1
Smallwood Gr ST1 . . . . 57 C3
Smallwood Rd WV8 . . . . . . 239 C1
Smarts Ave WS14 . . . . 258 A4
Smedley Ct D65 . . . . 148 A3
Smestow Bridge Ind Est
WV5 . . . . 269 B3
Smestow La DY3 . . . . 269 B2
Smestow Sch WV3 . . . . 255 A1
Smiston Way WV11 . . . . . . 209 C2
Smith Child St ST6 . . . . 41 B2
Smith Ho WS3 . . . . 243 B2
Smith St Longton ST3 . . . . . 283 C5
Wood End CV9 . . . . 262 B1
Smithfield Cl ST7 . . . . 228 B4
Smithfield Cl TF9 . . . . 97 B1
Smithfield Ct ST1 . . . . 282 B1
Smithfield Ctr The 18
ST13 . . . . 30 C3
Smithfield Rd
Market Drayton TF9 . . . . . . 97 B1
Uttoxeter ST14 . . . . 126 A4
Walsall WS3 . . . . 243 B1
Smithfield Rise WS13 . . . . . 231 B4
Smithpool Rd ST4 . . . . 72 B3
Smiths Bldgs 4 ST8 . . . . . . 74 A1
Smiths Pas ST4 . . . . 73 A3
Smithy Bank ST10 . . . . 78 C1
Smithy Croft ST20 . . . . 190 A4
Smithy St WS3 . . . . 244 A2
Smithy La
Acton Trussell ST17 . . . . . . 193 C4
Barthomley CW2 . . . . 38 B4
Biddulph ST8 . . . . 16 B1
Bosley SK11 . . . . 7 C3
Bradley ST18 . . . . 191 B4
Cheadle ST10 . . . . 92 B4
Clifton Campville B79 . . . . . 218 C1
Eccleshall ST21 . . . . 117 A1
Hixon ST18 . . . . 158 B4
Lichfield WS13 . . . . 214 A1
Longdon WS15 . . . . 212 C4
Longton ST3 . . . . 283 C3
Sedgley DY5 . . . . 271 A1
Seghford ST18 . . . . 154 A4
Tamworth B77 . . . . 251 A4
Weston CW2 . . . . 37 B3
Whitmore ST5 . . . . 85 C3
Woore TF9 . . . . 83 A3
Smithyfield Rd ST5 . . . . 42 B2
Smokies Way ST8 . . . . 16 B1
Smout Cres WV14 . . . . 266 C1
Snape Hall Rd ST5 . . . . 85 B3
Snape Hall Rd ST5 . . . . 85 B4
Snape Hollow CW2 . . . . 37 C2
Snape La ST21 . . . . 4 C2
Snape Rd WV11 . . . . 242 A1
Snapes La D66 . . . . 81 A1
Snead Cl ST16 . . . . 156 B2
Sneyd Ave Leek ST13 . . . . . 30 C3
Newcastle-u-L ST5 . . . . 70 C4
Sneyd Cl ST13 . . . . 45 B2
Sneyd Com Sch WS3 . . . . . 242 C1
Sneyd Cres ST5 . . . . 70 C4
Sneyd Green Prim Sch
ST6 . . . . 57 B4
Sneyd Hall Rd WS3 . . . . . . 243 A1
Sneyd Hill ST6 . . . . 57 B4
Sneyd Hill Ind Est ST6 . . . . 57 A4
Sneyd Ho WS3 . . . . 242 C1
Sneyd Ind Est ST6 . . . . 57 A4
Sneyd La Essington WV11 . . 242 B1
Walsall WS3 . . . . 242 C1
Sneyd Pl ST6 . . . . 41 B3
Sneyd St Hanley ST6,ST1 . . 57 B3
Leek ST13 . . . . 30 C3
Sneyd Terr ST5 . . . . 55 A1
Sneyd Wood View ST6 . . . . 57 B4
Sneydlands WS15 . . . . 178 C1
Snipe Cl WV10 . . . . 241 A4
Snow Hill Hanley ST1 . . . . . 282 A1
Stafford ST16 . . . . 155 C2
Snowberry Dr ST5 . . . . 271 B1
Snowden Way ST3 . . . . 74 A1
Snowdon Rd
Cannock WS11 . . . . 209 C3
Pattingham WV6 . . . . 252 A3
Snowdon Rise DY2 . . . . 271 B3
Snowdon Way WV12 . . . . . 242 A1
Snowdrop Cl WS8 . . . . 244 B3
Snows Yd ST16 . . . . 155 B2
Snowshill Gdns DY1 . . . . . 271 C2
Soames Cres ST4 . . . . 72 C3
Solent Cl WV9 . . . . 239 C1
Solney Cl DE11 . . . . 186 C2
Solway Cl B79 . . . . 250 A4
Solway Gr ST3 . . . . 73 C2
Somerfield Cl WS4 . . . . 244 B1
Somerford Cl
Brewood WV9 . . . . 224 A1
Great Wyrley WS6 . . . . 226 C1
Somerford Gdns WV10 . . . . 240 C1
Somerford La ST19 . . . . . . 223 C3
Somerley Rd ST1 . . . . 57 C3
Somerset Ave
Kidsgrove ST7 . . . . 25 C1
Rugeley WS15 . . . . 196 B3
Somerset Cl B78 . . . . 250 A1
Somerset Dr ST6 . . . . 279 B4
Somerset Pl WS11 . . . . 209 C2
Somerset Rd
Burton u T DE15 . . . . 185 B3
Hanley ST1 . . . . 57 C2
Walsall WS5 . . . . 230 A4
Somerton Rd ST19 . . . . 59 A2
Somerton Way ST3 . . . . 283 D5
Somervale ST17 . . . . 175 B3
Somerville Ave ST5 . . . . . . 56 B2

Somerville Ct B79 249 B3
Somerville Rd DE13 201 A1
Somerville Sq ST17 174 C3
Sonning Dr WV9 239 C1
Sophia Way ST5 56 A4
Sopwith Cl ST15 118 C3
Sorbus B77 251 A2
Sorrel B77 251 A3
Sorrel Ave ST10 92 C2
Sorrel Cl Bucknall ST2 58 A2
Featherstone WV10 241 A4
Uttoxeter ST14 126 A3
Sorrento Gr ST3 73 C2
Souldern Way ST3 73 B2
Soulthorpe Rd DY10 281 A1
South Ave DY8 279 C2
South Broadway St
DE14 185 B4
South Cl WS11 226 B4
South Cres WV10 241 B3
South Dr DE11 186 C3
South Gn WV4 265 B3
South Hill DE13 147 B2
South Oak St DE14 185 A4
South Oval DY3 271 C3
South Pl ST6 42 B3
South Rd Bucknall ST2 58 A3
Millmeece ST15 118 B3
Stourbridge DY8 279 C2
Wolv WV4 266 C2
South St
Mount Pleasant ST7 26 A3
Norton-in-t-M ST6 42 B3
Stafford ST16 155 B2
South Staffordshire Bsns Pk
WS11 226 B2
South Terr
Newcastle-u-L ST5 56 B3
Stoke-on-T ST4 72 A3
South Uxbridge St
DE14 185 A4
South View Biddulph ST8 27 B4
Mayfield DE6 81 B3
Uttoxeter ST14 126 A4
South View Cl
Codsall WV8 239 A1
Featherstone WV10 241 A3
South View Rd DY3 271 B4
South View Wlk ST14 95 C2
South Walls ST16 155 C2
South Wlk ST3 74 A1
South Wolf St ST4 72 A4
South Wood ST5 85 A4
Southall Way ST2 58 A1
Southampton St ST1 282 C4
Southbank St ST13 30 C3
Southbank View DY6 275 C2
Southborough Cres ST6 42 B2
Southbourne Pl WS11 209 B1
Southbourne Rd WV10 240 B2
Southdown Cl ST3 89 B4
Southern Cl DY6 275 C2
Southern Cross WS14 231 B4
Southern Way ST6 42 B1
Southerndown Rd DY3 271 A4
Southfield Cl WS9 256 A3
Southfield Gr WV3 265 B4
Southfield Way WS6 226 C1
Southfields Cl ST17 174 B3
Southfields Rd ST17 174 B3
Southgate Brewood ST19 223 B4
Cannock WS11 226 A4
Southgate Ave ST4 88 B3
Southgate End WS11 226 A4
Southlands Ave
Longton ST3 283 B1
Newcastle-u-L ST5 56 B3
Southlands Cl ST13 30 B3
Southlands Rd CW12 16 A4
Southlowe Ave ST9 59 C2
Southlowe Rd ST9 59 C2
Southwark Cl WS13 214 B2
Southway Ct DY6 275 C2
Southwell Est ST21 133 C3
Southwood Cl DY6 275 C3
Sovereign Dr
Burton u T DE14 185 A4
Sedgley DY1 271 C1
Sovereign La TF9 100 B3
Sovereign Works DY1 271 C2
Sowdley Gn ST19 205 A3
Sowdley La ST19 205 A2
Sowers Ct B75 258 B2
Spa St ST6 57 B4
Spalding Pl ST2 73 C4
Sparch Ave ST5 56 B2
Sparch Gr ST5 56 B2
Sparch Hollow ST5 56 B2
Spark St ST4 72 A4
Spark Terr ST4 72 A4
Sparrow Cl ST18 177 B4
Sparrow St ST6 42 B1
Sparrow Terr ST5 56 A3
Sparrowbutts Gr ST7 26 B1
Sparrows End La ST19 223 B3
Speakman St ST3 283 D2
Spearhill WS14 231 C4
Spedding Rd ST4 72 C4
Spedding Way ST8 27 C4
Speechley Dr WS15 178 B1
Speedwall St ST3 73 B3
Speedwell Cl WS9 256 A3
Speedwell Gdns WV10 241 A4
Speedwell Rd ST5 40 C1
Speedy Cl WS11 209 C3
Spencer Ave Endon ST9 43 C3
Leek ST13 30 C3
Spencer Cl
Burton u T DE13 147 B1
Sedgley DY3 271 A2
Uttoxeter ST14 126 B3
Weston ST18 138 B1
Spencer Pl ST5 55 C3
Spencer Rd
Lichfield WS14 231 A3
Stoke-on-T ST4 72 B4
Spencroft Rd ST5 56 A3
Spend La Mapleton DE6 66 C4
Thorpe DE6 51 C1
Spens St ST6 56 C4
Spenser Ave WV6 254 C2
Spenser Cl Stafford ST17 174 B4
Tamworth B79 250 A3
Sperry Cl ST3 90 A4
Spey Dr ST7 26 B1
Spiceal Mews ST14 126 B4
Spicer's Cl WV5 267 B4
Spills Mdw DY3 271 C3
Spindlewood Cl 5
WS11 210 B1
Spinney Cl
Burntwood WS7 212 A1
Endon ST9 43 C4
Kingswinford DY8 275 B2
Norton Canes WS11 227 C3
Polesworth B78 262 C4
Walsall WS3 244 A1
Spinney Dr CW2 37 A3
Spinney Farm Rd WS11 226 A4
Spinney La WS7 211 C1
Spinney Lodge DE13 145 C3
Spinney Rd DE14 184 C4
Spinney The Biddulph ST8 27 B3
Keele CW3 69 A4
Lawton-gate ST7 25 C2
Little Aston B74 257 A3
Newcastle-u-L ST5 71 B1
Sedgley DY3 271 B1
Wolv WV3 255 B1
Spinneyfields 9 ST17 175 B3
Spinning School La
B79 250 A3
Spiral Ct DY3 271 B2
Spire Cl ST6 42 C2
Spires Croft WV10 225 B1
Spires The WS14 231 C3
Spitfire Way ST6 41 B2
Splash La WS12 210 B2
Spode Ave
Armitage WS15 198 B2
Hopton ST18 156 A4
Spode Cl ST10 76 B1
Spode Gr ST5 71 A2
Spode Pl WS11 210 A1
Spode St ST4 72 A3
Spout La ST2 43 B1
Spoutfield Rd ST4 56 C1
Spragg House La ST6 42 C2
Spratslade Dr ST3 283 B2
Spreadoaks Dr ST17 175 B3
Sprengers Cl ST19 193 A1
Spring Bank ST7 26 A4
Spring Bank Flats ST16 155 B3
Spring Cl Hagley DY9 281 C2
Kinver DY7 277 C3
Swadlincote DE11 186 C1
Walsall WS4 244 B1
Spring Cres ST6 43 B4
Spring Garden Rd ST3 283 B2
Spring Gdns
Forsbrook ST11 91 A4
Leek ST13 30 B3
Stone ST15 120 A3
Spring La Walsall WS4 244 B1
Whittington WS14 232 C3
Spring Leasow ST20 151 A2
Spring Mdw WS6 226 B1
Spring Meadows Cl
WV8 239 A2
Spring Rd Lichfield WS13 214 B1
Longton ST3 73 C1
Walsall WS4 244 B1
Spring St Cannock WS11 226 C4
Stoke-on-T ST5 56 B1
Spring Terr WS7 228 C3
Spring Terr Rd DE15 166 C1
Spring Vale Prim Sch
WV4 266 C2
Spring View ST6 43 B4
Springbank Ave ST9 43 C3
Springcroft ST11 90 C3
Springcroft Prim Sch
ST11 90 C4
Springdale Jun Sch
WV4 265 B3
Springfarm Rd DE15 167 A1
Springfield Ashley TF9 99 C3
Blythe Bridge ST11 90 C3
Springfield Ave
Newport TF10 168 C1
Rugeley WS15 196 C4
Sedgley DY3 266 C1
Springfield Cl Leek ST13 31 A3
Newcastle-u-L ST5 55 C3
Springfield Cres ST3 283 B2
Springfield Ct Leek ST13 31 A3
Stafford ST17 174 C3
Wolv WV10 240 B2
Springfield Dr
Forsbrook ST11 91 A4
Leek ST13 31 A3
Stafford ST17 174 C3
Wheaton Aston ST19 205 B4
Springfield Gr
Biddulph ST8 27 B4
Springfield Gr *continued*
Sedgley DY3 266 B1
Springfield La WV10 240 B2
Springfield Prim Sch
ST4 71 C3
Springfield Rd
Biddulph ST8 27 B4
Leek ST13 31 A3
Tamworth B77 261 B4
Uttoxeter ST14 126 A4
Springfield Rise WS12 210 B3
Springfield Sch ST13 31 A3
Springfield Terr DE15 167 A1
Springfields Fst Sch
ST15 118 C3
Springfields Ind Est
TF10 168 C1
Springfields Rd
Rugeley WS15 178 B2
Stoke-on-T ST4 71 C3
Springhead Cl ST7 40 B3
Springhead Prim Sch
ST7 40 B3
Springhill Ave WV4 265 B2
Springhill Cl WS4 244 B1
Springhill Gr WV4 265 B2
Springhill La WV4 265 A2
Springhill Pk WV4 265 A2
Springhill Prim Sch
WS7 229 A3
Springhill Rd
Brownhills WS8 245 A4
Burntwood WS7 229 A3
Springhill Terr WS15 196 C4
Springle Styche La WS7 212 B1
Springpool ST5 70 B3
Springs Bank ST9 44 A1
Springside Pl ST3 88 C4
Springvale Prim Sch
WS11 226 C4
Springvale Rise ST16 155 B4
Springwood Dr ST15 120 B4
Springwood Rd ST5 55 B4
Sprink La CW12 6 B3
Sprinkbank Rd ST6 42 A3
Sprinkswoods La DE6 81 C3
Sprinkwood Gr ST3 74 A2
Sproston Rd ST6 41 C2
Spruce B77 251 A2
Spruce Rd WS12 195 A1
Spruce Way WV3 255 B1
Spruce Wlk WS15 178 B2
Spruces The DY9 281 C2
Spur Lea ST18 173 B1
Spur St ST1 282 C1
Spur Tree Ave WV3 255 A1
Square The
Aldridge WS9 256 A3
Caverswall ST11 74 C1
Codsall WV8 238 C2
Colwich ST18 158 A1
Elford B79 216 B1
Fazeley B78 261 A4
Marchington ST14 127 C1
Meir ST3 74 A1
Newcastle-u-L ST5 71 A3
Newport TF10 168 C2
Oakamoor ST10 78 A3
Pattingham WV6 253 B1
Wolv WV2 266 B4
Woore CW3 67 B1
Squires Gate WS7 229 B4
Squires View ST4 72 B4
Squirrel Cl
Cannock WS12 210 B1
Huntington WS12 209 B3
Lichfield WS13 230 C3
Squirrel Hayes Ave ST8 27 C3
Squirrel Hayes Fst Sch
ST8 27 B4
Squirrel Wlk
Little Aston B74 257 B3
Stafford ST17 174 C2
Wolv WV4 266 A3
Squirrel's Hollow WS7 212 A1
Squirrels The
Lichfield WS14 231 B4
Newcastle-u-L ST5 71 B2
Stable Ct DY3 271 C3
Stable La Alstonefield DE6 35 A1
Market Drayton TF9 97 A1
Shareshill WV10,ST19 225 A4
Stableford Bank ST5 86 A1
Stables The ST18 158 A1
Stacey Cl SK17 23 A1
Stackhouse Cl WS9 245 A2
Stackhouse Dr WS3 244 A2
Stackyard La TF10 168 A2
Stadium Ct ST6 57 A3
Stadmorslow La ST7 26 C2
Stafford Ave ST5 71 B3
Stafford Brook Rd
WS15 195 C4
Stafford Castle* ST16 155 A1
Stafford Cl Stone ST15 120 A4
Walsall WS3 243 A1
Stafford Coll ST16 155 B2
Stafford Cres
Newcastle-u-L ST5 71 B2
Whittington WS14 232 B2
Stafford Ct WV10 240 B3
Stafford Gram Sch
ST18 174 B3
Stafford La
Cannock WS12 210 A3
Codsall WV8 238 C1
Hanley ST1 282 B3
Stafford Rd
Brewood WV10 224 B3
Cannock WS11 209 B1
Eccleshall ST21 133 C3
Gnosall ST20 171 C3
Huntington WS11,WS12 209 B3
Lichfield WS13 213 C1
Newport TF10 169 A2
Stone ST15 120 A3
Uttoxeter ST14 125 C3
Walsall WS3 243 A2
Weston ST18 138 B2
Wolv WV10 240 B2
Stafford St
Brewood ST19 223 B3
Burton u T DE14 166 B3
Cannock WS12 210 C1
Eccleshall ST21 133 C4
Hanley ST1 282 B3
Market Drayton TF9 97 B1
Newcastle-u-L ST5 284 C2
Newport TF10 168 C2
Stafford ST16 155 C2
Stone ST15 120 A4
Stafford Sta ST16 155 B1
Staffordshire Coll (North
Walls Annexe) ST16 155 C2
Staffordshire Ct ST18 156 B2
Staffordshire General Hospl
ST16 156 A2
Staffordshire Regiment Mus
The* WS14 232 B1
Staffordshire Tech Pk
ST18 156 B3
Staffordshire Univ (Lichfield
Ctr) WS13 231 A4
Staffordshire Univ (Stafford
Campus) ST18 156 B3
Staffordshire Univ Stoke
Campus) ST4 72 B4
Stag Cl WS15 178 A1
Stag Cres WS11 228 A3
Stag Dr WS12 209 B3
Stagborough Way
WS12 210 A2
Staines Ct ST15 120 B4
Staite Dr DY10 280 A3
Staithe Terr DY10 280 A3
Stakenbridge La DY10 281 B2
Staley Croft WS12 209 B2
Stalling's La DY6 275 B4
Stallings La DY6 271 A1
Stallington Cl ST11 90 B2
Stallington Gdns ST11 90 C3
Stallington Rd ST11 90 B2
Stamer St ST4 72 A3
Stamford Cres WS7 229 A4
Stamford St DY8 279 C4
Stamford Way WS9 245 B1
Stamps Cl DE15 167 B2
Standard St ST4 72 B3
Standedge B77 262 A4
Standersfoot Pl ST6 42 A3
Standhills Rd DY6 275 C3
Standing Butts Cl DE12 202 B4
Stanfield Cres ST10 76 B1
Stanfield Rd ST6 42 A1
Stanfield St 4 ST3 73 B3
Stanford Cl ST19 192 C1
Stanford Rd WV2 266 B4
Stanhope Ho B79 250 A2
Stanhope St
Burton u T DE15 167 A2
Hanley ST1 282 A1
Stanier St Fenton ST4 72 C3
Newcastle-u-L ST5 284 B3
Stanley Bank ST9 44 A3
Stanley Cl DE12 219 C4
Stanley Cres ST14 111 A1
Stanley Ct WV6 254 C2
Stanley Dr
Newcastle-u-L ST5 40 B1
Swindon DY3 269 C1
Stanley Gr
Newcastle-u-L ST5 56 B1
Norton-in-t-M ST2 43 A1
Stanley Matthews Sports Ctr
ST4 72 B4
Stanley Matthews Way
Fenton ST4 72 B2
Trentham ST4 88 B4
Stanley Moss La ST9 43 C3
Stanley Moss Rd ST9 43 C3
Stanley Rd Bagnall ST9 43 C2
Biddulph ST8 16 B1
Cannock WS12 210 A3
Newcastle-u-L ST5 56 C1
Stoke-on-T ST4 71 C4
Stourbridge DY8 279 C2
Wolv WV10 240 B1
Stanley St Biddulph ST8 27 B4
Burton u T DE14 166 B1
Leek ST13 30 C3
Tunstall ST6 41 C2
Walsall WS3 243 B1
Stansgate Pl ST1 282 A4
Stanshope La DE6 35 B1
Stansmore Rd ST3 74 A1
Stanton Ave DY1 271 C3
Stanton Cl ST5 55 C1
Stanton La DE6 65 C1
Stanton Prim Sch DE15 186 A3
Stanton Rd
Burton u T DE15 185 C4
Meir ST3 74 A1
Stanway Ave ST6 57 B4
Stanway Cl ST14 126 A3
Stanways La ST8 17 A1
Stapenhill Rd DE15 166 C1
Stapleford Gdns WS7 229 B3
Stapleford Gr DY8 275 C1
Stapleton Cres ST3 73 A1
Star & Garter Rd ST3 89 C4
Star Bank ST10 78 B4
Star St WV3 265 C4
Starkey's La ST19 205 B4
Starling Cl ST7 26 B2
Startley La WS15 196 C1
Starwood Rd ST3 89 C4
Starwood Terr ST10 78 A3
Statfold La Alrewas DE13 200 C2
Alrewas, Fradley WS13 215 B4
Statham St ST1 282 A2
Station App Stone ST15 104 C1
Sutton Coldfield B74 257 C3
Station Bridge Rd ST4 72 C3
Station Cl WV8 238 C2
Station Cotts ST5 85 B3
Station Cres ST6 42 B1
Station Ct TF10 169 A1
Station Dr
Armitage WS15 198 A2
Blakedown DY10 281 B1
Keele ST5 69 B4
Penkridge WV10 224 B3
Station Gr ST2 43 A1
Station La
Rushton Spencer SK11 8 A1
Walton-on-T DE12 184 B1
Station Rd
Albrighton WV7 237 A3
Aldridge WS9 256 A3
Alton ST10 78 C1
Audley ST7 54 B4
Barlaston ST12 88 B1
Barton-u-N DE13 183 C1
Biddulph ST8 16 B1
Burntwood WS7 229 C2
Cannock WS12 210 B3
Cheadle ST10 76 B1
Chebsey ST15 118 C1
Cheddleton ST13 45 B3
Codsall WV8 238 C2
Endon ST9 43 C4
Gnosall ST20 171 B3
Great Wyrley WS6 226 C2
Haughton ST18 172 C4
Hixon ST18 139 B2
Keele ST5 69 C4
Kidsgrove ST7 25 C1
Kidsgrove, Newchapel ST7 26 C1
Lichfield WS13 231 A4
Madeley CW3 68 C3
Madeley, Onneley CW3 68 A1
Millmeece ST15 118 B3
Mow Cop ST7 26 B4
Newcastle-u-L ST5 55 A1
Newport TF10 168 C1
Penkridge ST19 192 C1
Penkridge, Four Ashes
WV10 224 B3
Rolleston DE13 147 B2
Rugeley WS15 178 C1
Scholar Green ST7,CW12 26 A4
Shenstone WS14 246 C3
Stafford ST16 155 B1
Standon ST21 102 B2
Stoke-on-T ST4 72 A4
Stone ST15 104 C1
Uttoxeter ST14 126 B4
Walsall WS3 244 A2
Wombourne WV5 270 A4
Station Rd DE6 144 B4
Station St Burslem ST6 56 B4
Burton u T DE14 166 B2
Cheslyn Hay WS6 226 C2
Leek ST13 30 B3
Station View ST3 74 A1
Station Wlks ST7 54 B4
Station Yd DE13 201 A1
Staunton Rd WS3 243 A2
Staveley Cl ST2 58 A2
Staveley Pl ST5 55 A1
Steadman Cres ST17 174 C3
Stedman St ST1 282 C4
Steel St ST4 71 C4
Steele Ave ST6 42 A1
Steele Cl ST13 45 B3
Steelhouse La WV2 266 C4
Steenwood La WS15 160 A1
Steere Ave B79 250 B4
Stellar St ST6 42 B1
Stenbury Cl WV10 240 C2
Step Row 12 ST13 30 C3
Stephen Ave ST10 61 B1
Stephens Rd DE14 185 A4
Stephens Way ST7 39 C1
Stephens Wlk WS13 214 A1
Stephenson Cl B77 251 A1
Stephenson Dr WV6 254 C3
Stephenson Way WS12 210 A3
Stepping Stones WS15 178 B1
Steps Gdns ST18 172 C3
Sterndale Dr Fenton ST4 73 A3
Newcastle-u-L ST5 71 A2
Sterndale Moor SK17 5 C3
Sterrymere Gdns DY7 278 A2
Stevens Dr WS12 210 B3
Stevens Gate 8 WV2 266 B4
Stevenson Dr ST17 174 B4
Stevenson Rd
Bucknall ST2 58 A2
Doveridge DE6 127 A4

Stevenson Rd *continued*
Tamworth B79 . . . . .250 A3
Stevenson Wlk WS14 . . . .231 A3
Steventon Pl ST6 . . . . .56 C4
Stewart Cl DE14 . . . . .185 A3
Stewart Ct ST12 . . . . .58 B1
Stewart Rd
Brownhills WS9 . . . . .245 A2
Kingswinford DY6 . . . . .275 B2
Stewart St Fenton ST4 . . . . .72 B3
Wolv WV2 . . . . .266 B4
Stewkins DY8 . . . . .279 C4
Stickley La DY3 . . . . .271 B2
Stile Cl Biddulph ST8 . . . . . .27 A3
Rugeley WS15 . . . . .196 C3
Stile Cop Rd WS15 . . . . . .196 B2
Stile House La ST13 . . . . . . .31 C3
Stirling Cl ST2 . . . . .73 C4
Stirling Pl WS11 . . . . .226 A4
Stirling Rise DE13 . . . . . . .166 B4
Stirling St 1 ST6 . . . . .57 A4
Stitchings The DE6 . . . . . . .65 B1
Stock La ST14 . . . . .143 A4
Stockbridge Cl WV6 . . . . .254 C1
Stockfield Rd 2 ST3 . . . . .89 C4
Stockford La WS17 . . . . . .216 A2
Stockhay La WS7 . . . . .229 B3
Stockholm Gr ST1 . . . . .57 C4
Stocking La ST18 . . . . .153 A3
Stocking-gate La ST18 . . .153 C1
Stockings La
Longdon WS15 . . . . .197 B1
Wheaton Aston ST19 . . . . .205 B3
Stocks La ST14 . . . . .125 B4
Stockton La ST17 . . . . .175 C4
Stockwell End WV6 . . . . . .255 B3
Stockwell Gr ST3 . . . . .73 B2
Stockwell Rd WV6 . . . . . . .255 B3
Stockwell St ST13 . . . . .30 C3
Stoke Bsns Pk ST14 . . . . . .72 A3
Stoke Rd ST4 . . . . .57 A1
Stoke Recn Ctr ST14 . . . . .72 A3
Stoke Ski Ctr ST4 . . . . .56 C3
Stoke's La WS11 . . . . .227 C4
Stoke-on-Trent Coll ST1 . .57 A1
Stoke-on-Trent Sta ST4 . . .72 A4
Stokebay Dr ST10 . . . . .76 C2
Stokesay Ave WV6 . . . . . .254 C2
Stokesay Gr ST6 . . . . .57 A4
Stokesay Rise DY1 . . . . . . .271 C2
Stone Bank Rd ST7 . . . . . . .41 A4
Stone Bsns Pk ST15 . . . . .120 A3
Stone Chair La ST7 . . . . . . .25 C4
Stone Cotts Clifton DE6 . . . .81 C4
Congleton CW12 . . . . .6 C1
Stone Cross ST9 . . . . .192 C1
Stone Ent Ctr ST15 . . . . . .120 A2
Stone La DY7 . . . . .278 A2
Stone Pine Cl WS12 . . . . .209 C4
Stone Rd Chedsey ST21 . . .134 A4
Eccleshall ST21 . . . . .133 C4
Stafford ST16 . . . . .155 B3
Stoke-on-T ST4 . . . . .71 C1
Tittensor ST4,ST12 . . . . .88 A1
Trentham ST4 . . . . .87 C4
Uttoxeter ST14 . . . . .124 A4
Stone St ST4 . . . . .72 A4
Stone Sta ST15 . . . . .104 C1
Stoneacre CI WV3 . . . . . . .255 A1
Stonebridge Rd ST19 . . . .223 B3
Stonecrop Cl WS8 . . . . . . .244 B3
Stonefield Sq ST15 . . . . . .105 A1
Stonehaven B77 . . . . .250 C3
Stonehaven Gr ST1 . . . . . .282 C1
Stonehill Wlk B77 . . . . . . .261 C3
Stonehouse Cres ST9 . . . . .59 A2
Stonehouse Dr B74 . . . . . .257 B2
Stonehouse Rd
Caverswall ST9 . . . . .59 A2
Rugeley WS15 . . . . .178 A1
Stoneleigh Cl ST18 . . . . . .174 B3
Stoneleigh Gdns WV8 . . .238 C2
Stoneleigh Rd ST6 . . . . . . .42 A3
Stoneleigh Way DY3 . . . . .271 B3
Stonepine Cl ST17 . . . . . . .175 B4
Stonepit B77 . . . . .250 B1
Stonewall Pl ST5 . . . . .55 B1
Stonewell La SK17 . . . . . . .24 B3
Stonewood Cl ST4 . . . . . . .71 C2
Stoney Brook Leys WV5 . .269 C3
Stoney Croft WS11 . . . . . .209 C1
Stoney Dale ST10 . . . . .77 C2
Stoney La Endon ST9 . . . . .43 C4
Hagley DY9 . . . . .281 C2
Walsall WS3 . . . . .243 B2
Waterhouses ST10 . . . . .63 B3
Wheaton Aston ST19 . . . . .206 B2
Wolv WV4 . . . . .266 A3
Stoney Lea Rd WS11 . . . . .209 C1
Stoneycroft ST2 . . . . .43 A1
Stoneydale Cl DE11 . . . . . .186 C3
Stoneydelph Prim Sch
B77 . . . . .251 A1
Stoneyfields ST8 . . . . .28 A4
Stoneyfields Ave ST2 . . . . .43 A1
Stoneyfields Cl 3
WS11 . . . . .209 C1
Stoneyfields Ct ST5 . . . . . .284 D4
Stoneyford Terr ST14 . . . .126 B3
Stoneywell La
Longdon WS15 . . . . .213 A3
Longdon WS15 . . . . .212 C3
Stonier Dr ST14 . . . . .141 B4

Stonnall Gate WS9 . . . . . .256 B4
Stonnall Rd WS9 . . . . .256 B4
Stonor Rd ST4 . . . . .57 A3
Stony La ST10 . . . . .49 B1
Stonydelph La B77 . . . . . . .262 A4
Stonyford La WS15 . . . . . .179 C2
Stormont Cl ST6 . . . . .42 B1
Stour B77 . . . . .262 A2
Stour Cl Burntwood WS7 . .229 B3
Hilton DE65 . . . . .147 C4
Stourbridge Coll DY8 . . . .279 C3
Stourbridge Rd
Blakedown DY9 . . . . .281 C1
Cookley DY10 . . . . .280 B1
Himley WV5,DY3 . . . . .270 A3
Kidderminster DY10 . . . . . .280 B1
Wombourne WV5,DY3 . . . . .270 A3
Stourton Cres DY7 . . . . . .278 A4
Stourton Dr WV4 . . . . .265 B3
Stowe Hill Gdns WS13 . . .214 B1
Stowe La ST18 . . . . .139 B1
Stowe Rd WS13 . . . . .231 B4
Stowe St WS13 . . . . .231 B4
Stovecroft WS13 . . . . .214 B1
Stowford Gr ST4 . . . . .88 A4
Stradbroke Dr ST13 . . . . . .73 A1
Straight Mile WV10 . . . . . .225 A3
Straits Gn DY3 . . . . .271 A2
Straits Prim Sch DY3 . . . .271 A3
Straits Rd DY3 . . . . .271 A2
Straits The DY3 . . . . .271 A2
Strand Cl ST2 . . . . .58 A1
Strand Pas ST13 . . . . .283 B4
Strand The ST13 . . . . .283 B3
Strangman St ST13 . . . . . . .30 C3
Stranraer Cl ST13 . . . . .74 A2
Stratford Ave ST5 . . . . .56 C2
Stratford Cl
Forsbrook ST11 . . . . .91 A4
Norton-in-H At ST6 . . . . . . .42 C1
Sedgley DY1 . . . . .271 C1
Stratford Dr WS9 . . . . .256 B4
Stratford Way WS11 . . . . .209 C3
Stratheden Rd ST6 . . . . . . .42 A1
Strathfield Wlk WV3,
WV4 . . . . .265 B3
Strathmore Cres WV5 . . . .265 A1
Strathmore Pl 6 WS11 . . .209 C1
Strawberry La WS6 . . . . . .224 C4
Strawmoor La WV8 . . . . . .238 B2
Stream Mdw WS4 . . . . . . .248 B1
Stream Pk DY6 . . . . .275 C2
Stream Rd DY6,DY8 . . . . . .275 B2
Streamside Cl ST19 . . . . . .207 C4
Streather Rd B75 . . . . .258 B1
Street The ST20 . . . . .150 C3
Streetly Cres ST4 . . . . .257 B2
Streetly Dr B74 . . . . .257 B2
Streetly La B74 . . . . .257 B1
Streetly Wood B74 . . . . . .257 A1
Streets Corner Gdns
WS9 . . . . .245 A2
Streets La WS6 . . . . .226 C1
Streetway Rd WS14 . . . . . .247 A4
Stretton Ave
Newport TF10 . . . . .168 C1
Stafford ST16 . . . . .155 A3
Stretton Brook Sch
DE13 . . . . .147 B1
Stretton Gdns WV8 . . . . . .238 C2
Stretton Rd
Newcastle-u-L ST5 . . . . . . .54 C1
Walsall WV12 . . . . .242 B1
Wheaton Aston ST19 . . . . .206 A3
Stretton St B77 . . . . .250 C2
Strine Way TF10 . . . . .168 C2
Stringer Cl B75 . . . . .258 A2
Stringer's St ST4 . . . . .27 B4
Stringers Hill WS12 . . . . . .210 B4
Strode Ho B79 . . . . .250 A2
Strode Rd WV2 . . . . .266 B3
Stroma Cl 4 ST6 . . . . .56 C4
Stross Ave ST6 . . . . .41 C3
Stroud Cl ST3 . . . . .90 A4
Stuart Ave
Draycott in t M ST11 . . . . . .91 B3
Trentham ST4 . . . . .88 A4
Stuart Cl ST15 . . . . .119 C3
Stuart Cl N ST15 . . . . .119 C3
Stuart Gr ST5 . . . . .56 B2
Stuart Rd ST11 . . . . .57 C1
Stuart Way TF9 . . . . .97 A1
Stubbers Green Rd
Aldridge WS9 . . . . .256 A4
Walsall WS4 . . . . .244 B1
Stubbs Dr ST15 . . . . .120 B4
Stubbs La ST1 . . . . .282 C2
Stubbs Rd WV3 . . . . .266 A3
Stubbs St ST6 . . . . .56 C4
Stubbs' Gate ST5 . . . . .284 C2
Stubbs Rd WV3 . . . . .266 A3
Stubbsfield Rd ST5 . . . . . .284 C1
Stubby La DE6 . . . . .144 A3
Stubwood Hollow ST14 . . .95 B3
Stubwood La ST14 . . . . . . .95 B2
Sud Farm Cotts B78 . . . . .249 C1
Studley Gate DY8 . . . . . . .279 B3
Studley Rd WV3 . . . . .265 B4
Sturgeon's Hill WS14 . . . .231 B4
Sturgess St ST4 . . . . .72 A3
Sturbrook Gdns WS13 . . . .214 A1
Stychfields ST17 . . . . .155 C1
Suckling Green La WV8 . .238 C1
Sudbourne Cl ST7 . . . . .41 C4
Sudbury Hall & Mus of
Childhood* DE6 . . . . .128 B3
Sudbury Pk DE6 . . . . .128 B4
Sudbury Pl ST5 . . . . .71 A1

Sudbury Prim Sch DE6 . . .128 C2
Sudbury Rd DE13 . . . . . . .182 A2
Sudeley B77 . . . . .261 B4
Sudeley Gdns DY7 . . . . . . .271 B1
Sudgrove Pl ST3 . . . . .90 A4
Sudlow St ST6 . . . . .57 A4
Suffolk Cl WV9 . . . . .256 A4
Suffolk Cl ST5 . . . . .71 B2
Suffolk Gr WS9 . . . . .256 A4
Suffolk Rd
Burton u T DE15 . . . . .185 B4
Meir ST3 . . . . .89 B4
Sugar Loaf La DY10 . . . . . .281 A4
Sugnall Bsns Ctr ST21 . . .116 B1
Sullivan Way ST13 . . . . . . .214 B1
Sullivan Wlk WS13 . . . . . .214 B1
Sunbeam Dr WS6 . . . . . . .226 C2
Summer Dr WV3 . . . . .271 B2
Summer Gr ST13 . . . . .214 B1
Summer Hill DY6 . . . . .275 B3
Summer La Sedgley DY3 . .271 B2
Walsall WS9 . . . . .244 B1
Summer Row ST3 . . . . . . .283 C2
Summer St
Kingswinford DY6 . . . . .275 B3
Stoke-on-T ST4 . . . . .72 A3
Stourbridge DY8 . . . . .279 C3
Summerbank Prim Sch
ST6 . . . . .41 B2
Summerbank Rd ST6 . . . . .41 B2
Summercourt Dr DY6 . . . .275 B3
Summercourt Sq DY6 . . . .275 B3
Summerfield ST7 . . . . .26 A1
Summerfield Ave DY6 . . . .275 B4
Summerfield Cl B77 . . . . . .250 B2
Summerfield Dr ST14 . . . .126 A4
Summerfield Rd
Burntwood WS7 . . . . .229 A3
Tamworth B77 . . . . .250 B2
Summerfields ST15 . . . . . .118 C3
Summergate DY3 . . . . .271 B2
Summerhill WS14 . . . . . . .245 C4
Summerhill Dr ST5 . . . . . . .40 B1
Summerhill Gdns TF9 . . . .112 B4
Summerhill La ST18 . . . . . .153 C3
Summerhill Sch DY6 . . . . .275 A3
Summerhouse Gr TF10 . . .168 C2
Summerside Ave ST21 . . . .211 B2
Summervale Rd DY9 . . . . .281 C3
Summerville Rd ST14 . . . . .71 C2
Summit Pl DY3 . . . . .271 A2
Sun St Cheadle ST10 . . . . . .76 C2
Hanley ST1 . . . . .282 A2
Sunbeam Cl B77 . . . . .250 C2
Sunbeam St WV2 . . . . .266 B4
Sunbury Ave WS14 . . . . . .231 A3
Sunbury Cl ST14 . . . . .88 B3
Sundorne Pl ST2 . . . . .58 A1
Sundour Cres WV11 . . . . .241 A1
Sundown Dr ST7 . . . . .174 A4
Sundridge Wlk WV4 . . . . .265 B3
Sunfield Rd WS3 . . . . .209 A1
Suningdale DE13 . . . . .147 B1
Sunley Dr WS12 . . . . .210 B4
Sunningdale Stone ST15 . .120 A4
Sunningdale Ave
Tamworth B77 . . . . .251 B3
Sunningdale Ave WS9 . . . .254 B3
Sunningdale Cl
Chell Heath ST6 . . . . .42 A2
Stourbridge DY8 . . . . .279 C1
Sunningdale Dr ST16 . . . . .156 B2
Sunningdale Gr ST5 . . . . . .55 C4
Sunningdale Rd DY3 . . . . .266 A1
Sunningdale Way WS3 . . .243 A2
Sunny Bank Burslem ST6 . .56 C3
Sunny Hill Cl WV5 . . . . . . .270 A3
Sunny Hollow ST5 . . . . . . .56 B2
Sunny Side ST10 . . . . .61 B2
Sunnybank Cl WV9 . . . . . .256 C1
Sunnybank Rd DY3 . . . . . .266 A2
Sunnycroft Ave ST3 . . . . . .283 A1
Sunnyfield Oval ST2 . . . . . .43 B1
Sunnyhills Rd ST13 . . . . . . .30 B2
Sunnymead Rd WS7 . . . . .212 A1
Sunnymede Rd 1 DY6 . . .275 C2
Sunnyside
Brownhills WS9 . . . . .245 A1
Swadlincote DE11 . . . . . . .186 C4
Sunnyside Ave ST6 . . . . . . .41 C2
Sunnyside Rd ST14 . . . . . .111 A1
Sunridge Ave WV5 . . . . . . .270 A4
Sunridge Cl ST2 . . . . .43 A1
Sunrise Hill WS13 . . . . . . .210 A3
Sunset Cl Brewood WV9 . .224 A2
Great Wyrley WS6 . . . . . . .226 C2
Sunset Pl WV4 . . . . .266 C2
Sunwell Gdns ST10 . . . . . . .76 C2
Surrey Cl Cannock WS11 . .226 C4
Rugeley WS15 . . . . .196 B3
Surrey Dr
Kingswinford DY6 . . . . .275 C2
Tamworth B78 . . . . .250 A1
Wolv WV3 3 DY8 . . . . .255 C1
Surrey Rd DY8 . . . . .279 C3
Surrey Rd Kidsgrove ST7 . .26 A1
Stafford ST17 . . . . .174 B4
Surrey Wlk WS9 . . . . .245 A1
Surtees St ST4 . . . . .73 A3
Sussex Ave WS9 . . . . .245 A4
Sussex Dr Cannock WS12 . .210 A3
Kidsgrove ST7 . . . . .25 C1
Wolv WV3 . . . . .255 C1
Sussex Pl ST3 . . . . .73 B1
Sussex Rd DE15 . . . . .185 C3

Sutherland Ave
Longton ST3 . . . . .283 B1
Wolv WV2 . . . . .266 C4
Sutherland Cres ST11 . . . . .90 C3
Sutherland Dr
Newcastle-u-L ST5 . . . . . . .70 C3
Wombourne WV5 . . . . .265 A1
Sutherland Gr WV6 . . . . . .255 B3
Sutherland Prim Sch
ST3 . . . . .72 C1
Sutherland Rd
Cheslyn Hay WS6 . . . . .226 C1
Longsdon ST9 . . . . .30 A1
Longton ST3 . . . . .283 C3
Stone ST15 . . . . .120 B4
Tittensor ST12 . . . . .88 A1
Wolv WV4 . . . . .266 A3
Sutherland St ST4 . . . . .72 B3
Sutton Ave B78 . . . . .250 A4
Sutton Cl WS15 . . . . .196 C3
Sutton Ct WV4 . . . . .266 C3
Sutton Dr Stafford ST16 . . .155 A2
Stoke-on-T ST4 . . . . .71 C2
Sutton La WS14 . . . . .112 B2
Sutton Pl ST6 . . . . .42 C3
Sutton Rd Aldridge WS9 . .256 A1
Drayton Bassett B78 . . . . .260 A4
Tamworth B78 . . . . .249 B1
Sutton St
Brierley Hill DY8 . . . . .275 C1
Newcastle-u-L ST5 . . . . . . .55 C3
Sutton Way TF9 . . . . .112 A4
Swadlincote La DE11 . . . . .186 C1
Swaffham Way ST2 . . . . . . .58 B1
Swaffield Pk WS11 . . . . . .210 A1
Swainsfield Rd DE13 . . . . .182 A1
Swainsley Cl BS 3 ST6 . . . .57 A4
Swaledale Ave CW12 . . . . . .6 A3
Swallow Cl
Huntington WS12 . . . . .209 B4
3 Kidsgrove ST7 . . . . .26 A1
Meir ST3 . . . . .90 A4
Rugeley WS15 . . . . .178 B1
Uttoxeter ST14 . . . . .126 A3
Swallow Croft Leek ST13 . .30 C2
Lichfield WS13 . . . . .214 A1
Swallow Wlk ST6 . . . . .27 B4
Swallowdale
Brownhills WS9 . . . . .245 A2
B 1 Stafford ST17 . . . . . . .175 B4
Wolv WV6 . . . . .254 C1
Swallowfall Ave WV8 . . . .279 B2
Swallowfield 2 B77 . . . . .249 C3
Swallowfields Dr ST12 . . .210 A2
Swallowfields Rd DY3 . . . .266 B1
Swallowmore View ST7 . . .40 B4
Swallows Cl WS3 . . . . .244 A3
Swan Bank Talke ST7 . . . . .40 B4
Wolv WV4 . . . . .265 C2
Swan Cl Blakedown DY10 . .281 A1
Cheslyn Hay WS6 . . . . .224 B3
Longdon WS15 . . . . .197 C1
Rugeley WS15 . . . . .197 A3
Stafford ST16 . . . . .155 B1
Talke ST7 . . . . .40 B4
Swan Corner Sh Ctr
WS7 . . . . .229 B3
Swan Cotts WS14 . . . . . . .232 C3
Swan Ct Burton u T DE14 . .166 C2
Church Eaton ST20 . . . . . .190 A4
Swan Farm La CW3 . . . . . .67 A1
Swan La
Abbots Bromley WS15 . . . .161 A3
Kingswinford DY8 . . . . .275 C1
Penkridge ST18 . . . . .192 C3
Shareshill WV10 . . . . .225 A3
Stoke-on-T ST4 . . . . .71 C2
Swan Mews WS13 . . . . . . .231 A4
Swan Pas ST11 . . . . .90 C4
Swan Pool Gr WS4 . . . . . .244 B1
Swan Rd
Draycott in t C DE6 . . . . . .144 B3
Lichfield WS13 . . . . .231 A4
Whittington WS14 . . . . .232 C3
Swan Sq ST6 . . . . .56 C4
Swan St Stoke-on-T ST4 . . .72 A4
Stourbridge DY8 . . . . .279 C3
Swan Village DY3 . . . . .266 A1
Swan Wlk DE14 . . . . .166 B1
Swanage Cl ST3 . . . . .90 A4
Swancote Dr WV4 . . . . . . .265 B3
Swanfield Rd DY8 . . . . . . .275 C1
Swanfields WS7 . . . . .229 B3
Swanholme Way ST5 . . . . . .85 B2
Swanland Gr ST3 . . . . .73 B2
Swanmere TF10 . . . . .168 C3
Swanmore Cl WV3 . . . . . . .265 C4
Swannymore Cl WV3 . . . . .265 A2
Swannington St DE13 . . . .166 A3
Swanton Pl ST14 . . . . .87 C4
Swarbourn Cl DE13 . . . . . .182 A1
Swaythling Gr ST2 . . . . .58 B1
Sweetbriar Way
Cannock WS12 . . . . .210 B1
Stafford ST17 . . . . .175 B3
Sweetbrier Dr 5 DY8 . . . .275 C1
Sweetman St WV6 . . . . . . .255 C2
Sweetlace La ST20 . . . . . . .189 C1
Sweetpool La DY9 . . . . . . .281 C3
Swift B77 . . . . .250 C2
Swift Cl Kidsgrove ST7 . . . .26 A1
Uttoxeter ST14 . . . . .126 A3
Swift Ho ST4 . . . . .27 C4
Swift Pl ST3 . . . . .73 C2
Swin Forge Way DY3 . . . . .269 C1
Swinburne Cl Longton ST3 .72 C1
Stafford ST17 . . . . .174 B4
Swindale B77 . . . . .261 A4
Swindon Rd DY6 . . . . .275 A4

Swinfen Broun Rd
WS13 . . . . .231 A4
Swinford Leys WV5 . . . . . .269 B3
Swingle Hill Rd ST3 . . . . . .72 C2
Swinscoe Hill DE6 . . . . . . .66 A1
Swinson Cl ST14 . . . . .96 A2
Swiss Dr DY8 . . . . .275 C1
Swiss Lodge Dr B78 . . . . .260 C4
Swithin Dr ST4 . . . . .73 A3
Swynnerton Dr WV11 . . . .241 C2
Sycamore B77 . . . . .250 C2
Sycamore Cl Biddulph ST8 .16 C1
Blythe Bridge ST3 . . . . .90 A3
Brereton WS15 . . . . .185 C3
Stourbridge DY8 . . . . .279 C4
Talke ST7 . . . . .40 C4
Uttoxeter ST14 . . . . .125 C4
Sycamore Cres WS11 . . . .197 A3
Sycamore Dr Hixon ST18 . .158 B4
Wolv WV3 . . . . .255 B1
Sycamore Gn
Cannock WS11 . . . . .209 C3
Dudley DY1 . . . . .271 C3
Sycamore Gr Fenton ST3 . .72 C2
Newcastle-u-L ST5 . . . . . . .55 A4
Sycamore Green Prim Sch
DY1 . . . . .271 C3
Sycamore Hill WS15 . . . . .211 C3
Sycamore La ST17 . . . . . . .174 A4
Sycamore Rd
Burntwood WS7 . . . . .228 C4
Burton u T DE15 . . . . .185 C3
Cannock WS12 . . . . .210 C2
Kingswinford DY6 . . . . .275 C3
Mayfield DE6 . . . . .81 B4
Stone ST15 . . . . .120 A4
Sycamore Way
Huntington WS12 . . . . .209 B4
Market Drayton TF9 . . . . . . .97 B1
Sycamores The
Hagley DY9 . . . . .281 C2
Lichfield WS14 . . . . .231 A3
Sutton Coldfield B74 . . . . .257 C1
Sydenham Pl ST3 . . . . .73 B4
Sydnall La TF9 . . . . .112 C1
Sydney St
Burton u T DE14 . . . . .166 B3
Newcastle-u-L ST5 . . . . .56 B1
Syerscote La
Clifton Campville B79 . . . . .218 A1
Wigginton B79 . . . . .234 B1
Sykesmoor B77 . . . . .262 A4
Sylvan Gr ST14 . . . . .71 C2
Sylvan Way ST17 . . . . .175 B3
Sylvester St ST6 . . . . .57 A4
Sytch La WV5 . . . . .270 A3
Sytch Rd ST6 . . . . .43 A4

T

Tack Farm Rd DY8 . . . . . . .275 B1
Tadgedale Ave TF9 . . . . . . .99 B3
Tag La TF9 . . . . .113 C2
Tagg La DE45 . . . . .14 C4
Talaton Cl WV9 . . . . .240 A1
Talbot B77 . . . . .250 C2
Talbot Ave B74 . . . . .257 A2
Talbot Cl TF10 . . . . .168 B1
Talbot Fst Sch ST14 . . . . .141 B4
Talbot Rd Rugeley WS15 . .196 C3
Stafford ST17 . . . . .155 C1
Wolv WV2 . . . . .266 B3
Talbot St Hanley ST1 . . . . .282 C1
16 Leek WS15 . . . . .30 C3
Rugeley WS15 . . . . .196 C4
Talke La ST7 . . . . .40 A3
Talke Rd
Newcastle-u-L ST5,ST7 . . . .55 A4
Newcastle-u-L, Red Street
ST7,ST5 . . . . .40 B2
Tall Ash Ave CW12 . . . . .6 A2
Tall Trees Cl B74 . . . . .257 B2
Talland Ave B77 . . . . .250 C3
Tallis Gr ST3 . . . . .57 C3
Tallpines ST17 . . . . .175 B4
Tally Cl ST2 . . . . .73 B4
Talsarn Gr ST4 . . . . .88 B3
Tamar Cl WS8 . . . . .228 B1
Tamar Dr DY3 . . . . .271 C3
Tamar Gr Cheadle ST10 . . .76 C1
Perton WV6 . . . . .254 C2
Stafford ST17 . . . . .174 A4
Tamar Rd Kidsgrove ST7 . .26 A1
Tamworth B77 . . . . .262 A3
Tame Ave WS7 . . . . .229 B3
Tame Cl ST18 . . . . .16 A1
Tame Ct Fazeley B78 . . . . .261 A4
Tamworth B79 . . . . .250 A3
Tame Dr WS3 . . . . .244 A1
Tame Rd WV13 . . . . .226 B4
Tame St WS3 . . . . .244 B3
Tame St E WS3 . . . . .244 B3
Tame St B77 . . . . .250 B2
Tame Valley Bsns Ctr
B77 . . . . .261 C3
Tame Valley Ind Est
B77 . . . . .261 C4
Tame Wlk ST3 . . . . .74 A2
Tamedrive B78,B79 . . . . . .250 A2
Tamworth & Lichfield Coll
B79 . . . . .250 A3
Tamworth Bsns Ctr B77 . .251 A2
Tamworth Bsns Pk B77 . . .251 A2
Tamworth Castle* B79 . . .250 A2
Tamworth Castle Mus*
B79 . . . . .250 A2
Tamworth Rd Elford B79 . .233 C4

Tamworth Rd continued
Fazeley B78 ....261 B1
Lichfield WS14 ....231 C3
Polesworth B78 ....251 C1
Sutton Coldfield B75 ....259 A1
Tamworth B77 ....250 B1
Whittington WS14 ....232 A2
Wood End CV9 ....262 B3
Tamworth Rd (Amington)
B77 ....250 C3
Tamworth Rd (Dosthill)
B77 ....261 B3
Tamworth St WS13 ....231 A4
Tamworth Sta B79 ....250 B3
Tan Bank TF10 ....168 C2
Tanfield CI WV6 ....255 A2
Tanglewood Gr DY3 ....266 B1
Tangmere CI WV6 ....254 C3
Tanhill B77 ....262 B4
Tanners Rd ST2 ....58 A4
Tannery CI WS15 ....178 C1
Tansey CI ST2 ....58 A2
Tansley Green Rd DY6 ....271 A1
Tansley View WV2 ....266 B4
Tansy
Sutton Coldfield B74 ....257 C2
Tamworth B77 ....250 B2
Tanyard WS13 ....231 B4
Tape St ST10 ....76 C2
Taplin CI ST10 ....155 B4
Taplow PI WS11 ....209 C2
Tapton CI WS3 ....243 B2
Tara Gr ST2 ....43 A2
Targate CI WS15 ....198 A3
Tarleton St ST1 ....40 C3
Tarlton Rd ST11 ....57 C2
Tarporley Gr ST4 ....71 C3
Tarragon Dr ST3 ....90 A3
Tarragona Dr ST17 ....175 A4
Tarrant B77 ....261 C4
Tarwin Gr ST6 ....41 C3
Tasman Dr ST16 ....156 A3
Tasman Gr WV6 ....254 C3
Tasman Sq ST1 ....57 C3
Tatenhill Comm DE13 ....164 C1
Tatenhill La
Branston DE14 ....184 B4
Tatenhill DE13 ....184 A4
Tatenhill, Rangemoore
DE13 ....164 B1
Tatlovfold La ST10 ....48 C2
Tattenhall Coll (The Drive Sch) WV6 ....255 B4
Tattenall Arc WV6 ....255 B3
Tatton CI ST13 ....30 A3
Tatton St ST3 ....283 C2
Taunton Ave WV10 ....240 B2
Taunton PI ST5 ....55 C4
Taunton Way ST2 ....58 B1
Taurus Gr ST6 ....41 C3
Taverners CI WV12 ....242 B1
Taverners Dr ST15 ....120 B3
Tavistock Ave ST17 ....156 B1
Tavistock CI B79 ....250 B4
Tavistock Cres ST5 ....71 A3
Tavistock PI ST4 ....56 C1
Tawney CI ST7 ....26 A1
Tawney Cres ST3 ....74 A1
Tay CI Biddulph ST8 ....16 C1
Kingsley ST10 ....76 C3
Longton ST3 ....56 B2
Taylor Ave ST5 ....56 B2
Taylor Rd Bucknall ST2 ....58 A2
Wolv WV4 ....266 C3
Taylor St
Newcastle-u-L ST5 ....
Tunstall ST6 ....41 B4
Taylor Wlk ST17 ....174 B4
Taylor's La WS15 ....178 C1
Taylors La ST14 ....95 B2
Taynton CI ST6 ....42 A4
Teal CI ST5 ....85 B3
Teal View ST5 ....42 A3
Tean CI Burntwood WS7 ....229 B3
Burton u T DE15 ....167 A1
Tean Rd ST10 ....76 B1
Teanhurst CI ST10 ....92 C1
Teanhurst Rd ST10 ....92 C1
Teasel Gr WV10 ....241 A4
Tebworth CI WV9 ....239 C1
Tedder Rd ST16 ....156 A3
Teddesley CI WS11 ....209 C2
Teddesley Rd
Acton Trussell ST17,ST19 ....193 A3
Penkridge ST19 ....192 C1
Teddesley Way ST13 ....209 B3
Teign B77 ....262 A3
Telegraph St ST17 ....155 C1
Telford CI
Albrighton WV7 ....237 A3
Great Wyrley WS6 ....226 C2
Telford CI
Burntwood WS7 ....229 B4
Congleton CW12 ....6 A1
Stone ST15 ....120 B3
Talke ST7 ....40 C4
Telford Dr ST16 ....155 C4
Telford Gdns
Wolv WV3 ....265 B4
Telford Gr WS12 ....210 A4
Telford La ST20 ....171 B3
Telford Rd B79 ....249 C4
Telford Way ST6 ....42 A2
Tellwright Gr ST5 ....56 A4
Tellwright St ST6 ....42 A1
Telford CI DE13 ....147 B1
Teme Rd DY8 ....279 C2

Temperence PI ST6 ....41 B4
Tempest St B79 ....250 A3
Templar Cres ST5 ....56 A3
Templar Terr ST5 ....56 A3
Templars Way ST19 ....207 C4
Temple CI DE14 ....166 C4
Temple St Fenton ST4 ....72 B3
Sedgley DY3 ....271 B2
Templeton Ave ST2 ....72 A3
Ten Butts Cres ST17 ....174 C3
Tenacre La DY3 ....271 C3
Tenbury Ct WV4 ....265 B3
Tenbury Dr WS9 ....256 B4
Tenbury Gdns WV4 ....265 B3
Tenbury Gro ST2 ....58 B1
Tenby Dr ST16 ....155 C3
Tenby Gr ST5 ....55 C4
Tenford La ST10 ....92 B3
Tennant PI ST5 ....56 A4
Tennscore Ave WS14 ....
Tennyson Ave
Burntwood WS7 ....212 A1
Kidsgrove ST7 ....41 A4
Sutton Coldfield B74 ....257 C3
Tamworth B79 ....250 A3
Tennyson CI Cheadle ST10 ....76 A1
Market Drayton TF9 ....112 A4
Tennyson Gdns ST11 ....72 C1
Tennyson Rd
Burton u T DE14 ....166 B4
Essington WV10 ....241 A1
Sedgley DY3 ....271 A2
Stafford ST17 ....174 B4
Tenterbanks ST16 ....155 B2
Tercel Gr ST3 ....90 A4
Terence Wlk ST8 ....27 A1
Tern Ave ST7 ....26 B1
Tern CI Biddulph ST8 ....27 C4
Wolv WV4 ....266 B2
Tern Gr TF9 ....99 C2
Tern Ridge TF9 ....97 B1
Tern View TF9 ....112 A4
Terrace The Cheadle ST10 ....76 B2
Wolv WV3 ....255 B1
Terrington Dr ST5 ....73 A1
Terry CI Lichfield WS13 ....213 C1
Meir ST3 ....74 A2
Terson Way ST13 ....73 C2
Tettenhall Coll WV6 ....255 B2
Tettenhall Rd WV1,WV3,
WV6 ....255 C2
Tettenhall Wood Sch
WV6 ....255 A2
Teveray Dr ST19 ....207 C4
Tewe PI WS13 ....231 A3
Tewkesbury Gr ST2 ....58 A2
Tewkesbury Rd WS3 ....242 C1
Tewnals La WS13 ....213 C3
Tewson Dr ST6 ....57 B4
Thackeray Dr Longton ST3 ....73 A1
Tamworth B79 ....250 A3
Thackeray Wlk ST17 ....174 B4
Thames Dr Biddulph ST8 ....27 C4
Cheadle ST10 ....76 C1
Thames Ho DY3 ....271 B2
Thames Rd
Newcastle-u-L ST5 ....71 A2
Walsall WS3 ....243 C1
Thames Way ST17 ....174 A4
Thanet CI DY6 ....275 B4
Thanet Gr ST3 ....283 A3
Thatcham Gn ST3 ....88 C4
Thatcher Gr ST8 ....27 A4
Thatchmoor La DE13 ....182 B4
The Richard Heathcote Prim Sch ST7 ....56 A3
Thelma Ave ST6 ....43 A4
Theodore Rd ST2 ....58 A2
Theresa CI ST4 ....72 A1
Thicknall La DY9 ....281 C2
Third Ave Branston DE14 ....
Brownhills WS8 ....229 A1
Bucknall ST2 ....58 B2
Kidsgrove ST7 ....25 C1
Kingswinford DY6 ....275 C4
Thirlmere CI
Cannock WS11 ....209 C1
Wolv WV6 ....255 B4
Thirlmere Dr WV11 ....242 A1
Thirlmere Gr Longton ST3 ....73 C2
Perton WV6 ....254 C2
Thirlmere PI ST5 ....71 A3
Thirlmere Rd WV6 ....255 B4
Thirlmere Way ST17 ....174 C4
Thirsk PI ST5 ....55 A1
Thistle CI Rugeley WS15 ....178 B1
Sedgley DY3 ....271 B2
Thistle Down CI B74 ....257 A1
Thistleberry Ave ST5 ....71 C2
Thistledown Ave WS7 ....229 A3
Thistledown Dr
Cannock WS11 ....210 B1
Featherstone WV10 ....241 A4
Thistledown Wlk DY3 ....266 B1
Thistles The ST5 ....71 C2
Thistley Hough ST4 ....71 C3
Thistley Hough High Sch
ST4 ....
Thistley Nook ST4 ....214 A1
Thomas Alleyne's High Sch
ST14 ....126 B4
Thomas Ave
Newcastle-u-L ST5 ....55 A2
Stone ST15 ....120 B3
Thomas Barnes Prim Sch
B78 ....249 A4

Thomas Greenway
WS13 ....214 A1
Thomas Hardy Ct B79 ....250 A4
Thomas Ho WV5 ....243 B2
Thomas Russell Inf Sch
DE13 ....183 C1
Thomas Russell Jun Sch
DE13 ....183 C1
Thomas St Biddulph ST8 ....16 B1
Leek ST13 ....30 B3
Packmoor ST7 ....26 C1
Talke ST7 ....40 B4
Tamworth B77 ....250 B2
Wolv WV2 ....266 B4
Thompson Ave WV2 ....266 C3
Thompson CI ST17 ....174 B4
Thompson Rd WS15 ....197 A3
Thompstone Ave ST5 ....55 C2
Thor CI WS11 ....210 A3
Thoresby B79 ....249 C3
Thoresby Croft DY1 ....271 C2
Thorley's Hill WS15 ....212 B3
Thorn CI WS15 ....197 A4
Thorn Tree La DE11, ...
DE15 ....186 C4
Thornbridge Gr WS9 ....244 C2
Thornburrow Dr ST4 ....71 C4
Thornbury Ct WV6 ....255 A2
Thornby Ave B77 ....261 C4
Thorncliff Gr ST1 ....57 C3
Thorncliff Rd ST13 ....31 A4
Thorncliffe View ST13 ....31 A4
Thorndyke St ST1 ....282 A1
Thorne PI ST13 ....74 A2
Thornes Croft WS9 ....245 C2
Thornescroft Gdns
DE14 ....185 A4
Thornewill Dr DE13 ....147 C1
Thorney CI WV11 ....241 C1
Thorney Lanes ST14, ...
DE13 ....142 C3
Thorney Rd B74 ....256 C1
Thorneycroft Ave ST6 ....42 A1
Thorneyfields La ST17 ....31 A3
Thornfield Ave ST13 ....31 A4
Thornfield Cres B78 ....16 B1
Thornfield Croft DY3 ....271 C4
Thornham CI ST5 ....71 A1
Thornham Gn ST2 ....58 B1
Thornhill Ave DE13 ....183 B1
Thornhill Dr ST5 ....68 C4
Thornhill Rd Bucknall ST2 ....73 C4
Cannock WS12 ....209 C4
Leek ST13 ....30 A4
Little Aston B74 ....257 A1
Thornleigh DY3 ....271 B3
Thornley Croft WS6 ....226 B1
Thornley Rd WV10 ....76 C1
Thornley Rd
Chell Heath ST6 ....42 A2
Essington WV11 ....241 C1
Thornley St WV1 ....166 B3
Thornton Rd ST4 ....72 B4
Thorny Lanes DE13 ....162 B3
Thorny Lanes DE13 ....143 A1
Thornyedge Rd
Bagnall ST9 ....44 A1
Bagnall, Thorneyedge ST9 ....44 A5
Thornyfields La ST17 ....174 A4
Thornyhurst La WS14 ....246 A3
Thorpe Ave WS7 ....228 B4
Thorpe CI
Burntwood WS7 ....228 B4
Burton u T DE15 ....167 B1
Thorpe Gn ST3 ....88 C4
Thorpe Rise ST10 ....76 C3
Thorpe St WS7 ....228 B4
Thorswood La DE6 ....65 A1
Three Mile La ST5 ....69 C2
Three Spires Sh Ctr
WS13 ....213 C1
Three Tuns La WV10 ....240 B1
Three Tuns Par WV10 ....240 B1
Thrift Rd DE14 ....185 A4
Thurlstone Dr WV4 ....265 C2
Thurlstone Rd WS3 ....243 A2
Thurlwood Dr ST16 ....42 C1
Thurne B77 ....261 C4
Thursfield Ave ST7 ....26 B2
Thursfield PI ST6 ....42 B2
Thursfield Prim Sch ST7 ....26 C2
Thursfield Wlk ST6 ....42 B3
Thurso B77 ....250 C3
Thurston Way ST17 ....73 B4
Thurvaston Rd DE6 ....96 C1
Thyme Gr ST3 ....90 A3
Tibberton CI ST5 ....39 C1
Tibberton CI WV3 ....265 B4
Tiber Dr ST5 ....55 B3
Tickhill La ST10 ....75 A4
Tidebrook PI ST7 ....41 C4
Tideswell Gn DE11 ....186 C3
Tideswell Rd ST3 ....283 C5
Tierney St ST1 ....282 C4
Tiffany La WV9 ....239 C1
Tilbrook CI ST2 ....73 B4
Tilbury CI WV3 ....265 A4
Tilcon Ave ST18 ....156 B1
Tildesley CI ST19 ....207 C4
Tilehurst PI ST3 ....90 A4
Tilery La ST3,ST4 ....88 B4
Tilford CI ST4 ....72 C1
Tilia Rd B77 ....251 A3
Till Wlk ST3 ....74 B2
Tiller Gr B75 ....258 A2
Tillet Gn ST3 ....74 A2
Tilling Dr ST15 ....120 A3

Tillington Manor Prim Sch
ST16 ....155 B3
Tillington St ST16 ....155 B3
Tilson Ave ST14 ....71 C4
Tilstone CI ST7 ....41 A4
Timber Gr ST19 ....223 B3
Timber La ST14 ....126 A3
Timber Pit La ST19 ....205 A2
Timberfields ST15 ....116 C4
Timberfields Rd ST16 ....155 B2
Timble CI ST2 ....73 B4
Times Sq ST3 ....283 B4
Timmis St ST1 ....57 A1
Timor Gr ST4 ....88 A4
Timothy CI ST3 ....73 B3
Tinacre Hill WV6 ....254 C1
Tinker's Castle Rd WV5 ....263 B1
Tinker's La ST14 ....143 A4
Tinkers Green Rd B77 ....262 A3
Tinkers La Ashley TF9 ....100 A2
Brewood ST19 ....223 C3
Tintagel CI
Burton u T DE13 ....147 C1
Perton WV6 ....254 C2
Tintagel Dr DY1 ....271 C1
Tintagel PI ST2 ....73 B4
Tintern Cres WS3 ....242 C1
Tintern Ho WV6 ....254 C2
Tintern PI WS5 ....55 C4
Tintern St ST1 ....57 C2
Tintern Way WS3 ....242 C1
Tipping Ave ST3 ....74 A1
Tipping St ST16 ....155 C2
Tipton Rd DY3 ....271 C4
Tipton St DY3 ....271 C4
Tirley St ST4 ....72 C3
Tissington PI ST3 ....90 B4
Titan Way WS13 ....231 C4
Titchfield CI WV10 ....240 C2
Tithe Barn CI ST16 ....156 A2
Tithe Barn La WS15 ....212 B3
Tithe Barn Rd ST16 ....156 A2
Tithebarn Rd WS15 ....178 C1
Tittensor CE Fst Sch
ST12 ....88 A1
Tittensor Rd
Barlaston ST12 ....104 A4
Newcastle-u-L ST5 ....71 B3
Titterton La ST13 ....33 A2
Titterton St ST14 ....126 A3
Tittesworth Ave ST13 ....31 A4
Tittesworth Rd ST13 ....20 C2
Tiverton Ave ST17 ....175 B4
Tiverton CI DY6 ....275 C2
Tiverton Rd ST2 ....73 B4
Tixall CI ST18 ....157 C2
Tixall Mews ST18 ....157 B2
Tixall Rd
Stafford ST16,ST18 ....156 B2
Tixall ST18 ....157 A1
Toby's Hill DE6 ....144 B3
Toft End Rd ST1 ....41 A1
Tolkien Way ST4 ....72 A4
Toll Bar Rd ST9 ....57 B2
Toll Gate La B79 ....233 C2
Toldish La ST18 ....158 B2
Tollgate Ave ST5 ....85 B3
Tollgate CI ST7 ....40 B4
Tollgate Cotts DE6 ....81 C4
Tollgate Dr ST16 ....155 C1
Tollgate Ind Est ST16 ....155 C4
Tollgate Rd ST12 ....29 B3
Tollhouse Way WV5 ....269 C4
Tolman Dr B77 ....250 B2
Tolson Ave B78 ....261 A4
Tolson CI B77 ....261 B3
Tolworth Gdns WV2 ....266 C4
Tom Fields ST7 ....39 C1
Tom La DY3,DY7 ....268 C3
Tom Williams Way B77 ....261 B4
Tomkin Rd ST9 ....44 A1
Tomkinson CI TF10 ....169 A2
Tomlinson St ST6 ....56 B4
Tommy's La CW12 ....6 A2
Tonadine CI WV11 ....242 A1
Tonbridge Ave ST6 ....42 A2
Toney PI ST2 ....58 B1
Tong CI ST19 ....221 C4
Tong Rd ST19 ....221 C4
Tongue La ST6 ....42 C1
Tontine Sq ST1 ....282 B3
Tontine St ST1 ....282 B3
Tontines Sh Ctr The
ST1 ....282 B3
Tony Waddington PI ST4 ....72 B2
Toothill Rd ST14 ....126 B2
Top Chapel La ST6 ....28 A1
Top Heath Row ST16 ....43 A4
Top La ST4 ....87 B1
Top Rd
Acton Trussell ST17 ....175 A1
Bednall ST17 ....17 B2
Top Station Rd ST18 ....130 B4
Topham PI ST12 ....57 C2
Tor St ST1 ....57 C3
Tor Way WS3 ....243 B3
Torbay B77 ....250 C3
Torc Ave B77 ....250 B2
Torc High Sch B77 ....250 C1
Torfield WS8 ....229 A1
Torrance CI DE14 ....185 A4
Torrance Gr ST14 ....110 C1
Torres Wlk ST1 ....57 C3
Torridge B77 ....262 A3
Torridge Dr ST17 ....174 C4
Torridon CI ST14 ....88 B3
Torridon Rd WV9 ....239 C1
Torrington Ave ST17 ....175 C4

Torside B77 ....262 A4
Torvale Rd WV6 ....255 A1
Torville Dr ST8 ....27 C4
Totnes CI DE13 ....166 B4
Tower Bsns Pk WS15 ....197 A3
Tower CI Biddulph ST8 ....27 A3
Market Drayton TF9 ....97 A1
Tower Hill Rd ST7 ....26 C4
Tower Rd Ashley TF9 ....99 C2
Cannock WS12 ....167 A1
Cannock WS12 ....194 C1
Sutton Coldfield B75 ....258 A2
Tower Sq ST5 ....41 B2
Tower St DY3 ....266 B1
Tower View Prim Sch
DE15 ....167 B2
Tower View Rd WS6 ....242 C4
Tower Yard Ind Est ST13 ....30 B3
Town End ST10 ....76 B2
Town Head ST10 ....78 C1
Town Hill DE13 ....182 A1
Town Meadows Way
ST14 ....126 B4
Town Rd ST1 ....282 B4
Townend CI ST6 ....41 C4
Townend ST11 ....106 C4
Townend La Swinscoe DE6 ....65 C3
Waterhouses ST10 ....48 C2
Townfield CI ST7 ....25 B1
Townfields WS13 ....231 A4
Townfold WS3 ....244 A2
Townsend Ave ST3 ....271 B4
Townsend CI B79 ....236 B2
Townsend Ho B79 ....250 A2
Townsend La ST7 ....25 A4
Townsend PI Bucknall ST2 ....58 A2
Kingsenford DY6 ....275 B3
Townsend Prim Sch ST2 ....58 B2
Toy CI WS15 ....178 B1
TP Riley Com Sch WS3 ....243 B1
Trade St ST14 ....72 A4
Trafalgar CI WS12 ....210 C2
Trafalgar Ct ST16 ....57 A4
Trafalgar Rd ST4 ....71 C4
Trafalgar St ST1 ....282 B4
Trafford CI ST13 ....31 A3
Transport La ST3 ....283 B3
Tranter Cres WS11 ....210 A2
Tranter Rd ST2 ....58 A3
Tranwell CI WV9 ....239 C1
Travellers CI WS7 ....229 A3
Travers Ct ST4 ....72 B3
Travers St ST6 ....56 C4
Treasure CI B77 ....250 C2
Trecastle Gr ST3 ....73 C1
Treetops 7 ST17 ....175 B4
Trefoil B77 ....251 A3
Tregaron Cr ST2 ....72 B2
Tregaron CI 1 ST3 ....90 A4
Tregew PI ST5 ....55 B1
Tregony Rise WS14 ....231 B3
Tregowan Ct ST6 ....42 A2
Trenance CI WS14 ....231 B4
Trenchard Ave ST16 ....156 A3
Trent CI Burntwood WS7 ....229 B3
Cheadle ST10 ....76 C1
Colwich ST18 ....158 A1
Stafford ST16 ....155 C4
Stafford ST17 ....174 C3
Stone ST15 ....119 C4
Trent Ct ST15 ....119 C4
Trent Gr Biddulph ST8 ....27 B3
Newcastle-u-L ST5 ....71 A2
Trent Ho Cannock WS12 ....210 B3
Sedgley DY3 ....271 C2
Trent Ind Est DE14 ....166 C4
Trent La Colwich ST18 ....158 A1
Hixon ST18 ....157 C4
Newton Solney DE15 ....167 C4
Trent Rd Cannock WS11 ....209 C3
Forsbrook ST11 ....91 A4
Stone ST15 ....104 C1
Walsall WS3 ....244 A1
Trent St Bucknall ST2 ....57 B2
Burton u T DE14 ....166 B1
Trent Terr
Burton u T DE14 ....166 C2
Norton-in-t-M ST6 ....43 A3
Trent Vale CE Prim Sch
ST5 ....71 C2
Trent Valley Cotts
WS13 ....214 C1
Trent Valley Rd
Lichfield WS13,WS14 ....231 B4
Stoke-on-T ST4 ....71 C3
Trent Valley Trad Est
WS15 ....178 C2
Trent View CI WS15 ....197 A4
Trent Wlk Hanley ST1 ....282 C1
Ingestre ST18 ....157 C4
Trentfield La ST18 ....137 B3
Trentfields Rd ST2 ....43 A1
Trentham Bsns Ctr ST4 ....88 B4
Trentham Rd WS11 ....210 A1
Trentham Ct ST4 ....87 B1
Trentham Gardens CI
ST4 ....87 C4
Trentham Gdns* ST4 ....87 C4
Trentham High Sch ST4 ....56 B2
Trentham Rd
Longton ST3,ST4 ....88 C4
Whitmore ST5 ....86 C4
Trentham Rise WV2 ....266 C4
Trentley Gr ST4 ....88 A4
Trentley Rd ST4 ....88 A4

328 Tre – Vin

Trentmill Rd ST1 57 C1
Trentside Rd ST6 43 A3
Trentway Cl ST2 58 A2
Tresham Rd 3 DY6 275 B4
Trevelyan's Gn ST16 155 B4
Trevelyn Cl DE15 167 B1
Trevithick Cl Bucknall ST2 73 B4
Burntwood WS7 229 B4
Trevitt Pl ST19 205 B3
Trevor Ave WS6 227 A2
Trevor Dr ST11 74 B2
Trevor Rd WS3 243 C2
Trevose Cl WS3 242 C2
Triangle WS7 229 A2
Trimley Way ST2 58 A1
Trimpley Gdns WV4 265 C2
Trimpos ST10 76 A2
Triner Pl ST6 42 C2
Tring Cl ST2 73 B4
Tring Ct WV6 255 C2
Trinity Cl Cannock WS11 226 C4
Kingswinford DY8 275 B1
Shenstone WS14 246 C3
Trinity Ct
4 Congleton CW12 6 A1
Kinver DY7 278 A2
Newcastle-u-L ST5 55 C4
Trinity Dr Stone ST15 104 C1
Tamworth B79 249 B3
Trinity Gorse ST16 155 A4
Trinity Pl Bucknall ST2 58 A2
Congleton CW12 16 A4
Trinity Rd Eccleshall ST21 133 B3
Sutton Coldfield B75 258 B1
Uttoxeter ST14 126 B4
Trinity Rise ST16 155 A4
Trinity Sq ST14 126 B4
Trinity St ST1 282 B3
Trinity Wlk ST14 126 B4
Tristram Gr DE13 147 C1
Triton Cl WS6 226 C1
Triton Wlk ST6 42 B1
Triumph B77 250 C2
Trojan B77 250 C2
Troon B77 251 B2
Troon Cl Burton u T DE13 147 B1
Walsall WS3 243 A2
Troon Ct WV6 254 B3
Troon Pl DY8 275 B2
Troutdale Cl ST4 73 A3
Trowbridge Cres ST2 58 B2
Trubshaw Cl ST18 177 C4
Trubshaw Cross ST6 56 B4
Trubshaw Ct ST7 26 B2
Trubshaw Pl ST7 26 A2
Trubshaw St ST6 56 B4
Truro Cl Congleton CW12 15 C4
Lichfield WS13 214 A2
Truro Pl Bucknall ST2 58 A1
Cannock WS12 227 B4
Truro Way ST17 156 B1
Trussel Grange ST17 175 A1
Trussell Cl ST17 175 A1
Trustley Cl DE14 185 A4
Trysull Gdns WV3 265 B4
Trysull Holloway WV5 264 B2
Trysull Rd Wolv WV3 265 B4
Wombourne WV5 269 C4
Tuckers Pl TF10 168 C2
Tudor Cl Burntwood WS7 229 B3
Cheslyn Hay WS6 226 C2
Lichfield WS14 231 C3
Newport TF10 169 A2
Stoke-on-T ST4 72 A3
Stone ST15 119 C3
Tudor Cres
Tamworth B77 250 C2
Wolv WV2 266 A3
Tudor Ct Essington WV11 241 C2
Newcastle-u-L ST5 56 A3
Sutton Coldfield B74 258 A1
Tudor Gdns DY8 279 C3
Tudor Gr ST5 56 B2
Tudor Hollow
Blythe Bridge ST11 90 C1
Burton u T DE13 166 B4
Tudor Park Ct B74 257 C2
Tudor Pl DY3 271 C3
Tudor Rd Burntwood WS7 229 B3
Cannock WS12 209 C4
Dudley DY3 271 C3
Tudor Rise
Clifton Campville B79 218 C1
Stafford ST16 155 B4
Tudor Rose Way ST6 42 C1
Tudor Vale DY3 271 C3
Tudor Way
Cheslyn Hay WS6 226 B1
Stafford ST17 155 A1
Tudors The ST6 41 C2
Tuke Pl WS13 213 C1
Tulip Gr ST5 284 C4
Tulley Pl ST2 58 A2
Tullis Cl ST16 155 B1
Tulsa Cl ST2 58 A1
Tunbridge Dr ST5 54 C1
Tunley St ST15 104 C1
Tunnicliffe Cl ST3 73 C2
Tunnicliffe Dr WS15 178 B1
Tunnicliffe Way ST14 110 C1
Tunstall La ST20 131 C1
Tunstall Rd Biddulph ST8 27 B3
Bosley SK11 7 B4
Congleton CW12 6 C1
Tunstall Road Ind Est
ST8 27 A2
Tuppenhurst La WS15 198 B2
Turf Cl WS11 228 A2
Turf Cotts WV4 265 C1
Turf Pitts La B75 258 C2
Turin Dr ST5 70 C3
Turls Hill Rd DY3 271 C4
Turls St DY3 271 C4
Turnberry B77 251 B3
Turnberry Dr ST4 88 A4
Turnberry Gr WV6 254 B3
Turnberry Rd WS3 243 A2
Turnbull Rd WS13 215 B3
Turnbury Cl DE14 185 A4
Turner Ave Audley ST7 40 A1
Wolv WV4,WV14 266 C1
Turner Cl WS11 210 B1
Turner Cres ST5 55 C3
Turner Croft WS13 215 B4
Turner Gr WV6 255 A2
Turner St Hanley ST1 57 C3
Sedgley DY3 271 B2
Turner's Gr DY3 271 B2
Turner's Hill Rd DY3 271 B2
Turners La TF10 168 A2
Turney Gr ST17 174 B4
Turney Rd DY8 279 C3
Turnham Gn WV6 254 C2
Turnhill Cl ST17 174 B3
Turnhill Gr ST5 56 A4
Turnhurst Rd ST6,ST7 41 C4
Turnlea Cl ST8 27 A3
Turnock St ST2 58 B2
Turnpike Way WV9 224 B1
Turnstone Dr WV10 241 A4
Turquoise Gr WS11 210 B2
Turton Cl Alrewas DE13 201 A1
Walsall WS3 243 A2
Tuscan Cl ST10 76 B1
Tuscan Ho ST3 283 B2
Tuscan St ST3 283 C4
Tuscan Way ST5 55 B3
Tutbury B77 261 B4
Tutbury & Hatton Sta
DE65 146 B4
Tutbury Ave WV6 255 A2
Tutbury Castle* DE13 146 A4
Tutbury Cl WS11 210 B2
Tutbury Gr ST3 73 B2
Tutbury Rd DE13 166 A4
Tutehill B77 262 A4
Twayblade DE14 185 A4
Tweed Gr ST5 71 A2
Tweed St ST4 72 C2
Twemlow Cl ST18 154 B1
Twemlow St ST1 57 A2
Twentylands DE13 147 B2
Twickenham Ct DY8 279 B4
Twigg St ST2 58 A1
Two Gates Com Prim Sch
Tamworth B77 250 B1
Tamworth B77 261 B4
Two Gates Ind Est B77 261 B4
Two Oaks Ave WS7 228 B4
Twyford Cl Aldridge WS9 256 A3
Swadlincote DE11 186 C1
Twyning Gn ST3 88 C4
Tylecote Cres ST18 158 A1
Tyler Gr 22 Burslem ST6 56 C4
Stone ST15 119 C4
Tyndall Pl ST4 71 C4
Tyne Cl WS8 228 B1
Tyne Way ST5 71 A2
Tynedale Cres WV4 266 C2
Tyneham Gr ST2 43 A1
Tyning Cl WV9 240 A1
Tyninghame Ave WV6 255 B4
Tynings La WS9 256 A3
Tynsel Parkes CE Fst Sch
ST14 111 A1
Tynsel Parkes Fst Sch
ST14 110 C1
Tynwald Grange ST5 56 A2
Tyrell Gr ST1 57 C4
Tyria Way 5 ST17 175 A4
Tyrley Cl WV6 255 A1
Tyrley Rd TF9 112 C3
Tyrol Cl DY8 279 B3
Tyson Gn ST2 73 B4
Tythebarn Dr DY6 275 A4

U

Ubberley Gn ST2 58 B1
Ubberley Rd ST2 58 B1
Uffington Par ST2 73 B4
Ufton Cres ST3 88 C4
Ullswater B77 262 A4
Ullswater Ave ST6 56 C4
Ullswater Dr
Cheadle ST10 76 C2
Stone ST15 120 B4
Ullswater Gdns DY6 275 B3
Ullswater Ho ST17 174 C3
Ullswater Pl WS11 209 C1
Ullswater Rd WV11 242 A1
Ulster Cl WS11 210 A2
Ulster Dr DY6 275 C2
Ulster Terr ST4 72 A3
Ulverston Rd ST3 88 C4
Umberleigh Rd ST3 88 C4
Under Rainow Rd CW12 6 C1
Under The Hill ST8 17 A1
Underhill Cl TF10 168 C2
Underhill La WV10 241 A1
Underhill Prim Sch
WV10 241 A1
Underhill Wlk DE14 166 B1
Underley Cl DY6 275 A4
Undertown La DE6 96 B3
Underwood Cl ST16 155 B4
Underwood Rd ST5 55 A1
Unicorn Ind Est ST5 56 B4
Unicorn Pl ST6 41 C3
Union Ct ST1 282 B4
Union La WV5 264 B1
Union St Burntwood WS7 228 C3
Burton u T DE14 166 B1
Cannock WS11 226 C3
Hanley ST1 282 B4
Leek ST13 30 C3
Unity Ave ST1 57 B4
Unity Way ST7 40 B4
Univ of Sheffield SK17 4 A4
Univ of Wolverhampton
Compton Park Campus
WV6 255 C1
University Ct ST18 156 B3
Unwin Cres DY8 279 C3
Unwin St ST6 42 A2
Upfield Cotts WS7 229 C4
Upfield Way WS15 178 B1
Uplands Ave
Caverswall ST9 59 A2
Chell Heath ST6 41 C3
Wolv WV3 265 B4
Uplands Cl
Cannock WS15 211 C3
Penkridge ST19 192 C1
Uplands Croft ST9 59 A2
Uplands Dr
Caverswall ST9 59 A2
Sedgley DY3 271 B4
Wolv WV3 265 C4
Wombourne WV5 270 A3
Uplands Gn WS15 196 B3
Uplands Jun Sch WV3 265 B4
Uplands Rd Bucknall ST2 58 A4
Stafford ST17 174 B3
Uplands The Biddulph ST8 16 C1
Colwich ST18 158 A1
Newcastle-u-L ST5 284 C4
Upmeadows Dr ST16 155 A1
Upper Bar TF10 168 C1
Upper Belgrave Rd ST3 73 B1
Upper Brook St 2
WS15 196 C4
Upper Cres ST4 71 C4
Upper Cross Rd WS15 196 C4
Upper Cross St ST3 283 C4
Upper Furlong St ST4 72 B3
Upper Gn WV6 255 B3
Upper Gungate B79 250 A3
Upper Hillchurch St
ST1 282 C3
Upper Huntbach St ST1 282 C3
Upper Landywood La
WS6 226 B1
Upper Lodge Rd WS15 197 C2
Upper Market Sq ST1 282 B3
Upper Marsh ST5 56 B2
Upper Normacot Rd
1 Longton, Longton ST3 73 B1
Longton, Normacot ST3 73 C1
Upper Sneyd Rd WV11 242 A1
Upper St WV6 255 B3
Upper St John St WS14 231 A3
Upper Villiers St WV2 266 B3
Upper Way WS15 197 A1
Upper Zoar St WV3 266 A4
Upton Ct TF9 97 B1
Upton Pl WS15 178 B1
Urmston Pl ST3 88 C4
Usam Trad Est WV10 240 B1
Usulwall Cl ST21 133 B3
Utterby Side ST2 73 B4
Uttoxeter Heritage Ctr*
ST14 126 B4
Uttoxeter Race Course
ST14 126 C3
Uttoxeter Rd
Abbots Bromley WS15 160 C3
Alton ST10 94 C4
Armitage WS15 198 B2
Blythe Bridge ST11 90 C4
Draycott in t M ST11 91 B3
Foston DE65 129 C2
Foston, HM Detention Ctr
DE65 129 B2
Hill Ridware WS15 198 A4
Hill Ridware, Blithbury
WS15 180 A3
Longton ST3 283 C3
Meir ST3 74 A1
Milwich ST18 122 B3
Sandon ST15 121 B4
Stone ST15 120 C4
Upper Tean ST10,ST14 109 B4
Uttoxeter Sta ST14 126 B4
Uxbridge Cl DY3 271 B1
Uxbridge Ct
Burntwood WS7 228 C3
Cannock WS12 210 B3
Uxbridge St
Burton u T DE14 166 B1
Cannock WS12 210 B2

V

Vale Ave Aldridge WS9 256 B2
Sedgley DY3 271 B3
Vale Cl WS13 214 A1
Vale Gdns ST19 207 C4
Vale Head Dr WV6 255 A1
Vale Park (Port Vale FC)
ST6 42 A1
Vale Pleasant ST5 55 B1
Vale Rise ST19 207 C4
Vale Row DY3 271 B3
Vale St
Newcastle-u-L, Chesterton
ST5 55 C4
Newcastle-u-L, Silverdale
ST5 55 A1
Sedgley DY3 271 B3
Stoke-on-T ST4 72 A4
Vale View Aldridge WS9 256 A2
Cheddleton ST13 45 B3
Newcastle-u-L ST5 56 B4
Valentine Rd ST7 26 A1
Valerian B74 257 C2
Valerian Way ST3 90 A3
Valley Dr ST13 30 A3
Valley Gn WS6 226 C1
Valley La Lichfield WS13 231 B4
Tamworth B77 261 C4
Valley Park Nature Reserve*
WV6 255 B2
Valley Park Sch WV6 255 C3
Valley Park Way ST3 72 C2
Valley Prim Sch ST10 78 A4
Valley Rd Cannock WS12 211 A3
Cannock, Hednesford
WS12 210 B3
Meir ST3 74 A2
Sedgley DY3 271 C3
Stone ST15 120 A3
Walsall WS3 243 B1
Valley Side WS3 243 C1
Valley View
Brownhills WS8 245 A4
Market Drayton TF9 112 A4
Valley View Wlk ST14 96 A2
Van Diemans Rd WV5 269 C3
Van Gogh Cl WS11 210 B1
Vanbrugh Ct WV6 254 C2
Vancouver Dr DE15 167 B2
Vanguard B77 261 B3
Vanity Cl ST15 105 B2
Vanity La ST15 105 B2
Varden Ct WS15 178 C1
Vardon Cl ST16 156 B2
Vaudrey Cres CW12 6 A2
Vaughan Cl B74 257 C3
Vaughan Gdns WV8 238 C2
Vaughan Way ST17 155 B1
Vaughan's La WS15 159 B3
Vauxhall Cres TF10 168 C1
Vauxhall Terr TF10 168 C2
Venice Ct ST5 70 C4
Venn Pl ST1 57 C1
Ventnor Gr ST3 88 C3
Venton Cl ST6 42 C2
Ventura Park Rd B78 249 C2
Ventura Pk B78 250 A2
Venture Way ST6 42 B2
Vercourt B74 257 A2
Verdi Ct WS13 214 B1
Verdon Cl ST19 208 A4
Verity Wlk DY8 275 C1
Vermont Gn 5 WS11 210 A2
Verney Cl ST14 125 B4
Verney Way ST3 88 C4
Vernon Ave Audley ST7 39 B1
Brownhills WS8 245 A4
Congleton CW12 15 C4
Vernon Cl Audley ST7 39 B1
Essington WV11 241 C2
Sutton Coldfield B74 257 C3
Vernon Ho ST14 126 B4
Vernon Lodge Prep Sch
ST19 206 B2
Vernon Rd ST4 72 A4
Vernon Terr DE14 166 B2
Vernon Way WS3 242 C1
Vernons Pl WV10 225 B1
Verona Gr ST3 73 C3
Veronica Ave WV4 266 C3
Verulam Rd ST16 155 C4
Verwood Cl ST16 156 B2
Vesey Cl B74 257 C1
Vessey Terr ST5 284 C2
Vestry Ct DY8 279 C3
Vicar St DY3 271 B4
Vicar's Cl Lichfield WS13 231 A4
Stone ST15 105 B2
Vicarage Bank ST18 138 C3
Vicarage Cl
Brownhills WS8 245 A4
Burton u T DE15 167 A2
Dordon B78 262 C3
Eccleshall ST21 133 B4
Vicarage Cres
Caverswall ST11 74 B2
Newcastle-u-L ST5 284 C1
Tittensor ST12 88 A1
Upper Tean ST10 92 C2
Vicarage Croft DE13 199 B3
Vicarage Ct DY7 278 A2
Vicarage Dr Kinver DY7 278 A2
Uttoxeter ST14 110 C2
Vicarage Field DE15 166 C1
Vicarage Hill B78 260 A1
Vicarage La
Acton Trussell ST17 193 C4
Barlaston ST12 88 C1
King's Bromley DE13 199 B3
Madeley CW3 68 C3
Stoke-on-T ST4 71 C2
Vicarage Rd
Brewood ST19 223 B3
Brownhills, Ogley Rd WS8 245 A4
Cheslyn Hay ST19 225 A4
Leek ST13 30 C3
Penkridge WV10 224 C4
Sedgley DY3 271 C3
Stoke-on-T ST4 71 C4
Stourbridge DY8 279 B4
Upper Tean ST10 92 C2
Walsall WS3 244 A1
Wolv WV2 266 B4
Wolv, Penn WV4 265 C2
Vicarage Way
Hixon ST18 139 B1
Stafford ST17 155 B1
Vicars Croft WS15 178 C1
Vichy Cl ST5 70 C4
Vickers Rd ST6 42 A3
Victor St Stone ST15 104 C1
Walsall WS3 244 A1
Victoria Ave Audley ST7 54 C4
Hanley ST1 282 B1
Kidsgrove ST7 25 C1
Walsall WS3 243 B1
Victoria Cl ST5 55 B1
Victoria Com Sch DE14 166 B2
Victoria Cotts ST10 61 A1
Victoria Cres DE14 166 B3
Victoria Ct Fenton ST4 72 C3
8 Kidsgrove ST7 26 A1
Market Drayton TF9 112 A4
Newcastle-u-L ST5 56 B2
Norton Canes WS11 228 A3
Victoria Dr B78 261 A4
Victoria Gdns WS13 230 C3
Victoria Gr WV5 270 A4
Victoria Hospl WS13 231 A3
Victoria Ind Complex
ST4 283 A5
Victoria Mdw DE13 199 B3
Victoria Park Rd ST6 41 C2
Victoria Pk TF10 168 C2
Victoria Pl Fenton ST4 72 C3
Newcastle-u-L, Chesterton
ST5 55 C4
Newcastle-u-L, Wolstanton
ST5 56 B3
Victoria Rd
Burton u T DE14 166 B2
Fenton ST4 72 C4
Market Drayton TF9 97 A1
Newcastle-u-L ST5 284 C2
Sedgley DY3 271 C4
Stafford ST16 155 B2
Tamworth B79 250 B3
Walsall WS3 244 A2
Wolv, Oxbarn WV3 265 C4
Wolv, Stockwell End WV6 255 C3
Victoria Row ST8 27 B2
Victoria Sq ST1 282 A1
Victoria St
Burton u T DE14 166 B2
Cannock WS11 226 B4
Cannock, Chadsmoor
WS11 209 C2
Cannock, Hednesford
WS12 210 B3
Cheadle ST10 76 C2
Kingswinford DY6 270 A1
Leek ST13 31 A3
Newcastle-u-L ST4 284 C2
Newcastle-u-L, Chesterton
ST5 55 C4
Newcastle-u-L, Silverdale
ST5 55 B1
Stafford ST16 155 C2
Stoke-on-T ST5 56 B1
Stone ST15 105 A1
Yoxall DE13 182 A2
Victoria Terr ST16 155 C3
Victoria Way ST17 175 C3
Victory Ave WS7 228 C4
Victory Cl WS12 210 C2
Victory Cres ST10 76 C2
Victory Terr B78 261 A4
Vienna Pl ST5 70 C3
Vienna Way ST3 73 C3
View St WS12 209 C3
Viewfield Ave WS12 209 C4
Viewfield Cres DY3 271 B3
Viewlands Dr WV6 255 A1
Viggars Pl ST5 55 C1
Vigo Cl WS9 244 C1
Vigo Pl WS9 256 A4
Vigo Rd WS9 244 C1
Vigo Terr WS9 244 C1
Viking B77 261 B4
Villa Cl Biddulph ST8 27 B4
Shareshill WV10 225 B1
Villa Melita ST11 90 B4
Villa Rd ST13 45 B4
Villa St ST4 72 A3
Village Gdns ST17 175 C4
Village Mews The WV6 255 B3
Village The Astbury CW12 15 A4
Endon ST9 29 A1
Keele ST5 69 C4
Kingswinford DY6 275 C4
Stafford ST17 175 C3
Villas The Ipstones ST10 62 B3
Stoke-on-T ST4 72 A3
Villiers Ho WV2 266 B4
Villiers Ind Est WV2 266 A4
Villiers St ST3 283 B1
Vincent St ST1 57 C3
Vine Bank Rd ST7 26 A1
Vine Cl ST18 158 A4

Vine La WS11 .... 226 B3
Vine Row ST4 .... 72 A3
Vine St DY8 .... 275 C1
Vinebank St ST4 .... 72 A3
Vineyard Dr TF10 .... 168 C2
Vineyard Rd TF10 .... 168 C2
Violet La DE15 .... 185 C4
Violet Lane Inf Sch
DE15 .... 185 C4
Violet Way ST16 .... 186 A4
Virginia Ave ST17 .... 175 A4
Virginia Dr WV4 .... 265 C2
Virginsalley La DE6 .... 81 B1
Viscount Rd WS7 .... 211 C1
Viscount Wlk 8 ST3 .... 90 A4
Vista The DY3 .... 266 B1
Vivian Rd ST4 .... 72 C3
Vowchurch Way ST2 .... 58 B1
Voyager Dr WS11 .... 226 C3
Vulcan Rd WS13 .... 214 C1

W

Waddell Cl WV14 .... 266 C1
Wadden La ST18 .... 138 C2
Wade Ave ST5 .... 56 B3
Wade Cl Cheadle ST10 .... 76 B1
  Hill Ridware WS15 .... 197 C4
Wade Croft WS15 .... 179 C1
Wade La WS15 .... 197 C4
Wade St Chell Heath ST6 .... 42 A1
  Lichfield WS13 .... 231 A4
Wadebridge Rd ST2 .... 58 A1
Wadesmill Lawns WV10 .... 240 C2
Wadham St ST4 .... 72 A4
Waggon La DY10 .... 280 C2
Waggoner's La B78 .... 259 C4
Wain Ave
  Newcastle-u-L ST5 .... 70 C4
  Nurton-in-M ST6 .... 42 C3
Wain Dr ST4 .... 71 C3
Wain St ST6 .... 41 C1
Waine Ho WS8 .... 245 A3
Wainrigg B77 .... 262 A4
Wainwood Rise ST4 .... 71 C3
Wainwright Cl DY6 .... 275 A4
Wainwright Wlk ST1 .... 282 C3
Wakefield Ave DE13 .... 146 A3
Wakefield Rd ST4 .... 71 C2
Wakeley Hill Wolv WV4 .... 265 C2
Wakeman Cl WV4 .... 266 A2
Wakeman Ct WV11 .... 241 C2
Walcot Cl B75 .... 258 A2
Walcot Gr ST2 .... 58 A1
Waldale Cl WV11 .... 242 B1
Walden Ave ST16 .... 155 B3
Walden Gdns WV4 .... 265 C3
Wales La DE13 .... 183 B1
Walford Ave WV3 .... 265 C4
Walford Back La ST21 .... 117 B4
Walford Rd DE13 .... 147 B2
Walhouse CE Jun Sch
  WS11 .... 209 B1
Walhouse Dr ST19 .... 207 C4
Walhouse St WS11 .... 226 C4
Walk La WV5 .... 270 A3
Walk The DY3 .... 266 B1
Walker Dr DY10 .... 280 A1
Walker Rd ST6 .... 41 C2
Walker St
  Burton u T DE14 .... 166 A1
  Tunstall ST6 .... 41 B1
Walkers Croft WS13 .... 214 B1
Walkers Rise WS12 .... 210 B4
Walkersgreen Rd ST5 .... 40 B1
Walklate Ave ST5 .... 56 B2
Walkley Bank TF10 .... 169 B2
Walkmill Bsns Pk WS11 .... 226 B3
Walkmill Dr TF10 .... 112 B4
Walkmill La WS11 .... 226 B3
Walkmill Marsh Nature
  Reserve* TF9 .... 112 B4
Walkmill Rd TF10 .... 112 B4
Walkmill Way WS11 .... 226 B3
Walks The ST13 .... 30 B3
Wall (Letocetvm) Roman Site
  (Town)* WS4 .... 230 C1
Wall Croft WS9 .... 256 A4
Wall Ditch DE6 .... 35 A1
Wall Dr B74 .... 257 C2
Wall Heath La WS14 .... 245 C3
Wall La WS13,WS14 .... 230 B2
Wall La Terr ST13 .... 45 B3
Wall Rd DE14 .... 185 A4
Wall Roman Site (Letocetvm)
  Mus* WS14 .... 230 B1
Wallace Cl WS11 .... 227 C3
Wallace Ct WS6 .... 226 B1
Wallace Rd WS8 .... 244 C4
Walland Gr ST16 .... 155 A2
Wallbridge Cl ST13 .... 30 B2
Wallbridge Dr ST13 .... 30 B2
Wallbridge Prec ST13 .... 30 B2
Wallbrook Rd ST18 .... 122 C2
Walley Dr ST6 .... 41 B3
Walley Pl ST6 .... 57 A4
Walley St Biddulph ST8 .... 27 B4
  Bursem ST6 .... 57 A4
Walley's Dr ST6 .... 56 B1
Wallfield Cl ST10 .... 92 B2
Wallheath Cres WS14 .... 245 C2
Wallington Cl WS13 .... 214 C1
Wallington Heath WS3 .... 243 A1
Wallis Pl ST4 .... 58 A3
Wallis St ST4 .... 72 C3

Wallis Way ST2 .... 43 A1
Wallows Wood DY3 .... 271 A2
Wallshead Way TF10 .... 168 C1
Walmer Mho WS9 .... 256 A4
Walmer Pl ST4 .... 283 B5
Walmers The WS9 .... 256 A4
Walmsley Ct DY7 .... 278 A2
Walney Gr ST1 .... 282 A4
Walnut Ave WV8 .... 239 A2
Walnut Cl Cannock WS11 .... 209 C1
  Newport TF10 .... 168 C1
Walnut Crest ST18 .... 158 B4
Walnut Ct WS15 .... 197 A3
Walnut Dr Cannock WS11 .... 209 C2
  Wolv WV3 .... 255 B1
Walnut Gr Lichfield WS14 .... 231 C4
  Newcastle-u-L ST5 .... 55 B4
Walnut Tree La TF10 .... 188 A4
Walpole St ST1 .... 283 C5
Walrand Cl B79 .... 234 A1
Walsall Rd Aldridge WS9 .... 256 A3
  Brownhills, Vigo WS9 .... 244 C1
  Cannock WS11 .... 227 A1
  Lichfield WS13 .... 231 A1
  Norton Canes WS11 .... 227 C2
  Shenstone WS14 .... 245 C4
  Sutton Coldfield B74 .... 257 B2
  Walsall WS3 .... 244 A1
Walsall Wood Rd WS9 .... 245 A2
Walsall Wood Sch WS9 .... 245 A2
Walsingham Gdns ST5 .... 71 A1
Walter St WS3 .... 244 A1
Walton Cres Fenton ST4 .... 72 B3
  ST5 .... 71 A1
Walton Gdns WV8 .... 238 C2
Walton Gr ST7 .... 40 A4
Walton Grange ST15 .... 120 A4
Walton Hall Sch ST21 .... 134 A3
Walton Heath WS3 .... 242 C2
Walton Hgh Sch ST17 .... 175 C3
Walton Ind Est ST15 .... 120 A3
Walton La ST17 .... 176 A3
Walton Lodge ST17 .... 175 C3
Walton Mead Cl ST17 .... 175 C4
Walton Pl ST5 .... 55 B4
Walton Priory Mid Sch
  ST15 .... 119 C3
Walton Rd Aldridge WS9 .... 245 C4
  Stoke-on-T ST4 .... 71 C2
  Swadlincote DE15 .... 185 B3
  Wolv WV4 .... 266 C3
Walton Way Stone ST15 .... 119 C4
  Talke ST7 .... 40 B4
Walton-on-Trent CE Prim
  Sch DE12 .... 202 B4
Waltonbury Cl ST17 .... 175 C3
Waltonhurst La ST21 .... 134 B2
Wanderers Ave WV2 .... 266 B3
Wandsbeck B77 .... 266 C4
Wannerton Rd DY10 .... 281 A1
Wansbeck Wlk DY3 .... 271 C3
Warburton Cl 20 ST6 .... 57 A4
Warburton St ST4 .... 57 A4
Ward Gr WV4 .... 266 C2
Ward Pl ST6 .... 42 A3
Ward Rd Codsall WV8 .... 238 C2
  Wolv WV4 .... 266 B3
Ward St WS12 .... 209 C3
Wardel Cres ST13 .... 30 C2
Wardel La ST7 .... 43 B1
Wardle Cl ST5 .... 258 A2
Wardle Pl WS11 .... 209 C3
Wardle St Tamworth B79 .... 250 A3
  Tunstall ST6 .... 41 C2
Wardles La WS6 .... 226 C1
Wardlow Cl WV4 .... 266 A3
Wardle La CW12 .... 16 B4
Warings The WV5 .... 269 C2
Warm Croft ST15 .... 120 B4
Warminster Pl ST3 .... 283 A3
Warmson Ct ST3 .... 73 B3
Warner Rd WV8 .... 238 C2
Warner St ST1 .... 282 B2
Warnford Wlk WV4 .... 265 B3
Warren Cl
  Burton u T DE13 .... 147 C1
  Cannock WS12 .... 211 A3
  Lichfield WS14 .... 231 C4
Warren Croft WS15 .... 198 B2
Warren Ct TF9 .... 37 C3
Warren Dr WV3 .... 266 B1
Warren Gdns DY6 .... 275 B3
Warren La DE14 .... 184 C4
Warren Pl
  Brownhills WS8 .... 245 A4
  Longton ST3 .... 283 D2
Warren Rd
  Burntwood WS7 .... 229 A3
  Chell Heath ST6 .... 42 A3
  Stoke-on-T ST4 .... 71 C1
Warrens La WS3 .... 155 A3
Warrilow Heath Rd ST5 .... 40 B1
Warrington Dr ST13 .... 30 B3
Warrington Rd ST1 .... 57 B1
Warrington St ST4 .... 72 C3
Warsill Gr ST3 .... 73 B3
Warstone Hill Rd WV6 .... 253 C2
Warstone Rd WS6 .... 242 B4
Warstones Cres WV4 .... 265 B3
Warstones Dr WV4 .... 265 B3
Warstones Gdns WV4 .... 265 B3
Warstones Jun & Inf Sch
  WV4 .... 265 C3
Warstones Rd WV4 .... 265 B3
Wartell Bank DY6 .... 275 B4

Wartell Bank Ind Est
  DY6 .... 275 B4
Warwick Ave 6 Meir ST3 .... 73 C1
  Newcastle-u-L ST5 .... 71 B2
  Perton WV6 .... 254 C2
Warwick Cl
  Branston DE14 .... 184 C4
  Cannock WS11 .... 226 C4
  Kidsgrove ST7 .... 26 A2
  Market Drayton TF9 .... 97 C1
Warwick Ct WV3 .... 271 B2
Warwick Dr WV8 .... 238 C2
Warwick Gr ST5 .... 56 C2
Warwick Rd
  Kingswinford DY8 .... 275 B1
  Stafford ST17 .... 175 A4
  Tamworth B77 .... 250 C2
Warwick St Biddulph ST8 .... 27 B4
  Burton u T DE13 .... 166 B3
  Hanley ST1 .... 57 A2
  Newcastle-u-L ST5 .... 55 C4
Warwick Way WS9 .... 245 A1
Wasdale Dr ST6 .... 275 C3
Wasdale Rd WS8 .... 244 B3
Wash Dale La ST15 .... 105 A3
Washbrook La
  Norton Canes WS11 .... 227 B3
  Tissington DE6 .... 51 C2
Washerwall La ST9 .... 59 A2
Washerwell St ST2 .... 73 B4
Washford Rd DE65 .... 147 C4
Washington Cl ST8 .... 16 B1
Washington Ct WV3 .... 255 B1
Washington Dr ST17 .... 175 A4
Washington St ST6 .... 41 C1
Waste La DE6,ST10 .... 79 B2
Wastwater Gr WV6 .... 254 C2
Wat Tyler Cl WS15 .... 178 B2
Watchfield Cl ST3 .... 73 C1
Water Dale WV4 .... 255 C1
Water Eaton La ST19 .... 207 C1
Water La Emvile DY7 .... 268 B1
  Newport TF10 .... 168 C2
Water Rd DY3 .... 271 B1
Water St Burntwood WS7 .... 228 C4
  Kingswinford DY6 .... 275 B4
  Newcastle-u-L ST5 .... 56 C2
Waterbeck Gr ST4 .... 88 B3
Waterbrook Cl ST19 .... 207 C4
Waterbrook Way WS11 .... 226 C3
Waterdale WV5 .... 269 C3
Waterdale Gr ST3 .... 73 C2
Waterfall La ST10 .... 48 C1
Waterford Dr TF10 .... 168 C1
Waterford Rd 5 DY6 .... 275 B4
Watergate St ST6 .... 41 B2
Waterhead Cl WV10 .... 241 A1
Waterhead Dr WV10 .... 241 A1
Waterhouse La ST3 .... 73 C1
Waterhouses CE Prim Sch
  ST10 .... 48 C1
Watering Cl ST5 .... 71 A4
Watering Trough Bank
  CW3 .... 69 A4
Waterlily Cl WS12 .... 210 C2
Waterloo Bvd WS12 .... 210 C2
Waterloo Gr ST17 .... 26 A1
Waterloo Rd
  Bursem ST6,ST1 .... 57 A3
  Edgmond TF10 .... 168 A3
Waterloo St
  Burton u T DE14 .... 166 B2
  Hanley ST1 .... 282 C2
  Leek ST13 .... 30 B3
Watermeadow Dr WS4 .... 244 B3
Watermint Cl WS12 .... 210 C2
Waterpark Rd DE6 .... 127 A4
Waters Dr B74 .... 257 B2
Waters Edge WS15 .... 198 B3
Waters Rd WS15 .... 160 C2
Waters View WS3 .... 244 A3
Waterside
  Burton u T DE15 .... 185 C4
  Rugeley WS15 .... 196 C3
Waterside Bsns Pk
  WS15 .... 197 A4
Waterside Cl
  Brewood WV10 .... 224 C1
  Newcastle-u-L ST5 .... 68 C3
Waterside Com Jun Sch
  DE15 .... 185 C4
Waterside Ct
  Branston DE14 .... 165 C1
  Codsall WV8 .... 171 B3
  Tamworth B77 .... 250 C3
Waterside Dr Longton ST3 .... 88 C4
  Market Drayton TF9 .... 97 C1
Waterside Mews TF10 .... 168 C2
Waterside Rd DE15 .... 185 B4
Waterside Way
  Abbots Bromley WS15 .... 160 B2
  Astbury CW12 .... 15 B3
  Clifton DE6 .... 81 C4
  Codsall WV8 .... 239 A3
  Ellastone DE6 .... 80 A2
  Haughton ST18 .... 172 C3

Watery La continued
  Kingswinford DY8 .... 275 C1
  Lichfield WS13 .... 214 B2
  Meir ST3 .... 73 B1
  Scropton DE65 .... 129 C1
  Swadlincote DE15 .... 186 B3
  Uttoxeter ST14 .... 110 B3
Watford Gap Rd WS14 .... 258 A4
Watford St ST4 .... 282 B4
Watkin Ave WV1 .... 266 C1
Watkin St ST4 .... 72 B3
Watkiss Dr WS15 .... 178 B1
Watlands Ave ST5 .... 56 B3
Watlands Rd ST7 .... 39 C1
Watlands View ST5 .... 56 B3
Watling St
  Brownhills WS8 .... 228 B1
  Cannock WS11 .... 226 B3
  Dordon B77,B78 .... 262 B3
  Hints B74 .... 248 B2
  Norton Canes WS11 .... 227 B2
  Tamworth B78 .... 249 C1
Watling Street Jun Mix Inf
  Sch WS8 .... 228 C1
Watson Cl Alrewas WS13 .... 215 C4
  Rugeley WS15 .... 178 B2
Watson Rd Stoke-on-T ST4 .... 71 C2
  Wolv, Cinder Hill WV10 .... 266 A4
  Wolv, Pendeford WV10 .... 240 A1
Watson St
  Burton u T DE14 .... 166 B1
  Stoke-on-T ST4 .... 72 A4
Watt Ho DY6 .... 275 C4
Watt Pl ST10 .... 76 B2
Wattfield Cl WS15 .... 197 A3
Wattles La ST17 .... 175 A1
Watts Cl ST17 .... 174 A4
Waveney Ave WV6 .... 254 C2
Waveney Gr
  Cannock WS11 .... 209 A1
  Newcastle-u-L ST5 .... 71 A2
Waveney Wlk N ST6 .... 42 A2
Waveney Wlk S ST6 .... 42 A2
Wavenham Cl B74 .... 257 C3
Waverley Cres
  Wolv, Cinder Hill WV4 .... 266 C2
  Wolv, Goldthorn Hill WV4 .... 266 A3
Waverley Gdns
  Rugeley WS15 .... 178 A1
  Wolv, New-bridge WV6 .... 270 A4
Waverley La DE14 .... 166 A2
Waverley Pl ST5 .... 71 A3
Waverley Rd WS3 .... 242 C1
Waverley St ST4 .... 72 A4
Wavertree Ave ST7 .... 25 C4
Waybutt La CW2 .... 52 B4
Wayfield Dr ST16 .... 155 B4
Wayfield Gr ST4 .... 71 B4
Wayside WV8 .... 239 A3
Wayside Acres WV8 .... 238 C1
Wayside Dr B74 .... 56 B2
Wayside Terr ST1 .... 282 C2
Wayte St ST1 .... 282 A4
Wealden Hatch WV10 .... 240 C2
Wealdstone Dr DY3 .... 271 B1
Weathercock La CW12 .... 6 C2
Weatheroaks WS9 .... 245 A2
Weaver Cl Biddulph ST8 .... 16 B1
  Cheadle ST10 .... 76 C3
Weaver Dr ST17 .... 174 A4
Weaver Pl ST5 .... 71 A2
Weaver Rd ST14 .... 111 A1
Weaver St ST14 .... 282 B3
Weavers La ST15 .... 120 B4
Weavers The ST14 .... 95 B3
Weaver Wlk ST15 .... 103 B2
Weaving Gdns 8 WS11 .... 209 C1
Web Cl WS13 .... 215 B3
Webb Ave WV6 .... 254 C3
Web St ST3 .... 74 A2
Webberley La ST3 .... 283 C3
Webley Rise WV10 .... 240 C2
Webster Ave ST3 .... 73 C3
Webster St ST5 .... 56 C3
Webster Wlk WS11 .... 210 A2
Wedgewood Ave WV5 .... 119 C3
Wedgwood Cl
  Burntwood WS7 .... 229 B4
  Burton u T DE13 .... 167 A1
Wedgwood Dr WS18 .... 156 A4
Wedgwood Ave
  Audley ST7 .... 40 A1
  Newcastle-u-L ST5 .... 284 A1
Wedgwood Ct WS11 .... 269 C4
Wedgwood Ct ST1 .... 57 A2
Wedgwood Dr ST12 .... 88 C2
Wedgwood Rd WS12 .... 211 B2
Wedgwood La
  Barlaston ST12 .... 88 C2
  Biddulph ST8 .... 16 B1
Wedgwood Meml Coll
  ST12 .... 88 C1
Wedgwood Pl 17 ST6 .... 56 C4
Wedgwood Rd
  Cheadle ST10 .... 76 B1
  Stoke-on-T ST4 .... 72 C3
  Talke ST7 .... 40 A4
Wedgwood St
  10 Burslem ST6 .... 56 C4
  Newcastle-u-L ST5 .... 56 B3
Wedgwood Visitor Ctr &
  Mus* ST12 .... 88 B2
Weeford Dell B75 .... 258 C2
Weeford Rd B75 .... 258 C2
Weeping Cross ST17 .... 175 B4
Weetman Cl ST14 .... 41 B4
Weighton Gr ST2 .... 58 A2

Weir Bank DE15 .... 185 C3
Weir Gr ST17 .... 26 A1
Weirside DE6 .... 81 B4
Welbeck Pl ST2 .... 58 B3
Welbury Gdns WV6 .... 255 C3
Welby St ST14 .... 72 B3
Welch St ST4 .... 72 A4
Weldon Ave ST3 .... 74 A2
Welford Gr B74 .... 257 C2
Welford Rd B77 .... 250 C2
Welford Rise DE13 .... 166 A3
Well La Biddulph ST8 .... 16 B2
  Great Wyrley WS6 .... 227 A1
  Norbury TF10 .... 150 B2
  Walsall WS3 .... 243 C1
  Warslow SK17 .... 22 A1
Well St Biddulph ST8 .... 27 B4
  Cheadle ST10 .... 76 C2
  Forsbrook ST11 .... 91 A4
  Hanley ST1 .... 282 C2
  Leek ST13 .... 30 C3
  Mow Cop ST7 .... 26 B4
  Newcastle-u-L ST5 .... 284 C2
Welland Cl DE15 .... 167 A3
Welland Gr ST5 .... 71 A2
Wellbury Ct ST4 .... 88 B3
Weller St ST4 .... 71 C4
Wellesbourne B79 .... 250 B4
Wellesbourne Cl WV3 .... 265 A4
Wellesley St ST1 .... 282 A1
Wellfield Cl WS11 .... 226 A4
Wellfield Rd
  Aldridge WS9 .... 256 A4
  Alrewas DE13 .... 201 A1
  Bucknall ST2 .... 58 B1
Wellington Ave WV3 .... 265 C4
Wellington Dr
  Kingswinford DY6 .... 275 C2
  Stafford ST16 .... 155 C3
Wellington Cres WS13 .... 215 A2
Wellington Ct
  Hanley ST1 .... 282 C3
  10 Leek ST13 .... 30 C3
Wellington Dr
  Cannock WS11 .... 226 A4
  Rugeley WS15 .... 196 C4
Wellington Mill 5 ST13 .... 30 C3
Wellington Rd
  Albrighton WV7 .... 220 C1
  Burton u T DE14 .... 166 A1
  Hanley ST1 .... 282 C2
  Kidsgrove ST7 .... 26 A1
  Newport TF10 .... 168 C1
Wellington St
  Burton u T DE14 .... 166 A2
  Hanley ST1 .... 282 C2
  Leek ST13 .... 30 C2
  11 Newcastle-u-L ST5 .... 56 B3
Wellington St W DE14 .... 166 A2
Wellington Terr ST1 .... 282 C2
Wells Cl Biddulph ST8 .... 27 B4
  Cannock WS11 .... 209 C3
  Perton WV6 .... 254 B2
Wells Dr ST17 .... 175 C4
Wells La ST18 .... 191 B4
Wells Rd WV4 .... 265 C3
Wellsfield Cl ST18 .... 138 B1
Wellwyn Gdns WV4 .... 240 A2
Welsh Cl ST3 .... 89 B4
Wem Gr ST5 .... 40 C1
Wembley La WS7 .... 228 B4
Wembury B77 .... 250 C3
Wemet CWW10 .... 240 C2
Wendling Cl ST21 .... 58 B1
Wendover Gr ST17 .... 175 C4
Wendover Rd WV4 .... 266 C1
Wendy Cl ST17 .... 52 A3
Wenger Cess ST4 .... 88 A4
Wenlock Dr ST3 .... 90 A4
Wenlock B77 .... 250 B2
Wenlock Ave WV3 .... 265 C4
Wenlock Cl
  Chell Heath ST6 .... 42 A4
  Newcastle-u-L ST5 .... 40 C1
  Sedgley DY3 .... 271 B4
Wenlock Dr TF10 .... 168 C1
Wensleydale Ave CW12 .... 6 A3
Wensleydale Cl ST1 .... 57 B4
Wentlows Ave ST12 .... 92 B3
Wentlows Rd ST10 .... 92 B3
Wentworth Cl WS7 .... 229 B4
Wentworth Ct B75 .... 258 C4
Wentworth Dr
  Burton u T DE13 .... 147 B1
  Kidsgrove ST7 .... 26 B2
  Lichfield WS14 .... 231 B3
  Perton WV6 .... 254 B3
Wentworth Gr Hanley ST1 .... 57 C4
  Perton WV6 .... 254 B3
Wentworth Rd
  Stourbridge DY8 .... 279 C2
  Walsall WV10 .... 242 C2
  Wolv WV10 .... 240 C2
Werburgh Dr ST4 .... 72 C3
Wereton Rd ST7 .... 39 B1
Wergs Dr WV6 .... 255 A4
Wergs Hall Rd
  Codsall WV8 .... 254 C4
  Wolv WV6 .... 254 C4
Wergs Rd Codsall WV8 .... 254 C4
  Wolv WV6 .... 255 A3
Werneth Gr WV3 .... 243 A2
Werrington Prim Sch
  ST9 .... 59 A2
Werrington Rd ST2 .... 58 A2

Wesker Pl ST3 .....73 C2
Wesley Ave
　Cheslyn Hay WS6 ....226 B2
　Codsall WV8 ....239 A1
Wesley Cl
　Burntwood WS7 ......211 C1
　Wombourne WV5 .....269 C3
Wesley Dr ST15 ....120 B3
Wesley Gdns **7** ST7 ...26 A1
Wesley Pl Audley ST7 ..54 B4
　Cannock WS12 ....210 B4
　Newcastle-u-L ST5 ....70 C4
Wesley Rd WV8 ....239 A1
Wesley St Audley ST7 ..40 A1
　Forsbrook ST11 ....91 A4
　Tunstall ST6 ....61 B2
Wesley Way B77 .....250 C2
Wesleyan Rd TF9 .....100 A3
Wessenden B77 ......262 A4
Wessex Cl WS8 ......244 C4
Wessex Cr ST9 ....251 C4
Wessex Dr
　Cannock WS11 ......209 C1
　Trentham ST4 ....88 A4
Wessex Rd WV2 .....266 C3
West Acres ST14 .....141 B4
West Ave Kidsgrove ST7 .25 B1
　Newcastle-u-L ST5 ....56 B1
　Stoke-on-T ST4 ....71 C4
　Stone CW7 ....37 A3
West Bank ST4 ....72 A3
West Beeches WV9 ..224 A1
West Brampton ST5 ..284 B3
West Butts Rd WS15 ..178 A1
West Cl Stafford ST16 .156 A2
　Stone ST15 ....119 C4
West Coppice Rd WS8 .244 B4
West Cres ST11 ....57 C4
West Dr Cheddleton ST13 .45 B4
　Tamworth B78 ......249 C1
West End Ave ST13 ....30 B3
West Gn WV4 ....265 B3
West Hill ST14 ....126 B3
West Hill Ave WS12 ..210 A3
West Hill Prim Sch
　WS12 ....210 A3
West Par ST4 ....72 B3
West Prec ST1 ....282 B2
West Rd WV4 ....266 C3
West St Biddulph ST8 ..27 B4
　Burton u T DE15 ......167 A2
　Cannock WS11 ......226 C3
　Leek ST13 ....30 C3
　Meir ST3 ....74 A3
　Mount Pleasant ST7 ...26 A3
　Newcastle-u-L ST5 ..284 C2
　Newcastle-u-L, Porthill ST5 .56 B4
　Newcastle-u-L, Silverdale
　　ST5 ....55 A1
　Stourbridge DY8 .....279 C3
　Tamworth B79 ....250 B3
　Tamworth, Kettlebrook
　　B77 ....250 B2
West Terr ST6 ....42 A3
West View Mayfield DE6 ..81 B3
　Newcastle-u-L ST5 ....56 A3
　Rocester ST14 ....96 A2
　Stone ST3 ....89 C2
　Uttoxeter ST14 ......125 B4
West View Dr DY6 ....275 C3
West Way Stafford ST17 .174 B4
　Uttoxeter ST14 ......110 C1
　Walsall WS4 ....244 A1
West Way Gn ST17 ...155 B1
West Winds WV10 ...241 B4
Westacre ST1 ....57 C2
Westacre Cres WV3 ..255 B1
Westacre Dr DE11 ...186 C1
Westacre Inf Sch WV3 .255 B1
Westbeech Rd WV6 ..253 B3
Westbrook Way WV5 ..269 C3
Westbourne Ave
　Cannock WS11 ......209 B2
　Cheslyn Hay WS6 ....226 C2
Westbourne Cl ST13 ...30 B3
Westbourne Cres WS7 .229 A4
Westbourne Gr ST4 ...71 C3
Westbourne Rd WV4 .266 A3
Westbury Cl ST1 ....57 C3
Westbury Hayes ST17 .174 A4
Westbury Rd ST5 .....71 A2
Westclife DY3 ....271 B4
Westcliffe Hospl ST6 ..41 C4
Westcott Cl DY6 .....275 C2
Westcott La TF9 .....130 A4
Westcroft Ave WV10 .241 A1
Westcroft Rd
　Perton WV6 ....254 C3
　Sedgley DY3 ....266 A1
Westcroft Sch WV10 .241 A1
Westerby Dr ST9 ......59 A2
Western La ST14 ......87 C4
Westerham Parkway
　WV10 ....240 C2
Western Ave DY3 ....271 A4
Western By Pass WS13 .213 C1
Western Rd
　Cannock WS12 ......210 A3
　Stourbridge DY8 .....279 C2
Western Springs Prim Sch
　WS15 ....178 B1
Western Springs Rd
　WS15 ....178 B1
Westfield Ave ST7 ....39 B1

Westfield Dr
　Aldridge WS9 ....256 A3
　Wombourne WV5 ....269 C4
Westfield Gr WV3 ....265 B4
Westfield Manor B75 .258 A2
Westfield Prim Sch
　WS5 ....269 C4
Westfield Rd Bucknall ST2 .58 A2
　Burton u T DE13 ....166 A3
　Mow Cop ST7 ....26 B4
　Sedgley DY3 ....266 C1
Westfields Cotton ST10 .63 C2
　Leek ST13 ....30 C3
Westfields Rd WS15 .197 C2
Westfields Rise CW3 ..67 B1
Westgate Brewood ST19 .223 B4
　Cannock WS12 ......211 A3
Westgate Cl DY3 .....221 C4
Westhall Cl ST10 .....223 B3
Westhall Gate WS3 ..243 A1
Westhead Ave ST16 ..156 A2
Westhead Rd DY10 ..280 A2
Westhead Rd N DY10 .280 A2
Westhead Wlk ST1 ..282 A2
Westhill WV3 ....255 B1
Westhouse La DE6,ST14 .79 C2
Westland Ave WV3 ..255 C1
Westland Gdns
　Brierley Hill DY8 ....279 C4
　Wolv WV6 ....255 C1
Westland Rd
　Market Drayton TF9 ...97 A1
　Wolv WV6 ....255 C1
Westland St ST14 .....70 C4
Westlands Audley ST7 ..39 C1
　Woore CW3 ....83 A4
Westlands Ave ST5 ...70 C4
Westlands Prim Sch ST5 .70 C3
Westlands Rd ST14 ..126 A3
Westlands The ST14 ..95 B3
Westleigh Rd WV5 ..269 C3
Westmarsh Gr ST6 ...42 A2
Westmead Rd DE13 .183 B1
Westmere Cl CW2 ....62 A3
Westmill St ST1 ......282 C1
Westminster Ave WV4 .266 A3
Westminster Cl ST17 .175 B4
Westminster Dr DE13 .166 B4
Westminster La ST14 ..72 A1
Westminster Rd
　Cannock WS11 ......209 C3
　Kingswinford DY8 ...275 B1
　Leek ST13 ....31 A4
Westmorland Ave ST7 .40 C4
Westmorland Cl
　Chell Heath ST6 ....42 A4
　Tamworth B78 ....250 A1
Weston Bank ST18 ..138 A1
Weston Cl Brewood ST19 .224 C1
　Cannock WS11 ......210 B1
　Caverswall ST12 ......59 A2
　Newcastle-u-L ST5 ....55 C2
Weston Coney Rd ST4 .74 A2
Weston Coney Inf Sch
　ST3 ....74 A3
Weston Coney Jun Sch
　ST3 ....74 A2
Weston Coney Rd ST3 .73 C2
Weston Cres WS9 ....256 A2
Weston Ct ST3 ....74 A2
Weston Dr
　Great Wyrley WS6 ...226 C1
　Meir ST3 ....74 A2
Weston Ho WV6 .....255 C3
Weston La Standon ST21 .102 A2
　Weston CW2 ....37 A3
Weston Park Ave DE14 .166 B4
Weston Pk* TF11 ....203 C1
Weston Rd
　Albrighton WV7 .....237 A3
　Hopton ST16 ....156 B2
　Lichfield WS13 ......214 A1
　Meir ST3 ....74 A2
　Weston CW1 ....37 A4
Weston Rd High Sch
　ST18 ....156 B3
Weston St Leek ST13 ..31 A3
　Longton ST3 ....74 A2
Weston Village Prim Sch
　ST3 ....37 B3
Westonfields Dr ST3 ..73 C2
Westonview Ave ST3 ..73 B3
Westport Lake Rd ST6 .41 B1
Westport Rd ST6 .....41 C1
Westridge DY3 ....271 B4
Westspnnk Cres ST13 ..73 C1
Westview Cl ST13 .....30 B3
Westward Cl ST14 ...111 A1
Westway Ho WS4 ...244 A1
Westwick Cl WS9 ...245 C2
Westwood Ave DY8 .279 B2
Westwood Cl
　Cheddleton ST13 ......45 B2
　Chorlton CW2 ....37 A1
Westwood Ct
　Hanley ST1 ....282 C3
　10 Leek ST13 ....30 B3
Westwood Fst Sch ST13 .30 B3
Westwood Gr **8** ST13 .30 B3
Westwood Heath Rd
　ST13 ....30 A3
Westwood High Sch
　ST13 ....30 A3
Westwood Holdings
　WS12 ....209 A3
Westwood Park Ave
　ST13 ....30 A3
Westwood Park Dr ST13 .30 A3

Westwood Pk DE11 ..186 C3
Westwood Rd Leek ST13 .30 B3
　Meir ST3 ....74 A1
　Newcastle-u-L ST5 ....56 B3
Westwood Sch WS15 .180 A2
Westwood Terr **6** ST13 .30 B3
Westwoods Hollow
　WS7 ....229 A4
Wetherall Cl WS15 ..178 B1
Wetherby Cl
　Kingsley ST10 ....76 C3
　Newcastle-u-L ST5 ....55 C4
　Wolv WV10 ....240 B3
Wetherby Ct DE14 ..184 C4
Wetherby Gr WS3 ...243 A2
Wetherby Rd ST14 ....88 A4
Wetherel Rd DE15 ...167 B1
Wetley Ave ST9 ......59 C2
Wetley La ST13 ....33 A1
Wetmore La DE14 ...166 C3
Wetmore Rd DE14 ..166 C3
Wettenhall Dr ST13 ...30 A2
Wetton Rd DE6,ST13 ..34 A3
Wexford Cl DY1 .....271 C1
Weybourne Ave ST2 ..43 A2
Weyhill Cl WV9 ......239 C1
Weymouth Dr B74 ..257 C2
Weymouth Ho B79 ..250 A3
Wharf Cl Lichfield WS14 .231 B4
　Uttoxeter ST14 ......126 B4
Wharf Hos DE13 .....184 A1
Wharf La Astbury CW12 .15 A2
　Brownhills WS8 ....228 C2
Wharf Pl ST4 ....72 B4
Wharf Rd Biddulph ST8 .27 B4
　Burton u T DE14 ....166 C3
　Gnosall ST20 ....171 B3
Wharf Rd Kingsley ST10 .196 C4
Wharf Road Ind Est
　DE14 ....166 C3
Wharf St ST5 ....284 D3
Wharf Terr ST3 ....69 A4
Wharfdale Cl DY6 ...275 A4
Wharfdale Rd CW12 ..6 A3
Wharfedale Wlk ST13 ..6 A3
Wharmadine La
　Ashley TF9 ....100 C4
　Maer ST5 ....84 C1
Wharwell La WS6 ...227 A1
Whateley La DE7 ....261 C2
Whateley Villas CV9 .262 A1
Whatmore St ST6 .....42 B1
Wheat Breach Cl DE13 .166 A3
Wheatcroft Cl
　Burntwood WS7 ......229 A3
　Penkridge ST19 .....207 C4
　Sutton Coldfield B75 .258 C2
Wheatfields Cl 42 B2
Wheathill Cl WV4 ...265 A3
Wheatlands Cl **21** WS11 .210 B1
Wheatlands Rd DE15 .185 C4
Wheatlands The WV6 .254 B2
Wheatley Ave ST14 ...71 C3
Wheatley Cl B75 .....258 B2
Wheatley La DE15 ...167 B2
Wheatley St WV2 ...266 C3
Wheatmill Cl DY10 ..281 A1
Wheatridge Cl DY6 ..275 A4
Wheatsheaf Rd WV8 .239 C1
Wheatstone Cl DY3 ..271 C3
Wheel Ave WS13 ....238 C2
Wheel La WS13 .....213 C1
Wheeler Cl WV8 ....238 C2
Wheeler St ST6 ....279 C3
Wheelfield WV8 ....238 C2
Wheelock Way **10** ST7 .26 A1
Whetstone Field Prim Sch
　WS9 ....256 A2
Whetstone Gn WV10 .240 B1
Whetstone La WV10 ..256 A2
Whetstone Rd ST18 ..16 B1
Whieldon Cres ST4 ..72 B3
Whieldon Rd ST4 ....72 B3
Whimpoll Cl WV10 ..241 A3
Whimple Side ST17 ..174 A4
Whimster Sq ST17 ..174 A4
Whinberry Rise DY5 .271 B1
Whinyates Rise WS11 .226 C4
Whisper La ST4,ST5 ...86 C4
Whiston Cl WV7 .....237 A3
Whiston Eaves La ST10 .62 B1
Whitacre La WS14 ..245 C4
Whitaker Mews ST14 ..95 C2
Whitaker Rd ST3 .....72 C2
Whitbeam Cl DY3 ...271 B2
Whitbread Dr ST8 .....27 C4
Whitburn Cl WV9 ...240 A1
Whitby Cl Stafford ST17 .174 B4
　Walsall WS3 ....242 C2
Whitby Way WS11 ..226 B4
Whitchurch Gr ST5 ...40 C1
Whitcliffe Pl ST3 .....72 C1
Whitcombe Rd ST3 ...74 A1
White Bark Cl WS12 .210 A4
White Farm Rd B74 .257 C2
White Hall DY7 .....277 C3
White Hollies WS3 ..243 C2
White Horse Rd WS8 .228 C1
White House La DY7 .268 C1
White Houses La WV10 .241 A3
White Lion St ST17 ..155 C1
White Oak Dr
　Kingswinford DY6 ...275 B3
　Wolv WV3 ....255 B1
White Oaks ST17 .....45 A4
White Row WV5 .....264 B1
White's Dr DY3 .....271 C4

White's Mdw ST18 ..153 B2
Whitebeam Cl
　Brownhills WS8 ......244 C3
Whitebeam Rd ST15 ..40 B1
Whitebridge Ind Est
　ST15 ....104 C1
Whitebridge La ST15 .104 C1
Whitechapel Cl WV8 .239 A1
Whitefields La ST10 ..49 A1
Whitehall Ave ST7 ....25 C1
Whitehall Cl ST14 ...141 B4
Whitehall Ct ST3 ....265 C3
Whitehall Rd
　Kingswinford DY6 ...275 B3
　Wolv WV4 ....266 A2
Whitehaven Dr ST11 ..282 B4
Whitehead Rd ST6 ....42 A3
Whitehill Rd ST7 .....26 A1
Whitehouse Cres B74 .256 B1
Whitehouse Ave WV3 .265 B4
Whitehouse Cres
　Burntwood WS7 ......229 A4
　Essington WV11 .....241 C1
Whitehouse La
　Codsall WV8 ....238 B4
　Sandon ST15 ....121 A4
　Swindon DY7,DY3 ...269 A1
Whitehouse Rd
　Bucknall ST2 ....58 A3
　Newcastle-u-L ST5 ....56 A2
　Polesworth B78 .....262 C4
Whitehouse Rd N ST5 .56 A2
Whitehurst La ST10 ...75 B3
Whitemill La ST15 ..119 C4
Whiteoaks Dr ST19 ..221 C4
Whiteridge Rd ST7 ...26 A1
Whites La CW2 ....37 A3
Whites Wood WV5 ..270 A3
Whitesands Cl B77 ..250 C3
Whitesands Gr ST3 ...90 A4
Whitesmith Cl DY3 ..271 B4
Whitestone Rd ST3 ...90 A3
Whitesytch La
　Hilderstone ST15 ....106 B1
　Sandon ST15 ....121 A4
Whitethorn Ave ST12 ..88 B1
Whitethorn Cl WS12 .210 A4
Whitethorn Rd **7** B78 .275 C1
Whitethorn Way ST5 ..40 C1
Whitfield Ave ST5 ...284 A1
Whitfield Rd
　Cannock WS11 ......210 B4
　Kidsgrove ST7 ....26 A1
　Norton-in-t-M ST6 ....42 B3
Whitfield Valley Prim Sch
　ST6 ....42 A4
Whitgreave Ave WV10 .241 A4
Whitgreave Ct
　Featherstone WV10 ..241 A3
　Stafford ST16 ......155 B3
Whitgreave La
　Rugeley WS15 ......196 C3
　Seighford ST18 .....135 B2
Whitgreave Prim Sch
　WV10 ....241 A4
Whiting B77 ....261 B4
Whitley Ave B77 ....250 C3
Whitley Cl WV6 .....255 A1
Whitley Rd ST6 ....42 B3
Whitmore Ave ST9 ...59 A2
Whitmore Rd
　Newcastle-u-L ST5 ....70 C2
　Stourbridge DY8 .....279 B3
　Trentham ST4,ST5 ....87 B4
Whitmore St ST7 .....57 A2
Whitney Ave DY8 ...279 B3
Whitridge Gr ST2 .....73 B4
Whittaker St WV2 ..266 C3
Whittingham Dr ST17 .174 A4
Whittington Common Rd
　WS14 ....232 C3
Whittington Grange Sch
　WS14 ....232 C3
Whittington Hall La
　DY7 ....279 A2
Whittington Ho WS13 .232 B2
Whittington Prim Sch
　WS14 ....232 C2
Whittington Rd DY8 .279 C2
Whittle Rd ST3 ....90 A4
Whitty La ST13 ....20 B3
Whitworth La WS15 .178 A1
Whygate Gr ST1 .....57 C3
Wickenstones Ct ST8 .27 B4
Wicket La DY7 ....277 C4
Wickets The DE15 ..185 C4
Wicksteed Row CW3 ..53 A3
Widecombe Ave ST17 .175 C4
Widecombe Rd ST3 ...57 C3
Widney Ave WS9 ...245 C4
Wigeon Gr WV10 ...241 A4
Wigford Rd B77 .....261 B3
Wiggin Ho WS12 ...243 B2
Wigginton Rd B79 ..250 A4
Wigmanal Cl WS14 ..231 C1
Wightwick Bank WV6 .255 A1
Wightwick Cl WS3 ..243 A1
Wightwick Gr WV6 ..255 A1
Wightwick Hall Rd WV6 .255 A1
Wightwick Hall Sch
　WV6 ....254 C1
Wigley Bank Rd DY7 .277 B3
Wigmore Pl ST3 ......73 B3
Wignall Rd ST6 ....41 C1
Wilbraham's Wlk ST7 .39 B1

Wilcox Ave WS12 ...210 A3
Wild Goose Ave ST7 ..26 B2
Wildacres DY6 ....279 B3
Wildfowl Wlk ST5 ....85 B2
Wildhay La DE6 ....80 B4
Wilding Rd ST6 ....42 B3
Wildtree Ave WV10 ..241 A1
Wildwood Dr ST17 ..175 B3
Wildwood Lawns ST17 .175 B4
Wileman Pl ST4 ....72 C3
Wileman St ST4 ......72 C3
Wilfred Owen Cl TF9 .112 A4
Wilfred Pl ST14 ....71 C4
Wilke's Wood ST18 ..154 C4
Wilkes Cl WS3 ....243 C2
Wilkes Croft DY3 ...271 B4
Wilkes Rd WV8 .....238 C2
Wilkin Rd WS8 ......228 B1
Wilkins Croft DE13 ..200 C1
Wilkins Ho WS3 ....243 A1
Wilkinson Cl WS7 ..229 A4
Wilkinson St ST6 .....41 B1
Wilks St ST6 ....41 C2
Wilm Pl ST7 ....43 A1
Willcock Rd
　Burton u T DE14 ....185 A4
　Wolv WV2 ....266 C3
Willdale Gr ST1 ......57 C3
Willerby Fold WV10 .240 C2
Willeton St ST12 .....58 A2
Willett Ave
　Brownhills WS7 .....228 C3
　Burntwood WS7 ....228 C3
Willey La ST10 ......171 B3
Willfield La ST16 .....43 B3
William Allitt Sch DE11 .186 C4
William Ave Biddulph ST8 .27 B4
　Meir ST3 ....90 B4
William Baxter Com Sch
　WS12 ....210 A3
William Birch Rd ST12 .58 A1
William Cl ST11 ....91 A4
William Clowes St ST6 .56 C4
William Coltman Way
　ST6 ....38 B1
William Fiske Ct ST14 .71 C2
William Hutson Jun Sch
　DE13 ....166 A4
William IV Rd DE13 .201 A2
William Lunn's Homes 23
　WS14 ....231 B4
William MacGregor Prim Sch
　B77 ....250 B2
William Mews WV10 .225 B1
William Morris Ct WS15 .178 B2
William Morris Gr
　WS11 ....209 C2
William Nadins Way
　DE11 ....186 C2
William Newton Cl
　DE65 ....148 A3
William Rd ST7 ....26 A1
William Rushton Rd ST6 .42 B1
William Shrewsbury Prim
　Sch DE13 ....147 C1
William St
　Burton u T DE14 ....166 B3
　Congleton CW12 ......6 A2
　Fenton ST4 ....72 C3
William Terr ST6 .....42 A3
William Wlk ST14 ...103 B2
Williamson Ave
　Cannock WS12 ......211 B2
　Norton-in-t-M ST6 ....42 C3
Williamson St ST6 ...41 C1
Willington Rd B79 ..250 A4
Williscroft Pl WS15 .179 A3
Willmott Terr ST7 ....26 A3
Willmott Cl B75 .....258 B2
Willotts Hill Rd ST5 ..40 B1
Willoughby Cl ST19 .207 C4
Willoughby Ct ST14 .125 B4
Willoughby Rd B79 .249 C4
Willow Ave ST9 ......41 B4
Willow Ave WS7 .....229 B2
Willow Bank WV3 ..255 B1
Willow Brook ST18 .154 C1
Willow Cl Alrewas WS13 .215 C4
　Brewood WV9 ....224 A1
　Hagley DY9 ....281 C3
　Kidsgrove ST7 ....41 A4
　Newcastle-u-L ST5 ....40 B1
　Penkridge ST19 .....207 C4
　Stafford ST17 ......175 C3
　Upper Tean ST10 .....92 B3
Willow Ct WS14 .....231 B3
Willow Dale ST15 ...120 B2
Willow Dr Codsall WV8 .239 A2
　Swadlincote DE11 ...186 C4
Willow Gr
　Essington WV11 .....242 A2
　Fenton ST3 ....72 C1
　Wolv WV10 ....244 B1
　Wolv WV10 ....241 C4
Willow Pl Biddulph ST8 ..17 A1
　Burton u T DE15 ....185 C4
Willow Rd
　Barton-u-N DE13 ...183 B1
　Kinver DY7 ....279 B2
　Stone ST15 ....120 A4
　Wolv WV3 ....265 B4
Willow Row ST3 .....283 B3
Willow Way ST11 .....91 A4
Willow Wlk WS12 ...209 B4

Willowbank B78 ...... 250 A1
Willowcroft ST20 ...... 151 C4
Willowherb Rise ST11 ...90 B4
Willowcroft Way ST7 ....26 C2
Willowdale Ave ST4 ....72 B3
Willowdale Grange
WV6 ...... 255 C3
Willowherb Cl WS11 ...210 B1
Willowmoor ST17 ...... 174 C3
Willowood Gr ST3 ....74 B1
Willows Dr ST3 ....90 A2
Willows Prim Sch
WS13 ...... 214 A1
Willows The
 Burton u T DE14 ......166 B1
 Cannock WS11 ...... 209 B1
 Leek ST13 ....30 B3
 Rugeley WS15 ......197 A3
 Stone ST15 ....120 A3
 Sutton Coldfield B74 ...257 C1
 Swynnerton ST15 ......118 C3
 Wombourne WV5 ......269 C3
Willowsmere Dr WS14 ...231 C4
Willowtree Cl WS13 ....214 A1
Willridding La DE6 .....80 B4
Willsford Ave ST14 .....126 B4
Wilmcote Dr B75 ......258 A2
Wilmore Ct ST18 ......137 B1
Wilmorehill La ST18 ...137 B1
Wilmot Cl ST5 ....55 C2
Wilmot Dr ST5 ....55 C2
Wilmot Gr ST3 ....73 B3
Wilmott Cl WS13 ......231 A4
Wilnecote High Sch
B77 ...... 261 C3
Wilnecote Jun Sch B77 .261 C4
Wilnecote La B77 .....250 B1
Wilnecote Sta B77 .....261 B4
Wilner's View WS3 .....243 C3
Wilson Gr WS11 ......210 B1
Wilson Keys Ct WS15 ...178 C1
Wilson Rd ST4 ....71 C1
Wilson St Chell Heath ST6 .42 A1
 Newcastle-u-L ST5 .....284 B3
Wilson Way ST6 ....41 B3
Wiltell Rd WS14 ......231 A3
Wilton Ave ST9 ....59 C2
Wilton Cl DY3 ....271 C4
Wilton St ST5 ....284 A4
Wiltshire Gr ST5 ....71 B2
Wiltshire Ho 4 DY8 ...279 C4
Wimberry Dr ST5 ....40 B1
Wimblebury Rd WS12 ..210 C1
Wimborne Ave ST3 .....88 C4
Wimshurst Mdw WV10 .250 C2
Winceby Rd WV6 ......254 C2
Winchcombe Cl DY1 ...271 C2
Winchcombe Dr DE15 ..167 A1
Winchester Ave ST7 ....58 B1
Winchester Cl
 Armitage WS15 ......198 A2
 Lichfield WS13 ......214 B2
Winchester Ct
 Stafford ST17 ......175 B3
 Sutton Coldfield B74 ...257 C1
Winchester Dr
 Burton u T DE14 ......185 B4
 Newcastle-u-L ST5 .....70 C2
Winchester Mews WS9 .256 A2
Winchester Rd
 Cannock WS11 ......210 A2
 Tamworth B78 ......249 C2
 Wolv WV10 ....240 B2
Wincote Dr WV6 ......255 B2
Wincote La ST21 ......133 B2
Windermere B77 ......262 A4
Windermere Dr
 Aldridge B74 ....256 C2
 Kingswinford DY6 .....275 B3
Windermere Ho ST6 ...155 C2
Windermere Pl WS11 ..209 C1
Windermere Rd
 Newcastle-u-L ST5 ....71 A2
 Wolv WV6 ....255 B4
Windermere St ST1 ....282 A4
Windermere Way ST10 ..76 C2
Windings The WS13 ...214 A1
Windmill Ave ST7 ......41 A4
Windmill Bank
 Longdon WS15 ......212 A3
 Wombourne WV5 ......270 A4
Windmill Cl
 Farewell WS13 ......213 C1
 Stone ST3 ....89 C2
 Tamworth B79 ......250 A4
 4 Uttoxeter ST14 .....111 A1
Windmill Cres WV3 ...255 A1
Windmill Dr ST14 .....127 C2
Windmill Gr DY6 ......275 A4
Windmill Hill ST3 .....89 C2
Windmill La
 Eccleshall ST21 ......116 A2
 Lichfield WS13 ......214 A1
 Longdon WS15 ......212 A2
 Snelston DE6 ....81 C1
 Wolv WV3 ....255 A1
Windmill View ST3 ....59 B2
Windmillhall La WV14 .232 C3
Windrow The WV6 .....254 B2
Windrush Cl Sedgley DY3 ..271 B2
 Trentham ST4 ....88 B3
Windrush Rd WS11 ....209 C3
Windsmoor St ST4 ....72 A3
Windsor Ave
 Cannock WS11 ......210 A3
 Longton ST3 ....283 D2

Windsor Ave continued
 Wolv WV4 ....265 C3
Windsor Cl
 Burntwood WS7 ......211 C1
 Sedgley DY3 ....271 A1
 Stone ST15 ....119 C3
 Tamworth B79 ......250 B4
Windsor Cres DY7 ....277 C2
Windsor Ct
 Cannock WS12 ......210 A3
 Lichfield WS14 ......231 A3
Windsor Dr
 Burton u T DE15 ......166 C1
 Leek ST13 ....31 A4
 Market Drayton TF9 ....97 C1
Windsor Gdns
 Codsall WV8 ....238 C2
 Wolv WV4 ....265 A4
Windsor Gr
 Kingswinford DY8 ....275 C1
 Walsall WS4 ....244 B1
Windsor Ho ST7 ....40 B3
Windsor Holloway DY7 .278 B1
Windsor Ind Est ST14 ..166 C2
Windsor Park CE Mid Sch
ST14 ...... 126 A4
Windsor Rd
 Albrighton WV7 ......237 A3
 Cheslyn Hay WS6 .....226 C2
 Pattingham WV6 ......253 B1
 Stafford ST17 ......175 A4
 Stourbridge DY8 ......279 C2
 Trentham ST4 ....72 A1
 Uttoxeter ST14 ......111 A1
 Wolv WV4 ....266 C3
 Wombourne WV5 ......269 C3
Windsor St ST5 ....284 C3
Windy Arbour ST10 .....76 C2
Windycote La ST19 .....60 A1
Windyridge SK17 ......13 A3
Winford Ave DY6 .....275 C2
Wingate Ct B74 ......257 C2
Wingate Wlk ST3 ......88 C4
Winghay Cl ST6 ....56 B4
Winghay Rd ST7 ......42 A3
Winghay Rd ST7 ......26 B1
Winghouse La ST12,
ST15 ...... 103 C4
Wingrove Ave 4 ST3 ...73 B1
Winifred Gdns ST13 ....88 C4
Winifred St ST11 ......282 A4
Winnipeg Cl ST14 .....88 A4
Winpenny Rd ST5 .....55 C4
Winscar Croft DY3 ....271 B2
Winsford Ave ST3 ......73 C1
Winsford Cres ST17 ...175 C3
Winshill Inf Sch DE15 ..167 A2
Winslow Dr WV6 .....255 C2
Winslow Gn ST3 ......73 C1
Winstanley Cl WS15 ...178 B1
Winstanley Pl WS15 ...178 B1
Winster Gn DE11 .....186 C3
Winston Pl ST2 ....58 A2
Winston Rd
 Codsall DY11 ....280 A3
 Swindon DY3 ....269 C1
Winston Terr ST5 ......56 B3
Winter Cl WS13 ......214 B1
Winterbourne Gr ST3 ...73 C2
Winterlea La DE6 .....51 C1
Winterfield La ST3 ....74 A4
Winterley Gdns DY3 ...271 C3
Winterside Cl ST5 ......40 B1
Winton Sq ST4 ....72 A4
Wintonfield St ST4 ....72 A4
Winwood Ct DY8 .....279 C2
Wiscombe Ave ST19 ...193 A1
Wise St ST3 ....283 C1
Wissage Ct WS13 .....231 B4
Wissage Rd WS13 .....231 A4
Wistmans Cl DY11 ....271 C1
Wistwood Hayes WV10 .240 C2
Witchford Cres ST13 ...88 C4
Witham Way ST8 ......16 C1
Withern Way DY3 .....271 B2
Withers Rd WV8 ......239 A2
Withies Rd ST4 ....71 C2
Within La ST18 ......137 B1
Withington Rd ST6 ....42 A3
Withnell Gn ST6 ......42 A3
Withymere La WV5 ...270 B4
Withystakes Rd ST9 ....59 B2
Withywood Cl WV12 ..242 B1
Witney Cl B79 ....249 C4
Witney Gr WV10 .....240 A2
Witney Rd ST17 ......156 A3
Witton St DY8 ....88 C4
Witton Rd WV4 ......266 A3
Witton St DY8 ....279 C2
Wobaston Rd
 Codsall WV9 ....239 C2
 Wolv WV9,WV10 ......240 A2
Woburn B77 ....250 B2
Woburn Cl ST4 ....88 B3
Woburn Dr CW12 .....16 A4
Wodehouse Cl WV5 ...269 C3
Woden Cl WV5 ......269 C4
Wogan St ST16 ......155 C3
Wold The WV5 ......267 B4
Wolfe St ST4 ....72 A3
Wolfscote Dale DE11 ..186 C1
Wolgarston High Sch
ST19 ...... 208 A4
Wolgarston Way ST19 .207 C4
Wollaston Cr DY8 ....279 B3
Wollaston Rd
 Brierley Hill DY8 ......279 C4

Wollaston Rd continued
 Kinver DY7 ....279 B4
Wolmer Rd WV11 .....242 A1
Wolmore La WV5 .....263 A1
Wolseley Rd ST5 ......250 C2
Wolseley Cl ST17 .....177 C4
Wolseley Rd
 Newcastle-u-L ST5 ....56 A3
 Rugeley WS15 ......177 C5
 Rugeley, Wolseley Park
 WS15 ...... 177 C1
 Stafford ST16 ......156 B2
 Stoke-on-T ST4 ....71 C2
Wolsey Rd WS13 .....213 C1
Wolstanton High Sch
ST5 ...... 56 B2
Wolstanton Rd ST5 ....55 C3
Wolstanton Ret Pk ST5 .56 C2
Wolstern Rd ST3 ......73 B3
Wolverhampton Bsns Airport
DY7 ...... 236 C4
Wolverhampton Coll Wulfrun
Campus WV6 ......255 C2
Wolverhampton Girls High
Sch WV6 ...... 255 C2
Wolverhampton Gram Sch
WV3 ...... 255 C1
Wolverhampton Rd
 Cheslyn Hay WV10,WS6 .226 A1
 Codsall WV8 ....239 A2
 Cookley DY10 ....280 A2
 Essington WV11 ......242 A2
 Kingswinford DY6 .....270 B1
 Penkridge ST19 ......278 C4
 Pattingham WV6 .....253 C2
 Penkridge ST19 ......207 C4
 Sedgley DY3 ....266 B1
 Stafford ST17 ......155 C1
 Walsall, Pelsall WS3 ...243 A1
Wolverhampton Rd E
WV4 ...... 266 B3
Wolverhampton Rd
WS11 ...... 226 A3
Wolverley Ave
 Stourbridge DY8 ......279 B3
 Wolv WV6 ....265 B3
Wolverley Ct WV7 ...237 A3
Wolverley Rd WV10 ..280 A1
Wolverson Rd WV9 ...245 A2
Wombourne Cl DY3 ...271 B4
Wombourne Ent Pk
DY3 ...... 269 B2
Wombourne Pk WV5 .269 C2
Wombourne Rd DY3 ..269 C2
Wombrook Dale WV5 .269 B3
Wombrook Ind Est WV5 269 C3
Wood Ave Brewood WV9 .224 A2
 Kingsley ST10 ....62 B3
Wood Bank La ST19 ...193 A1
Wood Bank Rd WV3 ..265 A4
Wood Common Grange
WS3 ...... 243 C2
Wood Cres Stafford ST16 ..155 A3
 Stone ST15 ....119 C3
Wood Ct DE14 ......166 B1
Wood Eaton Rd ST20 ..190 A4
Wood End La
 Airewas WS13 ......215 A3
 Cheadle ST10 ......61 A3
 King's Bromley WS13 ..214 C4
Wood End Prim Sch
CV9 ...... 262 B1
Wood End Rd WV11 ..241 A1
Wood End Way WS9 ..243 A4
Wood Hayes Rd WV11 .241 B1
Wood Hill Dr WV5 ...269 C3
Wood La Aldridge B74 ..256 C1
 Cannock WS12 ......210 B2
 Cheslyn Hay WS11 ...225 C3
 Hanbury DE13 ......144 C2
 Kingstone ST14 ......124 B1
 Maer ST5 ....84 B2
 Shenstone WS14 .....246 A1
 Stone ST15 ....186 C4
 Uttoxeter ST14 ......126 C3
 Walsall WS3 ....243 C2
 Wheaton Aston ST19 ..206 B2
 Wolv WV10 ....240 B1
Wood La ST4 ....182 A3
Wood Lane Prim Sch
ST7 ...... 40 A1
Wood Pl ST3 ....74 A1
Wood Rd Codsall WV8 .238 C2
 Longsdon ST9 ....45 A4
 Sedgley DY3 ....271 B2
 Wolv WV6 ....255 B2
 Wombourne WV5 ......270 A4
Wood Ridings WS13 ...214 A1
Wood St Audley ST7 ....39 C2
 Burton u T DE14 ......166 B1
 Leek ST13 ....30 C3
 Longton ST3 ....283 C4
 Mow Cop ST7 ....42 C2
 Stourbridge DY8 ......279 B3
 Wood End CV9 ......262 B1
Wood Terr ST11 .....282 A1
Wood The ST5 ....74 B1
Wood View Audley ST7 ..40 A1
Woodall St ST3 ....57 A3
Woodbank Rd DY3 ...271 B4
Woodbank St ST6 .....56 C4
Woodberry Ave ST14 ..71 C3
Woodberry Cl
 Stafford ST17 ......174 C2
 Stoke-on-T ST4 ....71 C3

Woodbine Way DE14 ..184 C3
Woodbridge Cl
 Walsall WS3 ....243 A2
 Walsall, Shelfield WS4 ..244 B1
Woodbridge Rd ST5 ...71 A1
Woodcock Gdns WV10 .241 A4
Woodcock La ST7 .....26 B3
Woodcock Rd WS15 ..178 B1
Woodcocks' Well CE Prim
Sch ST7 ...... 26 B3
Woodcote Rd WV4 ...255 B2
Woodcote The 3 ST17 .175 B4
Woodcroft ST7 ....40 A1
Woodcroft Ave ST13 ...30 B2
Woodcroft Lane ST13 ..30 A3
Woodcroft Fst Sch ST13 .30 B2
Woodcroft Rd ST11 ...30 B2
Woodcross La WV14 ..266 C1
Woodcross St WV14 ..266 C1
Wooddisse La ST13 ....33 C1
Woodedge La ST14 ...143 C3
Woodend Pl WV6 .....255 A2
Woodend St ST4 ....72 C3
Woodfield Ave WV4 ..265 C3
Woodfield Cl WS11 ...227 C4
Woodfield Ct ST13 .....31 A3
Woodfield Dr WS11 ...227 C4
Woodfield Ho WS3 ...244 A2
Woodfield Mts WV6 ..255 B2
Woodfield Jun Sch
WV4 ...... 265 C3
Woodfield Rd DY3 ....271 B2
Woodfields Dr WS14 ..231 C3
Woodford Croft WS9 ..256 A4
Woodford Cl WV9 ...239 C1
Woodford Cres WS7 ...229 A4
Woodford End WS11 ..209 C2
Woodford Gn WS9 ...269 B4
Woodford Way
 Cannock WS11 ......210 B1
 Wolverhampton WV6 .269 B3
Woodgate Ave ST7 ....25 A3
Woodgate St ST3 ......74 A1
Woodgate Way WV6 ..226 C3
Woodhall Pl ST5 ......54 C1
Woodhall Rd
 Kidsgrove ST7 ....26 B2
 Wolv WV4 ....265 A3
Woodham
 Cheslyn Hay WS11 ...226 A3
 Walsall WS4 ....244 B1
Woodseaves ST20 ....151 B4
Woodhead Rd ST2 ....56 C3
Woodhead Way ST10 ..76 C3
Woodheyes Lawns
ST3 ...... 73 B4
Woodhill Cl WV5 .....269 C3
Woodhouse High Sch
B77 ...... 250 C2
Woodhouse Jun Sch
ST3 ...... 283 C5
Woodhouse La
 Albrighton WV7 ......237 B2
 Biddulph ST8 ....16 C1
 Eccleshall ST21 ......42 C3
 Scropton DE65 ......129 C4
 Tamworth B77 ......251 A3
Woodhouse Mid Sch ST8 .16 C1
Woodhouse Rd WV6 .255 A2
Woodhouse St WV4 ..255 A2
Woodhouse St ST4 ....72 A3
Woodhouses La WS7 ..229 C3
Woodhouses Rd WS7 .230 A4
Woodhurst Cl B77 ...250 C2
Woodingdean Cl 12 ST3 .73 B3
Woodkirk Cl ST5 ......42 A4
Woodland Ave
 Hagley DY8 ....281 C3
 Newcastle-u-L ST5 ....56 B3
 Norton-in-H ST6 ....42 C2
 Wolv WV6 ....255 A2
Woodland Cl
 Albrighton WV7 ......237 A3
 Cannock WS12 ......210 A4
 Wolv WV6 ....255 B4
Woodland Cres
 Walsall WS3 ....243 C3
 Wolv WV3 ....255 B4
Woodland Ct
 Huntington ST17 ....209 B2
 Shenstone WS14 .....258 A4
Woodland Dr
 Cheslyn Hay WS6 .....226 C2
 Foston DE6 ....129 B2
Woodland Gr
 Chell Heath ST6 ......42 A1
 Cookley DY10 ....280 B2
 Sedgley DY3 ....271 A2
Woodland Hills CW3 ..68 C4
Woodland Rd
 Burntwood DE15 .....186 A2
 Tamworth B77 ......251 A2
 Wolv WV3 ....265 B4
Woodland St Biddulph ST8 .27 B3
 Tunstall ST6 ....41 C2
Woodland Views DY3 .269 B2
Woodland Views WS14 .127 C1
Woodland Way
 Burntwood WS7 .....229 A3
 Polesworth B78 ......262 C4
Woodlands Ave
 Cheddleton ST13 ....45 A1
 Kidsgrove ST7 ....25 B1
 Stone ST15 ....119 C4
Woodlands Cl
 Stafford ST17 ......155 B4
 Stone ST15 ....119 C4
 Thorpe DE6 ....51 B1

Woodlands Cotts WV4 .266 C2
Woodlands Dr
 Brewood WV9 ......224 A2
 Stone ST15 ....120 B2
Woodlands Gr ST3 .....90 A2
Woodlands La
 Cheslyn Hay WV10,WS11 .225 C1
 Forsbrook ST11 ......91 A3
Woodlands Paddock
WV4 ...... 265 C2
Woodlands Prim Sch
B77 ...... 250 C2
Woodlands Rd
 Cookley DY10 ....280 A2
 Stoke-on-T ST4 ......155 A4
 Stoke-on-T ST4 ......71 C2
 Wombourne WV5 ....270 A3
Woodlands The
 Lichfield WS13 ......231 B4
 Stoke-on-T ST4 ....71 C2
 Tatenhill DE13 ......184 A4
 Wood End CV9 ......262 B1
Woodlands Way WS15 .198 B2
Woodleigh Ave ST13 ..126 B3
Woodleighton Gr ST14 .126 B3
Woodleighton Rd ST14 .126 B3
Woodman La ST6 .....226 C2
Woodman St ST7 ......43 A1
Woodmill La WS15 ...161 A4
Woodpark La ST13 ....89 B4
Woodpecker View TF9 ..99 B2
Woodpecker Way WV11 .210 B2
Woodridge Cl TF10 ...168 A2
Woodroffe's Cliff ST14 .143 B3
Woodrow Way TF9 ...100 B3
Woodruff Cl ST8 ....27 A1
Woods Croft WS13 .....241 B4
Woods La DE15 ......167 A1
Woodseaves CE Prim Sch
ST20 ...... 151 C4
Woodsetton Specl Sch The
DY3 ...... 271 C3
Woodside Ave WS15 ..198 B2
Woodshurts St ST7 ....25 C1
Woodside
 Chapel Chorlton ST5 ..85 B2
 Lawton-gate ST7 ......25 C2
 Madeley CW3 ....68 C4
 Sutton Coldfield B74 .257 C1
Woodside Ave Endon ST6 .43 A3
 Kidsgrove ST7 ....25 C2
Woodside Cl
 Colwich ST18 ....177 B4
 Wood End CV9 ......262 B1
Woodside Cotts ST10 ..77 C4
Woodside Cres ST5 ....71 B1
Woodside Dr
 Blythe Bridge ST3 ....90 A2
 Little Aston B74 ......257 B3
Woodside Gr WV8 ....239 A1
Woodside La ST13 .....30 B1
Woodside Pl
 Cannock WS11 ......209 C3
 Norton-in-H ST6 ....42 C2
Woodside Villas ST3 ..283 D4
Woodside WV9 ......256 A3
Woodsorrel Rd DY1 ...271 C3
Woodside Cl B75 ....258 B2
Woodstock Cl
 Kingswinford DY8 ....275 B1
 Newcastle-u-L ST5 ....56 B2
Woodstock Dr
 Huntington ST17 ....209 B4
 Kingswinford DY8 ....275 B1
 Sutton Coldfield B74 .257 B2
Woodstock Rd
 Kidsgrove ST6 ....41 A4
 Stafford ST17 ......156 B1
Woodstock St ST4 .....41 B4
Woodthorne Cl ST19 ..207 C4
Woodthorne Cl
 Rugeley WS15 ......178 B1
 Sedgley DY3 ....271 B2
Woodthorne Prim Sch
WV6 ...... 255 C2
Woodthorne Rd WV6 .255 A3
Woodthorne Rd S WV6 .255 A3
Woodthorne Wlk DY6 .275 C4
Woodvale Cres ST13 ..126 C3
Woodville Dr DE11 ...186 C3
Woodville Gdns DY3 ..266 C1
Woodville Pl ST3 ......74 A1
Woodville St ST4 ......74 A1
Woodville Terr ST3 ....74 A1
Woodward St ST1 ......57 B3
Woody Bank WS6 ....226 C1
Woodyard Dr B77 ....217 B3
Woodyard La DE6 .....129 C2
Woolands Rise DE6 ...144 A4
Woolliscroft Ave ST5 ..56 B2
Woolliscroft Rd ST4 ...58 A2
Woolrich St ST6 ....56 C4
Woolston Ave CW12 ....6 A1
Worre Prim Sch CW3 ...67 A1
Woosnam Cl DE14 ...185 A3
Wootton Cl WS11 .....210 A1
Wootton Dr ST16 .....155 A4
Wootton La ST10 ......78 C2
Wootton Rd WV3 .....265 B4
Wootton St WS13 ....214 B3
Worcester Cl
 Cannock WS11 ......226 C4
 Lichfield WS13 ......214 B2

Worcester Cl continued
Sutton Coldfield B75 . . . . . .258 B2
Talke ST7 . . . . .40 B4
Worcester Ct WV3 . . . . . .266 A3
Worcester Gr WV6 . . . . .254 B2
Worcester La B75 . . . . . . .258 B2
Worcester Pl ST2 . . . . . . .58 B1
Worcester Rd
Burton u T DE15 . . . . .185 C3
Hagley DY9 . . . . .281 C2
Whittington WS14 . . . . . . .232 B2
Worcester St DY8 . . . . . .279 C2
Wordsley Green Sh Ctr
DY8 . . . . .275 B1
Wordsley Hospl DY8 . . . .275 C2
Wordsworth Ave
Stafford ST17 . . . . .174 B4
Tamworth B79 . . . . .250 A3
Wolv WV4 . . . . .266 C2
Wordsworth Cl
Armitage WS15 . . . . .198 A2
Burton u T DE14 . . . . .166 B3
Cannock WS11 . . . . .209 B2
Cheadle ST10 . . . . .76 B1
Lichfield WS14 . . . . .231 A3
Wordsworth Ct WV6 . . . .254 C2
Wordsworth Dr TF9 . . . .112 A4
Wordsworth Rd
Burntwood WS7 . . . . .229 A4
Sedgley DY3 . . . . .271 A3
Worfield Gdns WV3 . . . .265 C3
Worsley Dr CW12 . . . . .6 A1
Worston La ST15,ST18 . .135 A3
Worth Cl ST3 . . . . .73 B2
Worthing Pl ST3 . . . . . . .283 B3
Worthington Rd WS13 . .215 B3
Worthington Way DE14 . .166 B2
Wragby Cl WV9 . . . . .240 A2
Wragg's La ST18 . . . . .17 A1
Wrekin Ave TF10 . . . . . . .168 C1
Wrekin Ct B74 . . . . .257 C1
Wrekin Dr
Wolv, Bradmore WV3 . . . . .265 C4
Wolv, Wergs WV6 . . . . . . .255 A3

Wrekin Gr WV11 . . . . . . .242 A1
Wrekin La WV6 . . . . .255 A3
Wrekin View
Brownhills WS8 . . . . .245 A3
Huntington WS12 . . . . . . .209 B4
Wrekin View Rd DY3 . . .271 B4
Wren Ave WV8 . . . . .254 B2
Wren Cl ST8 . . . . .27 C4
Wren View Ashley TF9 . . . .99 B2
Longton ST3 . . . . .283 D2
Wrenbury Cl ST5 . . . . .40 B1
Wrenbury Cres ST2 . . . . . .58 A1
Wrenswood ST17 . . . . . . .175 B3
Wrexham Cl ST8 . . . . .16 B1
Wright Ave ST5 . . . . .55 C4
Wright St Kidsgrove ST7 . . .25 B1
Stafford ST16 . . . . .155 C3
Wright's Ave WS11 . . . . .209 C3
Wrighton Cl ST2 . . . . .57 C1
Wrighton Dr DY5 . . . . . .271 B1
Wrinehill Rd CW5 . . . . . . .52 A3
Wrottesley Park Rd
WV6,WV8 . . . . .254 B3
Wrottesley Rd WV6 . . . . .255 A3
Wrottesley Rd W
Perton WV6 . . . . .254 C3
Wolv WV6 . . . . .255 A3
Wroxham Way ST5 . . . . . .71 A1
Wulfad Ct ST15 . . . . .120 B4
Wulfric Cl ST19 . . . . .208 A4
Wulfruna Gdns WV3 . . . .255 C1
Wulstan Dr ST5 . . . . .56 B2
Wulstan Rd ST6 . . . . .57 A3
Wyatt St ST6 . . . . .41 B4
Wych Elm Rd WS8 . . . . . .244 C3
Wychall Dr WV10 . . . . . . .240 C2
Wychbold Cl WV12 . . . . .242 B1
Wychbold Way WV12 . . .242 B1
Wychbury Rd WV3 . . . . . .265 B4
Wycherwood Gdns
ST17 . . . . .175 B3
Wychwood Pk CW2 . . . . . .37 A1
Wycliffe Rd ST6 . . . . .56 C4
Wye Cl Cheadle ST10 . . . . .76 C1
Perton WV6 . . . . .254 C2
Wye Dale DE11 . . . . .186 C1
Wye Ho DY3 . . . . .271 B2

Wye Rd Newcastle-u-L ST5 . .71 A2
Walsall WS3 . . . . .243 C1
Wyggeston St DE13 . . . .166 B3
Wykeham Gr WV6 . . . . . .254 B2
Wymondley Gr ST4 . . . . . .88 A3
Wynbank Cl ST7 . . . . .54 C4
Wynchcombe Ave WV4 . .265 B2
Wynd The DY3 . . . . .266 B1
Wyndham Cres DE15 . . . .167 B2
Wyndham Rd ST3 . . . . . . .88 C4
Wyndham Wood Cl
WS13 . . . . .215 B4
Wynford Pl ST2 . . . . .58 A1
Wynn Rd WV4 . . . . .265 C3
Wynne Cres WV4 . . . . . . .265 B2
Wynstay Ave ST9 . . . . .59 A2
Wynstay Ct ST5 . . . . .71 B1
Wynyates B79 . . . . .249 C3
Wyre Cl WS9 . . . . .244 C2
Wyre Rd DY8 . . . . .279 C4
Wyrley Brook Pk
WS11 . . . . .226 B3
Wyrley Brook Ret Pk
WS11 . . . . .226 B3
Wyrley Cl
Brownhills WS8 . . . . .228 C2
Lichfield WS14 . . . . .231 A3
Wyrley La WS3 . . . . .243 C4
Wyrley Rd B75 . . . . .258 B1
Wyvern B77 . . . . .250 C2
Wyvern Gr WV12 . . . . . . .210 A3
Wyvis Cl WV6 . . . . .255 C1

Y

Yale St ST6 . . . . .56 C4
Yardley Pl ST3 . . . . .88 C3
Yardley St ST6 . . . . .42 C3
Yardley Wlk ST3 . . . . .88 C3
Yarlet Croft ST16 . . . . . . .155 B3
Yarlet La ST18 . . . . .136 B3
Yarlet Sch ST18 . . . . .136 B4
Yarmouth Wlk ST3 . . . . .283 D5
Yarnbrook Gr ST6 . . . . . . .42 B2
Yarner Cl DY1 . . . . .271 C1
Yarnfield Cl ST3 . . . . .74 A1

Yarnfield La Stone ST15 . .119 A4
Swynnerton ST15 . . . . . . .118 C3
Yarrow Cl WS3 . . . . .244 A3
Yateley Cl ST2 . . . . .58 A1
Yates Croft B74 . . . . .257 C3
Yates St ST1 . . . . .282 A2
Yaxley Ct ST5 . . . . .71 A1
Yaxley Pl ST3 . . . . .88 C3
Yeadon Gdns WV3 . . . . . .265 B4
Yeager Ct ST15 . . . . .118 C3
Yeaman St ST4 . . . . .72 A3
Yeatsall Rd WS15 . . . . . . .160 C3
Yeldham Pl ST3 . . . . .88 C3
Yelt La DE6 . . . . .127 B4
Yelverton Ave ST17 . . . . .175 B4
Yelverton Cl WS3 . . . . . . .243 A2
Yemscroft WS6 . . . . .243 A4
Yenton Cl B78 . . . . .250 A1
Yeoman Ind Est DE14 . . .166 C3
Yeoman Way WS15 . . . . .198 A2
Yeovil Pl ST3 . . . . .88 C3
Yeovilton B79 . . . . .250 B4
Yerley Hill DE6 . . . . .66 B3
Yew Cl WS15 . . . . .198 A2
Yew Pl ST5 . . . . .55 B4
Yew Tree Ave
Lichfield WS14 . . . . .231 C4
Longton ST3 . . . . .72 C1
Yew Tree Cl
Norton Canes WS11 . . . . .228 A3
Norton-in-t-M ST2 . . . . . . .43 B1
Seighford ST18 . . . . .154 C1
Yew Tree Ct ST17 . . . . . . .174 C2
Yew Tree Dr ST19 . . . . . .205 B3
Yew Tree Gdns WV8 . . . .239 A2
Yew Tree La
Astbury CW12 . . . . .15 B2
Bridgemere CW5 . . . . .67 A3
Wolv WV6 . . . . .255 A3
Yew Tree Pl WS3 . . . . . . .243 B2
Yew Tree Rd
Pattingham WV6 . . . . .253 B1
Rugeley WS15 . . . . .196 C3
Swadlincote DE11 . . . . . . .186 C4
Walsall WS4 . . . . .244 B1
Yew Tree Terr ST7 . . . . . . .41 A4
Yewtree Cres DE15 . . . . .185 C4

York Ave
Blythe Bridge ST11 . . . . . . .90 C1
Wolv WV3 . . . . .255 C1
York Cl Biddulph ST8 . . . . .16 B1
Forsbrook ST11 . . . . .91 A4
Lichfield WS13 . . . . .214 B2
Talke ST7 . . . . .40 B4
York Cres
Stourbridge DY8 . . . . .279 B4
Wolv WV3 . . . . .255 C1
York Gdns WV3 . . . . .255 C1
York Pl ST5 . . . . .284 B3
York Rd Cannock WS11 . .226 C4
Meir ST3 . . . . .74 A2
Stafford ST17 . . . . .175 A4
Wolv WV3 . . . . .265 A4
York St Burton u T DE14 . .166 B2
Hanley ST1 . . . . .282 B3
Leek ST13 . . . . .30 C3
Newcastle-u-L ST5 . . . . . .284 D3
Stone ST15 . . . . .105 A1
Yorkdale Cl DY3 . . . . .271 B2
Yorksand Rd B78 . . . . . . .260 C4
Youlgreave Ave ST2 . . . . .58 A1
Youlton Pl ST2 . . . . .58 A1
Young Ave ST16 . . . . .155 B3
Young St Cheadle ST10 . . .76 C2
Chell Heath ST6 . . . . .41 C3
Younger St ST4 . . . . .72 B3
Yoxall Ave ST4 . . . . .71 C4
Yoxall Rd
King's Bromley DE13 . . . . .199 B4
Newborough DE13 . . . . . .162 C4

Z

Zamenhof Gr ST6 . . . . .42 B1
Zennor Gr ST2 . . . . .58 A1
Zetland Pl ST3 . . . . .88 C3
Zetland Wlk ST3 . . . . .88 C3
Zion Cl WS6 . . . . .226 B2
Zion St ST6 . . . . .57 A4
Zoar St DY3 . . . . .271 B2
Zodiac Dr ST6 . . . . .41 C3
Zouche Cl DY8 . . . . .279 C4

Any feature in this atlas can be given a unique reference to help you find the same feature on other Ordnance Survey maps of the area, or to help someone else locate you if they do not have a Street Atlas.

The grid squares in this atlas match the Ordnance Survey National Grid and are at 1 kilometre intervals. The small figures at the bottom and sides of every other grid line are the National Grid kilometre values (**00** to **99** km) and are repeated across the country every 100 km (see left).

To give a unique National Grid reference you need to locate where in the country you are. The country is divided into 100 km squares with each square given a unique two-letter reference. Use the administrative map to determine in which 100 km square a particular page of this atlas falls.

The bold letters and numbers between each grid line (**A** to **C**, **1** to **4**) are for use within a specific Street Atlas only, and when used with the page number, are a convenient way of referencing these grid squares.

Example The railway bridge over DARLEY GREEN RD in grid square A1

Step 1: Identify the two-letter reference, in this example the page is in **SP**

Step 2: Identify the 1 km square in which the railway bridge falls. Use the figures in the southwest corner of this square: Eastings **17**, Northings **74**. This gives a unique reference: **SP 17 74**, accurate to 1 km.

Step 3: To give a more precise reference accurate to 100 m you need to estimate how many tenths along and how many tenths up this 1 km square the feature is. This makes the bridge about **8** tenths along and about **1** tenth up from the southwest corner.

This gives a unique reference: **SP 178 741**, accurate to 100 m.

Eastings (read from left to right along the bottom) come before Northings (read from bottom to top). If you have trouble remembering say to yourself "Along the hall, THEN up the stairs"!

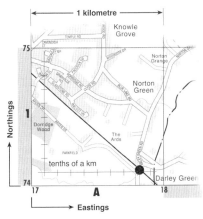

Name and Address	Telephone	Page	Grid reference

Street Atlases from Philip's

Philip's publish an extensive range of regional and local street atlases which are ideal for motoring, business and leisure use. They are widely used by the emergency services and local authorities throughout Britain.

Key features include:

◆ Superb county-wide mapping at an extra-large scale of 3½ inches to 1 mile, or 2½ inches to 1 mile in pocket editions

◆ Complete urban and rural coverage, detailing every named street in town and country

◆ Each atlas available in two handy sizes – standard spiral and pocket paperback

'The mapping is very clear... great in scope and value'

★★★★ BEST BUY   AUTO EXPRESS

1 Bedfordshire
2 Berkshire
3 Birmingham and West Midlands
4 Bristol and Bath
5 Buckinghamshire
6 Cambridgeshire
7 Cardiff, Swansea and The Valleys
8 Cheshire
9 Cornwall
10 Derbyshire
11 Devon
12 Dorset
13 County Durham and Teesside
14 Edinburgh and East Central Scotland
15 North Essex
16 South Essex
17 Glasgow and West Central Scotland
18 Gloucestershire
19 North Hampshire
20 South Hampshire
21 Herefordshire and Monmouthshire
22 Hertfordshire
23 East Kent
24 West Kent
25 Lancashire
26 Leicestershire and Rutland
27 Lincolnshire
28 London
29 Greater Manchest
30 Merseyside
31 Norfolk
32 Northamptonshire
33 Nottinghamshire
34 Oxfordshire
35 Shropshire
36 Somerset
37 Staffordshire
38 Suffolk
39 Surrey
40 East Sussex
41 West Sussex
42 Tyne and Wear an Northumberland
43 Warwickshire
44 Worcestershire
45 Wiltshire and Swin
46 East Yorkshire and Northern Lincolnshi
47 North Yorkshire
48 South Yorkshire
49 West Yorkshire

How to order

The Philip's range of street atlases is available from good retailers or directly from the publisher by phoning 01903 828503